D1124489

John P. O'Connell
1613 North 201st Street
Shoreline, WA 98133

THE FRENCH AND ITALIAN
NOTEBOOKS

EDITORS

General Editors

William Charvat, 1905–1966

Roy Harvey Pearce

Claude M. Simpson, 1910–1976

Thomas Woodson

Fredson Bowers, *General Textual Editor*

L. Neal Smith, *Associate Textual Editor*

James Rubino, *Assistant Textual Editor*

A PUBLICATION OF
THE OHIO STATE UNIVERSITY CENTER
FOR TEXTUAL STUDIES

NATHANIEL HAWTHORNE

THE
FRENCH AND ITALIAN
NOTEBOOKS

Edited by
Thomas Woodson

Ohio State University Press

CENTER FOR
SCHOLARLY EDITIONS
AN APPROVED EDITION
MODERN LANGUAGE
ASSOCIATION OF AMERICA

Copyright © 1980 by the Ohio State University Press
All Rights Reserved.

International Standard Book Number 0–8142–0256–X

Library of Congress Cataloguing in Publication Data
(Revised)

Hawthorne, Nathaniel, 1804–1864.
 The centenary edition of the works of Nathaniel Hawthorne.

 Half title; each vol. also has special t. p.
 "A publication of the Ohio State University Center for Textual Studies."
 Includes bibliographical references.
 CONTENTS: v. 1. The scarlet letter.—v. 2. The house of seven gables.—[etc.]—v. 14. The French and Italian notebooks.

 1. Charvat, William, 1905–1966, ed. II. Ohio State University, Columbus. Ohio State Center for Textual Studies.
PS1850.F63   813'.3   63–750

ACKNOWLEDGMENTS

The editors of this volume are indebted to its predecessor, "The French and Italian Notebooks by Nathaniel Hawthorne, edited with an introduction and notes," by Norman Holmes Pearson, and submitted as a doctoral dissertation to Yale University in 1941. This work was never published, but Professor Pearson generously made it available to many interested scholars, and it has had a considerable impact on the scholarship about Hawthorne's years in Europe. Nevertheless, he was not satisfied with his student work, and he welcomed the opportunity to redo it under the auspices of the Centenary Edition. Unfortunately, his death intervened.

Although the present edition draws much from Professor Pearson's example, readers familiar with his work will find that problems of text and annotation are freshly engaged here.

We are grateful to Professor Pearson's literary executors, Professor Louis L. Martz and Dr. Donald C. Gallup of the Beinecke Library, Yale University, for providing us with the notes and papers he had collected for revision of the dissertation: in particular, the typescripts of the almost daily letters to America by the Hawthornes' governess, Ada Shepard, and the typescript of passages from the manuscript diary of Maria Mitchell. We are also indebted to the annotation of Hawthorne's 1859 diary by William L. Reenan, privately distributed in 1931.

For the annotation of Hawthorne's interest in matters of art,

CONCORDIA UNIVERSITY LIBRARY
PORTLAND, OR 97211

achitecture, and design, we have had the benefit of conversation with two Hawthorne scholars working on an illustrated account of Hawthorne on art, Professor Rita Gollin of the State University of New York, Geneseo, and John L. Idol, Jr., of Clemson University. We are also grateful for the expert advice of Professors Francis L. Richardson and Barbara S. Groseclose of the Division of the History of Art, Ohio State University.

We acknowledge assistance from the libraries of Case Western Reserve University, the University of Chicago, Harvard University, the University of Illinois, Indiana University, the University of Michigan, Oberlin College, Pennsylvania State University, Rutgers University, and the Free Library of Philadelphia. The following librarians and scholars have provided assistance: Nina Myatt, Antioch College Library; Arthur Monke, Bowdoin College Library; Elizabeth Maxfield-Miller and Marcia Moss, Concord, Massachusetts; Irene Norton, the Essex Institute, Salem, Massachusetts; Barbara Bennett, the Georgia Historical Society; Raymona Hull, Indiana, Pennsylvania; William N. Copeley and Jane Johnson, the New Hampshire Historical Society; and Thomas Cooley, Edward Mancini, Julian Markels, John M. Muste, and Jacqueline Sisson, the Ohio State University.

Special acknowledgment is made for the work of Laurie Beringer-Yek, Joyce Heter, and Natalie Mann, undergraduate assistants at the Ohio State University. Jessica Rubinstein, graduate research assistant to the editors, is responsible for the index, and for many other felicities of the work.

For permission to edit the manuscript material of the *French and Italian Notebooks* and the Diaries of 1858 and 1859, we thank the Pierpont Morgan Library; the Henry W. and Albert A. Berg Collection, New York Public Library, Astor, Lenox and Tilden Foundations; the Henry E. Huntington

ACKNOWLEDGMENTS

Library; and the Bancroft Library, University of California, Berkeley. For allowing us to quote from other manuscripts we also thank them, as well as the libraries of Boston College, Bowdoin College, the Essex Institute, Harvard College, the New Hampshire Historical Society, St. Lawrence University, the University of Virginia, Yale University, and the Boston Public Library.

We gratefully acknowledge the support of the following divisions of the Ohio State University: the Department of English, the Graduate School, the University Libraries, and the Research Foundation.

The Editors.

CONTENTS

THE FRENCH AND ITALIAN
NOTEBOOKS

I

[112] Hôtel du Louvre, Paris, Jany 6th, Wednesday.

BENNOCH came to take tea with us on Monday evening, being his first visit since we came to London, and
likewise his [1st 114] farewell visit on our leaving for
the Continent. He keeps up a manly courage and aspect of
cheerfulness; but it is easy to see that he is a very different
man from the joyous one whom I knew a few months since;
and whatever may be his future fortune he will never get all
the sunshine back again. There is a more determinate shadow
upon him now, I think, than immediately after his misfor-
tunes; the cold, equable truth weighs down upon him, and
makes him sensible that the good days of his life have
probably all been enjoyed, and that the rest is likely to be an
endurance, not an enjoyment. His temper is still sweet and
warm, yet, I half fancy, not wholly unacidulated by his
troubles; but now I have written it, I decide that is not so, and
blame myself for surmising it. But it seems most unnatural
that so buoyant and expansive a character should have fallen
into the helplessness of commercial misfortune; it is most grievous to hear his manly and cheerful allusions to it, and even
his jokes upon it; as, for example, when we suggested how
pleasant it would be to have him accompany us to Paris, and
he jestingly spoke of the personal restraint under which he

now lived. On his departure, Julian [2nd 114] and I walked a good way down Oxford-street and Holborn with him, and I took leave of him with the truest wishes for his welfare.

On Tuesday morning (our dozen trunks, and half dozen carpet bags being all ready packed and labelled) we began to get up two or three hours before light. Two cabs were at the door by ½ past 6; and at seven, we set out for the London Bridge station, while it was still almost pitch dark, and bitter cold. There were already many people in the streets, growing more numerous as we drove city-ward; and in Newgate-street, there were such a number of market-carts that we almost came to a dead-lock with some of them. At the station, we found several persons sitting round the fire of the waiting-room, waiting apparently for the departure of the same train in which we were going. Since I came to England, there has hardly been a morning when I should less willingly have bestirred myself before daylight; so sharp and bitter was the atmosphere. We set out at ½ past eight, having taken through tickets to Paris, by way of Folkestone and Boulogne. A foot-[115]warmer (a long, flat, tin-utensil, full of hot-water) was put into the carriage, just before we started; but it did not make us more than half comfortable, and the frost soon began to cloud the windows and shut out the prospect; so that we could only glimpse at the green fields—immortally green, whatever winter can do against them—and at here and there a stream or pool with the ice forming on its borders. It was the first cold weather of a very mild season. The snow began to fall in scattered and almost invisible flakes; and it seemed as if we had staid our English welcome out, and were to find nothing genial and hospitable there, any more. At Folkestone, we were deposited at a railway-station close upon a shingly-beach, on which the sea broke in foam, and which Julian reported as strewn with shells and star-fish; behind, was the town, with, I believe, an old church in the midst; and, close at hand, the pier, where lay the steamer in which we were to embark. But the air was so wintry that I had no heart to explore the town or pick up shells with Julian on the beach; so we kept within doors, during the two hours of our stay, now and then looking out of the windows at a fishing-boat or two, as they pitched and rolled with an ugly and irregular motion, [116] such as this British channel generally communicates to the craft that navigate it.

At about one °clock we went on board, and were soon under steam, at a rate that quickly showed a long line of the white cliffs of Albion behind us. It is a very dusky white, by the by; and the cliffs themselves do not seem, at a distance, to be of very imposing height, and have too even an outline to be picturesque. As we increased our distance from England, the French coast came more and more distinctly in sight, with a low, wavy outline, not very well worth looking at, except because it was the coast of France. Indeed, I looked at it but little; for the wind was very bleak and boisterous; and, as my wife had to stay on deck with Rosebud (who would not go below for fear of sickness) I gave her one of my outside garments, and went below, after establishing her and the rest of the party amidships. She got a pea-jacket or two from the sailors, and was as comfortable as could be reasonably expected. She felt no sea-sickness; neither did Una; neither, as he affirms, did Julian, though his blustering assertion of enjoyment sounded rather suspicious; but Rosebud was a little sea-shaken, [117] and Miss Shepherd looked quite desolate and patiently miserable. As for me, I found the cabin-fire very comfortable, though there was an awful show of wash-bowls, and several people were stretched on sofas, in a state of placid wretchedness. I drank a glass of brandy-and-water, hot, with sugar, and found this sea-passage the only enjoyable part of the day. Indeed, I have never suffered from sea-sickness, but had been somewhat apprehensive of this rough strait between England

and France, which seems to have more potency over people's stomachs than ten times the extent of sea, in other quarters. Our passage was of two hours, a little more or less, at the end of which we landed on French soil, and found ourselves immediately in the clutches of the Custom House officers, who, however, merely made a momentary examination of my passport, and allowed us to pass without so much as opening one of our carpet-bags. The great bulk of our luggage had been registered through to Paris, for examination after our arrival there.

We left Boulogne (of which I saw very little, and have forgotten even that) in about an hour after our arrival; when it was already a darkening twilight. The weather had grown colder than ever, since our arrival in [118] sunny France, and the night was now setting in, wickedly bleak and dreary. The frost hardened upon the carriage-windows in such thickness that I could scarcely scratch a peep-hole through it; but, from such glimpses as I could catch, the aspect of the country seemed pretty much to resemble the December aspect of my dear native-land;—broad, bare, brown fields, with streaks of snow at the foot of ridges, and along fences, or in the furrows of ploughed soil. There was ice, wherever there happened to be water to form it. We had feet-warmers in the carriage, but the cold crept in nevertheless; and I do not remember, hardly, in my life, a more disagreeable piece of a journey than this, my first advance into French territory. My impression of France will always be, that it is an Arctic region. At any season of the year, the tract over which we passed yesterday must be an uninteresting one, as regards its natural features; and the only adornment (as far as I could observe) which art has given it, consists in straight rows of very stiff-looking and slender-stemmed trees. In the dusk, they resembled poplar-trees, but I suppose they were something else.

[119] Weary, and frost-bitten, morally, if not physically, we

reached Amiens in three or four hours; and here I underwent much botheration from the French railway-officials and attendants, who, I believe, did not mean to incommode me, but rather to forward my purposes as far as they well could. If they would speak slowly and distinctly, I might understand them well enough, being perfectly familiar with the written language, and knowing the principles of its pronunciation; but, in their customary speech, it sounds like a mere string of gabble. When left to myself, therefore, I get into great difficulties; but as Miss Shepard speaks the language well, and my wife likewise, though long out of practice, they soon come to my relief. Nevertheless, it gives a taciturn personage, like myself, a new conception as to the value of speech, even to him, when he finds himself unable either to speak or understand. Finally, being advised on all hands to go to the Hôtel du Rhin, we were carried thither by an omnibus, rattling over a rough pavement through an invisible and frozen town; and on our arrival were ushered into a handsome *salon*, as chill as a tomb. They made a little bit of a wood fire for us, in a low [120] and deep chimney-hole, which let a hundred times more heat escape up the flue than it sent into the room. We took the waiter's advice by going down into the dining-room, where we found a comfortable coal-fire, and ate a good supper of mutton-cutlets; then, returning to our frosty saloon, we shivered over the fire till bedtime, and shivered in feather-beds and under *duvets* (a strange kind of coverture, apparently half down or fine feathers, and half air) till morning. Really, I do not know when I have been so utterly miserable as on this journey; and sooty, misty England seemed a kind and genial region in comparison.

In the morning, I got up, and went through my dressing-operations, all in a shiver. We breakfasted in the warm dining-room, (the only warm place I had yet found in France,) and, shortly after, sallied out to see the Cathedral. The aspect of the old French town was very different from any thing English; whiter, infinitely cleaner; higher and narrower houses, the entrance to most of which seemed to be through a great gateway, affording admission into a central court-yard; a public square, with a statue in the middle, and another statue in a neighboring street. We [121] met priests, in three-cornered hats, long frock-coats, and knee-breeches; also, soldiers, and gens-darmes, and peasants and children, clattering over the pavements in wooden shoes. It makes a great impression of outlandishness, to see the signs over the shop-doors in a foreign tongue. If the cold had not been such as to dull my sense of novelty, and make all my perceptions torpid, I should have taken in a set of new impressions and enjoyed them very much. As it was, I cared little for what I saw, but yet had life enough left to enjoy the Cathedral of Amiens, which has many features unlike the English cathedrals, which alone I have hitherto seen.

The Cathedral stands in the midst of the cold, white town, and has a high-shouldered look to a spectator accustomed to English minsters, which cover a great space of ground in proportion to their height. The impression the latter give is of magnitude and mass; this French Cathedral strikes you as lofty. The exterior is venerable, though but little time-worn by the action of the atmosphere; and statues still keep their places in numerous niches, almost as perfect as when first placed there, in the thirteenth century, I suppose. [122] The principal doors are deep, elaborately-wrought, pointed arches; and the interior of the Cathedral seemed to us, at the moment, as grand as any that we had seen, and to afford as vast an idea of included space; it being of such an airy height, and there being no screen betwixt the chancel and nave, as in all the English cathedrals. I never saw such lofty arches as these that are supported by the tall, clustered columns of this cathedral. We saw the difference, too, betwixt a church in which the same form of worship, for which it was originally built, is still kept up, and those of England, where it has been superseded for centuries; for here, in the recess of every arch of the side aisles, beneath each lofty window, there was a chapel, dedicated to some saint, and adorned with great marble sculptures of the crucifixion, and with pictures—execrably bad, in all cases—and various kinds of gilding and ornamentation. Immensely tall wax candles stand before the altars of these chapels; and before one sat a woman with a great supply of tapers, one of which was lighted. I suppose these were to be lighted as offerings to the saints, by the true believers. Artificial flowers were hung at some of the shrines, or placed under glass. In every chapel, moreover, there was [123] a confessional, a little oaken structure about as big as a century-box, with a closed part for the priest to sit in, and an open one for the penitent to kneel in, and speak through the open work in the priest's closet. Monuments, mural and others, to long departed worthies, and images of the Savior, the virgin, and saints, were numerous everywhere about the church; and in the chancel there was a great deal of quaint and curious sculpture, fencing in the Holy of Holies, where the high altar stands. There is not much painted glass; one or two very rich and beautiful rose-windows however, that looked antique, and the great eastern window, which I think is modern. The pavement of the Cathedral has probably never been renewed, as one piece of work, since the structure was erected, and is footworn by the successive generations, though still in excellent repair. I saw one of the small, square stones in it, bearing the date of 1597, and no doubt there are a thousand older ones. It was gratifying to see the Cathedral in such good condition, without any traces of recent repair; and it is perhaps a mark of difference between French and English character, that the Revolution in the former country, though all religious worship disappeared [124] before it, does not seem to have caused

such violence to ecclesiastical monuments, as the Reformation
and the reign of Puritanism, in the latter. I did not see a
mutilated shrine, or even a broken-nosed image, in the whole
cathedral. But probably the very rage of the English fanatics
against idolatrous tokens, and their smashing blows at them,
was a symptom of sincerer religious faith than the French
were capable of. These last did not care enough about their
Savior to beat down his crucified image; and they preserved
the works of sacred art for the sake of what beauty there was
in them.

While we were in the Cathedral, we saw several persons (all
of them women, I think) kneeling at their devotions, on the
steps of the chancel and elsewhere. One dipt her fingers in the
holy water at the entrance; by the by, I looked into the stone
basin that held it, and saw it full of ice. Could not all that
sanctity at least keep it thawed? Priests—fat, jolly, mean-looking fellows, in white robes—went hither and thither, but did
not interrupt or accost us. There were other peculiarities, which
I suppose I shall see more of in my visits to other churches;
but now we were all glad to make [125] our visit as brief as
possible, the atmosphere of the Cathedral being so bleak,
and its stone pavement so icy cold beneath our feet. We
returned to the Hôtel; and having paid the bill, (amounting
to a little more than three Napoleons,) the chamber-maid
brought me a book, in which she asked me to inscribe my
name, age, profession, country, destination, and the authoriza-
tion under which I travelled. After the freedom of an English
hotel, (so much greater than even that of an American, where
they make you disclose your name,) this is not so pleasant.

We left Amiens at ½ past one; and I can tell as little of
the country between that place and Paris, as between Boulogne
and Amiens. The windows of our railway carriage were already frosted with dirty French breath, when we got into it;
and the ice grew thicker and thicker continually. I tried at

various times to scratch or rub a peep-hole through; but the ice immediately shot its crystallized tracery over it again; and, indeed, there was little or nothing to make it worth while to look out on so bleak a scene. Now and then a chateau, too far off for its characteristics to be seen; now and then a church, with a [126] tall gray tower, and a little peak on top; here and there a village, or a town, which we could not see. At sunset, there was just the clear, cold, wintry sky, which I remember so well in America, but have never seen in England. At five, we reached Paris, and were suffered to take a conveyance to the Hôtel du Louvre, without any examination of the little luggage we had with us. Arriving at the Hôtel we took a suite of apartments *au troisieme*, which will cost a little more than 25 francs per day; and the waiter immediately lighted a wax candle in each separate room, thereby saddling us with four francs more. We might have dined at the table d'hôte, but preferred the restaurant connected with the hotel. It is a terrible business, feeding so many mouths, and especially children, and most especially a boy, at a French table. We had a soup, some lamb-cutlets (and a very young and diminutive lamb it must have been,) and a chicken with truffles, ending with some ice-cream, which I little thought to have eaten in this Arctic weather. For drink, a half bottle of Burgundy. All the dishes were very delicate, and a vast change from the simple English sys[127]tem, with its joints, shoulders, beef-steakes and chops; but I doubt whether English cookery, for the very reason that it is so gross, is not better for man's moral and spiritual nature, than French. In the former case, you know that you are gratifying your coarsest animal needs and propensities, and are duly ashamed of it; but, in dealing with these French delicacies, you delude yourself into the idea that you are cultivating your taste while filling your belly. This last, however, it needs a good deal of perseverance to accomplish.

In the Cathedral at Amiens, there were printed lists of acts of devotion, posted on the columns, such as prayers at the shrines of certain saints, whereby plenary indulgencies might be gained. It is to be observed, however, that all these external forms were required to be accompanied with true penitence and religious devotion.

Hôtel du Louvre, Jany 8th, Friday.

It was so awfully cold that I really felt little or no curiosity to see Paris; and besides I had a cold in my head, which, probably, was the reason that my nose fell a-bleeding, the morning after our arrival. On this latter account, it was necessary that my wife and Miss Shepard should go with[128]out me to get our luggage (which had been registered through from London) passed through the Custom House. Until after one °clock, therefore, I knew nothing of Paris except the lights which I had seen beneath our window, the evening before, far, far downward, in the narrow Rue St Honoré; and the rumble of the wheels, which continued later than I was awake to hear it, and began again before light. I could see, too, tall houses, that seemed to be occupied in every story, and that had windows on the steep roofs; one of these houses is six stories high. This Rue St. Honoré is one of the old streets in Paris, and is that in which Henry IV was assassinated; but it has not, in this part of it, the aspect of antiquity.

After my wife's return, we all went out and walked along the Rue de Rivoli, in quest of our dinners; for we had determined, in consideration of the many mouths we have to feed, not to dine at the Restaurant of the Hotel, but at some less splendid one in the vicinity. We are here right in the midst of Paris, and close to whatever is best known to those who hear or read about it; the Louvre being right across the street; the

Palais Royal but a little way off; the Tuilleries joining on to the Louvre; the Place de la Concorde just beyond, verging on which is the [129] Champs Elysées. We looked about us for a suitable dining-place, and soon found the Restaurant des Echelles, (I am not sure that I spell it correctly) where we entered at a venture, and were courteously received by a waiter. It has a handsomely furnished saloon, much set off with gilding and mirrors; and (like, I presume, most of the eating-houses in this vicinity) it appears to be frequented by Englishmen or Americans, its carte—a bound volume—being printed in English as well as French. It was too late for dejeuners, and too early for dinner; so that there was but one other guest in the salôn. The waiter joined two tables together, to accommodate our large party; and the children immediately fell to work upon the long rolls of delicious bread which were placed at every plate. He recommended some cold *paté de foie gras*; and I think we all, except Julian and Rosebud, ate some and found it very good; and for the young people, we ordered some mutton-chops, of which Julian made no complaint, except that there was not half enough for his dinner. I really think he would eat a whole sheep. I had, moreover, a bottle of rather thin claret, which I found excellent for quenching thirst, and wholly ineffective on the brain. I had scarcely begun to eat and drink, before my nose set to bleeding [130] again; and thus my blood must be reckoned among the rivers of human gore which have been shed in Paris, and especially on the Place de la Concorde, where the guillotine used to stand.

I think the above-mentioned dishes made up our dinner, for which I paid eleven francs, and thought it a very reasonable charge. It was now nearly four °clock, and too late to visit the Louvre, or to do anything else but walk a little way along the street. The splendor of Paris, so far as I have seen, takes me altogether by surprise; such stately edifices, prolonging themselves in unwearying magnificence and beauty, and, ever and anon, a long vista of a street, with a column rising at the end of it, or a triumphal arch, wrought in memory of some grand event. The light stone, or stucco, wholly untarnished by smoke and soot, puts London to the blush, if a blush could be seen through its dingy face; but, indeed, London is paltry, despicable, not to be mentioned in the same day, nor compared even for the purpose of ridiculing it, with Paris. I never knew what a palace was, till I had a glimpse of the Louvre and the Tuilleries;—never had any idea of a city gratified, till I trod these stately streets. The life of the scene, too, [1st 132] is infinitely more picturesque than London, with its monotonous throng of smug faces and black coats; whereas, here, you see soldiers and priests; policemen in cocked hats; Zouaves, with turbans, long mantles, and bronzed, half-Moorish faces; and a great many people whom you perceive to be outside of your experience, and know them ugly to look at, and fancy them villainous. Truly, I have no sympathies towards the French people; their eyes do not win me, nor do their glances melt and mingle with mine. But they do grand and beautiful things, in the architectural way; and I am grateful for it. The Place de la Concord is the most splendid square, large enough for a nation to erect trophies of all its triumphs there; and one side of it is the Tuilleries, on the opposite side the Champ Elyssée, and on a third the Seine, adown which we saw large cakes of ice floating beneath the arches of a bridge. The Champ Elysée, so far as I saw it, had not a grassy soil beneath its trees, but the bare earth, white and dusty. The very dust, if I saw nothing else, would assure me that I was out of England. We had time only to take this little walk, when it began to grow dusk; and being so pitilessly cold, we hurried back to our Hôtel. Thus far, I think, what I have seen of Paris is wholly un[2nd 132]like what I expected, but very like an imaginary picture which I had conceived of Saint Petersburg;

new, bright, magnificent, and desperately cold. A great part of this architectural splendor is due to the present Emperor, who has wrought a great change on the aspect of the city within a very few years. A traveller, if he look at the thing selfishly, ought to wish him a long reign, and arbitrary power; since he makes it his policy to illustrate his capital with palatial edifices, which are better for a stranger to look at than for his own people to pay for.

We have spent to-day chiefly in seeing, or glimpsing, at some of the galleries of the Louvre. I will not be fool enough to attempt a description; but I must confess that the vast and beautiful edifice struck me far more than the pictures, sculpture, and curiosities which it contains; the shell more than the meat inside. I never saw (nor could have seen, as none such exist elsewhere) such noble suites of rooms and halls as those through which we first passed, containing Egyptian, and, farther onward, Greek and Roman antiquities; the walls cased with variegated marbles, the cielings glowing with beautiful pictures, the whole prolonged into infinite vis[133]tas by looking-glasses, that seemed like vacancy, and multiplied everything forever. The picture-rooms are not so splendid, and the pictures themselves did not greatly win upon me, in this one day. Many artists were employed in copying them, especially in the rooms hung with the productions of French painters; not a few of these copyists were females; most of them were young men, picturesquely moustached and bearded, but some were elderly, who, it was pitiful to think, had passed through life without so much success as now to paint pictures of their own.

From the pictures, we went into a suite of rooms, where are preserved many relics of the ancient and later kings of France; more relics of the elder ones, indeed, than I supposed had remained extant through the Revolution. The French seem to like to keep memorials of whatever they do, and of whatever their forefathers have done, even if it be ever so little to their credit; and perhaps they do not take matters sufficiently to heart to detest anything that has ever been. What surprised me most were the golden sceptre, and the magnificent sword, and the other gorgeous relics of Charlemagne, a personage whom I have always associated with a sheepskin cloak. There [134] were suits of armor and weapons that had been worn and handled by a great many of the French kings; and a religious book that had belonged to Saint Louis; a dressing-glass, most richly set with precious stones, which formerly stood on the table of Catherine de Medici, and in which I saw my own face where hers had been; and there were a thousand other treasures, just as well worth mentioning as these. If each monarch could have been summoned from Hades to reclaim his own relics, we should have had the halls full of the old Charleses and Childerics, Bourbons and Capets, Henrys and Louises, snatching with ghostly hands at sceptres, swords, armour, mantles; and Napoleon would have seen, apparently, almost everything that personally belonged to him; his coat, his cocked hats, his camp-desk, his field bed, his knives, forks and plates, and even a lock of his hair. I must let it all go; these things cannot be reproduced by pen and ink.

Hôtel du Louvre, Jan.ʸ 9ᵗʰ, Saturday.

Last evening, Mr. Husson, whom we had known in Liverpool, called; and, simultaneously, Miss McDaniel, a New England lady, of plain, Massachusetts manners and appearance, who has been living here with her mother, nearly two years. The daughter was for[135]merly at Brook Farm. The mother suffered so much from sea-sickness that she is afraid to return to America; and so this poor woman is kept here against her will, and without enjoyment, and, as I judge, in narrow circumstances. It is a singular misfortune. She told me that she had been at the Louvre but twice since her arrival, and did not know Paris at all. After their departure, Mr. Fezandie, an acquaintance of Miss Shepard, and her instructor during her residence in Paris, called. He spoke very freely respecting the Emperor, and the hatred entertained against him in France, but said that he is more powerful (that is, more firmly fixed as a ruler) than ever the first Napoleon was. We, who look back upon him as one of the eternal facts of the past, a great boulder in history, cannot well estimate how momentary and unsubstantial the Great Captain may have appeared, to those who beheld his rise out of obscurity. They never, perhaps, took the reality of his career fairly into their minds, before it was over. The present Emperor, I believe, has already been as long in possession of the supreme power as his uncle was. I should like to see him, and may perhaps do so, as he is our neighbor across the way.

[136] This morning, Miss Mitchell, the celebrated astronomical lady of Nantucket, called. She had brought a letter of introduction to me, while Consul; and her business now was, to see if we could take her as one of our party to Rome, whither she likewise is bound. We readily consented; for she seems to be a simple, strong, healthy-humored woman, who will not fling herself as a burden on our shoulders; and my only wonder is, that a person evidently so able to take care of herself should care about having an escort.

We issued forth, at about eleven, and went down the Rue St Honoré, which is narrow, and has houses of five or six stories on either side, between which runs the street like a gully in a rock. One face of our hotel borders on this street. After going a good way, we came to an intersection with another street, the name of which I forget; but, at this point, Ravaillac sprang at the carriage of Henry IV, and plunged his dagger into him. As we went down the Rue St. Honoré, it grew more and more thronged, and with a meaner class of people; the houses still were high, and without the shabbiness of exterior that distinguishes the old part of London, being of [137] light colored stone, or stucco; but I never saw anything that so much came up to my idea of a swarming city as this narrow, crowded and rumbling street. Thence we turned into the Rue de St Denis, which is one of the oldest streets in Paris, and is said to have been first marked out by the track of the Saint's footsteps, when, after his martyrdom, he walked along it without his head, in quest of a burial-place. This legend may account for any crookedness of the street; for it could not reasonably be asked of a headless man that he should walk straight. Through some other indirections, we at last found the Rue Bergere, down which I went with Julian in quest of Hottinguer & Co., the Bankers; while Mamma, Miss Shepard, Una, & Rosebud, went along the Boulevards towards the Church de la Madeleine. I found the bankers, with some difficulty, and not by any visible sign, but was directed to it, within a gateway, by a Concierge of whom I inquired; and a clerk, who spoke English, received my letter of credit and gave me fifty Napoleons upon it, done up in a neat and weighty little rouleau. This business accomplished, Julian and I threaded our way back, and overtook Mamma and the rest of the party, still a good distance from [138] the Madeleine. I know not why the Boulevards are called so. They seem to be a succession of broad walks through broad streets, and were much thronged with people, most of whom appeared to be more bent on pleasure than business. The sun, long before this, had come out brightly, and gave us the first genial and comfortable sensations which we have had in Paris.

Approaching the Madeleine, we found it a most beautiful church, that might have been adapted from heathendom

to Catholicism; for on each side there is a range of magnificent pillars, unequalled except by those of the Parthenon.
A mourning coach, splendidly arrayed in black and silver,
was drawn up at the steps; and the front of the church was
hung with black cloth, which covered the whole entrance.
However, seeing other people going in, we entered along
with them. I never saw anything—in the guise of a church,
at least—so glorious and gorgeous as the Madeleine; the
entrance to the nave is beneath a most stately arch; and three
arches of equal height, open from the nave to the side-aisles,
and at the end of the nave is another great arch, rising with
a vaulted half-dome over the high altar. The pillars, supporting these [139] arches, are Corinthian (I believe) with richly
sculptured capitals; and wherever gilding might adorn the
church, it is lavished like sunshine; and within the sweeps
of the arches, there are fresco paintings of sacred subjects,
and a beautiful picture covering the hollow of the vault over
the altar; all this besides much sculpture, and especially a
group above and around the high altar, representing the
Magdalen, smiling down upon angels and archangels, some
of whom are kneeling, and shadowing themselves with their
heavy marble wings. There is no such thing as making my
page glow with the most distant idea of the magnificence of
this church, in its details, and in its whole. It was founded
as a church, a hundred, or two hundred years ago; then
Buonaparte contemplated transforming it into a Temple of
Victory, or building it anew as one. The restored Bourbon
re-made it into a church; but it still has a heathenish look,
and will never lose it.

When we entered, we saw a crowd of people, all pressing
forward towards the high altar, before which burned fifty—
or it may be a hundred—wax lights, some of which were six
or seven feet high; and altogether [140] they shone like a
galaxy of stars. In the middle of the nave, moreover, there

was another galaxy of wax candles, burning around an immense pall of black velvet, embroidered with silver, which seemed to cover, not merely a coffin, but a sarcophagus, or something still more huge. The organ was grumbling forth a deep, lugubrious base, accompanied with heavy chanting of priests, out of which sometimes rose the clear, young voices of choristers, like light flashing out of the gloom. The church, between the arches along the nave, and round the altar, was hung with broad expanses of black cloth; and all the priests, or whatever were the holy personages who stood on the steps of the altar, had their sacred vestments covered with black. They looked exceedingly well. I never saw anything half so well got up upon the stage. Some of these ecclesiastical figures were very stately and noble, and knelt, and bowed, and bore aloft the cross, and swung the censer, in a way that I liked to see. These ceremonies of the Catholic church were a magnificent work of art, or perhaps a true growth of man's religious nature, and so long as men felt their original meaning, they must have [141] been full of awe and glory. Being of another parish, I looked on coldly, but not irreverently, and was glad to see a funeral service so well performed, and very glad when it was over. What struck me as very singular, the person who performed the part, usually performed by a verger, keeping order among the audience, had on a gold embroidered scarf, a cocked hat, and, I believe, a sword, and the air of a military man. Before the close of the service, a contribution-box, or, rather, a black velvet-bag, was handed about by this military verger; and I gave Julian a franc to put in, though I did not in the least know for what. Issuing from the church, we inquired of two or three persons who was the distinguished defunct at whose obsequies we had been assisting; for we had some hope that it might be Rachel, who died last week, and is still above ground. But it proved to be only a Madame Martel, or some such name, whom nobody had ever before heard of. I forgot to say that her coffin was taken from beneath the illuminated pall, and carried out of the church before us.

When we left the Madeleine, we took our way to the Place de la Concorde, and thence through the Elysian Fields (which I suppose is the French idea of [142] Heaven) to Bonaparte's Triumphal arch, in the Place d'Etoile. The Champs Elysées may look pretty in summer; though I suspect they must be somewhat dry and artificial at whatever season, the trees being slender and scraggy, never healthy, and requiring to be renewed, every few years. The soil is not genial to them. The strangest peculiarity of this place, however, to eyes fresh from moist and verdant England, is, that there is not one blade of grass in the whole Elysian fields; nothing but hard clay, apparently, now covered with white dust. It gives the whole scene the air of being a contrivance of man, in which Nature has either not been invited to take any part, or has declined to do so. There were merry-go-rounds, wooden horses, and such provision for children's amusements, among the trees; and booths, and tables of cake-and-candy women; and restaurants on the borders of the wood; but very few people there, and doubtless we can form no idea of what the scene might become, when alive with French gaiety and vivacity.

As we walked onward, our children nibbling gingerbread and cakes, the Triumphal Arch began to loom up in the distance, looking huge and massive, though still [143] a long way off. It was not, however, till we stood almost beneath it, that we really felt the grandeur and stateliness of this great arch, including so large a space of the blue sky in its airy sweep. At a distance, it impresses the spectator with its solidity; nearer, with the lofty vacancy beneath it. There is a spiral staircase within one of the immense legs of this four-fronted arch; and, climbing wearily upward, (lighted by a lanthern which the doorkeeper's wife gave us) we had a bird's eye view of Paris, much obscured by smoke or mist. Several interminable avenues shoot with painful directness right towards the arch.

On our way homeward, we visited the Place de Vendome, in the centre of which is a tall column, sculptured from top to bottom, all over the pedestal, and all over the shaft, and with Napoleon himself at the summit. The shaft is wreathed round and roundabout with representations of what, as far as I could distinguish up the height of the column, seemed to be the Emperor's victories. It has a very rich effect. At the foot of the column, we saw wreaths of artificial flowers, suspended there no doubt by some admirer of Napoleon, still ardent enough to expend a franc or two in this queer [144] way. By this time, we were all tired; and Rosebud's little legs, which had bestrode several miles during the day, could scarcely drag themselves one after the other. We went to the same Restaurant, in the Rue d'Echelle, where we had already dined twice, and there had another dinner; maccaroni soup, beefsteaks au pommes de terre, and volaille of fowl, with a bottle of Chablis, for seventeen francs and a half. This Parisian mode of living would have looked strangely to us, had we foreseen it out of the midst of our New England country-life; but it has its own enjoyment, and we take to it pleasantly enough for a time.

Hôtel du Louvre, Jany 10th, Sunday.

This morning, Paris looked as bleak as London, with clouds and rain; and when we issued forth, it seemed as if a cold, sullen agony were interposed between each separate atom of our bodies. In all my experience of bad atmospheres, methinks I never knew anything so atrocious as this. England has nothing to be compared with it. We had purposed going to the Cathedral of Notre Dame to-day; but the weather and walking were too unfavorable for a distant expedition; so Mamma, Julian, and I, merely went a[145]cross the street to the Louvre, while Una, who was much wearied with yesterday's rambles, staid at home in our saloon. Baby and Miss Shepard had gone together to visit Miss Macdaniel, intending to dine at a Restaurant by themselves.

Our principal object, to-day, was to see the pencil-drawings by eminent artists. Of these the Louvre has a very rich collection, occupying many apartments, and comprising sketches by Annibal Caracci, Claude, Raphael, Leonardo di Vinci, Michael Angelo, Rubens, Rembrandt, and almost all the other great masters, whether French, Italian, Dutch, or whatever else; the earliest dawnings of their great pictures, when they had the glory of their pristine idea directly before their mind's eye— that idea which inevitably became overlaid with their own handling of it, in the finished painting. No doubt, the painters themselves had often a happiness in these rude, off-hand sketches, which they never felt again in the same work, and which resulted in disappointment after they had done their best. To an artist, the collection must be intensely interesting; to myself, it was merely curious, and soon grew wearisome. In the same suite of apartments, [146] there is a collection of miniatures, some of them very exquisite, and absolutely life-like, on their small scale. I observed two of Franklin, both good, and picturesque; one of them especially so, with its cloudlike white hair. I do not think we have produced a man so interesting to contemplate, in many points of view, as he. Most of our great men are of a character that I find it impossible to warm into life by thought, and by lavishing any amount of sympathy upon them; not so Franklin, who had a great deal of common and uncommon human-nature in him. Much of the time, while my wife was looking at the drawings, I sat observing the crowd of Sunday visitors. They were generally of a lower class than those of week days; private soldiers, in a variety of uniforms, and for the most part ugly little men, but decorous and well-behaved. I saw medals on many of their breasts, denoting Crimean service; some wore the English medal, with Queen Victoria's head upon it. A blue coat, with red, baggy trowsers, was the most usual uniform. Some had short-breasted coats, made in the same style as those of the first Napoleon, which we had seen in the preceding rooms. The police-men, distributed pretty abundantly about the rooms, themselves looked mili[147]tary, wearing cocked-hats and swords. There were many women of the middling classes; some, evidently, of the lowest, but clean and decent, in colored gowns and caps; and laboring men, citizens, Sunday gentlemen; young artists, too, no doubt, looking with educated eyes at these art-treasures; and, I think, as a general thing, each male was mated with a female. The soldiers, however, came in pairs or little squads, unaccompanied by women. I did not much like any of these French faces; and yet I am not sure that there is not more resemblance between them and the American physiognomy, than between the latter and the English. The women are not pretty; but in all ranks above the lowest, they have a trained expression that supplies the place of beauty.

I was wearied to death with the drawings, and began to have that dreary and desperate feeling which has often come upon me, when the sights last longer than my capacity for receiving them. As our time in Paris, however, is brief and precious, we next enquired our way to the galleries of sculpture; and these alone are of astounding extent, reaching, I should think, all round one quadrangle of the Louvre, on the basement-floor. [148] Hall after hall opened interminably before us, and on either side of us, paved and encrusted with variegated and beautifully polished marble, relieved against which stand the antique statues and groups, interspersed with great urns, and vases, sarcophagi, altars, tablets, busts of historic personages, and all manner of shapes of marble, which consummate art has transmuted into precious stones. Not that I really did feel much impressed by any of this sculpture, nor saw more than two or three things which I thought very beautiful; but whether it be good or no, I suppose the world has nothing better, unless it be a world-renowned statue or two in Italy. At all events, it shamed the sculpture gallery of the British Museum out of sight; and I was even more struck by the skill and ingenuity of the French in arranging these sculptural remains, than by the value of the sculptures themselves. The galleries, I should judge, have been recently prepared, and on a most magnificent system, the adornments being yet by no means completed; for besides the floor and wall-casings of rich, polished marble, the vaulted cielings of some of the apartments are painted in fresco, causing them to glow as if the sky were opened. It must be owned, [149] however, that the statuary—often time-worn and darkened from its original brilliancy by weather-stains—does not suit well, as furniture, for such splendid rooms. When we see a magnificence of modern finish about them, we recognize that most of these statues were thrown down from their pedestals, hundreds of years ago, and have been battered and externally degraded; and though whatever spiritual beauty they ever had may still remain, yet this is not made more apparent by the contrast betwixt the new gloss of modern upholstery, and their rusty, even if immortal, grace. I rather think the English have given really the most hospitable reception to poor maimed Theseus, and his broken-nosed, broken-legged, headless companions, flouting them with no gorgeous fittings-up.

By this time, poor Julian (who, with his taste for art yet undeveloped, is [*word deleted*] the companion of all our visits to sculpture and picture galleries, [*three-quarters line deleted*])—Julian was woefully hungry, and for bread we had given him a stone,—not one stone, but a thousand. We returned to the Hôtel; and it being too damp and raw to go to our Restaurant d'Eschelle, we took Una and Julian down with us to the [150] Restaurant of the Hotel. In my opinion, it would require less time to cultivate one's gastronomic tastes, than taste of any other kind; and, on the whole, I am not sure that a man could do a better thing than to afford himself a little discipline in this line. It is certainly throwing away the bounties of Providence to treat them as the English do, producing, from better materials than the French have to work upon, nothing but sirloins, joints, joints, steaks, steaks, steaks, chops, chops, chops, chops! We ate a soup, in which twenty kinds of vegetables were represented, and manifested each its own aroma; a fillet of stewed beef, which was ordered principally for Julian's benefit; and a fowl, in some form of delicate fricassée. We had a bottle of Chablis, and renewed ourselves, at the close of the banquet, with a plate of Chateaubriand ice. It was all very good, and we respected ourselves far more than if we had gorged a quantity of red roast-beef; but I am not quite sure that we were right.

Among the relics of Kings and Princes, I do not know that there was anything more interesting than a little brass cannon, two or three inches long, which had been a toy of the unfortunate Dauphin, son of Louis XVI. There was [151] a map—a hemisphere of the world—which his father had drawn for this poor boy; very neatly done, too. The sword of Louis XVI—a magnificent rapier, with a beautifully damasked blade, and a jewelled scabbard, but without a hilt, is likewise preserved; as is the hilt of Henry IV's sword. But it is useless to begin a catalogue of these things. What a collection it is, including Charlemagne's sword and sceptre and the last Dauphin's little toy-cannon, and so much between the two!

Hôtel du Louvre, Jany 11th, Monday.

This was another chill, raw day, characterized by a spite-fulness of atmosphere which I do not remember ever to have experienced in my own dear country. We meant to have visited the Hôtel des Invalides; but when my wife, Miss Shepard, Rosebud, and Una, got into an omnibus to go thither, Julian and I remained behind for want of room. We two, therefore, walked the Rue Rivoli, the Place de la Concorde, and the Champs Elysées, to the Rue de Beaujon, to the residence of the American Minister, where I wished to arrange about my passport. After speaking with the Secretary of Legation, we were ushered into the Minister's private room, where he received me with great kindness. Judge Mason is a heavy old gentleman in a morning-gown, with a [152] white head and a large red face, which wears an expression of dull amiability, not unmingled with a certain dignity. He did not rise from his arm-chair to greet me; a lack of ceremony which I imputed to the gout, feeling it impossible that he should have wilfully failed in courtesy to one of his twenty-five million sovereigns. His pipe lay on the mantel-piece before him, and he had the air of a man indulging himself freely at meal-times, and sleeping in his arm-chair after dinner. In response to some remark of mine about the shabby way in which our government treats its officials, pecuniarily, he gave a detailed account of his own troubles on that score; then expressed a hope that I had made a good thing out of my consulate, and inquired whether I had received a hint to resign—to which I replied that, for various reasons, I had resigned of my own accord, and before Mr. Buchanan's inauguration. We agreed, however, in disapproving the system of periodical change in

our foreign officials; and I remarked that a consul or an ambassador ought to be a citizen both of his native country and
of the one in which he resided, and that his possibility of
beneficial influence depended largely on his being so. Apropôs
to which, [153] Judge Mason said that he had once asked
a diplomatic friend, of long experience, what was the first
duty of a minister. "To love his own country, and to watch
over its interests," answered the diplomatist. "And his second
duty?" asked Judge Mason. "To love, and to promote the
interests of the country to which he is accredited," said his
friend. This is a very Christian and sensible view of the matter; but it can scarcely have happened once in our whole
diplomatic history, that a minister can have had time to overcome his first rude and ignorant prejudice against the country
of his mission; and if there were any suspicion of his having
done so, it would be held abundantly sufficient ground for his
recal. I like Judge Mason; a fat-brained, good-hearted, sensible
old man. The newspapers, I see, announce that he has sent
home his resignation, and, from the tone of his remarks, I
take it to be true, and am afraid the poor gentleman is going
back, with narrow means, to seek some poor office at home
for his livelihood. He regretted that I was not staying long
enough in Paris to take a family-dinner, my wife and me,
with Mrs. Mason and himself; and desiring my compliments
to the latter lady, I took my leave. The Secretary of Legation
[154] is a man of very different aspect and address from the
Minister; about thirty years old, dark-complexioned, with a
black moustache, handsome, with a courteous, but decided
air, like a man of society and the world. I should think the
heavy old judge would often need some spirit more alert than
his own. By the by, the Secretary's advice respecting my passport was just contrary to that of the Minister, and I decided
to take it. On the whole (though I am sorry for him) there is
no good reason why Uncle Sam should pay Judge Mason

seventeen thousand dollars a year for sleeping in the dignified post of Ambassador to France. The true ground of complaint is, that, whether he slept or waked, the result would be the same.

Julian and I returned along the Champs Elysées, and crossing the Seine, kept on our way by the river's brink, looking at the titles of books on the long lines of stalls that extend between the bridges. Novels, fairy-tales, dream-books, treatises of behavior and etiquette, collections of bon-mots and of songs, were interspersed with volumes in the old style of calf and gilt-binding, the works of the elder classics of French literature. A good many persons, of the poor classes, and of those apparently well to do, stopt [155] transitorily to look at these books. On the other side of the street was a range of tall edifices, with shops beneath, and the quick stir of French life hurrying, and babbling, and swarming along the sidewalk. The city was livelier, on this sombre and misty day, than ever London was, in its gayest sunshine. We passed two or three bridges, occurring at short intervals, and at last re-crossed the Seine by a bridge which oversteps the river from a point near the National Institute, and reaches the other side, not far from the Louvre. During most of the walk, Julian had been munching French gingerbread, which he bought in the Champs Elyseès, and along the bridges; tasting which, I desired never to taste any more. We reached our hotel, and had scarcely sat down before Mamma and her party came in, full of admiration at the magnificence of the Hôtel des Invalides, and the tomb of Napoleon.

Though the day was so disagreeable, we thought it not best to lose the remainder of it, and therefore set out, (mamma, Miss Sheperd, Baby, and I) to visit the Cathedral of Notre Dame. Una was tired, and remained at home, as did Julian, who wanted to draw a vase on the mantel-piece. The rest of us took a fiacre in the Place de Carrousel, and drove to the

door of the Cathedral. On entering, we found [156] the interior terribly shut off from view by the stagings erected for
the purpose of repairs. Penetrating from the Nave towards
the Chancel, an official personage signified to us that we must
first purchase a ticket for each grown person, at the price of
half-a franc each. This expenditure admitted us into a Chapel,
where we were taken in charge by a guide, who came down
upon us with an avalanche or cataract of French, descriptive
of a great many treasures reposited in this chapel. <It was
the sacristy.> I understood hardly more than one word in ten,
but gathered doubtfully that a bullet (which was shown us)
was the one that killed the late Archbishop of Paris, on the
floor of this Cathedral; also, that some gorgeously embroidered
vestments, which he drew forth, had been used at the coronation of Napoleon. <A mistake; it was the archbishop killed in
the insurrection of 1848. Two joints of his back-bone were
also shown.> There were two large, full-length portraits,
hanging aloft in the chapel, and a gold, or silver-gilt, or, at all
events, gilt image of the Virgin, as large as life, standing on a
pedestal. The guide had much to say about these, but understanding him so imperfectly, I have little to record.

The guide's supervision of us seemed not to extend beyond
this chapel, on quitting which, he gave us permission to go
where we pleased, only intimating a hope that [157] we
would not forget him; so I gave him half a franc, though
thereby violating an inhibition on the printed ticket of entrance. We had been much disappointed, at first, by the apparently narrow limits of the interior of this famous church;
but now, as we made our way round the choir, gazing into
chapel after chapel, each with its painted window, its crucifix,
its pictures, its confessional, and afterwards came back into
the nave, where arch rises above arch to the lofty roof, we
came to the conclusion that it was the most magnificent
Gothic edifice we had ever seen. It is the greatest of pities

that its grandeur and solemnity should just now be so infinitely marred by the workmen's boards, timber, and ladders, occupying the whole centre of the edifice, and screening all its best effects. It seems to have been already most richly ornamented, its roof being painted, and the capitals of the pillars gilded and their shafts ornamented in fresco; and no doubt it will shine out gorgeously, when all the repairs and adornments shall be completed. Even now, it gave to my actual sight what I have often tried to imagine in my visits to the English Cathedrals; the pristine glory of those edifices when they stood glowing with gold and picture, fresh from the architect's and adorner's hands. [158] The interior loftiness of Notre Dame, moreover, gives it a sublimity, which would swallow up anything that might look gewgawy in its ornamentation, were we to consider it, window by window, or pillar by pillar. It is an advantage of these vast edifices, rising over us and spreading about us in such a firmamental way, that we cannot spoil them by any pettiness of our own, but that they receive our pettiness into their own immensity. Every little fantasy finds its place and propriety in them, like a flower on the earth's broad bosom.

When we emerged from the Cathedral, we found it beginning to rain, or snow, or both; and as we had dismissed our fiacre at the door, and could find no other, we were at a loss what to do. We stood a few moments on the steps of the Hotel Dieu, looking up at the front of Notre Dame, with its twin towers, and its three, deep, pointed arches, piercing through a great thickness of stone, and throwing a cavern-like gloom around these entrances. I never saw so rich a front as this. Being so huge, and all of gray stone, it is carved and fretted with statues and innumerable devices, as cunningly as any ivory casket in which relics used to be kept. Its size did not so much impress me. The wicked chill of the air, and the increasing rain, now compelled [159] us to set out homeward on foot. We looked anxiously for a cab, but saw none; and called to passing omnibusses, but found them all full, or going in wrong directions. We invaded the little shop of a second-hand bookseller (a dirty hole, and of ill-odour) and staid there a considerable time, hoping for some means of escape, but finally had to plunge forth and paddle onward, through rain and mud, amid this old, ugly, and dirty quarter of Paris, till we reached the arcade along the Rue Rivoli. Thence we were under shelter all the way to our Hôtel. We went out no more, to-day, but dined in the Restaurant below; and sitting in the saloon after dinner, were accosted by Mr. and Mrs. Pickman, two natives of our own native town.

Hôtel du Louvre, Jan.ᵞ 12ᵗʰ, Tuesday.

This has been a bright day, as regards weather; but Mamma had taken cold from yesterday's muddy and rainy expedition to Notre Dame; and it is her enterprise, much more than mine, that impels us to see new things. I have therefore done little or nothing worth recording. After breakfast, I set out in quest of the Consul, and found him (Mr. Henry Spencer) up a court, at 51, Rue Caumartin, in an office rather smaller, I think, than mine at Liverpool, but to say the truth, a little more handsomely [160] furnished. I was received in the outer apartment by an elderly, brisk looking man, in whose air, respectful and subservient, and yet with a kind of authority in it, I recognized the Vice-Consul. He introduced me to Mr. Spencer, who sat writing in the inner room; a very gentlemanly, courteous, cool man of the world, whom I should take to be an excellent person for Consul in Paris. He tells me that he has resided here some years, although his occupancy of the consulate dates only from November last. Consulting him respecting my passport, he gave me what appear good reasons why I should get all the necessary visés here; for example, that the visé of a minister carries more weight than that of a consul, and especially that an Austrian Consul will never visé a passport unless he sees his minister's name upon it. Mr. Spencer has travelled much in Italy, and ought to be able to give me sound advice. His opinion was, that, at this season of the year, I had better go by steamer to Civita Vecchia, instead of landing at Leghorn and thence journeying to Rome. On this point I shall decide when the time comes. As I left the office, the Vice Consul informed me that there was a charge of five francs and some sous (a dollar, I suppose) for the Consul's visé; a tax that surprised me, the whole business of passports having been taken from Consuls before I quit[161]ted office, and the consular fee having been annulled even earlier. However, no doubt Mr. Spencer had a fair claim to my five francs; but, really, it is not half so pleasant to pay a consular fee as it used to be to receive it.

Afterwards, Julian and I walked to Nòtre Dame, the rich and magnificent front of which I viewed with more attention than yesterday. There are whole histories, carved in stone-figures, within the vaulted arches of the three entrances in this west front, and twelve apostles in a row, above, and as much other sculpture as would take a month to see. We then walked quite round the Cathedral; but I had no sense of immensity from it—not even that of great height—as from many of the cathedrals of England. It stands very near the Seine; indeed, if I mistake not, it is on an island formed by two branches of the river. Behind the Cathedral, is what seems to be a small public ground, (or garden, if a space entirely denuded of grass or other green thing, except a few trees, can be called so) with benches, and a monument in the midst. This quarter of the city looks old, and appears to be inhabited by poor people, and to be busied about small and petty affairs; the most picturesque business that I saw being that of the old woman, who sells crucifixes of pearl and wood at the Cathedral door. We bought two of these, yesterday. I must again speak of the horrible mud[162]diness, not only of this part of the city, but of all Paris, so far as I have traversed it to-day. My ways, since I came to Europe, have often lain through nastiness; but I never before saw a pavement so universally overspread with mud-pudding as that of Paris. It is difficult to imagine where so much filth comes from.

We dined at the Restaurant de L'Echelle; but already we are getting to be connoisseurs in French cookery, and we found nothing very admirable in the dishes of to-day. After dinner, I walked through the gardens of the Tuileries; but, as dusk was coming on, and as I was afraid of being shut up within the iron-railing, I had not time to examine them particularly. There are broad, intersecting walks, fountains, broad basins, and many statues; but almost the whole surface of the gardens is barren earth, instead of the verdure that would beautify an English pleasure ground of this sort. In the summer, it has trees enough to throw doubtless an agreeable shade; but, at this season, their naked branches look meagre, and sprout from slender trunks. The trees in the Champs Elysées, and, I presume, in the gardens of the Tuileries, are said to need renewing, every few years. The same is true of the human race; families becoming extinct after a generation or two of residence in Paris. Nothing really thrives here; [163] and vegetables have but an artificial life, like flowers stuck in a little mould, but never taking root. I am quite tired of Paris, and never longed for a home so much.

Hôtel d'Angleterre, Marseilles, Jany 15th, Friday.

On Tuesday morning, I paid our bill at the Hôtel du Louvre (more than 450 francs for little more than lodging and break-

fasts for a week,) and we took our departure. It is a most
excellent and perfectly ordered Hotel; and I have not seen a
more magnificent hall, in whatever palace, than the dining
saloon, with its profuse gilding, and its cieling painted in compartments; so that when the chandeliers are all a-light, it
looks a fit place for princes to banquet in, and not very fit for
the few Americans (for they seemed to be chiefly my countrymen and countrywomen) whom I saw scattered at its long
tables. Most of the guests, I believe, dine either at the
Restaurant of the Hotel, or some similar establishment in the
vicinity; the table d'hôte (seven francs) being dearer than a
good dinner costs elsewhere.

It was a very chill morning, and the rain began to fall, as
we left the Hôtel. At the railway, there ensued much botheration about our tickets and luggage; but we got our seats in a
separate carriage, seven in all, Miss Mitchell being of the
party. By the by, as we drove [164] to the Railway, we passed
through the public square where the Bastille formerly stood;
and in the centre of it now stands a column, surmounted
by a golden figure of Mercury, I think, which seems to be
just on the point of casting itself from a gilt ball into the air.
This statue is so buoyant that the spectator feels quite willing
to trust it to the viewless element, being as sure that it would
be borne up, as that a bird would fly. Our first day's ride was
wholly without interest, through a country entirely flat, and
looking awfully brown and barren; there were rows of trees,
very slender, very prim and formal; there was ice, wherever
there happened to be any water to form it; there were occasional villages, compact little streets or masses of stone or
plastered cottages, very dirty, with gable ends and earthen
roofs; and a succession of this same landscape was all that we
saw, whenever we rubbed away the congelation of our breath
from the carriage-windows. Thus we rode on, all day long,
from eleven °clock, with hardly a five minutes' stop, till

long after dark, when we came to Dijon, where there was a halt of twenty-five minutes for dinner. Then we set forth again, and rumbled forward, through cold and darkness without, and carrying much trouble along with us, the children being tired, sleepy, and hard to please, un[165]til we reached Lyons at about ten °clock. We left our luggage at the railway station, and took an omnibus for the Hôtel de Provence, which we chose at a venture, among a score of other names of hôtels.

As our hôtel was a little off the direct route of the omnibus, the driver set us down at a corner of the street and pointed to some lights, which he said designated the Hôtel de Provence; and thither we proceeded, all seven of us, lugging along a few carpet-bags and shawls, our equipage for the night. The porter of the hôtel met us near its door-way, and ushered us through an archway into the inner quadrangle, and then up some old and worn stone steps, very broad, and appearing to be the principal staircase of the house. At the first landing-place, an old woman and a waiter or two received us; and we went up two or three more flights of the same broad and worn stone-staircase. What we could see of the house looked very old, and had the musty smell with which I first became acquainted at Chester. After ascending to the proper level, we were conducted along a corridor, paved with octagonal earthen tiles; on one side were windows looking into the courtyard; on the other doors, opening into the sleeping chambers. The corridor was of immense length, and [166] seemed still to lengthen itself before us, as the glimmer of our conductor's candle went farther and farther into its obscurity. Our own chamber was at a vast distance along this passage; those of the rest of the party were on the hither side; but all this immense suite of rooms appeared to communicate by doors from one to another like the chambers through which the reader wanders at midnight, in Mrs. Ratcliffe's romances. And they were really splendid rooms, though of an old fashion; lofty, spacious, with floors of oak or other wood, inlaid in squares and crosses, and waxed till they were slippery, but without carpets. Our own sleeping-room had a deep fireplace, in which we ordered a fire, and asked if there was not some room already warmed, where we could get a cup to tea. Hereupon, the waiter led us back along the endless corridor, and down the old stone staircases, and out into the quadrangle, and journeyed with us along an exterior corridor, and finally threw open the door of the Salle a Manger, which proved to be a room of magnificent height, with a vaulted roof, a stone floor, and interior spaciousness sufficient for a baronial hall; the whole bearing the same aspect of times gone-by, that characterized the rest of the house. There were two or three tables, covered with white [167] cloths; and our party sat down at one of them and had our tea. Finally, we wended our way back to our sleeping rooms, itself a considerable journey, so endless seemed this ancient hôtel. I should like to know its history.

The fire made our great chamber look comfortable, and the fireplace threw out the heat better than the little square hole over which we cowered in our room at the Hôtel du Louvre. We went to bed leisurely, but got up much sooner than we liked, and began our preparations for starting at ten. Issuing into the corridor, I found a soldier of the line pacing to-and-fro there, as sentinel. Another was posted in another corridor, into which I wandered by mistake; another stood in the inner-court yard; and another, I believe, at the porte-cochere. They were not there, the night before; and I know not whence or why they came, unless that some officer of rank may have taken up his quarters in the hôtel. Miss Mitchell says that she heard, at Paris, that a considerable number of troops had recently been drawn together at Lyons, in consequence of symptoms of dis-affection that have recently shown themselves here. Before breakfast, I went out to catch a momentary glimpse of Lyons. The street, in which our hôtel stands, is near a large public square, [168] in the centre of which is a bronze equestrian statue of Louis XIV; and the square itself is called the Place de Louis le Grand. I wonder where this statue hid itself while the Revolution was raging in Lyons and when the guillotine perhaps stood on that very spot. The square was surrounded by stately buildings, but had what seemed to be barracks for soldiers—at any rate, mean little buildings deforming its ample space—and a soldier was on guard before the statue of Louis le Grand. It was a cold, misty morning, and a fog lay throughout the square, so that I could scarcely see from one side of it to the other. Returning towards our hotêl, I saw that it had an immense front, along which ran, in gigantic letters, its title, HÔTEL DE PROVENCE ET DES AMBASSADEURS.

The excellence of the hôtel lay rather in the faded magnificence of its sleeping rooms, and the vastness of its salle a manger, than in anything very good to eat or drink. We left it after a poor breakfast (a little cutlet or two, about as big as a chicken's wing, and a thin slice of ham being the best of it) and went to the railway-station. Looking at the mountainous heap of our luggage, the night before, we had missed a great carpet-bag; and we now found that Miss Mitchell's trunk had been substituted for it; and, there being the [169] proper number of packages, as registered, it was impossible to convince the officials that anything was wrong. We, of course, began to generalize forthwith, and pronounced the incident characteristic of French morality; they love a certain system and external correctness, but do not trouble themselves to be deeply in the right; and Miss Mitchell suggested that there used to be parallel cases in the French revolution, when, so long as the assigned number were sent out of prison to be guillotined, the jailer did not much care whether they were the persons designated by the tribunal. At all events, we could get no satisfaction about the carpet-bag, and shall very probably be compelled to leave Marseilles without it.

This day's ride was through a far more picturesque country than that we saw yesterday; heights began to rise, imminent above our way, with sometimes a ruined castle-wall upon them; on our left, the rail-track kept close to the hills, on the other side there was the level bottom of a valley, with heights descending upon it, a mile, or a few miles, away. Farther off, we could see blue hills, shouldering high above the intermediate ones, and themselves worthy to be called mountains. These hills arranged themselves in beautiful groups, affording glimpses [170] between them, and vistas of what lay beyond, and gorges which, I suppose, held a great deal of romantic scenery. By and by, a river made its appearance, flowing swiftly in the same direction that we were travelling, a beautiful and cleanly river, with white pebbly shores, and itself of a peculiar blue. It rushed along very fast, sometimes whitening over shallow descents, and, even in its calmer intervals, its surface was all covered with whirls and eddies, indicating that it whirled onward in haste. I do not know the name of this river, but have set it down as the "arrowy Rhone." It kept us company a long while, and I think we did not part with it as long as daylight remained. I have seldom seen hill-scenery that struck me more than some that we saw to-day; and the old feudal towers, and old villages at their feet, and the old churches, with spires shaped just like extinguishers, gave it an interest accumulating from many centuries past. Still going southward, the vineyards began to border our track, together with what I at first took to be orchards, but soon found were plantations of olive-trees, which grow to a much larger size than I supposed, and look almost precisely like very crabbed and eccentric apple-trees. Nei[171]ther they nor the vineyards add anything to the picturesqueness of the landscape. On the whole, I should have been delighted with all this scenery, if it had not looked so bleak, barren, brown, and bare; so like the wintry scenes in New England, before the snow has fallen. It was very cold, too; ice along the borders of streams, even among the vineyards and olives. The houses are of rather a different shape here than farther northward; their roofs being not nearly so sloping. They are almost invariably covered with white plaster; the farmhouses have their outbuildings in connection with the dwelling, the whole surrounding three sides of a quadrangle.

We travelled far into the night, swallowed a cold and hasty dinner at Avignon, or some town within a hundred miles of it, and reached Marseilles, sorely wearied, at about eleven °clock. We took a cab to the Hôtel d'Angleterre (two cabs, to be quite accurate) and find it a very poor place. To go back a little, as the sun went down, we looked out of the window of our railway-carriage, and beheld a sky that reminded us of what we used to see, day after day, in America, and what we have not seen since; and, after sunset, the horizon burned and glowed with rich crimson and orange lustre, looking at once warm [172] and cold. After it grew dark, the stars brightened out, and Miss Mitchell, from her window, pointed out some of the planets to the children, she being as familiar with them as a gardener with his flowers. They were as bright as diamonds; as bright as in America; brighter than stars ever were, for a single moment, in English atmosphere.

This morning, there was a mist through the air, and it was very chill, the people appearing in the street in their great coats, shivery and frost-bitten; though I think there was hardly more than a hoar-frost, if so much. We had a wretched breakfast of bad coffee, chocolate, and bread and butter; and Miss Shepard, Julian, and I, then went to the railway to see about our luggage (which we had left there for the night)

and about the missing carpet-bag. Nothing was to be discovered respecting the latter; so we came away, resolving to
telegraph to Paris about it. On our way back, we went astray,
passing by a triumphal arch, of no great beauty, erected by the
Marsellaise in honor of Louis Napoleon; but we inquired our
way of old women and soldiers—who were very kind and
courteous, especially the latter—and were directed aright.
We came to a large, oblong, public place, set with trees, but
devoid of grass, like all public places in France. In the middle
of it was a bronze statue of an ecclesiastical personage, stretching forth his hands [173] in an attitude as if addressing the
people, or throwing a benediction over them; it was some
archbishop, who had distinguished himself by his humanity
and devotedness, during the plague of 1720. At the moment
of our arrival, the Place was quite thronged with people, who
seemed to be talking amongst themselves with considerable
earnestness, though without any actual excitement; they were
smoking cigars, and we judged that they were only loitering
here for the sake of the sunshine, having no fires at home,
and nothing to do. Some looked like gentlemen; others like
peasants; mostly, I should have taken them for loafers, the
lazzaroni of this southern city—men with cloth caps, like the
classic liberty-cap, or with wide-awake hats. There were one
or two women of the lower classes, without bonnets, the
elder ones with white caps, the younger, bareheaded. I have
hardly seen a lady in Marseilles; and I suspect, being a commercial city, and dirty to the last degree, ill-built, narrow-
streeted, and sometimes pestilential, there are few or no
families of gentility resident here.

Returning to the Hôtel, we found my wife and the rest
of the party ready to go out; so we all issued forth in a body,
and inquired our way to the telegraph office, in order to send
my message about the carpet-bag. In a street through which

we had to pass (and which seemed to be the Exchange, or its precincts) there [174] was a crowd even denser—yes, much denser—than that which we saw in the Square of the Archbishop's statue; and each man was talking to his neighbor in a vivid, animated way, as if business were very brisk to-day. At the telegraph office, we found out the cause that had brought out these many people; there had been an attempt on the Emperor's life, unsuccessful, as they seem fated to be, though it had done some mischief amongst those near him. I rather think the good people of Marseilles were glad of the attempt, as an item of news and gossip, and did not very greatly care whether it were successful or no; it seemed to have roused their vivacity, rather than their interest. The only account I have seen of it was in the brief public despatch from the Syndic, or whatever he be, of Paris, to the chief authority of Marseilles, which was printed and posted in various conspicuous places. The only chance of knowing the truth, with any fulness of detail, would be, to come across an English paper. We have had a banner hoisted half-mast in front of our hotel to-day, as a token, the head-waiter tells us, of sympathy and sorrow for the general and other persons who were slain by this treasonable attempt.

Julian and I parted from Mamma and her party, at the door of a shop; and we ourselves wandered along a circular line of Quais, having on one side of us a thick forest of masts; while [175] on the other was a long sweep of shops, bookstalls, sailor's restaurants and drinking-houses, fruit-sellers, candy-women, and all manner of open air dealers and pedlers, little children playing, and jumping the rope, and such a babble and bustle as I never saw or heard before; the sun lying along the whole sweep, very hot, and evidently very grateful to those who bustled and basked in it. Whenever I passed into the shade, immediately, from too warm, I became too cold.

The sunshine was like hot iron; the shade, like the touch of cold steel—sharp, hard, yet exhilarating. From this broad street of the quais, narrow thread-like lanes pierced up between the edifices, calling themselves streets, yet so narrow that a person in the middle could almost touch the houses on either hand; they ascended steeply, bordered on each side by long, contiguous walls of high houses, and from the time of their first being built, could never have had a gleam of sunshine in them—always in shadow, always unutterably nasty, often pestiferous. The nastiness—the human nastiness, as an abode of men—which I saw in Marseilles, exceeds my heretofore experience. There is dirt in the hotel, and everywhere else; and it evidently troubles nobody, no more than if all the people were pigs in a pig-stye. The water closet of the hotel, though it is in a nook hard by the salle-a-manger, is a place of horrors. All over [176] the town, people consult their necessities without a scruple, no matter what be the sex of the passer-by. The cabinets provided by public authority are scarcely so decent, as regards concealment, as none at all. Private enterprise seeks to accommodate the necessitous; and on the quai, I saw "Cabinets d'aisance" advertised, with a painting of the particular commodity offered to public patronage.

Passing by all this sweep of quais, Julian and I ascended to an elevated walk, overlooking the harbor, and far beyond it; for here we had our first view of the Mediterranean, blue as heaven, and bright with sunshine. It was a bay, widening forth into the open deep, and bordered with heights, and bold, picturesque headlands, some of which had either fortresses or convents on them. Several boats, and one brig, were under sail, making their way towards the port. I have never seen a finer sea-view, but will not give up the waters and coasts of New England as less beautiful than these, were they twenty

times the Mediterranean. Behind the town, there seemed to
be a mountainous landscape, imperfectly visible in consequence
of the intervening edifices.

Steamer Calabrese, Mediterranean Sea, Jany 17th. Sunday.

If I had remained at Marseilles, I might have found many
peculiarities and characteristics of that Southern city to notice;
but I fear that these will not be recorded, if I leave them till I
touch [177] the soil of Italy. Indeed, I doubt whether there is
anything really worth recording in the little distinctions between one nation and another; at any rate, after the first
novelty is over, new things seem equally common place with
the old. There is but one little interval when the mind is in
such a state that you can catch the fleeting aroma of a new
scene. And it is always so much pleasanter to enjoy this
delicious newness than to attempt arresting it, that it requires
great force of will to insist with oneself upon sitting down to
write. I can do nothing with Marseilles; especially here, on the
Mediterranean, long after night-fall, and when the steamer is
pitching in a pretty lively way.

I walked out with Julian, yesterday morning, and reached
the outskirts of the city, whence we could see the bold and
picturesque heights that surround Marseilles as with a semi-
circular wall; they rise into peaks; and the town, being on
their lower slope, descends from them towards the sea, with a
gradual slope. Adown the streets, that descend these slopes,
come little rivulets, running along over the pavement, close to
the side walks, as over a pebbly-bed; and though it looks
vastly like a kennel, I saw women [178] washing linen in
these streams, and others dipping up the water for household
purposes. The women appear very much in public, at
Marseilles. In the squares and Places, you see half a dozen

of them together, sitting in a social circle on the bottoms of up-turned baskets, knitting, talking together, and enjoying the public sunshine as if it were their own household fire. Not one in a thousand of them, probably, ever has a household fire for the purpose of keeping themselves warm, but only to do their little cookery; and when there is sunshine they take advantage of it; and in the short season of rain and frost, they shrug their shoulders, put on what warm garments they have, and get through the winter somewhat as grasshoppers and butterflies do,—being summer-insects, like them. They certainly do have a very keen and cutting air—sharp as a razor—and I saw ice along the borders of the little rivulets, almost at noon-day. To be sure, it is mid-winter, and yet, in the sunshine, I found myself uncomfortably warm; but, in the shade, the air was like the touch of death itself. I do not like the climate, and have not felt comfortable in it.

There are a great number of public Places in Marseilles, several of which are adorned with statues, or [179] fountains, or triumphal arches, or columns; and set out with trees, and otherwise furnished as a sort of drawing-room, where the populace may meet together and gossip. I never before heard from human lips anything like the bustle and babble, the thousand-fold talk, that you hear all roundabout you in the crowd of a public square; so entirely different is it from the dulness of a crowd in England, where, as a rule, every body is silent, and hardly half-a-dozen monosyllables will come from the lips of a thousand people. In Marseilles, on the contrary, a stream of unbroken talk seems to bubble from the lips of every individual. A great many interesting scenes take place in these Squares. From the window of our Hotel (which looks into the Place Royale,) I saw a juggler displaying his art to a crowd, who stood in a regular square about him, none pretending to press nearer than the prescribed limit. While the juggler wrought his miracles, his wife supplied him with his magic materials out of a box; and when the exhibition was over, she packed up the white cloth with which his table was covered, together with cups, cards, balls, and whatever else, and they took their departure.

I have been struck by the idle curiosity, and, at the [180] same time, the courtesy and kindliness of the populace of Marseilles; and I meant to exemplify it by recording how Miss Shepard and I attracted their notice, and became the centre of a crowd of at least fifty of them, while doing no more remarkable thing than merely settling with a cab-driver. But really this pitch and swell is getting too bad, and I shall go to bed, as the best chance of keeping my stomach in an equable state.

37, Via Porta Pinciana, Rome, Jany 24th, Sunday.

I think I did not record, under my last date, that we left Marseilles in the Neapolitan Steamer Calabrese, a week ago this morning. There was no fault to be found with the Steamer, which was very clean and comfortable; contrary to what we had understood beforehand. Except for the coolness of the air (and I know not this was greater than that of the Atlantic in July) our voyage would have been very pleasant; but for myself I enjoyed nothing, having a cold upon me, or a low fever, or something else that took the light and warmth out of everything.

I went to bed immediately after my last record, and was rocked to sleep pleasantly enough by the billows of the Mediterranean; and coming on deck about sunrise, next morning, found the steamer approaching [181] Genoa. We saw the city lying at the foot of a range of hills, and stretching a little way up their slopes; the hills sweeping round it in the segment of a circle, and looking like an island rising abruptly out of the sea; for no connection with the mainland was visible on either side. There was snow scattered on their summits, and streaking their sides a good way down; they looked bold and barren, and brown except where the snow streaked them. The city did not impress us with much expectation of size or magnificence. Shortly after coming into the port, our whole party landed, and found ourselves at once in the midst of a crowd of cab-drivers, hotel-runners, and commissionaires, who assaulted us with a volley of French, Italian, and broken English, which beat pitilessly about our ears; for really it seemed as if all the dictionaries in the world had been torn to pieces, and blown around us by a hurricane. I never heard such a pother. We took a commissionaire, a respectable-looking man in a cloak, who said his name was Salvator Rosa; and he engaged to show us whatever was interesting in Genoa. In the first place, he took us through narrow streets (mere gullies, as it were, between lines of tall stone houses, and chill as death with the eternal shade that broods in them) to an old church, [182] the name of which I have forgotten, and indeed its peculiar features; but I know that I found it more mag- nificent than anything I had before seen or imagined; its whole interior being cased in polished marble, of various kind and colors, its cieling painted, and its chapels adorned with pictures. However, this church was dazzled out of sight by the Cathedral of San Lorenzo, to which we afterwards were con- ducted, the exterior front of which is covered with alternate slabs of black and white marble, which were brought, either in whole or in part, from Jerusalem. Within, there was an immense richness of precious marbles, and a pillar, if I mistake not, from Solomon's Temple, and a picture of the Virgin by Saint Luke, and others (rather more intrinsically valuable, I imagine) by old Masters, set in magnificent marble frames, within the arches of the Chapels. I used to try to imagine how splendidly the English Cathedrals must have looked in their primeval glory, before the Reformation, and before the whitewash of Cromwell's time had overlaid their marble pillars; but I never imagined anything at all approaching what my eyes now beheld; this sheen of polished and variegated marble, covering every inch of the walls; this glow of brilliant frescoes all over [183] the roof, and up within the domes; these beautiful pictures by great masters, painted for the places which they now occupied, and making an actual portion of the edifice; this wealth of silver, gold, and gems, that adorned the shrines of the saints, before which wax candles burned, and were kept burning, I suppose, from years' end to years' end; in short, there is no imagining or remembering a hundredth part of this magnificence. And even the Cathedral (though I give it up as indescribable) was nothing in comparison with a church to which the Commissionaire afterwards led us; a church that had been built, four or five hundred years ago, by a pirate, in expiation of his sins and out of the profit of his rapine. This last edifice, in its interior, absolutely shone with burnished gold, and glowed with pictures; its walls were a quarry of precious stones, so valuable were the marbles out of which they were wrought; its columns and pillars were of inconceivable value; its pavement was a mosaic of wonderful beauty. There were four twisted pillars, made out of stalactites. I am ashamed of my folly in trying even to make myself remember how much I was dazzled by this church. Perhaps the best way to form some dim conception of [184] it, is to imagine a little casket, all inlaid, in its inside, with precious stones, so that there shall not a hair's breadth be left un-precious-stoned; and then imagine this little bit of a casket increased to the magnitude of a great church, without losing anything of the intense glory that was compressed into its original small compass, but all its pretty lustre made sublime and magnificent by the immensity. At any rate, nobody who has not seen a church like this (if there be another such) can imagine what a splendid religion it was that reared it. In the Cathedral, and in all the churches, we saw priests, and many persons kneeling at their devotions; and our Salvator Rosa, whenever we passed a chapel or shrine, failed not to touch the pavement with one knee, crossing himself the while; and once, when a priest was going through some form of devotion, he stopt a few moments to share in it.

He conducted us, too, to the Balbi palace, the stateliest and most magnificent residence that I had ever seen, but not more so than another which he afterwards showed us, nor perhaps than many others which exist in Genoa the superb. The painted cielings in these palaces are a glorious adornment; the walls of the saloons, encrusted [185] with various-colored marbles, give an idea of splendor which I never gained from anything else; the floors, wrought in mosaic, seem too precious to tread upon. In the royal palace, many of the floors were wrought of inlaid woods, by an English artist, and looked like a magnification of some exquisite piece of Tunbridge ware; but, in all respect, this palace was inferior to others which we saw. I say nothing of the immense pictorial treasures which hung upon the walls of all the rooms through which we passed; for I soon grew so weary of admirable things that I could neither enjoy nor understand them. My receptive faculty is very limited; and when the utmost of its small capacity is full, I become perfectly miserable, and the more so, the better worth seeing are the things I am forced to reject. I do not know a greater misery; to see sights after such repletion is, to the mind, what it would be to the body to have dainties forced down the throat long after the appetite was satiated.

All this while, whenever we emerged into the vault-like streets, we were wretchedly cold. The commissionaire took us to a sort of pleasure-garden, occupying the ascent of a hill, and presenting seven different views of the city [186] from as many stations. One of the objects pointed out to us was a large yellow house, on a hill-side in the outskirts of Genoa, which was formerly inhabited for six months by Charles Dickens. Looking down from the elevated part of the pleasure-garden, we saw orange-trees beneath us, with the golden fruit hanging upon them, though their trunks were muffled in straw; and still lower down there was ice and snow.

Gladly (so far as I myself was concerned) we dismissed the Commissionaire, after he had brought us to the Hôtel of the Cross of Malta, where we dined; needlessly, as it proved, for another dinner awaited us after our return on board the boat. We set sail for Leghorn before dark, and I went to bed early, feeling still more ill with my cold than the night before. The next morning, when I got up, we were in the crowded port of Leghorn. We all went ashore, with some idea of taking the rail for Pisa, which is within an hour's distance, and might have been seen in time for our departure with the steamer. But a necessary visit to a Banker's, and afterwards some unnecessary formalities about our passports, kept us wandering about the streets nearly all day; and we saw nothing in the slightest [187] interesting, except the tomb of Smollet, in the burial-place attached to the English chapel. It is surrounded by an iron railing, and marked by a slender obelisk of white marble, the pattern of which is many times repeated over surrounding graves. We went into a Jewish synagogue, the interior of which is cased with marble, and surrounded with galleries resting upon arches above arches. There were lights burning at the altar, and it looked very like a Christian church; but it was dirty, and had an odour not of sanctity. In Leghorn, as everywhere else, we were chilled to the heart except when the sunshine fell directly upon us; and we returned to the steamer with a feeling as if we were getting back to our home; for this miserable life of wandering makes a three days' residence seem like home. We found several new passengers on board, and among others a monk, in a long brown frock of woollen cloth, with an immense cape, and a little black covering over his tonsure. He was a tall figure with a grey beard, and might have walked, just as he stood, out of a picture by one of the old masters. This holy person addressed me very affably in Italian; but we found it impossible to hold much conversation.

[188] The evening was beautiful, with a bright young moonlight, not yet sufficiently powerful to overwhelm the stars; and as we walked the deck, Miss Mitchell showed the children the stars and constellations, and told their names. Julian made a slight mistake as to one of these, pointing it out to me as "O'Brian's Belt." Elba was in view before I went to bed; and we might have seen many other interesting points, had it not been for our steamer's practice of resting by day and only pursuing its voyage by night. The next morning, we found ourselves in the harbor of Civita Vecchia, and, going ashore with our baggage, went through a blind pother with Custom House officers, inspectors of passports, soldiers, vetturino-people, and the devil knows whom besides. My wife and I strayed a little through Civita Vecchia, and found its streets narrow, like clefts in a rock (as seems to be the fashion of Italian towns) and smelling nastily. I had made a bargain with a vetturino to send us to Rome, in a carriage with four horses, in eight hours, for three Napoleons, and as soon as the Custom House and passport people would let us, we started, lumbering slowly along, with our mountain of luggage. We had heard rumors of robberies lately [189] committed on this route, especially of a Nova Scotian bishop, who was detained on the road an hour and a half, and utterly cleaned out; and certainly there was not a single mile of the dreary and desolate tract of country, over which we passed, where we might not have been robbed and murdered with impunity. Now and then, at long distances, we came to a structure, that might have been either a prison, a tavern, or a barn, but did not look very

much like either, being strongly built of stone, with iron grated windows, and of ancient and rusty aspect. We kept along by the seashore a great part of the way, and stopt to feed our horses at a village, the wretched street of which stands close along the shore of the Mediterranean, the loose, dark sand of which was made nasty by the vicinity. The vetturino cheated us, one of the horses giving out (as he must have known it would) halfway on our journey; and we staggered onward through cold and darkness—and peril, too, if the banditti were not a myth—reaching Rome not much before midnight. I perpetrated unheard of briberies on the Custom House officers at the gates, and was permitted to pass through and established myself at Spillman's Hotel—where we were half-frozen, and have been so ever since. And this is sunny Italy, and genial Rome!

II

[1] 37, Via Porta Pinciana, Rome, February 3ᵈ, 1858, Wednesday.

WE HAVE BEEN in Rome, I believe, a fortnight to day; or rather at eleven °clock to night; and I have seldom or never spent so wretched a time anywhere. Our impressions were very unfortunate, arriving at midnight, half-frozen, in the wintry rain, and being received into a cold and cheerless hotel, where we shivered during two or three days; meanwhile, seeking lodging, amongst the sunless, dreary alleys which are called streets in Rome. One cold, bright day after another has pierced me to the heart and cut me in twain, as with a sword, keen and sharp, and poisoned at point and edge. I did not think cold weather could have made me so very miserable; upon my word, having caught a feverish cold, I was glad of being muffled up comfortably in the fever-heat. The atmosphere certainly has a peculiar quality of malignancy. After a day or two, we settled ourselves in a suite of ten rooms, comprehending one flat, or what is called the second piano of this house. The rooms, thus far, have been very cold and uncomfortable, it being impossible to warm them by means of the deep, old-fashioned, inartificial fireplaces, unless we had the great logs of a New England forest to burn in them; so I have sat in my corner by the fireside, with more clothes on than ever I wore before, and my thickest [2] great coat. In the middle of the day, I generally venture out for an hour or two, but have only once been warm enough even in the sunshine; and out of the sun, it is as chill as death. I understand, now, the force of that story of Alexander and Diogenes, when the latter asked the conqueror, as the only favor he could do him, to stand out of his sunshine; there being such a difference, in these Southern climes of Europe, between sun and shade. You stand within the sunshine, though on its very verge, and are comfortably warm; you make one step beyond, and are smitten as with the edge of cold steel. If my wits had not been too much congealed, and my fingers too numb, I should like to have kept a minute journal of my feelings and impressions, during the past fortnight; it would have shown up modern Rome in an aspect in which it has never yet been depicted. But I have now grown somewhat acclimated, and the first freshness of my discomfort has worn off; so that I shall never be able to express how I dislike the place, and how wretched I have been in it; and soon, I suppose, warmer weather will come, and perhaps reconcile me to Rome against my will. Cold, nastiness, evil smells, narrow lanes between tall, ugly, mean-looking, white-washed houses, sour bread, pavement, most uncomfortable to the feet, enormous prices for poor living, beggars, pickpockets, ancient temples and broken monuments with filth [3] at the base, and clothes hanging to dry about them, French soldiers, monks, and priests of every degree, a shabby population smoking bad cigars—these would have been some of the points of my description. Of course there are better and truer things to be said; but old Rome does seem to lie here like a dead and mostly decayed corpse, retaining here and there a trace of the noble shape it was, but with a sort of fungous growth upon it, and no life but of the worms that creep in and out.

It would be idle for me to attempt any sketches of these famous sites and edifices—Saint Peter's for example—which have been described by a thousand people, though none of them have ever given me an idea what sort of place Rome is. Saint Peter's disappointed me terribly by its want of effect, and the little justice it does to its real magnitude, externally; but the interior blazed upon me with altogether unexpected magnificence; so brilliant is it with picture, gilding, variegated and polished marbles, and all that splendor which I tried in vain to describe in the churches of Genoa. I had expected something vast and dim, like the great English Cathedrals, only more vast, and dim, and gray; but there is as much difference as between noonday and twilight. I never saw nor imagined so bright and splendid an interior as that of this immense church; but I am not sure that it [4] would not be more grand and majestic if it were less magnificent, though I should be sorry to see the experiment tried. The Coliseum was very much what I had pre-conceived it, though I was not prepared to find it turned into a sort of Christian church, with a pulpit on the verge of the open space. Right in the center, there is a great iron cross, on which is advertized, in Italian, an indulgence of two hundred days to whoever shall kiss it. While I sat on a stone, under one of the arches, I saw two women prick their way through the mud and kiss this cross, and then go away repeating their prayers aloud. The French soldiers (who keep guard within the Coliseum, as in most other public places in Rome) have an excellent opportunity to secure the welfare of their souls.

Rome, Feby 7th, Sunday.

I cannot get fairly into the current of my Journal, since we arrived in Rome; and already I perceive that the nice peculiarities of Roman life are passing from my notice before I have recorded them. It is a very great pity. During this past week, I have plodded daily, for an hour or two, through the narrow, stony streets, that look worse than the worst backside lanes of any other city; indescribably ugly and disagreeable they are; so cold, so alley-like, so uncomfortably paved with little square stones, without side walks, but provided with a line of larger squares, set corner-[5]wise to each other, along which there is somewhat less uneasy walking. Along these lanes, or gullies, a chill wind blows; down into their depths the sun never falls; they are bestrewn with horse dung and the filth of the adjacent houses, which rise on each side to the height of five or six stories, generally plastered and white-washed and looking neither old nor new. Probably these houses have the brick and stone of old Rome in them—the Coliseum, and many another stately structure—but they themselves look like magnified hovels. Ever and anon, even in the meanest streets (though, generally speaking, one can hardly be called meaner than another) we pass a palace, extending far along the narrow way on the line with the other houses, but distinguished by its architectural windows, iron-barred on the basement story, and by its portal arch through which we have glimpses sometimes of a filthy courtyard, or perhaps an ornamented one, with trees, a colonnade, a fountain and a statue in the vista; though, more likely, it resembles the entrance to a stable, and may perhaps really be one. The lower regions of palaces come to strange uses in Rome; a cobler or a tinker perhaps exercizes his craft under the archway; a work-shop may be established in one of the apartments; and in the basement story of the Barberini palace a regiment of French cavalry seems to be quartered, while, no doubt, princes have magnificent domiciles above. Be it palace or what[6]ever other dwelling, the inmates climb through stink and nastiness to the comforts, such as they may be, that await them above. I vainly try to get down upon paper the dreariness and ugliness, nastiness, discomfort, shabbiness, un-home-likeness, of a Roman street. It is also to be said, that you cannot go far, in any direction, without coming to a Piazza, which is often little more than a widening and enlarging of the dingy street, with the lofty facade of a church or basilica on one side, and a fountain in the middle, where the water squirts out of some fantastic piece of sculpture into a great stone basin. These fountains are sometimes of immense size and most elaborate design; one, for instance, occupying the whole side of a great edifice, and representing Neptune and his steeds, who seem to lunge atangle down with a cataract that tumbles over a ledge of rocks into a marble-bordered lake; the whole (except the fall of water itself) making up an exceedingly cumbrous and ridiculous affair. There is an immense variety of these fountain-shapes, constructed under the orders of one pope or another, in all parts of the city; and only the very simplest, such as a jet springing from a broad marble or porphyry vase, and falling back into it again, are really ornamental. If an antiquary were to accompany me through the streets, no doubt he would point out ten [7] thousand interesting objects, that I now pass over unnoticed, so general is the surface of plaster, white-wash, and shabbiness; but often I can see fragments of antiquity built into the walls, or perhaps a church that was a Roman temple, or a basement of ponderous stones, that were laid above twenty centuries ago. It is strange how our ideas of what antiquity is become altered here in Rome; the sixteenth century, in which many of the churches and fountains seem to have been built or re-edified, seems close at hand, even like our own days; a thousand years, or the days of the latter empire, is but a modern date; and scarcely interests us; and nothing is really venerable of a more recent epoch than the reign of Constantine. The Egyptian obelisks that stand in several of the piazzas, put even the Augustan or Republican antiquities to shame. I remember reading in a New York newspaper an account of one of the public buildings of that city—a relic of the "olden time," the writer called it; for it was erected in 1825! I am glad I saw the castles and Gothic churches and cathedrals of England before visiting Rome; or I never could have felt that delightful reverence for their gray and ivy-hung antiquity, after seeing these so much older remains. But indeed, old things are not so beautiful in this dry climate and clear atmosphere as in moist England. [8] The marble, it is true, grows black or brown, and shows its age in that manner; but it remains hard and sharp, and does not become again a part of Nature, as stone walls do in England; some dry and dusty grass sprouts along the ledges of a ruin, as in the Coliseum, but there is no green mantle of ivy kindly spreading itself over the gray dilapidation. Whatever beauty there may be in a Roman ruin is the remnant of what was beautiful originally, whereas an English ruin is more beautiful, often, in its decay than ever it was in its primal strength. If we ever build such noble structures as these Roman ones, we can have just as good ruins after two thousand years, in the United States; but we never can have a Furness Abbey or a Kenilworth.

The Corso, and perhaps some other streets, does not deserve all the vituperation which I have bestowed on the generality of Roman vias; though the Corso is a narrow street, not averaging more than nine paces, if so much, from sidewalk to sidewalk. But palace after palace stands along almost its whole extent; not that they make such architectural show as palaces should. The inclosed courts were perhaps the only parts of these edifices which the founders cared to enrich architecturally. I think Linlithgow Palace, of which I saw [9] the ruins during my last tour in Scotland, was built by an architect who had studied these Roman palaces. There was never any idea of domestic comfort—or of what we include in the name of home—at all implicated in such structures; they being generally built by wifeless and childless churchmen for the display of pictures and statuary in galleries and long suites of rooms.

I have not yet fairly begun the sight-seeing of Rome; the weather being so cold that I shiver at the thought of each new thing. I have been three or four times to Saint Peters' and always with pleasure, because there is such a delightful, summer-like warmth the moment we pass beneath the heavy, padded, leather curtains, that protect the entrances. It is almost impossible not to believe that this genial temperature is the result of furnace heat; but really it is the warmth of last summer, which will be included within those massive walls, and in that vast immensity of space, till, six months hence, this winter's chill will just have made its way thither. It would be an excellent plan for a valetudinarian to lodge during the winter in Saint Peter's, perhaps establishing his household in one of the papal tombs. I become, I think, more sensible of the size of Saint Peter's, but am as yet far from being overwhelmed by it; it is not so big as all out-doors, nor its [10] dome so immense as that of the firmament. It looked queer, however, the other day, to see a little ragged boy, the very least of human things, going round and kneeling at shrine after shrine, and a group of children standing on tiptoe to reach the vase of holy-water. Saint Peter's offers itself as a place of worship and religious comfort for the whole human race; and in one of the transepts I found a range of confessionals, where the penitent might tell his sins in the tongue of his own country, whether French, German, Polish, English, or what not. If I had had a murder on my conscience or any other great sin, I think I should have been inclined to kneel down there, and pour it into the safe secrecy of the confessional. What an institution that is! Man needs it so, that it seems as if God must have ordained it. This popish religion certainly does apply itself most closely and comfortably to human occasions; and I cannot but think that a great many people find their spiritual advantage in it, who would find none at all in our formless mode of worship. You cannot think it is all a farce when you see peasant, citizen, and soldier, coming into the church, each on his own hook, and kneeling for moments or for hours, directing his silent devotions to some particular shrine; too humble to approach his God directly, and therefore asking the mediation of some saint, who stands [11] beside his infinite presence. In the church of San Paulo yesterday I saw a young man standing before a shrine, writhing and wringing his hands in an agony of grief and contrition. If he had been a protestant, I think he would have shut all that up within his heart, and let it burn there till it seared him.

On coming out of Saint Peter's, at my last visit, I saw a great sheet of ice around the fountain on the left hand, and some little Romans awkwardly sliding on it. I, too, took a slide, just for the sake of doing what I never thought to do in Rome. This cold weather, I should suppose, must make the whole city very miserable; for the native Romans, I am told, never keep any fire except for culinary purposes, even in the severest cold. They seem to flee from their cheerless homes into the open air, and bring their firesides along with them in the shape of little earthen vases or pipkins, with a handle, by which they carry them up and down the streets, and so keep at least their hands warm with the lighted charcoal. I have had glimpses through open doorways into interiors and saw them as cold and dismal as a tomb. Wherever I pass my summers, let me spend my winters in a cold country.

My wife and I went yesterday to the Pantheon, which stands in the central intricacy and nastiness of Roman lanes. Its portico, with ranges of vast granite columns, is greatly [12] admired by architects, and no doubt justly. Its interior is most noble and beautiful, yet with a strange, half-heathenish aspect, which seems to be caused chiefly by a great circular opening in the center of its dome, through which comes all the light that illuminates the edifice. It is open to the sky, and, when we were there, the pavement beneath was plashy with the rain that had fallen through. All round the great circle of the Pantheon there are arches and stately altars, formerly dedicated to heathen gods and now to Saints, who step with ludicrous composure into every vacant niche in Rome, just as if it had been made for them. Up as far as the commencement of the curve of the dome, the walls are encrusted with precious marbles, which, together with the marble pillars and pilasters, must once have been most gorgeous; as also the mosaic pavement of colored marble and porphyry. I know not whether all this marble has laid over the walls, since the Pantheon became a christian church, or whether it has remained from old Roman times, but I think the latter can hardly have been the case. The Pantheon has been Christianized more than twelve centuries; so that there has been time for its Christian decorations to grow dingy and weather-worn, especially as the waters have had free access through [13] the circular skylight. The interior of the dome, which is now bare and stony, was formerly overlaid with bronze. The tomb of Raphael is in this church, or temple, but we did not see it, and must go again for that purpose. I think the Pantheon has impressed me more than anything else I have seen in Rome; the more for its dust and dinginess, and for that one circumstance of its gray roof open to the sky, so unlike the snugness of all our modern civilization. I must not forget, as characteristic of the spirit of modern Rome, that there are pasteboard statues, as large as life, aloft beneath the dome; so well done it is true, that they deceived me at first, in the dim cloudy light that came through the circular opening, on that rainy day. Also there are tin-hearts and other adornments of that kind hanging at the shrines of the Saints. I do not believe that the old heathen deities were ever cheated with similar sham jewellery. People were kneeling in devotion at several of the shrines. When I first came to Rome I felt embarrassed, and unwilling to pass with my heresy and unbelief, between a devotee and his saint; for they often shoot their prayers at a shrine almost quite across the church. But there seems to be no violation of etiquette in so doing. A woman begged of us in the Pantheon, and accused my wife of impiety, [14] for not giving her an alms. Beggars are extremely numerous in Rome; and people of very decent appearance are often unexpectedly converted into beggars, as you approach them, but, in general, they take a "No" at once.

Rome, February 9th, Tuesday.

For three or four days, it has been cloudy and rainy, which is the greater pity, as this should be the gayest and merriest part of the carnival. I go out but little; yesterday only as far as Pakenham & Hookers bank, in the Piazza di Espagna, where I read Galignani and the American papers. At last, after seeing more of my fellow citizens during four years than ever before, I really am dis-joined from my country.

To-day, I walked out along the Pincian Hill, whence there is the best view of Rome that I have yet found, and especially Saint Peter's does more justice to its real magnitude than at any nearer view. But there is certainly a lack of picturesque variety of outline. As the clouds still threatened rain, I deemed it my safest course to go to Saint Peter's for refuge. Heavy and dull as the day was, the effect of this great world of a church was still brilliant in the interior, as if it had a sunshine of its own, as well as its own temperature; and, by and by, the sunshine of the outward world came through the windows, hundreds of feet aloft, and fell upon the beautiful mosaic [15] pavement. On the whole, I think I am glad that

Saint Peter's is so rich, gorgeous, sunny, and fresh, so fadeless after centuries, so independent of the wear and tear of time; nor do I think that the very minutest of its million adornments is impertinent; for it is great enough to find room for them all, and you can easily overlook them if you like that best. It is strange to see what a multiplicity of ornament there is in some parts of the church; how cherubims flutter and kick upon the pilasters, bearing up medallions; how there are marble doves in unexpected places, with olive branches of green precious stones; how, in hundreds of places, there has been art and expense enough bestowed to have made a world-famous shrine, anywhere else, and how it all melts away into this great sunny breadth, and becomes of no account. The bronze statue of Saint Peter is a very mean-looking affair. He sits in a marble chair at the base of one of the pillars that support the dome (on the right hand as you enter,) and his foot extends partly over the marble pedestal which supports his chair. The toes of this foot are polished bright by the kisses of the faithful. Against the companion-pillar, on the other side of the nave, is the mosaic copy of Raphael's picture of the Transfiguration, fitly framed within a great arch of gorgeous marble; and, no doubt, the indestructible mosaic has preserved it far more com[16]pletely than the fading and darkening tints in which the artist painted it. At any rate, it seemed to me the one glorious picture that I have ever seen. The pillar nearest the great entrance, on the same side of the nave, supports the monument to the Stuart family, where two winged figures, with inverted torches, stand on either side of a marble door, which is closed forever. It is an impressive monument, for you feel as if the last of the race had passed through that door.

Emerging from the church, I saw a French sergeant drilling his men in the piazza. These French soldiers are prominent objects everywhere about the city, and make up more of its sight and sound than anything else that lives. They stroll about individually; they pace as sentinels in all the public places; and they march up and down in squads, companies, and batallions, always with an immense din of drum, fife, and trumpet; ten times the proportion of music that the same number of men would require elsewhere, and it reverberates with ten times the noise, between the high edifices of these narrow lanes, that it would make in broader streets. Nevertheless, I have no quarrel with the French soldiers; they are fresh, healthy, smart, honest-looking young fellows enough, in blue coats and red ɪ.ɔwsers; it seems as if they were nearer akin to me than these dingy and dusky [17] Romans; and at all events, they serve as an efficient police, making Rome as safe as London, whereas, without them, it would very likely be a den of banditti. On my way home, I saw a few tokens of the Carnival, which is now in full progress, though, as it was only about one ºclock, its frolics had not commenced for the day. Bouquets were bounteously for sale, in the shops and at the street-corners, and there were reservoirs of ammunition in the shape of sugar-plums and little pellets of paste or chalk. I question whether the Romans themselves take any great interest in the Carnival. The balconies along the Corso are almost entirely taken by English, Americans, or other foreigners.

As I approached the Bridge of St. Angelo, I saw several persons engaged, as I thought, in fishing in the Tiber, with very strong lines; but on drawing nearer, I found that they were trying to hook up the branches and twigs, and other drift wood, which the recent rains might have swept into the river. There was a little heap of what chiefly looked like willow-twigs; the poor result of their labor. The hook was a knot of wood with the lopped off branches projecting in three or four prongs. The Tiber has always the hue of a mud-puddle; but now, after a heavy rain which has washed the clay into it, it looks like pease soup. It is a broad and rapid stream, eddying along as if it were [18] in haste to disgorge its impurities into the sea. On the left side, where the city mostly stands, the buildings hang directly over the stream; on the other, where stand the Castle of Saint Angelo, and the church of Saint Peter, the town does not press so imminent upon the shore. The banks are clayey, and look as if the river had been digging them away for ages, but I believe its bed is higher than of yore.

Rome, February 10th, Wednesday.

I went out to-day, and going along the Via Felice and the Via delle Quattro Fontane, came unawares to the Basilica of Santa Maria Maggiore, on the summit of the Esquiline Hill. I entered it without in the least knowing what church it was, and found myself in a broad and noble nave, the simplest and grandest, it seems to me, that I have ever seen. There was a long row of Ionic columns of marble, twenty or thereabouts on each side, supporting a flat roof. There were vaulted side-aisles, and at the further end a bronze canopy over the high altar; and all along the length of the side-aisles were shrines, with pictures, sculpture, and burning lamps; the whole church, too, was lined with marble; the roof was gilded; and yet the general effect of severe and noble simplicity triumphed over all the ornament. I should have taken it for a Roman temple, retaining nearly its pristine aspect; but Murray tells me that it was founded A.D. 352, by Pope Liberi[19]us, on the spot precisely marked out by a miraculous fall of snow in the month of August, and it has undergone many alterations since his time. But it is very fine, and gives the beholder the idea of vastness, which seems harder to attain than anything else. On the right hand, approaching the high altar, there is a chapel separated from the rest of the church by an iron paling; and, being admitted into it with another party, I found it most elaborately magnificent—more so, I think, than any other church, or part of a church, that I was ever in. But one magnificence dazzles out another, and makes itself the brightest conceivable for the moment. However, this chapel was as rich as the most precious marble, in pillars, and pilasters, and broad, polished slabs, covering the whole walls (except where there were splendid and glowing frescoes, or where some monumental statuary or bas-relief, or mosaic picture, filled up an arched niche) could make it. Its architecture was a dome, resting on four great arches, and in size it would alone have been a church. In the center of the mosaic pavement, there was a flight of steps, down which we went, and saw a group in marble, representing the nativity of Christ, which, judging by the unction with which our guide talked about it, must have been of peculiar sanctity. I hate to leave this chapel and church, without being able to say any one [20] thing that may reflect a portion of their beauty, or of the feeling which they excite. But there is no help for it. Kneeling against many of the pillars, there were persons in prayer, and I stept softly, fearing lest my tread on the marble pavement should disturb them;—a needless precaution, however, for nobody seems to expect it, nor to be disturbed by the lack of it. The situation of this church, I should suppose, is the loftiest in Rome; it has a column at one end, and a fountain at the other, but I did not pay particular attention to either, nor to the exterior of the church itself.

On my return, I turned aside from the Via delle Quattro Fontane, into the Via Quirinales, I think, and was led by it into the Piazza di Monte Cavallo. The street through which I passed was broader, cleaner, and statelier than most streets in Rome, and bordered by palaces; and the Piazza had noble edifices around it, and a fountain, an obelisk, and two naked statues, in the centre. The obelisk was, as the inscription said, a relic of Egypt; the basin of the fountain was an immense bowl of oriental granite, into which poured a copious flood of water discolored by the rain; the statues were colossal, two beautiful young men, each holding a fiery steed. On the pedestal of one was this inscription—OPUS PHIDIAE; on the other —OPUS PRAXITILIS. What a city is this, when one may stumble by mere chance—at a street-corner, as it were—on the works of two [21] such sculptors. I do not know the authority on which these statues—Castor and Pollux, I presume—are attributed to Phidias and Praxitiles; but they impressed me as noble and godlike, and I feel inclined to take them for what they purport to be. On one side of this Piazza is the Pontifical Palace, but not being aware of it at the time, I did not particularly look at the edifice. I came home by way of the Corso, which seemed a little enlivened by Carnival time; though, as it was not yet two °clock, the fun had not yet begun for the day. The rain (which is always falling or threatening to fall) throws a terrible damper on the festivities.

Rome, February 13th, Saturday.

Day before yesterday, we took a carriage—Mamma, Julian, Rosebud and I—and went to see the Carnival by driving up and down the Corso. Una and Miss Shepard were spectators from a window with Miss Mitchell. It was as ugly a day, as respects weather, as has befallen us since we came to Rome, cloudy, with an indecisive little wet, which finally settled into a rain; and people say that such is generally the weather in Carnival-time. There is very little to be said about the spectacle. Sunshine would have improved it, no doubt; but a person must have very broad sunshine within himself to be very joyous on such shallow provocation. The street, at all events, would have looked rather brilliant under a sunny sky, the balconies being hung with bright-colored dra[22]peries,

which were also flung out of some of the windows. The balconies were mostly filled with ladies; some of whom sat nearly
on a level with the passers by, in full dress, with deep colored
Italian faces, ready to encounter whatever the chances of the
Carnival might bring them. The upper balconies (and there
was sometimes a third, if not a fourth tier) were occupied, I
think, chiefly by foreigners, English or Americans; nor, I
fancy, do the Roman ladies of rank and respectability generally display themselves at this time. At least, the festival seems
to me to have sunk from the upper classes to the lower ones;
and probably it is only kept alive by tradition, and the curiosity
which impels foreigners to join in it.

We entered the Corso between two and three °clock, from
the Piazza de Popolo. Bouquets were already flying to and fro
between the balconies, and the carriages in the street, and soon
I had my first experience of the Carnival in a handful of confetti right slap in my face. These confetti are very nasty
things, resembling sugar-plums as the apples of Sodom do
better fruit, but really made up of lime—or bad flour at best—
with oats or worthless seeds as a nucleus; and they readily
crumble and turn to dirty dust, making the hair irreverently
hoary, and giving a miller-like aspect to hat and cloathes.
Many of the ladies wore loose white sacks or dominoes, and
some of the gentlemen had on defensive armor of blouses, and
wire masks over the face were a [23] protection for both sexes,
not a needless one, for I received a shot in my right eye which
cost me many tears. It seems to be a point of courtesy (though
often disregarded) not to fling confetti at ladies or at non-
combatants, or quiet by-standers; and the engagements with
these missiles were generally between open carriages manned
with young men, who were provided with confetti for such
encounters, and with bouquets for the ladies. We had one real
enemy on the Corso; for our old friend Mrs. Tappan was
there, and as often as we passed and re-passed her, she favored

us with a handful of lime. Two or three times, somebody ran by the carriage and puffed forth a shower of winged seeds through a tube into our faces and over our clothes. Handfuls of flour and lime, or a mixture of both, in powder, were also thrown; and, in the course of the afternoon, we were hit with perhaps half a dozen sugar-plums. Possibly we may not have received our fair share of these last; for Julian had on a black mask which made him look like an imp of Satan, and drew many vollies of confetti that we might otherwise have escaped. A good many bouquets were flung at Rosebud, and at the party generally; but I hardly think them preferable to the confetti. They were composed of the most ordinary flowers, and were miserably wilted as if they had served two or three carnival-days already; they were muddy, too, having been picked up from the pavement, for there was a [24] crowd of men and boys, busy at picking up the bouquets that were aimed amiss, from carriage or balcony, and selling them over and over again. Such were the flowery favors—the bunches of sentiment—that flew to and fro along the Corso, from lady to knight and back again, and I suppose they aptly enough symbolized the poor battered, wilted, starved hearts, that had flown from one hand to another along the muddy pathway of life instead of being treasured in one faithful bosom. Really, it was great nonsense. Originally, I suppose, the youth or damsel made up their own bouquets of choice and virgin blossoms, and threw them with love and gentle aim to those whom they favored, with liking, at least, if not love; but when it comes to a purchased bouquet, at the original cost of half a baioccho, and this cheap article bought and sold at a reduced rate twenty times over, it is time to let the whole affair drop into the mud.

This was what is called masquing day, when it is the rule to wear masques in the Corso, but the great majority of people appeared without them. There were some queer shapes and faces, however, clowns, harlequins, apes' snouts, young men

in feminine guise, and vice versa, and several samples of
Italian costume, which might offer a picturesque variety.
Either the masques were not very funny, or I was in no funny
mood. There was little or nothing to laugh at except perhaps
two fantastic figures with enormous heads, as big round as
bushel-baskets, and [25] set round with frizzly hair. These
faces came and grinned into our carriage, and Julian tore out
a handful of hair (which proved to be sea-weed) from one
of their heads rather to the discomposure of the owner, who
muttered his indignation in Italian. Upon my honor, this
was all the fun, and I never in my life knew a shallower joke
than the Carnival at Rome; such a rainy and muddy day, too!
Greenwich Fair (at the very last of which I assisted) was
worth a hundred of it. While the bouquets and confetti were
flying, the Roman populace, or a good portion of them, stood
along the Corso, inactive spectators, seldom smiling; for I
cannot make it out to be their festival, or anybody's festival,
unless of the people in the carriages and balconies. The whole
affair is not worth this page or two. It was curious however to
see how safely the Corso was guarded; a strong patrol of the
papal dragoons, in steel helmets and white cloaks, were sta-
tioned at the street-corners, and rode up and down the thor-
oughfare, singly, or in a body. Detachments of the French
troops, stood by their stacked muskets in the Piazza de Popolo,
and at the other end of the Corso, and if the chained tiger-cat
(meaning thereby the Roman populace) had but shown the
tip of his claws, the bullets would have been flying along the
street. But the tiger-cat is a very harmless brute. In the course
of the afternoon, there came a full band of martial music
and then a body of [26] cavalry, escorting a number of carriages,
some of which, and especially one, were magnificent with
paint and gilding, and with gorgeous coachmen and footmen,
in wigs, gold lace, and silk coats and breeches. I should have
taken it to be a procession of His Holiness and the Cardinals;

but, if we rightly understood our driver, they were merely the heads of the Roman police. At any rate, with its martial show and its antique splendor of costume, it was the most effective masque of the day. A handful of confetti from one of the windows hit the coachman of the principal equipage, and hurt his dignity very much, though the lime and flour could hardly be distinguished from the official powder that had already been sprinkled over him. On comparing notes with Julian and Rosebud—indeed, with Una too—I find that they all enjoyed the Carnival much more than I did. Only the young ought to write descriptions of such scenes. My cold criticism chills the life out of it.

Rome, February 14th, Sunday.

Friday was a sunny day, the first that we had had for some time; and my wife and I went forth to see sights, as well as to make some calls that had long been due. We went first to the church of Santa Maria Maggiore, which I have already mentioned; and on our return, we went to the Piazza di Monte Cavallo, and saw those admirable old statues of Castor and Pollux, of which, [27] also, I have little more to say, though they seem to me sons of the morning, and full of life and strength. The atmosphere, in such a length of time, has covered the marble surface of these statues with a gray rust that envelopes both the men and horses as with a garment; besides which there are strange discolorations, such as patches of white moss on the elbows and reddish streaks down the sides; but the glory of form overcomes all these defects of color. It is pleasant to see how familiar some little birds are with these colossal statues, hopping about on their heads, and over their huge fists; very likely they have nests in their ears or among their hair.

We called into the Barberini Palace, where William Story
has established himself and family for the next seven years, on
the third piano, in apartments that afford a very fine look-out
over Rome, and (which is more important) have the sun in
them through most of the day. Mrs. Story invited us to her
fancy-ball, but we declined. On the staircase, ascending to
their piano, we saw the ancient Greek bas-relief of a lion,
whence Canova is supposed to have taken the idea of his
lions on the monument in Saint Peter's. Afterwards we made
two or three calls in the neighborhood of the Piazza d'Espagna
(finding only Mr. Hamilton Fish and family in the Hotel
d'Europe, at home,) and next visited the [28] studio of Mr.
C. G. Thompson, whom I knew in Boston. He has very
greatly improved since those days; and being always a man of
delicate mind, and earnestly desiring excellence for its own
sake, he has won himself the power of doing beautiful and
elevated works. He is now meditating a series of pictures from
Shakspeare's Tempest, the sketches of one or two of which he
showed us; likewise, a copy of a small Madonna by Raphael,
wrought with a minute faithfulness which it makes one a
better man to observe. He showed us, too, a Circassian Slave,
voluptuously beautiful, and a noble womanhood stirring
within her. Mr. Thompson is a true artist, and whatever his
pictures have of beauty comes from very far beneath the surface; and this, I suppose, is one great reason why he has but
moderate success. I should like his pictures for the mere color
even if they represented nothing. His Studio is in the Via
Sistina, and at a little distance, on the other side of the same
street, is William Story's, where we likewise went in, and
found him at work on a sitting statue of Cleopatra. William
Story looks thin and worn, already a little bald and a very
little gray, but quite as vivid—in a graver way—as when I
saw him last, a young man. He can yet, methinks, be scarcely
thirty-seven. His perplexing variety of talents and accomplish-

ments—a poet, a prose-writer, a lawyer, [29] a painter, a sculptor—seems now to be concentrating itself into this latter vocation; and I cannot see why he should not achieve something very good. He has a beautiful statue, already finished, of Goethe's Margaret pulling a flower to pieces to discover whether Faust loves her; a very type of virginity and simplicity. The statue of Cleopatra, now only fourteen days advanced in the clay, is as wide a step from the little maidenly Margaret as any artist could take; it is a grand subject, and he appears to be conceiving it with depth and power, and working it out with adequate skill. He certainly is sensible of something deeper in his art than merely to make beautiful nudities and baptize them by classic names. By the by, he told us several queer stories about American visitors to his studio; one of them, after long inspecting Cleopatra (into which he has put all possible characteristics of her time and nation and of her own individuality) asked "Have you baptized your statue yet?" as if the sculptor were waiting till his statue were finished before he chose the subject of it; as, indeed, I should think many sculptors do. Another remarked of a statue of Hero (who is seeking Leander by torchlight, and in momentary expectation of finding his drowned corpse,) "Is not the face a little sad?" Another time, a whole party of Americans filed into his studio and ranged themselves [30] round his father's statue, and after much silent examination the spokesman of the party inquired, "Well, Sir, what is this intended to represent?" William Story, in telling these little anecdotes, gave the Yankee twang to perfection, all the better, perhaps, because he has it somewhat obviously in his own customary tone.

The statue of his father—his first work—is very noble; as noble and fine a portrait statue as I ever saw. In the outer room of his studio, a stone-cutter (or whatever this sort of artizan is called) was at work transferring the statue of Hero

from the plaster-cast into marble; and already, though still in
some aspects a block of stone, there was a wonderful degree
of expression in the face. It is not quite pleasant to think that
the sculptor does not really do the whole labor on his statues,
but that they are all but finished to his hand by merely mechanical people. It is only the finishing touches that are given
by his own chisel.

Yesterday, being another bright day, my wife and I went
to the basilica of Saint John Lateran, which is the next basilica
in rank to Saint Peter's, and has the precedence of it as regards
certain sacred privileges. It stands on a most noble site, on
the outskirts of the city, commanding a view of the Sabine
and Alban Hills, blue in the distance, [31] and some of them
hoary with sunny snow. The ruins of the Claudian aqueduct
are close at hand. The church is connected with the Lateran
palace and museum, so that the whole is one edifice; but the
facade of the church distinguishes it, and is very lofty and
grand—more so, it seems to me, than Saint Peter's. Under the
portico is an old statue of Constantine, representing him as a
very stout and sturdy personage. The inside of the church
disappointed me, though no doubt I should have been wonder-
struck had I seen it a month ago. We went into one of the
chapels, and found it very rich in colored marbles, and going
down a winding staircase, found ourselves among the tombs
and sarcophagi of the Corsini family, and in presence of a
marble Pieta (a representation of the mother of Christ with
her son's dead body) very beautifully sculptured. On the other
side of the church we looked into the Torlonia chapel; it is
very rich, rather profusely gilded, but as it seemed to me, not
tawdry; though the snow white newness of the marble is not
perfectly agreeable, after being accustomed to the milder tint
which time bestows on sculpture. The tombs and statues
looked like shapes and images of new-fallen snow. The most
interesting thing which we saw in this church (and, admitting

its authenticity, there can scarcely be a more interesting relic [32] anywhere) was the table on which the last supper was eaten. It is preserved in a corridor on one side of the Tribune or chancel, and is shown by torch-light, suspended upon the wall, beneath a covering of glass. Only the top of the table is shown, presenting a broad flat surface of wood, evidently very old, and showing traces of dry rot in one or two places. There are nails in it; and the attendant said that it had formerly been covered with bronze. As well as I can remember, it may be five or six feet square and I suppose would accommodate twelve persons, though not if they reclined in the Roman fashion, nor if they sat as they do in Corregio's picture. It would be very delightful to believe in this table. There are several other sacred relics preserved in this church; for instance, the staircase of Pilate's house up which Jesus went; and the porphyry slab on which the soldiers cast lots for his garments. These, however, we did not see. There are very glowing frescoes on portions of the walls of this basilica; but, there being much white-wash, instead of incrusted marble, it has not the splendid effect which one's eye learns to demand in Roman churches. There is a good deal of statuary along the columns of the nave, and in the monuments of the side aisles. In reference to the interior splendors of Roman churches, I must say that I think it a [33] pity that painted windows are exclusively a Gothic ornament; for the elaborate ornamentation of these interiors puts the ordinary daylight out of countenance; so that a window, with only the white sunshine coming through it, or even with a glimpse of the blue Italian sky, looks like a portion left unfinished, and therefore a blotch in the rich wall. It is like the one spot in Aladdin's palace which he left for the king, his father-in-law, to finish, after his fairy architects had exhausted their magnificence on the rest; and the son, like the king, fails in the effort. I shall say nothing more about this church, except that it has what is called a Porta Sacra, which we saw, walled up, in the front of the church, on one side of the main-entrance. I know not what gives it its sanctity, but it appears to be opened by the pope on a year of jubilee, once every quarter of a century.

After our return my wife lay down, very much wearied, and I took Rosebud along the Pincian Hill; and finally (after witnessing what of the Carnival could be seen in the Piazza de Popolo, from that safe height) we went down into the Corso, and some little distance along it. Except for the sun-shine the scene was much the same as I have already described; perhaps fewer confetti and more boquets. Some Americans and English are said to have been brought be[34]fore the police authorities, and fined for throwing lime. It is remarkable that the jollity, such as it is, of the Carnival, does not extend an inch beyond the line of the Corso; there it flows along in a narrow stream, while in the nearest street, we see nothing but the ordinary Roman gravity.

Rome, February 15th, Monday.

Yesterday was a bright day, and Una, Miss Shepard, and Julian went to the Palace of the Caesars. I did not go out till the afternoon, when I took an hour's walk along the Pincian, stopping a good while to look at the old beggar who, for many years past has occupied one of the platforms of the flights of steps leading from the Piazza d'Espagna to the Trinita di Monti. Hillard commemorates him in his book. He is an un-lovely object, moving about on his hands and knees (princi-pally by aid of his hands which are fortified with a sort of wooden shoes) while his poor wasted lower shanks stick up in the air behind him loosely vibrating as he progresses. He is gray, old, ragged; a pitiable sight, but seems very active in his own fashion, and bestirs himself, on the approach of his vic-

tims, with the alacrity of a spider when a fly touches the remote circumference of his web. While I looked down at him,
he received alms from three persons, one of whom was a
young woman of the lower orders; the other two were gentlemen, probably either English or American. I could not [35]
quite make out the principle on which he let some persons
pass without molestation, while he shuffled from one end of
the platform to the other to intercept an occasional individual.
He is not persistent in his demands; nor, indeed, is this a usual
fault among Italian beggars. A shake of the head will stop
him, when wriggling towards you from a distance. I fancy
he reaps a pretty fair harvest, and no doubt leads as contented
and as interesting a life as most people, sitting there all day
on those sunny steps, looking at the world, and making his
profit out of it. It must be pretty much such an occupation
as fishing, in its effect upon the hopes and apprehensions;
and probably he suffers no more from the many refusals he
meets with, than the angler does, when he sees a fish smell
at his bait and swim away. One success pays for a hundred
disappointments, and the game is all the better for not being
entirely in his own favor. Walking onward, I found the
Pincian thronged with promenaders, as also with carriages,
which drove round the verge of the gardens in an unbroken
ring.

To-day has been very rainy. I went out in the forenoon,
and took a sitting at Miss Lander's studio, she having done
me the honor to request me to sit for my bust. Her rooms are
those formerly occupied by Canova; the one where she models
being large, high, and dreary, from the want of [36] carpet,
furniture, or anything but clay and plaster. A sculptor's studio
has not the picturesque charm of a painter's, where there is
color, warmth, cheerfulness, and where the artist continually
turns towards you the glow of some picture which is resting
against the wall. Miss Lander is from my own native town,

and appears to have genuine talent, and spirit and independence enough to give it fair play. She is living here quite alone, in delightful freedom, and has sculptured two or three things that may probably make her favorably known. "Virginia Dare" is certainly very beautiful. During the sitting, I talked a good deal with Miss Lander, being a little inclined to take a similar freedom with her moral likeness to that which she was taking with my physical one. There are very available points about her and her position; a young woman, living in almost perfect independence, thousands of miles from her New England home, going fearlessly about these mysterious streets, by night as well as by day, with no household ties, no rule or law but that within her; yet acting with quietness and simplicity, and keeping, after all, within a homely line of right. In her studio, she wears a sort of pea-jacket, buttoned across her breast, and a little foraging-cap, just covering the top of her head. She asked me not to look at the bust at the close of the sitting, and, of course, I obeyed; though I have a vague idea of a heavy-browed [37] physiognomy, something like what I have seen in the glass, but looking strangely in that guise of clay. Miss Lander has become strongly attached to Rome, and says that, when she dreams of home, it is merely of paying a short visit, and coming back before her trunk is unpacked. This is a strange fascination that Rome exercises upon artists; there is clay elsewhere, and marble enough, and heads to model; and ideas may be made sensible objects at home as well as here. I think it is the peculiar mode of life, and its freedom from the enthralments of society, more than the artistic advantages which Rome offers; and then, no doubt, though the artists care little about one another's works, yet they keep one another warm by the presence of so many of them.

The Carnival still continues; though I hardly see how it can have withstood such a damper as this rainy day. There were several people—three, I think—killed in the Corso, on Saturday; some accounts say that they were run over by the horses in the race, others, that they were ridden down by the dragoons in clearing the course.

After leaving Miss Lander's, I stept into the church of St. Luigi de' Franchesi, in the Via di Ripetta. It was built, I believe, by Catherine de Medici, and is under the protection of the French government, and the most shamefully dirty place of worship I ever saw; the beautiful [38] marble columns looking dingy for the want of loving and pious care. There are many tombs and monuments of French people, both of the past and present, artists, soldiers, priests, and others who have died in Rome. It was so dusky within the church that I could hardly distinguish the pictures in the chapels and over the altar, nor did I know that there were any worth looking for; nevertheless, there were frescoes of Domenichino, and oil paintings by Guido and others. I found it peculiarly touching to read the records, in Latin or French, of persons who had died in this foreign land, though they were not my own country-people, and though I was even less akin to them than they to Italy. Still, there was a sort of relationship in the fact that neither they nor I belonged here.

Rome, February 17th, Wednesday.

Yesterday morning was perfectly sunny; and my wife and I went betimes to see churches, going first to the Capuchin church (I forget its individual title) close by the Piazza Barbarini. It is now, I believe, the church of a convent of Capuchin monks. On entering, we found it not very large, but of good architecture, with a vaulted roof over the nave, and rows of chapels on either side, instead of aisles. The pavement seemed old and worn, and was much patched with brick tiles as well as with mediaeval tombstones; and we were startled to see—right [39] in the middle of the pavement, and in the centre of the nave, on a bier, with three candles burning on each side, and one at the head and another at the feet—a dead monk! He was dressed, as when alive, in the brown woollen frock of his order, with the hood drawn over his head, but so as to leave his face uncovered, as well as part of his gray beard. His beads and cross hung by his side; his hands were folded over his breast; his feet were bare both of shoes and stockings, and seemed to be tied together with a black ribbon. He certainly was a dead monk, and had once been alive; though, at first, I was in some doubt whether he might not be a wax figure, so strange was it to see him displayed in such guise. Meanwhile, his brother monks were singing or chanting some deep, lugubrious strain—a *de profundis*, I believe—in the vaults under the church, where the dead man was soon to be laid, in earth brought long ago from Jerusalem, but which has been the bed, over and over again, of deceased members of the fraternity. For it is the custom of this convent, when one of its monks dies, to take the bones that have been longest buried out of the oldest grave, and remove them to a common ossuary, putting the newly deceased into the vacant bed. It is rather hard upon these poor fathers, that they cannot call even their graves their own. We walked round the church, which contains pictures and fres[40]coes by Guido and Domenichino; but pictures in the side-chapels of churches are quite lost, in nine cases out of ten, by the bad light, or the no light, in which they must be seen. Much the most interesting object to me was still the dead monk, with his bare feet, those old, worn feet, that had walked to and fro over the hard pavements of Rome, and along the dreary corridors of his convent, for so many years, and now stuck forth so stiffly from beneath his frock. He had been a somewhat short and punchy personage, this poor monk, and perhaps had died of apoplexy; for his face did not look pale, but had almost, or quite, the natural flush of life, though the feet were of such a yellow, waxy hue. His gray eyebrows were very thick, and my wife had a fancy that she saw him contort them. There were a good many people in the church; some kneeling at one shrine or another; one pouring his soul through the open-work of the confessional, and some standing round the dead monk. The children, of whom there were several, stood about the bier in little groups, gazing at him with great interest and pity, rather awed; sometimes they knelt; and a woman knelt down and kissed his beads. By and by, as we moved round from chapel to chapel, still with our eyes turning often to the dead monk, we saw some blood oozing from his nostrils! Perhaps his murderer—or his doctor—had just then come into the [41] church and drawn nigh the bier; at all events, it was about as queer a thing as ever I witnessed. We soon came away and left him lying there; a sight which I shall never forget.

We next went to the Trinita di Monti, which stands at the head of the steps leading, in several flights, from the Piazza d'Espagna. It is now connected with a convent of French nuns, and when we rang at a side-door, one of the sisterhood answered the summons, and admitted us into the church. This, like that of the Capuchins, had a vaulted roof over the nave, and no side-aisles, but rows of chapels instead. Unlike the Cappuchins'—which was filthy, and really shameful to behold—the church was most exquisitely neat, as women alone would have thought it worth while to keep it. It is not a very splendid church—not rich in gorgeous marbles —but pleasant to be in, if it were only for the sake of this godly purity. There was only one person in the nave; a young girl, who sat perfectly still, with her face towards the altar, as long as we staid. Between the nave and the rest of the church, there is a high iron railing; and on the other side were two kneeling figures in black, so motionless that I at first thought them statues; but they proved to be two nuns at their devotions, and others of the sisterhood came by-and-by and joined them. Nuns—at least these nuns, who are French, and probably ladies of refinement, having the education of young girls—are far pleasanter objects to [42] see, and think about, than monks; the odour of sanctity, in the latter, not being an agreeable fragrance. But these holy sisters, with their black crape and white muslin, looked really pure and unspotted from the world. On the iron railing, above-mentioned, was the representation of a golden heart, pierced with arrows; for these are nuns of the Sacred Heart. In the various chapels, there are several paintings in fresco, mostly by Daniele da Volterra; and one of these—the Descent from the Cross—has been pronounced the third greatest picture in the world. Upon my word, I never should have had the slightest suspicion that it was a great picture at all; so worn and faded it looks, and so hard; so difficult to be seen, and so undelightful when one does see it.

From the Trinita we went to the San Maria del Popolo, a church built on a spot where Nero is said to have been buried, and which was afterwards made horrible by devilish phantoms. It being now past twelve, and all the churches closing from twelve till two, we had not time to pay much attention to the frescoes, oil pictures, and statues, by Raphael and other famous men, which are to be seen here. I remember dimly the magnificent chapel of the Chigi family, and little else; for we staid but a short time, and went next to Miss Lander's studio, where I had another sitting for my bust. [43] After Miss Lander had moulded me for above an hour, we turned homeward; but my wife concluded to hire a balcony for this last afternoon and evening of the Carnival, and she took possession of it, while I went home to send Miss Shepard and the two elder children. For my part, I took Rosebud, and walked, by way of the Pincian, to the Piazza del Popolo, and thence along the Corso, where, by this time, the warfare of boquets and confetti raged pretty fiercely. The sky being blue and the sun bright, the scene was much gayer and brisker than I had before found it, and I can conceive of its being rather agreeable than otherwise, up to the age of twenty. We got several volleys of confetti; Rosebud received a bouquet and a sugar-plum; and I, a resounding hit from something that looked more like a cabbage than a flower. Little as I have enjoyed the Carnival, I think I could make quite a brilliant sketch of it, without very widely departing from truth. Little Rosebud and I went home betimes; and Julian (who had gone with Miss Mitchell to the Baths of Caracalla, and afterwards had run wild along the Corso) came just about sunset; but Mamma, Miss Shepard, and Una, staid in their balcony to see the extinguishing of the tapers, which is the final frolic of the Carnival. They described the taper-spectacle as very picturesque, even as if the long avenue of the Corso were sown with stars.

[44] Rome, February 19th. Friday.

Day before yesterday, pretty early, my wife and I went to St Peter's, expecting to see the Pope cast ashes on the heads of the Cardinals, it being Ash Wednesday. On arriving, however, we found no more than the usual number of visitants and devotional people scattered through the broad interior of St Peter's, and thence concluded that the ceremonies were to be performed in the Sistine Chapel. Accordingly, we went out of the church through the door in the left transept, and went round the exterior, and through the vast courtyards of the Vatican, seeking for the Chapel. We had blundered into the carriage-entrance of the Vatican; there is an entrance from

some street near the front of the church, but this we did
not find. The papal guards (in the strangest, antique, and
antic, costume that was ever seen, a party-colored dress, striped
with black, red and yellow, with a doublet and ruff, and trunk
breeches, and armed with halberds) were on duty at the
gateways, but suffered us to pass without question. Finally,
we reached a large courtyard, where some cardinals' red equipages and other carriages were drawn up, but were still at a
loss as to the whereabouts of the chapel. At last, an attendant
kindly showed us the proper door, and led us up flights of
stairs, along passages and galleries, and through halls, till at
last we came to a spacious and lofty apartment, adorned with
frescoes. This was the Sala Regia, and the ante-chamber to
the Sistine Chapel. The [45] attendant, meanwhile, had informed us that my wife could not be admitted to the Chapel
in her bonnet, and that I myself could not be admitted at all,
for lack of a dress-coat; so my wife took off her bonnet, and
covering her head with her black veil, was readily let in; while
I remained in the Sala Regia, with several other people who
found themselves in the same predicament. There was a wonderful variety of costume to be seen and studied among the
persons around me, comprising garbs that have been elsewhere laid aside for at least three centuries;—the broad, fluted,
double ruff, and black velvet cloak, doublet, trunk breeches
and sword, of Queen Elizabeth's time; the papal guard, in
their striped & particolored dress, as before described, looking
not a little like harlequins; other soldiers in helmets & jack-
boots; French officers of various uniform; monks and priests;
attendants in old-fashioned and gorgeous livery; gentlemen,
some in black dress coats and pantaloons; others in wide-
awake hats and tweed overcoats; and a few ladies in the prescribed costume of black; so that, in any other country, the
scene might have been taken for a fancy ball. By and by, the
Cardinals began to arrive, and added their splendid purple

robes and red hats to make the picture still more brilliant. They were old men—one or two very aged and infirm—and generally men of bulk and substance, with heavy faces, fleshy about the chin. Their red hats, trimmed with gold lace, are a beautiful [46] piece of finery, and are identical in shape with the black, loosely cocked beavers, worn by the Catholic ecclesiastics generally. Wolsey's hat, which I saw at the Manchester Exhibition, might have been made on the same block, but apparently was never cocked, as the fashion now is. The attendants of the cardinals changed the upper portions of their masters' attire, and put a little cap of scarlet cloth on each of their heads, after which the cardinals (one by one, or two by two, as they happened to arrive) went into the Chapel; with an attendant behind each, holding up his purple train. In the meantime, within the chapel, we heard singing and chaunting; and whenever the voluminous curtains, that hung before the entrance, were partly drawn aside, we outsiders peeped through, but could see only a mass of people within, and beyond them, still another chapel, divided from the hither one by a screen. When almost everybody had gone in, there was a muster and stir among the guards and attendants, and a door opened, apparently communicating with the inner apartments of the Vatican. Through this door came—not the Pope, as I had partly expected—but a bulky old lady in black, with a red face, who bowed towards the spectators with an aspect of dignified complaisance, as she passed towards the entrance of the chapel. I took off my hat (unlike certain [47] English gentlemen who stood nearer) and found that I had not done amiss, as this was the ex-queen of Spain.

There was nothing else to be seen; so I went back through the ante chambers (which were noble halls, richly frescoed on the walls and cielings) endeavoring to get out through the same passages that had let me in. I had already tried to descend what I now suppose to be the Scala Sancta but had been turned back by a centinel. After wandering to and fro, a good while, I at last found myself in a long, long gallery, on each side of which were innumerable inscriptions, in Greek and Latin, on slabs of marble, built into the walls; and classic altars and tablets were ranged along the gallery, from end to end. At the extremity was a closed iron-grating, from which I was turning back; but a French gentleman accosted me, with the information that the Custode would admit us, if I chose, and would accompany us through the sculpture department of the Vatican. I acceded, and thus took my first view of those innumerable art-treasures, passing from one object to another, at an easy pace, pausing hardly a moment anywhere, and dismissing even the Apollo, and the Laocoon, and the torso of Hercules, in the space of half a dozen breaths. I was well enough content to do so, in order to get a general idea of the contents of the galleries, be[48]fore settling down upon individual objects. Most of these world-famous sculptures presented themselves to my eye with a kind of familiarity, through the copies and casts which I had seen; but I found the originals were different than I anticipated. The Apollo, for instance, has a face which I have never seen in any cast or copy. I must confess, however—taking such transient glimpses as I did—I was more impressed with the extent of the Vatican, and the beautiful order in which it is kept, and its great, sunny, open courts, with fountains, grass, and shrubs, and the views of Rome and the Campagna from its windows—more impressed with these, and with certain vastly capacious vases, and two great sarcophagi, than with the statuary. Thus we went round the whole, and were dismissed through the grated barrier into the gallery of inscriptions again; and after a little more wandering, I found my way out of the palace. I looked into St Peter's, a few moments, and thought that perhaps as grand effect of its great size, as any other, was the long bars of dusty sunshine, coming aslantwise through the windows in the dome, or through the windows of the transepts or side aisles, and travelling so far before they reached any resting-place. But my mind has not yet so adapted itself as to acknowledge the immensity of the church. Everybody talks of the diminutive appearance of [49] the six-foot cherubs that uphold the vase of holy water. To me, they look just six feet high, neither more nor less.

Yesterday, I went out betimes, and strayed through some portion of ancient Rome,—to the column of Trajan, to the forum, thence along the Tarpeian way, after which I lost myself among the intricacies of the streets, and finally came out at the bridge of St Angelo. The first observation which a stranger is led to make, in the neighborhood of Roman ruins, is, that the inhabitants seem to be strangely addicted to the washing of clothes; for all the precincts of Trajan's forum, and of the Roman forum, and wherever else an iron railing affords opportunity to hang them, were whitened with sheets and other linen and cotton, drying in the sun. It must be that washerwomen burrow among the old temples. The second observation is not quite so favorable to the cleanly character of the modern Romans; indeed, it is so very unfavorable that I hardly know how to express it. But the fact is, that, through the forum, and along the base of any ancient wall, and anywhere else, out of the commonest foot-track and road-way, you must look well to your steps, or they will be defiled with unutterable nastiness. If you tread beneath the triumphal arch of Titus or Constantine, you had better look downward than upward, whatever be the merit of the sculptures aloft; and, in my opinion, the Romans of to-day [50] consider these ancient relics as existing for no other purpose than that they may turn aside to them in their necessity. They appear to have no other places of need, and to need them ten times as much as other people. After awhile, the visitant finds himself getting accustomed to this horrible state of things, and the associations of moral sublimity and beauty seem to throw a veil over the physical meannesses to which I allude. Perhaps there is something in the mind of the people of these countries that enables them quite to dissever small ugliness from great sublimity and beauty. They spit on the glorious pavement of St Peter's, and wherever else they like; they place mean-looking wooden confessionals beneath its sublime arches, and ornament them with cheap little colored prints of the crucifixion; they hang tin hearts and other tinsel and trumpery at the gorgeous shrines of the saints, in chapels that are encrusted with gems, or marbles almost as precious; they put pasteboard statues of Saints beneath the dome of the Pantheon; in short they let the sublime and the ridiculous come close together, and are not in the least troubled by the proximity. It must be that their sense of the beautiful is stronger than in the Anglo Saxon mind, and that it observes only what is fit to gratify it.

To day (which was bright and cool) my wife and I set forth immediately after breakfast, in search of the Baths [51] of Diocletian, and the church of Santa Maria dei Angeli. We went too far along the Via di Porta Pia, and after passing by two or three convents, and their high garden walls, and the Villa Bonaparte on one side, and the Villa Torlonia on the other, at last issued through the city-gate. Before us, far away, were the Alban hills, the loftiest of which was absolutely silvered with snow and sunshine, and set in the bluest and brightest of skies. We now retraced our steps to the Fountain of the Termini, where is a ponderous heap of stone representing Moses striking the rock; a colossal figure, not without a certain enormous might and dignity, though rather too evidently looking his awfullest. This statue was the death of its sculptor, who broke his heart on account of the ridicule which it excited. There are many more absurd acquatic devices in Rome, and few better.

We turned into the Piazza di Termini, the entrance of

which is at this fountain; and after some enquiry of the French soldiers, a numerous detachment of whom appear to be quartered in the vicinity, we found our way to the portal of San Maria dei Angeli. The exterior of this church has no pretensions to beauty or majesty, or indeed to architectural merit of any kind, or to any architecture whatever; for it looks like a confused pile of ruined brickwork, with a façade resembling half the inner curve of a large oven. No one would imagine [52] that there was a church under that enormous heap of ancient rubbish. But the door admits you into a circular vestibule, once an apartment of Diocletian's baths, but now a portion of the nave of the church, and surrounded with monumental busts; and thence you pass into what was the central hall of the baths, now, with little change except of detail and ornament, transformed into the body of the church. This space is so lofty, broad, and airy, that the soul forthwith swells out, and magnifies itself, for the sake of filling it. It was Michael Angelo that contrived this miracle; and I feel even more grateful to him for rescuing this noble interior from destruction, than if he had originally built it himself. In the cieling above, you see the metal fixtures, whence the old Romans hung their lamps; and there are eight gigantic pillars of Egyptian granite, standing as they stood of yore. There is a grand simplicity about this church, more satisfactory than elaborate ornament; but the present Pope has paved and adorned one of the large chapels of the transept, in very beautiful style; and the pavement of the central part is likewise beautifully laid in marbles. In the choir, there are several pictures, one of which was veiled, as celebrated pictures frequently are, in churches. A person, who seemed to be at his devotions, withdrew the veil for us, and we saw a martyrdom of Saint Sebastian, by Domenichino, orig[53]inally, I believe, painted in fresco at Saint Peter's, but since transferred to canvas, and removed hitherto. Its place at St. Peter's is supplied by a mosaic copy. I was a good deal impressed by this picture—the dying saint, amid the sorrow of those who loved him, and the fury of his enemies, looking upward, where a company of angels, and Jesus in the midst, were waiting to welcome him and crown him;—and I felt what an influence pictures might have upon the devotional part of our nature. The nail-marks in the hands and feet of Jesus, ineffaceable even after he had passed into bliss and glory, touched my heart with a sense of his love for us. I think this really a great picture. We walked round the church, looking at the other pictures and frescoes, but saw none that greatly interested us. In the vestibule there are monuments to Carlo Maratti and Salvator Rosa; and there is a statue of Saint Bruno, by Houdon, which is pronounced to be very fine. I thought it good, but scarcely worthy of vast admiration. Houdon was the sculptor of the first statue of Washington, and the bust whence, I suppose, all subsequent statues have been, and will be, mainly modelled.

After emerging from the church, I looked back with wonder at the stack of shapeless old brickwork that hid the splendid interior of this church. I must go there again, and breathe freely in that noble space.

[54] Rome, February 20th, Saturday.

This morning, after breakfast, I walked across the city, making a pretty straight course to the Pantheon, and thence to the Bridge of St Angelo, and to Saint Peter's. It had been my purpose to go to the Fontana Paolina, but finding that the distance was too great, and being weighed down with a Roman lassitude, I concluded to go into St Peter's. Here I looked at Michael Angelo's *Pieta*; a representation of the dead Christ, naked in his mother's lap. Then I strolled round the great church, and find that it continues to grow upon me both in magnitude and beauty, by comparison with the many interiors of sacred edifices, which I have lately seen. At times, a single, casual, momentary glimpse of its magnificence gleams upon my soul, as it were, when I happen to glance at arch opening beyond arch, and I am surprised into admiration when I think least of it. I have experienced that a landscape, and the sky, unfold their deepest beauty in a similar way, not when they are gazed at of set purpose, but when the spectator looks suddenly through a peep-hole among a crowd of other thoughts. Passing near the confessionals for foreigners, to day, I saw a Spaniard, who had just come out of the one devoted to his native tongue, taking leave of his confessor, with an affectionate reverence which—as well as the benign dignity of the good Father—it was good to behold. The relation between the confessor and his penitent might, and ought to be, one of great [55] tenderness and beauty; and the more I see of the Catholic church, the more I wonder at the exuberance with which it responds to the demands of human infirmity. If its ministers were themselves a little more than human, they might fulfill their office, and supply all that men need.

I returned home early, in order to go with my wife to the Barberini Palace, at two °clock. We entered through two gateways, from the Via delle quatre Fontane, passing one or two French centinels; for there is, apparently, a regiment of dragoons quartered on the ground-floor of the palace, and I stumbled upon a room containing their saddles, the other day, when seeking for Mr. Story's staircase. The entrance to the picture gallery is by the door on the right hand, affording us a sight of a beautiful spiral staircase, which goes circling upward from the very basement to the very summit of the palace, with a perfectly easy ascent, yet confining its sweep within a moderate compass. We looked up through the interior of the spiral, as through a tube, from the bottom to the top. The pictures are contained in three contiguous rooms of the lower story, and are few in number, comprising barely half-a-dozen which I should care to see again, though doubtless all have value in their way. One that attracted our attention was a picture of Christ disputing with the Doctors, by Albert Durer, in which was represented the ugliest, most evil-minded, stubborn, pragmatical, and [56] contentious old Jew, that ever lived under the law of Moses; and he and the child Jesus were arguing not only with their tongues, but making hieroglyphics, as it were, by the motion of their hands and fingers. It is a very queer, as well as a very remarkable picture. But we passed hastily by this, and almost all the other pictures, being eager to see the two which chiefly make the collection famous.— These are Raphael's Fornarini, and Guido's portrait of Beatrice Cenci. These we found in the last of the three rooms; and as regards Beatrice Cenci, I might as well not try to say anything, for its spell is indefinable, and the painter has wrought it in a way more like magic than anything else I have known. It is a very youthful, girlish, perfectly beautiful face, with white drapery all around it, and quite enveloping the form. One or two locks of auburn hair stray out. The eyes are large and brown, and meet those of the spectator; and there is, I think, a little red about the eyelids, but it is very slightly indicated. The whole face is perfectly quiet; no distortion nor disturbance of any single feature; nor can I see why it should not be cheerful, nor why an imperceptible touch of the painter's brush should not suffice to brighten it into joyousness. Yet it is the very saddest picture that ever was painted, or conceived; there is an unfathomable depth and sorrow in the eyes; the sense of it comes to you by a [57] sort of intuition. It is a sorrow that removes her out of the sphere of humanity; and yet she looks so innocent, that you feel as if it were only this sorrow, with its weight and darkness, that keeps her down upon the earth and brings her within our reach at all. She is like a fallen angel, fallen, without sin. It is infinitely pitiful to meet her eyes, and feel that nothing can be done to help or comfort her; not that she appeals to you for help and comfort, but is more conscious than we can be that there is none in reserve for her. It is the most profoundly wrought picture in the world; no artist did it, or could do it again. Guido may have held the brush, but he painted better than he knew. I wish, however, it were possible for some spectator, of deep sensibility, to see the picture without knowing anything of its subject or history; for no doubt we bring all our knowledge of the Cenci tragedy to the interpretation of the picture.

Close beside Beatrice Cenci hangs the Fornarina, a brunette, with a deep, bright glow in her face, naked below the navel, and well pleased to be so for the sake of your admiration —ready for any extent of nudity, for love or money,—the brazen trollope that she is. Raphael must have been capable of great sensuality, to have painted this picture of his own accord and lovingly.

While we were looking at these pictures, Miss Mitchell had unexpectedly joined us; and we went all three together to the Rospigliosi palace, in the piazza di Monte Cavallo. A [58] porter, in a cocked hat, and with a staff of office, admitted us into a spacious courtyard before the palace, and directed us to a garden on one side, raised as much as twenty feet above the level on which we stood. The gardener opened the gate for us; and we ascended a beautiful stone staircase, with a carved balustrade, bearing many marks of time and weather. Reaching the garden-level, we found it laid out in walks, bordered with box and ornamental shrubbery, amid which were lemon-trees, and one large old tree, an exotic from some distant clime. In the centre of the garden, surrounded by a stone balustrade like that of the staircase, was a fish-pond, into which several jets of water were continually spouting; and on pedestals, that made part of the balustrades, stood eight marble statues of Apollo, Cupid, nymphs, and other such sunny and beautiful people of classic mythology. There had been many more of these statues, but the rest had disappeared, and those who remained had suffered grievous damage, here to a nose, there to a hand or foot, and often a fracture of the body, very imperfectly mended. There was a pleasant sunshine in the garden, and a springlike, or rather a genial autumnal atmosphere, though elsewhere it was a day of poisonous Roman chill.

At the end of this garden (which was of no great extent) [59] was an edifice, bordering on the piazza or street, called the Casino, which, I presume, means a garden-house. The front that looks into the garden is richly ornamented with bas-reliefs and statues in niches; as if it were a place for pleasure and enjoyment, and therefore ought to be beautiful. As we approached it, the door swung open, and we went into a large room on the ground-floor, and looking up to the cieling, beheld Guido's Aurora. The picture is as fresh and brilliant as if he had painted it with the morning sunshine which it represents; it could not have been more lustrous in its hues, if he had given it the last touch an hour ago. Three or four artists were copying it at that instant; and positively their colors did not look fresher—though a great deal rawer— than his. The alacrity and movement, briskness, and morning stir and glow, of the picture, are wonderful. What nonsense it is to write about it. It seems impossible to catch its glory even in a copy. Several artists, as I said, were making the attempt, and we saw two other attempts at copies leaning against the wall; but it was easy to detect failure in just the essential points. My memory, I believe, will be somewhat brightened by this picture hereafter; not that I remember it very distinctly, even now; but bright things leave a sheen and glimmer in the mind, like Christian's tremulous glimpse of the Celestial

City. In two other [60] rooms of the Casino, we saw pictures by Domenichino, Rubens, and other famous painters, which I do not mean to speak of, because I really cared little or nothing about them. Emerging into the garden (the sunny warmth of which was most genial, after the chill air and cold pavement of the Casino) we walked round the fish-pool, examining the statues, and looking down at some little fishes that swarmed at the stone margin of the pool. There were two little members of the Rospigliosi family, one a young child playing with a nurse and a head-servant, another, the very chubbiest and rosiest boy in the world, sleeping on its nurse's bosom. The nurse was a comely young woman enough, dressed in bright colors, which set off the deep coloring of her Italian face. An old painter very likely would have beautified and refined the pair into a Madonna with the child Jesus. An artist need not go far, in Italy, to find a picture ready composed and colored, needing little more than to be literally copied.

Miss Mitchell had gone away before us; but my wife and I, after leaving the Palazzo Rospigliosi, and on our way home, went into the church of St. Andrea, which belongs to a convent of Jesuits. I have long ago exhausted all my capacity of admiration for splendid interiors of churches; but methinks this little church (it is not more than fifty or [61] sixty feet across) has a more perfect and gem-like beauty than any I have seen. Its shape is oval, with an oval dome, and, above that, another little dome, both of which are magnificently frescoed. Around the base of the larger dome is wreathed a flight of angels, and the smaller and upper one is circled by a wreath of cherubs—cherub and angel all of pure white marble. The oval centre of the church is walled round with precious and lustrous marble, of a red-veined variety, interspersed with columns and pilasters of white marble; and there are arches opening through this rich wall, forming chapels, which the

architect seems to have striven hard to make even more magnificent than the main body of the church. They contain
beautiful pictures, not dark and faded, but glowing as if just
from the painter's hand; and the shrines are adorned with
whatever is most precious, and in one of them was the Great
Carbuncle—at any rate, a bright, fiery gem, as big as a turkey's
egg. The pavement of the church was one star of various
colored marble, and in the centre was a mosaic, covering, I
believe, the tomb of the founder. I have not seen, nor expect
to see, anything else so entirely and satisfactorily finished as
this little oval church; and I only wish I could pack it into a
large box, and send it home.

I must not forget, that, on our way from the Bar[62]berini
palace, we stopped an instant to look at the house (at the
corner of the street of the Four Fountains) where Milton
was a guest, while in Rome. He seems quite a man of our
own day, seen so nearly at the hither extremity of the vista
through which we look back, from the epoch of railways to
that of the oldest Egyptian obelisk. The house (it was then
occupied by Cardinal Barberini) looks as if it might have
been built within the present century; for mediaeval houses
in Rome do not assume the aspect of antiquity, perhaps because the Italian style of architecture, or something similar,
is the one now generally in vogue in most cities.

Rome, February 21st, Sunday.

This morning, soon after breakfast, I took my way through
the Porta del Popolo, intending to spend the forenoon in the
Campagna; but getting weary of the straight, uninteresting
street that runs out of the gate, I turned aside from it and
soon found myself on the shores of the Tiber. It looked, as
usual, like a saturated solution of yellow mud, and eddied

hastily along between deep banks of clay, and over a clay bed, in which doubtless are hidden many a richer treasure of antiquity than we now possess. The French once proposed to drain off the river for the purpose of recovering all the sunken statues and relics; but the Romans made strenuous objection on account of the increased virulence of malaria which would probably result. I saw a man on the imme[63]diate shore of the river, fifty feet or so beneath the bank on which I stood, sitting patiently with an angling rod; and lighting a cigar I waited to see what he might catch. Two other persons likewise sat down to watch him; but he caught nothing as long as I staid, and at last seemed to give it up. The banks and vicinity of the river are very bare and uninteresting, as I then saw them; no shade, no verdure, a rough, neglected aspect, and a peculiar shabbiness about the few houses that were visible. Farther down the stream, the dome of St Peter's showed itself on the other side, seeming to stand on the outskirts of the town. I walked along the bank, with some expectation of finding a ferry by which I might cross the river; but my course was soon interrupted by the city-wall, and I turned up a lane that led me straight back again to the Porta del Popolo. I stopt a moment, however, to see some young men pitching quoits, which they appeared to do with a good deal of skill.

I went along the Via di Ripetta, and through other streets, stepping into two or three churches, one of which was the Pantheon. When I last saw it, the sun was coming through the circular opening in its dome; now the sunshine fell side-long through it, and threw a large span of light on the hollow curve; and it seemed well to have such a skyward door for good spirits to float down through, and for prayers to ascend. It is truly a noble edifice; and it is curious to see how well the Hea[64]then temple has adapted itself to Christian and Catholic purposes, supplying more shrines and chapels than any other form of building possibly could. There are, I think,

seven deep, pillared recesses around the circumference, each
of which becomes a sufficiently spacious chapel; and, alternately with these chapels, there is a marble structure, like
the architecture of a doorway, beneath which is the shrine
of a saint; so that the whole circle of the Pantheon is filled
up with the seven chapels and seven shrines. A number of
persons were sitting or kneeling around; others came in while
I was there, dipping their fingers in the holy water, and bending their knee as they passed the shrines and chapels, until they
reached the one which, apparently, they had selected as the
particular altar for their devotions. Everybody seemed so
devout, and in a frame of mind so suited to the day and place,
that it really made me feel a little awkward not to be able to
kneel down along with them. Unlike the worshippers in our
own churches, each individual here seems to do his own
individual acts of worship, and I cannot but think it better
so than to make a joint-stock concern of it, as we do. It is my
opinion that a great deal of devout and reverential feeling
is kept alive in people's hearts by the Catholic mode of worship.
Soon leaving the Pantheon, a few minutes walk towards the
Corso brought [65] me to the church of St Ignazio, which
belongs to the College of the Jesuits. It is a spacious church, of
beautiful architecture, but not strikingly distinguished in the
latter particular from many others; a wide and lofty nave,
supported upon marble columns, between which arches open
into the side-aisles, and, at the junction of the nave and
transept, a dome, resting on four great arches. The church
seemed to be purposely somewhat darkened, so that I could
not well see the details of its ornamentation, except the frescoes
on the cieling of the nave, which were very brilliant, and done
in so effective a style that I really could not satisfy myself that
some of the figures did not actually protrude from the cieling
—in short, that they were not colored bas-reliefs instead of
frescoes. No words can express the beautiful effect (in an

upholstery point of view) of this kind of decoration. Here as at the Pantheon, there were many persons, sitting silent, kneeling, or passing from shrine to shrine.

I reached home at about twelve, and, at one °clock, set out again with my wife towards St Peter's, where we meant to stay till after vespers. We walked across the city, and through the Piazza di Navona, where we stopt to look at one of Bernini's absurd fountains, of which the water makes but the smallest part—a little squirt or two, amid a prodigious fuss of gods and monsters. Thence we passed by [66] the poor battered torso of Pasquin, and came by devious ways to the Bridge of St Angelo; the streets bearing pretty much their week-day aspect, many of the shops open, the market-stalls doing their usual business, and the people brisk and gay, though not indecorously so. I suppose there was hardly a man or woman who had not heard mass, confessed, and said their prayers; a thing which—the prayer, I mean—it would be absurd to predicate of London, or New York, or any Protestant city. In however adulterated a guise, the Catholics do get a draught of devotion to slake the thirst of their souls, and methinks it must needs do them good, even if not quite so pure as if it came from better cisterns, or from the original fountain-head.

Arriving at St Peter's shortly after two, we walked round the whole church, looking at all the pictures and most of the monuments. In passing by the confessionals for the different nations, we saw a priest open one of them, and take from the central part (which is a little closet, with openwork on each side to which the priest can apply his ear, while the penitent kneels without) a rod, which he stuck up, projecting slant-wise from the confessional, like a barber's pole. This is in token that a priest is in attendance to receive the confession of such as may wish to make them. I was not attracted by the face of this particular priest; it did not indicate the wise, [67] deep, and tender soul, into which I could choose to pour my own. We passed quite round the whole circumference of the church, and paused longest before Guido's picture (its mosaic copy, rather) of the archangel Michael overcoming Lucifer. This is surely one of the most beautiful things in the world; one of the human conceptions that are imbued most largely with the celestial. These old painters were wonderful men, and have done great things for the Church of Rome— great things, we may say, for the church of Christ and the cause of good; for the moral of this picture (the immortal youth and loveliness of virtue, and its irresistible might against evil) is as much directed to a Puritan as to a Catholic.

Having completed the circuit of the church, we sat down in one of the aisles and awaited the beginning of vespers, which we supposed would take place at half-past three. Four °clock came, however, and no vespers; and as our dinner hour is at five, and the children would ill abide to be kept waiting for us, we at last came away without hearing the vesper song. As my wife had eaten nothing since breakfast, she bought some roasted chestnuts in the street, and we came homeward, munching them most of the way from the Bridge of St Angelo to the Via de Condotti. It was a fine sunny afternoon: but the small, square stones of Roman pavements are most wearisome to the feet.

[68] Rome, February 23ᵈ, Tuesday.

Yesterday at noon, mamma and I set out for the Capitol, and after ascending the acclivity (not from the forum, but from the opposite direction) stopt to look at the statues of Castor and Pollux, which, with other sculptures, look down the ascent. Castor and his brother seem to me to have heads disproportionately large, and are not so striking, in any respect, as such great images ought to be. But we heartily admired the equestrian statue of Marcus Aurelius Antonius, which is full of grace and dignity, and makes the spectator love and reverence him even over this wide gap of ages—stretching forth his hand, as he does, with a gesture as if he were issuing a command that was in itself a benediction. Then we looked at a fountain, principally composed, I think, of figures representing the Nile and the Tiber, who loll upon their elbows and preside over the gushing water; and between them, against the facade of the Senator's palace, there is a statue of Minerva with a petticoat of red porphyry. Having taken note of these objects, we went into the Museum, in an edifice on our left, entering the Piazza, and here in the vestibule we found various old statues and relics of which there remains hardly the slightest trace in my memory. Ascending the stairs, we passed through a long gallery, of the contents of which I can make no better record, and turning to our left, examined somewhat more carefully [69] a suite of rooms running parallel with the gallery. The first of these contained busts of the Caesars and their kindred, from the epoch of the mightiest Julius downward, eighty-three, I believe, in all. I had seen a bust of Julius Caesar, in the British Museum, and was surprised at its thin and withered aspect; but this head is of a very ugly old man indeed, wrinkled, puckered, shrunken, lacking breadth and substance, care-worn, grim, as if he had fought hard with life, and had suffered in the conflict; a man of schemes, and of eager effort to bring his schemes to pass. His profile is by no means good, advancing from the top of his forehead to the tip of his nose, and retreating, at about the same angle, from the latter point to the bottom of his chin, which seems to be thrust forcibly down into his shrunken neck. Not that he pokes his head forward, for it is particularly erect. The head of Augustus is very beautiful, and appears to be that of a meditative, philosophic man, saddened with the sense that it is not very much worth while to be at the summit of human greatness, after all. It is a sorrowful thing to trace the decay of civilization through this series of busts, and to observe how the artistic skill, so exquisite at first, went on declining through the dreary dynasty of the Caesars, till at length the master of the world could not get his head carved in better style than the figure-head of a ship.

[70] In the next room, there were better statues than we had yet seen, but neither do I retain any vivid recollection of these, nor yet of those in the succeeding apartment; but, in the last room of the range, we found the Dying Gladiator, of which I had already caught a glimpse, in passing by the open door. It had made all the other treasures of the gallery tedious, in my eagerness to come to that. I was not in a very fit state to see it, for that most miserable sense of satiety—the mind's repletion when too much rich or delicate food has been forced upon it— had got possession of me, though I had really done little more than glance at objects. Still, I had life enough left to admire this statue, and was more impressed by it than by anything of marble that I ever saw. I do not believe that so much pathos is wrought into any other block of stone. Like all other works of the highest excellence, however, it makes great demands upon the spectator; he must make a generous gift of his sympathies to the sculptor, and help out his skill with all his heart, or else he will see little more than a skilfully wrought surface. It suggests far more than it shows. I looked long at this statue, and little at anything else, though, among other famous works, a statue of Antinous was in the same room.

I was glad when we left the Museum, which, by the by, was awfully chill, as if the multitude of statues radiated [71] cold out of their marble substance. We might have gone to see the pictures in the Palace of the Conservators; and my wife (whose receptivity is unlimited, and forever fresh) would willingly have done so; but I objected, and so we went towards the Forum. I had noticed, two or three times, an inscription over a mean looking door in the neighborhood, stating that here was the entrance to the prison of the holy apostles, Peter and Paul; and we soon found the spot, not far from the Forum, with two wretched frescoes of the apostles above the inscription. We knocked at the door without effect; but a lame beggar, who sat at another door of the same house (it looked exceedingly like a liquor shop) desired us to follow him, and began to ascend the acclivity of the Capitol, by the causeway leading from the Forum. A little way upward, we met a woman, to whom the beggar delivered us over, and she led us into a door (a church, or chapel-door, I think) and pointed to a long flight of steps, which descended through twilight into utter darkness. She called to somebody in the lower regions, and then went away, leaving us to go down this mysterious staircase by ourselves. Down we went, farther and farther from the daylight, and found ourselves anon in a dark chamber, or cell, or some sort of a place, the shape or boundaries of which we could not make out, though it seemed to be of stone, and black, and dungeon-like. Indistinctly, and from a still further depth [72] in the earth, we heard voices— one voice, at least, apparently not addressing ourselves, but some other persons; and soon, directly beneath our feet, we saw a glimmering of light through a round, iron-grated hole, in the bottom of the dungeon. For a few minutes, the glimmer and the voice came up through this hole, and the light disappeared, and it, and the voice, came glimmering and babbling up a flight of stone stairs, of which we had not hitherto been aware. It was the Custode, with a party of visitors to whom he had been showing Saint Peter's dungeons. Each visitor was provided with a wax taper, and the Custode gave one to each of us, bidding us wait a moment while he conducted the other party to the upper air. During his absence, we examined the cell, as well as our dim lights would permit, and soon found an indentation in the wall, with an iron-grate put over it for protection, and an inscription above, informing us that the Apostle Peter had here left the imprint of his visage; and, in honest truth, there is a profile there, forehead, nose, mouth, and chin, plainly to be seen, an intaglio in the solid rock. We touched it with the tips of our fingers, as well as saw it with our eyes. The Custode soon returned, and led us down the darksome steps, chattering in Italian all the time. It is not a very long descent to the lower cell, the roof of which is so low that I believe I could have touched it [73] with my hand. We were now in the deepest and ugliest part of the old Mamertine Prison, one of the few remains of the kingly period of Rome, and which served the Romans as a state-prison for hundreds of years before the Christian era. A multitude of criminals, or innocent persons, no doubt, have languished here in misery, and perished in darkness. Here Jugurtha starved; here Cataline's adherents were strangled; and methinks there cannot be in the world another such an evil den, so haunted with black memories, and indistinct surmises of guilt and suffering. In old Rome, I suppose, the citizens never spoke of this dungeon above their breath. It looks just as bad as it is,—round, only seven paces across, yet so obscure that our tapers could not illuminate it from side to side, the stones, of which it is constructed, being as black as midnight. The Custode showed us a stone post, at the side of the cell, with the hole in the top of it, into which, he said, St Peter's chain had been fastened; and he uncovered a spring of water, in the middle of the stone floor, which he told us had miraculously gushed up, to enable the Saint to baptize his jailer. The miracle was perhaps the more easily wrought, inasmuch as Jugurtha had found the floor of the dungeon oozy with wet. However, it is best to be as simple and childlike, as we can, in these matters; and whether St Peter stamped his visage into the stone, and wrought this other miracle or no—and whether or no he ever was in [74] the prison at all—still the belief of a thousand years, and more, gives a sort of reality and substance to such traditions. The Custode dipt an iron ladle into the miraculous water, and we each of us drank a sip; and what is very re-markable, to me it seemed hard water, and almost brackish, while my wife thought it the sweetest she had tasted in Rome. I suspect Saint Peter still dabbles in this water, and tempers its qualities according to the faith of those who drink it.

The staircase, descending into the lower dungeon, is com-paratively modern, there having been no entrance, of old, except through the small circular opening in the roof. In the upper cell, the Custode showed us an ancient flight of stairs, now built into the wall, which used to descend from the Capitol. The whole precincts are now consecrated, and, I believe, the upper portion—and perhaps both upper and lower—are now a shrine or a chapel.

Being altogether weary of sight-seeing, I left my wife in the forum, and went to call on Mr. J. P. Kennedy, at the Hotel d'Europe. I found him just about to ascend the stairs, on his return from a drive; a gentleman of about sixty, or more, with gray hair, a pleasant, intellectual face, and penetrating, but not unkindly eyes. He moved infirmly, being just on the recovery from an illness. We went up to his parlor together, and had a talk; or rather, he had it nearly [75] all to himself—and particularly sensible talk, too, and full of the results of learning and experience. In the first place, he settled the whole Kansas difficulty; then he made terrible work with Saint Peter, who came very shabbily out of his hands, as regarded his early character in the church and his claims to the position he now holds in it. Mr Kennedy also gave a curious illustration, from something that happened to himself, of the little dependence that can be placed on traditions purporting to be ancient; and

I capt his story by telling how the site of my Town Pump, so plainly indicated in the sketch itself, has already been mistaken in the city-council and in the public prints.

Rome, February 24th, Wednesday.

Yesterday, I crossed the Ponte Sisto, and took a short ramble on the other side of the river; and it rather surprised me to discover, pretty nearly opposite the Capitoline Hill, a quay, at which several schooners and barques, of two or three hundred tons burthen, were moored. There was also a steamer, armed with a large gun and two brass swivels on her forecastle, and I know not what artillery besides. Probably she may have been a revenue-cutter. Returning, I crossed the river by way of the island of San Bartolomeo, over two bridges. The island appears to be densely covered with buildings, and is a separate, small fragment of the city. It was a tradition of the ancient Romans that this island was formed by the aggregation of soil and [76] rubbish brought down by the river, and accumulating round the nucleus of some sunken baskets.

On reaching the hither side of the river, I soon struck upon the ruins of the theatre of Marcellus, which are very picturesque, and the more so from being close linked in—indeed, identified—with the shops, habitations, and swarming life of modern Rome. The most striking portion was a circular edifice, which seemed to have been composed of a row of Ionic columns standing upon a lower row of Doric; many of the antique pillars being yet perfect, but the intervening arches built up with brickwork, and the whole once magnificent structure now tenanted by poor and squalid people, as thick as mites within the round of an old cheese. From this point I cannot very clearly trace out my course; but I passed, I think, between the Circus Maximus and the Palace of the Caesars, and near the Baths of Caracalla, and went into the cloisters of the church of San Gregorio. All along, I saw massive ruins, not particularly picturesque or beautiful, but huge, mountainous piles chiefly of brickwork, somewhat weed-grown, here and there, but oftener bare and dreary. For Nature does not take a Roman ruin to her heart as she does the old feudal castles and abbeys of England, covering them up with ivy as tenderly as Robin Redbreast covered the dead babes with leaves. Besides, all the successive ages, since Rome began to decay, have done their best to ruin the very ruins by [77] taking away the marble and the hewn stone for their own structures, and leaving only the inner filling-up of brick-work, which the ancient architects never designed to be seen. The consequence of all this is that except for the lofty and poetical associations connected with it—and except, too, for the immense difference in magnitude—a Roman ruin may be in itself not more picturesque than I have seen an old cellar, with a shattered brick chimney half crumbling down into it, in New England.

By this time, I knew not whither I was going, and turned aside from a broad, paved road, (it was the Appian Way) into the Via Latina, which I supposed would lead to one of the city-gates. It was a lonely path; on my right hand, extensive piles of ruin, in strange shapes or shapelessness, built of the broad and thin old Roman bricks, such as may be traced everywhere, when the stucco has fallen away from a modern Roman house, for I imagine there has not been a new brick made, these thousand years. On my left, I think, was a high wall, and before me, grazing on the sward, a well-grown calf, who seemed frolicsome, shy, and sociable, all at the same time; for he capered, leaped to one side, and shook his head as I passed him, but soon came galloping behind me, and again started aside when I looked round. The road went boldly on, with a well-worn track, up to the very wall of the city; but there it abruptly terminated at an ancient, closed up gate-way. From a no[78]tice posted against a door, which appeared to be the entrance to the ruins on my left, I found that these were the remains of Columbaria, where the dead used to be put away in pigeon-holes. Reaching the paved road again, I kept on my course, passing the tomb of the Scipios, and soon came to the gate of San Sebastiano, through which I emerged into the Campagna. Indeed, the scene around me was so lonely and rural, that I had fancied myself already beyond the walls. As the afternoon was getting advanced, I did not proceed any further towards the blue hills which I saw in the distance, but turned to my left, following a well-beaten road that runs round the exterior of the city wall. It was very lonesome, not a house on the whole track, and very dreary, with the broad and shaggy campagna on one side, and the high, bare wall looking down over my head. It is not—any more than the other objects of the scene—a very picturesque wall, but is little more than a brick garden-fence seen through a magnifying glass—with now and then a tower, however, and frequent buttresses to keep its height of fifty feet from toppling over. The top was ragged, and fringed with a few weeds; there had been embrasures for guns, and eyelet holes for musquetry, but these were plastered up with brick or stone. I passed one or two walled-up gateways (by the by, the Porta Latina was the gate through which Belisarius first entered Rome) and [79] one of these had two high, round towers, and looked more Gothic, and venerable with antique strength, than any other portion of the wall. Immediately after this, I came to the Gate of San Giovanni, immediately within which is the Basilica of St John Lateran, entering which, I was glad to rest myself a little while upon a bench, before proceeding homeward.

There was a French centinel at this gateway, as at all the others; for the Gauls have always been a pest to Rome, and now gaul her worse than ever. I observed, too, that an official in citizen's dress stood at the gateway, and appeared to exercise a supervision over some carts, with country produce, that were entering just then.

Rome, February 25th, Thursday.

We went, this forenoon, to the Palazzo Borghese, which is situated on a street that runs at right angles with the Corso, and very near the latter. Most of the palaces in Rome, and the Borghese among them, were built somewhere about the six-teenth century; this, in 1590, I believe. It is an immense edifice, standing round the four sides of a quadrangle; and though the suite of rooms, comprising the picture gallery, forms an almost interminable vista, they occupy only a part of the ground floor of one side. We enter from the street into a large court-yard, round which runs a corridor, the arches of which support a second series of arches above. The picture-rooms open from one into another, and have many points of magnificence, being large and lofty, with vaulted [80] cielings, and beautiful frescoes, generally of mythological subjects, in the flat central part of the vault; the cornices are gilded; the deep embrasures of the windows are panelled with wood-work; the doorways are of polished and variegated marble; the floors are either marble, or covered with a sort of composition as hard and highly polished, and seemingly as durable. The whole has a kind of splendid shabbiness thrown over it, like a slight coating of rust; the furniture, at least the damask chairs, being a good deal worn, though there are marble and mosaic tables which may serve to adorn another palace, when this one crumbles away with age. One beautiful hall, with a cieling more richly gilded than the rest, is panelled all round with large looking-glasses, on which are painted pictures, both landscapes and human figures, in oils; so that the effect is somewhat as if you saw these objects represented in the mirrors. These glasses must be of old date, perhaps coeval with the first building of the palace; for they are so much dimmed that one's own figure appears indistinct in them, and more difficult to be traced than the pictures which cover them half over. It was very comfortless in these rooms—indeed, I suppose nobody ever thought of being comfortable there, since the house was built—but especially uncomfortable on a chill, damp day like that. My fingers were quite numb before I got halfway through the suite of apartments, in spite of a brazier of charcoal which was smouldering into ashes, in two or three [81] of the rooms. There was not, so far as I remember, a single fireplace in the suite. A considerable number—not very large, however—of visitors were there; and a good many artists, and three or four ladies among them, were making copies of the more celebrated pictures, and in all, or most cases, missing the especial points that made their celebrity and value. The Prince Borghese certainly acts like a kind and liberal gentleman in throwing open this invaluable collection to the public to see, and for artists to carry away with them and diffuse all over the world, so far as their own strength and skill will permit. It is open every day of the week, except Saturday and Sunday, without any irksome restriction or supervision; and the fee, which custom requires the visitor to pay to the Custode, has the good effect of making us feel that we are not intruders, nor even received in any exactly elemosynary way. The thing could not be better managed.

As to the pictures, I do not propose to say much about them. The collection is one of the most celebrated in the world, and contains between eight and nine hundred pictures, many of which are esteemed master-pieces. I think I was not in a frame for admiration, to-day, nor could achieve that free and generous surrender of myself, which I have already said is essential to the proper estimate of anything excellent. Besides, how is it possible to give one's soul, or any considerable [82] part of it, to a single picture, seen for the first time, among a thousand others, all of which set forth their own claims in an equally good light! Furthermore, there is an external weariness and sense of thousand-fold sameness to be overcome, before we can begin to enjoy a gallery of the old Italian masters. There is such a terrible lack of variety in their subjects. A quarter part of the Borghese collection, I should think, consists of Virgins and infant Christs, repeated over and over again, in pretty much the same spirit, and often with no more mixture of the divine in the picture, than just enough to spoil it as a representation of maternity, with which everybody's heart has something to do. Then, half of all the rest of the pictures are crucifixions, takings down from the cross, Pietás, Noli me tangeres, subjects from the Old Testament, or scenes in the lives of Saints, all probably painted as altar-pieces or for the shrines of chapels, and requiring, for their full effect, the accompaniment which the artist took into view, in conceiving them. There remains another quarter part, comprising mythological subjects, such as naked Venuses, Ledas, Graces, and a general apotheosis of nakedness, once fresh and rosy perhaps, but mostly yellow and dingy, in our day; often, it seems to me, retaining only a traditional charm. These old painters seldom treated their subjects in a homely way; they were above [83] life, or on one side of it; and if they ever touched the heart, it was by the help of the religious sentiment, which we Protestants can not call up, to eke out our profane admiration. I can hardly think they really had the sentiments themselves; for evidently they were just as ready, or more so, to paint a lewd and naked woman, and call her Venus, as to imagine whatever is purest in womanhood, as the mother of their Saviour. I remember but one painter—Francia—who seems really to have approached this awful class of subjects in a fitting spirit; his pictures are very queer and awkward things, if you look at them with merely an external eye, but full of the beauty of holiness, and evidently wrought out as acts of devotion, with the deepest sincerity, and veritable prayers upon canvas. Raphael, and other great painters, have done wonders with sacred subjects; but the greatest wonder is, how they could ever paint them at all, and always they paint from the outside, and not from within.

I was glad, in the very last of the twelve rooms, to come upon some Dutch and Flemish pictures, very few, but very welcome; Rubens, Rembrandt, Vandyke, Paul Potter, Teniers, and others—men of flesh and blood, with warm fists, and human hearts. As compared with them, these mighty Italian masters seem men of polished steel, not human, nor addressing themselves so much to human sympathies as to a formed intellectual taste.

[84] Rome, March 1ˢᵗ, Monday.

We have had very bad weather for a week past, sombre, chill, and sometimes (as yesterday, from morning till night) pouring cataracts of rain. To-day, too, began very unfavorably; but Mamma and I ventured out, at about eleven ᵒclock, intending to view the gallery of the Colonna Palace. Finding it closed, however, on account of the illness of the Custode, we determined to go to the picture-gallery of the Capitol; and on our way thither, we stept into St Gesu, the grand and rich church of the Jesuits, where we found a priest in white preaching a sermon, with vast earnestness of action and variety of tones, insomuch that I sometimes fancied that two priests were in the agony of sermonizing at once. He had a pretty large, and seemingly attentive audience, clustered around him from the entrance of the church half way down the nave; while, in the chapels of the transepts, and in the remoter distances, were persons occupied with their own individual devotions. We sat down near the Chapel of St. Ignazio, which is adorned with a picture over the altar (I do not know the subject nor could see the picture very satisfactorily) and with marble sculptures of the Trinity aloft, and of angels fluttering at the sides. What I particularly noted (for the angels were not very real personages, being neither earthly nor celestial,) was the great ball of lapis lazuli, the biggest in [85] the world, at the feet of the chief person in the Trinity. The church is a splendid one, lined with a great variety of precious marbles, and having the cieling of its arched nave, its domes, and chapels, beautifully frescoed; but—partly, perhaps, owing to the dusky light, as well as to the want of cleanliness—(monks never seem to keep their conventual churches clean)—there was a dingy effect, upon the whole. We made but a very short stay, our New England breeding causing us to feel shy of moving about the church in sermon-time.

It rained when we reached the Capitol; and as the museum was not yet open, we went into the Palace of the Conservators, on the opposite side of the piazza. Around the inner courtyard of the ground-floor, partly under two opposite arcades, and partly under the sky, are several statues and other ancient sculptures; among them a statue of Julius Caesar, said to be the only authentic one, and certainly giving an impression of him more in accordance with his character than the withered old face in the Museum; also a statue of Augustus, in middle age, still retaining a resemblance to the bust of him in youth; some gigantic heads, and hands, and feet, in marble and bronze; a stone lion and horse, which lay long at the bottom of a river, broken and corroded and were repaired by Michael Angelo; and other things [86] which it were wearisome to set down. We inquired of two or three French soldiers the way into the picture-gallery, but it is our experience that

French soldiers, in Rome, never know anything of what is around them, not even the name of the palace or public place over which they stand guard; and though invariably civil, you might as well put a question to a statue of an old Roman as to one of them. While we stood under the arcade, however, looking at the rain plashing into the courtyard, a soldier of the papal guard kindly directed us up the staircase, and even took pains to go with us to the very entrance of the picture-rooms. Thank heaven, there are but two of them, and not many pictures which one cares to look very long at.

Italian galleries are at a disadvantage as compared with English ones, inasmuch as the pictures are not nearly such splendid articles of upholstery, though very likely, having undergone less cleaning and varnishing, they may retain more perfectly the finer touches of the masters. Neverthless, I miss the mellow glow, the rich and mild external lustre, and even the brilliant frames, of the pictures I have seen in England. You feel that they have had loving care taken of them; even if spoiled, it is because they have been valued so much. But these pic[87]tures in Italian galleries look rusty and lustre-less, as far as the exterior is concerned, and really the splendor of the painting, as a production of intellect and feeling, has a good deal of difficulty in shining through such clouds. There is one picture at the Capitol—the Rape of Europa, by Paul Veronese—that would glow with wonderful brilliancy if it were set in a magnificent frame, and covered with a sunshine of varnish; and it is a kind of picture that would not be desecrated, as some deeper and holier ones might, by any splendor of external adornment that could be bestowed on it. It is deplorable and disheartening to see it in faded and shabby plight, this joyous, exuberant, warm, voluptuous piece of work. There is the head of a cow, thrust into this picture, and staring with wild, ludicrous wonder at the godlike bull, so as to introduce quite a new sentiment. I did not see much else in

the gallery, that remains on my mind. Here, and at the
Borghese Palace, there were some pictures by Garofalo, an
artist of whom I never heard before, but who seems to have
been a man of power. A picture by Maria Sublegras—a
miniature copy from one by her husband of the woman
anointing the feet of Christ—is most delicately and beautifully
finished, and would be an ornament to a drawing room; a thing
that could not truly be said of one [88] in a hundred of
these grim masterpieces. When they were painted, life was
not what it is now, and the artist had not the same ends in
view. There is something forced, if not feigned, in our tastes
for pictures of the old Italian schools.

I was not much in the mood for enjoying them to-day, at
all events, being chilled to the fingers' ends in those great
rooms, where a fire was never kindled; and besides, it depresses the spirits to go from picture to picture, leaving a
portion of your vital sympathy at every one, so that you come
with a kind of half-torpid desperation, to the end. On our
way down the staircase, we saw several noteworthy bas-
reliefs, and among them a very ancient one of Curtius plunging on horseback into the chasm in the Forum. It seems to me,
however, that old sculpture affects the spirits even more dole-
fully than old painting; it strikes colder to the heart, and lies
heavier upon it, being marble, than if it were merely canvass.
My wife went to re-visit the Museum, which we had already
seen, on the other side of the piazza; but being cold and
miserable, morally and physically, I left her there, and went
out to ramble in the sun; for it was now brightly, though
fitfully, shining again. I went through the forum, (where a
thorn thrust itself out and tore the sleeve of my talma) and
under the Arch of Titus, towards the Coliseum. About [89] a
score of French drummers were beating a long, loud roll-call,
at the base of the Coliseum and under its arches; and a score
of trumpeters responded to them from the rising ground, op-

posite the Arch of Constantine; and the echoes of the old Roman ruins, especially those of the Palace of the Caesars, responded to this martial uproar of the barbarians. There seemed to be no cause for it; but the drummers beat, and the trumpeters blew, as long as I was within hearing. I walked along the Appian Way, as far as the Baths of Caracalla. The Palace of the Caesars, which I have never yet explored, appears to be crowned by the walls of a convent, built, no doubt, out of some of the fragments that would suffice to build a city; and I think there is another convent among the Baths. The Catholics have taken a peculiar pleasure in planting themselves in the very citadels of Paganism, whether temples or palaces. There has been a good deal of enjoyment in the destruction of old Rome. I often think so, when I see the elaborate pains that have been taken to smash and demolish some beautiful column, for no purpose on earth, except the mere delight of annihilating a noble piece of work. There is something in the impulse with which one sympathizes; though I am afraid the destroyers were not sufficiently aware of the mischief they did, to enjoy it fully. Probably, too, the Early Christians were impelled by [90] religious zeal to destroy the Pagan temples, before the happy thought occurred to them of converting them into churches.

March 3ᵈ, Rome, Wednesday.

This morning was Una's fourteenth birth-day, and we celebrated it by taking a barouche, and driving (the whole family) out on the Appian Way, as far as the tomb of Cecilia Metella. For the first time since we came to Rome, the weather was really warm; a kind of heat producing languor and disinclination to active movement, though still a little breeze, which was stirring, threw an occasional coolness over us, and made us distrust the almost sultry atmosphere. I cannot think this Roman climate healthy in any of its moods that I have yet experienced.

The Appian way is a desolate and dreary avenue, generally between brick and plastered walls, very solid in their construction, and so high as almost to exclude the view of the surrounding country. The houses are of very interesting aspect, not picturesque, though most unhomelike and unsocial, built of brick, I suppose, stuccoed over, seldom with a door opening hospitably upon the way side, but only accessible from the rear, and often with iron-grated windows. The road is paved from side to side with the small square blocks that make every Roman street so exceedingly uncomfortable. At frequent intervals, [91] close by the roadside, uprises the ruin of an ancient tomb, an immensely high, broken mound of conglomerated brick and stone, all molten, as it were, by time, into a mass as solid and indestructible as if it were one boulder of granite. When first erected, these tombs were no doubt cased externally with hewn stones or marble, and made beautiful with architectural forms; but all this has long since been stript away to adorn other edifices. On the top of one of them, I saw what seemed to be a modern dwelling, perched on the lofty dilapidation of the tomb, which formed a precipice of at least fifty feet in height on all the four sides. Others wear a crown of grass, shrubbery, and even trees. One had been made the foundation of a tower, which itself was centuries old, and was rifted quite from top to bottom with a great crack, though the tomb-hillock will surely stand just as firm as now till the last trump shall rend it asunder for the dead to come forth. Even the pyramids are not stranger, nor more alien from modern sympathies, than these old Roman tombs. I had conceived no idea of them beforehand—their immense height and mass, their solidity, defying time and the elements, and too hard, I should think, for any ordinary earth-quake to crack. And after

all, except in one or two instances, [92] they have not availed
to keep so much as the name of an individual or a family from
utter oblivion; so that these dead people might just as well
have been buried each under his own little green hillock,
without a head-stone. It is rather agreeable than otherwise to
think so much idle pains have been thwarted.

About two miles or more from the gate of St. Sebastiano we
saw, right on the roadside, a large circular edifice, constructed
of great blocks of hewn stone, standing on a great square
foundation of rough, agglomerated bricks, stones, and rubbish,
such as compose the masses of the tombs heretofore mentioned.
This was the tomb of Cecilia Metella. On the summit of the
circular structure, was a battlemented wall, the remains of a
fortress, which was built six hundred years ago, when the tomb
was not more than a thousand or fifteen hundred years old.
As we drew nearer, we saw a great space of grass, with bushes,
and a few trees, on the top of the immense round tower, and
within the partly fallen walls of the mediaeval fortress; and if
there were any lack of land below, an industrious man might
well enough have made a moderate-sized garden there. The
tomb has a door (of modern construction, I presume) through
which we ought to have had [93] entrance; but the custode was
away, and we found nobody about the precincts. The mediaeval ruins in the vicinity are very extensive, consisting of what
apparently was a feudal castle, of which the tomb of Cecilia
Metella was the citadel or donjon-keep. The posthumous fate
of this poor lady was certainly very odd. I suppose her husband
expected to secure endless peace and undisturbed repose for
her ashes, but the very means adopted for that end—the vast
shelter which he built over her urn—made that little handful
of female dust the nucleus of battles and sieges, many ages
after her death. Close on the other side of the road are the
ruins of a Gothic Chapel, little more than a few bare walls
and pointed windows, and some other fragmentary structures,

which we did not particularly examine. Una and I clambered
through a gap in the wall, extending from the basement of the
tomb, and then getting into the field beyond, went quite round
the tomb and the remains of the castle connected with it. The
latter, though still high and stalwart, showed few or no
architectural features of interest, being built, I think, principally of large bricks, and not to be compared to English ruins,
as a beautiful or venerable object.

[94] A little way beyond Cecilia Metella's tomb, the road
still shows a specimen of the ancient Roman pavement, composed of broad, flat, flag-stones, a good deal cracked and worn,
but sound enough probably to outlast the little cubes which
make the other portions of the road so uncomfortable. We
turned back from this point, and soon re-entered the gate of
St Sebastian, which is flanked by two tall towers, and just
within which is the old triumphal arch of Drusus, a sturdy
construction, much dilapidated as regards its architectural
beauty, but rendered far more picturesque than it would have
been in its best days, by a crown of verdure on its head. Probably so much of the dust of the highway has risen in clouds
and settled there, that sufficient soil for shrubbery to root itself
has thus been collected, by small annual contributions, in the
course of two thousand years. A little farther towards the city,
we turned aside from the Appian way, and came to the site of
some ancient columbaria, close by what seemed to partake
of the characters of a villa and a farm-house. A man came out
of the house, and unlocked a door in a low, square building,
apparently quite modern; but on entering, we found ourselves
looking down into a large square chamber, sunk [95] entirely
beneath the surface of the ground. A very narrow and steep
staircase, of stone, and evidently antique, descended into this
chamber; and, going down, we found the walls hollowed on
all sides into little semi-circular niches, of which, I believe,
there were nine rows, one above another, and nine niches in

each row. Thus they looked somewhat like the little entrances to a pigeon-house; and hence the name of Columbarium. Each semi-circular niche was about a foot in its semi-diameter. In the centre of this subterranean chamber was a solid, square column, or pier, rising to the roof, and containing other niches of the same pattern, besides one high and deep niche, rising to the height of a man from the floor, on each of the four sides. In every one of the little semi-circular niches were two round holes, covered with an earthen plate, and in each hole were ashes and little fragments of bones—the ashes and bones of the dead, whose names were inscribed in Roman capitals on marble slabs, inlaid into the wall, over each individual niche. Very likely the great niches, in the central pier, had contained statues or busts, or large urns; indeed, I remember that some such things were there, as well as bas-reliefs in the walls; but little more than the general aspect of the strange place re[96]mains in my mind. It was the Columbarium of the con- nections or dependents of the Caesars; and the impression left on me was, that this mode of disposing of the dead was in- finitely preferable to any which has been adopted since that day. The handful or two of dry dust and bits of dry bone, in each of the little round holes, had nothing disgusting in them; and they are no drier now than they were when first deposited there. I would rather have my ashes scattered over the soil, to help the growth of the grass and daisies, but still I should not murmur much at having them decently pigeon-holed in a Roman tomb. After ascending out of this chamber of the dead, we looked down into another similar one, containing the ashes of the servants of the Pompey-family, which was discovered only a very few years ago. Its arrangement was the same as the one just described, except that it had no central pier with a pas- sage round it, as the former had. While we were down in the first chamber, the proprietor of the spot, a half gentlemanly

and very affable kind of person, came down to us, and explained the arrangements of the Columbarium; though, indeed, we understood them better by their own aspect than by
his explanation. The whole soil around his dwelling is elevated
much above [97] the level of the road, and it is probable that,
if he chose to excavate, he might bring to light many more
sepulchral chambers, and find his profit in them too, by disposing of the urns and busts. What struck me as much as
anything was the neatness of these subterranean chambers,
which were quite as fit to sleep in as most of those occupied
by living Romans; and having undergone no wear and tear,
they are in as good condition as the day they were built.

In this chamber, measuring about twenty-five feet square,
I roughly estimate that there have been deposited together the
remains of at least seven or eight hundred persons, reckoning
two little heaps of bones and ashes in each pigeon-hole, nine
pigeon-holes in each row, and nine rows in each side of the
chamber, besides those in the middle pier. All difficulty in
finding space for the dead would be obviated by returning to
the ancient fashion of reducing them to ashes; the only objection—though a very serious one—being, the quantity of fuel
that it would require. But perhaps future chemists may discover
some better means of consuming, or dissolving, this troublesome mortality of ours.

We got into the carriage again, and driving a little farther
towards the city, came to the tomb of the Scipios, of the exterior of which I retain no very definite idea. It [98] was close
upon the Appian Way, however, though separated from it
by a high fence, and accessible through a gateway leading into
a yard. I think the tomb is wholly subterranean, and that the
ground above it is covered with the buildings of a farm-house,
but of this I cannot be certain, as we were led immediately
into a dark, underground passage, by an elderly peasant of

cheerful and affable demeanor. As soon as he had brought us into the twilight of the tomb, he lighted a long wax taper for each of us, and led us groping into blacker and blacker darkness. Even little Rosebud took her taper, and followed courageously in the procession, which looked very picturesque, as we glanced backward or forward, and beheld a twinkling line of seven lights, glimmering faintly on our faces, and showing nothing beyond. The passages and niches of this tomb seem to have been hewn and hollowed out of the rock, not built by any art of masonry; but the walls were very dark, almost black, and our tapers so dim, that I could not gain a sufficient breadth of view to ascertain what kind of place it was. It was the darkest place I ever was in; the Mammoth Cave could not be darker. The rough-hewn roof was within touch, and sometimes we had to stoop to avoid hitting our heads; it was covered with damps, which collected and fell upon us in occasional dew-drops. The passages, besides being narrow, were so irregular and crooked, that, after going a little way, it would have been impossible to return [99] upon our tracks without the help of the guide; and we appeared to be taking quite an extensive ramble underground, though in reality, I suppose, the tomb includes no great space. At several turns of our dismal way, the guide pointed to inscriptions in Roman capitals, commemorating various members of the Scipio family who were buried here; among them, a son of Scipio Africanus, who himself had his death and burial in a foreign land. All these inscriptions, however, are copies, the originals, which were really found here, having been removed to the Vatican. Whether any bones and ashes have been left, or whether any were found, I do not know. It is not, at all events, a particularly interesting spot, being such a shapeless blackness, and a mere dark hole, requiring a stronger illumination than that of our tapers to distinguish it from any other cellar. I did, at one place, see a sort of frieze, rather roughly sculptured; and as we returned towards the twilight of the entering passage, I discerned a large spider, who fled hastily away from our tapers—the solitary inhabitant of the tomb of the Scipios.

One visit that we made—and I think it was before entering the city-gate—I forgot to mention. It was to an old edifice, formerly called the Temple of Bacchus, but now, I believe, supposed to have been the Temple of Honor and Virtue. The interior consists of one vaulted hall, which was converted from its Pagan con[100]secration into a church or chapel, by the early Christians, and the ancient marble pillars of the temple may still be seen, built in with the brick and stucco of the later occupants. There is an altar, and other tokens of a Catholic church, and high towards the cieling there are some frescoes of saints or angels, very curious specimens of mediaeval, and earlier than mediaeval art. Nevertheless, the place impressed me as still rather pagan than Christian. What is most remarkable about this spot, or this vicinity, lies in the fact that the fountain of Egeria was formerly supposed to be close at hand; indeed, the Custode of the chapel still claims the spot as the identical one consecrated by the legend. There is a dark grove of trees, not far from the door of the Temple; but Murray— a highly essential nuisance on such excursions as this—throws such overwhelming doubt, or rather incredulity, upon the site, that I seized upon it as a pretext for not going thither. In fact, my little capacity for sight-seeing was already more than satisfied. On my wife's account, I am sorry that we did not see the grotto; for her enthusiasm is as fresh as the waters of Egeria's well can be, and she has poetical faith enough to light her cheerfully through all these mists of incredulity.

Our visits to sepulchral places ended with Scipio's tomb, whence we returned to our dwelling (by the by, I do not know whether I have mentioned that our dwelling is a palace, [1st 101] the Palazzo Laza— I forget its name!) and Miss Mitchell and Miss Lander came to dine with us.

Rome, March 10th, Wednesday.

On Saturday last (a terribly rainy day) my wife and I went to the Sciarra Palace, on the Corso, nearly opposite to the Piazza Colonna. It has (Heaven be praised) but four rooms of pictures, among which, however, are several very celebrated ones. Only a few of these remain in my memory;—Raphael's Violin Player, which I am willing to accept as a good picture, and Leonardo da Vinci's Vanity and Modesty, which also I can bring up before my mind's eye, and find it very beautiful, although one of the faces has an affected smile, which I have since seen on another picture by the same artist—Joanna of Aragon. The most striking picture in the collection, I think, is Titian's Bella Donna—the only one of Titian's works that I have yet seen, that makes an impression on me corresponding with his fame. It is a very splendid and very scornful lady, as beautiful and as scornful as Gainsborough's Lady Lynedoch, though of an entirely different type. There were two Madonnas by Guido, of which I liked the least celebrated one best; and several pictures by Garofalo, who always produces something noteworthy. All the pictures lacked the charm (no doubt I am a barbarian to [2nd 101] think it one) of being in brilliant frames, and looked as if it were a long, long while since they were cleaned or varnished. The light was so scanty, too, on that heavily clouded day, and in those gloomy old rooms of the palace, that scarcely anything could be fairly made out. The palace is about two hundred and fifty years old, and looks as if it had never been a very cheerful place; most shabbily and scantily furnished, moreover, and as chill as any cellar. There is a little balcony, looking down on the Corso, which probably has often been filled with a merry little family party in the Carnivals of days long past; it has faded frescoes and tarnished gilding, and green blinds, and a few damask chairs still remain in it.

On Monday, my wife, Una, Julian, and I, went to the Sculpture Gallery of the Vatican, and saw as much of the sculpture as we could in the three hours during which the public are admissible. There were a few things which I really enjoyed, and a few moments during which I really seemed to see them; but it is in vain to attempt giving the impression produced by masterpieces of art, and most in vain when we see them best. They are a language in themselves; and if they could be expressed any way except by themselves, there would have been no need of expressing those particular ideas and sentiments by sculpture. I saw the Apollo Belvidere as something ethereal and godlike; only for a [1st 102] flitting moment, however, and as if he had alighted from heaven, or shone suddenly out of the sunlight, and then had withdrawn himself again. I felt the Laocoon, too, very powerfully, though very quietly; an immortal agony, with a strange calmness diffused through it, so that it resembles the vast rage of the sea, calm on account of its immensity, or the tumult of Niagara, which does not seem to be tumult because it keeps pouring on, forever and ever. I have not had so good a day as this (among works of art) since we came to Rome; and I impute it partly to the magnificence of the arrangements of the Vatican—its long vistas, and beautiful courts, and the aspect of immortality which marble statues acquire by being kept free from dust. Julian was very hungry, and seeing a vast porphyry vase, forty-four feet in circumference, he wished that he had it full of soup.

Yesterday, my wife and I went to the Doria Pamfili palace, which, I believe, is the most splendid in Rome. The entrance is from the Corso, into a courtyard surrounded by a colonnade, and having a space of luxuriant verdure and ornamental shrubbery in the middle. The apartments containing pictures and sculpture are fifteen in number, and run quite round the court yard, on the first piano; all of them (the rooms, halls, and galleries) of beautiful proportions, with vaulted roofs, some of which glow with frescoes, and all [2nd 102] are colder and more comfortless than can possibly be imagined without having been there. I was positively chilled to the heart. The pictures—most of them, at all events—interested me very little. In truth, I am of opinion that good painters are quite as rare as good poets; and I do not see why we should pique ourselves on admiring any but the very best. One in a thousand, perhaps, ought to live in the applause of men from generation to generation, till his colors fade or blacken out of sight, and his canvas rots away; the rest should be put up garret, or painted over by newer artists, just as tolerable poets are shelved when their little day is over. Nevertheless, there was one long gallery, containing many pictures that I should be glad to see again, under more favorable circumstances—that is, separately, and in a room not quite so chill as a sepulchre, and where I might contemplate them quite undisturbed, reclining in an easy chair. At one end of the long vista of this gallery is a bust of the present prince Doria—a smooth, sharp-nosed, rather handsome young man—and at the other end, his princess, an English lady of the Talbot family, apparently a blonde, with a simple and sweet expression enough. There is a noble and striking portrait of the old Venetian admiral, Andrea Doria, by Sebastian del Piombo, and some other portraits and busts of the family.

In the whole immense range of rooms, I saw but a [103] single fire-place, and that so deep in the wall that no amount of blaze would raise the atmosphere of the room ten degrees. If the builder of the palace, or any of his successors, have committed crimes worthy of Tophet, it would be a still worse punishment for him to wander perpetually through this suite of rooms, on the cold floors, of polished brick tiles, or marble, or mosaic, growing a little chiller and chiller through every moment of eternity—or, at least, till the palace crumbles down upon him. Neither would it assuage his torment in the least to be compelled to gaze up at the dark old pictures—the ugly ghosts of what may once have been beautiful. I am not going to try, any more, to receive pleasure from a faded, tarnished, lustreless picture; especially if it be a landscape. There were two or three landscapes of Claude's in this palace, which I doubt not would have been exquisite if they were in the condition of those in the British National Gallery, but here they looked most forlorn, and even the sunshine was sunless. The merits of historical painting may be quite independent of the attributes that give pleasure, and a superficial ugliness may even heighten the effect.

III

[1] 37, Via Porta Pinciana, Rome, March 11th, Thursday, 1858.

TO DAY, Mamma, Rosebud, and I, called at Mr. Thompson's studio (68, via Sistina) and found not only himself but his wife there. He had on the easel the little picture of Saint Peter released from prison by the angel, which I saw once before. It is very beautiful indeed, and deeply and spiritually conceived, and I wish I could afford to have it finished for myself. I looked again, too, at his Georgian Slave, and admired it as much as at first view; so very warm and rich it is, so sensuously beautiful, and with an expression of higher life and feeling within. I do not think there is a better painter than Thompson living—among Americans, at least, not one so earnest, faithful, and religious in his worship of art. I had rather look at his pictures than at any except the very finest of the old Masters; and—taking into consideration only the comparative pleasure to be derived—I would not except more than one or two of those. In painting, as in literature, I suspect, there is something in productions of the [2] day that takes the fancy more than the works of any past age;—not greater merit, nor nearly so great, perhaps, as former artists or writers have possessed, but better suited to this very present time. Miss Lander tells me that Mr. Thompson is an unhappy man, dissatisfied with his position among artists, and feeling himself unappreciated.

After leaving him, we went to the Piazza di Termini, near the baths of Diocletian, and found our way with some difficulty to Crawford's Studio. It occupies several great rooms, connected with the offices of the Villa Negroni, and all these rooms were full of plaster casts, and a few works in marble, principally portions of his huge Washington monument, which he left unfinished at his death. Close by the door at which we entered, stood a gigantic figure of Mason, in bag-wig, and the coat, waistcoat, breeches, and knee-and-shoe buckles of the last century—the enlargement of these unheroic matters to far more than heroic size having a very odd effect. There was a figure of Jefferson on the same scale; another of Henry; besides a horse's head, and other por[3]tions of the equestrian statue which is to cover the summit of the monument. In one of the rooms was a model of the monument itself, on a scale, I should think, of about an inch to a foot. It did not impress me as having grown out of any great and genuine idea in the artist's mind, but as being merely an ingenious contrivance enough. There were also casts of statues that seemed to be intended for some other monument, referring to Revolutionary times and personages; and with these were intermixed some ideal statues or groupes—a naked boy, playing marbles, very beautiful; a girl with flowers; the cast of his Orpheus, of which I long ago saw the marble statue; Adam and Eve; Flora; and several others, all with a good deal of merit, no doubt, but not a single one that justifies Crawford's reputation, or that satisfied me of his genius. They are but common-places in marble and plaster, such as we should not tolerate on a printed page. He seems to have been a respectable man, highly respectable, but no more; although those who knew him seem to have rated him much higher. Miss Lander tells me [4] that he exclaimed, not very long before his death, that he had fifteen years of good work still in him; and he appears to have considered all his life and labour, heretofore, as only preparatory to the great things that he was to achieve hereafter. I should say, on the contrary, that he was a man who had done his best, and had done it early in life; for his Orpheus is quite as good as anything else we saw in his rooms.

People were at work, chiselling several of the plaster-casts in marble, a very interesting process, and what I should think a doubtful and hazardous one; but the artists say that there is no risk of mischief, and that the model is sure to be accurately repeated in the marble. These people, who do what is considered the mechanical part of the business, are often themselves sculptors, and of higher reputation than those who employ them. It is rather sad to think that Crawford died before he could see his ideas in the marble, where they gleam with so pure and celestial a light, as compared with the plaster; there is almost as much difference as between flesh and spirit. The floor [5] of one of the rooms was burthened with immense packages, containing parts of the Washington monument ready to be forwarded to its destination. When finished and set up, it will probably make a very splendid appearance, by its height, its mass, its skilful execution, and will produce a moral effect through its images of illustrious men, and the associations that connect it with our Revolutionary history; but I do not think it will owe much to the artist's force of thought or depth of feeling. It is certainly, in one sense, a very foolish and illogical piece of work—Washington mounted on an uneasy steed, on a very narrow space, aloft in the air, whence a single step of the horse, backward, forward, or on either side, must precipitate him; and several of his contemporaries standing beneath him, not looking up to wonder at his predicament, but each intent on manifesting his own personality to the world around. They have nothing to do with one another, nor with Washington, nor with any great purpose which all are to work out together.

Rome, March 14th, Sunday.

On Friday evening, I dined at Mr. T. B. Reades', the poet and artist, with a [6] party composed of painters and sculptors —the only exceptions being Mr. Hooker, the American banker, and an American tourist who has given Mr. Reade a commission. Next to me at table sat Mr. Gibson, the English sculptor, who, I suppose, stands foremost in his profession at this day. He must be quite an old man now; for it was whispered about the table that he is known to have been in Rome forty-two years ago, and he himself spoke to me, I think, of spending thirty seven years here before he once returned home. I should hardly take him to be sixty, however; his hair being more dark than grey, his forehead unwrinkled, his features unwithered, his eye undimmed, though his beard is somewhat venerable. He must have been very handsome once; a Grecian face, the most regular that I ever saw in an Englishman, with even forehead and brows, a straight nose, the whole just such as he himself might like to carve out of marble. His eyes are brown and bright, under brows that impend a little, but not so as to give him a brooding look; he has a quiet, self-contained aspect; and being a bachelor, has doubtless spent a calm life among his clay and marble, meddling little [7] with the world, and entangling himself with no cares beyond his studio. He did not talk a great deal, but enough to show that he is still an Englishman in many sturdy traits, though his accent has something foreign about it;—not but what I detected the h, once at least, where it had no business to be. His conversation was chiefly about India, and other topics of the day, together with a few reminiscences of people in Liverpool, where he once resided; there was a kind of simplicity both in his manner and matter, and nothing very remarkable in the latter. Once, however, he got upon the topic of art; and the immediate silence and concentrated attention of the rest of the company showed, rather to my surprise, with what weight of admitted authority he spoke. The gist of what he said was condemnatory of the pre-Raphaelite modern school of painters, of whom he seemed to spare none, and of their works nothing; though he allowed that the old pre-Raphaelites had some exquisite merits, which the moderns entirely omit in their imitations. In his own art, he said the aim should be to find out the principles on which the Greek sculptors wrought, and to do the [8] work of this day on those principles, and in their spirit; a fair doctrine enough, I should think, but which Mr. Gibson can scarcely be said to practise, giving birth, as he has, and does, to a vast progeny of marble dream-work from the Grecian mythology. The difference between the pre-Raphaelites and himself is deep and genuine; they being literalists and realists, in a certain sense, and he a pagan idealist. Methinks they have hold of the best end of the matter. On the whole, however, I liked Mr. Gibson, and doubt not that he has a beautiful fancy, and a cunning art at his finger-ends, though so simple a man in his nature and intercourse. He appears to have full and quiet faith in his own opinions; and very frequently, in his talk, he says "Yes," in a gentle but emphatic way, as if giving his own assent to his own proposition, and thereby settling the point beyond the possibility of dispute.

As for the other sculptors and painters (with the exception of Mr. Thompson, of whom I have already spoken,) I was not impressed with the sense of there being a man—I will not say of genius, but of anything beyond mechanical ability—among them all. The sculp[9]tors especially, I suspect, are of the stone-mason and figure-head-carver fraternity. They appear to be a jovial set of people, on good terms with one another, but without education, refinement, poetic feeling, taste, or any of the attributes which one feels inclined to allow to an artist in such an exquisite material as marble, as a matter of course. Possibly, they can only express themselves in their own art, and what poets say in words, they must say in marble. If so, I will try to know them better in their Sculptures, of which I have as yet seen nothing. I heard nothing worth remembering or repeating, from anybody's lips, except the following, which is attributed to Thorwaldsen—"The Clay is the Life; the Plaster is the Death; and the Marble is the Resurrection." The perfect truth of these analogies can only be estimated by observing a piece of sculpture in its three stages.

Rome, March 18th, Thursday.

To-day, it being very bright and mild, my wife and I set out at noon on an expedition to the Temple of Vesta; though I did not feel much inclined for walking, having been [10] sick and feverish, for two or three days past, with a cold, which keeps renewing itself faster than I can get rid of it. We kept along on this side of the Corso, and crossed the forum, skirting along the Capitoline Hill, and thence towards the Circus Maximus. On our way, looking down a cross-street, we saw a heavy arch, and on examination, made it out to be the Arch of Janus Quadrifrons, standing in the Forum Boarium. Its base is now considerably below the level of the surrounding soil; and there is a church, or basilica, close by, and other mean edifices looking down upon it. There is something satisfactory in this arch, from the immense mass and solidity of its structure; it gives the idea, in the first place, of a solid mass, constructed of huge blocks of marble, which time can never wear away, nor earthquakes shake down; and then this mass is penetrated by two arched passages, meeting in the centre. There are empty niches, three in a row, and, I think, two rows, on each face of the arch; but there seems to have been very little effort to make it a beautiful object. On the top is some brick-work, the remains of a mediæval fortress built by the Frangipanis, looking [11] very frail and temporary, being brought thus in contact with the antique strength of the arch. A few yards off, across the street, and close beside the basilica, is what appears to be an ancient portal, with carved bas-reliefs, and an inscription which I could not make out. Some Romans were lying dormant, in the sun, on the steps of the basilica; indeed, now that the sun is getting warm, they seem to take advantage of every quiet nook to bask in, and perhaps to go to sleep.

We had gone but a little way from the arch, and across the Circus Maximus, when we saw the Temple of Vesta before us, right on the bank of the Tiber, which, however, we could not see behind it. It is the most perfectly preserved Roman ruin that I have yet seen, and very beautiful, though so very small, that, in a suitable locality, one would take it rather for a garden-house than an ancient temple. A circle of white marble pillars, much time-worn, and a little battered, though none of them broken, surround the solid structure of the temple, leaving a circular walk between it and the pillars; the whole covered by a modern roof, which looked like wood, and disgraces and de-forms the elegant little [12] structure. This roof resembles, as much as anything else, the round wicker cover of a basket, and gives a very squat aspect to the temple. The pillars are of the Corinthian order, and when they were new, and the marble snow-white, and sharply carved and cut, there could not have been a prettier object in all Rome; but so small an edifice does not figure well as a ruin. Within view of it (and, indeed, a very little way off) is the Temple of Fortuna Virilis, which appears likewise to retain its antique form in better preservation than we generally find a Roman ruin; although the Ionic pillars are now built up with blocks of stone and patches of brickwork, the whole constituting a church, which is stuck against the side of a tall edifice, the nature of which I do not know. I forgot to say that we got admittance into the temple of Vesta, and found the interior a plain cylinder of marble, about ten paces across, and fitted up as a Chapel, when the Virgin took the place of Vesta.

In very close vicinity, we came upon the Ponte Rotto, the old Pons Æmilius, which was broken down long ago, and has only recently been pieced out by connecting [13] a suspension-bridge with the old piers. We crossed by this bridge (paying a toll of a baiocco each) and stopt in the midst of the river to look at the Temple of Vesta, which shows well, right on the brink of the Tiber. We fancied, too, that we could discern, a little farther down the river, the ruined and almost submerged piers of the Sublician bridge, which Horatius Cocles defended. The Tiber here whirls rapidly along, and Horatius must have had a perilous swim for his life, and the enemy a fair mark at his head with their arrows. With the Aventine Hill rising on the left bank, I think this is the most picturesque part of the Tiber, in its passage through Rome.

After crossing the bridge, we kept along the right bank of the Tiber, through the dirty and hard-hearted streets of Tras-tevere (which have in no respect the advantage over those of hither Rome) till we reached St Peter's. We saw a family sitting before their door, on the pavement, in the narrow and sunny street, engaged in their domestic avocations; the old woman spinning with a wheel. I suppose the people now begin to live out of doors. We entered beneath the colonnade of St. Peter's, [14] and immediately became sensible of the evil smell—the bad odour of our fallen nature—which there is no escaping in any nook of Rome, or wherever a column, or the wall of a temple, or any sort of a corner, offers its temptation to the necessitous man. Under the Arch of Janus Quadrifons, as

I remember, we saw a whole hecatomb of oblation; and there is no place, whether of pagan or Christian sanctity, where such may not be found. Between the pillars of the colonnade, however, we had the pleasant spectacle of the two fountains sending up their lily-shaped gush, with rainbows shining on their falling spray. Parties of French soldiers, as usual, were undergoing their drill in the Piazza. When we entered the church, the long, dusty sunbeams were falling aslantwise through the dome, and through the chancel behind it; the interior looked gorgeous, but somewhat dingy and faded, as if it needed new gilding, new polishing, new varnishing, especially the pavement, which, having been spit upon for three centuries, has lost some of its original brilliancy. Being ornamented so elaborately as this church is, they are bound to keep it bright. I have come—I think, finally—to the conclusion, that there [15] was a better St Peter's in my mind, before I came to Rome, than the real one turns out to be—without definite outline, it is true, and with but misty architecture, dim, and gray, and vast, with an interminable perspective, and a dome like the cloudy firmament, and space beneath for the soul to feel its immensity, or the personal man his littleness. This gay piece of cabinet-work, big as it strives to be, cannot make up for what I have lost. It is a great prettiness:—only that. One feels its limits, much more than its extent. There is no use trying to reconcile myself to it. It would be but compelling myself to take the actual for the ideal; an exchange which is always to our loss, in things physical and moral. So I shall hope to remember St Peter's for what it is, but will still shut my eyes, when I get back across the sea, and try to see that illimitable interior which vanished when I first lifted the heavy leathern curtain. It was better than Michael Angelo could build; for I said of mine "How vast it is!"—and of his, "It is not so very big, after all!" The reality is a failure:—but so is Niagara.

[16] Rome, March 23ᵈ, Tuesday.

On Sunday, the whole family of us, with Miss Lander, went to the Coliseum, and enjoyed ourselves there in the bright, warm sun; so bright and warm that we were glad to get into the shadow of the walls and under the arches; though, after all, there was the freshness of March in the breeze that stirred now and then. Julian and baby found some beautiful flowers growing roundabout the Coliseum; and far up towards the top of the walls, we saw tufts of yellow wall-flowers, and a great deal of green grass growing along the ridges between the arches. The general aspect of the place, however, is somewhat bare, and does not compare favorably with an English ruin, both on account of the lack of ivy, and because the material is chiefly brick—the stone and marble having been stolen away by popes and cardinals, to build their palaces. While we sat within the circle, many people (of both sexes, but mostly women) passed through, kissing the iron cross which stands in the centre; thereby gaining an Indulgence, I believe, of seven years. In front of several churches, I have seen an inscription in Latin— INDULGENTIA PLENARIA ET PERPETUA [17] PRO CUNCTIS MORTUIS ET VIVIS; than which, it seems to me, nothing more could be asked or desired. The terms of this great boon are not mentioned.

Leaving the Coliseum, we went and sat down in the vicinity of the Arch of Constantine; and Julian and Rosebud went in quest of lizards. Julian soon caught a large one with two tails; one, a sort of after-thought or appendix, or corollary, to the original tail, and growing out from it, instead of from the body of the lizard. These reptiles are very abundant, and Julian has already brought home several, which make their escape, and appear occasionally darting to-and-fro on the carpet. Since we have been here, Julian has taken up various pursuits in turn; first, he devoted himself to gathering snail-shells, of which there are many sorts; afterwards, he had a fever for marbles, pieces of which he found on the banks of the Tiber, just on the edge of its muddy waters, and in the Palace of the Caesars, the Baths of Caracalla, and, indeed, wherever else his fancy led him—verd Antique, Rosso Antico, porphyry, giallo antico, serpentine, sometimes fragments of bas-[18]reliefs and mouldings; bits of mosaic, still firmly stuck together, on which the foot of a Caesar had perhaps once trodden; pieces of Roman glass, with the iridescence glowing on them; and all such things, of which the soil of Rome is full. It would not be difficult, from the spoil of his boyish rambles, to furnish what would be looked upon as a curious and valuable museum, in America.

Yesterday, mamma and I went to the sculpture-gallery of the Vatican. I think I enjoy these noble galleries, and their contents, and beautiful arrangement, better than anything else in the way of art; and, sometimes, I seem to have a deep feeling of something wonderful in what I look at. The Laocoon, on this visit, impressed me not less than before; there was such a type of human beings struggling with an inextricable trouble, and entangled in a complication which they can never free themselves from by their own efforts, and out of which Heaven will not help them. It was a most powerful mind, and one capable of reducing a complex idea to unity, that imagined this groupe. I looked at Canova's Perseus, and thought [19] it exceedingly beautiful, but found myself less and less contented, after a moment or two, though I could not tell why. Afterwards, looking at the Apollo, the recollection of the Perseus disgusted me; and yet I really cannot explain how one is better than the other. I was interested in looking at the busts of the Triumvirs, Antony, Augustus, and Lepidus. The two first are men of intellect, evidently, though they do not recommend themselves to one's affections by their physiognomy; but Lepidus has the strangest common-place countenance that can be imagined, small-featured, weak, such a face as you meet anywhere in a man of no mark, but are amazed to find in one of the three foremost men of the world. I suppose that it is these weak and shallow men, when chance raises them above their proper sphere, that commit enormous crimes without any such restraint as stronger men would feel, and without any retribution in the depths of their conscience. These old Roman busts, of which there are so many in the Vatican, have often a most life like aspect, a striking individuality. One [20] recognizes them as faithful portraits, just as certainly as if the living originals were standing beside them. The arrangement of the hair and beard, too, in many cases, is just what we see now; the fashions of two thousand years ago having come round again.

There were a good number of visitors in the galleries; chiefly, I should think, English, among whom we were recognized by Mr. & Mrs Daubeny, and had a chat with them. We likewise met with the Waterstons, with whom, likewise, we held a short confabulation; afterwards, we spoke with Miss Pickering, who, with another Salem lady and ourselves, made four people from that one stupid old town; finally, we saw Miss Bremer, but did not make ourselves known.

Rome, March 24th, Wednesday.

On Tuesday, Mamma, Una, and I, went to breakfast at William Story's, in the Palazzo Barberini, and had a very pleasant time. He is one of the most agreeable men I know, in society. He showed us a note from Thackeray, an invitation to dinner, written in hieroglyphics with great fun and [21] pictorial merit. He spoke of an expansion of the story of

Bluebeard, which he himself had either written or thought of writing, in which the contents of the several chambers which Fatima opened, before arriving at the fatal one, were to be described. This idea has haunted my mind ever since; and if it had but been my own, I am pretty sure that it would develope itself into something very rich. I mean to press William Story to work it out. The character of Bluebeard, too (and this was a part of his suggestion) might be so handled as to become powerfully interesting. Were I to take up the story, I would create an interest by suggesting a secret in the first chamber, which should develope itself more and more in every successive hall of the great palace, and lead the wife irresistibly to the chamber of horrors.

After breakfast, we went to the Barberini Library, in the other part of the palace, passing through the great hall, which appears to occupy the central part of the edifice. It is the most splendid domestic hall I ever saw; eighty feet in length at least, and of proportionate breadth and height; [22] and the vaulted cieling is entirely covered, to its utmost edge and remotest corner, with-a most brilliant painting in fresco, looking like a whole heaven of angelic people descending towards the floor of the hall. The effect is indescribably gorgeous. At one side of this hall, stands a Baldacchino, or canopy of state, covered with scarlet cloth and fringed with gold embroidery; the scarlet indicating that the palace is inhabited by a Cardinal. Green would be appropriate to a prince. In point of fact, the Palazzo Barberini is inhabited by a Cardinal, a Prince, and a Duke, all belonging to the Barberini family, and each having his separate portion of the palace; while their servants have a common territory and meeting-ground in this noble hall. After admiring it for a few minutes, we made our exit by the door on the opposite side, and went up the spiral staircase of marble to the library, where we were received by an ecclesiastic, who belongs to the Barberini household, and, I believe, was born in it. He is a gentle, refined, quiet-looking man; as well he may be, having spent all his life among these books, where few people intrude, and few cares can [23] come. He showed us a very old bible on parchment, a specimen of the earliest printing, beautifully ornamented with pictures; and some monkish illuminations, of indescribable delicacy and elaboration. No artist could afford to produce such work, if the life that he thus lavished on one sheet of parchment had any value to him, either for what could be done or enjoyed in it. There are about eight thousand volumes in this library, and judging by their outward aspect, the collection must be curious and valuable; but having another engagement, we could spend only a little time here. We had a hasty glance, however, of some poems of Tasso, in his own autograph.

We now went to the Palazzo Galizin (or some such name) where dwelt the Misses Weston, with whom we lunched, and where we met a French abbe, an agreeable man, and an anti-quarian, under whose auspices two of the Weston ladies and ourselves took carriage for the Castle of St Angelo. Being admitted within the external gateway, we found ourselves in the court of guard (as I presume it is called) where the French soldiers were playing with very dirty cards, or lounging about in military idleness. They were [24] very well behaved and courteous; and when we had intimated our wish to see the interior of the castle, a soldier soon appeared, with a large, unlighted torch in his hand, ready to guide us. I cannot describe the external defences of the fortress; there is an outer wall, surrounding the solid structure of Hadrian's tomb, to which there is access by one or two drawbridges; the entrance to the tomb (or castle, call it what you will) not being at the base, but near its central height. The ancient entrance, by which Hadrian's ashes and those of other imperial personages were probably brought into this tomb, has been walled up—perhaps ever since the last emperor was buried here. We were now in a vaulted passage, both lofty and broad, which circles round the whole interior of the tomb, from the base to the summit; during many hundred years, this passage was filled with earth and rubbish, and forgotten, and it is but partly excavated, even now, although we found it a long, long, and gloomy descent, by torch light, to the base of the vast mausoleum. The passage was once lined and [25] vaulted with precious marbles (which are now entirely gone) and paved with fine mosaics, portions of which still remain; and our guide lowered his flaming torch to show them to us, here and there amid the earthy dampness over which we trod. It is strange to think what splendor and costly adornment was here wasted on the dead. After we had descended to the bottom of this passage, and again retraced our steps to the highest part, the guide took a large cannon-ball, and sent it with his whole force rolling down the hollow arched way, rumbling and reverberating, and bellowing forth long, thunderous echoes, and winding up with a loud, distant crash, that seemed to come from the very bowels of the earth.

We saw the place, near the centre of the mausoleum, and lighted from above, through an immense thickness of stone and brick, where the ashes of the old Emperor and his fellow-slumberers were found. It is as much as twelve centuries, very likely, since they were scattered to the wind; for the tomb has been nearly or quite that space of time a fortress. The tomb itself is merely [26] the base and foundation of the castle; and being so massively built, it serves just as well for the purpose as if it were a solid granite rock. The mediæval fortress, with its antiquity of more than a thousand years, and having dark and deep dungeons of its own, is but a modern excrescence on the top of Hadrian's tomb. We now ascended towards this upper region, and were led into the vaults which used to serve as a prison, but which, if I mistake not, are situated above the ancient structure, although they seem as damp and subterranean as if they were fifty feet under the earth. We crept down to them through narrow and ugly passages, which the torch light would not illuminate; and stooping under a low, square entrance, we followed the guide into a small, vaulted room— not a room, but an artificial cavern, remote from light or air—where Beatrice Cenci was confined before her execution. According to the Abbé, she spent a whole year in this dreadful pit, her trial having dragged on through that length of time. How ghostlike she must have looked when she came forth! Guido never painted that beautiful picture from her blanched [27] face as it appeared after this confinement. And how rejoiced she must have been to die at last, having already been in a sepulchre so long! Adjacent to Beatrice's prison, but not communicating with it, was that of her mother-in-law; and next to the latter was one that interested me almost as much as Beatrice's—that of Benvenuto Cellini, who was confined here, I believe, for an assassination. All these prison-vaults are more horrible than can be imagined, without seeing them; but there are worse places here, for the guide lifted a trap-door in one of the passages, and held his torch down into an inscrutable pit beneath our feet. It was an oubliette, a dungeon where the prisoner might be buried alive, and never come forth again alive or dead. Groping about among these sad precincts, we saw various other things, that looked very dismal, but at last emerged into the sunshine, and ascended from one platform and battlement to another, till we found ourselves right at the feet of the Archangel Michael. He has stood there in bronze, for I know not how many hundred years, in the act of sheathing a rusty sword; such being the attitude in which he appeared [28] to one of the Popes in a vision, in token that a pestilence, which was then desolating Rome, was to be stayed.

There is a fine view from this lofty station, over Rome and the whole adjacent country; and the Abbe pointed out the site of Ardea, and Corioli, and other places renowned in story.

We were ushered, too, into the French commandant's quarters, in the Castle. There is a large hall, ornamented with frescoes by I forget whom; and, accessible from this, a drawing room, comfortably fitted-up, and where we saw modern furniture and a chess-board, and a fire burning clear, and other symptoms that the place had perhaps just been vacated by civilized and kindly people. But, in one corner of the cieling, the Abbe pointed out a ring, by which, in the times of mediæval anarchy, when popes, cardinals, and barons were all by the ears together, a certain Cardinal was hanged. It was not an assassination, but a legal punishment; and he was executed in the best apartment of the Castle, as an act of grace. I have no more space to spend upon the Castle; it is a straight-lined structure on the summit of the [29] immense round tower of Hadrian's tomb; and to make out the idea of it, we must throw in draw-bridges, esplanades, piles of ancient marble balls for cannon; battlements and embrasures, lying high in the breeze and sunshine, and opening views round the whole horizon; accommodations for the soldiers; many small beds in a large room. How much mistaken was the old Emperor in his expectation of a stately, solemn repose for his ashes, through all the coming centuries as long as the world should endure! Perhaps his ghost glides up and down, disconsolate, in that spiral passage which goes from top to bottom of the tomb; while the Gauls plant themselves on his very Mausoleum to keep the imperial city in awe.

Leaving the Castle of St Angelo, we drove, still on the same side of the Tiber, to the Villa Pamfili-Doria, which lies a short distance beyond the walls of the city. As we passed through one of the gates (I think it was that of San Pancrazio) the Abbé pointed out the spot where the Constable de Bourbon was killed, while attempting to scale the walls. If we are to believe Benvenuto Cellini, it was he who shot the constable. The road to the villa is not very interesting, lying (as the roads in the vicinity of Rome often [30] do) between very high walls, admitting not a glimpse of the surrounding country; the road itself white and dusty, with no verdant margin of grass, or border of shrubbery. At the gateway of the villa, we found many carriages in waiting; for the Prince Doria throws open the grounds to all comers, and, on a pleasant day like this, they are probably sure to be thronged. We left our carriage at the entrance, and rambled among these beautiful groves, admiring the live-oak trees, and the stone-pines, which latter are truly a majestic tree, with tall, columnar stems, supporting a cloudlike density of boughs far aloft, and not a straggling branch between them and the ground. They stand in straight rows, but are now so ancient and venerable as to have lost the formal look of a plantation, and seem like a wood that might have arranged itself almost of its own will. Beneath them is a flower-strewn turf, quite free of underbrush. We found open fields and lawns, moreover, all a-bloom with anemones, both white and rose-colored, and far larger than could be found, out of Italy, except in hot-houses. Violets, too, were abundant, and exceedingly fra[31]grant. When we consider that all this floral exuberance occurs in the midst of March, there does not appear much ground for complaining of the Roman climate; and, so long ago as the first week of February, I found daisies among the grass, on the sunny side of the church of St John Lateran. At this very moment, I suppose the country within twenty miles of Boston may be two feet deep with snow, and the streams solid with ice.

We wandered about the grounds, and found them very beautiful indeed; Nature having done much for them by an undulating variety of surface; and Art having added a good many charms, which have all the better effect, now that decay and neglect have thrown a natural grace over them likewise. There is an artificial ruin, so picturesque that it betrays itself; weather-beaten statues and pieces of sculpture, scattered here and there; an artificial piece of water, with up-gushing fountains, cascades, and broad-bosomed coves, and long, canal-like reaches, with swans taking their delight upon them. I never saw such a glorious and resplendent lustre of white as shone between the wings of two [32] of these swans. It was really a sight to see, and not to be imagined beforehand. Angels, no doubt, have just such lustrous wings as those. English swans partake of the dinginess of the atmosphere, and their plumage has nothing at all to be compared to this; in fact, there is nothing like it in the world, unless it be the illuminated portion of a fleecy, summer-cloud.

While we were sauntering along beside this piece of water, we were surprized to see Una on the other side; she had come hither with Edith Story and her two little brothers, and with our Rosebud, the whole under the charge of Mrs. Story's nursery-maids. Una and Edith crossed, not over, but beneath the water, through a grotto, and exchanged greetings with us. Then, as it was getting towards sunset, and cool, we took our departure, the Abbe, as we left the grounds, taking me aside to give me a glimpse of a Columbarium, which descends into the earth to about the depth to which an ordinary house might rise above it. These grounds, it is said, formed the country-residence of the Emperor Galba, and he was buried here after his assassination. It is a sad thought that so much natural beauty and long refinement of picturesque [33] culture is thrown away here, the villa being unhabitable during all the most delightful season of the year, on account of malaria. There is surely a curse on Rome, and all its neighborhood.

On our way home, we passed by the great Paolina Fountain, and were assailed by a good many beggars during the short time while we stopt to look at it. It is a very copious fountain, but not so beautiful as the Fountain of Trevi—taking into view merely the water-gush of the latter.

Rome, March 26th, Friday.

Yesterday, between twelve and one, our whole family went
to the Villa Ludovisi, the entrance to which is at the termination of a street which passes out of the Piazza Barberini, and
is at no very great distance from our own street. The grounds,
though very extensive, are wholly within the walls of the city
(which skirt them) and comprise a part of what were formerly
the gardens of Sallust. The villa is now the property of Prince
Piombini, a ticket from whom procured us admission. A little
within the gateway, to the right, is a Casino, containing two
large rooms filled with sculpture, much of which is very [34]
valuable. A colossal head of Juno, I believe, is considered the
greatest treasure of the collection, but I did not myself feel it
to be so, nor, indeed, received any strong impression of its excellence. There is no use in telling what I did admire; nothing
so much, I think, as the face of Penelope (if it be her face) in
the groupe supposed to represent Penelope and Telemachus.
The sitting statue of Mars is very fine; so is the groupe of Arria
and Pætus; so are many other busts and figures; but, after a
while, I found that peculiar lassitude and despondency coming
upon me, which has so often afflicted me while viewing works
of art. So I sat down wearily upon a chair, and left my wife
to see and admire, to her heart's content.

By and by, we left the Casino, and wandered about among
the grounds, threading interminable allies of cyprus, through
the long vistas of which we could see here and there a statue,
an urn, a pillar, a temple, or garden-house, a bas-relief against
the wall. It seems as if there must have been a time—and not
so very long ago—when it was worth while to spend money
and thought [35] upon the ornamentation of grounds in the

neighborhood of Rome. That time is past, however, and the result is very melancholy; for great beauty has been produced, but it can be enjoyed, in its perfection, only at the peril of one's life. Generation after generation has lavished its care upon these grounds, as we see it lavished on an English country-seat; but if you stay here through the summer, Fever walks arm in arm with you through these long, shadowy avenues, and Death waits for you at the end of the vista. It is a great pity. For my part, and judging from my own experience, I suspect that the Roman atmosphere is never wholesome, always more or less poisonous.

In a part of the grounds remote from the gateway, we came to another and larger Casino, in which the Prince, I believe, resides during two months of the year. It was now under repair, but we found admission—as did several other visitors—and saw, in the entrance hall, the Aurora of Guercino, painted in fresco on the cieling. There is beauty in the design; but the painter certainly was most unhappy in his black shadows, and, in the work [36] before us, they give the impression of a cloudy and lowering morning, which is likely enough to turn to rain by-and-by. After viewing the fresco, we mounted by a spiral staircase to a lofty terrace, and found Rome at our feet, and, far off, the Sabine and Alban Mountains, some of them still capt with snow. In another direction, there was a vast plain, on the horizon of which, could our eyes have reached to its verge, we might perhaps have seen the Mediterranean. After enjoying the view, and the warm sunshine, we descended, and went in quest of the Gardens of Sallust, but found no satisfactory remains of them.

One of the most striking objects in the first Casino was a groupe by Bernini—Pluto (an outrageously masculine and strenuous figure, heavily bearded, and with a prodigious muscular developement in mad activity) ravishing away a little tender Proserpine, whom he holds aloft, while his strong gripe impresses itself into her soft, virgin flesh. It is very disagreeable; but it makes one feel that Bernini was a man of great ability. There are some works in literature that bear an analogy to his works in sculpture—where great power is lavished, a little outside of nature, and therefore proves [37] to be only a fashion, and not permanently adapted to the tastes of mankind.

Rome, March 27th Saturday.

Yesterday forenoon, my wife and I went to St Peter's, to see the Pope pray at the chapel of the Holy Sacrament. We found a good many people in the church, but not an inconvenient number; indeed, not so many as to make any remarkable show in its great nave, nor even in front of the chapel. A detachment of the Swiss guard, in their strange, picturesque, harlequin-like costume, were on duty before the chapel, in which the wax tapers were all lighted; and a desk, or other convenience for praying, was arranged in front of the shrine, and covered with scarlet velvet. On each side, along the breadth of the side-aisle, were placed seats, covered with rich tapestry or carpeting; and some gentlemen and ladies— English, probably, or American—had comfortably deposited themselves here, but were compelled to move by the guards, before the Pope's entrance. His Holiness should have appeared precisely at twelve; but we waited nearly or quite half an hour beyond that time, and it seemed to me particularly ill-mannered in the Pope, who owes the courtesy of being punctual to the people, if not [38] to St Peter and the Deity. By and by, however, there was a stir; the guard motioned to us to stand away from the benches, against the backs of which we had been leaning; the spectators in the nave looked towards the door, as if they beheld something approaching; and first there appeared some cardinals, in scarlet scull caps and purple robes, intermixed with some of the Noble Guard, and other attendants. It was not a very formal and stately procession, but rather straggled onward, with ragged edges, the spectators standing aside to let it pass, and merely bowing, or perhaps slightly bending the knee, as good Catholics are accustomed to do when passing before the shrines of Saints. Then, in the midst of the purple Cardinals, all of whom were gray haired men, appeared a stout old man, with a white scull-cap over his grey hair, a scarlet, gold-embroidered cape falling over his shoulders, and a white silk robe, the train of which was borne up by an attendant. He walked slowly, with a sort of dignified waddle, stepping out broadly, and planting his feet (on which were red shoes) flat upon the pavement, as if he were not much accustomed to locomotion, and perhaps had known a twinge of the gout. His face seemed kindly, and [39] venerable, but was not particularly impressive. Arriving at the scarlet-covered desk, he kneeled down and took off his white scull-cap; the Cardinals also kneeled behind and on either side of him, taking off their scarlet scull-caps; while the Noble Guard remained standing, six on one side of his Holiness, and six on the other. The Pope bent down his head upon the desk, and seemed to spend three or four minutes in prayer; then rose, and all the purple Cardinals, and bishops, and priests of whatever degree, rose behind and beside him. Next, he went to kiss St Peter's toe; at least, I believe he kissed it, but was not near enough to be certain; and lastly, he knelt down and directed his devotions towards the high altar. This completed the ceremonies; and his Holiness left the church by a side entrance, making a short cut into the Vatican. I am very glad I have seen the Pope, because now he may be crossed out of my list of sights to be seen. His proximity impressed me kindly and favorably towards him; and I did not see one face among all the Cardinals—in whose number, doubtless, is his successor—which I would so soon trust as Pio Nono's.

This morning, I walked as far as the gate of [40] San Paolo, and on approaching it, I saw the gray, sharp pyramid of Caius Cestius, pointing upward in close proximity to the two dark-brown, battlemented, Gothic round towers of the gateway, each of these very different pieces of architecture looking the more picturesque for the contrast of the other. Before approaching the gateway and pyramid, I walked onward, and soon came in sight of the Monte Testaccio, the artificial hill made of pot-sherds. There is a gate admitting into the grounds around the hill, and a road passing round its base. At a distance, the hill looks greener than any other part of the landscape, and has all the rounded outlines of a natural hill, resembling in shape a headless Sphinx, or Saddleback mountain, as I used to see it from Lenox. It is of very considerable height—two or three hundred feet, at least, I should say—and well entitled, both by its elevation and the space it covers, to be reckoned among the hills of Rome. The base is almost entirely surrounded with small structures, which seem to be used as farm-buildings. On the summit is a large iron cross; the Church having thought it expedient to redeem these shattered pipkins from the power of paganism, as it has so many other Roman ruins. There was a [1st 41] pathway up the hill, but I did not choose to ascend it, under the hot sun, so steeply did it clamber up:—There appears to be a good depth of soil on most parts of Monte Testaccio; but, on some of the sides, you observe precipices, bristling with fragments of red or brown earthenware, or pieces of vessels of white, unglazed clay; and it is evident that this immense pile is entirely composed of broken crockery, which I should hardly have thought would have aggregated to such a heap, had it all been thrown here—vases, tea-cups, porcelain, earthen, or Wedgewood—since the beginning of the world.

I walked quite round the hill, and saw, at no great distance from it, the enclosure of the Protestant burial ground, which lies so close to the pyramid of Caius Cestius, that the latter may serve as general monument to the dead. Deferring, for the present, a visit to the cemetery, or to the interior of the pyramid, I returned to the gateway of San Paolo, and passing through it, took a view of the pyramid from the out-side of the city-wall. It is itself a portion of the wall, having been built into it by the Emperor Aurelian, so that about half of it lies within, and half with[42]out. The brick or red stone material of the wall being so unlike the marble of the pyramid, the latter is as distinct, and seems as insulated, as if it stood alone in the centre of a plain; and really I do not think that there is a more striking architectural object in Rome. It is in perfect condition; just as little ruined or decayed as on the day when the builder put the last, peaked piece of marble on the summit; and it ascends steeply from its base into a peak so sharp that it looks as if it would hardly afford foothold to a bird. The marble was once white, but is now covered with a gray coating, like that which has gathered upon the statues of Castor and Pollux at the Monte Cavallo. Not one of the great blocks is displaced, nor seems likely to be through all time to come; they rest one upon another in straight and even lines, and present a vast, smooth triangle, ascending from a base of a hundred feet, and narrowing to a point at the height of a hundred and twenty-five; the junctures of the marble blocks being so close, that, in all these twenty centuries, only a few little tufts of grass, and a trailing plant or two, have succeeded in [2nd 41] rooting themselves into the interstices. It is good and satisfactory to see anything, which, being built for an enduring monument, has endured so faithfully, and has a prospect of such an interminable futurity before it. Once, indeed, it seemed likely to be buried; for, three hundred years ago, it had become covered to the depth of sixteen feet, but the soil has since been dug away from its base, which is now lower than that of the road which passes through the neighboring gate of San Paolo. Midway up the pyramid, cut in the marble blocks, is an inscription in great Roman letters, still almost as legible as when first cut.

I did not return through the San Paolo gateway, but kept onward round the exterior of the wall, till I came to the gate of San Sebastiano. It was a hot, and not a very interesting walk, with only the high, bare wall of brick, broken by frequent square towers, on one side of the road, and a high bank and hedge, or a garden wall, on the other. Roman roads are most inhospitable, offering no shade, and no seat, and no pleasant views of rustic domiciles; nothing but the wheel track of white dust, without a footpath run[44]ning by its side; and seldom any grassy margin to refresh the wayfarer's feet.

April 3ᵈ. Saturday. Rome.

A few days ago, my wife and I visited the studio of Mr. Mozier, an American, who seems to have a good deal of vogue as a sculptor. We found a figure of Pocahontas, which he has repeated several times; another which he calls the "Wept of Wish-ton-Wish"; a figure of a smiling girl playing with a cat and dog; and a school-boy mending a pen. These two last were the only ones that gave me any pleasure, or that really had any merit; for his cleverness and ingenuity appear in homely subjects, but are quite lost in attempts at a higher ideality. Nevertheless, he has a groupe of the Prodigal Son, possessing more merit than I should have expected from Mr. Mozier; the son reclining his head on his father's breast, with an expression of utter weariness, at length finding perfect rest, while the father bends his benign visage over him, and seems to receive him calmly into himself. This groupe (the plaster-cast standing beside it) is now taking shape out of an immense block of marble, and will be as indestructible as the Laocoon; an idea at once awful [45] and ludicrous, when we consider that it is at best but a respectable production. Miss Lander tells me that Mr Mozier has stolen—adopted, we will rather say—the attitude and general idea of this groupe from one executed by a student of the French Academy, and to be seen there in plaister.

Mr. Mozier has now been seventeen years in Italy; and, after all this time, he is still intensely American in everything but the most external surface of his manners; scarcely Euro-peanized, or much modified, even in that. He is a native of Ohio, but had his early breeding in New York, and might—for any polish or refinement that I can discern in him—still be a country shopkeeper in the interior of New York or New England. How strange! For one expects to find the polish, the close grain, and white purity of marble, in the artist who works in that noble material; but, after all, he handles clay, and, judging from the specimens I have seen here, is apt to be clay, not of the finest, himself. Mr. Mozier is sensible, shrewd, keen, clever; an ingenious workman, no doubt, with tact enough, and not destitute of taste; very agreeable and lively in his conversation, [46] talking as fast and as naturally as a brook runs, without the slightest affectation. His naturalness is, in fact, a rather striking characteristic, in view of his lack of culture, while yet his life has been concerned with idealities, and a beautiful art. What degree of taste he pretends to, he seems really to possess; nor did I hear a single idea from him that struck me as otherwise than sensible.

He called to see us last night, and talked for about two hours in a very amusing and interesting style; his topics being taken from his own personal experience, and shrewdly treated. He spoke much of Greenough, whom he described as an excel-lent critic of art, but possessed of not the slightest inventive

genius. His statue of Washington, at the Capitol, is taken precisely from the Phidian Jupiter; his Chanting Cherubs are
copied in marble from two figures in a picture by Raphael. He
did nothing that was original with himself. From Greenough,
Mr. Mozier passed to Margaret Fuller, whom he knew well,
she having been an inmate of his during a part of her residence
in Italy. His developements about poor Margaret were very
[47] curious. He says that Ossoli's family, though technically
noble, is really of no rank whatever; the elder brother, with
the title of Marquis, being at this very time a working brick-
layer, and the sisters walking the streets without bonnets—
that is, being in the station of peasant-girls, or the female
populace of Rome. Ossoli himself, to the best of his belief, was
Margaret's servant, or had something to do with the care of her
apartments. He was the handsomest man whom Mr. Mozier
ever saw, but entirely ignorant even of his own language,
scarcely able to read at all, destitute of manners; in short, half
an idiot, and without any pretensions to be a gentleman. At
Margaret's request, Mr Mozier had taken him into his studio,
with a view to ascertain whether he was capable of instruction
in sculpture; but, after four months' labor, Ossoli produced a
thing intended to be a copy of a human foot; but the "big
toe" was on the wrong side. He could not possibly have had
the least appreciation of Margaret; and the wonder is, what
attraction she found in this boor, this hymen without the
intellectual spark—she that had always [48] shown such a
cruel and bitter scorn of intellectual deficiency. As from her
towards him, I do not understand what feeling there could
have been, except it were purely sensual; as from him towards
her, there could hardly have been even this, for she had not
the charm of womanhood. But she was a woman anxious to
try all things, and fill up her experience in all directions; she
had a strong and coarse nature, too, which she had done her
utmost to refine, with infinite pains, but which of course could

only be superficially changed. The solution of the riddle lies in this direction; nor does one's conscience revolt at the idea of thus solving it; for—at least, this is my own experience —Margaret has not left, in the hearts and minds of those who knew her, any deep witness for her integrity and purity. She was a great humbug; of course with much talent, and much moral reality, or else she could not have been so great a humbug. But she had stuck herself full of borrowed qualities, which she chose to provide herself with, but which had no root in her.

Mr. Mozier added, that Margaret had quite [49] lost all power of literary production, before she left Rome, though occasionally the charm and power of her conversation would re-appear. To his certain knowledge, she had no important manuscripts with her when she sailed, (she having shown him all she had, with a view to his procuring their publication in America;) and the History of the Roman Revolution, about which there was so much lamentation, in the belief that it had been lost with her, never had existence. Thus there appears to have been a total collapse in poor Margaret, morally and intellectually; and tragic as her catastrophe was, Providence was, after all, kind in putting her, and her clownish husband, and their child, on board that fated ship. There never was such a tragedy as her whole story; the sadder and sterner, because so much of the ridiculous was mixed up with it, and because she could bear anything better than to be ridiculous. It was such an awful joke, that she should have resolved—in all sincerity, no doubt—to make herself the greatest, wisest, best woman of the age; and, to that [50] end, she set to work on her strong, heavy, unpliable, and, in many respects, defective and evil nature, and adorned it with a mosaic of admirable qualities, such as she chose to possess; putting in here a splendid talent, and there a moral excellence, and polishing each separate piece, and the whole together, till it seemed to

shine afar and dazzle all who saw it. She took credit to herself
for having been her own Redeemer, if not her own Creator;
and, indeed, she was far more a work of art than any of Mr.
Mozier's statues. But she was not working on an inanimate
substance, like marble or clay; there was something within her
that she could not possibly come at, to re-create and refine it;
and, by and by, this rude old potency bestirred itself, and undid
all her labor in the twinkling of an eye. On the whole, I do not
know but I like her the better for it;—the better, because she
proved herself a very woman, after all, and fell as the weakest
of her sisters might.

To-day, my wife, Rosebud, and I, went to see Miss Hosmer;
and as her studio seems to be mixed [51] up with Gibson's,
we had an opportunity of glancing at some of his beautiful
works. We saw a Venus and a Cupid, both of them tinted, and,
side by side with them, other statues identical with these, except that the marble was left in its pure whiteness. The tint of
the Venus seemed to be a very delicate, almost imperceptible,
shade of yellow, I think, or buff; that of the Cupid was a
more decided yellow; and the eyes and hair of both, and
especially the Cupid, were colored so as to indicate life rather
than imitate it. The apple in Venus's hand was brightly gilt.
I must say, there was something fascinating and delectable in
the warm, yet delicate tint of the beautiful nude Venus, although I should have preferred to dispense with the colouring
of the eyes and hair; nor am I at all certain that I should not,
in the end, like the snowy whiteness better for the whole
statue. Indeed, I am almost sure I should; for this lascivious
warmth of hue quite demoralizes the chastity of the marble,
and makes one feel ashamed to look at the naked limbs in the
com[52]pany of women. There is not the least question about
the eyes and hair; their effect is shocking, in proportion to
the depth of tint.

We found Miss Hosmer in a little up-stairs room. She is a small, brisk, wide-awake figure, of queer and funny aspect, yet not ungraceful, nor to be rejected from one's good graces without further trial; and she seems so frank, simple, straightforward, and downright, that there can be little further trial to make. She had on petticoats, I think; but I did not look so low, my attention being chiefly drawn to a sort of man's sack of purple or plum-colored broadcloth, into the side-pockets of which her hands were thrust as she came forward to greet us. She withdrew one hand, however, and presented it cordially to my wife (whom she already knew) and to myself without waiting for an introduction. She had on a male shirt, collar, and cravat, with a brooch of Etruscan gold; and on her curly head was a picturesque little cap of black velvet; and her face was as bright and funny, and as small of feature, as a child's. It looked, in one aspect, youthful, and [53] yet there was something worn in it, too, as if it had faced a good deal of wind and weather, either morally or physically. There never was anything so jaunty as her movement and action; she was indeed very queer, but she seemed to be her actual self, and nothing affected nor made-up; so that, for my part, I give her full leave to wear what may suit her best, and to behave as her inner woman prompts. I don't quite see, however, what she is to do when she grows old; for the decorum of age will not be consistent with a costume that looks pretty and excusable enough in a young woman.

She led us into a part of the extensive studio, or collection of studios, where some of her own works were to be seen; Beatrice Cenci, which did not very greatly impress me; and a monumental design, a female figure, wholly draped even to the stockings and shoes, in a quiet sleep. I like this last. There was also a Puck, doubtless full of fun; but I had hardly time to glance at it. Miss Hosmer evidently has good gifts in her profession, and doubtless she derives great advantage from her close association [54] with a consummate artist like Gibson; nor yet does his influence seem to interfere with the originality of her own conceptions. In one way, at least, she can hardly fail to profit—that is, by the opportunity of showing her works to the throngs of people who come to see Gibson's own; and these are just such people as an artist would most desire to come in contact with, and might never see in a lifetime, if left to himself. I shook hands with this frank and pleasant little woman—if woman she be, as I honestly suppose, though her upper half is precisely that of a young man—and took leave, not without purpose of meeting her again.

Within a few days past, there have been many pilgrims in Rome, who come hither to attend the ceremonies of the Holy Week, and to perform their vows and undergo their penances. I saw two of them near the forum, yesterday, with their pilgrim staves, in the fashion of a thousand years ago. I likewise saw, in the open forum, a husband and wife occupied with a small-tooth comb, which was applied to the good purpose of ridding the husband's head [55] of its redundant population. Entering a church to escape a shower, I sat down on a bench near one of the chapels, and a woman immediately came up to me to beg. I at first refused, but she knelt down by my side, and instead of praying to the Saint, prayed to me; and being thus treated as a canonized personage, I thought it incumbent on me to be gracious, to the extent of half a Paul. I know not whether I recorded that my wife, sometime ago, came in contact with a pickpocket at the entrance of a church; and, failing in his enterprise upon her purse, he passed in, dipped his thieving fingers into the holy water, and paid his devotions at a shrine. Missing the purse, he said his prayers, in the hope perhaps that the Saint would send him better luck another time.

Rome, April 10ᵗʰ, Saturday.

I have made no entries in my journal recently, being exceed-ingly lazy, partly from indisposition, as well as from an atmos-phere that takes the vivacity out of everybody. Not much has happened or been effected. Last [56] Sunday (Easter Sunday) I went with Julian to St. Peter's, where we arrived at about 9 °clock, and found a multitude of people already assembled in the Church. The interior was arrayed in festal guise, there being a covering of scarlet damask over the pilasters of the Nave, from base to capital, giving an effect of splendor, yet with a loss as to the apparent dimensions of the interior. A guard of soldiers occupied the nave, keeping open a wide space for the passage of a procession that was momently ex-pected, and soon arrived. The crowd was too great to allow of my seeing it in detail; but I could perceive that there were priests, cardinals, Swiss guards, (some of them with corslets on;) and, by and by, the Pope himself was borne up the nave, high over the heads of all, sitting under a canopy, with his tiara on his head. He floated slowly along, and was set down, I believe, in the neighborhood of the High Altar; and the procession being broken up, some of its scattered members might be seen here and there about the church; officials in antique Spanish dresses, Swiss guards in polished [57] steel breastplates, serving men in richly embroidered liveries, of-ficers in scarlet coats and military boots; priests; and divers other shapes of men; for the papal ceremonies seem to forego little or nothing that belongs to times past, while it includes everything appertaining to the present. I ought to have waited to witness the papal benediction from the balcony in front of the church; or, at least, to hear the famous silver trumpets sounding from the dome; but Julian grew weary (to say the truth, so did I,) and we went on a long walk, out of the nearest city-gate, and back through the Janiculum gate—and, finally, homeward over the Ponte Rotto. Standing on the bridge, I saw the arch of the Cloaca Maxima, close by the Temple of Vesta, with the water (the river being high) rising apparently within two or three feet of its key-stone.

The same evening we went to Monte Cavallo, where, from the gateway of the Pontifical Palace, we saw the illumination of St Peter's. Mr. Akers, the sculptor, had recommended this position to us, and accompanied us thither, as the best point [58] from which the illumination could be witnessed, at a distance, without the incommodity of such a crowd as would be assembled at the Pincian. The first illumination (the Silver one, as it is called,) was very grand and delicate, describing the outline of the great edifice and crowning dome, in light; while the daylight was not yet wholly departed. As my wife finely remarked, it seemed like the glorified spirit of the church made visible; or, as I will add, it looked as this famous and never-to-be-forgotten structure will look, to the imaginations of men, through the waste and gloom of future ages, after it shall have gone quite to decay and ruin—the brilliant, though scarcely distinct gleam of a statelier dome than ever was seen, shining on the back-ground of the night of time. This simile looked prettier in my fancy than I have made it look on paper. After we had enjoyed this Silver Illumination a good while, and when all the daylight had passed out of the starry night, the distant outline of St Peter's burst forth, in the twinkling of an eye, into a starry blaze, being quite the [59] finest effect that I ever witnessed. I staid to see it, however, only a few minutes; for I was quite sick and feverish with a cold— which, indeed, I have seldom been free from, since my first breath of the genial atmosphere of Rome. This plague kept me within doors, all the next day, and prevented me from seeing the beautiful fireworks that were exhibited, in the evening, from the platform on the Pincian, above the Piazza del Popolo.

On Thursday, I paid another visit to the Sculpture Gallery of the Capitol, where I was particuarly struck with a bust of Cato the Censor, who must have been the most disagreeable, stubborn, ugly-tempered, pig-headed, narrow-minded, strong-willed old Roman that ever lived. The collection of busts here and at the Vatican are most interesting; many of the individual busts being full of character, and commending themselves by intrinsic evidence as faithful portraits of the originals. These stone faces have stood face to face with Caesar, and all the other Emperors, and with statesmen, soldiers, Phi[60]losophers, and poets, of the antique world, and have been to them like their reflections in a mirror. It is the next thing to seeing the men themselves. We went afterwards into the Palace of the Conservators and saw, among various other interesting things the bronze she-wolf suckling Romulus and Remus, who sit beneath her dugs, with open mouths to receive the milk.

On Friday, we all went to see the Pope's palace on the Quirinal, whereof I shall not trouble myself to give any long description. There was a vast hall (the largest, I think, that I ever saw) and an interminable suite of rooms, cased with marble, or fair imitations of it, floored with marble, or mosaics, or inlaid wood, adorned with frescoes on the vaulted cielings, and many of them lined with Gobelin tapestry, not woefully faded, like almost all that I have hitherto seen, but brilliant as pictures. Indeed, some of them so closely resembled pictures that I could hardly believe they were not so; and the effect was even richer than that of an oil-painting. In every room there was a cruci[61]fix; but I did not see a single nook or corner where anybody could have dreamed of being comfortable. Nevertheless, as a stately and solemn residence for His Holiness, it is quite a satisfactory affair. Afterwards, we went into the Pontifical Gardens, connected with the Palace. They are very extensive, and laid out in straight avenues, bordered with walls of box, as impervious as if of stone, not less than twenty feet high, and pierced with lofty archways cut in the living wall. Some of the avenues were overshadowed with trees, the tops of which bent over and joined one another from either side, so as to resemble a side-aisle of a Gothic Cathedral. Pieces of marble sculpture, much weather-stained, and generally broken-nosed, stood along these stately walks; there were many fountains gushing up into the sunshine; we likewise found a rich flower-garden, containing rare specimens of exotic flowers, and gigantic cactusses, and also an aviary, with vultures, doves, and singing-birds. We did not see half the garden; but, stiff and formal as its general arrangement is, it [62] is a beautiful place,—a delightful, sunny, and serene seclusion. Whatever it may be to the Pope, two young lovers might find the Garden of Eden here, and never desire to stray out of its precincts—for the honeymoon, at least. They might fancy angels standing in the long glimmering vistas, of the avenues. It would suit me well enough to have my daily walk along such straight paths; for I think them favorable to thought; which is apt to be disturbed by variety and unexpectedness.

Rome, April 12th, Monday.

We went to-day (Mamma, Una, Julian, & I) to the Vatican, where we found our way to the Stanze of Raphael; these being four rooms, or halls, painted with frescoes. No doubt, they were once very brilliant and beautiful; but they have encountered hard treatment since Raphael's time, especially when the soldiers of the Constable de Bourbon occupied these halls, and made fires on the mosaic floors. The entire walls and cielings of the rooms are covered with pictures; but the handiwork or designs of Raphael consist of paintings on the four sides of each apartment, and include several famous works of art. [63] The School of Athens is perhaps the most celebrated; and the longest side of the largest hall is occupied by a battle-piece, of which the Emperor Constantine is the hero, and which covers almost space enough for a real battle-field. There was a wonderful light in one of the pictures— that of St. Peter awakened, in his prison, by the angel; it really seemed to throw a radiance into the hall below. I shall not pretend, however, to have been sensible of any particular rapture at sight of these frescoes; so faded as they are, so battered by the mischances of years, insomuch that, through all the power and glory of Raphael's designs, the spectator cannot but be continually sensible that the groundwork of them is an old plaster-wall. They have been scrubbed, I suppose—brushed, at least—a thousand times over, till the surface, brilliant or soft, as Raphael left it, must have been quite rubbed off; and with it all the consummate finish, and everything that made them originally delightful. The sterner features remain; the skeleton of thought, but not the beauty that once clothed it. In truth, the frescoes—excepting a few figures—never had the real touch of Raphael's [64] own hand upon them, having been merely designed by him, and finished by his scholars, or by other artists.

The halls themselves are specimens of antique magnificence, paved with elaborate mosaics; and wherever there is any woodwork, it is richly carved with foliage and figures. In their newness, and probably for a hundred years afterwards, there could not have been so brilliant a suite of rooms in the world. Connected with them—at any rate, not far distant—is the little chapel of San Lorenzo, the very site of which, among the thousand apartments of the Vatican, was long forgotten, and its existence only known by tradition. After it had been walled up, however, beyond the memory of man, there was still a rumour of some beautiful frescoes by Fra Angelico, in an old chapel of Pope Nicholas V, that had strangely disappeared out of the palace; and search at length being made, it was re-discovered and entered through a window. It is a small, lofty room, quite covered over with frescoes of sacred subjects, both on the walls and cieling, a good deal faded, yet pretty distinctly preserved. It would have been no misfortune to me, if the little old chapel had remained still hidden. We next [65] issued into the Loggie of Raphael, which consist of a sort of long gallery, or arcade, or colonnade, the whole extent of which was once adorned with beautiful frescoes by Raphael. These are almost quite worn away, and so defaced as to be untraceable and unintelligible, along the side wall of the gallery; although traceries of Arabesque, and compartments where there seem once to have been rich pictures, but now only an indistinguishable waste of dull colour, are still to be seen. In the coved cieling, however, there are still some bright frescoes, in better preservation than any that we had yet seen; not particularly beautiful, nevertheless. I remember to have seen (indeed, we ourselves possess them) a series of very spirited and energetic engravings, old and coarse, of these frescoes, the subjects being the creation, and the early Scripture history; and I really think that their translation of the pictures is better than the original. On reference to Murray, I find that little more than the designs of the frescoes is attributable to Raphael, the execution being by Giulio Romano and other artists.

Escaping from these forlorn splendors, we went into the Sculpture Gallery, where I was able to enjoy, [66] in some small degree, two or three wonderful works of art, and had a perception that there were a thousand other wonders around me. It is as if the statues kept, for the most part, a veil around them, which they sometimes withdrew, and let their beauty glow upon my sight;—only a glimpse, or two or three glimpses, or a little space of calm enjoyment; and then I see nothing but a discolored marble image again. The Minerva Medica revealed herself to-day. I wonder whether other people are more fortunate than myself, and can invariably find their way to the inner soul of a work of art. I doubt it; they look at these things for just a minute, and pass on, without any pang of remorse, such as I feel, for quitting them so soon and so willingly. I am partly sensible that some unwritten rules of taste are making their way into my mind; that all this Greek beauty has done something towards refining me, who am still, however, a very sturdy Goth.

I met to-day, a groupe of two or three monks, in their coarse brown habits of woollen cloth; and it being pretty warm weather, I was disagreeably made aware of a certain frowzy fragrance exhaling [67] from these good fathers, in the sunshine. Probably they have but one habit for all seasons and weathers, and no linen beneath it.

Rome, April 15th, Thursday.

Yesterday, I went with Julian to the Forum, and descended into the excavations at the base of the Capitol, and on the site of the Basilica of Julia. The essential elements of old Rome are there; columns, single, or in groupes of two or three, still erect, but battered and bruised, at some forgotten time, with infinite pains and labor; fragments of other columns lying prostrate, together with rich capitals and friezes; the bust of a colossal female statue, showing the bosom and upper part of the arms, but headless; a long, winding space of pavement, forming part of the ancient ascent to the Capitol, still as firm and solid as ever; the foundation of the Capitol itself, wonderfully massive, built of immense square blocks of stone, doubtless nearly three thousand years old, and durable for whatever may be the lifetime of the world; the Arch of Septimus Severus, with bas-reliefs of Dacian captives sculptured round it; the column of Phocas, with the rude series of steps ascending on four sides to its pedestal; the floor of beautiful and precious marbles in the Basilica of [68] Julia, the slabs cracked across, the greater part of them torn up and removed, the grass and weeds growing up through the chinks of what remain; heaps of bricks, shapeless bits of marble and granite, and other ancient rubbish, among which old men are lazily rummaging for specimens that a stranger may be induced to buy; this being an employment that suits the indolence of a modern Roman. The level of these excavations is about fifteen feet, I should judge, below the present level along which the street passes through the forum, and only a very small part of this alien surface has been removed, though there can be no doubt that it hides immense treasures of art and monuments of history. Yet these remains do not make that impression of antiquity upon me, which Gothic ruins do. Perhaps it is because they belong to quite another system of society and epoch of time; and in view of them, we forget all that has intervened betwixt them and us, being morally unlike, and disconnected with them, and not belonging to the same train of thought; so that we look across a gulf to these Roman times, and do not realize how [69] wide the gulf is. Yet in that intervening valley, lie Christianity, the dark ages, the feudal system, chivalry and Romance, and a deeper life of the human race than Rome brought to the verge of the gulf.

To-day, Mamma, Una, and I, went to the Colonna Palace, where we saw some fine pictures, but, I think, no master-pieces. They did not depress and dishearten me so much as the pictures in Roman palaces usually do; for they were in remarkably good order as regards frames and varnish;—indeed, I rather suspect some of them had been injured by the means

adopted to preserve their beauty. The palace is now in the occupancy of the French Ambassador, who probably looks upon
the pictures as articles of furniture, and household adornment,
and does not choose to have squares of black and forlorn
canvass upon his walls. There were a few noble portraits by
Vandyke, a very striking one by Holbein, one or two by
Titian, also by Guercino, and some pictures by Rubens and
other forestieri painters, which refreshed my weary eyes. But
what chiefly interested me was the magnificent and stately
hall of the palace, [70] fifty-five of my paces in length, besides
a large apartment at either end, opening into the hall through
a pillared space, as wide as the gateway of a city. The pillars,
two at either end of the hall, are of giallo antico, and there
are pilasters of the same all the way up and down the walls,
forming a perspective of the richest aspect; especially as the
broad cornice blazes with gilding, and the spaces between the
pilasters are emblazoned with heraldic achievements and emblems in gold; and there are Venetian looking-glasses, richly
decorated over the surface with beautiful pictures of flowers
and Cupids, through which you catch the gleam of the mirror;
and two rows of splendid chandeliers extend from end to end
of the hall, which, when lighted up—if ever it is lighted up,
now-a-nights—must be the most brilliant interior that ever
mortal eye beheld. The cieling glows with pictures in fresco,
representing scenes connected with the history of the Colonna
family; and the floor is paved with beautiful marbles, polished,
and arranged in square and circular compartments; and [71]
each window (of which there is a row on each side of the
hall) is set in a great architectural frame of precious marble,
as large as the portal of a door. The apartment at the farther
end of the hall is elevated above it, and is attained by several
marble steps, whence it must have been glorious, in former
days, to have looked down upon a gorgeous throng of princes,
cardinals, warriors, ladies, in such rich attire as might be worn

when this palace was built. It is singular how much freshness and brightness it still retains; and the only objects to mar the effect were some ancient statues and busts, not very good in themselves, and now made dreary of aspect by their corroded surfaces, the result of long burial under ground.

In the room at the entrance of the hall, are two cabinets, each a wonder in its way; one being adorned with precious stones, the other with ivory carvings of Michael Angelo's Last Judgment, and of the frescoes of Raphael's loggie. The world has ceased to be so magnificent as it once was. Men make no such marvels now-a-days. The [72] only defect, I remember in this hall, was in the marble steps that ascend to the elevated apartment at the end of it; a large piece had been broken out of one of them, leaving a rough, irregular gap in the polished marble stair. It is not easy to conceive what violence can have done this, without also doing mischief to all the other splendor around it.

Rome, April 16th, Friday.

My wife and I went, this morning, to the Academy of St Luke (the Fine Arts Academy of Rome,) in the Via Bonella, close by the Forum. We rang the bell at the house-door; and, after a few moments, it was unlocked or unbolted by some unseen agency from above stairs; no one making his appearance to admit us. We ascended two or three flights of stairs, and entered a hall, where was a young man, the Custode, and two or three artists engaged in copying some of the pictures. The collection not being immensely large, and the pictures being in more presentable condition than usual, I enjoyed them more than I generally do; particularly a Virgin and Child, by Vandyke, where two angels are [73] singing and playing, one on a lute and the other on a violin, to remind the Holy Infant of the strains he used to hear in Heaven. It is one of the few pictures that there is really any pleasure in looking at. There were several pictures by Titian, mostly of a voluptuous character, but not very charming; also, two, or more, by Guido, one of which, representing Fortune, is celebrated. They did not impress me much; nor do I find myself strongly drawn towards Guido, though there is no other painter who seems to achieve things so magically and inscrutably as he sometimes does. Perhaps it requires a finer taste than mine to appreciate him; and yet I do appreciate him so far as to see that his Michael, for instance, is perfectly beautiful; but I also seem to see that there is something dainty in the foot which treads on Satan, and that a warrior-angel ought not to be quite so delicate. In the gallery, there are whole rows of portraits of members of the Academy of St. Luke, most of whom, judging by their physiognomies were very common-place people; a fact which makes itself visible in a portrait, however much the painter may try to flatter his sitter. Several of the pictures by Titian, Paul [74] Veronese, and other artists, now exhibited in this gallery, were formerly kept in a secret cabinet at the Capitol, being considered of a too voluptuous character for the public eye. I did not think them noticeably indecorous, as compared with a hundred other pictures that are shown and looked at without scruple;—Calypso and her nymphs, a knot of naked women by Titian, is perhaps as objectionable as any. But even Titian's flesh cannot keep, and has not kept, its warmth through all these centuries. The illusion, and life-likeness, effervesces and exhales out of a picture, as it grows old; and we keep talking traditionally of a charm that has forever vanished.

From St Luke's, we went to San Pietro in Vincoli, which was at no great distance, occupying a fine position on or near the summit of the Esquiline Mount. A little abortion of a man (and, by the by, there are more diminutive and ill-shapen men

and women in Rome than I ever saw elsewhere; a phenomenon
to be accounted for, perhaps, by their custom of wrapping
the new-born infant in swaddling-clothes) this little two-foot
abortion, hastened before us, as we drew nigh, to summon the
Sacristan to open the church-door. It was a [75] needless piece
of service, for which we rewarded him with two baiocchi.
St Peter's is a simple and noble church, consisting of a nave,
divided from the Side-aisles by rows of columns that once
adorned some ancient temple; and its wide, unincumbered
interior affords better breathing space than most churches in
Rome. The statue of Moses occupies a niche in one of the side-
aisles, on the right, and not far from the high-altar. I found it
grand and sublime, with a beard flowing down like a cataract,
a truly majestic figure, not so benign as it were desirable that
such strength should be. The horns, about which so much
has been said, make no very prominent feature of the statue,
being merely two diminutive tips, sticking straight up over
his forehead, neither adding to the grandeur of the head, nor
detracting sensibly from it. The whole force of this statue is
not to be felt in one brief visit; but I agree with an English
gentleman (the paterfamilias of a large party who entered the
church while we were there) in thinking that Moses has
"very fine features"—a compliment for which the colossal
Hebrew ought to have made the Englishman a bow. Besides
the Moses, this church contains some [76] attractions of a
pictorial kind, which are reposited in the Sacristy, into which
we passed through a side-door. The most remarkable of these
pictures is a face and bust of Hope, by Guido, with beautiful
eyes, lifted upward; it has a grace which artists are continually
trying to get into their innumerable copies, but always without
success; for, indeed—though nothing is more true than the
existence of this charm in the picture—yet if you try to analyze
it, or even look too intently at it, it vanishes, till you look
again with more trusting simplicity.

Leaving the church, we wandered to the Coliseum, and to the public grounds contiguous to them, where a score of French drummers, and more, were beating, each man his drum, without reference to any rub-a-dub but his own. This seems to be a daily or periodical practice and point of duty with them. After resting ourselves on one of the marble benches we came slowly home, through the Basilica of Constantine, and along the shady side of the streets and piazzas, sometimes perforce striking boldly though the white sunshine, which, however, was not so hot as to shrivel us up bodily. It has [77] been a most beautiful and perfect day, as regards weather, clear and bright, very warm in the sunshine, yet freshened throughout by a quiet stir of the air. Still there is something in this air, malevolent, or at least not friendly. The Romans lie down and fall asleep in it in any vacant part of the streets, and wherever they can find any spot sufficiently clear of filth, among the ruins of temples. I would not sleep in the open air for whatever my life may be worth.

On our way home, sitting in one of the narrow streets, we saw an old woman spinning with a distaff; a far more ancient implement than the spinning-wheel, which the housewives of other nations have long since laid aside.

Rome, April 18th 1858, Sunday.

Yesterday, at noon, the whole family of us set out on a visit to the Villa Borghese and its grounds, the entrance to which is just outside of the Porta del Popolo. After getting within the grounds, however, there is a long walk before reaching the Casino, and we found the sun rather uncomfortably hot, and the road dusty and white in the sunshine;—nevertheless, a foot-path ran along side of it, most of the way, through the grass and among the young trees. It seems [78] to me that the trees do not put forth their leaves with nearly the same magical rapidity, in this southern land, at the approach of summer, as they do in more northerly countries. In these latter, having a much shorter time to develope themselves, they feel the necessity of making the most of it. But the grass, in the lawns and enclosures along which we passed, looked already fit to be mowed, and it was interspersed with many flowers.

Saturday being, I believe, the only day of the week on which visiters are admitted to the Casino, there were many parties in carriages, artists on foot, gentlemen on horseback, and miscellaneous people, to all of whom the door was opened by a Custode, on ringing a bell. The whole of the basement floor of the Casino, comprising a suite of beautiful rooms, is filled with statuary. The entrance-hall is a very splendid apartment, brilliantly frescoed, and paved with ancient mosaics, representing the combats with beasts and gladiators, in the Coliseum; curious, though very rudely and awkwardly designed, apparently after the arts had begun to decline. Many of the specimens of Sculpture, displayed in these rooms, are fine, but none of them, [79] I think, possess the highest merit; an Apollo is beautiful; a group of a fighting Amazon, and her enemies trampled under her horse's feet, is very impressive; a Faun, copied from that of Praxiteles, and another, who seems to be dancing, are exceedingly pleasant to look at. I like these strange, sweet, playful, rustic creatures, almost entirely human as they are, yet linked so prettily, without monstrosity, to the lower tribes by the long, furry ears, or by a modest tail; indicating a strain of honest wildness in them. Their character has never, that I know of, been wrought out in literature; and something very good, funny, and philosophical, as well as poetic, might very likely be educed from them. In my mind, they connect themselves with that ugly, bearded woman, who was lately exhibited in England, and by some supposed to have been engendered betwixt a human mother and an orang-outang; but she was a wretched monster—the faun, a natural and delightful link betwixt human and brute life, and with something of a divine character intermingled.

The gallery, as it is called, on the basement floor of the Casino, is sixty feet in length, by perhaps a third as much in breadth, and is (after all I have seen [80] at the Colonna Palace and elsewhere) a more magnificent hall than I imagined to be in existence. It is floored with rich marbles, in beautifully arranged compartments, and the walls are almost entirely cased with marble of various sorts, the prevailing variety being giallo antico, intermixed with verde antique, and I know not what else; but the splendor of the giallo antico gives the character to the room, and the large and deep niches, along the walls, appear to be lined with the same material. Without coming to Italy, one can have no idea of what beauty and magnificence are produced by these fittings up of polished marble. Marble, to an American, means nothing but white limestone. This hall, moreover, is adorned with pillars of oriental alabaster; and wherever there is a space vacant of precious and richly colored marble, it is frescoed with arabesque ornaments; and over the whole is a coved and vaulted cieling, glowing with picture. There never can be anything richer than the whole effect. As to the Sculpture here, it was not very fine, so far as I remember, consisting chiefly of busts of the Emperors in porphyry; but they served a good [81] purpose in the upholstery way. There were also magnificent tables, each composed of one great slab of porphyry, and also vases of nero antico, and other rarest material. It remains to be mentioned, that, on this almost summer day, I was quite chilled in passing through these glorious halls; no fireplace anywhere; no possibility of comfort; and, in the hot season, when their coolness might be agreeable, it would be Death to inhabit them.

Ascending a long, winding staircase, we arrived at another suite of rooms, containing a good many not very remarkable pictures, and a few more pieces of statuary. Among the latter is Canova's statue of Pauline, the sister of Bonaparte, who is represented with but little drapery, and in the character of Venus, holding the apple in her hand. It is admirably done, and, I have no doubt, a perfect likeness; very beautiful, too; but it is wonderful to see how the artificial elegance of the woman of the world makes itself perceptible in spite of whatever simplicity she could find in almost utter nakedness. The statue does not afford pleasure in the contemplation. In one of these upper rooms are some [82] works of Bernini; two of them Æneas and Anchises, and David on the point of slinging a stone at Goliath, have great merit, and do not tear and rend themselves quite out of the laws and limits of marble, like his later sculptures. Here is also his Apollo, overtaking Daphne, whose feet take root, whose finger-tips sprout into twigs, and whose tender body roughens roundabout with bark, as he embraces her. It did not seem very wonderful to me; not so good as Hillard's description of it made me expect; and one does not enjoy these freaks in marble.

We were glad to emerge from the Casino into the warm sunshine; and, for my part, I made the best of my way to a large fountain, surrounded by a circular stone seat, of wide sweep, where, sitting down in a sunny segment of the circle, I solaced myself with a cigar. Around grew a solemn company of old trees—ilexes, I believe—with huge, contorted trunks, and evergreen branches. It was a very beautiful scene, both immediately around me, and in whatever direction a vista was opened; for these Borghese grounds are as wild and sweet as if Nature had been left to herself, and yet have all the charm [83] that the art of man can give;—deep groves, sunny openings, the airy gush of fountains, marble statues dimly visible in recesses of foliage, great urns and vases, terminal figures, pillars, temples; all these works of art looking as if they had stood there long enough to feel at home, and to be on friendly and familiar terms with the grass and trees;—so long that Nature has given them tokens of her motherly kindness in the guise of lichens and moss. It is a most beautiful place, so near the gate del Popolo too!—and the Malaria is its true master and inhabitant!

Rome, April 22ᵈ, Thursday.

We have been, recently, to the studio of G. L. Brown, the American landscape painter, and were altogether surprised and delighted with his pictures. He is a very plain, homely, Yankee sort of a man, quite unpolished by his many years residence in Italy; he talks ungrammatically, and in Yankee idioms, walks with a strange, awkward gait, and stooping shoulders; is altogether unpicturesque, but wins one's confidence by his very lack of grace. It is not often that we see an artist so entirely free from affectation in his aspect and deportment. His pictures were views of Swiss and Italian scenery, and were most beauti[84]ful and true. One of them—a moonlight picture—was really magical, the moon shining so brightly that it seemed to throw a light even beyond the limits of the picture; and yet his sunrises, and sunsets, and his noontides too, were nowise inferior to this, although their excellence required somewhat longer study to be fully appreciated. I seemed to receive more pleasure from Brown's pictures than from any of the landscapes by old masters; and the fact serves to strengthen me in the belief that the most delicate, if not the highest charm of a picture is evanescent; and that we continue to admire pictures prescriptively and by tradition, after the qualities that first won them their fame have vanished. I suppose Claude was a greater landscape painter than Brown; but, for my own pleasure, I would prefer one of the latter artist's pictures; those of the former being quite changed from what he intended them to be, by the effect of time on his pigments. Mr. Brown showed us some drawings from Nature, done with incredible care and minuteness of detail, as studies for his pictures. We complimented him on his patience; but he said "Oh, it's not patience;—it's love!" In fact, it was [85] a patient and most successful wooing of a beloved object, which at last rewarded him by yielding herself wholly.

We have likewise been to Mr. Bartholomew's studio, where we saw several pretty statues and busts, and among them an Eve, after the fall, with her wreath of fig-leaves lying across her poor nudity; pretty in some points, but with an awful volume of thighs and calves. I do not altogether see the necessity of ever sculpturing another nakedness. Man is no longer a naked animal; his clothes are as natural to him as his skin, and sculptors have no more right to undress him than to flay him. Also, we have seen again William Story's Cleopatra; a work of genuine thought and energy, representing a terribly dangerous woman, quiet enough for the moment, but very likely to spring upon you like a tigress. It is delightful to escape from this universal prettiness, which seems to be the highest conception of the herd of modern sculptors, and which they almost invariably attain.

Miss Bremer called on us, the other day. We find her very little changed from what she was when [86] she came to spend an evening at our little red cottage among the Berkshire hills, and went away so dissatisfied with my conversational performances, and so laudatory of my brow and eyes, while so severely criticising my poor mouth and chin. She is the funniest little old fairy, in person, whom one can imagine, with a huge nose, to which all the rest of her is but an insufficient appendage; but you feel at once that she is most gentle, kind, womanly, sympathetic, and true. She talks English fluently, in a low, quiet voice, but with such an accent that it is impossible to understand her without the closest attention. This was the real cause of the failure of our Berkshire interview; for

I could not guess, half the time, what she would be at, and of course had to take an uncertain aim with my responses. A more intrepid talker than myself would have shouted his ideas across the gulf; but, for me, there must first be a close and unembarrassed contiguity with my companion, or I cannot say one real word. I doubt whether I have ever really talked with half a dozen persons in my life, either men or women.

To-day, my wife and I have been at the Pic[87]ture and Sculpture Galleries of the Capitol. I rather enjoyed looking at several of the pictures, though, at this moment, I particularly remember only a very beautiful face of a man, one of two heads on the same canvass, by Vandyke. Yes; I did look with new admiration at Paul Veronese's Rape of Europa. It must have been, in its day, the most brilliant and rejoicing picture, the most voluptuous, the most exuberant, that ever put the sunshine to shame. The bull has all Jupiter in him, so tender and gentle, yet so hot and passionate with desire that you feel it indecorous to look at him; and Europa, under her thick, rich stuffs and embroideries, is as much a woman as if she were naked. What a pity that such a picture should fade, and perplex the beholder with such splendor shining through such forlornness.

We afterwards went into the Sculpture Gallery, where I looked at the faun of Praxitiles, and was sensible of a peculiar charm in it; a sylvan beauty and homeliness, friendly and wild at once. Its lengthened, but not preposterous ears, and the little tail which we infer, behind, have an exquisite effect, and make the spectator smile in his very heart. This [88] race of fauns was the most delightful of all that antiquity imagined. It seems to me that a story, with all sorts of fun and pathos in it, might be contrived on the idea of their species having become intermingled with the human race; a family, with the faun-blood in them, having prolonged itself from the classic era till our own days. The tail might have disappeared by dint of constant intermarriages with ordinary mortals; but the pretty, hairy ears should occasionally reappear in members of the family; and the moral instincts and intellectual characteristics of the faun might be most picturesquely brought out, without detriment to the human interest of the story. Fancy this combination in the person of a young lady!

I have spoken, I think, of Mr. Gibson's colored statues. It seems (at least, so Mr. Nichols, the painter, tells me) that he stains them with tobacco-juice; his Cupids, at all events, though his Venuses, I think, have a pinkish hue, which could not have been thus produced. Were he to send a Cupid to America, he need not trouble himself to stain it beforehand.

IV

[1] Rome, April 25th, Sunday.

NIGHT before last, my wife and I took a moonlight ramble through Rome; it being a very beautiful night, warm enough for comfort, and with no perceptible dew or dampness. We set out at about nine °clock, and our general direction being towards the Coliseum, we soon came to the Fountain of Trevi, full on the front of which the moonlight fell, making Bernini's sculptures look stately and beautiful; though the semi-circular gush and fall of the cascade, and the many jets of the water, pouring and bubbling into the great marble basin, are of far more account than Neptune and his steeds, and the rest of the figures. We descended to the edge of the basin, and bent over the parapet, in order to ascertain the possibility of Lord Nelville's having seen Corinne's image in the water, or if she could have seen his (for I forget which it was,) at their moonlight interview. It could not have happened. The transparency of the water, permitting the bottom of the basin to be clearly seen, its agitation, and the angle at which one looks into it, prevent any reflection from being visible. The moon, shining brightly over head and a little behind us, threw our black shadows on the water; and this is what Lord Nelville or Corinne would have seen, but nothing else.

Thence we went through several streets, and through the Piazza of the Holy Apostles, to Trajan's column and forum, skirting along which latter, we tried to imagine its plan and immense extent, only partly indicated by the rows of broken granite columns, that still mark out the direction of the great nave and side aisles of the edifice. The tall, shabby structures of modern Rome now cover much of the space over which Trajan's temples and courts extended; and I wish they might be pulled [2] down for the sake of what they hide. On the left of the iron railing, at the edge of the deep hollow space in which what of Trajan's forum lies, is a nearly entire specimen of the immense granite pillars, such as those of which the bases and fragments now stand in rows beneath. It lies at its length close by the side-walk, a great, solid fact of the past, making the spectator and handler very sensible of the reality of the Romans; there is still (except where violence has shattered it, ages ago) a polish over its hard substance, remaining in spite of weather and underground burial; and, moreover, when I put my hand on it, I still felt some of the warmth of the noon-day sun, which had done its best to heat it through. This pillar, like a thousand other things that the Romans left, seems likely to last forever; so that the polish of eighteen centuries ago, and the warmth of to-day's sunshine, lingering into the night, are both ephemeral in reference to it.

We passed along the Via Alessandria, I think, and turned aside a little to look at the white marble columns (much weather-stained and time-gnawed now, however) of the temple of Mars Ultor, the massive walls of which still remain, or a large portion of them, and enclose a convent. We passed, too, a temple of Minerva, the columns of its portal buried midway in the ground, and within the temple a baker's shop. It is a great pity, and a great wonder, that an excavation is not made hereabouts, though to be sure—so closely packed are these modern six-story hovels—a row of medi-æval houses would be brought down by the unearthing of a single temple. Thence we pursued our way through one of the three vast arches of the Basilica of Constantine, which now gives passage to a street leading in the direction of the [3] Coliseum. Between Constantine's Basilica and the Coliseum, we met not a single person; but as we approached the latter place we heard voices, and saw several carriages waiting at the principal entrance. A French sentinel was of course on guard there; but he at once gave us permission to go in; and we found the whole interior flooded with the bright moonshine—so bright, indeed, that it took away the dimness and mystery which the spectator desires to find, in viewing the Coliseum by moonlight. Moreover, being familiar with its aspect at noonday, there was little scope left for imagination, in my own case. We sat down to rest ourselves on two fragments of marble, near one of the shrines that are ranged around the circle. The Coliseum was by no means a solitary spot; for some Roman youths and girls were running merry races across the open space; groups were sitting, as we did, on fragments of pillars; and the steps of the great iron cross, in the very centre, where the gladiators fought, and the martyrs were tortured to death, were occupied by a company of persons, gossiping in quiet tones. I did not suppose that the Romans would have made so free with a spot so deeply sanctified, and with the steps of such a very holy cross, each kiss bestowed on which (as the inscription says) ensures an indulgence of seven years. Looking up over the slope of arches, on the side of the Coliseum opposite to us, we discerned here and there the twinkling of a light, or its broader gleam coming up from some abyss among the ruins, and glimmering higher and higher, till it reached the upper ranges and passages of the structure. It was a party of English or Americans, probably, trying to realize Byron's description of the Coliseum by moonlight.

[4] From the Coliseum, we went to the Arch of Constantine,

which looked very stately and beautiful in the moonlight, with its richly sculptured and pillared front. We returned along the old Roman pavement and passed beneath the Arch of Titus, and thence through the Forum, meeting pairs and groupes of people, some talking English, others chattering in Italian or French; and one party of young men awoke the echoes of the old Roman temples with loud singing. We looked down into the Basilica of Julia, and at the column of Phocas, and at the various ruins that strew the base of the Capitol; but I must here record my opinion that Roman ruins, however morally and historically interesting, are not to be compared with English ones, as picturesque objects. We ascended the Capitoline Hill, and I felt a satisfaction in placing my hand on those immense blocks of stone, the remains of the Ancient Capitol, which form the foundation of the present edifice, and will make a sure basis for as many edifices as posterity may choose to rear upon it, till the end of the world. It is wonderful, the solidity with which those old Romans built; one would suppose that they contemplated the whole course of time as the only limit of the individual lifetime. This is not so strange in the time of the Republic, when probably they believed in the permanence of their institutions; but they still seemed to build for eternity, in the days of the Emperors, when neither rulers nor people had any faith or moral substance, or laid any earnest grasp on life.

Reaching the top of the Capitoline Hill, we ascended the steps of the portal of the Palace of the Senator, and looked down into the Piazza, with the equestrian statue of Marcus Aurelius [5] in the centre of it. The architecture that surrounds this Piazza is very ineffective; and so, in my opinion, are all the other architectural works of Michael Angelo, including Saint Peter's itself, of which he has made as little as could possibly be made of such a vast pile of material. He balances everything in such a way that it seems but half of itself. We soon descended into the Piazza, and walked round and round the statue of Marcus Aurelius, contemplating it from every point, and admiring it in all. I have a singular feeling of love and reverence for this old heathen Emperor, derived chiefly from his aspect and attitude of grand beneficence, as exhibited in this statue. Descending the acclivity of the Capitol, we passed by the church of the Jesuits, and so into the Corso, where I bought a cigar of an old man who still sat at a street-corner, although it was now past eleven °clock. On these beautiful moonlight nights, Rome appears to keep awake and stirring, though in a quiet and decorous way. It is, in fact, the pleasantest time for promenades, and both my wife and myself felt far less wearied than by any promenade in the daytime, of similar extent, since our residence in Rome. In future, I mean to walk often after nightfall.

Yesterday, we set out betimes, and ascended the dome of Saint Peter's; an exploit which I do not feel moved to describe at any great length. The best view of the interior of the church, I think, is from the first gallery, beneath the dome. The whole inside of the dome is set with mosaic-work, the separate pieces being, so far as I could see, about half an inch square. Emerging on the roof, we had a fine view of all the roundabout of Rome, including the Medi[6]terranean Sea in the far distance. Above us still rose the whole mountain of the great dome, and it made an impression on me of greater height and size than I had yet been able to receive. The copper ball at the summit looked hardly bigger than a man could lift; and yet, a little while afterwards, Una, Julian, and I, stood all together in that ball, which could have contained a dozen more along with us. The esplanade of the roof is of course very extensive; and along the front of it are ranged the statues which we see from below, and which, on nearer examination, prove to be roughly hewn giants. There is a small house on the roof, where, probably, the custodes of this part of the edifice reside; and there is a fountain gushing abundantly into a stone trough, that looked like an old sarcophagus. It is strange where the water comes from, at such a height. The children tasted it, and pronounced it very warm and disagreeable. After taking in the prospect, on all sides, we rang a bell, which summoned a man who directed us towards a door, in the side of the dome, where a Custode was waiting to admit us. Hitherto the ascent had been easy, along a slope without stairs, up which, I believe, people sometimes ascend on donkeys. The rest of the way was up steep and narrow staircases, winding round within the wall, or between the two walls, of the dome, and growing narrower and steeper, till finally there is but a perpendicular iron ladder, by means of which to climb into the copper ball. Except through small windows and peepholes, there is no external prospect at a higher point than the roof of the church. Just beneath the ball, there is a circular room capable of containing a large company, and a door which ought to give access to a gallery [7] on the outside; but the Custode informed us that this door is never opened. As I have said, Una, Julian, and I, clambered into the copper ball, which we found as hot as an oven, and, after putting our hands on its top, and on the very summit of Saint Peter's, were glad to clamber down again. I have made some mistake, after all, in my narration; there certainly is a circular balcony at the top of the dome; for I remember walking round it, and looking not only across the country, but downward along the ribs of the dome, to which are attached the iron contrivances by which the dome is illuminated on Easter Sunday.

We descended without accident or adventure, meeting several parties on their way up, as we had met others coming down. Before leaving the church, we went to look at the mosaic copy of the Transfiguration, because we were going to see the original, in the Vatican, and wished to compare the two. Going round to the entrance of the Vatican, we went first to the manufactory of mosaics, to which we had a ticket of admission. We found it a long series of rooms, in which the mosaic artists were at work, chiefly in making some medallions of the heads of saints, for the new church of St Paul's. It was rather coarse work, and it seemed to me that the mosaic copy was somewhat stiffer and more wooden than the original, the bits of stone not flowing into color quite so freely as paint from a brush. There seemed to be no large picture now in process of being copied; but two or three artists were employed on small and delicate subjects; one had a holy family of Raphael in hand; and the Sybils of Guercino and Domeni-chino were hanging on the wall, apparently ready to be put into mosaic. Wherever great skill and delicacy, [8] on the artist's part, were necessary, they seemed quite adequate to the occasion; but, after all, a mosaic from any celebrated picture is but a copy of a copy. The substance employed is a sort of stone paste, of innumerable different hues, and in bits of vari-ous sizes, quantities of which were seen in cases, along the whole series of rooms.

We next ascended an amazing height of staircases, and walked along I know not what extent of passages, under my wife's guidance, till we reached the picture gallery of the Vatican, into which I had never been before. There are but three rooms, all lined with red velvet, on which hang about fifty pictures, each one of them, no doubt, worthy to be con-sidered a master-piece. In the first room, were three Murillos, all so beautiful that I could have spent the day happily in looking at either of them; for methinks, of all painters, he is the tenderest and truest. I could not enjoy these pictures now, however, because in the next room, and visible through the open door, hung the Transfiguration. Approaching it, I felt that the picture was worthy of its fame, and was far better than I could at once appreciate; admirably preserved, too, though, I fully believe, it must have possessed a charm when it left Raphael's hand that has now vanished forever. As an article of church furniture and external adornment, the mosaic copy is preferable to the original; but no copy could ever reproduce all the life and expression which we see here. It is useless to say any more about this picture. Opposite to it hangs the Communion of St Jerome; the aged, dying Saint, half torpid with death already, partaking of the sacrament, and a sunny garland of cherubs [9] in the upper part of the picture, looking down upon him, and quite comforting the spectator with the idea that the old man needs only to be quite dead in order to flit away with them. As for the other pictures, I did but glance at, and have forgotten them.

The Transfiguration is finished with great minuteness and detail; the weeds and blades of grass in the foreground being as distinct as if they were growing in a natural soil. A partly decayed stick of wood, with the bark, is likewise given in close imitation of nature. The reflection of one of the apostles' foot is seen in a pool of water, at the verge of the picture. One or two hands and arms seem almost to project from the canvass; there is great lifelikeness and reality, as well as higher qualities. The face of Jesus, being so high aloft, and so small in the distance, I could not well see, but am impressed with the idea that it looks too much like human flesh and blood to be in keeping with the celestial aspect of the figure, or with the probabilities of the scene, when the divinity and immortality of the Savior beamed from within him through the earthly features that ordinarily shaded him. As regards the composition of the picture, I am not convinced of the propriety of its being in two so distinctly separate parts; the upper portion not thinking of the lower, and the lower portion not being aware of the higher. It symbolizes, however, the spiritual shortsightedness of mankind, that, amid the trouble and grief of the lower picture, not a single individual, either of those who seek help or those who would willingly afford it, lifts his eyes to that region one glimpse of which would set everything right. One or two of the disciples point upward, but without really knowing what abundance of help is to be had there.

[10] Rome, April 27th, Tuesday.

To day we have all been with Mr. Akers to some studios of painters; first to that of Mr. Wilde, an artist originally from Boston. His pictures are principally of scenes in Venice, and are miracles of color, being as bright as if the light were transmitted through rubies and sapphires. And yet, after contemplating them awhile, we became convinced that the painter had not gone in the least beyond nature, but, on the contrary, had fallen short of brilliancies which no palette, or skill or boldness in using color, could attain. I do not quite know whether it is best to attempt these things. They may be found in nature, no doubt, but always so tempered down by what surrounds them—so put out of sight, even while they seem full before our eyes—that we question the accuracy of a faithful reproduction of them on canvass. There was a picture of sunset, the whole sky of which would have outshone any gilded frame that could have been put around it. There was a most brilliant sketch of a handful of weeds and leaves, such as may be seen strewing acres of forest-ground, in an American autumn. I doubt whether any other man has ever ventured to paint a picture like either of these two—the Italian sunset, or the American autumnal foliage. Mr. Wilde (who is still young) talked with genuine feeling and enthusiasm of his art, and is certainly a man of genius.

We next went to the studio of an elderly Swiss artist (named Muller, I believe) where we looked at a great many water color and crayon drawings of scenes in Italy, Greece, and Switzerland. The artist was a quiet, respectable, somewhat heavy-looking old gentleman, from whose aspect [11] one would expect a plodding pertinacity of character, rather than quickness of sensibility. He must have united both these qualities, however, to produce such pictures as these; such faithful transcripts of whatever Nature has most beautiful to show, and which she shows only to those who love her deeply and patiently. They are wonderful pictures, compressing plains, seas, and mountains, with miles and miles of distance, into the space of a foot or two, without crowding anything, or leaving out a feature, and diffusing the free, blue atmosphere throughout. The works of the English water-color artists, which I saw at the Manchester exhibition, seemed to me no wise equal to these. Now, here are three artists—Mr. Brown, Mr. Wilde, and this Mr. Müller—who have smitten me with vast admiration, within these few days past, while I am continually turning away disappointed from the landscapes of the most famous among the old masters, unable to find any charm or illusion in them. Yet I suppose Claude, Poussin, and Salvator Rosa must have won their renown by real achievements. But the glory of a picture fades like that of a flower.

Contiguous to Mr. Müller's studio was that of a young German artist, not long resident in Rome, and Mr. Akers proposed that we should go in there, as a matter of kindness to the young man, who is scarcely known at all, and seldom has a visiter to look at his pictures. His studio comprises his whole establishment; for there was his little bed, with its white drapery, in a corner of the small room, and his dressing-table with its brushes and combs; while the easel and the few sketches of Italian scenes and figures [12] occupied the foreground. I did not like his pictures very well, but would gladly have bought them all, if I could have afforded it, the artist looked so cheerful, patient, and quiet, doubtless amidst huge discouragement. He is probably stubborn of purpose, and is the sort of man who will improve, with every year of his life.

We could not speak his language, and therefore were spared the difficulty of paying him any compliments, but Miss Shepard said a few kind words to him in German, and seemed quite to win his heart, insomuch that he followed her with bows and smiles a long way down the staircase. It is a terrible business, this looking at pictures (whether good or bad) in the presence of the artists who painted them; it is as great a bore as to hear a poet read his own verses. It takes away all my pleasure in seeing the pictures, and even makes me question the genuineness of the impressions which I receive from them.

After this latter visit, Mr. Akers conducted us to the jeweller's shop of Castellani, who seems to be a great reproducer of ornaments in the old Roman and Etruscan fashion. These antique styles are very fashionable just now, and some of the specimens which he showed us were certainly very beautiful, though I doubt whether their quaintness and old-time curiosity, as patterns of gewgaws dug out of immemorial tombs, be not their greatest charm. We saw the toilette-case of an Etruscan lady—that is to say, a modern imitation of it—with her rings for summer and winter, and for every day of the week; and for thumb and fingers; her ivory comb, her bracelets, and more knicknacks than I can half remember. Splendid things of our own time, were likewise [13] shown us; a necklace of diamonds, worth eighteen thousand scudi, together with emeralds, and opals, and great pearls. Finally, we came away, and my wife and Miss Shepard were taken up by the Misses Weston, who drove with her to visit the Villa Albani. On their way, my wife happened to raise her arm, and Miss Shepard espied a little Greek cross of gold which had attached itself to the lace of her sleeve, thus making an involuntary pilferer of my poor wife. Pray Heaven the jeweller may not discover his loss before we have time to restore the spoil! He is apparently so free and careless in displaying his precious wares—putting inestimable gems, and pins and brooches great and small, into the hands of strangers like ourselves, and leaving scores of them strewn on the top of his counter—that it would seem easy enough to pocket a diamond or two; but I suspect there must needs be a sharp eye somewhere. Before we left the shop, he requested me to honor him with my autograph, in a large book that seemed full of the names of his visitors. This is probably a measure of precaution.

Rome, April 30th, Friday.

I went yesterday to the Sculpture Gallery of the Capitol, and looked pretty thoroughly through the busts of the Illustrious Men, and less particularly at those of the Emperors and their relatives. I likewise took particular note of the Faun of Praxitiles; because the idea keeps recurring to me of writing a little Romance about it, and for that reason I shall endeavor to set down a somewhat minutely itemized detail of the statue and its surroundings. The faun is the image of a young man, leaning with one arm upon the trunk or stump of a tree; he has a pipe, or some such [14] instrument of music, in the hand which rests upon the tree, and the other, I think, hangs carelessly by his side. His only garment falls half way down his back, but leaves his whole front, and all the rest of his person, exposed, displaying a very beautiful form, but clad in more flesh, with more full and rounded outlines, and less developement of muscle, than the old sculptors were wont to assign to masculine beauty. The figure is not fat, but neither has it the attribute of slender grace. The face has a character corresponding with that of the form; beautiful and most agreeable features, but rounded, especially about the throat and chin; a nose almost straight, yet very slightly curving inward, a voluptuous mouth, that seems almost (not quite) to smile outright;—in short, the whole person conveys the idea of an amiable and sensual nature, easy, mirthful, apt for jollity, yet not incapable of being touched by pathos. The faun has no principle, nor could comprehend it, yet is true and honest by virtue of his simplicity; very capable, too, of affection. He might be refined through his feelings, so that the coarser, animal part of his nature would be thrown into the back ground, though liable to assert itself at any time. Praxitiles has only expressed this animal nature by one (or rather two) definite signs—the two ears—which go up in a little peak, not likely to be discovered on slight inspection, and, I suppose, are covered with fine, downy fur. A tail is probably hidden under his garment. Only a sculptor of the finest imagination, most delicate taste, and sweetest feeling, could have dreamed of representing a Faun in this guise; and if you brood over it long enough, all the pleasantness of sylvan life, and all the genial and happy characteristics of the brute creation, seemed to be mixed in him with humanity—trees, grass, flowers, cattle, deer, and unsophisticated man.

The Faun stands in the room nearest to the head of the [15] staircase, close beside a window, from which is seen the staircase of the Ara Coeli, behind the Capitol, and, right beneath you, the descent into the Forum towards the Arch of Septimus Severus. Beyond, you glance along the side of the Forum, over temples that have been transformed into domed churches, and a confusion of modern edifices built out of ancient brick and stone—with the old heathen pillars holding up the christian roofs—to the Coliseum, through some of the arches of which glows the blue sky. Miles farther onward, in the same direction, are seen the Alban Hills. The room is called the Hall of the Faun; but the Faun is by no means the object likely to attract the visitor's eye when he first enters;—no, I am mistaken; it is the Hall of the Dying Gladiator, which latter famous sculpture occupies the centre of the room, with a wooden railing round it, leaving not much more than space enough for comfortable passage. Round the walls, besides the Faun, stand other admirable statues, the Antinous, the Juno, a Minerva, an Apollo, a Roman matron, a little girl holding a dove and frightened by a snake. The marble of the Faun is somewhat discolored by time; not so much, however, as all the other statues.

We have had beautiful weather, for two or three days past, very warm in the sun, yet always freshened by the gentle life of a breeze, and quite cool enough the moment you pass within the limit of the shade. I generally go to the garden of the Pincian and smoke a cigar at least once a day; sometimes twice. In the morning there are few people there, except the gardeners, lazily trimming the borders, or filling their watering pots out of the marble-brimmed basin of the fountain; French soldiers, in their long, mixed blue surtouts and wide scarlet pantaloons, chatting with here and there a nursery-maid and playing with the child; and perhaps a few [16] smokers like myself, choosing each his marble seat or wooden bench, in sunshine or shade as best suits him. In the afternoon, especially within an hour or two of sunset, the gardens are much more populous, and the seats—except when the sun falls full upon them—are hard to come by. Ladies come in carriages, splendidly dressed; children are abundant, much impeded in their frolics, and rendered stiff and stately, by the finery which they wear; English gentlemen, and Americans, with their wives and families; the flower of the Roman population, too, both male and female, mostly dressed with great nicety; but a large intermixture of artists, shabbily picturesque, and other persons not of the first stamp. A French band, comprising a great many brass instruments, by-and-by begins to play; and what with music, sunshine, a delightful atmosphere, flowers, grass, well kept pathways bordered with box-hedges, pines, cypresses, horse-chesnuts, flowering shrubs, and all manner of cultivated beauty, the scene is a very lively and agreeable one. The fine equipages, that drive round and round through the carriage paths, are another noticeable item. The Roman aristocracy are magnificent in this respect, driving abroad with beautiful horses, and footmen in rich liveries, sometimes as many as three behind, and one sitting by the coachman.

Rome, May 1st, Saturday.

This morning, I wandered, for the thousandth time, through some of the narrow intricacies of Rome, stepping here and there into a church. I do not know the name of the first one; nor had it anything remarkable here; though, till I came to Rome, I was not aware that any such churches existed —a marble pavement, in variegated compartments; a series of shrines and chapels, round the whole floor of the church, each with its own adornment of sculpture and pictures, its [17] own altar, with tall wax tapers before it, some of which were burning; a great picture over the high altar; the whole interior of the church ranged round with pillars and pilasters, and lined, every inch of it, with rich yellow marble, or an excellent imitation of it; finally, a frescoed cieling over the nave and transepts, and a dome rising high over the central part, and filled with frescoes, wrought to such perspective illusion that the edges seem to project into the air. Two or three persons are kneeling at separate shrines; there are several wooden confessionals placed against the walls, at one of which kneels a lady, confessing to a priest who sits within; the tapers are lighted at the high altar, and at one of the shrines; an attendant is scrubbing the marble pavement with a broom and water—a process, I should think, seldom practised in most of the Roman churches. By and by, the lady finishes her confession, kisses the priest's hand, and sits down in one of the chairs which are set about the floor; while the priest (in a black robe, with a short, loose, white jacket over his shoulders) disappears by a side-door out of the church. I, likewise, finding nothing attractive in the pictures, take my departure. But, really, to good Catholics, it must be a blessed convenience—this facility of finding a cool, quiet, silent, beautiful place of worship in even the hottest and most bustling street, into which they may step, leaving the fret and trouble of the world at the threshold, purifying themselves with a touch of holy water as they enter, and kneeling down to hold communion with some saint, their awful friend; or perhaps confessing all their sins to a priest, laying the whole dark burthen at the foot of the cross, and coming forth in the freshness and elasticity of innocence. It is for Protestants to inquire whether some of these inestimable advantages are not compatible with a purified faith, and do not indeed belong to Christianity, making part of the blessings it was meant to bring. It [18] would be a good time to suggest and institute some of them, now that the American public seems to be stirred by a Revival, hitherto unexampled in extent. Protestantism needs a new Apostle to convert it into something positive.

After leaving this church, I soon saw before me the great, dark, pillars, forming the portico of the Pantheon. I went in, and was impressed anew with the large, free space of the interior, wholly unencumbered from side to side of the vast circle; and, above, that great eye continually gazing straight upward to the seventh heaven. The world has nothing else like the Pantheon. It is very grand; so grand, that the pasteboard statues, between the rotunda and the commencement of the dome, do not in the least disturb the effect, any more than the tin crowns and hearts and the faded artificial flowers, and all manner of trumpery gewgaws, hanging at some of the shrines. The pavement of the Pantheon is very admirable, with its great squares and circles of porphyry, marble, and granite, and not the less so, that most of the compartments are cracked crosswise, and in a hundred ways, showing how all the troublesome centuries have trampled rough-shod over this floor. Under the opening in the dome, there is a grated-opening for the rain-water to pass off; and the marble, in that part of the pavement, is green with a small, fine moss, like that which gathers on tombstones in damp places. The sun came out fitfully, at intervals, while I stood in the Pantheon, throwing a great, broad beam, a sloping cataract of light, down upon the shrine at the right hand, as you enter the church; and going thither to look at the picture over the altar, thus strongly illuminated, I beheld a tabby cat, exceedingly fat and comfortable, reposing on the altar itself, among the holy tapers. She (or rather he, for I believe it was a ram-cat) [19] seemed to have just waked up, and sat blinking in the sunshine, yet with a certain dignity and self-possession, as if conscious of representing a saint. I waited to see if any worshipper would kneel at that shrine, but nobody came near it except two ladies, who whispered together and smiled. I suppose this is the first cat that has ever been a saint, or an object of worship, since the days of ancient Egypt.

From the Pantheon, I found my way to the Piazza Navona, which is at no great distance. It is to me the most interesting Piazza in Rome; a large, oblong space surrounded with tall, shabby houses, among which there are none that seem to be palaces. The sun falls broadly over the area of the Piazza, and shows the fountains in it; one a large basin, with great sea-monsters, probably of Bernini's invention, squirting very small streams of water into it; another of the fountains I do not at all remember; but the central one is an immense basin, over which is reared an old Egyptian obelisk, elevated on rock which is cleft into four arches. Monstrous devices in marble, I know not of what purport, are clambering about the cloven rock or burrowing beneath it, but one and all of them are superfluous and impertinent; the only essential thing being the abundant supply of water in the fountain. This whole Piazza Navona is usually the scene of more business than seems to be transacted anywhere else in Rome; in some parts of it, rusty iron is offered for sale, locks and keys, old tools, and all such rubbish; in other parts, vegetables, comprising, at this season, green peas, onions, cauliflower, radishes, lettuce, artichokes, and others with which I have never made acquaintance; also, stalls or wheelbarrows, containing apples, chestnuts (the meats dried and taken out of the shells,) green almonds in their husks, and squash-seeds salted and dried in an oven—apparently a favorite delicacy of the Romans. [20] There are also lemons and oranges; stalls of fish, mostly about the size of smelts, taken from the Tiber; cigars of various qualities, the best at a baioccho and a half apiece; bread, in loaves, or in small rings, a great many of which are strung together on a long stick, and thus carried round for sale. Women and men sit with these things for sale, or carry them about in trays or on boards, on their heads, crying them with shrill and hard voices. There is a shabby crowd, and much babble; very little picturesqueness of costume or figure, however; the chief exceptions being, here and there, an old, white-bearded beggar. A few of the men have the peasant costume; a short jacket and breeches of light blue cloth, and white stockings—the ugliest dress I ever saw. The women go bare-headed, and seem fond of scarlet and other bright colors, but are homely, and clumsy in build. The Piazza is dingy in its general aspect, and very dirty, being strewn with straw, vegetable-tops, and the rubbish of a week's marketing; but there is more life in it than one sees elsewhere in Rome.

On one side of this Piazza is the Church of St. Agnes, traditionally said to stand on the site of the house where that holy maiden was exposed to infamy by the Roman soldiers, and where her modesty and innocence were saved by miracle. I went into the church, and found it very splendid with rich marble columns, all as brilliant as if just built; a frescoed dome above; beneath, a range of chapels all round the church, ornamented not with pictures but bas-reliefs, the figures of which almost step and struggle out of the marble. They did not seem very admirable as works of art, none of them explaining themselves, or attracting me long enough to study out their meaning; but as part of the architecture of the church, they had a good effect. Out of the busy square, two or three persons had stept into this bright and calm seclusion, to pray and be devout for a little while; and between [21] sunrise and sunset of the bustling market-day, many doubtless snatch a moment to refresh their souls.

In the Pantheon, it was pleasant, looking up to the circular opening, to see the clouds flitting across it; sometimes covering it quite over, then permitting a glimpse of sky, then showing all the circle of sunny blue. Then would come the ragged edge of a cloud, brightened throughout with sunshine; all, whether sun or shadow, passing and changing quickly, not that the divine smile was not always the same, but continually variable through the medium of earthly influences. The great slanting beam of sunshine was visible all the way down to the pavement, falling upon motes of dust or a thin smoke of incense, imperceptible in the shadow. Insects were playing to-and-fro in the beam, high up toward the opening. There is a wonderful charm in the naturalness of all this; and it is natural enough to fancy a swarm of cherubs coming down through the opening, and sporting in the broad sunbeam, to gladden the faith of worshippers on the pavement beneath; or angels, bearing prayers upward, or bringing down responses to them, visible with dim brightness as they pass through that pathway of heaven's radiance, even the many hues of their wings discernible by a trusting eye; though, as they pass into the shadow, they vanish as the motes do. So the sunbeam would represent those rays of divine intelligence which enable us to see wonders, and to know that they are natural things.

The effect of light and shade in a church, when the windows are open and darkened with curtains, which are occasionally lifted by a breeze, letting in the sunshine, which whitens a carved tombstone in the pavement of the church—disclosing, perhaps the letters of the name and inscription, a death's head, a crosier, or other emblems; then the curtain falls, and the bright spot vanishes.

[22] May 8th, Saturday, Rome.

This morning my wife and I went to breakfast with Mr. & Mrs. Story, at the Barberini Palace, expecting to meet Mrs. Jameson, who has been in Rome for a month or two past. We had a very pleasant breakfast, but Mrs. Jameson was not present, on account of indisposition, and the only other guests were Mrs. Apthorp and Miss Hunter, two sensible American ladies. Mrs. Story, however, received a note from Mrs. Jameson, asking her to bring us to see her at her lodgings; so, in the course of the afternoon, she called for us and took us thither in her carriage. Mrs. Jameson lives on the first piano of an old palazzo on the Via di Ripetta, nearly opposite the ferry-way, across the Tiber, and affording a pleasant view of the yellow river and the green bank and fields on the other side. I had expected to see an elderly lady, but not quite so venerable a one as Mrs. Jameson proved to be; a short, or shortish, round and massive personage, of benign and agreeable aspect, with a sort of black scull-cap on her head, beneath which appeared her hair, which seemed once to have been fair, and was now almost white. I should take her to be not much short of seventy years old. She began to talk to us with affectionate familiarity, and was particularly kind in her manifestations towards myself, who, on my part, was equally gracious towards her. In truth, I have found great pleasure and profit in her works, and was glad to hear her say that she liked mine. We talked about art, and she showed us a picture standing up against the wall of the room; a quaint old Byzantine painting, with a gilded background, and two stiff figures (our Savior and St Catherine) standing shyly at a sacred distance from one another, and going through the marriage ceremony. There was a great deal of expression in their faces and figures, and [23] the spectator feels, moreover, that the artist must have been a devout man; an impression which we seldom receive from pictures, however awfully sacred the subject, or however holy the place they hang in. Mrs. Jameson seems to be familiar with Italy, its people and life, as well as its picture-galleries. She is said to be rather irascible in her temper; but nothing could be sweeter than her voice, her look, and all her manifestations, to-day. To finish off this meagre sketch of her, she had on the shabbiest old dressing gown that ever a decent woman wore, girded round her waist with a cord. When we were coming away, she clasped my hand in both of hers, and again gave vent to her pleasure at having seen me, and her gratitude to me for coming to call on her; nor did I refrain from responding anew to these effusions. Were we to meet often, I should be a little bit afraid of her embracing me outright—a thing to be grateful for, but by no means to be glad of.

Taking leave of Mrs Jameson, we drove through the city, and out of the Lateran gate; first, however, waiting a long while at Monaldi's bookstore, in the Piazza d'Espagna, for Mr. Story, whom we finally took up in the street, after losing nearly an hour. Just two miles beyond the gate, is a space on the green Campagna where, for some time past, excavations have been in progress, which, thus far, have resulted in the discovery of several tombs, and the old, buried, and almost forgotten church, or basilica, of (I believe) San Stefano. It is a beautiful spot, that of the excavations, with the Alban Hills in the distance, and some heavy, sun-lighted clouds hanging above, or recumbent at length upon them; and, behind, the city, and its mighty dome. The excavations are an object of great interest both to the Romans and to strangers; and there were many carriages, and a great many visitors viewing the progress of the works, [24] which appear to be carried forward with greater energy than anything else I have seen attempted in Rome. A short time ago, the ground in the vicinity was a green surface, level, except here and there a little hillock, or scarcely perceptible swell; the tomb of Cecilia Metella showing itself a mile or two distant, and other rugged ruins of great tombs, rising here and there on the plain. Now the whole site of the basilica is uncovered and made apparent, and they have dug into the depths of several tombs, bringing to light precious marbles, pillars, a statue, and elaborately wrought sarcophagi; and if they were to dig into almost any other inequality that frets the surface of the Campagna, I suppose the result might be the same. You cannot dig six feet downward anywhere into the soil—deep enough to hollow out a grave—without finding some precious relic of the past; only they lose somewhat of their value, when you think that you can almost spurn them out of the ground with your foot. It is a very wonderful arrangement of Providence, that these things should have been preserved for a long series of coming generations by that accumulation of dust, and soil, and grass, and trees, and houses, over them, which will keep them safe, and cause their re-appearance above ground to be gradual; so that the rest of the world's lifetime may have for one of its enjoyments the uncovering of old Rome.

The tombs were accessible by long flights of steps, going steeply downward; and they were thronged with so many visitors that we had to wait some little time for our own turn

to descend. In the first into which we descended, we found
two tombs side by side, with only a partition-wall between;
the outer tomb being, as is supposed, a work and burial place
of the early Christians, while the adjacent and inner one was
a work of pagan Rome, about the second century after Christ.
The former was much less in[25]teresting than the latter. It
contained some large Sarcophagi, with sculpture upon them,
of rather heathenish aspect; and in the centre of the front of
each sarcophagus was a bust in bas-relief, the features of
which had never been wrought, but were left almost blank,
with only the faintest indications of a nose, for instance. It is
supposed that sarcophagi were kept on hand by the sculptors,
and were bought ready made, and that it was customary to work
out the portrait of the deceased upon the blank face in the
centre; but when there was a necessity for sudden burial, as
may have been the case in the present instance, this was dis-
pensed with. The inner tomb was found without any earth
in it, just as it had been left when the last old Roman was
buried there; and it being only a week or two since it was
opened, there was very little intervention of persons—though
much of time—between the departure of the friends of the
dead and our own visit. It is a square room, with a mosaic
pavement, and is six or seven paces in length and breadth, and
as much in height to the vaulted roof. The roof and upper
walls are beautifully ornamented with frescoes, which were
very bright when first discovered, but have rapidly faded
since the admission of the air; though the graceful and joyous
designs, flowers, and fruits, and figures, are still perfectly discernible. The room must have been anything but sad and
funereal; on the contrary, as cheerful a saloon, and as brilliant,
if lighted up, as one could desire to feast in. It contained
several marble sarcophagi, covering indeed almost the whole
floor, and each of them as much as three or four feet in length,
and two much larger. The larger ones I did not particularly

examine, and they seemed comparatively plain; but the smal[26]ler sarcophagi were covered with the most delicately wrought and beautiful bas-reliefs that I ever beheld; a throng of glad and lovely shapes in marble, clustering thickly and chasing one another round the sides of these old stone coffins. The work was as perfect as when the sculptor gave it his last touch; and if he had wrought it to be placed in a frequented hall, to be seen and admired by continual crowds, as long as the marble should endure, he could not have chiselled with better skill and care; though his work was to be shut up in the depths of a tomb, forever. This seems to me the strangest thing in the world; the most alien from modern sympathies. If they had built their tombs above ground, one could understand the arrangement better; but no sooner had they adorned them so richly, and furnished them with such exquisite productions of art, than they annihilated them with darkness. It was an attempt, no doubt, to render the physical aspect of death cheerful; but there was no good sense in it.

We went down also into another tomb, close by, the walls of which were ornamented with medallions in stucco. These works presented a numerous series of graceful designs; wrought with the hands in the short space (Mr. Story said it could not have been more than five or six minutes) while the wet plaster remained capable of being moulded; and it was marvellous to think of the fertility of the old artist's fancy, and the rapidity and accuracy with which he must have given substantial existence to his ideas. These, too—all of them such adornments as would have suited a festal hall—were made to be buried forthwith, in eternal darkness. I saw and handled, in this tomb, a great thigh-bone, and measured it with my own; it was one of many such relics of the guests who were laid to sleep in these rich chambers. The sarcophagi, that served [27] them for coffins, could not now be put to a more appropriate use than as wine coolers in a modern dining-room;

and it would heighten the enjoyment of the festival to look at them.

We would gladly have staid much longer, but it was drawing towards sunset, and the evening, though bright, was unusually cool; so we drove home, and, on the way, Mr. Story told us of the horrible practices of the modern Romans with their dead—how they place them in the church, where, at midnight, they are stript of their last rag of funeral attire, put into the rudest wooden coffins, and thrown into a trench—a half a mile, for instance, of promiscuous corpses. This is the fate of all, except those whose friends choose to pay an exorbitant sum to have them buried under the pavement of a church. The Italians have a terrible dread of corpses, and never meddle with those of their nearest and dearest relatives. They have a horror of death too, especially of sudden death, and most particularly of apoplexy; and no wonder, as it gives no time for the last rites of the church, and so exposes them to a fearful risk of perdition forever. On the whole, the ancient practice was perhaps the preferable one; but Nature has made it very difficult for us to do anything pleasant and satisfactory with a dead body. God knows best; but I wish He had so ordered it that our mortal bodies, when we have done with them, might vanish out of sight and sense, like bubbles. A person of delicacy hates to think of leaving such a burthen as his decaying mortality, to be disposed of by his friends; but, I say again, how delightful it would be, and how helpful towards our faith in a blessed futurity, if the dying could disappear like vanishing bubbles, leaving perhaps a sweet fragrance, diffused for a minute or two throughout the death-chamber. This would be the odour of sanctity! [28] And if sometimes the evaporation of a sinful soul should leave a smell not so delightful, a breeze through the open windows would soon waft it quite away.

Apropos of the various methods of disposing of dead bodies,

William Story recalled a newspaper paragraph respecting a ring, with a stone of a new species in it, which a widower was observed to wear upon his finger. Being questioned as to what the gem was, he answered—"It is my wife." He had procured her body to be chemically resolved into this stone. I think I could make a story on this idea; the ring should be one of the widower's bridal gifts to a second wife, and of course it should have wondrous and terrible qualities, symbolizing all that disturbs the quiet of a second marriage—on the husband's part, remorse for his inconstancy, and the constant comparison between the dead wife of his youth, now idealized, and this grosser reality which he had now adopted into his bed and hers; while, on the new wife's finger, it should give pressures, shooting pangs into her heart, jealousies of the past, and all such miserable emotions.

By the by, the tombs which we looked at and entered may have been originally above ground, like that of Cecilia Metella, and a hundred others along the Appian Way; though, even in this case, the beautiful chambers must have been shut up in darkness. Had there been windows, letting in the light upon the rich frescoes and exquisite sculpture, there would have been a satisfaction in thinking of the existence of so much visual beauty, though no eye had the privilege to see it. But darkness, to objects of sight, is annihilation, as long as the darkness lasts.

Rome, May 9th, Sunday.

Mrs. Jameson called this forenoon to ask us to come and see her this evening. My wife happened to be lying down, wearied out with the toils of yesterday; so that I had to receive her alone, only devolving part of the burthen on Miss Shepard and the three children, all of whom I introduced to her notice.

Finding that [29] I had not been further beyond the walls of Rome than the tomb of Cecilia Metella, she invited me to take a drive of a few miles with her, this afternoon; and after some small conversation with Miss Shepard and Una (who are full of her books, just now) she took her leave. The poor old lady seems to be very lame; and I am sure I was grateful to her for having taken the trouble to hobble up the seventy steps of our staircase, and felt pain at seeing her hobble down again. It looks awfully like the gout, the affection being apparently in one foot. Her hands, by the way, are white and must once have been—perhaps now are—beautiful. She must have been the whole of a pretty woman in her day; a blue-or-gray-eyed, fair-haired beauty. I think that her hair is not white, but only flaxen in the extreme.

At half-past four, according to appointment, I arrived at her lodgings, and had not long to wait before her little one-horse carriage drove up to the door, and we set out, rumbling along the Via Scrofa, and through the densest part of the city, past the theatre of Marcellus, and thence along beneath the Palatine Hill, and by the Baths of Caracalla, through the gate of San Sebastiano. After emerging from the gate, we soon came to the little church of "Domine, quo vadis?" standing on the spot where St Peter is said to have seen a vision of our Savior bearing his cross. Mrs Jameson proposed to alight, and going in, we saw a cast from Michael Angelo's statue of the Savior; and, not far from the threshold of the church (yet perhap in the centre of the edifice, which is extremely small) a circular stone is placed, a little raised above the pavement of the church, and surrounded by a low wooden railing. Pointing to this stone, Mrs. Jameson showed me the prints of two feet, side by side, impressed into its surface, as if a person had stopt short while pursuing his way to Rome. These, she informed me, were supposed to be the miraculous prints [30] of the Savior's feet; but on looking into Murray, I am mortified to find that they are merely facsimiles of the original impressions, which are treasured up among the relics of the neighboring Basilica of San Sebastiano. The marks of sculpture seemed to me, indeed, very evident on these prints, nor did they indicate such beautiful feet as should have belonged to the bearer of the best of glad tidings.

Hence we drove on a little way further, and came to the Basilica of San Sebastiano, where also we alighted, and, leaning on my arm, Mrs. Jameson went in. It is a stately and noble interior, with a spacious, unencumbered nave, and a flat cieling, frescoed and gilded. In a chapel at the left of the entrance is the tomb of St Sebastian; a sarcophagus containing his remains, raised on high before the altar, and beneath it a recumbent statue of the saint, pierced with gilded arrows. The sculpture is of the school of Bernini—done after the design of Bernini himself, Mrs. Jameson said—and is more agreeable and in better taste than most of his works. We walked round the Basilica, glancing at the pictures in the various chapels, none of which seemed to be of remarkable merit, although Mrs Jameson pronounced rather a favorable verdict on one of St. Francis. She says that she can read a picture like the page of a book; in fact, without perhaps assuming more taste and judgment than really belong to her, it was impossible not to perceive that she gave her companion no credit for knowing one single, simplest thing about art. Nor, on the whole, do I think she under-rated me; the only mystery is, how she came to be so well aware of my ignorance on artistical points. In the Basilica, the Franciscan monks were arranging benches on the floor of the nave, and some peasant-children, and grown people besides, were assembling, probably to undergo an examination in the Catechism; and we hastened to depart, lest our pres[31]ence should interfere with their arrangements. At the door, a monk met us, and asked for a contribution in aid of his church, or some other religious purpose; and I gave him a half a Paul. Boys, as we drove on, ran stoutly along by the side of the chaise, begging as often as they could find breath, but were constrained finally to give up the pursuit. The great ragged bulks of the tombs along the Appian Way now hove in sight, one with a farm-house on its summit, and all of them preposterously huge and massive. At a distance across the green Campagna, on our left, the Claudian Aqueduct strode away over miles of space, and doubtless reached even to that circumference of blue hills, which stand afar off, girdling Rome about. The tomb of Cecilia Metella came in sight a long while before we reached it, with the warm, buff hue of its travertine, and the gray, battlemented wall which the Gaetanis erected on the top of its circular mound, six hundred years ago. After passing it, we saw an interminable line of tombs on both sides of the way, each of which might, for aught I know, have been as massive as that of Cecilia Metella, and some perhaps still more monstrously gigantic, though now dilapidated and much reduced in size. Mrs. Jameson had an engagement to dinner at ½ past six; so that we could go but a little further along this most interesting road, the borders of which are strewn with broken marble, fragments of capitals, and nameless rubbish that once was beautiful. Methinks the Appian Way should be the only entrance to Rome—through an avenue of tombs.

The day had been cloudy, chill, and windy, but was now grown calmer and more genial, and brightened by a very pleasant sunshine, though great, dark clouds were still lumbering up the sky. We drove homeward, looking at the distant dome of St Peter's, and talking [32] of many things—painting, sculpture, America, England, spiritualism, and whatever else came up. She is a very sensible old lady, and sees a great deal of truth; a good woman too, taking elevated views of matters; but I doubt whether she has quite the finest and highest perceptions in the world. At any rate, however, she pronounced a good judgment on the American sculptors now in Rome, condemning them in the mass, as men with no high aims, no worthy conception of the purposes of their art, and desecrating marble by the things they wrought in it. William Story, I presume, is not to be included in this censure, as she had already spoken highly of his sculpturesque faculty in our previous conversation. On my part, I suggested that the English sculptors were little or nothing better than our own; to which she acceded generally, but said that Gibson had produced works equal to the antique—which I did not dispute, but still questioned whether the world needed Gibson or was any the better for him. We had a great dispute about the propriety of adopting the costume of the day, in modern sculpture; and I contended that either the art ought to be given up (which possibly would be the best course) or else should be used for idealizing the man of the day to himself; and that, as Nature makes us sensible of the fact when men and women are graceful, beautiful, and noble, through whatever costume they wear, so it ought to be the test of a sculptor's genius that he should do the same. Mrs. Jameson decidedly objected to buttons, breeches, and all other items of modern costume; and indeed they do degrade the marble and make high sculpture utterly impossible. Then let the art perish, as one that the world has done with, as it has done with many other beautiful things that belonged to an earlier time.

It was long past the hour of Mrs Jameson's dinner-engage[33]ment when we drove up to her door in the Via di Ripetta. I bade her farewell, with much good feeling on my own side, and, I hope, on hers; excusing myself, however, from keeping the previous engagement to spend the evening with her; for, in point of fact, we had mutually had enough of one another for the time being. I am glad to set down that she expressed a very favorable opinion of our friend Mr. Thompson's pictures.

Rome, May 10th, Monday.

To-day, Mamma, Una, Julian, and I, have been to the Villa Albani, to which we had a ticket of admission through the agency of Mr. Cass. We set out between ten and eleven °clock, and walked through the Via Felice, the Piazza Barberini, and a long, heavy, dusty range of streets beyond, to the Porta Salara, whence the road extends, white, sunny, and dusty, between two high blank walls, to the gate of the Villa, which is luckily at no great distance. We were admitted by a girl, and went first to the Casino, along an aisle of overshadowing trees, the branches of which met above our heads. In the portico of the Casino, which extends along its whole front, there are many busts and statues, and among them one of Julius Caesar, representing him at an earlier period of life than others which I have seen. His aspect is not particularly impressive; there is a lack of chin, though not so much as in the elder statues and busts. Within the edifice, there is a beautiful hall, not so brilliant, perhaps, with frescoes and gilding as those at the Villa Borghese, but lined with the most beautiful variety of marbles that I have ever seen. But, in fact, each new splendor of this sort out-dazzles the last, and unless we could pass from one into another, all in the same suite, we cannot remember them well enough to compare the Borghese with the Albani; the effect being more on the fancy than on the intellect. I do not recall any of the Sculpture, except a colossal [34] bas-relief of Antinous, crowned with flowers, and holding flowers in his hand, which was found in the ruins of Hadrian's Villa. This is said to be the finest relic of antiquity, next to the Apollo and the Laocoon, but, I could not feel it to be so—partly, I suppose, because the features of Antinous do not seem to me beautiful in themselves; and that heavy, downward look is repeated till I am more weary of it

than of anything else in sculpture. We went up stairs and
down stairs, and saw a good many beautiful things, but none,
perhaps, of the very best and beautifullest; and second-rate
statues, with the corroded surface of old marble that has lain
dozens of centuries under a ground, depress the spirits of the
beholder. The bas-relief of Antinous has at least the merit of
being almost as white and fresh, and quite as smooth, as if it
had never been buried and dug up again. The real treasures
of this Villa, to the number of nearly three hundred articles,
were removed to Paris by Napoleon; and, except the Antinous,
not one of them ever came back.

There are some pictures in one or two of the rooms, among
which I recollect one by Perugino, in which is a Saint Michael,
very devout and very beautiful; indeed, the whole picture
(which is in compartments, representing the three principal
points of the Savior's history) impresses the beholder as being
painted devoutly and earnestly by a religious man. In one of
the rooms of the Casino, there is a small bronze Apollo, supposed by Winckelmann to be an original of Praxitiles; but I
could not make myself in the least sensible of its merit. The
rest of the things in the Casino, I shall pass over, as also those
in the Coffee-house, an edifice which stands a hundred yards,
or more, distant from the Casino, with an ornamental garden,
laid out in walks and flower-plats, between. The Coffee-house
has a semi-circular sweep of porch, with a good many statues
and busts beneath [35] it, chiefly of distinguished Romans.
In this building, as in the Casino, there are curious mosaics,
large vases of rare marble, and many other things worth
long pauses of admiration; but I think we were all happier
when we had done with the works of art, and were at leisure
to ramble about the grounds. The Villa Albani itself is an
edifice separate from both the Coffee-house and the Casino,
and is not opened to strangers; it rises palace-like in the midst
of the gardens, and, it is to be hoped, has some possibility of

comfort amidst its splendors. Comfort, however, would be thrown away upon it; for, besides that the site shares the curse that has fallen upon every pleasant place in the vicinity of Rome, and is uninhabitable during the finest season of the year, it really has no occupant except the servants who take care of it. The Count of Castelbarco, its present proprietor, resides at Milan. The grounds are laid out in the old fashion of straight paths, with borders of box, which form hedges of great height and density, cut as even as a brick wall, at the top and sides. There are also allies forming long vistas between the trunks and beneath the boughs of oaks, ilexes, and olives; and there are shrubberies, and tangled wildernesses of palm, cactus, rhododendron, and I know not what; and a profusion of roses, that bloom and wither with nobody to pluck and few to look at them. They climb about the sculpture of fountains, rear themselves against pillars and porticos, run brimming over the walls, and strew the paths with their falling leaves. We stole a few, and feel that we have wronged our consciences in not stealing more. In one part of the grounds, we saw a field actually a-blaze with scarlet poppies. There are great pools; fountains presided over by Naiads, who squirt their little jets into basins; sunny lawns; a temple so artificially ruined that we half-believed it a veritable antique; [36] and at its base, a reservoir of water, in which stone swans seemed positively to float; groves of crypress; balustrades, and broad flights of stone stairs, descending to lower levels of the garden; beauty, peace, sunshine, and antique repose, on every side; and, far in the distance, the blue hills that girdle in the Campagna of Rome. The day was very fine for our purpose, cheerful, but not too bright, and tempered by a breeze that seemed even a little too cool when we sat long in the shade. We enjoyed it till three °clock, and then came home, along the same dry and dusty way that had brought us thither.

Referring to sarcophagi, and to my remarks on the joyous

subjects which are usually represented in the bas-reliefs around them, Mrs Jameson said that there is almost always some allusion to death in the subject chosen. For instance, the story of Meleager is a favorite one for the purpose. On a visit to the Vatican, day before yesterday, I looked at a good many sarcophagi, and found that their bas-reliefs are often of battles; the rush of men and horses, and the ground strewn with dead; in some cases, a dying person seems to be represented, with the friends weeping all along the side of the sarcophagus; but oftener, I think, the allusion to death is very remote, if it exist at all. At the Capitol, there is a sarcophagus, with a most beautiful bas-relief of the discovery of Achilles by Ulysses, in which there is even an expression of mirth on the faces of many of the spectators; and to day, at the Albani, a sarcophagus was ornamented with the nuptials of Pelieus and Thetis. Death strides behind every man, to be sure, at more or less distance, and sooner or later enters upon any event of his life; so that, in this point of view, they might each and all serve for bas-reliefs on a sarcophagus; but the Romans seem to have treated death as lightly and playfully as they could, and tried to cover his dart with flowers, because they hated it so much.

[37] Rome, May 16th, Sunday.

My wife and I went yesterday to the Sistine Chapel, it being my first visit. It is a room of noble proportions, lofty and long, though divided in the midst by a screen or partition of white marble, which rises high enough to break the effect of spacious unity. There are six arched windows on each side of the chapel, throwing down their light from the height of the walls, with as much as twenty feet of space (more I should think) between them and the floor. The entire walls and cieling of this stately chapel are covered with paintings in fresco, except the space about ten feet in height from the floor; and that portion was intended to be covered by tapestries from pictures by Raphael, but the design being prevented by his immature death, the projected tapestries have no better substitute than paper hangings. The roof (which is flat at top, and coved or vaulted at the sides) is painted in compartments, by Michael Angelo, with designs representing the whole progress of the world, and of mankind, from its first formation by the Almighty out of his solitude, till after the flood; on one of the sides of the chapel are pictures by Perugino, and other old masters, of subsequent events in Sacred History; and the whole wall behind the altar, a vast expanse, from the cieling to the floor, is taken up with Michael Angelo's summing up of the world's history and destinies—his Last Judgment.

There can be no doubt that, while these frescoes remained in their perfection, there was nothing else in the world to be compared with the magnificent and solemn beauty of this chapel. Enough of ruined splendour still remains to convince the spectator of all that has departed; but methinks I have seen hardly anything else so forlorn and depressing as it is now; all dusky and dim, even the very lights having passed into shadows, [38] and the shadows into utter blackness; so that it needs a sunshiny day, under this bright Italian sky, to make the designs perceptible at all. As we sat in the chapel, there were clouds flitting across the sky; when the clouds came, the pictures vanished; when the sunshine broke forth, the figures sadly glimmered into something like visibility—the Almighty bestirring himself in Chaos, the noble shape of Adam, the beautiful Eve; and, beneath, where the roof curves, the mighty figures of Sybils and Prophets, looking as if they were necessarily so gigantic, because the thought within them was so massive. In the Last Judgment, the scene of the greater part of the picture lies in the upper sky, the blue of which glows through betwixt the groups of naked figures; and above sits Jesus, not looking in the least like the Savior of the world, but with uplifted arm denouncing eternal misery on those whom he came to save. I fear I am myself among the wicked, for I found myself inevitably taking their part, and asking for at least a little pity, some few regrets, and not such a stern denunciatory spirit on the part of Him who had thought us worth dying for. Around him stand grim Saints, and, far beneath, people are getting up sleepily out of their graves, not well knowing what is about to happen; many of them, however, finding themselves clutched by demons before they are half-awake. It would be a very terrible picture to one who should really see Jesus, the Savior, in that inexorable Judge; but it seems to me very undesirable that he should ever be represented in that aspect, when it is so essential to our religion to believe him infinitely kinder and better towards us than we deserve. At the Last Day, I presume—that is, in all future days, when we see ourselves as we are—man's only inexorable Judge will be himself, and the punishment of his sins will be the perception of them.

In the lower corner of this great picture, at the right of the [39] spectator, is a hideous figure of a damned person girdled about with a serpent, the folds of which are carefully knotted between his thighs, so as, at all events, to give no offence to decency. This figure represents a man who suggested to Pope Paul III. that the nudities of the Last Judgment ought to be draped; for which offence Michael Angelo at once consigned him to Hell. It shows what a debtor's prison and dungeon of private torment men would make of hell, if they had the control of it. As to the nudities, if they were ever more nude than now, I should suppose, in their fresh glow, they might well have startled a not very squeamish eye. The effect, such as it is, of this picture, is much injured by the high altar and its canopy, which stands close against the wall, and intercepts a considerable portion of the sprawl of nakedness with which Michael Angelo has filled his sky. However, I am not unwilling to believe (with faith beyond what I can actually see) that the greatest pictorial miracles, ever yet achieved, have been wrought upon the walls and cieling of the Sistine Chapel.

In the afternoon, I went with Mr Thompson to see what bargain could be made with veturrinos for taking myself and family to Florence. We talked with three or four, and found them asking prices of various enormity, from a hundred and fifty scudi down to little more than ninety; but Mr. Thompson says that they always begin in this way, and will probably come down to somewhere about seventy-five. Mr. Thompson took me into the Via Portoghese, and showed me an old palace; above which rose—not a very customary feature of the architecture of Rome—a tall, battlemented tower. At one angle of the tower we saw a shrine of the virgin, with a lamp, and all [40] the appendages of those numerous shrines which we see at the street corners, and in hundreds of places about Rome. Three or four hundred years ago, this palace was inhabited by a nobleman who had an only son and a large pet monkey; and one day the monkey caught the infant up in his arms, and clambered with him to this lofty turret, and sat there with him in his arms, grinning and chattering like the devil himself. The father was in despair, but was afraid to pursue the monkey, lest he should fling down the child from the height of the tower, and make his escape. At last, he vowed that if the boy were safely restored him, he would build a shrine at the summit of the tower, and cause it to be kept as a sacred place forever. By and by, the monkey came down and deposited the child on the ground; the father fulfilled his vow, built the shrine, and made it obligatory on all future possessors of the palace to keep the lamp burning before it. Centuries have passed; the property has changed hands; but still there is the shrine on the giddy top of the tower, far aloft over the street, on the very spot where the monkey sat; and there burns the lamp in memory of the father's vow. This being the tenure by which the estate is held, the extinguishment of that flame might yet turn the present owner out of his palace.

Rome, May 21ˢᵗ, Friday.

Mamma, Julian, and I, went yesterday forenoon to the Spada Palace, which we found among the intricacies of central Rome; a dark and massive old edifice, built around a court-yard, the fronts looking on which are adorned with statues in niches, and sculptured ornaments. A woman led us up a stair-case, and ushered us into a great, gloomy hall, square, and lofty, and wearing a very gray and ancient aspect, its walls being painted in chiaro-oscuro, apparently a great many years ago. The hall was lighted by small windows, high upward from the floor, and admitting only a dusky light. The only [41] furniture or ornament, so far as I recollect, was the colossal statue of Pompey, which stands on its pedestal, at one side of the hall, certainly the sternest and severest figure, and producing the most awful impression on the spectator, of any that I have yet beheld. Much of this effect no doubt is due to the sombre obscurity of the hall, and to the loneliness in which the great, naked statue stands. It is entirely nude, ex-cept for a cloak that hangs down from the left shoulder; in the left hand it holds a globe; the right arm is extended. The whole expression is such as the statue might have assumed, if, during the tumult of Caesar's murder, it had stretched forth its marble hand and motioned the conspirators to give over their attack, or to be quiet, now that their victim had fallen at its feet. On the left leg, about midway above the ancle, there is a dull red stain, said to be Caesar's blood; but of course it is just such a red stain in the marble as may be seen on the statue of Antinous at the Capitol. I could not see any resemblance in the face of the statue to that of the bust of Pompey, shown as such in the Capitol, in which there is not the slightest moral dignity or sign of intellectual eminence. I am glad to have seen this statue, and glad to remember it in that gray, dim, lofty hall; glad that there were no bright frescoes on the walls, and that the cieling was wrought with massive beams, and the floor paved with ancient brick.

From the hall, we passed through several saloons containing pictures, some of which were by eminent artists; the Judith of Guido, a copy of which used to weary me to death, year after year, in the Boston Athenaeum, and many portraits of Cardinals of the Spada family, and other pictures, by the same. There were some portraits, also of the family, by Titian; some good pictures by Guercino; and many others, which I should have been glad to examine more at leis[42]ure; but, by-and-by, the Custode made his appearance and began to close the shutters, under pretence that the sunshine would injure the paintings—an effect, I presume, not very likely to follow, after two or three centuries of exposure to light, air, and whatever else might hurt them. However, the pictures seemed to be in much better condition, and more enjoyable, so far as they had merit, than in most Roman picture-galleries; although the Spada palace itself has a decayed and impoverished aspect, as if the family had dwindled from its former state and grandeur, and now perhaps smuggled itself into some out-of-the-way corner of the old edifice. If such is the case, there is something touching in their still keeping possession of Pompey's statue, which makes their house famous, and the sale of which might give them the means of building it up anew; for surely it is worth the whole sculpture-gallery of the Vatican.

In the afternoon, Mr. Thompson and I went, for the third

or fourth time, to negotiate with vetturinos for the conveyance of myself and family to Florence. In common with
all the rest of their countrymen, so far as I know them, the
vetturini are a very tricky set of people, bent on getting as
much as they can, by hook or by crook, out of the unfortunate
individual who falls into their hands. They begin by asking
about twice as much as they ought to receive; and anything
between this extortionate amount and the just price, is just
what they thank God for, as so much clear gain. Nevertheless,
I am not quite sure that the Italians are worse than other
people, even in this matter. In other countries, it is the custom
of persons in trade to take as much as they can get from the
public, fleecing one man to exactly the same extent as another;
here, they take what they can get from the individual cus-
tomer. In fact, tradesmen do not pretend to deny that they
ask and receive different prices from [43] different people,
taxing them according to their supposed means of payment;
the article supplied being the same in one case as in another.
A shopkeeper looked into his books to see if we were of the
class who paid two pauls, or only a paul and a half, for candles;
a charcoal dealer said that seventy baiocchi was a very reasonable sum for us to pay for charcoal, and that some persons paid
eighty; and Mr. Thompson, recognizing the rule, told the
vetturino that a hundred and fifty scudi was a very proper
charge for carrying a prince to Florence, but not for carrying
me, who was merely a very good artist. The result is well
enough; the rich man lives expensively, and pays a larger
share of the profits which people of a different system of
trade-morality would take equally from the poor man. The
effect on the conscience of the vetturino, however, and of
tradesmen of all kinds, cannot be good; their only intent
being, not to do justice between man and man, but to go as
deep as they can into all pockets, and to the very bottom of
some. We had all but concluded a bargain, a day or two ago,

with a vetturino to take or send us to Florence, via Perugia, in eight days, for a hundred scudi; but he now drew back, under pretence of having misunderstood the terms, though, in reality, no doubt, he was in hopes of getting a better bargain from somebody else. We concluded a bargain with another man, whom Mr. Thompson knows and highly recommends, and immediately made it sure and legally binding by exchanging a formal written contract, in which everything is set down, even to milk, butter, bread, eggs, and coffee, which we are to have for breakfast; the vetturino being to pay every expense for himself, his horses, and his passengers, and include it within ninety-five scudi, and five crowns additional for buonamano.

[44] In the evening, Mamma, Una, and I, went to see Mr. Thompson and his wife. They are a very kind and agreeable family, both grown people and children. During the evening, Mr Ropes and his wife came in, he being an American landscape painter, from my own old town indeed; and likewise Mr. Rothermel, another American artist, with his wife. I suppose there is a class-feeling among the artists who reside here, and they create a sort of atmosphere among themselves, which they do not find anywhere else, and which is comfortable for them to live in. Nevertheless, they are not generous or gracious critics of one another; and I hardly remember any full-breathed and whole-souled praise from sculptor to sculptor, or from painter to painter. They dread one another's ill-word, and scrupulously exchange little attentions for fear of giving offence; they pine, I suspect, at the sight of another's success, and would willingly keep a rich stranger from the door of any studio save their own. Their public is so much more limited than that of the literary men, that they have the better excuse for these petty jealousies. I do not mean to include Mr. Thompson in the above remarks; for I believe him to be an excellent man, and know him to be most friendly

towards me, and, as an artist, earnestly aiming at beautiful things, and achieving them. In the course of our visit, he produced several rich portfolios; one containing some sketches from nature by an eminent German landscape painter, long resident in Rome, and now deceased; another contained the contributions of many artists, his friends, little pencil-drawing and water-color sketches, bits of landscapes, likenesses, in short, an artistic album; the other was a most curious collection of sketches, many of them very old, and by celebrated painters, which he had partly picked up at the shops of dealers in such things, but had bought the greater [45] part in a lump, for about two dollars. He conjectures that they were part of the collection of some old Cardinal, at whose death the servants had stolen them, and sold them for what they would fetch. Here were pen-and-ink sketches, and pencil-drawings, on coarse and yellow paper of centuries ago, often very bold and striking; the 'motives,' as artists say, or first hints and rude designs, of pictures which were afterwards painted, and very probably were never equal to these original conceptions. Some of the sketches were so rough and hasty that the eye could hardly follow the design; yet, when you caught it, it proved to be full of fire and spirit. Others were exceedingly careful and accurate, yet seemed hardly the less spirited for that; and in almost all cases, whether rough or elaborate, they gave me a higher idea of the imaginative scope and toil of artists than I generally get from their finished pictures.

Rome, May 22ᵈ, Saturday.

Yesterday, while we were at dinner, (we dine at two °clock, so as to have the decline and coolness of the day for walks,) Mr. W. C. Bryant called. I never saw him but once before; and that was at the door of our little red cottage in Lenox; he

sitting in a wagon, with some of the Sedgwicks, merely exchanging a greeting with me from under the brim of his
straw-hat, and driving on. He presented himself now with a
long white beard, such as a palmer might have worn, as the
growth of his long pilgrimages; a brow almost entirely bald,
and what hair he has quite hoary; a forehead impending, yet
not massive; dark, bushy eyebrows, and keen eyes, without
much softness in them; a dark and sallow complexion; a
slender figure, bent a little with age, but at once alert and
infirm. It surprised me to see him so venerable; for, as poets
are Apollo's kins[46]men, we are inclined to attribute to them
his enviable quality of never growing old. There was a
weary look in Bryant's face, as if he were tired of seeing things
and doing things, though with activity enough still to see and
do, if need were. My family gathered about him, and he
conversed with great readiness and simplicity about his
travels, and whatever other subject came up; telling us that
he had been abroad five times, and was now getting a little
home sick, and had no more eagerness for sights, though
his "gals" (as he called his daughter and another young lady)
dragged him out to see the sights of Rome again. His manners
and whole aspect are very particularly plain, though not af-
fectedly so; but it seems as if, in the decline of life, and the
security of his position, he had put off whatever artificial polish
he may have heretofore had, and resumed the simple habits
and deportment of his early New England breeding. Not but
what you discern, nevertheless, that he is a man of refinement,
who has seen the world, and is well aware of his own place
in it. He spoke with great pleasure of his recent visit to Spain.
I introduced the subject of Kansas; and methought his visage
forthwith assumed something of the bitter keenness of the
Editor of a political newspaper, while speaking of the triumph
of the administration over the free-soil opposition. I inquired
whether he had seen Sumner recently; and he gave a very

sad account of him as he appeared at their last meeting, which was in Paris. Sumner, he thought, had suffered terribly, and would never again be the man he was; he was getting fat; he talked continually of himself, and trifles concerning himself, and seemed to have no interest for other matters; and Bryant feared that the shock [47] upon his nerves had extended to his intellect, and was irremediable. He said that Sumner ought to retire from public life, but had no friend true enough to tell him so. This is about as sad as anything can be. I hate to have Sumner undergo the fate of a martyr; because he was not naturally of the stuff that martyrs are made of, and it is altogether by mistake that he has thrust himself into the position of one. He was merely (though with excellent abilities) one of the best fellows in the world, and ought to have lived and died in good-fellowship with all the world.

Bryant was not in the least degree excited about this or any other subject. He uttered neither passion nor poetry, but excellent good-sense and accurate information on whatever subject came up; a very pleasant man to associate with, but rather cold, I should imagine, if one should seek to touch his heart with one's own. He shook hands kindly all round, but not with any warmth of gripe, although the ease of his deportment had put us all on sociable terms with him.

At seven °clock, Mamma, Miss Shepard, and I, went by invitation to take tea with Miss Bremer. After much search, and lumbering painfully up two or three staircases in vain, and at last going up stairs and down, in a strange circuity, we found her in a little chamber of a large old building, situated a little way from the brow of the Tarpeian Rock. It was the smallest and humblest domicile that I have seen in Rome, just large enough to hold her narrow bed, her tea-table, and a table covered with books, photographs of Roman ruins, and some pages written by herself.—I wonder whether she is poor. Probably so; for she told us that her expense of living here is only five Pauls a day. She [48] welcomed us, however, with the greatest cordiality and lady-like simplicity, making no allusion to the humility of her environment, and making us also lose sight of it (only that we had hardly room enough to sit down) by the absence of all apology, any more than if she were receiving us in a palace. There is not a better-bred woman in the world; and one does not think whether she has any breeding or no. Her little bit of a round table was already spread for us with some blue earthenware tea-cups; and after she had got through an interview with the Swedish Consul (about her passport, I believe) and dismissed him with a hearty pressure of his hand between both her own, she gave us our tea, and some bread, and a mouthful of cake. Meanwhile, as the day declined, there had been the most beautiful view over the Campagna, out of one of her windows, and from the other, looking towards Saint Peter's, the broad glow of a mildly glorious sunset, not so pompous and magnificent as many that I have seen in America, but softer and sweeter, in all its changes, than I almost ever saw. As its beautiful hues died slowly away, the half-moon shone out brighter and brighter; for there was not a cloud in the sky, and it seemed like the moonlight of my younger days, which has vanished for many a long year. In the garden beneath her window, verging upon the Tarpeian Rock, there was shrubbery, and one large tree, softening the brow of the famous precipice adown which the old Romans used to fling their traitors, or sometimes their patriots.

Miss Bremer talked plentifully in her strange gibberish; good English enough, for a foreigner, but so oddly intonated and accented that it is impossible to be sure of more than one word in ten. Being so little comprehensible, it is very singular [49] how she contrives to make her auditors so perfectly certain, as they are, that she is talking the best sense in the world, and in the kindliest spirit. There is no better heart than hers, and not many sounder heads; and a little touch of sentiment comes delightfully in, mixed up with a quick and delicate sense of humour, and the most perfect simplicity. There is a very pleasant atmosphere of old-maidishness about her; we are sensible of a freshness and smell of the morning, still, in this little withered rose—its recompense for never having been worn in anybody's bosom, but only smelt at on the stem. I forget mainly what we talked about; a good deal about art, of course, although that is a subject of which Miss Bremer evidently knows nothing. Once we talked of fleas; animals that, in Rome, come home to everybody's business and bosom, and are so common and inevitable that no delicacy is felt about alluding to the sufferings they inflict. Poor little Miss Bremer was tormented with one while turning out our tea, and positively had to indicate the fact, and the spot too, by rubbing it. She talked, among other things, of the winters in Sweden, and said that she liked them, long and severe as they are; and this made me feel ashamed of dreading the winters of New England, as I did before coming away, and do now still more, after five or six mild English Decembers.

By and by two young ladies came in, her neighbors, it seemed, fresh from a long walk on the Campagna—fresh and weary at the same time. One apparently was German and the other French, and they brought her an offering of flowers, and chattered to her with affectionate vivacity; and, as we were about taking leave, Miss Bremer asked them to accompany her [50] and us on a visit to the edge of the Tarpeian Rock. Before we left the room, she took a bunch of roses, that were in a tumbler, and gave them to Miss Shepard, who told her that she should make each of her six sisters happy by giving them one a-piece. We went down the intricate stairs, and emerging into the garden, walked round the brow of the hill, which plunges down with exceeding abruptness, but, so far as I could see in the moonlight, is no longer quite a precipice. Then we re-entered the house, and went up stairs and down again, through intricate passages, till we got into the street, which was still peopled with the ragamuffins who infest and burrow in that part of Rome. We returned through an archway and down the broad flight of steps into the piazza of the Capitol; and from the extremity of it, just at the head of the long descent, where Castor and Pollux and the old mile-stones stand, we turned to the left, and followed a somewhat winding way till we came into the court-yard of a palace. This court-yard is bordered by a parapet, leaning over which, we saw a sheer precipice of the Tarpeian Rock, about the height of a four-story house; not that the precipice was a bare face of rock, but appeared to be cased in some sort of ancient stone-work, through which the primeval rock, here and there, looked grimly and doubtfully. Bright as the Roman moonlight was, it could not show the front of wall, or rock, so well as I should have liked to see it, but left it in pretty much the same degree of dubiety and half-knowledge, in which the antiquaries leave almost all the Roman ruins. Perhaps this last precipice may have been the traitors' leap; perhaps the one on which Miss Bremer's garden verges; possibly, neither of the two. At any rate, it was a good idea of the stern [51] old Romans, to fling political criminals down from the very height of that Capitoline hill on which stood the temples and public edifices, symbols of the institutions which they sought to violate.

On the edge of the Tarpeian Rock, before we left the court-yard of the palace, Miss Bremer bade us farewell, kissing my wife most affectionately on each cheek, "because," she said, "you look so sweetly"; kissing Miss Shepard too; and then turning towards myself. I was in a state of some little tremor, not knowing what might be about to befal me; but she merely pressed my hand, and we parted, probably never to meet again. God bless her good heart, and every inch of her little body, not forgetting her red nose, preposterously big as it is in proportion to the rest of her! She is a most amiable little woman, worthy to be the maiden-aunt of the whole human race. I suspect, by-the-by, that she does not like me half so well as I do her; it is my impression that she thinks me un-amiable, or that there is something or other not quite right about me. I am sorry if it be so, because such a good, kindly, clear-sighted, and delicate person is very apt to have reason at the bottom of her harsh thoughts, when, in rare cases, she allows them to harbour within her.

To-day, and for some days past, we, especially my wife, have been in quest of lodgings for next winter; a weary search, up interminable staircases, which seduce us upward to no success-ful result. It is very disheartening not to be able to place the slightest reliance on the integrity of the people we are to deal with; not to believe in any connection between their words and their purposes; to know that they are certainly telling you lies, while you are [52] not in a position to catch hold of the lie and hold it up in their faces.

This afternoon, my wife and I called on Mr. and Mrs. Bryant, at the Hotel d'Europe, but found only the former at home. We had a pleasant visit, but I made no observations of his character save such as I have already sufficiently recorded; and when we had been with him a little while, Mrs. Chapman, the artist's wife, Mr Terry, the painter, and my friend Mr. Thompson came in. Bryant received them all with the same good degree of cordiality that he did ourselves, not cold, not very warm, not bothered, not ecstatically delighted; a man, I should suppose, not likely to have warm individual pref-erences, though perhaps capable of stern individual dislikes. But I take him, at all events, to be a very upright man, and pursuing a narrow track of integrity; at any rate, he is a man whom I would never forgive (as I might a thousand other men) for the slightest moral delinquency. I would not be bound to say, however, that he has not the little sin of a fretful and peevish habit; and yet, perhaps, I am a sinner myself for thinking so.

Rome, May 23ᵈ, Sunday.

This morning, I breakfasted at William Story's, and met there Mr. Bryant, Mʳ Twisden (an English gentleman), Mʳ and Mrs. Apthorp, Miss Hosmer, and one or two other ladies. Bryant was very quiet, and made no conversation audible to the general table. Mr. Twisden talked of English politics and public men, the Times, and other newspapers, English clubs, and social habits generally; topics in which I could well enough bear my part of the discussion. After breakfast, and apart from the ladies, he mentioned (in illustration of Lord Ellenborough's lack of administrative ability) a proposal seriously made by his lordship [53] in reference to the refractory Sepoys; it was nothing less than to emasculate them!! We had a very pleasant breakfast, and certainly the meal is much preferable to a dinner, not merely in the enjoyment while it is passing, but in the freedom from headache afterwards. I made a good suggestion to Miss Hosmer for the design of a fountain—a lady 'bursting into tears,' water gushing from a thousand pores, in literal translation of the phrase; and to call the statue 'Niobe all tears.' I doubt whether she adopts the idea, but Bernini would have been delighted with it. I should think the gush of water might be so arranged as to form a beautiful drapery about the figure, swaying and fluttering with every breath of wind, and re-arranging itself in the calm; in which case the lady might be said to have a 'habit of weeping.' Apart with

William Story, he and I talked of the unluckiness of Friday, and both acknowledge that this nonsense has a certain degree of influence with us. We spoke, also, and more seriously, of the idea (which has been realized in my own experience) that a piece of good fortune is apt to be attended by an equivalent misfortune, as its shadow, or black twin. There seems to be a vein of melancholy in William Story, which I was not aware of in my very slight previous acquaintance with him, before meeting him now in Rome. He acknowledged that, for three years past, he had lived in dread that some sorrow would come to counterbalance the prosperity of his present life. I hope not; for I like him particularly well; and indeed it is very hard if we cannot enjoy a little sunshine in this short and hard life, without a deadly shadow gliding close behind. Old age, and death in its due time, will surely come; let those suffice. The notion, however, [54] is a comfortable one or otherwise, according to your point of view. If the misfortune comes first, it is consolatory to think of the good that is soon to follow; in the other category, it is exceedingly disagreeable. Miss Hosmer, to-day, had on a neat little jacket, a man's shirt-bosom, and a cravat with a brooch in it; her hair is cut short, and curls jauntily round her bright and smart physiognomy; and sitting opposite me at table, I never should have imagined that she terminated in a petticoat, any more than in a fish's tail. However, I do not mean to speak disrespectfully of Miss Hosmer, of whom I think very favorably; but, it seems to me, her reform of the female dress commences with its least objectionable part, and is no real improvement.

We have been plagued to-day with our preparations for leaving Rome tomorrow, and especially with verifying the inventory of furniture, before giving up the house to our landlord. He and his daughter have been, examining every separate article, down even to the kitchen-skewers, I believe, and charging us to the amount of several scudi for cracks and breakages, which very probably existed when we came into possession. It is very uncomfortable to have dealings with such a mean people; mean in their business transactions; mean even in their beggary, for the beggars seldom ask for more than a mezzo-baiocchi, though they sometimes grumble when you suit your gratuity exactly to their petition. It is pleasant to record that they, the Italians, have great faith in the honor of the English and Americans, and never hesitate to trust entire strangers, to any reasonable extent, on the strength of their being of the honest Anglo Saxon breed.

This evening, Una and I took a farewell walk in the Pincian gardens, to see the sunset, and found the hill crowded [55] with people, promenading, and listening to the music of the French band. It was the feast of Whitsunday, which probably brought a greater throng than usual abroad. When the sun was down, we descended into the Piazza del Popolo, and thence into the Via di Ripetta, and emerged through a gate to the shore of the Tiber, along which there is a pleasant walk beneath a grove of trees. We traversed it once, and back again, looking at the rapid river, which still kept its mud-puddly aspect even in the clear twilight and beneath the brightening moon. The great bell of Saint Peter's tolled with a deep boom, a grand and solemn sound; the moon gleamed through the branches of the trees above us; and Una spoke with somewhat alarming fervor of her love for Rome and regret at leaving it. We shall have done the poor child no good office in bringing her here, if the rest of her life is to be a dream of this 'city of the soul,' and an unsatisfied yearning to come back. On the other hand, nothing elevating and refining can be really injurious; and so I hope she will always be the better for Rome, even if her life should be spent where there are no pictures, no statues, nothing but the dryness and meagreness of a New England village.

Civita Castellana, May 24th, Monday.

We left Rome this morning, after troubles of various kinds, and a dispute in the first place with Lalla, our female servant, and her mother; the first claiming a week's extra-wages, and the latter the same extent of extra pay for bringing water; but as we had given them both more than the fortnight's warning, which Lalla said was requisite, we declined to make any over-payment; especially as we had tax above six scudi by the Padrone for [56] Lalla's breakage of glass and crockery. Mother and daughter exploded into a livid rage, and cursed us plenti-fully, wishing that we might never come to our journey's end, that we might all break our necks, and that we might die of the apoplexy—the most awful curse that an Italian knows how to invoke upon his enemies, because it precludes the possibility of extreme unction. However, as we are heretics and certain of damnation anyhow, it does not much matter to us; and also we hope that the anathemas were blown back upon those who invoked them, like those which were flung out from the balcony of Saint Peter's, during last Holy Week, and wafted by Heaven's breezes right into the faces of some Priests. Next we had a dispute with two men who brought down our baggage and put it on the vetturo, and who asked five francs for the job, but were forced to content themselves with three Pauls and a half a-piece. Lastly we were infested by beggars, who hung round the carriage, with doleful petitions till we began to move away; but the previous warfare had put me into too stern a mood for charity; so that they also were doubtless inclined to curse more than to bless, and I am persuaded that we drove off under a perfect shower of anathemas.

We emerged from the gate del Popolo at about eight °clock;

and after a moment's delay, while the passport was examined, began our journey along the Flaminian Way, between two such high and inhospitable fences of brick or stone as seem to shut in all the avenues to Rome. We had not gone far, before we heard military music in advance of us, and saw [57] the road blocked up with people, and then the glitter of muskets; and soon appeared the drummers, fifers, and trumpeters, and then the first batallion of a French regiment marching into the city, with two mounted officers at their head. Then appeared another batallion; then a third, the whole seeming to make almost an army, though the number on their caps showed them all to belong to one regiment, the 1st. Then came a battery of artillery; then a detachment of horse, these last, by the cross-keys on their helmets, being apparently papal troops. All were young, fresh, good-looking men, in excellent trim as to uniform and equipments, and marched rather as if they were setting out on a campaign than returning from it; the fact being, I believe, that they have been encamped or in barracks within a few miles of the city. Nevertheless it reminded me of the military processions of various kinds, which so often, two thousand years ago and more, have entered Rome over the Flaminian Way, and over all the roads that led to the famous city; triumphs oftenest, but sometimes the down cast train of a defeated army, like those who retreated before Hannibal. On the whole I was not sorry to see the Gauls still pouring into Rome; but, after all, I begin to find that I have a strange affection for Rome, and so did we all, the rest of the family in a greater degree than myself. It is very singular, the sad embrace with which Rome takes possession of the soul. Though we intend to return in a few months, and for a longer residence than this has been, yet we felt the city pulling at our heart strings far more than London did, where we shall proba[58]bly never spend much time again. It may be because the intellect finds a home there, more than in any other spot in the world, and wins the heart to stay with it, in spite of a great many things strewn all about to disgust us.

The road, in the earlier part of the day, was not particularly picturesque; the country undulated, but scarcely rose into hills, and was destitute of trees; there were a few shapeless ruins, too indistinct for us to make out whether they were Roman or mediaeval. Nothing struck me so much, in the forenoon, as the spectacle of a peasant-woman riding on horseback astride. The houses were few, and those of a dreary aspect, built of gray stone, and looking bare and desolate, with not the slightest promise of comfort within doors. We passed two or three locandas, or inns; and finally came to the village (if village it were, for I remember no houses except our osteria) of Castel Nuova di Porto, where we were to take a dejeuner a la fourchette, which was put upon the table between twelve and one. On this journey, according to the custom of travellers in Italy, we pay the vetturino a sum in the lump, and live at his expense; and this meal was the first specimen of his catering on our behalf. It consisted of a beef-steak, rather dry and hard, but not unpalatable, for each of us six, and a large omelette, and for beverage two quart bottles of red wine, which, being tasted, had an agreeable acid flavor and possibly a drop of alcohol to the bottle. The locanda was built of stone, and had what looked like an old Roman altar in the basement-hall, and a shrine with a lamp before it on the staircase; and the large public chamber, in which we ate, had a brick floor, a cieling with cross-beams, meagrely painted in fresco, and a scanty supply of chairs and settees. After lunch, we wan[59]dered out into a valley or ravine, near the house, where we gathered some flowers, and Julian stole a nest, with the young birds in it; which, however, we made him put back into the bush where he found it.

Our afternoon's drive was more picturesque and noteworthy. Soracte (or Monte de Sant Oreste) rose before us, bulging up

quite abruptly out of the plain, and keeping itself entirely distinct from a whole horizon of hills. Byron well compares it to
a wave just on the bend, and about to break over towards the
spectator. As we approached it nearer and nearer, it looked like
the barrenest great rock that ever protruded out of the hard substance of the earth, with scarcely a strip or a spot of verdure
upon its steep and gray declivities. The road kept trending
towards the mountain, following the line of the old Flaminian
Way, which we could see, at frequent intervals, close beside
the modern track. It is paved with large flag-stones, laid so
accurately together that it is still, in some places, as smooth
and even as the floor of a church; and everywhere the tufts
of grass find it difficult to root themselves into the interstices.
Its course is straighter than that of the road of to-day, which
often turns aside to avoid obstacles which the ancient one
surmounted. Much of it, probably, is covered with the soil
and over-growth deposited in later years; and now and then
we could see its flag-stones partly protruding from the bank
through which our road has been cut, and thus showing that
the thickness of this massive pavement was more than a foot
of solid stone. We lost it over and over again; but still it re-
appeared, now on one side of us, now on the other, perhaps
from beneath the roots of old trees [60] or the pasture land of
a thousand years old, and leading on towards the base of
Soracte. I forget where we finally lost it. Passing through a
town called Rignano, we found it dressed out in festivity, with
festoons of foliage along both sides of the street, which ran beneath a triumphal arch, bearing an inscription in honor of a
ducal personage of the Massimi family. I know no occasion
for the feast, except that it is Whitsuntide. The town was
thronged with peasants in their best attire, and we met others
on their way thither, particularly women and girls, with heads
bare in the sunshine; but there was no tiptoe-jollity, nor, indeed, any more show of festivity than I have seen in my own

country, at a cattle-show or muster. Really, I think, not half so much.

The road still grew more and more picturesque, and now lay along ridges, at the bases of which were deep ravines and hollow vallies. Woods were not wanting; wilder forest than I have seen since leaving America, of oak-trees chiefly; and among the green foliage grew golden tufts of broom, making a gay and lovely combination of hues. I must not forget to mention the poppies, which burned like live-coals along the wayside, and lit up the landscape, even a single one of them, with wonderful effect. At other points, we saw olive-trees, hiding their eccentricity of boughs under thick masses of foliage of a livid tint, which is caused, I believe, by their turning their reverse sides to the light and to the spectator. Vines were not wanting, but were of little account in the scene. By and by, we came in sight of the high, flat table land on which stands Civita Castellana, and beheld, straight downward, between us and the town, a deep, level valley, with a river winding through it. It was the valley of the Tre[61]ja. A precipice, hundreds of feet in height, falls straight down upon this valley from the site of Civita Castellana; there is an equally abrupt one, probably, on the side from which we beheld it; and a modern road, skilfully constructed, goes winding down to the stream, crosses it by a narrow stone bridge, and winds upward into the town. After crossing the bridge, I alighted, as did Julian, Miss Shepard, and Rosebud, and made the ascent on foot, passing along walls of natural rock, in which old Etruscan tombs were hollowed out. There are likewise antique remains of masonry, whether Roman or of what earlier period, I cannot tell. At the summit of the ascent, which brought us close to the town, our vetturino took us into the carriage again, and quickly brought us to what appears to be really a good hotel, where the whole family are accommodated with sleeping-chambers in a range, beneath an arcade entirely secluded from the rest of the population of the hotel. After a splendid dinner (that is, splendid, considering that it was ordered by our hospitable vetturino,) Una, Miss Shepard, Julian, and I, walked out of the little town, in the opposite direction from our entrance, and crossed a bridge at the height of the table-land, instead of at its base. On either side we had a view down into a profound gulf, with sides of precipitous rock, and heaps of foliage in its lap, through which ran the snowy track of a stream; here snowy, there dark, here hidden among the foliage, there quite revealed in the broad depths of the gulf. I have not seen anything finer than this. Walking on a little further, Soracte came fully into view, starting with bold abruptness out of the middle of the country; and before we got back, the bright Italian moon was throwing a shower [62] of silver over the scene, and making it so beautiful that it seems miserable not to know how to put it into words; a foolish thought, however, for such scenes are an expression in themselves, and were never meant to be translated into any feebler language. On our walk, we met parties of laborers, both men and women, returning from the fields, with rakes and wooden forks over their shoulders, singing in chorus. It is very customary for women to be laboring in the fields.

Terni May 25th, Tuesday.

We were aroused at four °clock, this morning, had some eggs and coffee, and were ready to start between five and six; being thus matutinary, in order to get to Terni in time to see the falls. The road was very striking and picturesque; but I remember nothing particularly, till we came to Borghetto, which stands on a bluff, with a broad valley sweeping round it, through the midst of which flows the Tiber. There is an old castle on a projecting point; and we saw other battlemented fortresses, of mediæval date, along our way, forming more beautiful ruins than any of the Roman remains to which we have become accustomed. This is partly, I suppose, owing to the fact that they have been neglected, and allowed to mantle their decay with ivy, instead of being cleaned, propt up, and restored. The antiquarian is apt to spoil the objects that interest him. Sometimes we passed through wildernesses of various trees, each contributing a different hue of verdure to the scene; the vine, also, marrying itself to the fig-tree, so that a man might sit in the shadow of both at once, and temper the luscious sweetness of the one fruit with the fresh flavor of the other. The wayside incidents were such as meeting a man and woman borne along as prisoners, handcuffed, and in a cart; two men reclining across one another, asleep, and lazily lifting their [63] heads to gaze at us, as we passed by; a woman spinning with a distaff, as she walked along the road. An old tomb or tower stood in a lonely field; and several caves were hollowed in the rocks, which might have been either tombs or habitations. Soracte kept us company, sometimes a little on one side, sometimes behind, looming up again and again, when we thought that we had done with it, and so becoming rather tedious at last, like a friend who presents himself for another and another leave-taking, after the one which ought to have been final. Honeysuckles sweetened the hedges along the road.

After leaving Borgheto we crossed the broad valley of the Tiber, and skirted along one of the ridges that border it, looking back upon the road we had passed, lying white behind us. We saw a field so covered with buttercups, or some other yellow flower, that it looked like the field of the cloth of gold. Poppies burned along the roadside, as they did yesterday; and there were flowers of a delicious blue, as if the blue Italian sky had been broken into little bits and scattered down upon the green earth. Ottricoli by and by appeared, situated on

a bold promontory above the valley, a village of a few gray
houses and huts, with one edifice gaudily painted in white and
pink; it looked more important at a distance, than we found
it on our nearer approach. As the road kept ascending, and as
the hills grew to be mountains, we had taken two additional
horses, making five in all, with a man and boy running beside
them, to keep the team in motion. The boy had two club-
feet, so inconveniently disposed that it seemed almost inevitable
for him to stumble over them at every step; besides which
he seemed to tread upon his ancles, and moved [64] with
such a disjointed gait, as if each of his legs and thighs had
been twisted round together with his feet. Nevertheless, he
had a bright, cheerful, intelligent face, and was exceedingly
active keeping up with the horses at their trot, and inciting
them to better speed when they lagged. I conceived a great
respect for this poor boy, who had what most Italian peasants
would consider an enviable birth-right in those two club-feet,
as giving him a right to live on charity, but yet took no
advantage of them; on the contrary, putting his poor, mis-
shapen hoofs to such good use as might have shamed many a
better-provided biped. When he quitted us, he asked no
charity of the travellers, but merely applied to Gaetano for
some slight recompense of his well-performed service. This
behavior contrasted most favorably with that of some other
boys and girls, who ran begging beside the carriage-door, keeping up a low, miserable murmur, like that of a kennel-stream,
for a long, long way. Beggars, indeed, started up at every point
when we stopt for a moment, and wherever a hill imposed a
slower pace upon us; each village had its deformity or its
infirmity, offering his wretched petition at the step of the
carriage; and once a venerable white-bearded patriarch—the
grandfather of all the beggars—seemed to grow up by the roadside, but was left behind, from inability to join in the race
with his light-footed juniors. No shame is attached to beggary

in Italy. In fact, I rather imagine it to be held an honorable profession, inheriting some of the odour of sanctity that used to be attached to a mendicant and idle life in the days of early Christianity, when every Saint lived upon Providence and deemed it meritorious to do nothing for his living.

Murray's guide-book is exceedingly vague and unsatisfactory, along this route; and whenever we asked Gaetano the name [65] of a village or a castle, he gave some one which we had never heard before, and could find nothing of in the book. We made out the river Nar, however, or what I suppose to be such, though he called it Nera. It flows through the most tremendous mountain-gorge I ever beheld, winding its narrow passage between high hills, the broad sides of which descend steeply upon it, covered with trees and shrubbery, that mantle a host of rocky roughnesses and make all look smooth. Here and there a precipice juts sternly forth. We saw an old castle on a hill-side, frowning down into the gorge; and, farther on, the gray town of Narni stands upon a height, imminent over the depths below, and with its battlemented castle above, now converted into a prison, and therefore kept in excellent repair. A long, winding street passes through Narni, broadening at one point into a market-place, where an old Cathedral showed its venerable front, and the great dial of its clock, the figures on which were numbered in two semi-circles of twelve points each; one, I suppose, for noon, and the other for midnight. The town has, so far as its principal street is concerned, a city-like aspect, with large, fair edifices and shops as good as most in Rome, the smartness of which contrasts strikingly with the rude and lonely scenery of mountain and stream, through which we had come to reach it. We kept through Narni without stopping, and emerged from it on the other side, where a broad, level valley opened before us, most unlike the wild, precipitous gorge which had brought us to the town. The road went winding down into the peaceful vale, through the midst of which flowed the same stream that cuts its way betwixt the impending hills, as already described. We passed a monk and a soldier—the [66] two curses of Italy, each in his way—walking sociably side by side; and, from Narni to Terni, I remember nothing that need be recorded. Terni, like so many other towns in this neighborhood, stands on a high and commanding position, chosen doubtless for its facilities of defense, in days long before the mediæval warfares of Italy made such sites desirable. I suppose that, like Narni and Otricoli, it was a city of the Umbrians. We reached it between eleven and twelve °clock, intending to employ the afternoon in a visit to the famous falls of Terni; but, after lowering all day, it has begun to rain, and we shall probably have to give them up.

8½ °clock.

It has rained in torrents during the afternoon, and we have not seen the Cascade of Terni; considerably to my regret, for I think I felt the more interest in seeing them, on account of their being artificial. Methinks nothing was more characteristic of the energy and determination of the old Romans, than thus to take a river, which they wished to get rid of, and fling it over a giddy precipice, breaking it into ten million pieces by the fall. We spent the afternoon moping in our bed-chambers; for it seems not to be the system of vetturino-travelling to allow parlours to the passengers. We are in the Hotel delle tre Colonne, and find it reasonably good, though not, so far as we are concerned, justifying the rapturous commendations of previous tourists, who probably travelled at their own charges. However, there is nothing really to be complained of, either in our accommodations or table, and the only wonder is how Gaetano contrives to get any profit out of our contract, since the hotel-bills would alone cost us more than we pay him for the journey and all. For breakfast, this morning, we had coffee, eggs, and bread and butter; for lunch, an omelette, some stewed veal, and a dessert of figs and grapes, be[67]sides two decanters of a light-colored acid wine, tasting very like indifferent cider; for dinner, an excellent vermicelli-soup, two young fowls stewed or fricasseed, and a hind-quarter of roast lamb, with fritters, oranges, and figs, and two more decanters of the wine aforesaid. This hotel of the Three Columns is an edifice with a gloomy front upon a narrow street, and enterable through an arch, which admits you into an enclosed court, around which, on each story, run the galleries with which the parlours and sleeping apartments communicate. The whole house is dingy, probably old, and seems not very clean, but yet bears traces of former magnificence; for instance, in our sleeping-room, the door of which is ornamented with gilding, and the cornices with frescoes, some of which appear to represent the cascade of Terni; the roof is crossed with carved beams, and is painted in the interstices; the floor has a carpet, but rough bricks under-neath it, which show themselves at the margin. The windows admit the wind; the door shuts so loosely as to leave great cracks; and, during the rain to-day, there was a heavy shower through our cieling, which made a flood upon the carpet. We see no chamber-maids; nothing of the comfort and neatness of an English hotel, nor of the smart splendors of an American one; but still this dilapidated palace affords us a better shelter than I expected to find in the decayed country-towns of Italy. In the Album of the hotel, I find the names of more English travellers than of any other nation except the Americans, who, I think, even exceed the former; and the route being the favorite one for tourists between Rome and Florence, what-ever merit the inns have is probably owing to the demands of the Anglo Saxons. I doubt not, if we chose to pay for it, this hotel could supply us with any luxury we might ask for, [68] and perhaps even a gorgeous saloon and state-bedchamber.

After dinner, Julian and I walked out, in the dusk, to see what we could of Terni. We found it compact and gloomy (but the latter characteristic might well enough be attributed to the dismal sky) with narrow streets paved from wall to wall of the houses, like those of all the towns in Italy; the blocks of paving-stone larger than the little square enormities of Rome. The houses are covered with dingy stucco, are mostly low, compared with those of Rome, and inhospitable as regards their dismal aspects and uninviting doorways. The streets are intricate, as well as narrow; insomuch that we quickly lost our way, and could not find it again, though the town is of so small dimensions that we passed through it in two directions, in the course of our brief wanderings. There are no lamp-posts in Terni; and as it was growing dark, and beginning to rain, we at last inquired our way of a person in the principal piazza, and found our hotel, as I expected, within two minutes' walk of where we stood.

Foligno, May 26ᵗʰ, Wednesday.

At six o'clock this morning, we packed ourselves into our vetturo, my wife and I occupying the coupé (or whatever the seat in front is called,) and drove out of the city-gate of Terni. There are some old towers near it, ruins of I know not what, and care as little, in the plethora of antiquities and other interesting objects. Through the arched gateway, as we approached, we had a view of one of the great hills that surround the town, looking partly bright in the early sunshine, and partly catching the shadows of the clouds that floated about the sky. Our way lay now through the vale of Terni, as I believe it is called, where we saw somewhat of the fertility of Italy; vines trained on poles, or twining round mulberry and other trees, ranged regularly like orchards; groves of olives, and fields of grain. There are innumerable shrines [69] in all sorts of situations; some under arched niches, or little pent-houses with a brick tiled roof, just large enough to cover them; or perhaps in some bit of old Roman masonry, on the wall of a wayside-inn, or in a shallow cavity of the natural rock, or high upward in the deep cuts of the road; everywhere, in short, so that nobody need be at a loss when he feels the religious sentiment stir within him. The road soon began to wind among the hills, which rose steep and lofty from the scanty level space that lay between; they continually thrust themselves across the passage, and appeared as if determined to shut us completely in; a great hill would put its foot right before us, but, at the last moment, would grudgingly withdraw it, and allow us just room enough to creep by. Adown their sides we discerned the dry beds of mountain torrents, which had lived too fierce a life to let it be a long one. On here and there a hill-side or a promontory, we saw a ruined castle or a convent, looking down from its commanding height upon the road, which very likely some robber-knight had formerly infested with his banditti, retreating with his booty to the security of such strongholds. We came, once in a while, to wretched villages, where there was no token of prosperity or comfort, but perhaps may have been more than we could appreciate; for the Italians do not seem to have any of that sort of pride which we find in New England villages, where every man, according to his taste and means, endeavors to make his homestead an ornament to the place. We miss nothing in Italy more than the neat door-steps and pleasant porches and thresholds, and delightful lawns or grass-plats, which hospitably invite the imagination into a sweet domestic interior. Everything—however sunny and lux-uriant may be the scene around—is especially dreary [70] and disheartening in the immediate vicinity of an Italian home.

At Strettura (which, as the name indicates, is a very narrow part of the valley) we added two oxen to our team of horses,

and began to ascend the Monte Somma, which, according to
Murray, is nearly 4000 feet high where we crossed it. When
we came to the steepest part of the ascent, Gaetano (who exercises a pretty decided control over his passengers) allowed us
to walk; and we all, except Mamma, alighted, and began to
climb the mountain on foot. I walked on briskly, and soon
left the rest of the party behind, reaching the top of the pass
in such a short time that I could not believe it, and kept
onward, expecting still another height to climb. But the road
began to descend, winding among the depths of the hills, as
heretofore, now beside the dry gravelly bed of a departed
stream, now crossing it by a bridge, and perhaps passing
through some other gorge, that yet gave no decided promise of
an outlet into the world beyond. A glimpse might occasionally
be caught, through a gap between the hill-tops, of a company
of distant mountain-peaks, pyramidal, as these hills are apt to
be, and resembling the camp of an army of giants. The landscape was not altogether savage; sometimes a hill-side was
covered with a rich field of grain, or an orchard of olive trees,
looking not unlike puffs of smoke, from the peculiar hue of
their foliage; but oftener, there was a vast mantle of trees and
shrubbery from top to bottom, the golden tufts of the broom
shining out amid the verdure, and gladdening the whole.
Nothing was dismal except the houses; those were always so,
whether the compact gray lines of village hovels, with a narrow
street between, or the lonely farm-house, standing far apart
from the [71] road, built of stone, with window-gaps high in
the wall, empty of glass, or the half-castle, half-dwelling, of
which I saw a specimen or two, with what looked like a defensive rampart drawn around its courtyard. I saw no look of
comfort anywhere; and continually, in this wild and solitary
region, I met beggars, just as if I were still in the streets of
Rome. Boys and girls kept beside me, till they delivered me into
the hands of others like themselves; hoary grandsires and

grandmothers caught a glimpse of my approach, and tottered as fast as they could to intercept me; women ran out of the cottages with rotten cherries on a plate, entreating me to buy them for a mezzo-baioccho; a man, at work on the road, left his toil to beg, and was grateful for the value of a cent; in short, I was never safe, as long as there was a house or a human being in sight.

We arrived at Spoleto before noon, and, while our dejeuner was being prepared, looked down from the window of the inn into the narrow street beneath, which, from the throng of people in it, I judged to be the principal one; priests, papal soldiers, women with no bonnets on their heads; peasants in breeches and mushroom hats, maids and matrons drawing water at a fountain; idlers smoking on a bench under the window; a talk, a bustle, but no genuine activity. After lunch, we walked out to see the lions of Spoleto, and found our way up a steep and narrow street that led us to the city-gate, at which, it is traditionally said, Hannibal sought to force an entrance, after the battle of Thrasimene, and was repulsed. The gateway has a double arch, on the inner one of which is a tablet, recording the above tradition as an unquestioned historical fact. From the gateway, we went in quest of the Duomo or Cathedral, and were kindly directed thither by an [72] officer, who was descending into the town from the citadel, which is an old castle, now converted into a prison. The Cathedral seemed small, and did not much interest us either by its Gothic front or its modernized interior. We saw nothing else in Spoleto, but went back to the inn and resumed our journey, emerging from the city into the classic valley of the Clitumnus, which we did not view under the best of auspices, because it was overcast, and the wind as chill as if it had the east in it. The valley, though fertile, and smilingly picturesque perhaps, is not such as I should wish to celebrate, either in prose or poetry; it is of such breadth and extent, that its frame

of mountains and ridgy hills hardly serves to shut it in sufficiently, and the spectator thinks of a boundless plain, rather
than of a secluded vale. After passing Le Vene, we came to
the little temple which Byron celebrates, and which is supposed
to be the one immortalized by Pliny. It is very small, and stands
on a declivity that falls immediately from the road, right upon
which stands the pediment of the temple, while the columns
of the other front find sufficient height to develope themselves
on the lower ground. A little further down than the base of
the temple, we saw the Clitumnus, so recently from its source
in the marble-rock, that it was still as pure as a child's heart,
and as transparent as truth itself. It looked airier than nothing,
because it had substance enough to brighten, and clearer than
the atmosphere. I remember nothing else of the valley of
Clitumnus, except that the beggars in this region of proverbial
fertility are well-nigh profane, in the urgency of their petitions; they absolutely fall down on their knees as you approach,
in the same attitude as if they were praying to their Maker,
and beseech you for alms with a fervency which, I am [73]
afraid, they seldom use before an altar or shrine. Being denied,
they run lustily beside the carriage, but get nothing, and
finally give over.

I am so very tired and sleepy, that I mean to mention
nothing else, to night, except the city of Trevi, which, on the
approach from Spoleto, seems completely to cover a high
peaked hill from its pyramidal tip-top to its base. It was the
strangest situation in which to build a town, where, I should
suppose, no horse can climb, and whence no inhabitant would
think of descending into the world, after the approach of age
should begin to stiffen his joints. On looking back on this most
picturesque of towns (which the road of course did not enter,
as evidently no road could) I saw that the highest part of the
hill was quite covered with a crown of edifices, terminating in a
church tower, while a part of the northern side was apparently

too steep for building, and a cataract of houses flowed down the western and southern slopes. There seemed to be palaces, churches, everything that a city should have; but my eyes are heavy, and I can write no more about them; only that I suppose the summit of the hill was artifically terraced, so as to prevent its crumbling down, and enable it to support the platform of edifices which crowns it.

Perugia, May 27th Thursday.

We reached Foligno in good season, yesterday afternoon, but I forget at precisely what hour. Our inn seemed ancient; and under the same roof, on one side of the entrance, was the stable, and on the other, I think, the coach-house. The house is built round a narrow court, with a well of water at bottom, and an opening in the roof at top, whence the staircases are lighted that wind round the sides of the court, up to the highest story. Our dining-room [74] and bed-rooms were in the latter region, and were all paved with brick, and without carpets; and the characteristic of the whole was an exceeding plainness and antique clumsiness of fitting up. We found ourselves sufficiently comfortable, however, and, as has been the case throughout our journey, had a very fair and well-cooked dinner. It shows (as perhaps I have already remarked) that it is still possible to live well, in Italy, at no great expense, and that the high prices charged to the forestieri, at Rome and elsewhere, are artificial, and ought to be abated. I should like to know the sum Gaetano pays for our accommodation at one of these hotels; at all events, it cannot be much.

The day had darkened, since morning, and was now ominous of rain; but as soon as we were established, we sallied out to see whatever was worth looking at. A beggar-boy, with one leg, followed us, without asking for anything, but apparently only for the pleasure of our company; though he kept at too great a distance for conversation, and, indeed, did not attempt to say anything. We went first to the Cathedral, which has a Gothic front, of no great beauty, and a modernized interior, stuccoed and white-washed, looking as neat as a New England meeting-house, and very mean, after our familiarity with the gorgeous churches. There were some pictures in the chapels, but, I believe, all modern, and I do not remember a single one of them. Next we went, without any guide, to a church attached to a convent of the Dominican monks, with a Gothic exterior, and two hideous pictures of Death, the skeleton, leaning on his scythe, one on each side of the door. This church, likewise, was white-washed; but we understood that it had been originally frescoed all over, and by famous hands, but these pictures having become much injured, they were all obliterated, [75] as we saw;—all, that is to say, except a few specimens of the best preserved, which had been spared to show the world what the whole had been. I thanked my stars that the obliteration of the rest had taken place before our visit; for if anything is dreary, and calculated to make the beholder utterly miserable, it is a faded frescoe, with spots of the white plaister dotted over it. Our one-legged boy had followed into the church, and stood near the door till he saw us ready to come out, when he hurried out before us, and waited a little way off to see whither we should go. We still went on at random, taking the first turn that offered itself, and soon came to another old church—that of St. Mary within the Walls, into which we went, and found it white-washed like the other two. This was especially fortunate; for the door-keeper informed us that, till two years ago, the whole church (except, I suppose, the roof, which is of timber) had been covered with frescoes by Pinturichio, all of which had been ruthlessly obliterated, except a very few fragments. These he proceeded to show us; poor dim ghosts of what may once have been beautiful, now so far gone towards nothingness that I was hardly sure whether I saw a glimmering of the design or not. By the by, it was not Pinturrichio, as I have written above, but Giotto, assisted, I believe, by Cimabue, who painted these frescoes. Our one-legged attendant had followed us also into this church, and again hastened out of it before us; and still we heard the dot of his crutch upon the pavement, as we passed from street to street. By and by, a sickly-looking man met us and begged for 'qualche cosa'; but the boy shouted out to him, 'Niente!'; whether intimating that we would give him nothing, or that he himself had a prior claim to all our charity, I cannot tell. However, the beggar-man turned round and likewise followed our devious [76] course. Once or twice we missed him; but it was only because he could not walk so fast as we; for he turned up again, begging miserable, as we emerged from the door of another church. Our one-legged friend we never missed for a moment; he kept pretty near us—near enough to be amused by our indecision whither to go; and he seemed much delighted when it began to rain, and he saw us at a loss how to find our way back to the hotel. Nevertheless, he did not offer to guide us, but stumped on behind with a faster or slower dot of his crutch according to our pace. I began to think that he must have been engaged as a spy upon our movements by the police, who had taken away my passport at the city-gate. In this way he attended us to the door of the hotel, where, if I remember right, the beggar-man had already arrived; the latter again put in his doleful petition; the one-legged boy said not a word, nor seemed to expect anything; and both had to go away without so much as a mezzo-baioccho out of our pockets. The multitude of beggars in Italy makes the heart as obdurate as a paving-stone.

We left Foligno at about ½ past six this morning, and, all ready for us at the door of the hotel, as we got into the carriage, were our friends the beggar-man and the one-legged boy, the latter holding out his ragged-hat, and smiling with as confident an air as if he had done us some very particular service, and were certain of being paid for it, as per contract. It was so very funny, so impudent, so utterly absurd, that I could not help giving him a trifle; but the beggar-man got nothing—a fact that gives me a twinge or two, for he looked sickly and miserable. But where everybody begs, everybody, as a general rule, must be denied; and besides, they act misery so well that you are never sure of the genuine article.

[77] Perugia, May 28th, Friday.

As I said last night, we left Foligno betimes in the morning, which was bleak, chill, and very threatening; there being very little blue sky anywhere, and the clouds lying heavily on some of the mountain ridges. The wind blew sharply right in Una's face and mine, as we occupied the front-seat; so that there must have been a great deal of the North in it. We drove through a wide plain, the Umbrian valley, I suppose, and soon passed the old town of Spello, just touching its skirts, and wondering how people, who had this rich and convenient plain to choose a site from, could think of covering a huge island of rock with their dwellings; for Spello tumbles its crooked and narrow streets down a steep descent, and cannot well have a yard of even space within its walls. It is said to contain some rich treasures of ancient pictorial art. I do not remember much that we saw, on our road; the plain and the lower hill-sides seemed fruitful of everything that belongs to Italy, especially the olive and the vine. As usual, there were a great many shrines, and frequently a cross by the way side. Hitherto, it had been merely a plain wooden cross; but now almost every cross was hung with various instruments, represented in wood, apparently symbols of the crucifixion of our Savior; the spear, the sponge, the crown of thorns, the hammer, a pair of pincers, and always St. Peter's cock made a prominent figure, generally perched on the summit of the cross. From our first start, this morning, we had seen mists in various quarters, betokening that there was rain on those spots; and now, it began to spatter in our own faces; although, within the wide extent of our prospect, we could see the sunshine falling on portions of the valley. A rainbow, too, shone out, and remained so long visible that it appeared to have made a permanent stain in the sky.

[78] By and by we reached Assissi, which is magnificently situated for pictorial purposes; with a gray castle above it, and a gray wall around it; itself on a mountain, and looking over the great plain which we had been traversing, and through which lay our onward way. We drove through the Piazza Grande (I think it was called) to an ancient house a little beyond, where a hospitable old lady receives travellers for a consideration, without exactly keeping an inn. In the piazza, we saw the beautiful front of a temple of Minerva, consisting of several marble pillars, fluted and with rich capitals, supporting a pediment; it was as fine as anything I had seen in Rome, and is now, of course, converted into a Catholic church. I ought to have said, that, instead of driving straight to the old lady's, we alighted at the door of an old church, near the city gate, and went in to inspect some melancholy frescoes; and thence clambered up a narrow street to the Cathedral, which has a Gothic front, old enough, but not very impressive. I really remember not a single object that we saw within, but am pretty certain that the interior had been stuccoed and white-washed. The ecclesiastics of old time did an excellent thing in covering the interiors of their churches with brilliant frescoes, thus filling the holy place with saints and angels, and almost with the presence of the Divinity; the modern ecclesiastics do the next best thing in

obliterating the wretched remnants of what has had its day, and done its office. These frescoes might be looked upon as the symbol of the living spirit that made Catholicism a true religion, and glorified it so long as it did live; now, this glory and beauty have departed from one and the other.

My wife, Una, and Miss Shepard, now set out with a Cicerone to visit the great Franciscan Convent, in the church of which are pre[79]served some miraculous specimens, in fresco and in oils, of early Italian art; but as I had no mind to suffer any further in this way, I staid behind, with Julian and Rosebud, who were equally weary of these things. After they were gone, we took a ramble through the city, but were almost swept away by the violence of the wind, which struggled with me for my hat, and whirled Rosebud before it like a feather. The people in the public square seemed much tickled at our predicament, being, I suppose, accustomed to these rude blasts, in their mountain home. However, the wind seemed to blow in momentary gusts, and then to become more placable, till another fit of fury came and passed as suddenly as before. We went out of the same gate through which we had entered, (an ancient gate, but recently stuccoed and white-washed, in wretched contrast to the gray, venerable wall through which it affords entrance,) and I stood gazing at the magnificent prospect of the great valley beneath. It was so vast, that there appeared to be all varieties of weather in it at the same instant; fields of sunshine, tracts of storm, here the coming tempest, there the departing one. It was a picture of the world, on a vast canvass; for here was rural life and city-life, within that great expanse, and the whole set in a frame of mountains, the nearest bold and distinct, with the rocky ledges showing through their sides, the distant ones blue and dim, so far stretched this wide valley.

When I had looked long enough—no, not long enough, for it would take a great while to read that page—we returned within the gates, and clambered up past the cathedral, and into the narrow streets above it. The aspect of everything was awfully old; a thousand years would be but a middle age for one of those houses, built so massively, with great stones, and solid arches, that I do not see [80] how they ever are to tumble down, or to be less fit for human habitation than they are now. The streets crept between them, and beneath arched passages, and up and down steps of stone or ancient brick; for it would be altogether impossible for a carriage to ascend above the Great Piazza, though possibly a donkey or a charman's mule might find foothold. The city seems like a sort of stony growth out of the hill-side, or a fossilized city, so old and strange it is, without enough life and juiciness in it to be susceptible of decay. An earthquake is the only chance of its ever being ruined, beyond its present ruin. Nothing is more strange than to think that this now dead city—dead, as regards the purposes for which men live, now-a-days—was, centuries ago, the seat, and birth-place almost, of art, the only art in which the beautiful part of the human mind then developed itself. How came that flower to grow among these wild mountains? I do not conceive, however, that the people of Assissi were ever much more enlightened, or cultivated on the side of art, than they are at present. The ecclesiastics were then the only patrons; and the flower grew here, because there was a great ecclesiastical garden in which it was sheltered and fostered. But it is very curious to think of Assisi, a school of art within, and mountains and wilderness without.

My wife, and the rest of the party, returned from the Convent before noon, delighted with what they had seen, as I was delighted, not to have seen it. We ate our dejeuner, and resumed our journey, passing beneath the great Convent, after emerging from the gate opposite to that of our entrance. The edifice made a very grand spectacle, being of great extent, and standing on a double row of high and narrow arches, on

[81] which it is built up from the declivity of the hill. We soon reached the church of St Mary of the Angels, which is a modern structure, and a very spacious one, built in place of one that was destroyed by an earthquake. It is a very fine church, opening out a magnificent space in its nave and open aisles; and beneath the great dome stands the small old chapel, with its rude stone walls, in which St Francis founded the order of the Franciscan. This chapel, and the dome, appear to have been the only portions of the ancient church that were not destroyed by the earthquake. The dwelling of St. Francis is said to be also preserved within the church; but we did not see it, unless it were a little dark closet, into which we squeezed to see some frescoes by Lo Spagna. It had an old wooden door, of which Una picked off a little bit of a chip, to serve as a relic. There is a fresco in the church (over the high altar, if I remember) by Overbeck, representing the Assumption of the Virgin. It did not strike me as wonderfully fine. The other pictures, of which there were many, were modern, and of no great merit.

We pursued our way, and came by and by to the foot of the high hill on which stands Perugia, and which is so long and steep that Gaetano took a yoke of oxen to aid his poor horses in the ascent. We all, except mamma, walked a part of the way up, and I myself, with Julian for my companion, kept on even to the city-gate, a distance, I should think, of two or three miles at least. The lower part of the ascent was on the edge of the hill, with a narrow valley on our left; and as the sun had now broke forth, its verdure and fertility, its foliage and cultivation, shone forth in miraculous beauty, as green as England, as bright as only Italy. Perugia ap[82]peared above us, crowning its mighty hill, the most picturesque of cities; and the higher we ascended, the more the view opened before us, as we looked back on the course that we had come, and saw the wide valley sweeping down and spreading out, and bounded afar by mountains, sleeping in sun and shadow. Nor language, nor any art of the pencil, can give an idea of the scene; when God expressed Himself in this landscape to mankind, He did not intend that it should be translated into any tongue save His own immediate one. Julian, meanwhile, (whose heart is now wholly in snail-shells) was rummaging for them among the stones and hedges by the roadside, yet doubtless enjoyed the prospect more than he knew. The coach lagged far behind us; and when it came up, we entered the gate, where a soldier appeared and demanded my passport. We drove to the Grand Hotel de France, which is near the gate, and two fine little boys ran beside the carriage, well-dressed and well-looking enough to have been gentlemen's sons, but claiming Gaetano for their father. He is an inhabitant of Perugia, and had therefore reached his own home, though we are still little more than midway to our journey's end. Our hotel proves, thus far, to be the best that we have yet met with. We are only in the outskirts of Perugia, the bulk of the city, where the most interesting churches and the public edifices are situated, being far above us on the hill. My wife, Una, Miss Shepard, and Rosebud, streamed forth immediately and saw a church; but Julian—who hates them, for the pictures' sake, I believe—and I, remained behind; and, for my part, I added several pages to this volume of scribble.

This morning was as bright as morning could be, even [83] in Italy, and in the transparent mountain-atmosphere. We at first declined the services of a Cicerone, and went out in the hopes of finding our way to whatever we wanted to see, by our own instincts. This proved to be a mistaken hope, however; and we wandered about the upper city, much persecuted by a shabby old man who wanted to guide us; so, at last, Miss Sheperd went back in quest of the Cicerone at the hotel, and, meanwhile, we climbed to the summit, I believe, of the hill of Perugia, and leaning over a wall, looked forth upon

a more magnificent view of mountain and valley than we had
yet seen, terminating in some peaks, lofty and dim, which
surely must be the Appenines. Here, again, a young man accosted us, offering to guide us to the Cambio, or Exchange;
and as this was one of the places which we especially wished
to see, we accepted his services. By-the-by, I ought to have
mentioned that we had already entered a church, (San Luigi,
I believe,) the interior of which we found very impressive,
dim with the light of stained and pictured windows, insomuch
that it at first seemed almost dark, and we could only see
the bright twinkling of the tapers at the shrines; but, after
a few minutes, we discerned the tall octagonal pillars of the
nave, marble, or covered with a polished imitation that looked
exactly like it, and supporting a beautiful roof of crossed
arches. The church was neither Gothic nor classic, but a
mixture of both, and most likely a barbarous one; but it had a
grand effect, in its colored twilight, and convinced me more
than ever how desirable it is that religious edifices should have
painted windows.

[86] The door of the Cambio proved to be one that we had
passed several times, while seeking for it, and was very near
the church just mentioned, which fronts on one side of the
same piazza. We were received by an old gentleman, who appeared to be a public officer; and found ourselves in a small
room, wainscoted with beautifully carved oak, roofed with
a coved cieling, painted with symbols of the planets, and
arabesqued in rich designs, by Raphael, and lined with
splendid frescoes of subjects scriptural and historical, by
Perugino. When this room was in its first glory, I can conceive
that the world had not elsewhere to show, within so small a
space, such magnificence and beauty as were then displayed
here. Even now, I enjoyed (to the best of my belief, for we
can never feel sure that we are not bamboozling ourselves in
such matters) some real pleasure in what I saw; and especially

seemed to feel, after all these ages, the old painter's devout sentiment still breathing forth from the religious pictures, the work of a hand that had so long been dust. When we had looked long at these, the old gentleman led us into a chapel, of the same size as the former room, and built in the same fashion, wainscotted likewise with old oak. The walls were also frescoed all over, and retained more of their original brightness than those we had already seen, although the pictures were the productions of a somewhat inferior hand, a pupil of Perugino. They seemed to me very striking, however; not the less so, that one of them provoked an unseasonable smile. It was the decapitation of John the Baptist; and this holy personage was represented as still on his knees, with his hands clasped in prayer, although the execu[87]tioner was already depositing the head in a charger, and the blood was spouting from the headless trunk, directly, as it were, into the face of the spectator.

While we were in the first room, the Cicerone, who first offered his services at the Hotel, had come in; so we paid our chance-guide, and expected him to take his leave. It is characteristic of this idle country, however, that if you once speak to a person, or connect yourself with him by the slightest possible tie, you will hardly get rid of him by anything short of main force. He still lingered in the room, and was still there when I came away; for having had as many pictures as I could digest, I left my wife and Una with the Cicerone, and set out on a ramble with Julian. We plunged from the upper city down through some of the strangest passages that ever were called streets; some of them, indeed, being arched all over, and going down into the unknown darkness, looked like caverns; and we followed one of them doubtfully, till it opened out upon the light. The houses on each side were divided only by a pace or two, and communicated with one another, here and there, by arched passages; they looked very ancient, and may have been inhabited by Etruscan princes, judging from the massiveness of some of the foundation stories. The present inhabitants, nevertheless, are by no means princely; shabby men, and the care-worn wives and mothers of the people, one of whom was guiding a child in leading-strings through these antique passages, where a hundred generations have trod before those little feet. Finally we emerged through a gateway, and walked round the city-wall, till we reached our hotel by the same gate at which we entered last night.

[88] I ought to have mentioned, in the narrative of yesterday, that we crossed the Tiber shortly before reaching Perugia, already a broad and rapid stream, and already distinguished by the same turbid and mud-puddly quality of water that we see in it at Rome. I think it will never be so disagreeable to me hereafter, now that I find this turbidness to be its native color, and not (like that of the Thames) accruing from city-filth or any impurities of the low-lands.

The painting of Overbeck's, mentioned above, as I now remember, was not over the high altar of Santa Maria dei Angeli, but on the pediment of the chapel of St Francis; both ends of that little edifice being apparently modern, and only the side-walls ancient. This chapel seems to have been originally the house of St Francis.

Perugia, May 29th, Saturday.

This morning, at about 9 °clock, my wife and I, with Julian and Rosebud, went out and visited the church of the Dominicans, where we saw some quaint pictures by Fra Angelico, with a good deal of religious sincerity in them; also, a picture of Saint Columba by Perugino, which unquestionably is very good. To confess the truth, I took more interest in a fair Gothic monument, in white marble, of Pope Benedict 12th, representing him reclining under a canopy, while two angels draw aside the curtain; the canopy being supported by twisted columns, richly ornamented. I like this overflow and gratuity of device, with which Gothic sculpture works out its designs, after seeing so much of the simplicity of classic art in marble. We then tried to find the church of San Pietro in Martyre, but without success, although every person, of whom we inquired, immediately attached himself or herself to us, and could [89] hardly be got rid of by any efforts on our part. Nobody seemed to know the church we wanted, but all directed us to another church of San Pietro, which contains nothing of interest; whereas, the right church is supposed to contain a celebrated picture by Perugino. Finally, we ascended the hill into the city proper of Perugia (for our hotel is in one of the suburbs) expecting, or rather partly hoping, to find Miss Shepard and Una, who had gone together to see the frescoes in the Cambio, and were afterwards to have met us in San Pietro Martyre. We did not meet them, however; and Mama and Rosebud left us, purposing to make another search for the true San Pietro, while Julian and I set out on a ramble about the city.

It was market day, and the principal piazza, with the neighboring streets, was crowded with people, and blocked up with petty dealers and their merchandize; baskets of vegetables, donkeys and mules with panniers, stalls, some of which had books for sale, chiefly paper-covered little volumes in Italian, and a few in French, as Paul de Kock's novels, for example; also, ink and writing materials. Cheap jewelry and cutlery made a considerable show; shoes, hats, and caps; and I know not what else. The scene was livelier than any I have seen in Rome, the people appearing more vivacious, in this mountain air, than the populace of the eternal city, and the whole piazza babbling with a multitudinous voice. I noticed to-day, more than yesterday, the curious and picturesque architecture of the principal streets, especially that of the grand piazza; the great

Gothic arch of the door of the vast edifice in which the Exchange is situated, elaborately [90] wreathed around with one sculptured semi-circle within another; an open gallery running along the same edifice, on the second story, looking out on the piazza through arched and stone-mullioned windows. The quaint old front, too, of the Cathedral-church of San Lorenzo (it is the same which we visited yesterday, and which I called the church of San Luigi) is in keeping with the Gothic aspect of the piazza; as is likewise a large and beautiful fountain, consisting of a great marble basin, carved all round with angels, I believe. Within a short distance, there is a bronze statue of Pope Julius III, in his pontificals; one of the best statues, I think, that I ever saw in a public square. He seems to have life and observation in him, and impresses the spectator as if he might rise up from his chair, should any public exigency demand it, and encourage or restrain the people by the dignity and awe of his presence. I wish I could in any way catch and confine within words my idea of the venerableness and stateliness, the air of long-past time subsisting into the present, which remains upon my mind with the recollection of these mediæval antiquities of Perugia. When I am absolutely looking at them, I do not feel it so much as when remembering them; for there is, of course, a good deal of the modern and common-place that obtrudes into the actual scene. The people themselves are not very picturesque; though there are some figures with cloaks (even in this summer weather) and broad-brimmed, slouching hats that a painter might make something of.

The best part of Perugia—that on which the grand piazza and the principal public edifices stand—seems to be a nearly level plateau on the summit of the hill; but it is of no very [91] great extent, and the streets rapidly run downward on either side. Julian and I followed one of these descending streets, and were led a long way by it, till we at last emerged from one of the gates of the city, and had another view of the mountains and vallies, the fertile and sunny wilderness, in which this ancient civilization stands. On the right of the gate there was a rude country-path, partly overgrown with grass, bordered by a hedge on one side, and on the other by the gray city-wall, at the base of which the track crept onward. We followed it, hoping that it would lead us to some other gate by which we might re-enter the city; but it soon grew so indistinct and broken that it was evidently on the point of melting into somebody's olive-orchard, or wheat-field, or vineyard, all of which lay on the other side of the hedge; and a kindly old woman, of whom I inquired, told me (if I rightly understood her Italian) that I should find no further passage in that direction. So we turned back, much broiled in the hot sun, and only now and then relieved by the shadow of an angle or a tower. A lame beggar-man sat by the gate, and as we passed him, Julian gave him two baiocchi (which he himself had begged of me, to buy an orange with) and was loaded with the pauper's prayers and benedictions as we entered the city. A great many blessings can be bought for very little money, anywhere in Italy; and whether they avail anything or no, it is pleasant to see that the beggars have gratitude enough to bestow them in such abundance.

Of all beggars, I think that a little fellow, who rode beside our carriage on a stick—his bare feet scampering merrily, while he managed his steed with one hand and [92] held out the other for charity—howling piteously the while, amused me most.

Pasignano, May 29th, Saturday.

We left Perugia at about three °clock to-day, and went down a pretty steep descent; but I have no particular recollection of the road, till it again began to ascend before reaching the village of Magione. We all, except mamma, walked up this long hill, while the vettura was dragged after us, with the aid of a yoke of oxen. Arriving first at the village, I leaned over the wall to admire the beautiful paese (the 'bel piano,' as a peasant called it who scraped acquaintance with me) that lay at the foot of the hill, so level, so bounded within moderate limits by a frame of hills and ridges, that it looked like a green lake. In fact, I think it was once a real lake, which made its escape from its bed, as I have known some lakes to do in America. Passing through and beyond the village, I saw, on a height above the road, a half ruinous tower, with great cracks running down its walls, half-way from top to bottom. Some little children had mounted the hill with us, begging all the way; they were recruited by additional numbers in the village; and here, beneath the ruinous tower, a madman, as it seemed, assaulted us, and ran almost under the carriage-wheels in his earnestness to get a baioccho. Ridding ourselves of these annoyances, we drove on, and, between five and six °clock, came in sight of the Lake of Thrasimene, obtaining our first view of it, I imagine, in its longest extent. There were high hills, and one mountain with its head in the clouds, visible on the farther shore, and on the horizon beyond it; but the nearer banks were long ridges, and hills of only moderate height. The declining sun threw a broad sheen of brightness across the surface of the lake, so that we could not well see for excess of light, but had a vision of head-lands, and islands, floating about [93] in a flood of gold, and blue, airy heights bounding it afar. When we first drew near the lake, there was but a narrow tract, covered with vines and olives, between it and a hill that rose on the other side. As we advanced, this tract grew wider, and was very fertile, as was the hill-side, with wheat-fields, and vines, and olives, especially the latter, which, symbol of peace as it is, seemed to find something congenial to it in this soil, stained long ago with blood. Farther onward, the space between the lake and hill grew narrower than ever, the road skirting along almost close to the water side; and when we reached the town of Pasignano, there was but room enough for its dirty and ugly street to stretch along the shore. I have seldom beheld a lovelier scene than that of the lake and the landscape around it; never an uglier one than that of this idle and decaying village, where we were immediately surrounded by beggars of all ages, and by men vociferously proposing to row us out upon the lake. We declined their offers of a boat, for the evening was very fresh and cool, insomuch that I should have liked an outside garment—a temperature that I had not anticipated, so near the beginning of June, in sunny Italy. Instead of a row, we took a walk through the village, hoping to come upon the shore of the lake in some secluded part; but an incredible number of beggar children, both boys and girls, but more of the latter, rushed out of every door, and went along with us, all howling their miserable petitions at the same moment. The village street is long; and our escort waxed more numerous at every step, till Miss Shepard actually counted forty of these little reprobates, and more were doubtless added afterwards. At first, no doubt, they begged in earnest hope of getting some baiocchi; but by and by, perceiving that we had determined not to give them anything, they made [94] a joke of the matter, and began to laugh, and babble around us, and turn heels over head, still keeping about us like a swarm of flies, and now and then begging again with all their might. There were as few pretty faces as I ever saw among the same number of children; and they were as ragged and dirty little imps as any in the world, and moreover tainted the air with a very disagreeable fragrance from their rags and dirt; rugged and healthy enough, nevertheless, and sufficiently intelligent; certainly bold and persevering, too; so that it is hard to say what they needed to fit them for success in life. Yet they begin as beggars, and no doubt will end so, as all their parents and grand-parents do; for, in our walk through the village, every old woman, and many younger ones, held out their hands for alms, as if they had all been famished. Yet these people kept their houses over their heads; had firesides in winter, I suppose, and food out of their little gardens, every day; pigs to kill, chickens, olives, sour wine, and a great many things to make life comfortable. The children, desperately as they begged, looked in good bodily case, and happy enough; but certainly there was a look of earnest misery in the faces of some of the old women, either genuine or exceedingly well acted.

I could not bear this persecution, and went into our hotel, determining not to venture out again, till our departure; at least, not in the daylight. My wife and the rest of the party, however, continued their walk, and at length were relieved from their little pests by three police-men (the very images of those in Rome, in their blue, long-skirted coats, cocked chapeau-bras, white shoulder-belts and swords) who boxed their ears and dispersed them. Meanwhile, they had quite driven away all sentimental effusion (of which I really felt more than I expected) about the Lake of Thrasimene.

V

[1] Florence, June 2^d 1858.

THE INN at Pasignano promised little from its outward appearance; a tall, dark, old house with a stone staircase leading us up from one sombre story to another into a brick-paved eating-room, with our sleeping-chambers on each side. There was a fire-place of tremendous depth and height, fit to receive big forest-logs, and with a queer, double pair of ancient andirons, capable of sustaining them; and, in a handful of ashes, lay a small stick of olive-wood, a specimen, I suppose, of the sort of fuel which had made the chimney black, in the course of a good many years. There must have been much shivering and misery of cold, around that fire-place. However, we needed no fire now; and there was promise of good cheer in the spectacle of a man cleaning some lake-fish for our dinner, while the poor things flounced and wriggled under the knife. The dinner made its appearance, after a long while, and was most plentiful; a rice-soup, a large dish of fried fish, some chops, and some chickens, besides, I think, a pudding, maccaroons, and fruit; so that, having measured our appetites in anticipation of a paucity of food, we had to make more room for such overflowing abundance. [2] When dinner was over, it was already dark; and before going to bed, I opened the window and looked out on Lake

Thrasimene, the margin of which lies just on the other side of the narrow village-street. The moon was a day or two past the full, just a little clipt on the edge; but gave light enough to show the lake and its nearer shores, almost as distinctly as by day; and there being a ripple on the surface of the water, it made a sheen of silver over a wide space.

We started at 6 °clock, and left the one ugly street of Pasignano before most of the beggars were awake. Immediately in the vicinity of the village, there is very little space between the lake in front, and the ridge of hills in the rear; but the plain widened as we drove onward, so that the lake was scarcely to be seen, or perhaps quite hidden among the intervening trees, although we could still see the summits of the mountains that rise far beyond its shores. The country was fertile, presenting, on each side of the road, vines trained on fig-trees, wheat-fields, and olives, in greater abundance than any other product. On our right, with a considerable width of plain between, was the bending ridge of hills that shut in the Roman army by its close approach to the lake at Pasignano. In perhaps half an hour's drive, [3] we reached the little bridge that throws its arch over the Sanguinetto, and alighted there. The stream has but about a yard across of water; and its whole course, between the hills and the lake, might well have been reddened and swollen with the blood of the multitude of slain Romans. Its name put me in mind of the Bloody Brook, in Deerfield, where a company of Massachusetts men were massacred by the Indians. The Sanguinetto flows over a bed of pebbles; and Julian crept under the bridge and got one of them for a memorial; while Una, Miss Shepard, and Rosebud, plucked some olive-twigs and oak-leaves, and made them into wreaths together—symbols of victory and peace. The tower, which is traditionally named after Hannibal, is seen on a height that makes part of the line of enclosing hills; it is a large, old castle, apparently of the middle-ages, with a square front, and a battlemented sweep of wall. The town of Torres (if I remember its name) where Hannibal's main-army is supposed to have lain, while the Romans came through the pass, was in full view; and I could understand the plan of the battle better than any system of military operations which I have hitherto tried to fathom. Both last night and to-day, I found myself stirred more sensibly than I expected by the influences of this [4] scene; the old battle-field is still fertile in thought and emotions, though it is so many ages since the blood spilt there has ceased to make the grass and flowers grow more luxuriantly. I doubt whether I should feel so much on the field of Saratoga or Monmouth; but these old classic battle-fields belong to the whole world, and each man feels as if his own forefathers fought there. Mine, by the by, if they fought there at all, must have been on the side of Hannibal; for certainly I sympathized with him, and exulted in the defeat of the Romans on their own soil. They excite much the same emotion of general hostility that the English do. Byron has written some very fine stanzas on this battle field; not so good as others that he has written on classical scenes and subjects, yet wonderfully impressing his own perception of the subject on the reader. Wherever he has to deal with a statue, a ruin, a battle-field, he pounces upon the topic like a vulture, and tears out its heart in a twinkling; so that there is nothing more to be said.

If I mistake not, our passport was examined by the Papal officers, at the last Custom House in the Pontifical territory, before we traversed the path through which the Roman army marched to [5] its destruction. Lake Thrasimene, of which we now took our last view, is not deep set among the hills, but is bordered by long ridges, with loftier mountains receding into the distance. It is not to be compared with Windermere or Loch-Lomond for beauty, nor with Lake Champlain and many a smaller lake in my own country; none of which, I hope, will ever become so historically interesting as this famous spot. A few miles onward, our passport was counter-signed at the Tuscan Custom House, and our luggage permitted to pass without examination, on payment of a fee of ten pauls, besides two pauls to the Porters. There appears to be no concealment on the part of the officials, in thus waiving the exercise of their duty; and I rather imagine that the thing is recognized and permitted by their superiors. At all events, it is very convenient for the traveller. We saw Cortona, sitting, like so many other cities in this region, on its hill, and arrived about noon at Arrezzo, which also stretches up a high hillside, and is surrounded, as they all are, by its wall, or the remains of one, with a fortified gate across every entrance. I remember one little village, somewhere in the neighborhood of the Clitumnus, which we entered [6] by one gateway, and, in the course of two minutes at the utmost, left by the opposite one; so diminutive was this walled town. Everything, hereabouts, bears the traces of times when war was the prevalent condition, and peace only a rare gleam of sunshine.

At Arrezzo, we put up at the Hotel Royal, which has the appearance of a grand old house, and proved to be a tolerable inn enough. After lunch, we wandered forth to see the town, which did not greatly interest me, after Perugia, being much more modern and less picturesque in its aspect. We went to the Cathedral, a Gothic edifice, but not of striking exterior. As the doors were closed, and not to be opened till three °clock, we went and seated ourselves under the trees, on a high, grassy space, surrounded and intersected with gravel-walks—a public promenade, in short—near the Cathedral; and after resting ourselves here, we went in search of Petrarch's house, which Murray's mentions as being in this neighborhood. We inquired of several people, who knew nothing about the matter; one woman misdirected us, out of mere fun, I believe, for she afterwards met us and asked how we had succeeded; but, finally, through my wife's [7] enterprise and perseverance, we found the spot, not a stone's throw from where we had been sitting. Petrarch's house stands just below the public promenade which I have just mentioned, and within hearing of the reverberations between the strokes of the Cathedral. It is two stories high, covered with a light-colored stucco, and has not the slightest appearance of antiquity, more than many a modern and modest dwelling-house in an American city. Its only remarkable feature is a pointed arch of stone, let into the plastered wall, and forming a frame-work for the doorway. I set my foot on the door steps—ascended them, I believe —and Miss Shepard and Julian gathered some weeds or blades of grass that grew in the chinks between the steps. There is a long inscription on a slab of marble, set in the front of the house, as is the fashion in Arrezo, when a house has been the birth-place or residence of a distinguished man.

Right opposite Petrarch's birth-house—and it must have been the well whence the water was drawn that first bathed him—stands, or lies, or whatever is the phrase for a hollow place, a well which Boccaccio has introduced into one of his stories, I forget which. It is surrounded [8] with a stone-curb octagonal in shape, and evidently as ancient as Boccacio's time; it has a wooden cover, through which is a square opening, and, looking down, I saw my own face in the water far beneath. There is no familiar object, connected with daily life, so interesting as a well; and this well of old Arrezzo, whence Petrarch had drunk, around which he had played in his boyhood, and which Boccaccio has made famous, really interested me more than the Cathedral. It lies right under the pavement of the street, under the sunshine, without any shade of trees about it, or any grass, except a little that grows in the crevices of its stones; but the shape of its stonework would make it a pretty object in an engraving. As I lingered round it, I thought of my own Town Pump, in old Salem, and wondered whether my townspeople would ever point it out to strangers, and whether the stranger would gaze at it with any degree of such interest as I felt in Boccaccio's well. Oh, certainly not; but yet I made that humble Town-Pump the most celebrated structure in the good town; a thousand and a thousand people had pumped there, merely to water oxen, or fill their tea-[9]kettles; but when once I grasped the handle, a rill gushed forth that meandered as far as England, as far as India, besides tasting pleasantly in every town and village of our own country. I like to think of this, so long after I did it, and so far from home, and am not without hopes of some kindly local remembrance on this score.

Petrarch's house is not a separate and insulated building, but stands in contiguity and connection with other houses on each side; and all, when I saw them, as well as the whole street, extending down the slope of the hill, had the bright and sunny aspect of a modern town.

As the Cathedral was not yet open, and as Julian and I had not so much patience as my wife, we left her with Miss Shepard, and set out to return to our Hotel. We lost our way, however, and finally had to return to the Cathedral to take a fresh start, and as the door was now open, we went in. We found the Cathedral very stately, with its great arches, and darkly magnificent, with the dim, rich light coming through its painted windows, some of which are reckoned the most beautiful that the whole world has to show. The hues are far more brilliant than those of [10] any painted glass I saw in England, and a great wheel window looks like a constellation of many colored gems. The old English glass gets so smoky, and dim with dust, that its pristine beauty cannot any longer be even imagined; nor did I imagine it, till I saw these Italian windows. We saw nothing of my wife and Miss Shepard, but found afterwards that they had been much pestered by the attentions of a priest who wanted to show them the Cathedral; till they finally told him that they had no money about them, and he left them, without another word. The attendants in the churches seem to be quite as venal as most other Italians, and, for the sake of their little profit, they do not hesitate to interfere with the great purposes for which their churches were built and decorated; hanging curtains, for instance, before all the celebrated pictures, or hiding them away in the sacristy, so that they cannot be seen without a fee.

Returning to the hotel, we looked out of the window, and, in the street beneath, there was a very lively scene, it being Sunday, and the whole population, apparently, being astir, promenading up and down the smooth flag-stones, which made the breadth of the street one side-walk, or at their windows, or sitting before their doors. The vivacity of the population [11] in these parts is very striking, after the gravity and lassitude of Rome, and the whole air was made cheerful with the talk and laughter of a hundred voices. I think the women are prettier than the Roman maids and matrons, who (as I think I have said before) have chosen to be very ugly since the rape of their ancestresses, by way of wreaking a terrible spite and revenge. I have nothing more to say of Arrezzo, except that, finding the ordinary wine very bad (as black as ink, and tasting as if it had tar and vinegar in it) we called for a bottle of Monte Pulciano, and were exceedingly gladdened and mollified thereby.

We left Arrezzo at twenty minutes past five on Monday morning, the sun throwing the long shadows of the trees across the road, which at first, after we had descended the hill, lay over a plain. As the morning advanced, the country grew more hilly. We saw many bits of rustic life, such as old women tending pigs or sheep, by the roadside, and spinning with a distaff; women sewing under a tree, or at their own doors; children leading goats, tied by the horns, while they browse; sturdy, sunburnt creatures (in petticoats, but otherwise manlike) [12] at work side by side with male laborers in the fields. The broad-brimmed, high-crowned hat of Tuscan straw is the customary female-headdress, and is as unbecoming as can possibly be imagined, and of little use, one would suppose, as a shelter from the sun; the brim continually blowing upward from the face. Some of the elder women wore felt-hats, likewise broad-brimmed, and the men wore felt-hats, shaped a good deal like a mushroom, with hardly any brim at all. The scenes in the villages through which we passed were very lively and characteristic, all the population seeming to be out of doors; some at the butcher's shop, others at the well; a tailor sewing in the open air, with a young priest sitting sociably beside him; children at play; women mending clothes, embroidering, spinning with the distaff, at their own door-steps; many idlers, letting the pleasant morning pass in the sweet do-nothing; all assembling in the street as in the common-room of one large household, and thus brought close together and made familiar with one another, as they can never be in a different system of society. As usual, along the road, we passed multitudes of shrines, where the virgin was painted in fresco, or sometimes represented in bas-reliefs, within niches, or under [13] more spacious arches. It would be a good idea to place a comfortable and shady seat beneath all these wayside shrines, where the wayfarer might rest himself and thank the Virgin for her hospitality; nor can I believe that it would offend her (any more than other incense) if he were to regale himself, even in such consecrated spots, with the fragrance of a pipe or cigar. In the wire-work screen, before many of the shrines, hung offerings of roses and other flowers, some wilted and withered, some fresh with that morning's dew, some that never bloomed and never faded, being artificial. I wonder that they do not plant rose-trees and all kinds of fragrant and flowering shrubs under the shrines, and twine and wreathe them all around, so that the Virgin may dwell within a bower of perpetual freshness; at least put flower-pots, with living plants, into the niche. There are many things, in the customs of these people, that might be made very beautiful, if the sense of beauty were as much alive, now, as it must have been when these customs were first imagined and adopted. I must not forget—among these little descriptive items—the spectacle of women and girls bearing huge bundles of twigs and shrubs, or grass, with scarlet [14] poppies and blue flowers intermixed; the bundle sometimes so huge as almost to hide the bearer's figure, from head to heel, so that she looked like a locomotive mass of verdure and flowers; sometimes reaching only half way down her back, so as to show the crooked knife, slung behind, with which she had been reaping this strange harvest-sheaf. A pre-Raphaelite painter (the one, for instance, who painted the heap of autumnal leaves, which we saw at the Manchester Exhibition) would find an admirable subject in one of these girls, stepping with a free, erect, and graceful carriage, her burthen on her head; and the miscellaneous herbage and flowers would give him all the scope he could desire for minute and various delineation of nature.

The country-houses which we passed had sometimes open galleries or arcades, on the second story and above, where the inhabitants might perform their domestic labor in the shade and in the air. The houses were often ancient, and most picturesquely time-stained, the plaster dropping in spots from the old brick-work; others were tinted of pleasant and cheerful hues; some were frescoed with designs in arabesque, or with imaginary windows; some had escutcheons of arms painted on the front. Wherever there was a pigeon-house [15] a flight of doves were represented as flying into the holes, doubtless for the invitation and encouragement of the real birds. Once or twice, I saw a bush stuck up before the door of what seemed to be a wine-shop. If so, it is the ancient custom, so long disused in England, and alluded to in the proverb—'Good wine needs no bush.' Several times, we saw grass spread to dry on the road, covering half the track, and concluded it to have been cut by the roadside for the winter forage of his ass, by some poor peasant, or peasant's wife, who had no grass-land except the margin of the public-way. A beautiful feature of the scene—to-day and the preceding day—were the vines growing on fig-trees, and often wreathed in rich festoons from one tree to another, by and by to be hung with clusters of purple grapes. I suspect the vine is a pleasanter object of sight, under this mode of culture, than it can be in countries where it produces a more precious wine, and therefore is trained more artificially. Nothing can be more picturesque than the spectacle of an old grape-vine, with almost a trunk of its own, clinging round its tree, imprisoning within its strong embrace the friend that supported its tender infancy, converting the tree wholly [16] to its own selfish ends, (as seemingly flexible natures are apt to do,) stretching out its innumerable arms on every bough, and allowing hardly a leaf to sprout except its own. I must not quit this hasty sketch, without throwing in, both in the early morning and later in the forenoon, the mist that dreamed among the hills, and which—now that I have called it mist—I feel almost more inclined to call light, being so quietly cheerful with the sunshine through it. Put in, now and then, a castle on a hill-top; a rough ravine; a smiling valley; a mountain stream, with a far wider bed than it at present needs, and a stone bridge across it, with ancient and massive arches;—and I shall say no more, except that all these particulars, and many better ones which escape me, made up a very pleasant whole.

About noon, we drove into the village of Incisa, and alighted at the albergo where we were to lunch. It was a gloomy old house, as much like my idea of an Etruscan tomb as anything else that I can compare it to; we pass into a wide and lofty entrance-hall, paved with stone, and vaulted with a roof of intersecting arches, supported by heavy columns of stuccoed brick, the whole as sombre and dingy as can well be. This entrance-[17]hall is not merely the passage-way into the inn, but is likewise the carriage-house, into which our vetturo is wheeled; and it has on one side the stable, fragrant with the litter of horses and cattle, and on the other the kitchen and a common sitting-room. A narrow stone staircase leads from it to the dining-room and chambers above, which are paved with brick, and adorned with rude frescoes instead of paper-hangings. We look out of the windows, or step into a little iron-railed balcony before the principal window, and observe the scene in the village-street. The street is narrow, and nothing can exceed the tall, grim ugliness of the village-houses, many of them four stories high, contiguous all along, from house to house, and paved quite across, so that Nature is as completely shut out from the precincts of this little village as from the heart of the widest city. The walls of the houses are plastered, gray, dilapidated; the windows small, some of them drearily closed with wooden shutters, others flung wide open, and with women's heads protruding, others merely frescoed for a show of light and air. It would be a hideous street to look at in a rainy day, or when no human life pervaded it; now, it has vivacity enough to keep it cheerful. People lounge round the door of the alber[18]go, and watch the horses as they drink from a stone trough, which is built against the wall of the house, and filled by the unseen gush of a spring. At first, there is a shade entirely across the street, and all the within-doors of the village empties itself there, and keeps up a babblement that seems quite disproportioned even to the multitude of tongues that make it. So many words are not spoken in a New England village in a whole year, as here in this single day. People talk about nothing, as if they were terribly in earnest, and laugh at nothing, as if it were an excellent joke. As the hot, noon sunshine encroaches on our side of the street, it grows a little more quiet. The loungers now confine themselves to the

shady margin (growing narrower and narrower) of the other
side, where, directly opposite our albergo, there are two caffés
and a wine-shop—vendita di pane, vino, ed altri generi—all
in a row, with benches before them. The benchers joke with
the women passing by, and are joked with back again. The sun
still eats away the shadow, inch by inch, beating down with
such intensity, that finally everybody disappears, except a few
passers-by. Doubtless the village snatches this half-hour for its
siesta. There is a song, however, inside one of the caffés, with a
burthen in which sev[19]eral voices join. A girl goes through
the street, sheltered under her great bundle of freshly cut
grass. By and by, the song ceases, and two young peasants come
out of the caffé, a little the better for liquor, in their shirt-sleeves
and bare feet, with their trowsers tucked up; they resume their
song in the street, and dance along, one's arm around his fellow's neck, his own waist grasped by the other's arm. They
whirl one another quite roundabout, and come down upon
their feet. Meeting a village-maid, coming quietly along, they
dance up and intercept her for a moment, but give way to her
sobriety of aspect. They pass on, and the shadow soon begins to
spread from our side of the street, which gradually fills again,
and becomes once more, for its size, the noisiest place I ever
knew.

We had quite a tolerable dinner at this ugly inn, where
many preceding travellers had written their condemnatory
judgments (as well as a few their favorable ones) in pencil, on
the walls of the dining-room. At setting-off, we were surrounded by beggars, as usual, the most interesting of whom
were a little blind boy and his brother, who had besieged us
with gentle pertinacity during our whole stay here. There was
likewise a man with a maimed hand and [20] other hurts or de-
formities; also, an old woman, who, I suspect, only pretended
to be blind, keeping her eyes tightly squeezed together, but
directing her hand very accurately where the copper-shower

was expected to fall. Besides these, there were a good many sturdy little rascals, vociferous in proportion as they needed nothing. It was touching, however, to see several persons— themselves beggars, for aught I know—assisting to hold up the little blind boy's tremulous hand, so that he, at all events, might not lack the pittance which we had to give. Our dole was but a poor one, after all, consisting of what Roman copper we had brought into Tuscany with us; and as we drove off, some of the boys ran shouting and whining after us, in the hot sunshine, nor stopt till we reached the summit of the hill which rises immediately from the end of the village-street. We heard Gaetano once say a good thing to a swarm of beggar-children who were infesting us—"Are your fathers all dead?"—a proverbial expression, I suppose. The pertinacity of beggars does not, I think, excite the indignation of an Italian, as it is apt to do that of Englishmen or Americans; the Italians probably sympathize more, though they give less. Gaetano is very gentle in his modes of repel[21]ling them, and, indeed, never interferes at all, as long as there is a prospect of their getting anything.

Immediately after leaving Incisa, we saw the Arno, already a considerable river, rushing between deep banks, with the greenish hue of a duck-pond diffused through its water. Nevertheless, though the first impression was not altogether agreeable, we soon became reconciled to this hue, and ceased to think it an indication of impurity; for, in spite of it, the river is still to a certain degree transparent, and is at any rate a mountain-stream, and comes uncontaminated from its source. The pure, transparent brown of the New England rivers is the most beautiful color; but I am content that it should be peculiar to them.

Our afternoon's drive was through scenery less striking than some which we had traversed, but still picturesque and beautiful; we saw deep vallies and ravines, with streams at the bottom; long, wooded hill-sides, rising far and high, and dotted with white dwellings, well towards the summits. By and by, we had a distant glimpse of Florence, showing its great dome and some of its towers out of a side-long valley, as it were between two great waves of the tumultuous sea of hills; while, far beyond, rose out [22] of the distance the blue peaks of three or four of the Appenines, just on the remote horizon.— There being a haziness in the atmosphere, however, Florence was little more distinct to us than the Celestial City was to Christian and Hopeful, when they spied at it from the Delectable Mountains. Keeping stedfastly onward, we ascended a winding road, and passed a grand villa, standing very high, and surrounded with extensive grounds. It must be the residence of some great noble; and it has an avenue of poplars or aspens, very light and gay, and fit for the passage of the bridal procession, when the proprietor or his heir brings home his bride; while, in another direction from the same front of the palace, stretches an avenue or grove of cypresses, very long, and exceedingly black and dismal, like a train of gigantic mourners. I have seen few things more striking, in the way of trees, than this grove of cypresses.

From this point, we descended, and drove along an ugly, dusty avenue, with a high brick wall on one side or both, till we reached the gate of Florence, into which we were admitted with as little trouble as Custom-House officers, soldiers, and policemen, can possibly give. They did not examine our baggage, and even declined a fee, as we had already paid one at the frontier Custom-[23]House. Thank Heaven, and the Grand Duke, or the Emperor of Austria, or whoever it may be that has the government of this country! As we hoped that the Casa del Bello had been taken for us, we drove thither in the first place, but found that the bargain had not been concluded. As the house and studio of Mr. Powers were just on the opposite side of the street, I went thither, but found him too much engaged to see me at the moment; so I returned to the vettura, and we told Gaetano to carry us to a Hotel. He established us at the Albergo della Fontana, a good and comfortable house, and, as it proved, very moderate in its charges. Mr. Powers called in the evening—a plain, homely personage, characterized by strong simplicity and warm kindliness, with an impending brow, and large, light eyes, which kindle as he speaks. He is gray and slightly bald, but does not seem elderly, nor past his prime. I accept him at once as an honest and trustworthy man, and shall not vary from this judgment. Through his good offices, the next day, we engaged the Casa del Bello at a rent of fifty dollars a month; and I shall take another opportunity (my fingers and head being tired now) to write about the house, and Mr. Powers, and what appertains to him, and about the beautiful city [24] of Florence. At present, I shall only further say, that this journey from Rome has been one of the brightest and most uncareful interludes of my life; we have all enjoyed it exceedingly; and I am happy that our younger companions have it to look back upon.

Florence June 4th, Friday.

At our visit to Powers's studio, on Tuesday, we saw a marble copy of the fisher-boy, holding a shell to his ear, and of the bust of Proserpina, and two or three other ideal busts; besides casts of most of the ideal statues and portrait-busts which he has executed. He talks very freely about his works, and is no exception to the rule that an artist is not apt to speak in a very laudatory style of a brother-artist. He showed us a bust of Mr. Sparks by Persico—a lifeless and thoughtless thing enough, to be sure—and compared it with a very good one of the same gentleman by himself; but his chiefest scorn was bestowed on a wretched and ridiculous image of Mr. King, of Alabama, by Clark Mills, of which he said he had been employed to make several copies for Southern gentlemen. The consciousness of power is plainly to be seen, and the assertion of it by no means withheld, in his simple and natural character; nor does it give one the idea of vanity on his part, to see and hear it. He appears to [25] consider himself neglected by his country—by the Government of it, at least—and talks with indignation of the by-ways and political intrigue which, he thinks, win the rewards which ought to be bestowed exclusively on merit. An appropriation of twenty-five thousand dollars was made, some years ago, for a work of sculpture by him, to be placed in the Capitol; but the intermediate measures, necessary to render it effective, have been delayed, while the above-mentioned Clark Mills—certainly the greatest bungler that ever botched a block of marble—has received an order for an equestrian statue of Washington. Not that Powers is made sour or bitter by these wrongs, as he considers them; he talks of them with the frankness of his disposition, when the topic comes in his way, and seems to be pleasant, kindly, and sunny when he has done with it. His long absence from our country has made him think worse of us than we deserve; and it is an effect of which I myself am sensible, in my shorter exile,—the most piercing shriek, the wildest yell, and all the ugly sounds of popular turmoil, inseparable from the life of a republic, being a million times more audible than the peaceful hum of prosperity and content, which is going on all the while. He talks of going home, but says that he [26] has been talking of it every year since he first came to Italy; and between his pleasant life of congenial labor here, and his idea of moral deterioration in America, I think it doubtful whether he ever crosses the sea again. Like most twenty-year exiles, he has lost his native country without finding another; but then it is as well to recognize the truth, that an individual country is by no means essential to one's comfort.

Powers took us into the farthest room, I believe, of his very extensive studio, and showed us a statue of Washington that has much dignity and stateliness; he expressed, however, great contempt for the coat and breeches, and masonic emblems, in which he had been required to drape the figure. What the devil would the man do with Washington, the most decorous and respectable personage that ever went ceremoniously through the realities of life! Did anybody ever see Washington naked! It is inconceivable. He had no nakedness, but, I imagine, was born with his clothes on and his hair powdered, and made a stately bow on his first appearance in the world. His costume, at all events, was a part of his character, and must be dealt with by whatever sculptor undertakes to represent him. I wonder that so very sensible a man as Powers should not see the necessity of accepting drapery; and [27] the very drapery of the day, if he will keep his art alive. It is his business to idealize the tailor's actual work. But he seems to be especially fond of nudity, none of his ideal statues—so far as I know them—having so much as a rag of clothes. His statue of California (lately finished, and as naked as Venus) seemed to me a very good work; not an actual woman, capable of exciting passion, but evidently a little out of the category of human nature. In one hand, she holds a divining rod, which luckily does the office of a fig-leaf. "She says to the emigrants," observed Powers, "here is the gold, if you choose to take it." But in her face, and in her eyes, very finely expressed, there is a look of latent mischief—rather grave than playful; yet somewhat impish, or spritelike—and in the other hand, behind her back, she holds a bunch of thorns. Powers calls her eyes Indian. The statue is true to the present fact and history of California, and includes the age-long truth as respects the 'auri sacra fames.'

While we were in the Studio, Mrs. Powers and one of her daughters made their appearance; the former a respectable,

cheerful, capable, housewifely matron, very sensible in common matters, and very suitable to the outward presentment
of Powers himself. I liked her much for what she evidently
was, [28] and for so quietly showing herself forth as such, and
nothing more. It is very queer, the life of these two people in
a foreign land, where they retain all their homely characteristics, losing nothing homelike, and taking nothing from
the manners around them. Had it been in England, twenty
years' residence would have changed them; but, in Italy, they
are hermetically sealed in a foreign substance, and cannot begin to assimilate with it. Powers speaks very little Italian; his
wife only enough to drive her bargains with trades-people, and
cannot read it at all. The children, however (all but one of
them born in Florence) speak both French and Italian as
readily as English, and learned both those languages earlier
than the latter. The daughter, whom we saw (a girl of nineteen) was one of the pleasantest young people I ever met,
charmingly frank and simple, and putting much warmth into
the grasp of her hand. Being her country-people, (for, though
born here, she acknowledges no country but America) her
heart probably warms to us more than if she had actually been
brought up on our soil. I cannot but feel some pity and
anxiety for her, lest she should never find a home anywhere.
It is dangerous to have been born in this beautiful land. At
present (except for one little voyage to Leghorn) she knows
only Florence.

[29] When we had looked sufficiently at the sculpture,
Powers proposed that we should now go across the street and
see the Casa del Bello. We did so, in a body, Powers in his
dressing-gown and slippers, and his wife and daughter without assuming any street costume. The Casa del Bello is a
palace of three pianos, the topmost of which is occupied by
an English lady, and an Italian count, her husband; the two
lower pianos are to let, and we looked at both. The upper one

would have suited us well enough, and might have been had
for forty dollars a month; but the lower has a terrace, with a
rustic summer-house over it, and is connected with a garden,
where there are arbors, and a willow-tree, and a little wilderness
of shrubbery and roses, with a fountain in the midst. It has
likewise an immense suite of rooms round the four sides of
a small court, spacious, lofty, with frescoed cielings and rich
paper hangings, and abundantly furnished with arm-chairs,
sofas, marble-tables, and great looking-glasses. Not that these
last are a great temptation; but, in our wandering life, I
wished to be perfectly comfortable myself, and to make my
family so, for just this summer; and so I have taken the lower
piano, the price being only fifty dollars per month. Certainly,
this is something like the Paradise of cheapness which we were
told of, and [30] which we vainly sought in Rome. As for our
other domestic arrangements, we pay six dollars a month for
a servant; twelve pauls (a dollar and twenty cents) a day for
dinner from a cook-shop; and about a paul a bottle for a very
tolerable red wine, which I like as well as claret, unless it were
of a special vintage. Cigars, too, are cheap; and cherries and
strawberries. What can man desire more! My wife has assigned me the pleasantest room (looking into the garden) for
my study; and when I like, I can overflow into the summer-
house, or an arbour, and sit there dreaming of a story, amid
the fumes of my cigar. The weather is delightful; too warm
to walk, but perfectly fit to do nothing in, in the coolness of
these great rooms. Every day I shall write a little, perhaps—
and probably take a brief nap, somewhere between breakfast
and tea—but go to see pictures and statues occasionally, and
so assuage and mollify myself a little, after that uncongenial
life of the Consulate, and before going back to my own hard
and dusty New-England.

   After concluding the arrangement for the Casa del Bello,
we stood talking a little while with Powers and his wife and

daughter, before the door of their house; for they seem so far to have adopted the habits of the Florentines as to feel themselves at home on the shady side of the street. This out-of-door life, and free com[31]munication with the pavement, habitual apparently among the middle classes, reminds one of the plays of Moliere and other old dramatists, in which the street or the square becomes a sort of common parlour, where most of the talk and scenic business is carried on.

Florence, June 5th, Saturday.

For two or three mornings, after breakfast, I have rambled a little about the city, till the shade grows narrow beneath the walls of the houses, and the heat makes it uncomfortable to be in motion. To-day, I went over the Ponte Carraja, and thence into and through the heart of the city, looking into several churches, in all of which I found people taking advantage of the cool breadth of these sacred interiors to refresh themselves and say their prayers. Florence at first struck me as having the aspect of a very new city, in comparison with Rome; but on closer acquaintance, I find that many of the buildings are antique and massive, though still the clear atmosphere, the bright sunshine, the light cheerful hues of the stucco, and— as much as anything else perhaps—the vivacious character of the human life in the streets, take away the sense of its being an ancient city. The streets are delightful to walk in, after so many penitential pilgrimages as I have made over those little square, [32] uneven blocks of the Roman pavement, which wear out the boots and torment the soul. I absolutely walk on the smooth flags of Florence for the mere pleasure of walking, and live in its atmosphere for the mere pleasure of living, and, warm as the weather is getting to be, I never feel that inclination to sink down in a heap and never stir again, which was my dull torment and misery as long as I staid in Rome. I hardly think there can be a place in the world where life is more delicious for its own simple sake than here.

I went to-day into the Baptistery, which stands near the Duomo, and, like that, is covered externally with slabs of black and white marble, now grown brown and yellow with age. The edifice is octagonal, both within and out; and, on entering, one immediately thinks of the Pantheon, the whole space within being free from side to side, with a dome above; but it differs from the severe simplicity of the former edifice, being elaborately ornamented with marble and frescoes, and lacking that great eye in the roof, that looks so nobly and reverently heavenward from the Pantheon. I did little more than pass through the Baptistery, glancing at the famous bronze doors, some perfect and admirable casts of which I had already seen at the Chrystal Palace. The entrance of the Duomo being just across the Piaz[33]za, I went in there after leaving the Baptistery, and was struck anew (for this is my third or fourth visit) with the dim grandeur of the interior, lighted as it is almost exclusively by painted windows, which seem to me worth all the variegated marbles and rich cabinet-work of St Peter's. The Florentine cathedral has a spacious and lofty nave, and side aisles divided from it by pillars; but there are no chapels along the aisles, so that there is far more breadth and freedom of interior, in proportion to the actual space. It is woeful to think how the vast capacity within St Peter's is thrown away, and made to seem smaller than it is by every possible device, as if on purpose. The pillars and walls of the Duomo are of a uniform, brownish, neutral tint; the pavement, a mosaic work of marble; the cieling of the dome itself is covered with frescoes, which, being very imperfectly lighted, it is impossible to trace out. Indeed, it is but a twilight region that is enclosed within the firmament of this great dome, which is actually larger than that of Saint Peter's, though not lifted so high from the pavement. But, looking at the painted windows, I little cared what dimness there might be elsewhere; for certainly the art of man has never contrived any other beauty and glory at all to be compared with this. The dome sits, as it [34] were, on three smaller domes (smaller, but still great) beneath which are three vast niches forming the transepts of the Cathedral, and the tribune behind the high altar. All round these hollow, dome-covered arches, or niches, are high and narrow windows, crowded with saints, angels, all manner of blessed shapes, that turn the common daylight into a miracle of richness and glory as it passes through their heavenly substance. And just beneath the swell of the great central dome is a wreath of circular windows, quite round it, as brilliant as the tall and narrow ones below. It makes me miserable with a hopeless sense of inefficiency to write about these things; but it is a pity anybody should die without seeing an antique painted window, with the bright Italian sunshine glowing through it. This is the 'dim, religious light' that Milton speaks of; but I doubt whether he saw these windows when he was in Italy, or any but those faded, or dusty and dingy ones, of the English cathedrals; else he would have illuminated that word 'dim' with some epithet that should not chase away the dimness, yet should make it shine like a million of rubies, sapphires, emeralds, and topazes— bright in themselves, but dim with tenderness and reverence, because God Himself was shining through them. I hate what I have said.

[35] All the time that I was in the cathedral, the space around the high altar (which stands right under the dome) was occupied by priests or acolytes, in white garments, chaunting a religious service. After coming out, I took a view of the edifice from a corner of the street, nearest to the dome, where it and the smaller domes could be seen at once. It is greatly more satisfactory than St. Peter's, in any view I ever had of

it; striking in its outline, with a mystery, yet not a bewilderment, in its masses, and curves, and angles, and wrought out with a richness of detail that gives the eye new arches, new galleries, new niches, new pinnacles, new beauties great and small, to play with, when wearied with the vast whole. The hue—black and white marble, like the Baptistery, turned also yellow and brown—is greatly preferable to the buff, (like General Washington's waistcoat and small-clothes) of St. Peter's.

From the Duomo, it is but a moderate street's length to the Piazza del Gran Duca, the principal square of Florence. It is a very interesting place, and has on one side the old Governmental Palace—the Palazzo Vecchio—where many scenes of historic interest have been enacted; for example, conspirators have been hanged from its windows, or precipitated from them upon the [36] pavement of the square below. It is a pity we cannot take as much interest in the history of these Italian republics as in that of England; for the former is much the most picturesque and full of curious incident. The sobriety of the Anglo Saxon race (in connection, too, with their moral sense) keeps them from doing a great many things that would enliven the page of history; and their events seem to come in great masses, shoved along by the agency of many, rather than to result from individual will and character. A hundred plots of a tragedy might be found in Florentine history, for one in English. At one corner of the Palazzo Vecchio is a bronze equestrian statue of Cosmo de Medici, the first Grand Duke, very stately and majestic; there are other marble statues (one of David, by Michael Angelo) at each side of the palace-door; and entering the court, I found a rich, antique corridor or arcade within, surrounded by marble pillars, most elaborately carved, supporting arches that were covered with faded frescoes. I went no further, but stept across a little space of the square to the Loggia de' Lanzi, which is a broad and

noble corridor of three vast arches, at the end of what I take
to be a part of the Palazzo Uffizi, and fronting on the Piazza.
I should call it a portico, if it stood before the palace-door;
but it seems to have been constructed merely for it[37]self,
and as a shelter for the people from sun and rain, and to contain some fine specimens of sculpture, as well antique as of
more modern times. Benvenuto Cellini's Perseus stands here;
but it did not strike me so much as the cast of it in the Crystal
Palace. A good many people were under these great arches,
some of whom were reclining, half or quite asleep, on the
marble seats that are built against the back of the Loggia. A
group were reading an edict of the Great Duke, which appeared to have been just pasted on a board, at the farther end
of the Loggia; and I was surprised at the interest which they
ventured to manifest, and the freedom with which they
seemed to discuss it. A soldier was on guard under the arches,
and doubtless there were spies enough to carry every word
that was said to the ear of absolute authority. Glancing myself
at the edict, however, I found it referred only to the further-
ance of a project, got up among the citizens themselves, for
bringing water into the city; and on such topics I suppose
there is freedom of discussion.

Florence, June 7th, Monday.

Saturday evening, Mamma, Una, Julian, & I, walked into
the city, and looked at the exterior of the Duomo with new
admiration. Since my former view of it, I have noticed (which,
strangely enough, did not strike me before) that the façade is
[38] but a great, bare, ugly space, roughly plastered over, with
the brickwork, peeping through it in spots, and a faint, almost
invisible fresco of columns upon it. This front was once nearly
finished with an encrustation of black and white marble, like

the rest of the edifice; but one of the city magistrates, Benedetto Uguccione, demolished it, three hundred years ago, with the idea of building it again in better style. He failed to do so, and ever since the magnificence of the great church has been marred by this unsightly roughness of what should be its principal front; nor is there, I suppose, any hope that it will ever be finished now. The Campanile, or bell-tower, stands within a few paces of the Cathedral, but entirely disconnected from it, rising to the height of nearly three hundred feet, a square tower of white marble, now discolored by time. It is impossible to give an idea of the richness of effect produced by its elaborate finish; the whole surface of the four sides, from top to bottom being decorated with all manner of statuesque and architectural sculpture. It is like a toy of ivory, which some ingenious and pious monk might have spent his life time in adorning with scriptural designs and figures of Saints; and when it was finished, seeing it so beautiful, he prayed that it might be miraculously magnified from the size of one foot to that of three hundred. This idea somewhat satisfies [39] me, as conveying an impression how gigantesque the Campanile is in its mass and height, and how minute and various in its detail. Surely these mediæval works have an advantage over the classic; they combine the telescope and the microscope.

The city was all alive in the summer evening, and the streets humming with voices. Before the doors of the caffes were tables at which people were taking refreshment; and it went to my heart to see a bottle of English ale, some of which was poured foaming into a tumbler;—at least, it had exactly the amber hue and the foam of English bitter ale, but perhaps it may have been merely a Florentine imitation. As we returned home over the Arno, crossing the Ponte di Santa Trinitá, we were struck by the beautiful scene of the broad, calm river, with the palaces along its banks repeated in it, on either side, and the neighboring bridges, too, just as perfect in the tide beneath as in the air above—a city of dream and shadow so close to the actual one. God has a meaning, no doubt, in putting this spiritual symbol continually beside us. Along the shore of the river, on both sides, as far as we could see, there was a row of brilliant lamps, which, in the far distance, looked like a cornice of golden light; and this also shone as brightly out of the river's depths. The hues of the eve[40]ning, in the quarter where the sun had gone down, were very soft and beautiful, though not so gorgeous (as no Italian sunsets have been, within my experience) as thousands that I have seen in America. But I believe I must fairly confess that the Italian sky, in the daytime, is bluer and brighter than our own, and that the atmosphere has a quality of showing objects to better advantage. It is more than mere daylight; the magic of moonlight is somehow mixed up with it, although it is so transparent a medium of sight.

Last evening, about sunset or sooner, Mr. Powers called to see us, and sat down to talk in a friendly and familiar way. I do not know a man of easier intercourse, nor with whom one so easily gets rid of ceremony. His conversation, too, is interesting, though perhaps not so original (as regards conveying new ideas) as it may appear to himself; for he thinks his own thoughts, and knowing that they are the product of his own mind, does not inquire whether they may have occurred to anybody else. Thus, he occasionally says things that many a man of borrowed ideas might not think it worth while to say, because they have often been said before. He is somewhat slow and ponderous, moreover, in drawing out his train of thought, so that an auditor of quick intelligence runs a risk of treading upon his [41] heels, and perhaps snatching his idea out of his mouth. He talked, to begin with, about Italian food, as poultry, mutton, beef, and their lack of savoriness as compared with our own; and mentioned an exquisite

dish of vegetables which they prepare from squash or pump-
kin-blossoms; likewise, another dish which it will be well
for us to remember when we get back to the Wayside, where
we are overrun with acacias. It consists of the acacia-blossom,
in a certain stage of its development, fried in oil. I shall get
the recipe from Mrs. Powers, and mean to deserve well of my
country by first trying it and then making it known; only I
doubt whether American lard, or even butter, will produce
the dish quite so delicately as Florence oil. Meanwhile, I like
Powers all the better because he does not put his life wholly
into marble. We had much talk, nevertheless, on matters of
sculpture; for he drank a cup of tea with us, and staid a good
while.

He passed a condemnatory sentence on classic busts in general, saying that they were conventional, and not to be depended upon as true representations of the men. He particularly excepted none but the bust of Caracalla; and, indeed,
everybody that has seen this bust must feel the justice of the
exception, and so be the more inclined to [42] accept his
opinion about the rest. There are not more than half-a-dozen—
that of Cato the Censor among the rest—in regard to which
I should like to ask his judgement individually. He seems to
consider the faculty of making a bust an extremely rare one;
Canova put his own likeness into all the busts he made;
Greenough could not make a good one, nor Crawford, nor
can Gibson. Mr. Harte, he observed (an American sculptor,
now resident in Florence) is the best man of the day for
making busts. Of course, it is to be presumed that he excepts
himself; but I would not do Powers the great injustice to
imply that there is the slightest professional jealousy in his
estimate of what others have done, or are now doing, in his
own art. If he saw a better man than himself, he would recognize him at once, and tell the world of him; but he knows
well enough that, in this line of art, there is no better, and

probably none so good. It would not accord with the simplicity of his character to blink a fact that stands so broadly before him.

We asked him what he thought of Mr. Gibson's practice of coloring his statues; and he quietly and slyly said that he himself had made wax figures in his earlier days, but had left off making them now. In short, he objected to the practice wholly, and said that a letter of his, on the subject, had been published in [43] the London Athenaeum, and had given great offence to some of Mr. Gibson's friends. It appeared to me, however, that his arguments did not apply quite fairly to the case; for he seems to think Gibson aims at producing an illusion of life in the statue—whereas, I think his object is merely to give warmth and softness to the snowy marble, and so bring it a little nearer to our hearts and sympathies. Even so far, nevertheless, I doubt whether the practice is defensible; and I was glad to see that Powers scorned, at all events, the argument drawn from the use of color by the antique sculptors, on which Gibson relies so much. It might almost be implied from the contemptuous way in which Powers spoke of color, that he considers it an impertinence on the face of visible nature, and would rather the world had been made without it; for he said that everything in intellect or feeling can be expressed as perfectly (or more so) by the sculptor in colorless marble, as by the painter with all the resources of his palette. I asked him whether he could model the face of Beatrice Cenci from Guido's picture, so as to retain the subtle expression; and he said he could, for that the expression depended entirely on the drawing, the picture being a 'badly colored thing.' I inquired whether he could model a blush, and he said 'Yes!'— and that he had [44] once proposed to an artist to express a blush in marble, if he would express it in picture. On consideration, I believe one to be as impossible as the other; the life and reality of the blush being comprehended in its tremulousness coming and going. It is lost in a settled red, just as much as in a settled paleness; and neither sculptor nor painter can do more than represent the circumstances of attitude and expression that accompany the blush. There was a great deal of truth in what Powers said about this matter of color; and, in one of our interminable New-England winters, it ought to comfort us to think how little real necessity there is for any hue but that of the snow. Mr. Powers, nevertheless, had brought us a beautiful bunch of roses, and seemed as capable of appreciating their delicate blush as we were. The best thing he said against the use of color in marble, was, to the effect that the whiteness removed the object represented into a sort of spiritual region, and so gave chaste permission to those nudities which would otherwise be licentious. I have myself felt the truth of this, in a certain sense of shame as I looked at Gibson's colored Venus.

He took his leave at about eight °clock, being to make a call on the Bryants, (who are at the Hotel de New York) and also on Mrs. Browning at the Casa Guidi.

[45] Florence, June 8ᵗʰ, Tuesday.

I went this morning to the Uffizzi Gallery. The entrance is from the great court of the palace, which communicates with Lung Arno at one end, and with the Grand Ducal Piazza at the other, the door being on the right side as you approach the Piazza. The gallery is in the upper story of the palace; and in the vestibule are some busts of the princes and cardinals of the Medici family—none of them very beautiful, one or two so ugly as to be ludicrous; especially one who is all but buried and smothered in his own wig.

I at first travelled slowly through the whole extent of this long, long gallery, which occupies the whole length of the palace on both sides of the court, and is full of sculpture and pictures. The latter, being opposite to the light, are not seen to the best advantage; but it is the most perfect collection, in a chronological series, that I have seen, comprehending specimens of all the masters since painting began to be an art. Here are Giotto, and Cimabue, and Botticcelli, and Fra Angelico, and Phillippo Lippi, and a hundred others, who have haunted me in churches and galleries ever since I came to Italy, and who ought to interest me a great deal more than they do. Occasionally, to-day, I was sensible of a certain degree of emotion in looking at an old picture; as, for example, [46] by a large, dark, ugly picture of Christ bearing the cross, and sinking beneath it, where, somehow or other, a sense of his agony, and the fearful wrong that mankind did to its Redeemer, and the scorn of his enemies and sorrow of those that loved him, came knocking at my heart, and partly got entrance. Once more, I deem it a pity that Protestantism should have entirely laid aside this mode of appealing to the religious sentiment.

I chiefly paid attention to the sculpture, and was interested in a long series of busts of the Emperors, and the members of their families, and of some of the great men of Rome. There is a bust of Pompey the Great, bearing not the slightest resemblance to that vulgar and unintellectual one in the gallery of the Capitol; altogether a different cast of countenance. I could not judge whether it resembled the face of the statue, having seen the latter so imperfectly in the duskiness of the hall of the Spada Palace. These, I presume, are the busts which Mr. Powers condemns, from internal evidence, as unreliable and conventional. He may be right—and is far more likely, of course, to be right than I am—yet there certainly seems to be character in these marble faces, and they differ as much among themselves as the same number of living faces might. The bust of Caracalla, how[47]ever, which Powers excepted from his censure, certainly does give stronger assurance of its being an individual and faithful portrait than any other in the series. All the busts of Caracalla, of which I have seen many, give the same evidence of their truth; and I should like to know what it was, in this abominable emperor, that made him insist upon having his actual likeness perpetuated, with all the ugliness of its animal and moral character. I rather respect him for it, and still more the sculptor, whose hand, methinks, must have trembled as he wrought the bust. Generally, these wicked old fellows, and their wicked wives and daughters, are not so hideous as we might expect. Messalina, for instance, has small and pretty features, though with rather a sensual developement of the lower part of the face. The busts, it seemed to me, are generally superior as works of art to those at the Capitol, and either better preserved, or more thoroughly restored. The bust of Nero might almost be called handsome here, though bearing his likeness unmistakeably. I wish some competent person would undertake to analyze and develope his character, and how and by what necessity—with all his elegant tastes, his love of the beautiful, his artist nature—he grew to be such a monster. Nero [48] has never yet had justice done him, nor have any of the wicked Emperors; not that I suppose them to have been any less monstrous than history represents them; but there must surely have been something in their position and circumstances to render the terrible moral disease, which seized upon them so generally, almost inevitable. A wise and profound man, tender and reverent of the human soul, and capable of appreciating it in its height and depth, has a great field here for the exercize of his powers. It has struck me, in reading the history of the Italian republics, that many of the tyrants, who sprung up after the destruction of their liberties, resembled the worst of the Roman emperors. This subject of Nero and his brethren has often perplexed me with vain desires to come at the truth.

There were many beautiful specimens of antique, ideal sculpture, all along the gallery; Apollos, Bacchuses, Venuses, Mercuries, Fauns, with the general character of all of which I was familiar enough to recognize then at a glance. The mystery and wonder of the gallery, however—the Venus de Medici—I could nowhere see, and indeed was almost afraid to see it: for I somewhat apprehended the extinction of another of those lights that shine along a man's pathway, and go out in a snuff the instant he comes within [49] eye-shot. My European experience has blown out a great many such. I was pretty well contented, therefore, not to find the famous statue, in the whole of my long journey from end to end of the gallery, which terminates on the opposite side of the court from that where it commences. The cieling, by the by, through the entire length, is covered with frescoes, and the floor paved with a composition of stone, smooth and polished, like marble. The final piece of sculpture, at the end of the gallery, is a copy of the Laocoon, considered very fine. I know not why, but it did not impress me with the sense of mighty and terrible repose— a repose growing out of the infinitude of trouble—that I had felt in the original.

Parallel with the gallery, on both sides of the palace-court, there runs a series of rooms devoted chiefly to pictures, although statues and bas-reliefs are likewise contained in some of them. I remember an unfinished bas-relief by Michael Angelo, of a Holy Family, which I touched with my finger, because it seemed as if he might have been at work on it only an hour ago. The pictures I did little more than glance at, till I had almost completed again the circuit of the gallery, through this series of parallel rooms; and then I came upon a [50] collection of French, and Dutch, and Flemish, masters, all of which interested me more than the general run of the Italians, who have tired me to-death in so many other galleries. There was a beautiful picture by Claude, almost as good as those in the British National gallery, and very like in subject; the sun near the horizon, of course, and throwing its line of light over the ripple of some water, with ships at the strand, and a palace or two of stately architecture on the shore. Landscapes by Rembrandt; fat Graces ("greases," rather) and other plump nudities, by Rubens; brass pans and earthen pots, and herrings, by Teniers and other Dutchmen; none by Gerard Duow, I think, but several by Mieris; all of which were like bread, and beef, and ale, after having been fed too long on made-dishes. This is really a wonderful collection of pictures; and, from first to last—from Giotto to the man of yesterday—they are in admirable condition, and may be appreciated for all the merit that they ever possessed.

I could not quite believe that I was not to find the Venus de Medici; and still, as I passed from one room to another, my breath rose and fell a little, with the half-hope, half-fear, that she might stand before me. Really, I did not know that I cared so much about Venus, or any possible woman [51] of marble. At last—when I had come from among the Dutchmen, I believe, and was looking at some works of Italian artists, chiefly Florentines—I caught a glimpse of her, through the door of the next room. It is the best room of the whole series, octagonal in shape, and hung with red damask; and the light comes down from a row of windows passing quite round, beneath an octagonal dome. The Venus stands somewhat aside from the centre of the room, and is surrounded by an iron-railing, a pace or two from her pedestal in front, and less behind. I think she might safely be left to the reverence her womanhood would win, without any other protection. She is very beautiful; very satisfactory; and has a fresh and new charm about her, unreached by any cast or copy that I have seen. The hue of the marble is just so much mellowed by time as to do for her all that Gibson tries, or ought, to try, to do for his statues by color; softening her, warming her almost imperceptibly, making her an inmate of the heart as well as a spiritual existence. I felt a kind of tenderness for her; an affection, not as if she were one woman, but all womankind in one. Her modest attitude—which, before I saw her, I had not liked, deeming that it might be an artificial shame—is partly what unmakes her as the heathen goddess, and softens her into woman. There is a slight [52] degree of alarm, too, in her face; not that she really thinks anybody is looking at her, yet the idea has flitted through her mind and startled her a little. Her face is so beautiful and intellectual, that it is not dazzled out of sight by her body. Methinks this was a triumph for the sculptor to achieve. I may as well stop here. It is of no use to throw heaps of words upon her; for they all fall away, and leave her standing in chaste and naked grace, as untouched as when I began.

The poor little woman has suffered terribly by the mishaps of her long existence in the marble. Each of her legs has been broken into two or three fragments; her arms have been broken off; her body has been broken quite across at the waist; her head has been snapt off at the neck. Furthermore, there have been grievous wounds and losses of substance in various tender parts of her body. But, partly by the skill with which the statue has been restored, and partly because the idea is perfect and indestructible, all these injuries do not in the least impair the effect, even when you see where the dissevered fragments have been re-united. She is just as whole as when she left the hands of the sculptor. I am glad to have seen this Venus, and to have found her so tender and so chaste. On the wall of the room, and to be taken in at the same glance, [53] is a painted Venus by Titian, reclining on a couch, naked and lustful.

The room of the Venus seems to be the treasure place of the whole Uffizzi palace, containing more pictures by famous masters than are to be found in all the rest of the gallery. There were several by Raphael, and the room was crowded with the easels of artists. I did not look half enough at anything, but merely took a preliminary taste, as a prophecy of enjoyment to come.

As we were at dinner to-day (we dine at half-past-three) there came a ring at the door, and a minute after, our servant brought in a card; it was Mr. Robert Browning's, and on it was written, in pencil, an invitation for us to go to their house, this evening. He had left the card and gone away; but very soon, the bell rang again, and he had come back, having forgotten to give his address. This time, we made him come in; and he shook hands with all of us, children and grown people, and was very vivacious and agreeable. He looked younger and handsomer than when I saw him in London, two years ago, and his gray hairs seemed fewer than those that had then strayed into his youthful head. He contrived to talk a wonderful quantity in a little time, and told us—among other things that we should never have dreamed of—that [54] Italian people will not cheat you if you construe them generously, and put them upon their honor. Mr Browning was very kind and warm in his expressions of pleasure at seeing us; and, on our part, we were all very glad to meet him. He must be an exceedingly likeable man; but I somewhat question whether an intimate acquaintance with him would flow on quite smoothly and equably enough to be sure of lasting a great while. They are to leave Florence very soon, and are going to Normandy, I think he said, for the rest of the summer.

The Venus de Medici has a dimple in her chin.

Florence, June 9th, Wednesday.

Mamma, Miss Shepard, and I, went last evening, at eight
°clock, to see the Brownings; and after some search and inquiry, we found the Casa Guidi, which is a palace in a street
not very far from our own. It being dusk, I could not see the
exterior, which, if I remember, Browning has celebrated in
song; at all events, he has called one of his poems the 'Casa
Guidi Windows.' The street is a narrow one; but on entering
the house, we found a spacious staircase, and ample accommodations of vestibule and hall; the latter opening on a balcony, where we could hear the chaunting of priests in a church
close by. Browning told us that this was the first church
where an oratorio had ever been performed. He came into the
ante-room to greet us; as did his little boy, Robert, whom they
nick[55]name Penny for fondness. This latter cognomen is a
diminutive of Appennine, which was bestowed upon him at
his first advent into the world, because he was so very small;
there being a statue in Florence nicknamed Appennine, because it is so huge. I never saw such a boy as this before; so
slender, fragile, and spritelike, not as if he were actually in
ill-health, but as if he had little or nothing to do with human
flesh and blood. His face is very pretty and most intelligent,
and exceedingly like his mother's, whose constitutional lack
of stamina I suppose he inherits. He is nine years old, and
seems at once less childlike and less manly than would befit
that age. I should not quite like to be the father of such a boy;
and should fear to stake so much interest and affection on him
as he cannot fail to inspire. I wonder what is to become of
him;—whether he will ever grow to be a man;—whether it is
desirable that he should. His parents ought to turn their
whole attention to making him gross and earthly, and giving

him a thicker scabbard to sheathe his spirit in. He was born in Florence, and prides himself on being a Florentine, and is indeed as un-English a production as if he were native in another planet.

Mrs Browning met us at the door of the drawing-room and greeted us most kindly; a pale little [56] woman, scarcely embodied at all; at any rate, only substantial enough to put forth her slender fingers to be grasped, and to speak with a shrill, yet sweet, tenuity of voice. Really, I do not see how Mr. Browning can suppose that he has an earthly wife, any more than an earthly child; both are of the elfin-breed, and will flit away from him, some day, when he least thinks of it. She is a good and kind fairy, however, and sweetly disposed towards the human race, although only remotely akin to it. It is wonderful to see how small she is; how diminutive, and peaked, as it were, her face, without being ugly; how pale her cheek; how bright and dark her eyes. There is not such another figure in this world; and her black ringlets cluster down into her neck and make her face look the whiter by their sable profusion. I could not form any judgement about her age; it may range any where within the limits of human life, or elfin-life. When I met her in London, at Mr. Milnes's breakfast-table, she did not impress me so strangely; for the morning light is more prosaic than the dim illumination of their great, tapestried drawing-room; and besides, sitting next to her, she did not then have occasion to raise her voice in speaking, and I was not sensible what a slender pipe she has. It is as if a grasshopper should speak. It is marvellous to me how so extraordinary, so acute, so [57] sensitive a creature, can impress us, as she does, with the certainty of her benevolence. It seems to me there were a million chances to one that she would have been a miracle of acidity and bitterness.

We were not the only guests. Mr. & Mrs. Eckers, Americans, recently from the East, and on intimate terms with the

Brownings, arrived after us; also, Miss Fanny Howarth, an English literary lady, whom I have met several times in Liverpool; and lastly came the white head and palmer-like beard of Mr. Bryant, with his daughter. Mr. Browning was very efficient in keeping up conversation with everybody, and seemed to be in all parts of the room and in every group at the same moment; a most vivid and quick-thoughted person, logical and common-sensible, as I presume poets generally are, in their daily talk. Mr. Byrant, as usual, was homely and plain of manner, with an old-fashioned dignity, nevertheless, and a remarkable deference and gentleness of tone, in addressing Mrs. Browning. I doubt, however, whether he has any high appreciation either of her poetry or her husband's; and it is my impression that they care as little about his.

We had some tea and some strawberries, and passed a pleasant evening. There was no very noteworthy conversation; the most interesting topic being that disagreeable, and now wearisome one, of [58] spiritual communications, as regards which Mrs. Browning is a believer, and her husband an infidel. Bryant appeared not to have made up his mind on the matter, but told a story of a successful communication between Cooper, the novelist, and his sister, who had been dead fifty years. Browning and his wife had both been present at a spiritual session held by Mr. Hume, and had seen and felt the unearthly hands; one of which had placed a laurel wreath on Mrs. Browning's head. Browning, however, avowed his belief that these aforesaid hands were affixed to the feet of Mr. Hume, who lay extended in his chair, with his legs stretching far under the table. The marvellousness of the fact, as I have read of it, and heard it from other eye-witnesses, melted strangely away, in his rude, hearty gripe, and at the sharp touch of his logic; while his wife, ever and anon, put in a little shrill and gentle word of expostulation. I am rather surprised that Browning's conversation should be so clear, and so much to the purpose of the moment; since his poetry can seldom proceed far without running into the high grass of latent meanings and obscure allusions.

Mrs. Browning's health does not permit late hours; so we began to take leave at about ten °clock. I heard her ask Mr. Bryant if he did not mean to re-visit Europe, and heard him answer, not uncheerfully taking hold of his white hair, "It is [59] getting rather too late in the evening now." If any old age can be cheerful, I should think his might be; so good a man, so cool, so calm—so bright, too, we may say—his life has been like the days that end in pleasant sunsets. He has a great loss, however—or what ought to be a great loss—soon to be encountered in the death of his wife, who, I think, can hardly live to reach America. He is not eminently an affectionate man. I take him to be one who cannot get closely home to his sorrow, nor feel it so sensibly as he gladly would; and in consequence of that deficiency, the world lacks substance to him. It is partly the result, perhaps, of his not having sufficiently cultivated his animal and emotional nature; his poetry shows it, and his personal intercourse—though kindly—does not stir one's blood in the least.

Little Penny, during the evening, sometimes helped the guests to cake and strawberries; joined in the conversation when he had anything to say, or sat down upon a couch to enjoy his own meditations. He has long curling hair, and has not yet emerged from his frock and drawers. It is funny to think of putting him into breeches. His likeness to his mother is strange to behold.

Florence, June 10th, Thursday.

Mamma and I went to the Pitti Palace to-day; and first entered a court where, yesterday, she had seen a carpet of flowers, arranged for some great ceremony. It must have [60] been a most beautiful sight, the pavement of the court being entirely covered by them, in a regular pattern of brilliant hues, so as really to be a living mosaic. This morning, however, the court had nothing but its usual pavement, and the show of yesterday seemed so much the more inestimable as having been so evanescent. Around the walls of the court there were still some pieces of splendid tapestry, which had made part of yesterday's magnificence. We went up a staircase, of regally broad and easy ascent, and made application to be admitted to see the grand ducal apartments. An attendant accordingly took the keys, and ushered us first into a grand hall, with a vaulted cieling, and thence through a series of noble rooms, with rich frescoed ceilings and mosaic floors, hung with damask, adorned with gilded chandeliers, and glowing, in short, with more magnificence than I could have imagined beforehand, or can now remember. In many of the rooms, there were those gorgeous, antique cabinets, which I admire more than any other furniture ever invented; only these were of unexampled art and glory, inlaid with precious stones and with beautiful Florentine mosaics, both of flowers and landscapes—each cabinet worth a lifetime's toil to make it, and the cost a whole palace to pay for it. Many of the rooms were covered with Arras tapestry, of landscapes, hunting scenes, mythological sub[61]-jects, or historical scenes, equal to pictures in truth of representation, and possessing an indescribable richness that makes them preferable as a mere adornment of princely halls and chambers. Some of the rooms, as I have said, were laid in mosaic of stone and marble; others were in beautiful patterns of various woods; others were covered with carpets, delightful to tread upon, and glowing like the pavement of flowers which mamma saw yesterday. There were tables, too, of Florentine mosaic, the mere materials of which—lapis lazuli, malachite, pearl, and a hundred other precious things—were worth a fortune, and made a hundred times more valuable, and a thousand times, by the artistic skill of the manufacturer. I toss together brilliant words by the handfull, and make a rude sort of patch work, but can record no adequate idea of what I saw in this suite of rooms; and the taste, the subdued splendor, so that it did not shine too high, but was all tempered into an effect at once grand and soft—this was quite as remarkable as the gorgeous material. I have seen quite as dazzling an effect produced in the principal cabin of an American clipper-ship.

After making the circuit of the grand ducal apartments, we went into a door in the left wing of the palace, and ascended a narrow flight of stairs—[62] several tortuous flights, indeed— to the picture-gallery. It fills a great many stately halls, which themselves are well worth a visit for their architecture and frescoes; only these matters become common-place after travelling through a mile or two of them. The collection of pictures (as well for their number as for the celebrity and excellence of many of them) is the most interesting that I have seen, and I do not yet feel in a condition, nor perhaps ever shall, to speak of a single one. It gladdened my very heart to find that they were not darkened out of sight, nor apparently at all injured by time, but were well-kept and varnished, brilliantly framed, and, no doubt, restored by skilful touches, if any of them needed it. The artists and amateurs may say what they like; for my part, I know no drearier feeling than that inspired by a ruined picture; ruined, that is, by time, damp, or rough treatment, and I would a thousand times rather an artist should do his best towards reviving it, than have it left in such a condition. I do not believe, however, that these pictures have been sacrilegiously interfered with; at all events, I saw, in the master-pieces, no touches but what seemed worthy of the master-hand. The most beautiful picture in the world, I am convinced, is Raphael's Madonna della Seggiola. I was familiar with it in a hun[63]dred engravings, and copies; and therefore it shone upon me as with a familiar beauty, though infinitely more divine than I had ever seen it before. An artist was copying it, and producing certainly something very like a fac-simile, yet leaving out, as a matter of course, that mysterious something that renders the picture a miracle. It is my present opinion that the pictorial art is capable of something more like magic— more wonderful and inscrutable in its methods—than poetry, or any other mode of developing the beautiful. But how does this accord with what I have been saying only a minute ago? How then can the decayed picture of a great master ever be restored by the touches of an inferior hand? Doubtless, it never can be restored; but let some devoted worshipper do his utmost, and the whole inherent spirit of the divine picture may pervade his restorations likewise.

I saw the Three Fates of Michael Angelo, which were also being copied, as were many other of the best pictures. Miss Fanny Howarth, whom I met in the gallery, told me that, to copy the Madonna della Seggiola, application must be made at least three years beforehand; so many are the artists who aspire to copy it. Michael Angelo's Fates are three very grim and pitiless old women, who [64] respectively spin, hold, and cut, the thread of human destiny, all in a mood of sombre gloom, but with no more sympathy than if they had nothing to do with us. I remember seeing an etching of this picture, when I was a child, and being struck, even then, with the terrible, stern, passionless severity, neither loving us nor hating us, that characterizes these ugly old women. If they were angry, or had the least spite against humankind, it would render them the more tolerable. They are a great work, containing and representing the very idea that makes a belief in Fate such a cold torture to the human soul. God give me a sure belief in his Providence!

In a year's time, with the advantage of access to this magnificent gallery, I think I might come to have some little knowledge of pictures. At present, I still know nothing, but am glad to find myself capable, at least, of loving one picture better than another. I cannot always 'keep the heights I gain,' however; and after admiring and being moved by a picture, one day, it is within my experience to look at it, the next, as little moved as if it were a tavern-sign. It is pretty much the same with statuary; the same, too, with those pictured windows of the Duomo, which I described so rapturously a few days ago. I looked at them again, the next morning; and thought they would have been hardly worthy of my eulogium, [65] even had all the separate windows of the Cathedral combined their narrow lights into one grand, resplendent, many-colored arch, at the eastern end. It is a pity they are so narrow. England has many a great Chancel window that, though dimmer in its hues, dusty, and perhaps made up of heterogeneous fragments, eclipses these by its spacious breadth.

From the gallery, I went into the Boboli Gardens, which are contiguous to the palace, but found them too sunny for enjoyment. They seem to consist partly of a wilderness; but the portion into which I strayed was laid out with straight walks, lined with high box-hedges, along which there was only a narrow margin of shade. I saw an amphitheater, with a wide sweep of marble seats around it, enclosing a grassy space, where doubtless the Medicis may have witnessed splendid spectacles.

Florence, June 11th Friday.

I paid another visit to the Uffizzi gallery, this morning, and found that the Venus is one of the things, the charm of which does not diminish on better acquaintance. The world has not grown weary of her in all these ages; and mortal man may look on her with new delight from infancy to old age, and keep the memory of her, I should imagine, as one of the treasures of spiritual existence hereafter. Surely, it makes one more ready to believe in the high destinies of the human race, to [66] think that this beautiful form is but Nature's plan for all womankind, and that the nearer the actual woman approaches to it, the more natural she is. I do not, and cannot, think of her as a senseless image, but as a being that lives to gladden the world, incapable of decay and death; as young and fair to day as she was three thousand years ago, and still to be young and fair, as long as a beautiful thought shall require physical embodiment. I wonder how any sculptor has had the impertinence to aim at any other presentation of female beauty. I mean no disrespect to Gibson, or Powers, or a hundred other men who people the world with nudities, all of which are abortive as compared with her; but I think the world would be all the richer if their Venuses, their Greek Slaves, their Eves, were burnt into quick-lime, leaving us only this statue as our image of the beautiful. I observed to day (what my wife had already remarked) that the eyes of the statue are slightly hollowed out, in a peculiar way, so as to give them a look of depth and intelligence. She is a miracle. The sculptor must have wrought religiously, and have felt that something far beyond his own skill was working through his hand. I mean to leave off speaking of the Venus hereafter, in utter despair of saying what I wish; especially as the contemplation of the statue will refine [67] and elevate my taste, and make it continually more difficult to express my sense of its excellence, as the perception of it grows upon me. If, at any time, I become less sensible of it, it will be my deterioration, not any defect in the statue.

I looked at many of the pictures, and found myself in a favorable mood for enjoying them. It seems to me that a work of art is entitled to credit for all that it makes us feel in our best moments; and we must judge of its merits by the impression it

then makes, and not by the coldness and insensibility of our less
genial moods.

After leaving the Uffizzi palace (and making a visit to
Messrs Emmanuel Fenzi & Co, my bankers) I went into the
Museum of Natural History, near the Pitti Palace. It is a very
good collection of almost everything that Nature has made,
(or exquisite copies of what she has made,) stones, shells,
vegetables, insects, fishes, animals, man; the greatest wonders
of the museum being some models in wax of all parts of the
human frame. It is good to have the wholeness and summed-up
beauty of woman in the memory, when looking at the details
of her system as here displayed; for these last, to the natural
eye, are by no means beautiful. But they are what belong only
to our mortality; the beauty that makes them invisible is our
im[68]mortal type, which we shall take away with us. Under
glass cases, there were some singular and horribly truthful representations, in small wax figures, of a time of pestilence; the
hasty burial, or tossing into one common sepulchre, of discolored corpses; a very ugly piece of work indeed. I think
Murray says that these things were made for the Grand Duke
Cosmo; and if so, they do him no credit, indicating something
dark and morbid in his character.

Florence, June 13ᵗʰ, Sunday.

Wife and I called at the Powers', yesterday morning, to leave
Rosebud there for an hour or two's play with the children; and
it being not yet quite time for the Pitti Palace, we stept into the
studio. Soon, Mr. Powers made his appearance, in his dressing-
gown and slippers, and sculptor's cap, smoking a cigar, which
by the by was none of the best. He was very cordial and
pleasant, as I have always found him, and began immediately

to be communicative about his own works or on any other subject that came up. There were two casts of the Venus de Medici
in the studio, which he said were valuable in a commercial
point of view, being genuine casts from the mould taken
from the statue. He then gave us a quite unexpected but most
interesting lecture on the Venus, demonstrating it as he proceeded by [69] reference to the points which he criticized.
The figure, he seemed to allow, was admirable, though I
rather think he hardly classes it so high as his own Greek
Slave or Eve; but the face, he began with saying, was that of
an idiot. Then, leaning on the pedestal of the cast, he continued—"It is rather a bold thing to say, isn't it, that the sculptor of the Venus de Medici did not know what he was about?"
Truly, it appeared to me so; but Powers went on remorselessly,
and showed, in the first place, that the eye was not like any
eye that Nature ever made; and, indeed, being examined
closely, and abstracted from the rest of the face, it has a very
queer look—less like a human eye than a half-worn button-
hole. Then he attacked the ear, which he affirmed, and demonstrated, was placed a great deal too low on the head, thereby
giving an artificial and monstrous height to the portion of the
head above it. The forehead met with no better treatment in
his hands, and as to the mouth, it was altogether wrong, as well
in its general make, as in such niceties as the junction of the
skin of the lips to the common skin around them. In a word, the
poor face was battered all to pieces and utterly demolished; nor
was it possible to doubt or question that it fell by its own
demerits—all that could be urged in its [70] defense (and
even *that* I did not urge) being that this very face had
affected me, only the day before, with a sense of higher beauty
and intelligence than I had ever till then received from sculpture, and that its expression seemed to accord with that of
the whole figure, as if it were the sweetest note of the same
music. There must be something in this; the sculptor dis-

regarded technicalities and the imitation of actual nature, the better to produce the effect which he really does produce, in somewhat the same way as a painter works his magical illusions by touches that have no relation to the truth, if looked at from the wrong point of view. But Powers considers it certain that the old sculptor had bestowed all his care on the study of the human figure, and really did not know how to make a face. I myself used to think that the face was a much less important thing with the Greeks, among whom the entire beauty of the form was familiarly seen, than with ourselves, who allow no other nudity.

After annihilating this poor visage, Powers showed us his two busts of Proserpine and Psyche, and continued his lecture by showing the truth to nature with which these are modelled. I freely acknowledge the fact; there is no sort of comparison to be made between the beauty, intelligence, feeling, and accuracy of representation, in these two faces, and in that of the [71] Venus de Medici. A light—the light of a soul proper to each individual character—seems to shine from the interior of the marble and beam forth from the features, chiefly from their eyes. Still insisting upon the eye, and hitting the poor Venus another, and another, and still another blow on that unhappy feature, Mr. Powers, turned up, and turned inward, and turned outward, his own Titanic orb (the biggest by far that ever I saw in mortal head) and made us see and confess that there was nothing right in the Venus, and everything right in Psyche and Proserpine. To say the truth, their marble eyes have life, and, placing yourself in the proper position towards them, you can meet their glances, and feel theirs mingle with your own. Powers is a great man, and also a tender and delicate one, massive and rude of surface as he looks; and it is rather absurd to feel how he impresses his auditor, for the time being, with his own evident idea that nobody else is worthy to touch marble. Mr Bryant told me that Powers has had many difficulties and quarrels, on professional grounds, as I understood him, and with his brother-artists. No wonder! He has said enough, in my hearing, to put him at swords' points with sculptors of every epoch, and every degree, between the two inclusive extremes of Phidias and Clark Mills.

[72] He has a bust of the reigning Grand-duchess of Tuscany, who sat to him for it. The bust is that of a noble-looking lady; and Powers remarked that royal personages have a certain look that distinguishes them from other people, and is seen in individuals of no lower rank. They all have it; the Queen of England and Prince Albert have it; and so likewise has every other Royalty, although the possession of this kingly look implies nothing whatsoever as respects kingly and commanding qualities. He said that none of our public men, whatever authority they may have held, or for whatever length of time, possess this look; but he added, afterwards, that Washington had it. Commanders of armies sometimes have it, but not in the degree that royal personages do. It is—as well as I could make out Powers's idea—a certain coldness of demeanor, and especially of eye, that surrounds them with an atmosphere through which the electricity of human brotherhood and sisterhood cannot pass. From their youth upward, they are taught to feel themselves apart from the rest of mankind; and this manner becomes a second nature to them in consequence, and as a safeguard to their conventional dignity. They put themselves under glass, as it were, (the illustration is my own,) so that though you see them, and see them looking no more noble and dignified [73] than other mortals, nor so much so as many, still they keep themselves within a sort of Sanctity, and repel you by an invisible barrier. Even if they invite you, with a show of warmth and hospitality, you cannot get through. I, too, recognize this look in the portraits of Washington; in him, a mild, benevolent coldness and apartness, but indicating that formality which seems to have been deeper in him than in any other

mortal, and which built up an actual fortification between himself and human sympathy. I wish, for once, Washington could come out of his envelopment, and show us what his real dimensions were.

Among other models of statues heretofore made, Powers showed us one of Melancholy, or rather of Contemplation, from Milton's Penseroso; a female figure, with unlifted face and 'rapt look commercing with the skies.' It is very fine, and goes deeply into Milton's thought; but, as far as the outward form and action is concerned, I remember seeing a rude engraving, in my childhood, that probably suggested the idea; it was prefixed to a cheap American edition of Milton's poems, and was probably as familiar to Powers as to myself. It is very remarkable how difficult it seems to be to strike out a new attitude in sculpture; a new group, or a new single figure. One [74] piece of sculpture Powers exhibited, however, which was very exquisite, and such as I never saw before. Opening a desk, he took out something carefully enclosed between two layers of cotton wool; on removing which, there appeared a little baby's hand, most delicately represented in the whitest marble, all the dimples where the knuckles were to be, all the creases in the plump flesh, every infantine wrinkle of the soft skin, being lovingly recorded. "The critics condemn minute representation," said Powers; "but you may look at this through a microscope—and see if it injures the general effect!" Upon my word, Nature herself never made a prettier or truer little hand. It was the hand of his daughter—'Luly's hand,' Powers called it —the same that gave my own such a frank and friendly grasp. The sculptor made it only for himself and his wife, but so many people, he said, had insisted on having a copy, that there are now as much as forty scattered about the world. At sixty years (though Powers will long ere then have laid aside his chisel) Luly ought to have her hand sculptured again, and give it to her grandchildren with the baby-hand of five months old. The baby-hand that had done nothing, and felt only its mother's kiss; the old woman's hand, that had exchanged the love-pressure, worn the marriage-ring, closed dead eyes, done a life[75]time's work, in short. The sentiment is rather obvious, but true, nevertheless.

Before we went away, Powers took us into a room apart— apparently the secretest room he had—and showed us some tools and machinery, all of his own contrivance and invention. "You see, I am a bit of a Yankee," he observed. This machinery is chiefly to facilitate the process of modelling his works; for (except in portrait-busts) he makes no clay-model, as other sculptors do, but models directly in the plaster; so that instead of being crumbled, like clay, the original model remains a permanent possession. He has also invented a certain open file, which is of great use in finishing the surface of the marble; and likewise a machine for making these files, and for punching holes through iron; and he demonstrated its efficacy by punching a hole through an iron bar, with a force equivalent to ten thousand pounds, by the mere application of a part of his own weight. These inventions, he says, are his amusement; and the set of his nature towards sculpture must indeed have been strong, to counteract, in an American, such a capacity for the contrivance of steam-engines. His wife regrets that he had not allowed the latter talent to make the business of his life. "In that case, we should not have been here now, she tells me!" said he.

[76] I had no idea of filling so many pages of this journal with the sayings and characteristics of Mr. Powers; but the man and his talk are fresh, original, and full of bone and muscle, and I enjoy him much. We now proceeded to the Pitti Palace, and spent several hours pleasantly in its saloons of pictures. I never enjoyed pictures so much anywhere else, as I do in Florence. There is an admirable 'Judith' in this gallery, by Allori; a face of great beauty and depth; and her hand clutches

the head of Holofernes by the hair in a way that startles the spectator. There are two peasant Madonnas by Murillo; simple women, yet with a thoughtful sense of some high mystery connected with the baby in their arms. Raphael grows upon me; several other famous painters—Guido, for instance—are fading out of my mind. Salvator Rosa has two really wonderful landscapes, looking from the shore seaward; and Rubens two, likewise on a large scale, of mountain and plain. It is very idle and foolish to talk of pictures; yet, after poring over them and into them, it seems a pity to let all the thought excited by them pass into nothingness. The copyists of pictures are very numerous both in the Pitti and Uffizzi galleries; and, unlike sculptors, they appear to be on the best of terms with one another, chatting sociably, exchanging [77] friendly criticism, and giving their opinions as to the best mode of attaining the desired effects. Perhaps, as mere copyists, they escape the jealousy that might spring up between rival painters, attempting to develope original ideas. Miss Howarth says that the business of copying pictures, especially those of Raphael, is a regular profession, and she thinks it exceedingly obstructive to the progress or existence of a modern school of painting; there being a regular demand and sure sale for all copies of the old masters, at prices proportioned to their merit; whereas, the effort to be original ensures nothing, except long neglect, at the beginning of a career, and probably ultimate failure, and the necessity of becoming a copyist at last. Some artists employ themselves from youth to age, in nothing else but the copying of one single and self-same picture of Raphael's, and grow at last to be perfectly mechanical, making, I suppose, the same identical stroke of the brush on fifty successive pictures.

The weather is very hot now; hotter in the sunshine, I think, than a mid-summer day usually is in America, but with rather a greater possibility of being comfortable in the shade. The nights, too, are warm; and the bats fly forth at dusk, and the fireflies quite light up the green depths of our little garden. The atmosphere, or something else, [78] causes a sort of alacrity in my mind, and an affluence of ideas, such as they are; but it does not thereby make me the happier. I feel an impulse to be at work, but am kept idle by the sense of being unsettled, with removals to be gone through, over and over again, before I can shut myself into a quiet room of my own, and turn the key. I need monotony, too—an eventless exterior life—before I can live in the world within.

Florence, June 15th, Tuesday.

Yesterday, my wife and I went to the Uffizzi gallery; and of course I took the opportunity to look again at the Venus de Medici, after Powers' attack upon her face. Some of the defects he attributed to her I could not see in the statue; for instance, the ear appeared to be in accordance with his own rule; the lowest part of it being about in a straight line with the upper lip. The eyes must be given up, as not, when closely viewed, having the shape, the curve outwards, the formation of the lids, that eyes ought to have; but still, at a proper distance, they seemed to have intelligence in them, beneath the shadow cast by the brow. I cannot help thinking that the sculptor intentionally made every feature what it is, and calculated them all with a view to the desired effect. Whatever rules may be transgressed, it is a noble and beautiful face; more so, perhaps, than if all rules had [79] been obeyed. I wish Powers would do his best to fit the Venus de Medici's figure (which he does not deny to be admirable) with a face which he would deem equally admirable, and in accordance with the sentiment of the form.

We looked pretty thoroughly through the gallery, and I saw many pictures that impressed me; but, among such a multitude, with only one poor mind to take note of them, the stamp of each new impression helps to obliterate a former one. I am sensible, however, that a process is going on—and has been, ever since I came to Italy—that puts me in a state to see pictures with less toil, and more pleasure, and makes me more fastidious, yet more sensible of beauty where I saw none before. It is the sign, I presume, of a taste still very defective, that I take singular pleasure in the elaborate imitations of Van Mieris, Gerard Duow, and other old Dutch wizards who painted such brass-pots that you can see your face in them, and such earthen jugs that they will surely hold water; and who spent weeks and months in turning a foot or two of canvass into a perfect, microscopic illusion of some homely scene. For my part, I wish Raphael had painted the Transfiguration in this style, at the same time preserving his breadth and grandeur of design; nor do I believe that there is any real impediment to the combination of the two [80] styles, except that no possible span of human life would suffice to cover a quarter part of the canvas of the Transfiguration with such touches as Gerard Duow's. But one feels the vast scope of this wonderful art, when we think of two excellences so far apart as that of this last painter and Raphael. I pause a good while, too, before the Dutch paintings of fruit and flowers, where tulips and roses acquire an immortal bloom; and grapes have kept the freshest juice in them for two or three hundred years. Often, in these pictures, there is a bird's nest, every straw perfectly represented, and the stray feather, or the down that the mother-bird plucked from her bosom, with the three or four small, speckled eggs, that seem as if they might be yet warm. These petty miracles have their use in assuring us that painters really can do something that takes hold of us in our most matter of fact moods; whereas, the merits of the grander style of art may be beyond our ordinary appreciation, and leave us in doubt (nine times out of ten that we look at them) whether we have not befooled ourselves with a false admiration. Until we learn to appreciate the cherubs and angels that Raphael scatters through the blessed air, in a picture of the Nativity, it is not amiss to look at a Dutch fly settling on a peach, or a humble-bee burying himself in a flower.

It is another token of imperfect taste, no doubt, [81] that queer pictures, and absurd pictures, remain in my memory, when better ones pass away by the score. There is a picture of Venus combing her son Cupid's head with a small-tooth comb, and looking with maternal care among his curls; this I shall not forget. Likewise, a picture of a broad, rubicund Judith, by Bordone—a widow of fifty, of an easy, lymphatic, cheerful temperament, who has just killed Holofernes, and is as self-complaisant as if she had been carving a goose. What could possibly have stirred up this pudding of a woman (unless it were a pudding-stick) to do such a deed! I looked with much pleasure at an ugly, old, fat, jolly Bacchus, astride on a barrel, by Rubens; the most natural and lifelike representation of a tipsy rotundity of flesh, that it is possible to imagine. And sometimes, amid these sensual images, I caught the divine pensiveness of a Madonna's face, or the glory and majesty of the babe Jesus in her lap, with his Father shining through him. This is a sort of revelation, whenever it comes.

This morning, immediately after breakfast, I walked into the city, meaning to make myself better acquainted with its appearance, and to go into various churches; but it soon grew so hot that I turned homeward again. The interior of the [82] Duomo was deliciously cool, to be sure, cool and dim, after the white-hot sunshine; but an old woman began to persecute me so that I came away. A male beggar drove me out of another church; and I took refuge in the street, where the beggar and I would have been two cinders together, if we had stood long enough on the sunny side. After my five summers' experience of England, I may have forgotten what hot weather is; but it does appear to me that an American summer is not so fervid as this. Besides the direct rays, the white pavement throws a furnace-heat up into one's face; the shady margin of the street is barely tolerable; but it is like going through the ordeal of fire to cross the broad, bright glare of an open piazza. The narrow streets prove themselves a blessing, at this season, except when the sun looks directly into them; the broad eaves of the houses, too, make a selvage of shade almost always. I do not know what becomes of the street-merchants, at the noontide of these hot days. They form a numerous class in Florence, displaying their wares—linen or cotton cloth, threads, combs, and all manner of haberdashery—on moveable counters that are borne about on wheels. In the shady morning, you see a whole side of a street or a piazza occupied by them, all offering their merchandize at full [83] cry. They dodge, as long as they can, from shade to shade; but at last the sunshine floods the whole space, and they seem to have melted away, leaving not a rag of themselves or what they dealt in.

Cherries are very abundant now (and have been so ever since we came here) in the markets and all about the streets. These are of various kinds, some exceedingly large, insomuch that it is almost necessary to disregard the old proverb about making two bites of a cherry. Fresh figs are already spoken of, though I have seen none; but I saw some peaches, this morning, looking as if they might be ripe.

Florence, June 16th, Wednesday.

Mr. Powers and his wife called in to see us last evening, about nine °clock. Mr. Powers, as usual, was full of talk, and gave vent to a good many instructive and entertaining ideas. As an instance of the little influence the religion of the Italians has upon their morals, he told a story of a servant of theirs, who desired leave to set up a small shrine of the Virgin in their room (a cheap print, or bas-relief, or image, such as are sold everywhere at the shops) and to burn a lamp before it; she engaging, of course, to supply the oil at her own expense. By-and-by, her oil-flask appeared to possess a miraculous property of re[84]plenishing itself, and Mr. Powers took measures to ascertain where the oil came from. It turned out that the servant had all the time been stealing the oil from them, and keeping up her daily sacrifice and worship to the Virgin by this constant theft.

His talk soon turned upon sculpture; and he spoke once more of the difficulty imposed upon an artist by the necessity of clothing portrait statues in the modern costume. I find that he does not approve either of nudity or of the Roman toga for a modern statue; neither does he feel it right to shirk the difficulty (as Chantrey did in the case of Washington) by enveloping him in a cloak; but acknowledges the propriety of taking the actual costume of the age and doing his best with it. He himself did so in the case of Washington, and also in a statue that he made of Daniel Webster. I suggested that, though this costume might not appear ridiculous to us now, yet, two or three centuries hence, it would create, to the people of that day, an impossibility of seeing the real man through the absurdity of his envelopment, after it shall have entirely gone out of fashion and remembrance; and Webster would seem as ridiculous to them then, as he would to us now, in a masquerade of some by-gone day. It might be well, therefore, to adopt some conventional costume, never actual, but always graceful and noble. Be[85]sides, Webster for example had other costumes than that which he wore in public, and perhaps it was in those that he lived his most real life; his dressing gown, his shirt-sleeves, his drapery of the night, the dress that he wore on his fishing-excursions; in these other costumes he spent three-fourths of his time, and most probably was thus arrayed when he conceived the great thoughts that afterwards, in some formal and outside mood, he gave forth to the public. I scarcely think I was right, but am not sure of the contrary. At any rate, I know that I should have felt much more sure that I knew the real Webster, if I had seen him in any of the above mentioned dresses, than either in his swallow-tailed coat or frock.

Talking of a taste for painting and sculpture, Powers observed that it was something very different and quite apart from the moral sense, and that it was often, perhaps generally, possessed by unprincipled men of ability and cultivation. I have had this perception myself; a genuine love of painting and sculpture, and perhaps of music, seems often to have distinguished men capable of every social crime, and to have formed a hard and fine enamel over their characters. Perhaps it is because such tastes are artificial, the product of cultivation, and, when highly developed, imply a great remove from natural simplicity.

This morning, I went with Miss Shepard and Una [86] to the Uffizzi gallery, and again looked with more or less attention at almost every picture and statue. I saw a little picture of the Golden Age (I forget by whom; Allori, or Albano, I believe) in which the charms of youths and virgins are depicted with a freedom that the Iron Age can hardly bear to look at. The Cabinet of Gems happened to be open for the admission of a privileged party; and we likewise went in, and saw a brilliant collection of goldsmiths' work, among which, no doubt, were specimens from such hands as those of Benvenuto Cellini. Little busts, with diamond eyes; boxes of gems; cups carved out of precious material; crystal vases, beautifully chased and engraved, and sparkling with jewels; great pearls, in the midst of rubies and other precious stones; opals, rich with all manner of lovely lights. I remember, Benvenuto Cellini, in his memoirs, speaks of manufacturing such playthings as these.

I observed another characteristic of the summer streets of Florence to-day; tables, moveable to and fro on wheels, and set out with cool, iced drinks and cordials which looked and smelt very tempting.

Florence, June 17th, Thursday.

My wife and I went, this morning, to the Academy of Fine Arts, and, on our way thither, went into the Duomo, where we found a deliciously cool twilight, through which shone the mild gleam of the painted windows. I cannot [87] but think it a pity that Saint Peter's is not lighted by such windows as these; although I by no means saw the glory in them now, that I have spoken of in my record of a former visit. We found out the monument of Giotto, a tablet and portrait in bas-relief, on the wall, near the entrance of the Cathedral, on the right hand; also, a representation in fresco of a knight on horseback, the memorial of one John Hawkwood, close by the door to the left. The priests were chaunting a service of some kind or other in the Choir; terribly inharmonious and out of tune, my wife said.

On reaching the Academy, the soldier or policeman at the entrance directed us into a large hall, the walls of which were covered on both sides with pictures, arranged as nearly as possible in a progressive series, with reference to the date of the painters; so that here the origin and procession of the art may be traced, through the course of at least two hundred years. Giotto, Cimabue, and others, of unfamiliar name to me, are among the earliest; and, except as curiosities, I should never desire to look once at them, nor think of looking twice. They seem to have been executed with great care and conscientiousness; and the heads are often wrought out with minuteness and fidelity, and have so much expression that they tell their own story [88] clearly enough; but it seems not to have been the painter's aim to effect a lifelike illusion, the background and accessories being conventional. The trees are no more like real trees than the feather of a pen; and there is no perspective, the figures of the picture being shadowed forth on a surface of burnished gold. The effect, when these pictures (some of them very large) were new, and freshly gilded, must have been exceedingly brilliant, and much resembling, on an immensely large scale, the rich illuminations in an old monkish missal. In fact, we have not now, in pictorial ornament, anything at all comparable to what their splendor must have been. I was most struck with a picture (by Fabricio Gentile, or Gentileschi, or some such name) of the Adoration of the Magi, where the faces and figures have a great deal of life and action, and even grace, and where the jewelled crowns, the rich embroidered robes and cloth of gold, and all the magnificence of the Three Kings, is represented with the vividness of the real thing; a gold sword-hilt, for instance, or a pair of gold spurs, being actually embossed on the picture. The effect is very powerful, and though produced in what modern painters would pronounce an unjustifiable way, there is yet pictorial art enough to reconcile it to the spectator's mind. Certainly, the people of the middle ages [89] knew better than ourselves what is magnificence, and how to produce it; and what a glorious work must that have been; both in its mere sheen of burnished gold and in its illuminating art, which shines thus through the gloom of perhaps four centuries.

Fra Angelico is a man much admired by those who have a taste for the pre-Raphaelite painters; and though I take little or no pleasure in his works, I can see that there is a great delicacy of execution in his heads, and that generally he produces such a Christ, and such a Virgin, and such Saints, as he could not have foreseen, except in a pure and holy imagination, nor have wrought out without saying a prayer between every two touches of his brush. I might come to like him, in

time, if I thought it worth while; but it is enough to have an
outside perception of his kind and degree of merit, and so to
let him pass into the garret of oblivion, where many things as
good or better are piled away, that our own age may not
stumble over them. Perugino is the first painter whose works
seem really worth preserving for the genuine merit that is in
them, apart from any quaintness and curiosity of an ancient
and new-born art. Probably, his religion was more genuine
than Raphael's, and therefore the Virgin often re[90]vealed
herself to him in a loftier and sweeter face of divine womanhood than all the genius of Raphael could produce. There is
a Crucifixion by him, in this gallery, which made me partly
feel as if I were a far-off spectator; no, I did not mean a
Crucifixion, but a picture of Christ, dead, lying with a calm,
sweet face, on his mother's knees. The most inadequate and
utterly absurd picture, here, or in any other gallery, is a head
of the Eternal Father, by Carlo Dolce; it looks like a feeble
Saint, on the eve of martyrdom, and very doubtful how he
shall be able to bear it—very finely and prettily painted,
nevertheless.

After getting through the principal gallery, we went into a
smaller room, in which are contained a great many small
specimens of the old Tuscan artists, among whom Fra
Angelico makes the principal figure. These pictures are all on
wood, and seem to have been taken from the shrines and
altars of ancient churches; they are predellas, and triptyches,
or pictures on three folding tablets, shaped quaintly, in Gothic
peaks or arches, and still gleaming brightly with backgrounds
of antique gold. The wood is much worm-eaten, and the colors
have often faded or changed from what the old artists meant
them to be; a bright angel darkening into what looks quite
as much like the devil. In one of Fra Angelico's pictures (a
representa[91]tion of the Last Judgement) he has tried his
saintly hand at making devils indeed, and showing them

busily at work, tormenting the poor, damned souls in fifty ghastly ways. Above sits Jesus, with the throng of blessed saints around him, and a glow of tender and powerful love in his own face, that ought to suffice to redeem all the damned, and convert the very fiends, and quench the fires of hell by its holier light. At all events, Fra Angelico had a higher conception of his Saviour than Michael Angelo did.

Florence, June 19th, Saturday.

My wife and I, this forenoon, have been to the church of St. Lorenzo, which stands on the site of an ancient Basilica, and was itself built more than four centuries ago. The facade is still an ugly height of rough brickwork, as is the case with the Duomo, and, I think, some other churches in Florence; the design of giving them an elaborate and beautiful finish having been delayed, from cycle to cycle, till at length the day for spending mines of wealth on churches is gone by. The interior has a nave with a flat roof, divided from the side-aisles by Corinthian pillars; and, at the further end, a raised space around the high altar. The pavement is a mosaic of squares of black and white marble, the squares meeting one another cornerwise; the pillars, pilasters, and other architectural material, is dark brown [92] or greyish stone; and the general effect is very sombre, especially as the church is somewhat dimly lighted, and as the shrines along the aisles, and the statues, and the monuments of whatever kind, look dingy with time and neglect. The nave is thickly set with wooden seats, brown and worn. What pictures there are, in the shrines and chapels, are dark and faded. On the whole, the edifice has a shabby aspect. On each side of the high altar, elevated on four pillars of beautiful marble, is what looks like a great sarcophagus of bronze; they are in fact pulpits, and are ornamented with mediæval bas-reliefs representing scenes in the life of our Savior. Murray says that the resting place of the first Cosmo de Medici, the old banker (who so managed his wealth as to get the posthumous title of Father of his Country, and to make his posterity its reigning princes) is in front of the high-altar, marked by red and green porphyry and marble, inlaid into the pavement. We looked, but could not see it there.

There were worshippers at some of the shrines, and persons sitting here and there along the nave or in the aisles, wrapt in devotional thought, doubtless, and sheltering themselves here from the white sunshine of the piazzas. In the vicinity of the choir and the high altar, workmen were busy [93] repairing the church, or perhaps only making arrangements for celebrating the great festival of Saint John.

On the left hand of the choir is what is called the Old Sacristy, with the peculiarities or notabilities of which I am not acquainted. On the right hand is the New Sacristy (otherwise called the Capella dei Depositi, or Chapel of the Buried, I suppose) built by Michael Angelo to contain two monuments of the Medici family. The interior is of somewhat severe and classic architecture, the walls and pilasters being of dark stone and surmounted by a dome, beneath which is a row of windows, quite round the building, throwing their light down far beneath upon niches of white marble. These niches are ranged entirely around the chapel (which is octagonal, I think, and perhaps twenty paces across) and might have sufficed to contain more than all the Medici monuments that the world would ever care to have. Only two of the niches are filled, however. In one of them sits Giuliano de Medici, sculptured by Michael Angelo, a figure of dignity, which would perhaps be very striking in any other presence than that of the statue which occupies the corresponding niche. At the feet of Giuliano recline two allegorical statues, Day and Night, whose business [94] there I do not know, and perhaps Michael Angelo knew as little. As the great sculptor's statues are apt to do, they sprawl, and fling their limbs abroad with adventurous freedom. Below the corresponding niche, in the opposite side of the chapel, recline two similar statues, representing Morning and Evening, sufficiently like Day and Night to be their brother and sister, all in truth having sprung from the same father. I think he must have begotten them for some other purpose, and put his allegorical progeny here only for lack of other house-room.

But the statue that sits above these two latter allegories, Morning and Evening, is like no other that ever came from a sculptor's hand; it is the one work worthy of Michael Angelo's reputation, and grand enough to vindicate for him all the genius that the world gave him credit for. And yet it seems a simple thing enough to think of, or to execute; merely a sitting figure, the face partly overshadowed by a helmet, one hand supporting the chin, the other resting on the thigh. But after looking at it a little while, the spectator ceases to think of it as a marble statue; it comes to life, and you see that this princely figure is brooding over some great design, which, when he has arranged in his own mind, the world will be fain to execute [95] for him. No such majesty and grandeur has elsewhere been put into human shape. It is all a miracle; the deep repose, and the deep life within it; it is as much a miracle to have achieved this, as to make a statue that would rise up and walk. The face, when one gazes earnestly into it, beneath the shadow of its helmet, is seen to be calmly sombre, a mood which I think is generally that of the rulers of mankind except in moments of vivid action. This statue is one of the things which I look at with highest enjoyment, but also with grief and impatience, because I feel that I do not come at all which it involves, and that by-and-by I must go away and leave it forever. How wonderful! To take a block of marble and convert it wholly into thought; and to do it through all the obstructions and impediments of drapery; for there is nothing nude in this statue but the face and hands. The rest is the costume of Michael Angelo's century. This is what I always thought that a sculptor of true genius should be able to do— to show the man of whatever epoch nobly and heroically through the costume which he might actually have worn.

The statue sits within a square niche of white marble, and completely fills it. It seems [96] to me a pity that it should be thus confined. At the Crystal palace, if I remember, the effect is improved by a free surrounding space. It is a shame for me to write about such a great work, and leave out everything that really characterizes it; its naturalness, for example, as if it came out of the marble of its own accord, with all its grandeur hanging heavily about it, and sat down there beneath its weight. I cannot describe it. It is like trying to stop the ghost of Hamlet's father by crossing a spear before it.

Communicating with the Sacristy is the Medicean Chapel, which was built more than two centuries ago for the reception of the Holy Sepulchre; arrangements having been made, about that time, to steal this most sacred relic from the Turks. The design failing, the chapel was converted by Cosmo II into a place of sepulture for the princes of his family. It is a very grand and solemn edifice, octagonal in shape, with a lofty dome, within which are a series of brilliant frescoes, painted not more than twenty five or thirty years ago. These pictures are the only portion of the adornment of the chapel which interfere with the sombre beauty of the general effect; for though the walls are encrusted, from pavement to dome, with marbles of inesti[97]mable cost, and a Florentine mosaic on a grander scale than was ever executed elsewhere, the result is not gaudy, as in many of the Roman chapels, but a dark and melancholy richness. The architecture strikes me as extremely fine; each alternate side of the octagon being an arch, rising as high as the cornice of the lofty dome, and forming the frame of a vast niche. All the dead princes, no doubt, according to the original design, were to have been honored with statues within this stately mausoleum, but only two—those of Ferdinand I and Cosmo II—seem ever to have been placed here. They were a bad breed, and few of them deserved any better monument than a dunghill; and yet they have this grand chapel for the family at large, and yonder grand statue for one of its most worthless members. I am glad of it; and as for the statue, Michael Angelo wrought it through the efficacy of a kingly idea, which had no reference to the individual whose name it bears.

In the piazza adjoining the church, is a statue of the first Cosmo, the old banker, in Roman costume, seated, and looking like a man fit to hold authority. No, I mistake; the statue is of John de Medici, the father of Cosmo, and himself no banker, but a soldier.

[98] Florence, June 21st, Monday.

Yesterday, after dinner, Mamma, Una, Julian, and I, went to the Boboli Gardens, which are open to the public on Thursdays and Sundays. We entered by a gate nearer to our house than that by the Pitti Palace, and found ourselves almost immediately among embowered walks of box and shrubbery, and little wildernesses of trees, with here and there a seat under an arbor, and here and there a marble statue, grey with ancient weather-stains. The site of the garden is a very uneven surface, and the paths go upward and downward, and ascend, at their ultimate point, to the base of what appears to be a fortress, commanding the city. A good many of the Florentines were rambling about the gardens, like ourselves; little parties of school boys, fathers and mothers with their youthful progeny, young men in couples, looking closely into every female face, lovers, with a maid or two in attendance on the young lady. All appeared to enjoy themselves, especially the children, dancing on the esplanades, or rolling down the slopes of the hills; and the loving-pairs, whom it was rather embarrassing to come upon unexpectedly, sitting close together on the stone-seat of an arbor, with clasped hands, a passionate solemnity on the young man's face, and a downcast pleasure on the lady's. Policemen, in cocked hats, epaulets, cross-belts, and swords, were scattered about the grounds, but interfered with [99] nobody, though they seemed to keep an eye on all. A sentinel stood in the hot sunshine, looking down over the garden from the ramparts of the fortress. For my part, in this foreign country, I have no objection to policemen or any other ministers of authority; though I remember, in America, I had an innate antipathy to constables, and always sided with the mob against law. This was very wrong and foolish, considering that I was one of the sovereigns; but a sovereign, or any number of sovereigns, or the twenty-millionth part of a sovereign, does not love to find himself—as an American must—included within the delegated authority of his own servants.

There is a sheet of water somewhere in the Boboli gardens, inhabited by swans; but this we did not see. We found a smaller pond, however, set in marble and surrounded by a parapet, and alive with multitudes of fish. There were minnows, by the thousand, and a good many gold fish; and Julian, who had brought some bread to feed the swans, threw in handsful of crumbs for the benefit of these finny people. They seemed to be accustomed to such courtesies on the part of visitors; and immediately the surface of the water was blackened, at the spot where each crumb fell, with shoals of minnows, thrusting one another even above the surface in their eagerness to snatch it. Within the depths of the pond, the [100] yellowish-green water (its hue being precisely that of the Arno) would be reddened duskily with the larger bulk of two or three gold fishes, who finally poked their great snouts up among the minnows, but generally missed the crumb. Beneath the circular margin of the pond, there are little arches, into the shelter of which, no doubt, the fish retire, when the noonday sun burns straight down into their duck puddle.

We went on, through the garden-paths, shadowed quite across by the high walls of box, and reached an esplanade, whence we had a good view of Florence, with the bare, brown ridges on the northern side of the Arno, and glimpses of the river itself, flowing like a street between two rows of palaces. A great way off, too, we saw some of the cloudlike peaks of the Appenines, and above them the clouds into which the sun was descending, looking quite as substantial as the distant mountains. The city does not present a particularly splendid aspect; though its great Duomo was seen in the middle distance, sitting on its circle of little domes, with the tall Campanile close by; and, within a hundred or two of yards of it, the tall, cumbrous bulk of the Palazzo Vecchio, with its lofty, machicolated and battlemented tower, very picturesque, yet looking exceedingly like a martin-box on a pole. There were [101] other domes, and towers, and spires, and here and there the distinct shape of an edifice; but the general picture was of a contiguity of red earthen roofs, filling a not very broad or extensive valley, among dry and ridgy hills, with a river-gleam lightening up the landscape a little. Una took out her pencil and tablet-book, and began to sketch the tower of the Palazzo Vecchio; in doing which, she immediately became an object of curiosity to some little boys and larger people, who failed not (under such pretences as taking a grasshopper off her dress, or no pretence at all) to come and look over her shoulder. There is a kind of familiarity among these Florentines, which is not meant to be discourteous, and ought to be taken in good part.

We continued to ramble through the gardens in quest of a good spot to see the sunset from, and at length found a stone-bench, on the slope of a hill, where the entire cloud and sun-scenery was fully presented to us. At the foot of the hill were statues, and among them a Pegasus with wings outspread; and, a little beyond, the garden-front of the Pitti Palace, which looks a little less like a state-prison here, than as it fronts the street. Girls, and children, and young men and old, were taking their pleasure in our neighborhood, and, just in front of us, a lady stood talking with her maid. By and by, we dis[102]covered her to be Miss Howarth. The sunset, after all, did not turn out a hundredth part so brilliant as may be seen, almost any June evening, in America. There may have been a misty light, streaming down just on the hither side of the ridge of hills, that was rather peculiar; but the most remarkable thing was the shape into which the clouds gathered themselves after the disappearance of the sun. It was like a tree, with a broad and heavy mass of foliage, spreading high upward on the sky, and a dark and well defined trunk, which rooted itself on the verge of the horizon.

This morning, my wife and I went to the Pitti Palace. The air was very sultry; and the pavements, already heated with the sun, made the space between the buildings seem like a close room. The earth, I think, is too much stoned out of the streets of an Italian city, paved, like those of Florence, quite across, with broad flagstones, to the line where the stones of the houses on each side are piled up. Thunder rumbled over our heads, however, and the clouds were so dark that we scarcely hoped to reach the palace without feeling the first drops of the shower. The air still darkened and darkened; so that, by the time we reached the suite of picture-rooms, the pictures seemed all to be changed to Rembrandt's, the shadows as black as midnight, with only some [103] highly illuminated portion gleaming out. This obscurity of the atmosphere made us sensible how splendid is the adornment of these apartments; for the gilded cornices shone out, as did the gilding of the arches and wreathed circles that divide the cieling into compartments, within which the frescoes are painted, and whence the figures looked dimly down, like gods out of a mysterious sky. The white marble sculptures also gleamed down from their height, where winged Cupids or cherubs gambolled aloft, in bas-reliefs, or allegoric shapes reclined along the cornices, hardly noticed when the daylight comes brightly into the halls. On the walls, all the rich picture-frames glimmered in gold, as did the framework of the chairs, and the heavy, gilded pedestals of the marble, alabaster, and mosaic-tables. These are very magnificent saloons; and since I have begun to speak of their splendor, I may as well add, that the doors are framed in polished, richly veined marble, and the walls hung with scarlet-damask.

It was useless to try to see the pictures; all the artists, engaged in copying, laid aside their brushes; and we all looked out of the windows into the square before the palace, where a mighty wind sprang up, and quickly raised a prodigious cloud of dust. It hid the opposite side of the street, [104] and was carried in a great dusky whirl higher than the roofs of the houses, higher than the tip top of the Pitti Palace itself. The thunder muttered and grumbled; the lightning emitted now and then a flash; and a few raindrops pattered against the windows; but, for a long time, the shower held off. At last, it came down in a stream, and lightened the air to such a degree that we could see some of the pictures, especially those of Rubens, and the illuminated parts of Salvator Rosa's, and best of all, Titian's Magdelene, the one with the golden hair clustering round her naked body. The golden hair, indeed, seemed to throw out a glory of its own. This Magdelene is very coarse and sensual, with only an impudent assumption of penitence and religious sentiment, scarcely so deep as the eyelids; but it is a splendid picture, nevertheless, with those naked, lifelike arms, and the hands that press the rich locks about her, and so carefully let those two voluptuous breasts be seen. She a penitent! She would shake off all pretence to it, as easily as she would shake aside that clustering hair and offer her nude front to the next comer. Titian must have been a very good-for-nothing old man.

I looked again at Michael Angelo's Fates to-day, but cannot satisfactorily make out what he meant by them. One of them —she who holds the dis[105]taff—has her mouth open, as if uttering a cry, and might be fancied to look somewhat irate. The second, who holds the thread, has a pensive air, but is still, I think, pitiless at heart. The third sister looks closely and coldly into the eyes of the last-mentioned, meanwhile cutting the thread with a pair of shears. Michael Angelo, if I may presume to say so, wished to vary the expression of these three sisters, and give each a different one, but did not see precisely how; inasmuch as all the fatal Three are united, heart and soul, in one purpose. It is a very impressive group. But, as regards the interpretation of this, or any other profound picture, there are likely to be as many as there are spectators. It is very curious to read criticisms upon pictures, and upon the same face in a picture, and by men of taste and feeling, and to see what different conclusions they arrive at. Each man interprets the hieroglyphic in his own way; and the painter, perhaps, had a meaning which none of them have reached; or possibly he put forth a riddle without himself knowing the solution. There is such a necessity, at all events, of helping the painter out with the spectator's own resources of feeling and imagination, that you never can be sure how much of the picture you have yourself made. There is no doubt that the pub[106]lic is, to a certain extent, right and sure of its ground, when it declares, through a series of ages, that a certain picture is a great work. It is so; a great symbol, proceeding out of a great mind; but if it means one thing, it seems to mean a thousand, and often opposite things.

Florence, June 27ᵗʰ, Sunday.

I have had a heavy cold and fever almost throughout the past week, and have thereby lost the great Florentine festivity, the feast of St. John, which took place on Thursday last, with the fireworks and illuminations the evening before, and the races and court ceremonies on the day itself. However, unless it were more characteristic and peculiar than the Carnival, I have not missed anything very valuable.

Mr. Powers called in to see me one evening, and poured out, as usual, a stream of talk, both racy and oracular in its character. Speaking of human eyes, he observed that they did not depend for their expression upon color, nor upon any light of the soul beaming through them, nor any glow of the eyeball, nor upon anything but the form and action of the surrounding muscles. He illustrated it by saying that if the eye of a wolf, or of whatever fiercest animal, could be placed in another setting, it would be found capable of the [107] utmost gentleness of expression. "You yourself," said he, "have a very bright and sharp look sometimes; but it is not in the eye itself." His own eyes, as I could have sworn, were glowing, all the time he spoke; and remembering how many times I have seemed to see eyes glow, and blaze, and flash, and sparkle, and melt, and soften; and how all poetry is illuminated with the light of ladies' eyes; and how many people have been smitten by the lightning of an eye, whether in love or anger; it was difficult to allow that all this subtlest and keenest fire is illusive, not even phosphorescent, and that any other jelly in the same socket would serve as well as the brightest eye. Nevertheless, he must be right; of course he must, and I am rather ashamed ever to have thought otherwise. Where should the light come from! Has a man a flame inside of his head? Does his spirit manifest itself in the semblance of flame? The moment we think of it, the absurdity becomes evident. I am not quite sure, however, that the outer surface of the eye may not reflect more light in some states of feeling than in others; the state of the health certainly has an influence of this kind.

I asked Powers what he thought of Michel [108] Angelo's statue of Lorenzo de Medici. He allowed that its effect was very grand and mysterious; but added that it owed this to a trick—the effect being produced by the arrangement of the hood, as he called it, or helmet, which throws the upper part of the face into shadow. The niche in which it sits has, I suppose, its part to perform in throwing a still deeper shadow. It is very possible that Michael Angelo may have calculated upon this effect of sombre shadow, and legitimately, I think; but it really is not worthy of Mr. Powers to say that the whole effect of this mighty statue depends, not on the positive efforts of Michel Angelo's chisel, but on the absence of light in a space of a few inches. He wrought the whole statue in harmony with that little part of it which he leaves to the spectator's imagination, and if he had erred at any point, the miracle would have been a failure; so that, working in marble, he has positively reached a point of excellence above the capability of marble, sculpturing his highest touches upon air and duskiness.

Mr. Powers gave some amusing ancedotes about his early life, when he was a clerk in a little provision-store, in Cincinnati, I believe. There was a museum opposite, the proprietor [109] of which had a peculiar physiognomy that struck

Powers, insomuch that he felt impelled to make continual caricatures of it. He used to draw them upon the door of the museum, and became so familiar with the face that he could draw them in the dark; so that, every morning, here was this absurd profile of himself, greeting the museum-man when he came to open his establishment. Often, too, it would reappear within an hour after it was rubbed out. The man was infinitely annoyed, and made all possible efforts to discover the unknown artist, but in vain; and finally concluded, I suppose, that the likeness broke out upon the door of its own accord, like the nettle rash. Some years afterwards, the proprietor of the museum engaged Powers himself as an assistant; and one day the latter asked him if he remembered this mysterious profile. "Yes," said he; "did you know who drew them?"— Powers took a piece of chalk, and touched off the very profile again before the man's eyes. "Ah," said he, "if I had known it at the time, I would have broken every bone in your body!"

Before he began to work in marble, Powers had great practice and success in making wax figures, and he produced a work of this kind [110] called the 'Infernal Regions,' which, he seemed to imply, had been very famous. He said that he once wrought a face in wax which was life itself, having made the eyes on purpose for it, and put in every hair of the eye brows individually, and finished the whole with similar minuteness; so that, within the distance of a foot or two, it was impossible to tell that the face did not live.

I have hardly ever before felt an impulse to write down a man's conversation, as I do that of Mr. Powers. The chief reason is, probably, that it is so possible to do it, his ideas being square, solid, and tangible, and therefore readily grasped and retained. He is a very instructive man, and sweeps one's empty and dead notions out of the way with exceeding vigor; but when you have his ultimate thought and perception, you feel inclined to think and see a little further for yourself. It must be added that he is especially wise in his own conceit, seeing too clearly what is within his range to be aware of any region of mystery beyond. Probably, however, this latter remark does him injustice. I like the man, and am always glad to encounter the mill-stream of his talk, though it sometimes comes down upon me at not very convenient [111] times and places. Yesterday, for instance, he met me in the street—(he was dressed, by the by, in his linen blouse and slippers, with a little bit of a sculptor's cap on the side of his head, as queer a figure as was then abroad in Florence)—he met me, and gave vent to a theory of colds, and a dissertation on the bad effects of draughts, whether of cold air or hot, and the dangers of transfusing blood from the veins of one living subject into those of another. On the last topic, he remarked that, if a single particle of air found its way into the veins, along with the transfused blood, it caused convulsions and inevitable death; otherwise, the process might be of excellent effect.

Last evening, my wife, Una, and I, went to pass the evening with Miss Blagden, who inhabits a villa at Bellosguardo, about a mile outside of the walls. The situation is very lofty, and there are good views from every window of the house, and an especially fine one of Florence and the hills beyond, from the balcony of the drawing-room. It was too far on the edge of evening, however, to see it so distinctly as might be desired. By and by came Mr. Browning, Mr. Trollope, Mr. Boot of Boston and a young daughter, and two or three [112] other gentlemen whom I do not know; and besides there was Miss Blagden's companion, a very pretty and pleasant young lady. Miss Blagden seems to be a likeable and intelligent person, with literary culture and affinities, being a friend, for example, of Sir Lytton Bulwer. Browning, too, evidently knows her well and likes her proportionably. He was very genial and full of life, as usual; but his conversation has the effervescent aroma which you cannot catch, even if you get the very words that seem to be imbued with it. He spoke most rapturously of a portrait of his wife, which an Italian artist is painting for the wife of an American gentleman, as a present from her husband. The success was already perfect, although there had been only two sittings as yet, and both on the same day; and in this relation, Mr. Browning remarked that Page, the American artist, had had no less than seventy-three sittings of him for a portrait. In the result, every hair and speck of him was represented; yet—as I inferred from what he did not say—this accumulation of minute truths did not, after all, amount to the true whole.

I do not remember much else that Browning said, except in playful abuse of a little King [113] Charles's spaniel, named Frolic, Miss Blagden's lapdog, whose venerable age (he is eleven years old) ought to have pleaded in his behalf.— Browning's nonsense is of very genuine and excellent quality, the true bubble and effervescence of a bright and powerful mind, and he lets it play among his friends with the faith and simplicity of a child. He must be an amiable man. I should like him much (and should make him like me) if opportunities were favorable.

I conversed principally with Mr. Trollope, a gentleman about forty years old, the son, I believe, of Mrs Trollope, to whom America owes more for her shrewd criticisms than we are ever likely to pay. Mr. Trollope is a very sensible and cultivated man, and, I suspect, an author; at least, there is a literary man of repute, of this name, though I have never read his works. He has resided in Florence, or other parts of Italy, eighteen years. It seems a pity to do this. It needs the native air to give life a reality; a truth which I do not fail to take home regretfully to myself, though without feeling much inclination to go back to the reality of my own. We had a pleasant cup of tea, and took a moonlight view of Florence from the balcony; and set out for home a little past ten.

[2nd 108] Florence, June 28th, Monday.

Yesterday afternoon, Julian and I went to a horse-race, which took place in the Corso and contiguous line of streets, in further celebration of the Feast of St. John. A considerable crowd of people was already collected, all along the line of the proposed race, as early as six °clock, and there were a great many carriages driving amid the throng, open barouches mostly, in which the beauty and gentility of Florence were freely displayed. It was a repetition of the scene in the Corso at Rome, at Carnival-time, without the masks, the fun, and the confetti. The Grand Duke and Duchess, and the Court, likewise made their appearance, in as many as seven or eight coaches-and-six, each with a coachman,—three footmen, and a postillion, in the royal-livery, and attended by a troop of horsemen in scarlet coats and cocked hats. I did not particularly notice the Grand Duke himself, but, in the carriage behind him, there sat only a lady, who favored the people along the street with a constant succession of bows, repeated at such short intervals and so quickly as to be little more than nods; therefore not particularly graceful or majestic. Having the good fortune to be favored with one of these nods, I lifted my hat in re[2nd 109]sponse, and may therefore claim a bowing acquaintance with the Grand Duchess. She is a Bourbon, of the Naples family, and seemed to be a pale, handsome woman, of princely aspect enough. The crowd evinced no enthusiasm nor the slightest feeling of any kind, in acknowledgement of the presence of their rulers; and indeed I think I never saw a crowd so well-behaved—that is, with so few salient points, so little ebullition, so absolutely tame—as this Florentine one. After all, and much contrary to my expectations, an American crowd has incomparably more life than any other; and meeting on any casual occasion, it will talk, laugh, roar, and be diversified with a thousand characteristic incidents, and gleams and shadows, that you see nothing of here. This people seems to have no part even in its own gatherings; it comes together merely as a mass of spectators, and must not so much as amuse itself by any activity of mind.

The race, which was the attraction that drew us all together, turned out a very pitiful affair. When we had waited till nearly dusk, the street being thronged quite across, insomuch that it seemed impossible that it should be cleared as a racecourse, there came sud[2nd 110]denly from every throat a quick, sharp exclamation, combining into a general roar. Immediately, the crowd pressed back on each side of the street; a moment afterwards, there was a rapid pattering of hoofs, over the earth with which the pavement was strewn, and I saw the head and back of a horse rushing past. A few seconds more, and another horse followed; and at another little interval, a third. This was all that we had waited for; all that I saw, or anybody else, except those who stood on the utmost verge of the course, at the risk of being trampled down and killed. Two men were killed in this way, on Thursday; and certainly human life was never spent for a poorer object. The spectators at the windows, to be sure, having the horses in sight for a longer time, might get a little more enjoyment out of the affair. By the by, the most picturesque aspect of the scene was the life given to it by the many faces, some of them fair ones, that looked out from window and balcony, all along the curving line of lofty palaces and edifices between which the racecourse lay; and from nearly every window, and over every balcony, was flung a silken texture, or cloth of brilliant hue, or piece of tapestry, or carpet, or whatever adornment of [2nd 111] the kind could be had, so as to dress up the street in gala-attire. But the Feast of St. John, like the Carnival, is but a meagre semblance of festivity, kept alive factitiously, and dying a lingering death of centuries. It takes the exuberant mind and heart of a people to keep its holidays alive.

I do not know whether there is any populace in Florence, but I saw none that I recognized as such, on this occasion. All the people were respectably dressed and perfectly well-behaved, and soldiers and priests were scattered abundantly among the throng. On my way home, I saw the Teatro Goldoni, which is in our street, lighted up for a representation on this Sunday evening. It shocked my New England prejudices a little.

This forenoon, Mamma and I went to the church of Santa Croce, the great monumental place of Florentine worthies. The piazza before it is a wide gravelled square, where the liberty of Florence (if it really ever had any genuine liberty) came into existence, some hundreds of years ago, by the people's taking its own rights into its hands, and putting its own immediate will into operation. The piazza has not much appearance of an[2nd 112]tiquity, except that the façade of one of the houses is quite covered with ancient frescoes, a good deal faded and obliterated, yet with traces enough of old glory to show that the colours must have been well laid on. The front of the church, the foundation of which was laid six centuries ago, is still waiting for its casing of marble, and I suppose will wait till Doomsday; though a carpenter's staging is now erected in front, as if with the purpose of doing something. The interior is spacious; the length of the church being between four and five hundred feet. There is a nave, roofed with wooden cross-beams, lighted by a clerestory, and supported on each side by seven great, pointed arches, which rest upon octagonal pillars. The octagon seems to be a favorite shape in Florence. These pillars were clad in yellow and scarlet damask, in honor of the Feast of St. John. The aisles, on each side of the nave, are lighted with high and somewhat narrow windows of painted glass, the effect of which, however, is much diminished by the flood of common daylight that comes in through the windows of the clerestory. It is like admitting too much of the light of reason and worldly intelligence into the mind, instead of illuminating it wholly through a [2nd 113] religious medium; the many-hued saints and angels lose their mysterious effulgence, when we get white light enough, and find we see all the better without their help.

The main pavement of the church is brickwork, but it is inlaid with many sepulchral slabs of marble, on some of which knightly or priestly figures are sculptured in bas-relief. In both of the side-aisles, there are saintly shrines, alternating with mural monuments, some of which record names as illustrious as any in the world. As you enter the church, the first monument in the aisle on your right is that of Michael Angelo, occupying the ancient burial site of his family. The general design is a heavy sarcophagus of colored marble, with the figures of Sculpture, Painting, and Architecture, as mourners, and Michael Angelo's bust above, the whole assuming a pyramidal form. You pass a shrine, within its frame-work of marble pillars and a pediment, and come next to Dante's monument, a modern work, with likewise its sarcophagus, and some huge, cold, images weeping and sprawling over it, and an unimpressive statue of Dante sitting above. Another shrine intervenes; and next you see the tomb of Alfieri, erected to his memory by the Countess of Albany, who pays, [114] out of a woman's love, the honor which his country owed him. Her own monument is in one of the chapels of the transept. Passing the next shrine, you see the tomb of Macchiavelli, which, I think, was constructed not many years after his death. The rest of the monuments, on this side of the church, commemorate people of less than world-wide fame; and though the opposite aisle has likewise a monument alternating with each shrine, I remember only the names of Raphael Morghen, and of Galileo. The tomb of the latter is right over against that of Michael Angelo, being the first large monument on the left-hand wall, as you enter the church. It has the usual heavy sarcophagus, surmounted by a bust of Galileo, in the habit of his time, and is of course duly provided with mourners, in the shape of Science, or Astronomy, or some such cold-hearted people. I wish every sculptor might be at once put to death, who shall hereafter chisel an allegoric figure; and as for those who have sculptured them heretofore, let them be kept in purgatory till the marble shall have crumbled away. It is especially absurd to assign to this frozen sisterhood of the Allegoric family the office of weeping for the dead, inasmuch as [115] they have incomparably less feeling than a lump of ice, which might contrive to shed a tear if the sun shone on it. But they seem to let themselves out, like the hired mourners at an English funeral, for the very reason that, having no interest in the dead person, nor any affections or emotions whatever, it costs them no wear and tear of heart.

All round both transepts of the church, there is a series of chapels, into most of which we went, and generally found an inscrutably dark picture over the altar, and often a marble bust or two, or perhaps a medi-æval statue of a saint, or a modern monumental bas-relief, in marble as white as new-fallen snow. A chapel of the Bonapartes is here, containing memorials of two female members of the family. In several of the chapels, moreover, there were some of those horrible frescoes by Giotto, Cimabue, or their compeers, which whenever I see—poor, faded relics, looking as if the devil had been rubbing and scrubbing them for centuries, in spite against the Saints—my heart sinks and my stomach sickens. There is no other despondency in the world like this; it is a new shade of human misery, akin

to the physical disease that comes from dry-rot in a wall. These
[116] frescoes are to a church what dreary, old remembrances
are to a mind, the drearier because they were once bright;
Hope fading into Disappointment, Joy into Grief, and festal
splendor passing into funereal duskiness, and saddening you all
the more by the grim identity that you find to exist between
gay things and sorrowful ones. Only wait long enough, and
they turn out to be the very same.

All the time we were in the church some great religious ceremony had been going forward; the organ playing (finely, my
wife said,) and the white-robed priest bowing, gesticulating,
and making Latin prayers at the High Altar, where at least a
hundred wax-tapers were burning in constellations. Everybody
knelt, except ourselves, yet seemed not to be troubled by the
echoes of our passing footsteps, nor to require that we should
pray along with them. They consider us already damned ir-
revocably, no doubt, and therefore right enough in taking no
heed of their devotions; not but what we take so much heed as
to give the smallest possible disturbance. By and by, we sat
down in the nave of the church, till the Ceremony should be
concluded; and then my wife left me to go in quest of yet another chapel, where either Giotto or Cimabue, or both, [117]
have left some of their ghastly decorations. While she was
gone, I threw my eyes about the church, and came to the conclusion, that—in spite of its antiquity, its size, its architecture,
its painted windows, its tombs of great men, and all the reverence and interest that broods over them—it is not an impressive edifice. Any little Norman church in England would
impress me as much, or more. There is something—I do not
know what, but it is in the region of the heart rather than the
intellect—that Italian architecture, of whatever age or style
never seems to reach.

Leaving the church, we went next (skirting along the shady
margins of the piazzas, and taking narrow streets in preference,

but now and then forced to pass through fiery sunshine,) in quest of the Riccardi palace. On our way, in the rear of the Grand Ducal piazza, we passed by the Bargello, formerly the palace of the Podestá of Florence, and now converted into a prison. It is an immense, square edifice of dark stone, with a tall, lank tower rising high above it, at one corner. Two stone lions, symbols of the city, lash their tails and glare at the pass-ers-by; and all over the front of the building windows are scattered irregularly, and grated with rusty iron bars; also, there are many square holes, which [118] probably admit a little light and a breath or two of air into prisoners' cells. It is a very ugly edifice, but looks antique, and as if a vast deal of history might have been transacted within it, or have beaten like fierce blasts against its dark, massive walls, since the thirteenth century. When I first saw the city, it struck me that there were few marks of antiquity in Florence; but I am now inclined to think otherwise, although the bright Italian atmosphere, and the general squareness and monotony of Italian architecture, have their effect in apparently modernizing everything. But everywhere we see the ponderous Tuscan basements, that never can decay, and which will look five hundred years hence as they look now; and one often passes beneath an abbreviated remnant of what was once a lofty tower, perhaps three hundred feet high, such as used to be numerous in Florence, when each noble of the city had his own warfare to wage; and there are patches of sculpture that look old on houses, the modern stucco of which causes them to look almost new. Here and there, an unmistakeable antiquity stands in its own impressive shadow; the Church of Or' St. Michel, for instance, once a market, but which grew to be a church by some [119] inherent fitness and inevitable consecration, the story of which I forget. It has not in the least the aspect of a church, being high and square like a mediæval palace; but deep and wide niches are let into its walls; within which stand great statues of Saints by Donatello and other sculptors of that age, before sculpture began to be congealed by the influence of Greek art.

The Riccardi palace stands at the corner of the Via Larga and another narrower street. It was built by the first Cosmo de Medici, the old Banker, more than four centuries ago, and was long the home of the good-for-nothing race of princes which he left behind him. It looks still fit to be the home of a princely race, being nowise dilapidated or decayed, externally, nor likely to be so; its high Tuscan basement being as solid as a ledge of rock, and its upper portion not much less so, though smoothed into another order of stately architecture. Entering its court-yard, from the Via Larga, we found ourselves beneath a pillared arcade, passing round the court like a cloister; and on the walls of the palace, under this succession of arches, were statues, bas-reliefs, and sarcophagi in which first dead pagans had slept, and then dead Christians, before their sculptured coffins were brought [120] hither to adorn the palace of the Medicis. In the most prominent place was a Latin inscription, of great length and breadth, chiefly in praise of old Cosmo, and his deeds and wisdom. This mansion, indeed, gives the visitor a stately notion of the life of a commercial man, in the days when merchants were princes; not that it seems to be so wonderfully extensive, nor so very grand, for I suppose there are a dozen Roman palaces that excel it in both these particulars. Still we cannot but be conscious that it must have been, in some sense, a great man who thought of founding a homestead like this, and was capable of filling it with his personality, as the hand fills a glove. It has been found spacious enough, since Cosmo's time, for an Emperor, a Pope, and a King, all of whom have been guests in the house. After being the family mansion of the Medicis for nearly two centuries, it was sold to the Riccardis, but was subsequently bought of them by the Government, and is now occupied by public offices and societies.

After sufficiently examining the court and its antiquities,

we ascended a noble staircase that passes, by broad flights and square turns, to the region above the basement. Here, the [121] palace seems to be cut up and portioned off into little rooms and passages, and everywhere there were desks, inkstands, and men with pens in their fingers or behind their ears. We were shown into a little antique chapel, quite covered with frescoes of the Giotto and Cimabue style, but painted by a certain Gozzoli. They were in pretty good preservation; and, in fact, I am wrong in comparing them to Giotto's works, inasmuch as there must have been nearly two hundred years between the two artists. However, I care almost as little for one as the other. The chapel was furnished with curiously carved old chairs, and looked surprisingly venerable within its little precinct. We were next shown into what is called the grand gallery, a hall of respectable size, with a frescoed cieling, on which is represented the blue sky, and various members of the Medici family ascending through it, by the help of angelic personages, who seem only to have waited for their society in order to be perfectly happy. At least, this was the meaning, so far as I could make it out. Along one side of the gallery were oil-pictures on looking-glass, rather good than otherwise; but Rome, with her palaces and villas, takes the shine out of all this sort of thing.

[122] On our way home, and on our own side of the Ponte Vecchio, we passed (in the street leading to the Pitti Palace) the Palazzo Guicciardini, the ancient residence of the historian of Italy, who was a politic statesman of his day, and probably as cruel and unprincipled as any of those whose deeds he has recorded. Right opposite, across the narrow way, stands the house of Macchiavelli, who was his friend, and, I should judge, an honester man than he. The house is distinguished by a marble tablet, let into the wall, commemorative of Macchiavelli, but has nothing antique or picturesque about it, being in a contiguous line with other smooth-fronted and stuccoed edifices.

Florence, June 30th Wednesday.

Yesterday, at 6 °clock, P. M., I went to see the final horse-race of the Feast of St John; or rather to see the concourse of people and grandees whom it brought together. I took my stand in the vicinity of the spot whence the Grand Duke and his courtiers view the race; and from this point the scene was rather better worth looking at than from the street-corners whence I saw it before. The vista of the street, stretching far adown between two rows of lofty edifices, was really gay and gorgeous with the silks, damasks, and tapestries, of all bright hues, that flaunted from windows and [123] balconies, whence ladies looked forth and looked down, themselves making the liveliest part of the show. The whole capacity of the street swarmed with moving heads, leaving scarce room enough for the carriages which, as on Sunday, passed up and down, until the signal for the race was given. Equipages, too, were constantly arriving at the door of the building which communicates with the open loggia where the Grand Ducal party sit to see and be seen. Two sentinels were standing at the door, and presented arms as each courtier or ambassador, or whatever dignity it might be, alighted. Most of them had on gold embroidered court-dresses; some of them had military uniforms, and medals in abundance at the breast; and ladies also came, looking like heaps of lace and gauze in the carriages, but lightly shaking themselves into shape as they went up the steps. By-and-by, a trumpet sounded, a drum-beat, and again appeared a succession of half-a dozen royal equipages, each with its six-horses, its postillion, coachman, and three footmen, grand with cocked hats and embroidery, and the grey-headed, bowing Grand Duke, and his nodding Grand Duchess, as before. The Noble Guard ranged themselves on horseback, opposite the loggia;

but there was no irk[124]some and impertinent show of ceremony and restraint upon the people. The play-guard of volunteer-soldiers, who escort the President of the United States in his northern progresses, keep back their fellow citizens much more sternly and immitigably, than the Florentine populace was kept back from its despotic sovereign.

This morning, Julian and I have been to the Uffizzi Gallery. It was his first visit there, and I believe he passed a sweeping condemnation upon everything he saw, except a fly, a snail-shell, a caterpillar, a lemon, a piece of bread, and a wine-glass, in some of the Dutch pictures. The Venus de Medici met with no sort of favour. His feeling of utter distaste re-acted upon me, and I was sensible of the same weary lack of appreciation that used to chill me through and through, in my earlier visits to picture-galleries; the same doubt, moreover, whether we do not bamboozle ourselves in the greater part of the admiration which we learn to bestow. I looked with some pleasure, however, at one of Raphael's Madonnas, in the Tribune; no divine and deep-thoughted mother of the Savior, but a young woman playing with her [125] first child, as gay and thoughtless as it itself. I looked at Michel Angelo's Madonna, in which William Ware saw such prophetic depth of feeling; but I suspect it was one of the many instances in which the spectator sees more than the painter ever dreamed of.

Straying through the city, after leaving the gallery, we went into the church of Or' St. Michele, and saw in its architecture the traces of its transformation from a market into a church. In its pristine state, it consisted of a double row of three great open arches, with the wind blowing through them, and the sunshine falling aslantwise into them, while the bustle of the market, the sale of fish, flesh, or fruit, went on within them, or brimmed over into the streets that enclosed them on every side. But, four or five hundred years ago, the broad arches were built up with stonework,—windows were pierced through, and filled with painted glass; a high-altar, in a rich style of pointed Gothic, was raised; shrines and confessionals were set up; and here it is, a solemn and antique church, where a man may buy his salvation instead of his dinner. At any rate the Catholic priests will insure it to him, and take the price. The sculpture, within the [126] beautifully decorated niches, on the outside of this church, is very curious and interesting. The statues of those old Saints seem to me to have that charm of earnestness which so attracts the admirers of the pre-Raphaelite painters.

It appears that a picture of the Virgin used to hang against one of the pillars of the market-place, while it was still a market; and in the year 1291, several miracles were wrought by its efficacy, insomuch that a Chapel was consecrated there. So many worshippers came to the shrine that the business of the market was impeded, and ultimately the Virgin and St. Michael won the whole space for themselves. The upper part of the edifice was at that time a granary, and is still used for other than religious purposes. This church was a spot to which the inhabitants betook themselves much for refuge and divine assistance during Boccaccio's great plague.

Florence, July 2ᵈ, Friday.

Mamma, Una, I, set out, yesterday morning, to visit the Palazzo Buonarotti, Michael Angelo's ancestral home. After much wandering through the hot sunshine and narrow shade, and after resting awhile in the cool church of Santa Croce, and after going through a street of tanners (where we saw a man almost as naked as the Apollo Belvidere) we came to the house, in the [127] Via Ghibellina. It is an ordinary-looking, three-story house, with broad-brimmed eaves, a stuccoed front, and two or three windows painted in fresco, besides the real ones. Adown the street, there is a glimpse of the hills outside of Florence. The sun shining heavily right down upon the front of the house, we rang the door bell, and then drew back into the shadow that fell from the opposite side of the street. After we had waited some time, a man looked out from an upper window, and a woman from a lower one, and informed us that we could not be admitted now, nor for two or three months to come; the house being under repairs. It is a pity; for I wanted to see Michael Angelo's sword, and walking-sticks, and old slippers, and whatever other of his closest little personalities are to be seen.

We came back towards the Grand Ducal Piazza, and, on our way, looked into the court-yard of the Bargello, where we saw a venerable stone-staircase, with a heavy balustrade, ascending in the open air. The four walls of the ancient edifice, looking into this court, were sculptured with escutcheons, and black with age; the sun of Italy could not make them bright. A sentinel stood in the arched gateway, and others were lounging near; but they could not tell us whether anything was seen within, nor whether we could have ad[128]mittance, nor, in fact, whether the Bargello is a palace or a prison. This has always been our experience with soldiers, in Rome and elsewhere; they never know even the name and character of the place where they are standing guard. Possibly, they are forbidden to make communications to strangers; but I rather take it to be sheer, genuine ignorance and sluggishness of mind.

We passed into the Piazza of the Grand Duke, and looked into the court of the Palazzo Vecchio, with its beautifully embossed pillars; and seeing, just beyond the court, a staircase of broad and easy steps, we ascended it at a venture. We saw people going up, and coming down, and inquired of one of them whether we could be permitted to see the palace. He pointed upward; and upward we went, flight after flight of stairs, and through passages, and peeping into doorways, till at last we found an official who showed us into a large saloon. He told us

it was the Hall of Audience. Its heavily embossed cieling, rich
with tarnished gold, was a feature of antique magnificence, and
the only one, I think, that it retained; the floor being paved
with brick, and the furniture scanty or none. There were, however, three cabinets, standing against the wall, two of which
contained very curious and exquisite car[1st 129]vings and cut-
tings in ivory; some of them in the Chinese style of hollow,
concentric balls; others, really beautiful works of art, little crucifixes, statues, saintly and knightly, and cups, enriched with
delicate bas-reliefs. The Custode pointed to a little figure of
St Sebastian, and also to a vase, around which the bas-reliefs
seemed to assume life. Both these specimens, he said, were by
Benvenuto Cellini; and there were many others that might
well have been wrought by his famous hand. The third cabinet
contained a great number and variety of crucifixes, chalices,
and whatever other vessels are needed in altar-service, exquisitely carved out of amber. They belong to the chapel of the
Palace; and into this holy closet we were now shown. It is large
enough to accommodate comfortably perhaps thirty worshippers, and is quite covered with frescoes by Ghirlandajo, in good
preservation, and with remnants enough of gilding and bright
color to show how splendid the chapel must have been, when
the Medicean Grand Dukes used to pray here. The altar is still
ready for service, and I am not sure that some of the wax tapers
were not burning; but Lorenzo the Magnificent was nowhere
to be seen.

The Custode now led us back through the Hall of [2nd 129]
Audience, and along some passages, hung with pictures chiefly
of the Medici and their connections, among whom I remember
the famous Catherine, an intelligent and pretty little girl.
There was nothing else to show us, except the great hall of the
palace, which we saw first from a stone gallery above, and afterwards from its brick pavement. It is a very noble and most
spacious hall, lighted by two large windows at each end, com-

ing down level with the floor, and by a row of windows on all sides, just beneath the cornice. A gilded frame-work divides the cieling into squares, circles, and octagons, the compartments of which are filled with pictures in oil; and the walls are covered with immense frescoes, representing various battles and triumphs of the Florentines. Statues, by Michael Angelo, John of Bologna, and Bandinello, as well historic as ideal, stand round the hall; and it is really a fit theatre for the historic scenes of a country to be acted in. It was built, moreover, with the idea of its being the council-hall of a free people; but our own little Faneuil—which was meant, in all simplicity, to be merely a spot where the townspeople should meet to choose their select-men—but served the world better in that respect. I wish I had room to speak more of this vast, dusky, historic hall.

VI

[1] Florence, July 4th, 1858. Sunday.

YESTERDAY forenoon, my wife and I went to see the church of Santa Maria Novella. We found the Piazza, on one side of which the church stands, still encumbered with the amphitheatrical ranges of wooden seats, that had been erected to accommodate the spectators of the chariot-races, at the recent feast of St John. The front of the church is composed of black and white marble, which, in the five centuries that it has stood there, has turned brown and yellow. There is a broad flight of steps along the whole façade; and on the right hand, as you approach, is a long colonnade of arches, extending on a line with the front, and having a tomb beneath every arch. This colonnade, I believe, forms one of the enclosing walls of a cloister. We found none of the three entrances in the façade of the church open; but, on our left, in a wall at right angles with the church, there was an open gateway, approaching which, we saw within the four-sided colonnade and enclosed green space of a cloister. This is what is called the Chiostro [2] Verde: so named from the prevailing color of the frescoes with which the walls, beneath the arched walk, are adorned.

This Cloister is the reality of what I used to imagine, when I saw the half-ruinous colonnades connected with English cathedrals, or endeavored to trace out lines along the broken wall of some old abbey. Not that the extant cloister, still perfect, and in daily use for its original purposes, is nearly so beautiful as the crumbling ruin, which has ceased to be trodden by monkish feet for more than three centuries. This cloister of Santa Maria has not the seclusion that seems desirable, being open by its gateway, as I have said, to the public square; and several of the neighbors, women as well as men, appeared to be loitering within its precincts. The Convent, however, has another and larger cloister, which I suppose is kept free from interlopers. The Chiostro Verde is a walk round the four sides of a square, beneath an arched and groined roof; one side of the walk looks upon an enclosed green space, with either a fountain or a tomb, I forget which, in the centre; the other side is orna[3]mented all along with a succession of ancient frescoes, representing subjects of scripture-history. These were painted about the year 1348, by Uccello and some other artist, and are of a sort of uniform brownish tint (that was once green) on a dark red ground. In the days when the designs were more distinct than now, it must have been a very effective way for a monk to read bible-history, to see its personages and events thus passing visibly beside him in his morning and evening walks. Beneath the frescoes, on one side of the cloistered walk, and along the low stone fence that separates it from the grass-plat, on the other, are inscriptions to the memory of the dead, who are buried underneath the pavement. Most of these appeared to be modern, and recorded the names of persons of no particular note. Older monumental slabs were inlaid with the pavement itself. Two or three Dominican monks, belonging to the convent, passed in and out of this cloister, while we were there, in their white habits.

We went round three sides of the cloister, and [4] coming to the side formed by the wall of the church, we heard the voice of a priest behind a curtain that fell down before a door. Lift-

ing it aside, we went in, and found ourselves in the ancient
Chapter House, a large interior formed by two great pointed
arches, crossing one another in a groined roof. The broad spaces
of the walls were entirely covered with frescoes, that are rich
even now, and must have glowed with inexpressible splendor,
when fresh from the artist's hand, five hundred years ago.
There is a long period during which frescoes illuminate a
church or a hall, in a way that no other adornment can; when
that epoch of brightness is past, they become the dreariest ghosts
of perished magnificence. I could not make out the subjects of
any of these pictures, except that of the one on the wall around
the high altar; this was the crucifixion, as large as life, and with
the Savior's cross elevated high over that of the two thieves.
This Chapter House seems to be the only part of the church
that is now used for the purposes of public worship. There
were several confessionals, and two [5] chapels or shrines, each
with its lighted tapers. A priest performed mass while we were
there; and several persons, as usual, stept in to do a little devotion, either praying on their own account, or joining in with
the ceremony that was going forward. One man was followed
by two little dogs; and in the midst of his prayers, as one of the
dogs was inclined to stray about the church, he kept snapping
his fingers to call him back. The cool, dusky refreshment of
these holy places, affording such a refuge from the hot noon
of the streets and piazzas, probably suggests devotional ideas to
the people; and it may be, when they are praying, they feel a
breath of Paradise fanning them. If we could only see any
good effects in their daily life, we might deem it an excellent
thing to be able to find incense and a prayer always ascending, to which every individual may join his own. I really
wonder that the Catholics are not better men and women.

When we had looked at the old frescoes, as well as the
scanty light would permit, and rested [6] ourselves, we emerged
into the cloister again, and thence ventured into a passage,

which I suspect would have led us into the Chiostro Grande, where strangers, and especially ladies, have no right to come. It was a secluded corridor, very neatly kept, and with a cheerful aspect enough, though bordered with sepulchral monuments; and at the end appeared a vista of cypress-trees, which indeed was but an illusory perspective, being painted in fresco. While we loitered along, looking at the busts and other sculptures upon the tomb-stones, the Sacristan or some such official (he was not a monk, but in lay-garments) appeared, and offered to show us the church. We consented; and he led us into the transept, on the right of the high altar, and ushered us into the Sacristy, where we found two artists, copying some of Fra Angelico's pictures. These were painted on the three wooden leaves of a triptyche, and, as usual, were glorified with a great deal of gilding, so that they seemed to float in the brightness of a heavenly element. Solomon speaks of "apples of gold in pictures of silver." The pictures of Fra [7] Angelico, and other artists of that age, are really pictures of gold; and it is wonderful to see how rich the effect, and how much delicate beauty is attained (by Fra Angelico, at least,) along with it. His miniature heads appear to me much more successful than his larger ones. In a monkish point of view, however, the chief value of the triptyche, of which I am speaking, does not lie in Fra Angelico's pictures; for they merely serve as the frame-work of some reliques, which are set all round the edges of the three leaves. They consist of little bits and fragments of bones, and of little packages carefully tied up in silk, the contents of which are signified in Gothic letters, appended to each parcel. I could not possibly make out what they were. The sacred vessels of the church are likewise kept in the sacristy, and there are several pictures, which did not look very interesting, and a great black crucifix over the entrance-door; but I forget whether it was the one carved by Brunelleschi, or by Donatello, or either of them.

Re-entering the transept, our guide showed us [8] the
Chapel of the Strozzi family, which is accessible by a flight of
steps from the floor of the church. The walls of this chapel are
covered with frescoes by Orgagna, representing, around the altar, the Last Judgment, and, on one of the walls, Heaven and
the assembly of the Blessed, and on the other, of course, Hell.
I cannot speak as to the truth of representation; but, at all
events, it was purgatory to look at this poor, faded rubbish.
Thank Heaven, there is such a thing as white-wash; and I shall
always be glad to hear of its application to old frescoes, even
at the sacrifice of remnants of real excellence. We passed next
into the choir, which occupies the extreme end of the church,
behind the great, square mass of the high altar, and is surrounded with a double row of ancient oaken seats, of venerable
shape and carving. The choir is illuminated by a threefold
Gothic window, full of richly painted glass, worth all the frescoes that ever stained a wall or cieling; but these walls, nevertheless, are adorned with frescoes by Ghirlandaio, and, it is easy
to see, must once have made a magnificent appearance. There
is a [9] tradition that Michael Angelo had a hand in them. I
really was sensible of a sad and ghostly beauty in many of the
figures; but all the bloom and grace, the magic of the painter's
touch, his topmost art, have long ago been rubbed off; the whi-
plaister shows through the colours in spots and even in large
spaces. It is time that the whole should vanish. Any other sort
of ruin acquires a beauty, proper to its decay, and often superior
to that of its pristine state, but the ruin of a picture, especially
of a frescoe, is wholly unredeemed; and, moreover, it dies out
so slowly that many generations are likely to be saddened by it.

We next saw the famous picture of the Virgin, by Cimabue,
which was deemed a miracle in its day, being a step in advance
of all that had thitherto been known in the pictorial art. The
picture was brought to the church in triumphal procession, in
which all Florence joined; and here it has hung, in the Chapel

of the Rucellai family, for five centuries, and still brightens the sombre walls with the lustre of its gold ground. As for its artistic merits, [10] it seemed to me that the Babe Jesus had a certain air of state and dignity, but I could see no charm whatever in the broad-faced Virgin; and it would relieve my mind and rejoice my spirit, if the picture were borne out of the church, in another triumphal procession, and reverently burnt. This should be the final honour, paid to all human works that have served a good office in their day; for, when their day is over, if still galvanized into false life, they do harm instead of good.

I remember little or nothing else in the church of Santa Maria Novella. Its interior is spacious, and in the Gothic style, though differing considerably from English churches of that architecture. Apparently, it is not now kept open to the public, nor were any of the shrines and chapels, nor even the high altar itself, adorned and lighted for worship. The pictures, or whatever else had decorated the shrines along the side-aisles, have been removed, leaving bare, blank spaces of brick-work, very dreary and desolate to behold. Upon my word, this is almost worse than a [11] black oil-painting or faded frescoe. The church was much injured by the French, and afterwards by the Austrians, both of which powers, I believe, quartered their troops within the holy precincts. Its old walls, however, are yet stalwart enough to outlast another set of frescoes, and to see the beginning and the end of a new school of painting, as long-lived as Cimabue's. I should be sorry to have the church go to decay, because it was here that Boccaccio's dames and cavaliers encountered one another, and formed their plan of retreating into the country during the plague. When we had seen all, we emerged again into the Chiostro Verde. A man was sitting by the door, under the shelter of the cloister, selling rosaries, crucifixes, (some of which, he said, came from the Holy Land) and

little books of devotion; and we bought a string of beads, with
a small gilt crucifix appended, in memory of Santa Maria Novella. The beads seem to be made of a grayish, pear-shaped
seed; and the seller assured us that they were the tears of Saint
Job. They were cheap, [12] probably because Job shed so many
tears in his lifetime; the price being only a Paul.

It being still early in the day, we went to the Uffizzi Gallery,
and after loitering a good while among the pictures, were so
fortunate as to find the rooms of the Bronzes open. Usually, I
believe, admittance can be obtained only by special permission.
The first object that attracted us was John of Bologna's Mercury, poising himself on his toes, and looking not merely buoyant enough to float, but as if he possessed more than an eagle's
power of lofty flight. It seems a wonder that he did not absolutely fling himself into the air, when the artist gave him the
last touch. No bolder work was ever achieved; nothing so full
of life has been done since. I was much interested, too, in the
original little wax model (about two feet high) of Benvenuto
Cellini's Perseus. The wax seems to be laid over a wooden
frame-work, and is but roughly finished off. There is a shield
and helmet, highly decorated, supposed to have been made for
Francis I.; and a great many other things worthy of minute
in[13]spection, including bronze copies (looking as unworn as
a new copper-kettle) of the Wrestlers, the Knife-sharpener, and
the Venus de Medici. In an adjoining room, are innumerable
specimens of Roman and Etruscan bronzes, great and small. A
bronze Chimera did not strike me as very ingeniously conceived, the goat's head being merely an adjunct, growing out
of the back of the monster, without possessing any original and
substantive share in its nature. The snake's head was at the end
of the tail. The article most really interesting was a Roman
eagle, the standard of the Twenty-fourth Legion, about as big
as a blackbird.

Florence, July 8th, Thursday.

My wife and I went on Tuesday to the church of the Annunziata, which stands in the Piazza of the same name. On the
corner of the Via dei Servi, by which we entered the Piazza,
stands the palace which I suppose to have been the one which
Browning makes the scene of his poem, "The Statue and the
Bust"; and the Statue of Duke Ferdinand sits stately [14] on
horseback, with the face turned towards the window where the
lady ought to appear. Neither she nor her bust, however, was
visible; at least not to my eyes. The church occupies one side
of the Piazza; and in front of it, as likewise on the two adjoining sides of the square, there are pillared arcades, constructed
by Brunelleschi or some of his scholars. After passing through
these arches, and still before entering the church itself, you
come to an ancient cloister, which is now quite enclosed in
glass as a means of preserving some frescoes of Andrea del
Sarto and others, which are considered valuable.—Peeping at
them through the glass, I did not find them much more attractive than frescoes generally are; rather better than Giotto's, to
be sure, but not quite so good as a plain white wall.

Passing the threshold of the church, we were quite dazzled
by the splendor that shone upon us from the cieling of the
nave, the great parallelogram of which, viewed from one end,
looks as if it were richly embossed all over with gold. The
whole [15] interior, indeed, has an effect of brightness, and
magnificence; the walls being covered mostly with white, or
light-colored marble, into which are inlaid compartments of
rarer and richer marbles. The pillars and pilasters, too, are of
variegated marble, with corinthian capitals that shine just as
brightly as if they were of solid gold; so faithfully have they
been gilded and burnished. The pavement is laid in squares

of black and white marble. There are no side-aisles; but ranges of chapels, with communication from one to another, stand round the whole extent of the nave and choir; all in marble; all decorated with pictures, statues, busts, and mural monuments; all worth separately a day's inspection. The high-altar is of great beauty and richness; but its particular design and architecture has escaped my memory; and, indeed I remember nothing distinctly, in that quarter, except seeing the tomb of John of Bologna, in a chapel at the remotest extremity of the church. In his chapel there are some bas-reliefs by him, and also a large [16] black crucifix with a marble Christ upon it; and John of Bologna's memorial-slab, with an inscription, is built into the wall beneath. I think there has been no better sculptor since the days of Phidias. The tomb of the sculptor Bandinelli, whose quarrels with Benvenuto Cellini make him rather interesting, is in another chapel; but I had forgotten the fact, and did not look particularly for his monument.

This church was founded in 1233, by seven gentlemen of Florence who formed themselves into a religious order called "Servants of Mary." Many miraculous cures were wrought here; and the church, in consequence, was so thickly hung with votive offerings of legs, arms, and such things, in wax, that they used to tumble upon people's heads; so that, finally, they were all cleared out as rubbish. The church is still, I should imagine, looked upon as a place of peculiar sanctity; for, while we were there, it had an unusual number of kneeling worshippers, and persons were passing from shrine to shrine, all round the nave and choir, praying awhile at each, and thus performing a [17] pilgrimage at little cost of time and shoe-leather. One old gentleman, I observed, carried a cushion or pad, just big enough for one knee, on which he carefully adjusted his genuflections before each altar. An old woman in the choir prayed alternately to us and to the saints—with most success, I hope, in her petitions to the latter, though certainly her prayers to ourselves seemed the more fervent of the two.

When we had gone entirely round the church, we came at last to the Chapel of the Annunziata, which stands on the floor of the nave, on the left hand as we enter. It is a very beautiful piece of architecture, a sort of canopy of marble supported upon pillars; and its magnificence within, in marble, and silver, and all manner of holy decoration, is quite indescribable. It was built four hundred years ago, by Pietro de Medici, and has probably been growing richer ever since. The altar is entirely overlaid with silver, richly embossed. As many people were kneeling on the steps, before it, as could find room; and most of [18] them, when they finished their prayers, ascended the steps, kissed over and over again the margin of the silver altar, laid their foreheads upon it, and then deposited an offering in a box placed upon the altar's top. From the dullness of the chink, in the only case when I heard it, I judged it to be a small copper-coin. In the inner part of this chapel is preserved a miraculous picture of the Annunciation, painted by angels, and held in such holy repute that forty thousand dollars have lately been expended in providing a new crown for the sacred personage represented. The picture is now veiled behind a curtain; and, as it is a fresco, and is not considered to do much credit to the angelic artists, I was well contented not to see it.

We found a side-door of the church, admitting us into the great cloister, which has a walk of intersecting arches round its four sides, paved with flat tomb-stones, and broad enough for six people to walk abreast. On the walls, in the semicircle of each successive arch, are frescoes, representing incidents in the lives of the Seven Founders of the church; [19] and all the lower part of the wall is incrusted with marble inscriptions to the memory of the dead, and mostly of persons who have died not very long ago. The space enclosed by the cloistered walk (usually made cheerful by green grass) has a pavement of tombstones, laid in regular ranges. In the centre is a stone octagonal monument, which I at first supposed to be the tomb of some deceased mediæval personage; but, on approaching, I found it a well, with its bucket hanging within the curb, and looking as if it were in constant use. The surface of the water lay deep beneath the deepest dust of the dead people, and thence threw up its picture of the sky; but I think it would not be a moderate thirst that would induce me to drink of that well.

On leaving the church, we bought a little gilt crucifix of a woman who kept one of several stalls, under the porch, for the sale of such things.

On Sunday evening, I paid a short visit to [20] Mr. Powers, and, as usual, was entertained and instructed with his conversation. It did not, indeed, turn upon artistical subjects; but the artistic is only one side of his character, and, I think, not the principal side. I agree with his wife in thinking that he might have achieved more valuable success as an engineer and mechanician, than as a sculptor. He gave a dissertation on flying-machines, evidently from his own experience, and came to the conclusion that it is impossible to fly by means of steam or any other motive power now known to man. No force, hitherto attained, would suffice to lift the engine which generates it. He appears to anticipate that flying will be a future mode of locomotion, but not till the moral condition of mankind is so improved as to obviate the bad uses to which the power might be applied. Another topic discussed was a cure for complaints of the chest, by the inhalation of nitric acid; and he produced his own apparatus for that purpose, being merely a tube inserted into a bottle contain[21]ing a small quantity of the acid, just enough to generate the gas for inhalation. He told me, too, a remedy for burns, accidentally discovered by himself;—viz. to wear a wash leather glove, or something equivalent, over the burn, and keep it constantly wet. It prevents all pain, and cures by the exclusion of the air. He evidently has a great tendency to empirical remedies, and would have made a natural Doctor, of mighty potency, possessing the shrewd sense, inventive faculty, and self-reliance, that such persons require. It is very singular that there should be an ideal vein in a man of this character. This morning, he called to see me, with intelligence of the failure of the new attempt to lay the electric cable between England and America; and here, too, it appears, the misfortune might have been avoided if a plan of his own for laying the cable had been adopted. He explained his process, and made it seem as practicable as to put up a bell-wire. I do not remember how or why (but [22] appositely) he repeated some verses from a pretty little ballad about Fairies, that had struck his fancy; and he wound up his talk with some acute observations on the characters of General Jackson and other public men. He told an anecdote, illustrating the old General's little acquaintance with astronomical science, and his force of will in compelling a whole dinner-party of better instructed people to knock under to him, in an argument about eclipses, and the planetary system generally. Powers witnessed the scene himself. He thinks that General Jackson was a man of the keenest and surest intuitions, in respect to men and measures, but with no power of reasoning out his own conclusions, or of imparting them intellectually to other men. Men who have known Jackson intimately, and in great affairs, would not agree as to this intellectual and argumentative deficiency, though they would fully allow the intuitive faculty. I have heard General Pierce tell a striking instance of Jackson's power of presenting his own view of a subject, with irre[23]sistible force, to the mind of his auditor. President Buchanan has likewise expressed to

me as high admiration of Jackson as I ever heard one man
award to another. Surely, he was the greatest man we ever had;
and his native strength, as well of intellect as character, compelled every man to be his tool that came within his reach; and
the cunninger the individual might be, it served only to make
him the sharper tool.

Speaking of Jackson, and remembering Raphael's picture
of Pope Julius II.—the best portrait in the whole world, and
excellent in all its repetitions—I wish it had been possible for
Raphael to paint General Jackson!

Referring again to General Jackson's intuitions, and to
Powers' idea that he was unable to render a reason to himself
or others for what he chose to do, I should have thought that
this might very probably be the case, were there not such
strong evidence to the contrary. The highest, or perhaps any
high, administrative ability is intuitive, and precedes argument,
and [24] rises above it. It is a revelation of the very thing to
be done; and its propriety and necessity are felt so strongly,
that, ten to one, it cannot be talked about; if the doer can
likewise talk, it is an additional and gratuitous faculty, as
little to be expected as that a poet should be able to write an
explanatory criticism on his own poem. The English overlook
this, in their scheme of government, which requires that the
members of the national executive should be orators, and the
readiest and most fluent orators that can be had. The very fact
(on which they are selected) that they are men of words, makes
it improbable that they are likewise men of deed. And it is only
tradition and old custom, founded on an obsolete state of
things, that assigns any value to parliamentary oratory; the
world has done with it, except as an intellectual pastime. The
speeches have no effect till they are converted into newspaper
paragraphs; and they had better be composed as such, in the
first place, and oratory reserved for churches, courts of law,
and public dinner-tables.

[25] Florence, July 10th, Saturday.

My wife and I went, yesterday forenoon, to see the church
of San Marco, with which is connected a Convent of Dominicans. I quite forget what is the architectural character of the
façade; it is not of older date, however, than the latter half of
the last century, though the interior of the church is not less
than three or four hundred years old. It is in the classic style,
with a flat cieling, gilded, and a lofty arch, supported by pillars,
between the nave and choir. There are no side-aisles, but ranges
of shrines on both sides of the nave, each beneath its own pair
of pillars and pediments. The pavement is of brick, with here
and there a marble tomb-stone inlaid. It is not a magnificent
church, but looks dingy with time and apparent neglect,
though rendered sufficiently interesting by statues of mediæval
date, by John of Bologna and other old sculptors, and by monumental busts and bas-reliefs; also, there is an old wooden
crucifix by Giotto, with ancient gilding on it, and a painting
of Christ, which [26] was considered a wonderful work in its
day. Each shrine—or most of them, at any rate—has its dark
old picture, and there is a very ancient and hideous mosaic of
the Virgin and two saints, which I looked at very slightly, with
the purpose of immediately forgetting it. Savonarola, the reforming monk, was a brother of this convent, and was torn
from its shelter in 1498, to be subsequently hanged and burnt
in the Grand Ducal piazza. A large chapel in the left transept
is now dedicated to him; no, this is a foolish mistake, the chapel
being of the Salviati family, and dedicated to St Anthony. Be
it whose it may, the chapel is decorated with several statues
of Saints, and with some old frescoes, not less dreary and disheartening than other works of the same class. When we had
more than sufficiently examined these, the Custode of the
church proposed to show us some frescoes by Fra Angelico,

and conducted us into a large cloister, under the arches of which, and beneath a covering of glass, he pointed to a picture of St Dominic kneeling at the cross. There are two or three other frescoes by Fra Angelico, in differ[27]ent parts of the cloister, and a regular series, filling up all the arches, by other artists. The four-sided, cloistered walk, surrounds a square, open to the sky, as usual, and paved with gray stones that seem to have no inscriptions, but probably are laid over graves. The walls, however, are incrusted, and the walk itself is paved, with monumental inscriptions on marble, none of which, so far as I observed, were of ancient date. Either the fashion of thus commemorating the dead is not ancient in Florence, or the old tomb-stones have been removed to make room for new ones. I do not know where the monks themselves have their burial place; perhaps in an inner cloister, which we did not see. All the inscriptions, here, I believe, were in memory of persons not connected with the Convent.

A door in the wall of the Cloister admitted us into the Chapter House, an interior moderately spacious, with a roof formed by intersecting arches. Three sides of the walls were covered with blessed white-wash; but on the fourth [28] side, opposite the entrance, was a great frescoe of the Crucifixion, by Fra Angelico, surrounded with a border, or pictured framework, in which were represented the heads of saints, prophets, and Sybils, as large as life. The Crosses of the Savior and the thieves were painted against a dark red sky; the figures upon them were lean and attenuated, evidently the vague conceptions of a man who had never seen a naked figure. Beneath was a multitude of people, most of whom seemed to be Saints, who had lived and been martyred long after the crucifixion; and some of them had wounds, from which gilded rays shone forth, as if the inner glory and blessedness of the saint burst through the holes in the flesh. It is a very ugly picture, and its ugliness is not that of strength and vigour, but of weakness and incompetency. Fra Angelico should have confined himself to miniature-heads, in which his delicacy of touch and minute labour often produce an excellent result. The custode informed us that there were some more frescoes by this pious artist, in the interior of the Convent, into which [29] I might be allowed admittance, but not my wife. I declined seeing them, and heartily thanked Heaven for my escape.

Returning through the church, we stopped to look at a shrine on the right of the entrance, where several wax-candles were lighted, and the steps of which were crowded with worshippers. It was evidently a spot of special sanctity; and approaching the steps, we saw, behind a gilded frame-work of stars, and protected by glass, a wooden image of the Savior, naked, covered with spots of blood, crowned with thorns, and expressing all the human wretchedness that the carver's skill could represent. The whole shrine, within the glass, was hung with offerings, as well of silver and gold as of tinsel and trumpery; and the naked body of Christ himself glistened with gold chains and ornaments, and with watches of silver and gold, some of which appeared to be of very old manufacture, and others might be new from the shop. Amid all this glitter, the face of pain and grief looked forth, not a whit comfort[30]ed. While we stood there, a woman, who had been praying, arose from her knees and laid an offering of a single flower upon the shrine. The corresponding shrine, on the opposite side of the entrance, contained a wax-work, within a large glass case, representing the birth of the Saviour. I do not remember how the blessed infant looked; but the Virgin was gorgeously dressed in silks, satins, and gauzes, with spangles and ornaments of all kinds, and, I believe, brooches of real diamonds on her bosom. Her attire, judging from its freshness and new glitter, might have been put on that very morning. By the by, I suppose (and trust there is no irreverence in saying it) that it was from the real and historical circumstances of this sacred birth-scene that the saying originated—a woman "in the straw."

Florence, July 13th, Tuesday.

Mamma and I went this morning, for the second time, to the Academy delle Belle Arti; and I looked pretty thoroughly at the pre-Raphaelite pictures, few of which are really worth looking at, now-a-days. Cimabue and Giotto might cer[31]-tainly be dismissed, henceforth and forever, without any detriment to the cause of good art. There is what seems to me a better picture than either of these have produced, by Bonamico Buffalmacco, an artist of apparently about their date, or not long after. The first real picture in the series is the Adoration of the Magi, by Gentile de Fabriano; a really splendid work in all senses, with some noble and beautiful figures in it, and a crowd of personages, managed with great skill. Three pictures by Perugino are the only other ones I cared to look at. In one of these, the face of the Virgin, who holds the dead Christ on her knees, has a deeper expression of woe than, I think, can ever have been painted since. After Perugino, the pictures cease to be interesting; the art has come forward with rapid strides, but the painters and their productions do not take nearly so much hold of the spectator as before. They all paint better than Giotto and Cimabue—in some respects better than even Perugino—but they paint in vain, probably because they were not nearly so much in earnest, and meant far less, though pos[32]sessing the dexterity to express far more. Andrea del Sarto appears to have been a good painter; yet I always turn away readily from his pictures. I looked again, and for a good while, at Carlo Dolce's portrait of the Eternal Father; for it is a miracle and master-piece of absurdity, and almost equally a miracle of pictorial art. It is the All-powerless; a fair-haired, soft, consumptive Deity, with a mouth that has fallen open through very weakness; he holds one hand on his stomach, as if the wickedness and wretchedness of mankind made him qualmish; and he seems to be looking down out of heaven, with an expression of pitiable appeal, or as if seeking somewhere for assistance in his heavy task of ruling the Universe. You might fancy such a being falling on his knees before a strong-willed man, and beseeching him to take the reins of Omnipotence out of his hands. No wonder that wrong gets the better of right, and that good and ill are confounded, and everything gone higgledy-piggledy, if the Supreme Head were as here depicted; for I never saw—and nobody else ever saw—so perfect a representation of a person burth[33]ened with a task infinitely above his strength. If Carlo Dolce had been wicked enough to know what he was doing, the picture would have been most blasphemous—a satire, in the very person of the Almighty, against all incompetent rulers, and against the ricketty machine and crazy action of the Universe which He contrived. Heaven forgive me for such thoughts as this picture has suggested! It must be added, that the great original defect, in the character of the personage represented, would appear to have been an easy good-nature. I wonder what Michael Angelo would have said to this picture.

In the large enclosed courtyard, connected with the Academy, there are a number of statues, bas-reliefs, and casts, and what was especially interesting, the vague and rude commencement of a statue of Saint Matthew, by Michael Angelo. The conceptions of this great sculptor were so godlike, that he appears to have been discontented at not likewise possessing the godlike attribute of creating and embodying them with an instantaneous thought; and therefore [34] we often find sculptures from his hand, left at the critical point of their struggle to get out of the marble. This statue of Saint Matthew looks like the antediluvian fossil of a human being, of an epoch when humanity was mightier and more majestic than now, long ago imprisoned in stone, and half-uncovered again.

Florence, July 16th, Friday.

We went (my wife and I), yesterday forenoon, to see the Bargello, or old Palace of the Podesta, now converted into a prison. I do not know anything more picturesque in Florence than the great interior court-yard of this ancient palace (dating back to the 13th Century) with the lofty height of the edifice looking down into the inclosed space, dark and stern, and the armorial bearings of a long succession of magistrates carved in stone upon the walls; a garland, as it were, of these Gothic devices extending quite round the court. The best feature of the whole is the broad stone staircase, with its heavy balustrade, ascending externally from the court-yard to an iron-grated door in the second-story. We passed the sentinels under the lofty archway that communicates with the [35] street, and went up the staircase without being questioned or impeded. At the iron-grated door, however, we were met by two officials in uniform, who courteously informed us that there was nothing to be seen in the Bargello except an old chapel, containing some frescoes by Giotto, and that these could be seen only by making a previous appointment with the Custode; he not being constantly on hand. I was not sorry to escape the frescoes, though one of them (if it have not been utterly destroyed by cleaning and attempted restoration) is a portrait of Dante.

We next went to the Church of the Badia, which is but the width of a street distant from the Bargello. It is built in the form of a Greek cross, with a flat-roof, embossed, and once splendid with now tarnished gold. The pavement is of brick, and the walls of dark stone, similar to the interior of the Cathedral; and there being, according to Florentine custom, but little light, the effect was sombre, though the cool, gloomy twilight was refreshing after the hot turmoil and dazzle of the adjacent [36] street. Here we found two or three Gothic tombs, with figures of the deceased persons stretched in marble slumber upon them. There were likewise a picture or two, which, in the dim light, it was impossible to see; indeed, I have hardly ever met with a picture in a church, that was not utterly wasted and thrown away, in the deep shadows of the chapel it was meant to adorn. If there is the remotest chance of its being seen (and often if there is none) the sacristan hangs a curtain before it, for the sake of his fee on withdrawing it. In the chapel of the Bianco family, we saw (if it could be called seeing) what is considered the finest oil-painting of Fra Lippo Lippi. It appears to have been hung with reference to a lofty window on the other side of the church, whence sufficient light might fall upon it to show a picture so vividly painted as this seems to be, and as most of Fra Lippo Lippi's are. The window was curtained, however, and the chapel so full of duskiness that I could make out nothing. On the wall of this chapel is a bas-relief of the Virgin and child, done in china or crockery, by Luca della Robbia. Sev[37]eral persons came in to say their prayers, during the little time that we remained in the church; and as we came out, we passed a good woman who sat knitting in the coolness of the vestibule, which was lined with mural tombstones. Probably she spends her day thus, keeping up the little industry of her fingers, slipping into the church to pray whenever a devotional impulse swells into her heart, and asking an alms as often as she sees a person of charitable aspect.

From the church we went to the Ufizzi gallery, and re-inspected the greater part of it pretty faithfully. We had the good fortune, too, again to get admittance into the cabinet of Bronzes, where we admired anew the wonderful airiness of John of Bologna's Mercury, which, as I now observed, rests on nothing substantial, but on the breath of Boreas beneath him. We also saw a bronze bust of one of the de Medici (Cosmo II., I think,) by Benvenuto Cellini, and a thousand other things, the curiosity of which is overlaid by their multitude. The Roman eagle, which I have record[38]ed to be about the size of a blackbird, I now saw to be as big as a pigeon. On our way towards the door of the gallery, on our departure, we saw the cabinet of gems open, and again feasted our eyes with its concentrated brilliancies and magnificences. Among them were two crystal cups, with engraved devices, and covers of enamelled gold, wrought by Benvenuto Cellini, and wonderfully beautiful. But it is idle to mention one or two things, when all are so beautiful and curious; idle, too, because language is not burnished gold, with here and there a brighter word flashing like a diamond, and therefore no amount of talk will give the slightest idea of one of these elaborate handiworks.

Florence, July 27th, Tuesday.

I seldom go out now-a-days; having already seen Florence tolerably well, and the streets being very hot, and myself having been engaged in sketching out a Romance—which whether it will ever come to anything, is a point yet to be decided. At any rate, it leaves me little heart for journalizing and describing new things; and six months of un-interrupted monotony would be more valuable to me, [39] just now, than the most brilliant succession of novelties. Yesterday, I spent a good deal of time in watching the setting-out of a wedding-party from our door; the bride being the daughter of an English lady, the wife of an Italian count, who inhabits the third piano of this house. After all, there was nothing very characteristic. The bridegroom is a young man of English birth—at least, of

English blood—who occupies a position, I believe, in the Grand Duke's noble guard, and whose father is said to be Chamberlain to the Pope. The only curious part of the spectacle was the swarm of beggars who haunted our street all day; the most wretched mob conceivable, chiefly women, with a few blind people, and some old men and boys. Among these, the bridal party distributed their beneficence in the shape of some handsful of copper, with here and there a half-paul inter-mixed; whereupon the whole wretched mob flung themselves in a heap upon the pavement, struggling, fighting, tumbling one over another—and then looking up to the windows with petitionary ges[40]tures for more and more, and still for more. Doubtless, they had need enough; for they looked thin, sickly, ill-fed, and the women ugly to the last degree. The wedding-party had a breakfast above stairs, which lasted till four ºclock; and then the bridegroom took his bride in a barouche and pair, which was already crammed with his own luggage and hers—carpet-bags, dressing-cases, a steel hilted and steel-scabbarded broad-sword, a double-barrelled fowling-piece, some loose female trumpery, two or three over-coats, &c &c &c. and drove off. The poor fellow will find his journeyings henceforth not quite so simple a matter as heretofore. He was a well-looking young man enough, in a uniform of French gray with silver epaulets; more agreeable in aspect than his bride, who, I think, will have the upper hand in their domestic life. I observed, that, on getting into the barouche, he sat down on her gown, (as he could not well help doing) and received apparently a slight reprimand in consequence. After their departure, the wedding guests took their leave; the most noteworthy being the Pope's Nuncio, an [41] ecclesiastical personage in purple stockings, attended by two young priests, all of whom got into a coach, the driver and footman of which wore gold-laced cocked hats and other splendours.

To-day, I paid a short visit to the gallery of the Pitti Palace, with the pictures of which I am now reasonably well acquainted. I looked longest at a Madonna of Raphael's, the one which is usually kept in the Grand Duke's private apartments, being only brought into the public gallery for the purpose of being copied. It is the holiest of all Raphael's Madonnas, with a great reserve in the expression, a sense of being apart, and yet with the utmost tenderness and sweetness; although she hangs her eyelids before her like a veil, as it were, and has a primness of eternal virginity about the mouth. It was one of Raphael's earlier works, when he mixed more religious sentiment with his paint than afterwards. Perugino's pictures give the impression of greater sincerity and earnestness than Raphael's, though the genius of the latter often gave him a miraculous vision.

[42] Florence, July 28th, Wednesday.

Last evening, my wife, Una, and I, went over to the Powers', and sat with them on their terrace, at the top of the house, till nearly 10 °clock. It was a delightful, calm, summer evening, and we were elevated high above all the adjacent roofs, and had a prospect of the greater part of Florence and its towers, and the surrounding hills; while right beneath us rose the trees of a garden, and hardly sent their tops higher than we sat. At a little distance, with only a house or two between, was a theatre in full act; the Theatro Goldoni, which is an open amphitheatre, in the ancient fashion, without any roof or other covering on top. We could see the upper part of the proscenium, and, had we been a little nearer, might have seen the whole performance, as did several boys and other rogues who crept along the roofs of the adjacent houses. As it was, we heard the music and the applause, and now and then an actor's stentorian tones, when we chose to listen. The female Powers, and my wife and Una, and Master Bob, sat in a group together and chatted, in one corner of our aerial drawing-room; while Mr. Powers and myself leaned a[43]gainst the parapet, and talked of innumerable things. When the clocks struck the hour, or the bells rung from the steeples (as they are continually doing, reason or none) I spoke of the sweetness of the Florence bells, the tones of some of which are as if the bell were full of liquid sweetness, and shed it through the air on being upturned. I had supposed, in my lack of musical ear, that the bells of the Campanile were the sweetest; but Mr. Powers says that there is a defect in their tone, and that the bell of the Palazzo Vecchio is the most melodious he ever heard. Then he spoke of his having been a manufacturer of organs, or, at least, of reeds for organs, at one period of his life. I wonder what he has not been! He told me of an invention of his, in the musical line; a jewsharp with two tongues; and by and by he produced it for my inspection. It was carefully kept in a little wooden case, and was very neatly and elaborately constructed, with screws to tighten it, and a silver centre-piece between the two tongues. Evidently a great deal of thought had been bestowed on this little harp; but the inventor told me that it was an utter failure, because the tongues were apt [44] to interfere and jar with one another; although the strain of music was very sweet and melodious (as he proved, by playing on it a little) when everything went right. It was a youthful production; and he said that its failure had been a great disappointment to him at the time; whereupon I congratulated him that his failures had been in small matters, and his successes in great ones. We talked, furthermore, about instinct and reason, and whether the brute creation have souls, and, if they have none, how justice is to be done them for their sufferings here; and came finally to the conclusion (at least, Mr Powers did) that brutes suffer only in appearance, and that God enjoys for them all that they seem to enjoy, and that man is the only intelligent and sentient being, except his Creator. We reasoned high about other states of being; and I suggested the possibility that there might be beings inhabiting this earth, contemporaneously with us, and close beside us, but of whose existence and whereabout we could have no perception, nor they of ours, because we are endowed with different sets of senses; for certainly it was within God's power to create be[45]ings who should communicate with nature by innumerable other senses than these few which we possess. Mr. Powers gave hospitable reception to this idea, and said that it had occurred to himself; and he has evidently thought much and earnestly about such matters, but is rather too apt, in my opinion, to let his ideas crystallize into a theory, before he can have sufficient data for it. He is a Swedenborgian in faith.

The moon had risen behind the trees, while we were talking; and Powers intimated his idea that beings analogous to men—men in everything except the modifications necessary to adapt them to their physical circumstances—inhabited the planets, and peopled them with beautiful shapes. Each planet, however, must have its own standard of the beautiful, I suppose; and probably his sculptor's eye would not see much to admire in the proportions of an inhabitant of Saturn.

The atmosphere of Florence (at least, when we ascend a little way into it) seems to suggest planetary speculations. Galileo found it so; and Mr. Powers [46] and I pervaded the whole Universe, but finally crept down his garret-stairs, and parted, with a friendly pressure of the hand.

Villa Montauto, August 2ᵈ, Monday.

We had grown weary of the heat of Florence, within the walls; and the children did not flourish, nor any of us, indeed;

there being little opportunity for air and exercise except within
the precincts of our little garden; which, also, we feared might
breed malaria or something akin to it. We had therefore taken
this suburban villa for the two next months; and, yesterday
morning, we all came out hither. Julian had preceded us, on
foot, in company with Bob Powers; and Una and I followed,
also on foot, leaving Mamma, Miss Shepard, and Rosebud,
with the servant, to come after us in a carriage. The villa is on
the hill called Bellosguardo, about a mile beyond the Porta
Romana; and we found it a hot, disagreeable walk, through
narrow, dusty lanes, which climb the hillside between the high
garden walls of the many villas hereabouts. Less than half-an-
hour's walk, however, brought us to the iron [47] gate of our
villa, which we found shut and locked. We shouted to be let
in; and while waiting for somebody to appear, there was a good
opportunity to contemplate the external aspect of the villa.
About thirty yards from the gate, rises an old, square tower,
machicolated and battlemented, with two or three iron-grated
windows up and down its height, besides smaller apertures
through the stone-work. It dates, no doubt, from the middle-
ages, and looks as old as the Palazzo Vecchio itself. The tower
is gray and mossy with age, and is venerable of aspect; but
the main body of the villa, appended to it, is covered with
fresh modern stucco, and looks as new as an American country-
house; although I think I can see that the part of the edifice,
immediately adjoining the tower, is more ancient than the
rest.

After we had waited a few minutes, Julian came racing
down to the gate, laughing heartily, and said that Bob Powers
and he had been in the house, but had come out without their
coats, shutting the door behind them; and as the door closed
with [48] a spring-lock, they could not get in again. Now
the key of the outer-gate, as well as that of the house itself,
was in one of their pockets; so that here we were shut out of

our own castle, and compelled to carry on a siege against it, and without much likelihood of taking it, although the garrison were willing to surrender. But Bob Powers called in the assistance of the Contadini who cultivate the ground, and who live in the farm-house, close by; and one of them got into the chamber-window, by means of a ladder; so that the keys were got, the gate opened, and we finally admitted. Before examining any other part of the house, I believe, we climbed to the top of the tower, which, indeed, is not very high in proportion to its massive square. Very probably, its original height was abbreviated in compliance with the law that lowered so many of the fortified towers of noblemen within the walls of Florence. We ascended a succession of crazy staircases, passing through several dreary old rooms, each occupying the whole area of the tower, unfurnished, paved with brick, lighted by grated windows [49] or by rude holes through the wall, and looking very much like ancient guard-rooms or prisoners' cells, both of which purposes they may have served in their day. In two or three of them, however, there are rows of pigeon-holes; and, I suppose, for the last two or three hundred years, the old warlike tower may have been turned into a dove-cote, although we found none of these peaceable inhabitants here now. There is a story that Savonarola, the famous reforming friar, was once a prisoner in one of the chambers of the tower. I do not remember that he ever was confined anywhere, except in the short period between his being taken from his convent by a mob, and burnt in the Granducal Piazza; and then, it would seem more probable that he should be kept prisoner within the city-walls. Nevertheless, it is as well to suppose that there is some foundation for the tradition; and, if so, there is one of the chambers where I can locate the ghost of the reverend prisoner.

The stairs (they were not of stone, built in with the original mass of the tower, as in English castles, but [50] of decayed wood, which shook beneath us,) grew more and more crazy as we ascended. It will not be many years, before the height of the tower becomes unattainable. At last, we emerged upon the top, and had a fine view, between the battlements, of Florence, seated low among the surrounding hills, with the Duomo, and the Campanile close beside it, bearing, I think, about due east of us. Towards the west lay the Valdarno, a great plain stretching away for miles, and bounded in the distance by misty hills, which set it in a frame-work on all sides; and over this wide extent were scattered white villas, and church towers, and villages near and afar, and great tracts of cultivation, rich with the fig, the vine, the olive, besides Indian corn, and other grains; while the Arno, though it nowhere opens its eye in the landscape, seemed to be flowing near the bases of the hills, on one side, where its course was shaded with trees. The line of a road could be traced through the middle of the great plain by the white villas or houses which stood almost connectedly along it, and which here and [51] there, like the widening of a stream, spread out into a village-street or little town. The shadows of clouds were flung upon portions of this fertile and elsewhere sunny tract of level country, as also upon the great hills which fenced it in, and which themselves are brown and sunburnt, and without a tree on all their broad backs. The mist softens them a little; else their outlines would be exceedingly distinct and hard.

Nearer at hand, in the vicinity of the city, we saw the Convent of Monte Olivetto, and other structures that looked like convents, being built round an enclosed square; also, numerous white villas, many of which had towers, like that on which we were standing, square and massive, some of them battlemented on the summits, and others apparently modernized for domestic purposes. Among them, Una pointed out what she believes to be Galileo's tower, whither she made an excursion, the other day. It looked lower than our own, but seemed to stand on a higher elevation. We also saw the Duke's villa, the Poggio, with a long avenue of cypresses [52] leading from it as if a funeral were going forth. And having wasted thus much of description on the landscape, I will finish with saying that it lacked only water, to be a very fine one. It is strange what a difference the gleam of water makes, and how a scene awakens and comes to life wherever it is seen. This landscape, moreover, gives the beholder (at least, this beholder) a sense of oppressive sunshine and scanty shade, and does not incite a longing to wander through it on foot, as a really delightful landscape should. The vine, too, being cultivated in so trim a manner, does not suggest that idea of luxuriant fertility which is the poetical notion of a vineyard. The olive-orchards have a pale and unlovely hue. An English view would have been incomparably richer in its never-fading green; and, in my own country, the wooded hills would have been a hundred times more delightful than these peaks and ridges of dreary and barren sunshine, and there would have been the bright eyes of half-a dozen little lakes, looking heavenward, within an extent like that of the Valdarno.

By and by, mamma's carriage came along the [53] dusty road, and passed through the iron gateway, which we had left open for their reception. We shouted down to them, and they waved their handkerchiefs upward to us; and on my way down, leaving Una, Julian, and Bob Powers on the tower, I met Rosebud and the servant coming up through the ghostly rooms.

The rest of the day was spent mostly in exploring the premises. The house itself is of almost bewildering extent, insomuch that we might each of us have a suite of rooms individually. I have established myself on the ground floor, where I have a dressing-room, a large vaulted saloon, and a square writing-closet, about five paces across, the walls and cielings of the two latter being ornamented with angels and cherubs aloft, in fresco, and with temples, pillars, statues, vases, broken columns, peacocks, parrots, vines, sunflowers (all in fresco) below. I know not how many more saloons, ante-rooms, and sleeping-chambers, there are on this same basement-story, besides an equal number above, and a great subterranean establishment, that seems to have been [54] a kitchen, below. I saw some immense jars there, which I suppose were intended to hold oil, and great iron kettles, for what purpose I know not. There is also a chapel in the house; but it is locked up, and we cannot with certainty find the door of it, nor ever (in this great wilderness of a house) decide absolutely what space the holy precincts occupy. Adjoining Una's chamber, there is a little oratory, hung round with a score or two of sacred prints, of very ancient date, and with crucifixes, holy-water pots, and other consecrated things; and here, within a glass-case, there is the representation of a naked little boy, in wax, very prettily made, and holding up a heart that looks like a bit of red sealing-wax. If I had found him anywhere else, I should have taken him for Cupid; but, being in an oratory, I presume him to have some religious signification. In the servant's room, a crucifix hangs on one side of the bed and a little vase for holy water (overgrown with a cobweb) on the other; and no doubt all the other sleeping-apartments would have been equally well provided, only that their occu[55]pants were to be heretics.

The lower floor of the house is tolerably furnished, and looks cheerful with its frescoes; although the bare brick pavements (universal throughout every room and chamber, from the cellar-kitchen to the topmost attic of the tower) give an impression of disarray and discomfort. But carpets are universally taken up, in Italy, during summer-time. The upper rooms are scantily and shabbily furnished, and have a neglected look, as if it were a long while since anybody lived in them. It must have been an immense family that could ever have filled such a house with life. We go on voyages of discovery, and, when in quest of any particular point, are likely enough to fetch up at some other. This morning, I had difficulty in finding my way again to the top of the tower. One of the most peculiar rooms (which I have not seen elsewhere than in Tuscany) is constructed close to the tower, under the roof of the main-building, but with no external walls on the two sides; it is left thus open to the air, I presume, for the [56] sake of coolness in summer. A parapet runs round the exposed sides, for the sake of security. Some of the palaces in Florence have such open apartments in their upper stories, and I saw others on our journey hither, after arriving in Tuscany. They must make excellent smoking-rooms.

The grounds immediately around the house are laid out in gravel-walks, and ornamented with shrubbery, and with what ought to be a grassy lawn; but the Italian sun is quite as little favorable to beauty of that kind, as our own. I have enjoyed the luxury, however, (almost for the first time since I left my own hill-top, at the Wayside,) of flinging myself at full length on the ground, without any fear of catching cold. Moist England would punish a man soundly for taking such liberties with her bosom. A Podere, or cultivated tract, comprising several acres, belongs to the villa, and seems to be fertile, like all the surrounding country, with vines, olives, figs, Indian-corn, and pumpkins. The possessions of different proprietors are not separated by fences, but only [57] marked out by ditches; and it seems possible to walk miles and miles by the intersecting paths, without obstruction. The rural laborers, so far as I have observed, go about in their shirt-sleeves, and look very much like tanned and sun-dried Yankees.

Last night, it was really a work of time and toil to go about, making our defensive preparations for the night; first closing the iron gate, then the ponderous and complicated fastenings of the house-door, then the separate barricadoes of each iron-barred window on the lower floor, with a somewhat slighter arrangement above. There are bolts and shutters, however, for every window in the house, and I suppose it would not be amiss to put them all in use. Our garrison is so small, that we must depend more upon the strength of our fortifications, than upon our own active efforts, in case of an attack. In England, in an insulated country-house, we should need all these bolts and bars; and Italy is not thought to be the safer country of the two.

[58] It deserves to be recorded that the Count Montauto, a nobleman, and seemingly a man of property, should deem it worth while to let his country seat, and reside during the hot months in his palace in a sweltering street or piazza of the city—for the consideration of twenty-eight scudi a month. He seems to contemplate returning hither for the autumn and winter, (when the situation must be dreadfully windy and bleak, and the cold deathlike in these great, cheerless halls;) and then, it is to be supposed, he will let his palace in town. The Count (through the agency of his son, a young man of good manners and appearance) bargained very stiffly for, and finally obtained, three dollars in addition to the sum which we at first offered him. This indicates that even a little money is still a matter of great moment, in Italy. Signor del Bello (who, I believe, is also a nobleman) haggled with us about some cracked crockery, at our late residence, and finally demanded and received fifty cents in compensation. But this poor gentleman has been a spendthrift, and now acts as the agent of an[59]other. Nevertheless, it is not easy to avoid the impression that the Italians are a particularly mean people.

Villa Montauto, August 3ᵈ, Tuesday.

Yesterday afternoon, William Story called on me; he being on a day or two's excursion from Sienna, where he is spending the summer with his family. He was very entertaining and conversative, as usual, and said (in reply to my question whether he was not anxious to return to Cleopatra) that he had already sketched out another subject for sculpture, which would give him employment during next winter. He told me —what I was glad to hear—that his sketches of Italian life, intended for the Atlantic Monthly, and supposed to be lost, have been recovered. Speaking of the superstitiousness of the Italians, he said that they universally believe in the influence of the Evil Eye; and from Mr. Story's manner, I rather suspect that he has a kind of belief in it, himself, classifying it with the phenomena of Mesmerism. The evil influence is supposed not to be dependent [60] on the will of the possessor of the Evil Eye; on the contrary, the persons to whom he wishes well are the very ones to suffer by it. The Evil Eye is oftener found in monks than in any other class of people; and on meeting a monk, and encountering his eye, an Italian usually makes a defensive sign, by putting both hands behind him with the forefingers and little fingers extended; although it is a controverted point whether it be not more efficacious to extend the hand with its stuck-out fingers towards the suspected person. It is considered an evil omen, at any rate, to meet a monk on first going out for the day. The Italians (especially the Neapolitans) very generally wear amulets. Pio Nono (perhaps as being the chief of all monks and other religious people) is supposed to have an Evil Eye of tenfold malignancy; and its effect has been seen in the ruin of all schemes for the public good, so soon as they are favored by him. When the pillar in the Piazza d'Espagna, commemorative of his Dogma of the Immaculate Conception, was to be erected, the people of Rome refused to be pres[61]ent, or to have anything to do with it, unless the Pope promised to abstain from interference. His Holiness did promise, but so far broke his word as to be present, one day, while it was being erected; and, on that day,

a man was killed. A little while ago, there was a Lord
Clifford, an English Catholic nobleman, residing in Italy; and
happening to come to Rome, he sent his compliments to Pio
Nono, and requested the favor of an interview. The Pope,
as it happened, was indisposed, or, for some reason, could not
see his lordship, but very kindly sent him his blessing. Those
who knew of the affair shook their heads, and intimated that it
would go ill with his lordship, now that he had been blessed
by Pio Nono; and, sure enough, the very next day, poor Lord
Clifford was dead! His Holiness had better construe the
scriptural injunction literally, and take to blessing his enemies.

I walked into town, with Julian, this morning; and meeting
a monk in the Via Fornace, I thought it no more than reasonable (especially as the good Father fixed his eyes upon me)
to provide against the [62] worst, by putting both hands behind me, with the forefingers and little fingers stuck out.

In speaking of the little Oratory, connected with Una's
chamber, I forgot to mention the most remarkable object in
it. It is a skull, the size of life, (or death, I suppose I should
say) carved out of gray alabaster, and very perfectly done; the
sutures, the little fragile bones of the nose, and the teeth,
being represented with startling fidelity. It reposes upon a
sculptured cushion of white marble, in which the weight of
the skull seems to make an impression. There is a large, old
engraving of Titian's Magdalen (the one veiled in her own
hair, in the Pitti Palace) looking a great deal more lugubrious
than the original. This part of the house must be very old;
probably coeval with the tower, contiguous to which it stands.
The cieling of Una's apartment is vaulted, with intersecting
arches; and adjoining it is a great saloon (we use it as a school-
room) likewise with a vaulted and groined cieling, and having
a cushioned divan running all round the walls. The windows
of these rooms look out on the Valdarno.

[63] The room above the saloon, just mentioned, is of

the same size, and is hung with engraved portraits, printed on large sheets, by the score and hundred together, and enclosed in wooden frames. They comprise the whole series of Emperors of Rome, the succession of Popes, the Kings of Europe, the Doges, and the Sultans of Turkey. The engravings bear different dates, between 1685 and twenty or thirty years later, and appear to have been executed at Rome.

Villa Montauto, August 4th, Wednesday.

Mamma and I, with Miss Shepard and Julian, climbed our tower, yesterday afternoon, to see the sunset. The sky was soft and bright, not so gorgeous as often in America, but tenderly magnificent, with golden clouds; not a metallic gold neither, or, if so, like the dream of an alchymist. The sun went down behind the dim hills at the farther extremity of the Valdarno, shooting his level beams along its length to the top of our tower. There was a mist—scattered, probably, through the whole of the valley, but only making itself visible in the distant parts; [64] indeed, there always seems to be a slight misty veil between us and the hills at the farther end, and also among the defiles of the hills themselves; nor have I seen the landscape without the shadows of clouds that float in white masses about the sky. In my first sketch of Valdarno, I said that the Arno seemed to hold its course near the bases of the hills. I now observe that the line of trees, which marks its current, appears to divide the valley into two pretty equal parts, and the river runs nearly east and west.

In the pavement, at the summit of our tower, a little plant has rooted itself, and seems to be in a thriving state. It has no soil to nourish it; nothing, that I could see, but the lime in the crevice out of which it grows; but its leaves are green and glossy, and it appears to like its situation, for Rosebud tried to pull it up, and its sturdy little roots refused to give way. This is the only vegetation on the tower, except lichens and dry yellow moss, both of which are sufficiently abundant. In England, it would have been completely mantled, with ivy, [65] centuries ago. Owls are said to haunt the tower, making their entrance, I suppose, through the pigeon holes, and taking up their abode in Savonarola's chamber; but I have seen none, nor heard them, unless a strange sound in the shrubbery, last night, was the hooting of an owl.

Soon after sunset, the breeze across the valley grew so fresh that Mamma and Miss Shepard descended, but Julian and I remained, looking down from our height, and flinging down pieces of stone and lime from the battlements, to watch how long they would be in falling, and where they would strike. At last, when it was growing dusk, we too went down, groping our way down the shaky staircases, and peeping into each dark chamber as we passed. I gratified Julian exceedingly by hitting my nose against the wall. Reaching the bottom, I went into the school-room, and stood at a window, watching the lights twinkle forth, near and far, in the Valdarno, and listening to the convent-bells that sounded from Monte Olivetto, and more remotely. The stars came out, and the constellation of the [66] Dipper (I know not what Galileo called it, espying it from his neighboring tower) hung right over the valley, pointing to the North Star above the hills on my right.

Villa Montauto, August 12th Thursday.

My wife and I drove into town, yesterday afternoon, with Miss Blagden and Miss Bracken, to call on Mr. Kirkup, an old Englishman who has resided a great many years in Florence. He is noted as an antiquarian, and has the reputation of being a necromancer; not undeservedly, inasmuch as he is deeply interested in spirit-rappings, and holds converse, through a medium, with dead poets and emperors. He lives in an old house, formerly a residence of the Knights Templars, hanging over the Arno, just as you come upon the Ponte Vecchio; and going up a dark staircase, and knocking at a door on one side of the landing-place, we were received by Mr. Kirkup into the opposite door. He had had notice of our visit, and was prepared for it; being dressed in a blue frock coat, of rather an old fashion, with a velvet collar, and a thin waistcoat and pantaloons, fresh from the drawer; looking very sprucely, in short, and [67] unlike his customary guise; for Miss Blagden hinted to us that the poor old gentleman is generally so unclean that it is not quite pleasant to take him by the hand. He is rather low of stature, with a pale, shrivelled face, and hair and beard perfectly white, and the former of a particularly soft and silken texture. He has a high, thin nose, of the English aristocratic type; his eyes have a queer, rather wild look, and the eyebrows are arched above them, so that he seems all the time to be seeing something that strikes him with surprise. I judged him to be somewhat crackbrained, chiefly on the strength of this expression. His whole make is delicate; his hands white and small; and his appearance and manners those of a gentleman, with rather more embroidery of courtesy than belongs to an Englishman. He appeared to be very nervous; tremulous, indeed, to his fingers' ends, without being in any degree disturbed or embarrassed by our presence. Finally, he is almost as deaf as a post; an infirmity that quite took away my pleasure in the interview because it is impossible to think of anything worthwhile to say, when one is compelled to raise one's voice above its ordinary level.

[68] He ushered us through two or three large old rooms, dark, dusty, hung with antique-looking pictures, and lined

with bookcases, containing, I doubt not, a very curious library. Indeed, he directed my attention to one case, and said that he had collected those works, in former days, merely for the sake of laughing at them. They were books of magic and occult sciences. What he seemed really to value, however, were some manuscript copies of Dante, of which he showed us two; one a folio, on parchment, beautifully written in German text, the letters as clear and accurately cut as printed type; the other a small volume, fit, as Mr. Kirkup said, to be carried in a capacious medi-aeval sleeve. This also was on vellum, and as elegantly executed as the larger one; but the larger had beautiful illuminations, the vermillion and gold of which looked as brilliant now as they did five centuries ago. Both of these books were written early in the fourteenth century. Mr. Kirkup has also a plaster-cast of Dante's face, which he believes to be the original one, taken from his face after death; and he has likewise an accurate tracing [69] from Giotto's fresco of Dante, in the chapel of the Bargello. This fresco was discovered through Mr. Kirkup's means; and the tracing is particularly valuable, because the original has been almost destroyed by rough usage in drawing out a nail that had been driven into its eye. It represents the profile of a youthful, but melancholy face, and has the general outline of Dante's features in other portraits. Dante has held frequent communications with Mr. Kirkup, through a medium; the poet being described by the medium as wearing the same dress seen in the youthful portrait, but as bearing more resemblance to the cast taken from his dead face, than to the picture from his youthful one.

There was a very good picture of Savonarola in one of the rooms, and many other portraits, paintings, and drawings, some of them ancient, and others the work of Mr. Kirkup himself. He has the torn fragment of an exquisite drawing of a nude figure by Rubens, and a portfolio of other curious drawings. And besides books and works of art, he has no end of antique knick-knackeries, none of which [70] we had any time to look at; among others (though I did not see them) some instruments with which nuns used to torture themselves in their convents, by way of penance. But the greatest curiosity of all—and no antiquity neither—was a pale, large eyed little girl, about four years old, who followed the conjuror's footsteps wherever he went. She was the brightest and merriest little thing in the world, and frisked through these shadowy old chambers, among the dead people's trumpery, as gaily as a butterfly flits among flowers and sunshine.

This child's mother was a beautiful girl, named Regina, whose portrait Mr. Kirkup showed us on the wall. I never saw a more beautiful and striking face, claiming to be a real one. She was a Florentine, I believe, of low birth; and she lived with the old necromancer as his spiritual medium. He showed us a journal, kept during her lifetime, and read from it his notes of an interview with the Czar Alexander, when that potentate communicated to Mr. Kirkup that he had been poisoned. The necromancer set a great value upon Regina; nor [71] were their communications, as it appears, exclusively spiritual; for, by and by, the medium produced this little girl, whom she declared, upon her death-bed, kissing the cross, to be the child of Mr. Kirkup. The poor old man seems to have had doubts respecting this paternity; indeed, if I interpret the story right, he did not quite know that he had done anything to bring the matter about. Nevertheless, he could not withstand the solemnity of Regina's declaration on the crucifix; and when the mother died, he received the poor baby into his heart, and now believes it to be absolutely his own—as perhaps it is. At any rate, it is a happy belief for him, since he has nothing else in the world to love, and loves the child entirely, and enjoys all the bliss of fatherhood, though he must have lived as much as seventy years before he began to taste it. By the by, where there is a very great difference betwixt the ages of father and mother, the offspring is usually a boy.

This child inherits her mother's gift of communication with the spiritual world; so that the necromancer can still talk with Regina through [72] the baby which she left him, and not only with her, but with Dante, and any other great spirit that may choose to visit him. It is a very queer story; and the child might be put at once into a Romance, with all her history and environment;—the ancient, knight-templar-palace, with the Arno flowing under the iron-barred windows, and the Ponte Vecchio, covered with its jewellers' shops, close at hand; the dark, lofty chambers, with faded frescoes on the cielings, black pictures hanging on the walls, old books on the shelves, and hundreds of musty antiquities, emitting an atmosphere of past centuries; the shrivelled, white bearded old man, thinking all the time of ghosts, and looking into the child's eyes to seek them;—and the child herself, springing so freshly out of the old soil, so pretty, so intelligent, so playful, with never a playmate save the conjuror and a kitten. It is a Persian kitten, and lay asleep in a window; but when I touched it, it started up at once in as gamesome a mood as the child herself.

The child looks pale; and no wonder, seldom or never stirring out of that old house, or away from the [73] River-atmosphere. Miss Blagden advised the father to go with her to the seaside or into the country; and he did not deny that it might do her good, but seemed to be hampered by an old man's sluggishness and dislike of change. I think he will not live a great while; for he seems very frail. When he dies, the little girl will inherit what property he may leave; a Lady Catherine Fleming, an Englishwoman, and a friend of Mr. Kirkup, has engaged to take her in charge. She followed us merrily to the door, and so did the Persian kitten, and Mr.

Kirkup shook hands with us, over and over again, with vivacious courtesy; his manner having been characterized by a great deal of briskness, throughout the interview. He expressed himself delighted to have met me (whose books he had read,) and said that the day would be a memorable one to him;—which I did not in the least believe.

Mr. Kirkup is an intimate friend of Trelawney, author of 'Adventures of a Younger Son'; and, long ago, the latter promised him that, if he ever came into possession of the family estate, he would [74] divide it with him. Trelawney (I know not how long since) did really succeed to the estate, and lost no time in forwarding to his friend the legal documents, entitling him to half of the property. But Mr. Kirkup declined the gift, as he himself was not destitute, and Trelawney had a brother. There were two pictures of Trelawney in the rooms, one a slight sketch on the wall, the other a half-length portrait in a Turkish dress; both handsome, but indicating no very amiable character. It is not easy to forgive Trelawney for uncovering dead Byron's legs and telling that terrible story about them—equally disgraceful to himself, be it truth or a lie.

It seems that Regina had another love, and a sister who was very disreputable. The child was born some time before her death (of consumption,) but she never imputed the paternity to Mr Kirkup till she lay on her death-bed, when, naturally, she was considering how to provide for the future of the little girl; and, I suppose, Catholic and Italian morality would think a false oath even on the crucifix a venial crime, the ob[75]ject being to secure the welfare of an orphan child. Mr. Kirkup is a very credulous man, and would be likely to believe the story all the more readily, the more improbable it was. It rather adds than otherwise to the romance of the affair—the idea that this pretty little elf has no right whatever in the asylum which she has found. Mr. Kirkup has named her Imogen.

The small manuscript copy of Dante, which he showed me,

was written by—I forget the name—but by a Florentine gentleman of the fourteenth century, one of whose ancestors the poet had met and talked with in Paradise.

August 19th (Villa Montauto) Thursday.

Here is a good Italian incident, which I find in Vasary:— Andrea del Castagno was a painter at Florence, in the 15th century; and he had a friend, likewise a painter, Domenico of Venice. The latter had the secret of painting in oils, and yielded to Castagno's entreaties to impart it to him. Desirous of being the sole possessor of this great secret, Castagno waited only till night to assassinate Domenico, who so little suspected his treachery, that he besought those who found him, bleeding and dying, to take him to [76] his friend Castagno, that he might die in his arms. The murderer lived to be seventy-four years old, and his crime was never suspected, till he himself revealed it on his death-bed. Domenico did actually die in Castagno's arms. This death-scene would have been a good one for the latter to paint in oils.

Villa Montauto, September 1st, Wednesday.

Few things journalizable have happened during the past month, because Florence and the neighborhood have lost their novelty; and, furthermore, I usually spend the whole day at home, having been engaged in planning and sketching out a Romance. I have now done with this for the present, and mean to employ the rest of the time we stay here chiefly in re-visiting the galleries, and seeing what remains to be seen of Florence.

Last Saturday, I went with my wife to take tea at Miss Blagden's, who has a weekly reception on that evening. We found Mr. Powers there; and, by and by, Mr. Boot and Mr. Trollope came in. Miss Shepard has lately been exercising her faculties as a spiritual-writing medium; and the conversation [77] turning on that subject, Mr. Powers related some things that he had witnessed through the agency of Mr. Hume, who had held a session or two at his house. He described the apparition of two mysterious hands, from beneath a table round which the party were seated. These hands purported to belong to the aunt of Countess Cotterel (who was present) and were a pair of thin, delicate, aged, lady-like hands and arms, appearing at the edge of the table, and terminating at the elbow in a sort of white mist. One of the hands (I know not whether at the request of anybody, or of their own accord) took up a fan and began to use it. The Countess then said, "Fan yourself as you used to, dear Aunt";—and forthwith the hands waved the fan back and forth in a peculiar manner, which the Countess recognized as her dead aunt's fashion. The spirit was then requested to fan each member of the party; and, accordingly, each separate individual round the table was fanned in turn, and felt the breeze sensibly upon his face. Finally, the hands (I think Mr. Powers [78] said) sank beneath the table; but I am not quite sure that they did not appear to melt into the air. During this apparition, Mr. Hume sat at the table, but not in such a position or within such distance that he could have put forth, or managed, the spectral hands; and of this Mr. Powers satisfied himself by taking precisely the same position after the party had retired.

Mr. Powers did not feel the hands, at this time, but he afterwards felt the touch of infant hands, which were at the time invisible. He told of many other wonders, which seem to have as much right to be set down as facts as anything else that depends on human testimony. For example, Mr. Kinney, one of the party, gave a sudden start and exclamation; he had felt on his knee a certain token, which could have been given him only by a friend long ago in his grave. Mr. Powers inquired what was the last thing that had been given as a present to a deceased child; and suddenly both he and his wife felt a prick as of some sharp instrument, on their knees. The present had been a [79] pen-knife. I have forgotten other incidents quite as striking as these; but (with the exception of the spiritual hands) they seemed to be akin to those that have been produced by mesmerism, returning the inquirer's thoughts and veiled recollections to himself, as answers to his queries. The hands are certainly an inexplicable phenomenon. Of course, they are not portions of a dead body, nor any other kind of substance; they are impressions on the two senses, sight and touch, but how produced I cannot tell. Even admitting the fact of their appearance (and certainly I do admit it, quite as freely and fully as if I had seen them myself) there is no need of supposing them to come from the world of departed spirits.

Powers seems to put full faith in the verity of spiritual communications, while acknowledging the difficulty of identifying spirits as being what they pretend. He is a Swedenborgian, and so far prepared to put faith in many of these phenomena. As for Hume, Powers gives a decided opinion that he is a knave, but thinks [80] him so organized, nevertheless, as to be a particularly good medium for spiritual communications. Spirits, I suppose, like earthly people, have to use such instruments as will answer their purposes; but rather than receive a message from a dead friend through the organism of a rogue and a charlatan, methinks I would choose to wait till we meet. But what most astonishes me is, the indifference with which I listen to these marvels. They throw old ghost stories quite into the shade; they bring the whole world of spirits down amongst us, visibly and audibly; they are absolutely proved to be sober facts by evidence that would satisfy us of any other alleged realities; and yet I cannot free my mind to interest itself in them. They are facts to my understanding (which, it might have been anticipated, would have been the last to acknowledge them,) but they seem not to be facts to my intuitions and deeper perceptions. My inner soul does not in the least admit them. There is a mistake somewhere. So idle and empty do I feel these stories to be, that [81] I hesitated long whether or no to give up a few pages of this not very important journal, to the record of them.

Here, at home, we have had written communications, through Miss Shepard, with several spirits; my wife's father, mother, two brothers, and a sister who died long ago in infancy; a certain Mary Hall, who announces herself as the guardian spirit of Miss Shepard; and, queerest of all, a Mary Runnel, who seems to be a wandering spirit, having relations with nobody, but thrusts her finger into everybody's mass. My wife's mother is the principal communicant; she expresses strong affection, and rejoices in the opportunity of conversing with her daughter. She often says very pretty things, (for instance, in a dissertation upon heavenly music;) but there is a lack of substance in her talk, a want of gripe, a delusive show, a sentimental surface with no bottom beneath it. The same sort of thing has struck me in all the poetry and prose that I have read, from spiritual sources. I should judge [82] that these effusions emanated from earthly minds, but had undergone some process that deprived them of solidity and warmth. In the communications between my wife and her mother, I cannot help thinking, that (Miss Sheperd being unconsciously in a mesmeric state) all the responses are conveyed to her fingers from my wife's mind; for I discern in them much of her beautiful fancy and many of her preconceived ideas, although thinner and weaker than at first hand. They are the echoes of her own voice, returning out of the lonely chambers of her heart, and mistaken by her for the tones of her mother.

We have tried the spirits by various test questions, on every one of which they have failed egregiously. Here, however, the aforesaid Mary Runnel comes into play. The other spirits have told us that the veracity of this spirit is not to be depended upon; and so, whenever it is possible, poor Mary Runnel is thrust forward to bear the odium of every mistake or falsehood. They have avowed themselves responsible, however, [83] for all statements signed by themselves, and have thereby brought themselves into more than one inextricable dilemma; but it is very funny—where a response on a matter of fact has not been thus certified—how invariably Mary Runnel is made to assume the discredit of it, on its turning out to be false. It is the most ingenious arrangement that could possibly have been contrived; and, somehow or other, the pranks of this lying spirit give a reality to the conversations, which the more respectable ghosts quite fail in imparting.

This whole matter seems to me a sort of dreaming awake, my wife being, in the present instance, the principal dreamer. It resembles a dream, in that the whole material is, from the first, in the dreamer's mind, though concealed at various depths beneath the surface; the dead appear alive, as they always do in dreams; unexpected combinations occur, as continually in dreams; the mind speaks through the various persons of the drama, and sometimes as[84]tonishes itself with its own wit, wisdom, and eloquence, as often in dreams—but, in both cases, the intellectual manifestations are really of a very flimsy texture. Mary Runnel is the only personage who does not come evidently from Dream-land; and she, I think, represents that lurking skepticism, that sense of unreality, of which we are often conscious amid the most vivid phantasmagoria of a dream. I should be glad to believe in the genuineness of these spirits, if I could; but the above is the conclusion to which my soberest thoughts tend. There remains, of course, a great deal for which I cannot account, and I cannot sufficiently wonder at the pig-headedness both of metaphysicians and physiologists, in not accepting the phenomena so far as to make them the subject of investigation.

In writing these communications, Miss Shepard holds the pencil rather loosely between her fingers; it moves rapidly, and with equal facility whether she fixes her eyes on the paper or not. The handwriting has far more freedom than her own. [85] At the conclusion of a sentence, the pencil appears to lay itself down. She sometimes has a perception of each word before it is written; at other times, she is quite unconscious what is to come next. Her integrity is absolutely indubitable, and she herself totally disbelieves in the spiritual authenticity of what is communicated through her medium.

Villa Montauto, Sept 3ᵈ, Friday.

Mamma and I walked into Florence, yesterday, betimes after breakfast; it being comfortably cool, and a grey, English sky; though, indeed, the clouds had a tendency to mass themselves more than they do on an overcast English day. We found it warmer in Florence, but not inconveniently so, even in the sunniest streets and squares. People say that this has been an uncommonly cool season, and now there is an evident autumnal quality in the atmosphere; though no doubt there may be a good deal of warm weather to come.

We went to the Ufizzi Gallery, the whole of [86] which, with its contents, is now familiar to us, except the rooms containing drawings; and our to-day's visit was especially to them. The door giving admittance to them is the very last in the gallery; and the rooms, three in number, are, I should judge, over the Loggia of Lanzi, looking on the Granducal piazza. The drawings hang on the walls, framed and glazed, and number perhaps from one to two hundred in each room;

but this is only a small portion of the collection, which amounts, it is said, to twenty-five thousand, and is reposited in portfolios. The sketches on the walls are changed, from time to time, so as to exhibit all the most interesting ones in turn. Their whole charm is artistic, imaginative, and intellectual, and in no degree of the upholstery kind; their outward presentment being, in general, a design hastily shadowed out, by means of light-colored crayons, on tinted paper; or perhaps scratched rudely in pen-and-ink; or drawn in pencil, or charcoal, and half-rubbed out;—very rough things indeed, in many instances, and the [87] more interesting on that account; because as it seems as if the artist had bestirred himself to catch the first glimpse of an image that did but reveal itself, and vanish. The sheets—or sometimes scraps—of paper on which they are drawn, are discolored with age, creased, soiled; but yet you are magnetized by the hand of Raphael, Michael Angelo, Leonardo, or whoever may have jotted down those rough-looking master-touches. They certainly possess a charm that is lost in the finished picture; and I was more sensible of forecasting thought, skill, and prophetic design, in these sketches, than in the most consummate works that have been elaborated from them. There is something more divine in these; for, I suppose, the first idea of a picture is real inspiration, and all the subsequent elaboration of the master serves but to cover up the celestial germ with something that belongs to himself. At any rate, the first sketch is the more suggestive, and sets the spectator's imagination at work; whereas, the picture, if a good one, leaves him nothing to [88] do; if bad, it confuses, stupefies, disenchants, and disheartens him. First thoughts have an aroma and fragrance in them that they do not lose in three hundred years; for so old, and a good deal more, are some of these sketches.

None interested me more than some sketches, on separate pieces of paper, by Perugino, for his picture of the mother and friends of Jesus round his dead body, now at the Pitti palace. The attendant figures are distinctly made out, as if the Virgin, and John, and Mary Magdalen, had each favored the painter with a sitting; but the body of Jesus lies in the midst, dimly hinted with a few pencil-marks. There were several designs by Michael Angelo, none of which made much impression on me; the most striking was a very ugly demon, afterwards painted in the Sistine Chapel. Raphael shows several sketches of Madonnas, one of which seems to have flowered into the Grand Duke's especial Madonna, at the Pitti palace, but with a different face. His sketches were mostly very rough in execution; but there were two or three designs [89] for frescoes, I think, in the Vatican, very carefully executed;—perhaps because their works were mainly to be done by other hands than his own. It seemed to me that the old fellows—the pre-Raphaelite artists—made more careful drawings than the later ones; and it rather surprised me to see how much science they possessed.

We looked at few other things in the gallery; and, indeed, it was not one of the days when works of art find me impressible. We stopt a little while in the Tribune; but the Venus de Medici seemed little more than any other piece of yellowish-white marble. How strange that a goddess should stand before us absolutely unrecognized, even when we know by previous revelations that she is nothing short of divine! It is queer, too, that, unless when one feels the ideal charm of a statue, it becomes one of the most tedious and irksome things in the world; either it must be a celestial thing, or an old lump of stone, dusty and time-soiled, and tiring out your patience with eternally looking just the same. Once in a while, [90] you penetrate through this crust of old sameness, and see the statue forever new and immortally young.

Leaving the gallery, we walked towards the Duomo, and, on our way, stopt to look at the beautiful Gothic niches, hollowed into the exterior walls of the church of San Michele. They are now in the process of being cleaned; and each niche appears to be elaborately inlaid with precious marbles, and some of them magnificently gilded, and they are all surmounted with marble canopies, as light and graceful as frostwork. Within stand statues, quaint, and not very beautiful—Saint George, and many other saints, by Donatello and others—but taking a sort of hold upon one's sympathies, even if they be ugly. Classic statues escape you with their slippery beauty, as if they were made of ice. Rough and ugly things can be clutched. This is nonsense, but yet it means something. We went into a cake-shop and refreshed ourselves with six crazias worth of cakes and buns, and then went on; while the streets were thronged and vociferous with more life and [91] outcry than usual. It must have been market-day in Florence; for the commerce of the streets was in great vigor, narrow tables being set out in them and in the squares, burthened with all kinds of small merchandize, such as cheap jewellery, glistening as brightly as what we had just seen in the gem-room of the Uffizi; crockery-ware; toys; books, Italian and French; silks; slippers; old iron; and I know not what else—all advertized by the dealers with terribly loud and high voices, that reverberated harshly from side to side of the narrow streets. Italian street-cries go right through the head, not that they are so very sharp, but exceedingly hard, like a blunt iron bar.

We stood at the base of the Campanile, and looked at the bas-reliefs which wreathe it around in two rows; and, above them, a row of statues; and from bottom to top a marvellous minuteness of inlaid marbles filling up the vast and beautiful design of this heaven-aspiring tower. Looking upward to its lofty summit (where angels might alight, lapsing downward from heaven, and gaze [92] curiously at the bustle of men below) I could not but feel that there is a moral charm in this

faithful minuteness of Gothic architecture, filling up its outline with a million of beauties that perhaps may never be
studied out by a single spectator. It is the very process of
Nature, and, no doubt, produces an effect that we know not
of. Classic architecture is nothing but an outline, and affords
no little points, no interstices, where human feelings may
cling and overgrow it like ivy. The charm, as I said, seems to
me moral, rather than intellectual; for in the gem-room of the
Ufizzi, you may see fifty designs, elaborated on a small scale,
that have just as much merit as the design of the Campanile.
If it were only five inches long, it might be a tooth-pick case;
being two hundred feet high, its prettiness developes into
grandeur as well as beauty, and it becomes really one of the
wonders of the world. The design of the Pantheon, on the
contrary, would retain its sublimity, on whatever scale it
might be represented.

Returning homeward, we crossed the Ponte [93] Vecchio,
and went to the Museum of Natural History, where we gained
admittance into the rooms dedicated to Galileo. They consist
of a vestibule, a saloon, and a semi-circular tribune, covered
with a frescoed dome, beneath which stands a colossal statue
of Galileo, long-bearded, and clad, I think, in a student's
gown, or some voluminous garb of that kind. Around the
tribune, beside and behind the statue, are six niches, in one
of which is preserved a forefinger of Galileo, fixed on a sort
of little gilt pedestal, and pointing upward, under a glass
cover. It is very much shrivelled and mummy-like, of the
color of parchment, and seems to be little more than a finger-
bone, with the dry skin or flesh flaking away from it; on the
whole, not a very delightful relic; but Galileo used to point
heavenward with this finger, and, I hope, has gone whither
he pointed. Another niche contains two telescopes, wherewith
he made some of his discoveries; they are perhaps a yard
long, or rather more, and of very small calibre. Other astro-

nomical instruments are displayed in the [94] glass-cases that line the rooms; but I did not understand their use any better than did the monks, who wanted to burn Galileo for his heterodoxy about the planetary system.

My wife went into the Boboli gardens to rest herself, and I pursued my way homeward; winding up the weary hill at the summit of which our villa stands. After dinner, I climbed our tower and smoked a cigar, gazing, the while, at the scene beneath and around me. To the west and northwest, there was a mist (as there always is, in the Valdarno) through which the hills that border it were dimly seen, and those at the farther end of the valley, not at all. The sky was heavy with lumbering clouds, but illuminated with peeps of vivid blue between. Towards the east, and on the left of Florence, there was a dusky region of cloud and sullen mist, in which some of the hills appeared of a dark purple hue, and others became so indistinct that you could not tell hill from cloud. Far into this cloud-region, however—within the domain of Chaos, as it were—there were seen hills bright[95]ened by the sunshine, so that they looked like fragments of the world broken adrift, and based on nothingness; or as if only so much of the world had as yet been compacted. The cloud-scenery gives such a variety to our landscape, that it would be worth while to journalize its aspects, from day to day; but the difficulty is, a cloud is apt to grow solid as soon as you take it in hand.

Florence lay in the sunshine, level, compact, and small of compass. Above the tiled roofs rose the tower of the Palazzo Vecchio, the loftiest I ever saw, and the most picturesque, though built, I suppose, with no idea of making it so. But it attains, in a singular degree, the end of causing the imagination to fly upward and alight on its airy battlements. Near it I beheld the square mass of Or' San Michele, and farther to the left, the bulky Duomo, and the Campanile close beside it. like a slender bride or daughter; the dome of San Lorenzo, too, and one or two other emerging objects. The Arno is no-where visible. Beyond, and on all sides of the city, the hills pile themselves lazily [96] upward, in ridges, here and there de-veloping into a peak; towards their bases, white villas were strewn numerously; but the upper region was lonely and bare.

As we passed under the arch of the Porta Romana, this morning, on our way into the city, we saw a queer object; it was what we at first took for a living man, in a garb of a light-reddish, or yellowish red color, of antique or priestly fashion, and with a cowl falling behind. His face was of the same hue, and seemed to have been powdered, as the faces of masquers sometimes are. He sat in a cart, which he seemed to be driving into the city, with a load of earthen jars and pipkins, the color of which was precisely like his own. On closer inspection, this priestly figure proved to be likewise an image of earthen ware; but his lifelikeness had a very strange and rather ghastly effect. Adam, perhaps, was made of just such red earth, and had the complexion of this figure.

Villa Montauto, Sept 7th, Tuesday.

I walked into town, yesterday morning, by way of the Porta St. [97] Frediano. The gate of a city (Rome or Florence, or many others, doubtless) might be a good locality for a chapter in a novel, or for a little sketch by itself, whether by painter or writer. The great arch of the gateway, piercing through the depth and height of the massive masonry, beneath the battlemented summit; the shadow brooding beneath, in the immense thickness of the wall; and beyond it the vista of the street, sunny, and swarming with life; outside of the gate, a throng of carts, laden with fruits, vegetables, small, flat barrels of wine, and such rustic produce, waiting to be examined by the custom-house officers; carriages, too, and foot-passengers, entering, and others swarming outward; beneath the shadowy arch, appear to be the offices of the police and customs, and probably the guard-room of the soldiers, all hollowed out in the mass of the gateway; civil officers loll on chairs in the shade, perhaps with an awning over their heads, where the sun falls aslantwise under the arch; a centinel, with musket and bayonet, paces to-and-fro in the entrance, and other soldiers lounge close by. The life of the city seems to be compressed [98] and made more intense by this barrier; and on passing within it, you do not breathe quite so freely, yet are sensible of an enjoyment in the close, elbowing throng, the clamor of high voices from side to side of the street, and the million of petty sights, actions, traffics, and personalities, all so squeezed together as to become a great whole.

The street by which I entered led me to the Carraja bridge, crossing which, I kept straight onward till I came to the church of Santa Maria Novella. Doubtless, it looks just the same as when Boccacio's party stood in a cluster on its broad steps, arranging their excursion to the villa. Thence, I went to the church of San Lorenzo, which I entered by the side-door, and found the organ playing, and a religious ceremony going forward. It is a church of sombre aspect, with its gray walls and pillars, but was decked out for some festivity with hangings of scarlet damask and gold. I sat awhile, to rest my-self, and then emerged by the front entrance and pursued my way to the Duomo. There is a fair [99] now in progress, in Florence, and its central locality seems to be in the piazza of the Duomo, where the dealers were making vast vociferation at their several tables; but really there is very little life and picture in an Italian scene of this sort. I entered the Duomo, looked at Sir John Hawkwood's painted effigy, and at several busts and statues, and at the windows of the chapels sur-rounding the dome, through which the sunshine glowed, white

in the outer air, but a hundred-hued splendour within. I tried
to bring up the scene of Lorenzo de Medici's attempted assassination, but with no great success; and after listening a
little while to the chaunting of the priests and acolytes, I left
the Cathedral and went to the Bank. It is in a palace of which
Raphael was the architect, in the Piazza Granduca. Here I
received a letter from General Pierce, and another from Mr.
Thompson, and read Galignani.

I next went, as a matter of course, to the Ufizzi gallery,
and, in the first place, to the Tribune, where the Venus de
Medici deigned to reveal herself rather more satisfactorily
than at my last visit. [100] In other respects, it was not a very
successful day; though all such rooms as are usually closed
were now thrown open, probably on account of the fair. I
looked into them all—Bronzes, Drawings, and Gem-room—
but have no particular observations to make, though a volume
might easily be written upon either subject. The contents of
the gem-room especially require to be looked at separately,
in order to convince oneself of their minute magnificences; for,
among so many, the eye slips from one to another with only
a vague, outward sense that here are whole shelves full of
little miracles both of Nature's material and man's workmanship. Greater things can be reasonably well appreciated with
a less scrupulous, though broader attention; but in order to
estimate the brilliancy of the diamond eyes of a little agate
bust, for instance, you have to screw your mind down to them,
and nothing else. You must sharpen your faculties of observation to a point, and touch the object exactly on the right
spot; or you do not appreciate it at all. It is a troublesome
process, when there are a thousand such objects to be seen.

[101] I stood at the open window in the transverse corridor,
and looked down upon the Arno, and across at the range of
edifices that impend over it, on the opposite side. The river,
I should judge, may be a hundred, or hundred and fifty yards

wide, in its course between the Ponte Grazie (I doubt whether I have its name correctly) and the Ponte Vecchio; that is, the width between strand and strand is at least so much. The river, however, leaves a broad margin of mud and gravel on its right bank, on which water-weeds grow pretty abundantly, and creep even into the stream. On my first arrival in Florence, I thought the goose-pond green of the water rather agreeable than otherwise; but its hue is now that of unadulterated mud, as yellow as the Tiber itself, yet not impressing me as being enriched with city filth, like that other famous river. From the Ponte Grazie downward, halfway towards the Ponte Vecchio, there is an island of gravel; and the channel on each side is so shallow as to allow the passage of men and horses wading not over-leg. I have seen fisher[102]men wading the main channel from side to side, their feet sinking into the dark mud, and thus discoloring the yellow water with a black track, visible step by step through its shallowness. But still the Arno is a mountain-stream, and liable to be tetchy and turbulent, like all its kindred; and, no doubt, it often finds its borders of hewn stone not too far apart for its convenience. Along the right shore, beneath the Ufizzi and the adjacent buildings, there is a broad, paved way, with a parapet; on the opposite shore, the edifices are built right upon the river's edge, and impend over the water, supported upon arches and machicolations, as I think that peculiar arrangement of buttressing arcades is called. The houses are picturesquely various in height, from two or three stories to seven; picturesque in hue, likewise, pea-green, yellow, white, and of aged discoloration, but all with green blinds; picturesque, also, in the courts and galleries that look upon the river, and in the wide arches that open beneath, intended, perhaps, to afford a haven for the household boat. Nets were suspended before one or two of the [103] houses, as if the inhabitants were in the habit of fishing out of windows. As a general effect, the houses, though often palatial in size and height, have a shabby, neglected aspect, and seem jumbled too closely together. Behind their range, the town swells upward on a hill-side, which rises to a green height above, forming, I believe, a part of the Boboli gardens.

I returned homeward over the Ponte Vecchio, which is a continuous street of ancient houses, except over the central arch; so that a stranger might easily cross the river without knowing it. In these small, old houses, there is a community of goldsmiths, who set out their glass cases and hang their windows with rings, bracelets, necklaces, strings of pearl, ornaments of malachite and coral, and especially with Florentine mosaics; watches, too, and snuff-boxes, of old fashion, or bran-new; offerings for shrines, also, such as silver hearts pierced with swords;—in short, an infinity of pretty things, the manufacture of which is continually going on in the little back-room of each little shop. This gew-gaw business has been established on the Ponte [104] Vecchio for centuries, although, long since, it was an art of far higher pretentions than now. Benvenuto Cellini had his workshop here, probably in one of these self-same little nooks. It would have been a ticklish affair to be Benvenuto's fellow-workman within such narrow limits.

Going out of the Porte Romana, I walked for some distance along the city-wall, and then turning to the left, toiled up the hill of Bellosguardo, through narrow, zig zag lanes, between high walls of stone or plastered brick, where the sun had the fairest chance to frizzle me. There were scattered villas and houses, here and there concentrating into a little bit of a street, paved with flag-stones from side to side, as in the city, and shadowed quite across its narrowness by the height of the houses. Mostly, however, the way was inhospitably sunny, and shut out by the high walls from every glimpse of a view, except, in one spot, where Florence spread itself before my eyes, with, I think, every tower, dome, and spire, which it contains. A little way farther on, my own gray tower rose before me, [105] the most welcome object that I had seen in the course of the day.

Villa Montauto, Sept 10th, Friday.

I went into town again, yesterday, by way of the Porta San Frediano, and observed that the gate (like the other gates of Florence, so far as I know them) is a tall, square structure of stone or brick, or both, rising high above the adjacent wall, and having a range of open loggia in the upper story. The arch externally is about half the height of the structure; inside, towards the town, it rises nearly to the roof. On each side of the arch, there is much room for offices, apartments, store-houses, or whatever else. On the outside of the gate, along the base of the structure, are those iron rings, and sockets for torches, which are said to be the distinguishing symbol of illustrious houses. As contrasted with the vista of the narrow, swarming street, through the arch from without, the view from the inside might be presented, with a glimpse of the free blue sky. And now I think I have sufficient data for a picture of a gate, if ever needed.

[106] I strolled a little about Florence, and went into two or three churches; into that of the Annunziata for one. I think I have already described this church, with its general magnificence, and the profuse gilding and elaborate fretwork of the cieling, the central ornament of which is an oval picture, not a fresco apparently, but painted in oils. The church was more magnificent than ever, to-day, being hung with scarlet silk, and gold embroidery. A great many people—mostly from the surrounding hills, I presume—were at their devotions, thronging principally around the Virgin's shrine. I went into the

cloisters, which, also, I have probably described; but I was struck now with the many bas-reliefs and busts (dating from two or three centuries back, down to the present time,) in the costume of their respective ages, and seemingly with great accuracy of portraiture, in the passage leading from the front of the church into the cloisters. The marble was not at all abashed, nor degraded, by being made to assume the guise of the medi-æval furred robe, or the close-fitting tunic, with elaborate ruff, or the [107] breastplate and gorget, or the flowing wig, or whatever the actual costume might be; and one is sensible of a rectitude and reality in the affair, and respects the dead people for not putting themselves into an eternal masquerade. The dress of the present day will look equally respectable, in one or two hundred years.

The Fair, which I have already noticed, is still going on; and one of its principal centres is before this church, in the piazza of the Annunziata. Cloth is the chief commodity offered for sale, and none of the finest; coarse, unbleached linen, I think, and cotton-prints, for country-people's wear, together with yarn, stockings, and all that kind of stuff, and here and there an assortment of bright-colored ribbons. Playthings, of a very rude fashion, were also displayed; likewise, books, in Italian and French; and a great deal of iron-work, both old and new. Both here and in Rome, they have this odd custom of offering rusty iron implements for sale, spread out on the pavements. There was a good deal of tin-ware, too, glittering in the sunshine, es[108]pecially around the pedestal of the bronze statue of Duke Ferdinand, who curbs his horse and looks down upon the bustling piazza in a very stately way; as if he himself were anything better than tin or old iron, being but a copper-captain, after all. The people, attending the fair, had mostly a rustic appearance; sunburnt faces, thin frames; no bloom, no beauty, no joyousness of young or old; an anxious aspect, as if life were no easy or holiday

matter with them; but still I should take them to be of a kindly
nature, and reasonably honest. Except the broad-brimmed
Tuscan hats of the women, there was no peculiarity of
costume. At a careless glance, I could very well have mistaken
most of the men for Yankees; as for the women, there is very
little resemblance betwixt them and ours, the old ones being
absolutely hideous, and the young ones very seldom pretty. I
never saw so dull a crowd in my life. They do not appear
to generate any warmth among themselves by contiguity; they
have no pervading sentiment, such as is continually breaking
out in rough merri[109]ment from an American crowd; they
have nothing to do with one another; they are not a crowd,
considered as one mass, but a collection of individuals. A
despotic government has perhaps destroyed their principle of
cohesion, and crumbled them to atoms. Italian crowds are
noted for their civility;—possibly they deserve credit for native
courtesy and gentleness;—possibly, on the other hand, the
crowd has not spirit and self-consciousness enough to be
rampant. I wonder whether they will ever hold another
parliament in the Piazza of Santa Croce!

I went to the Bank and read some newspapers, and then
paid a visit to the gallery of the Pitti Palace. There is too
large an intermixture of Andrea del Sarto's pictures in this
gallery; everywhere you see them, cold, proper, and uncriticiza-
ble, looking so much like first-rate excellence that you inevitably quarrel with your own taste for not admiring them.
None of the pictures made a deep impression on me, at this
visit; it was one of the days when my mind misgives me
whether the pictorial art be not a humbug, and when [110]
the minute accuracy of a fly, in a Dutch picture of fruit and
flowers, seems to me something more reliable than the master-
touches of Raphael. The gallery was considerably thronged,
and many of the visitors appeared to be from the country, and
of a class intermediate betwixt gentility and labor. Is there

such a rural class, in Italy? I saw—what I have often seen in New England—a respectable-looking man, feeling awkward and uncomfortable in a new and glossy pair of pantaloons, not yet bent and creased to his natural movement. Nothing pleased me better, to-day, than some amber-cups, in one of the cabinets of curiosities; they are richly wrought, and the material is as if the artist had compressed a great deal of sunshine together, and when sufficiently solidified, had moulded these cups out of it, and let them harden. This simile, or something like it, was suggested by my wife.

Leaving the palace, I entered the Boboli Gardens, and wandered up and down a good deal of its uneven surface, through broad, well-kept hedges of box, sprouting loftily, trimmed evenly, and strewn [111] between with cleanly gravel; skirting along plantations of aged trees, throwing a deep shadow within their precincts; passing many statues, not of the finest art, yet approaching so near it as to serve just as good a purpose, for garden-ornament; coming now and then to the borders of a fish-pool, or a pond where stately swans circumnavigated an island of flowers;—all very fine, and very wearisome. I never have enjoyed this garden; perhaps because it suggests dress-coats and such elegant formalities.

Villa Montauto, Sept 11th, Saturday.

We have heard a good deal about spiritual matters of late, especially of wonderful incidents that attended Mr Hume's visit to Florence, two or three years ago. Mrs. Powers told my wife a very marvellous thing;—how that, when Mr. Hume was holding a séance in her house, and several persons present, a great scratching was heard in a neighboring closet. She addressed the spirit, and requested it not to disturb the company then, as they were busy with other affairs, promising to converse with it on a future occasion. On a subsequent night, accordingly, [112] the scratching was renewed, with the utmost violence; and in reply to Mrs. Powers's questions, the spirit assured her that it was not *one*, but legion, being the ghosts of twenty seven monks, who were miserable and without hope! The house, now occupied by Powers, was formerly a convent, and I suppose these were the spirits of all the wicked monks that had ever inhabited it;—at least, I hope that there were not such a number of damnable sinners extant at any one time. These ghostly Fathers must have been very improper persons in their life-time, judging by the indecorousness of their be- havior even after death, and in such dreadful circumstances; for they showed a disposition to make free with Mrs. Powers' petticoats, and once went so far as to lift them as high as her knees. It was not ascertained, I believe, that they desired to have anything done for their eternal welfare, or that their situation was capable of amendment anyhow; but, being ex- horted to refrain from further disturbances, they took their departure, after making the sign of the cross on the breast of each person present. This was [113] very singular in such rep- robates, who, by their own confession, had forfeited all claim to be benefitted by that holy symbol; it curiously suggests that the forms of religion may still be kept up, in Purgatory and Hell itself. The sign was made in a way that conveyed the sense of something devilish and spiteful; the perpendicular line of the cross being drawn gently enough, but the transverse one sharply and violently, so as to leave a painful impression. Perhaps the monks meant thus to express their contempt and hatred for heretics; and how queer, that this antipathy should survive their own damnation! But I cannot help hoping that the case of these poor devils may not be so desperate as they think. They cannot be wholly lost, because their desire for communication with mortals shows that they need sympathy—

therefore are not altogether hardened—therefore, with loving treatment, may be restored.

A great many other wonders took place, within the knowledge and experience of Mrs. Powers. She saw, not one pair of hands only, but many. The head of one of her dead children—a little boy—was laid [114] in her lap, not in ghastly fashion, as a head out of the coffin and the grave, but just as the living child might have laid it on his mother's knees. It was invisible, by the by; and she recognized it by the features and the character of the hair, through the sense of touch. Little hands grasped hers;—in short, these soberly attested incredibilities are so numerous that I forget nine-tenths of them, and judge the others too cheap to be written down. Christ spoke the truth, surely, in saying that men would not believe, "though one rose from the dead." In my own case, the fact makes absolutely no impression.

Within a mile of our villa, stands the Villa Columbaia, a large house, built round a square court-yard. Like Mr Powers's residence, it was formerly a convent. It is now inhabited by Major Gregorie, an old soldier of Waterloo and various other fights; and his family consists of Mrs Crossman, (the widow of one of the Major's friends) and her two daughters, one of whom is married, but separated from her husband. We have become acquainted with the family; and Mrs. Baker (the married daughter) has [115] lent us a written statement of her experiences with a ghost, who has haunted the Villa Columbaia for many years back. He had made Mrs Baker aware of his presence in her room by a sensation of extreme cold, as if a wintry breeze were blowing over her; also by a rustling of the bed-curtains; and at such times she had a certain consciousness, as she says, that she was not ALONE. Through Mr. Hume's agency, the ghost was enabled to explain himself, and declared that he was a Monk, named Giannana, who died a very long time ago in Mrs. Baker's present bed-chamber. He appears to have been a murderer, and had been in a restless and miserable state, ever since his death, wandering up and down the house, but especially haunting his own death-chamber, and a staircase that communicates with the chapel of the villa. All the interviews with this lost spirit were attended with a sensation of severe cold, which was felt by every one present; he made his communications by means of table-rapping, and by the movements of chairs and other articles, which often assumed an angry character. The poor old fellow [116] does not seem to have known exactly what he wanted with Mrs. Baker, but promised to refrain from disturbing her any more, on condition that she would pray that he might find some repose. He had previously declined having any masses said for his soul. Rest—rest—rest—appears to be the continual craving of unhappy spirits; they do not venture to ask for positive bliss—perhaps, in their utter weariness, would rather forego the trouble of active enjoyment—but pray only for rest. The cold atmosphere around this latter monk suggests new ideas as to the climate of Hades. If all the twenty-seven other monks had a similar one, the combined temperature must have been that of a polar winter.

Mrs Baker saw, at one time, the fingers of her monk, long, yellow, and skinny; these fingers grasped the hands of other individuals of the party, with a cold, clammy, and horrible touch. After the departure of this ghost, other séances were held in her bed-chamber, at which good and holy spirits manifested themselves, and behaved in a very comfortable and encouraging way. It appeared to be their benevo[117]lent purpose to purify her apartments from all traces of the evil spirit, and to reconcile her to what had been so long the haunt of this miserable monk, by filling it with happy and sacred associations;—in which, as Mrs. Baker intimates, they entirely succeeded.

These stories remind me of an incident that took place at the Old Manse, in the first summer of our marriage. One night, about eleven °clock, before either my wife or I had fallen asleep, (we had been talking together, just before) she suddenly asked me why I had touched her shoulder. The next instant, she had a sense that the touch was not mine, but that of some third *presence* in the chamber. She clung to me in great affright, but I got out of bed and searched the chamber and adjacent entry, and, finding nothing, concluded that the touch was a fancied one. My wife, however, has never varied in her belief that the incident was supernatural, and connected with the apparition of old Dr Harris, who used to show himself to me, daily, in the Reading Room of the Boston Athenaeum. I am still incredulous, both as to the Doctor's ghostly identity and as [118] to the reality of the mysterious touch. That same summer of our honeymoon, too, George Hillard and his wife were sitting with us in our parlour, when a rustling as of a silken robe passed from corner to corner of the room, right among my wife and the two guests, and heard, I think, by all the three. Mrs. Hillard, I remember, was greatly startled. As for myself, I was reclining on a sofa, at a little distance, and neither heard the rustle nor believed in it.

Villa Montauto, Sept 17th, Friday.

Mamma and I, with Una, walked yesterday to Florence, and visited the church of San Lorenzo, where we saw (for the second time) the famous Medici statues of Michael Angelo. I found myself not in a very appreciative state; and being a stone myself, the statue of Lorenzo (or Giulian, is it?) was at first little more to me than another stone; but I think it was beginning to assume life, and would have impressed me as it did before, if I had gazed long enough. There was a better light upon the face, under the helmet, than at my former visit, although still the features were enough over[119]shadowed to produce that mystery, on which, according to Mr. Powers, the effect of the statue depends. I observe that the costume of the figure (instead of being mediæval, as I believe I have stated) is Roman; but, be it what it may, the grand and simple character of the figure imbues the robes with its individual propriety. I still think it the greatest miracle ever wrought in marble.

We crossed the church, and entered a cloister on the opposite side, in quest of the Laurentian Library. Ascending a staircase, we found an old man blowing the bellows of the organ, which was in full blast in the church; nevertheless, he found time (with what interruption of the sacred music, I know not) to direct us to the library-door. We entered a lofty vestibule, of ancient aspect and stately architecture, and thence were admitted into the Library itself; a long and wide gallery or hall, lighted on each side by a row of windows on which were painted the arms of the Medici. The cieling was [120] inlaid with dark and aged wood, in an elaborate pattern, which was exactly repeated in marble or stucco, on the pavement beneath our feet. Long desks, much like the old-fashioned ones in schools, were ranged on each side of the hall, in a series from end to end, with seats for the convenience of students; and on these desks were rare manuscripts, carefully preserved under glass, and books, fastened to the desks by iron chains, as the custom of studious antiquity used to be. Along the centre of the hall, between the two ranges of desks, were tables and chairs, at which two or three scholarly persons were seated, diligently consulting volumes in manuscript or aged type. It was a very quiet hall, imbued with a cloistered sanctity, and remote from all street-cries and rumble of the city—smelling of old literature—a spot where the commonest ideas ought not to be expressed in less than Latin.

The Librarian—or Custode, he ought rather to be termed; for he was a man not above the fee of a Paul—now presented himself, and [121] showed us some of the literary curiosities; a vellum manuscript of the Bible, I think, with a splendid illumination by Ghirlandaio, covering two folio-pages, and just as brilliant in its colors as if finished yesterday. Other illuminated manuscripts (or, at least, separate pages of them, for the volumes were kept under glass, and not to be turned over) were shown us—very magnificent—but not to be compared with this of Ghirlandaio. Looking at such treasures, I could almost say that we have left behind us more splendor than we have kept alive into our own age. We publish beautiful editions of books, to be sure, and thousands of people enjoy them; but, in ancient times, the expense that we spread thinly over a thousand volumes was all compressed into one; and it became a great jewel of a book, a heavy folio worth its weight in gold. Then what a spiritual charm it gives to a book, to feel that every letter has been individually wrought, and that the pictures glow for that individual page alone. Certainly, the ancient reader had a lux[122]ury which the modern one lacks. I was surprised, moreover, to see the clearness and accuracy of the chirography. Print does not surpass it, in these respects.

The Custode showed us an ancient manuscript of the Decameron; likewise a volume containing the portraits of Petrarch and of Laura, each covering the whole of a vellum-page, and very finely done. They are authentic portraits, no doubt, and Laura is depicted as a fair-haired beauty, with a very satisfactory amount of loveliness. I do not remember what else we saw; except some choice old editions of books in a small separate room; but as these were all ranged in wired book-cases, and as each volume, moreover, was in a separate cover, or modern binding, this exhibition did us very little good. By-the-by, there is a conceit struggling blindly in my mind about Petrarch and Laura, suggested by those two life-like portraits, which have been sleeping cheek to cheek through all these centuries. But I cannot lay hold of it.

[123] After leaving the Library, we went into the shops of one or two manufacturers of Florentine Mosaics, with a purpose of selecting a specimen. We saw none exactly to our mind, however—at least, within a reasonable limit as to price.

Villa Montauto, Sept 21ˢᵗ, Tuesday.

Yesterday morning, the Valdarno was entirely filled with a thick fog, which extended even up to our windows, and concealed objects within a very short distance. It began to dissipate itself betimes, however, and was the forerunner of an unusually bright and warm day. Mamma and I set out, after breakfast, and walked into town, where we did some shopping and looked at mosaic brooches. These are very pretty little bits of manufacture; but there seems to have been no infusion of fresh fancy into the work, and the specimens present little variety. It is the characteristic commodity of the place; the central mart and manufacturing locality being on the Ponte Vecchio, from end to end of which they are displayed in cases; but there are other [124] mosaic-shops scattered about the town. The principal devices are roses, pink, yellow, or white, and jasmyns, lilies of the valley, forget-me-nots, tulips, and I know not what other flowers, single, or in sprigs, or twined into wreaths; parrots, too, and other birds of gay plumage—often exquisitely done, and sometimes with precious materials, such as lapis lazuli, malachite, and still rarer stones. Bracelets, with several different, yet relative designs, are often

very beautiful. We find, at different shops, a great inequality
of prices for mosaics that seem to be of much the same quality.
In bargaining for them, as for everything else, the dealers
leave themselves a considerable margin to abate upon, and
only come down to their true price at the last moment.

We went into the Ufizzi gallery, and found it much
thronged with the middle and lower classes of Italians; and
the English, too, seemed more numerous than I have lately
seen them. Perhaps the tourists have just arrived here, starting at the close of the London season. We were [125] amused
with a pair of Englishmen who went through the gallery;
one of them criticising the pictures and statues audibly, for
the benefit of his companion. The critic I should take to be
a country-squire, not wholly untravelled; a tall, well-built,
rather rough, but gentlemanly man enough; his friend, a small
personage, exquisitely neat in dress, and of artificial deportment, every attitude and gesture appearing to have been
practised before a glass. Being but a small pattern of a man,
physically and intellectually, he had thought it worth while
to finish himself off with the elaborateness of a Florentine
mosaic; and the result was something like a dancing-master,
though without the exuberant embroidery of such characters.
Indeed, he was a very quiet little man, and though so
thoroughly made-up, there was something particularly green,
fresh, and simple in him. Both these Englishmen were elderly,
and the smaller one had perfectly white hair, glossy and
silken. It did not make him in the least venerable, however,
but took his own character of neatness and prettiness. He
[126] carried his well-brushed and glossy hat in his hand, in
such a way as not to ruffle its surface; and I do wish I could
put into one word, or one sentence, the pettiness, the minikin,
finical effect of this little man; his self-consciousness, so lifelong that, in some sort, he forgot himself even in the midst of

it; his propriety, his cleanliness and unruffledness; his prettiness and nicety of manifestation, like a bird hopping daintily
about.

His companion, as I said, was of a completely different type;
a tall, gray-haired man, with the rough English face, a little
tinted with Port-wine; careless, natural manners, betokening
a man of position in his own neighborhood; a loud voice,
not vulgar, nor outraging the rules of society, but betraying a
character incapable of much refinement. He talked continually, in his progress through the gallery, and audibly
enough for us to catch almost everything he said, at many
yards' distance. His remarks and criticisms, addressed to his
small friend, were so entertaining that we strolled behind him
for the sake of being bene[127]fitted by them; and I think
he soon became aware of this, and addressed himself to us as
well as to his more immediate friend. Nobody but an Englishman, it seems to me, has just this kind of vanity; a feeling
mixed up with scorn and good-nature; self-complacency on his
own merits and as an Englishman; pride at being in foreign
parts; contempt of everybody around him; a rough kindliness
towards people in general. I liked the man, and should be glad
to know him better. As for his criticisms, I am sorry to remember only one; it was upon the picture of the nativity, by
Corregio, in the Tribune, where the mother is kneeling before the child, and adoring it in an awful rapture, because she
sees the Eternal God in its baby-face and figure. The Englishman was highly delighted with this picture, and began to
gesticulate as if dandling a baby, and to make a chirruping
sound; it was to him merely a representation of a mother
fondling her child. He then said, "If I could have my choice
of the pictures and statues in the Tribune, I would take this
[128] picture, and that one yonder" (it was a good enough
Enthronement of the Virgin, by Andrea del Sarto,) "and the
Dancing Faun, and let the rest go!" A delightful man! I love

that wholesome coarseness of mind and heart, which no education nor opportunity can polish out of the genuine Englishman; a coarseness without vulgarity. When a Yankee is coarse (which is not the case half so often as with an Englishman) he is pretty sure to be vulgar too.

The two critics seemed to be considering whether it were practicable to go from the Ufizzi to the Pitti Gallery; but, "It confuses one," remarked the little man, "to see more than one gallery in a day!" I should think so—the Pitti Palace tumbling into his small receptacle, on the top of the Ufizzi.

Villa Montauto, Sept 23ᵈ, Thursday.

The vintage has been going on in our Podere for about a week past, and I saw a part of the process of making wine, under one of our back windows. It was on a very small scale, —the grapes being thrown [129] into a barrel, and crushed with a sort of pestle; and as each estate seems to make its own wine, there are probably no very extensive or elaborate appliances in general use for the manufacture. The cider-making of New-England is far more picturesque—the great heap of golden and rosy apples under the trees; and the cider-mill, worked by a circumgiratory horse, and all a-gush with sweet juice. Indeed, nothing connected with the grape culture and the vintage is picturesque, except the huge inverted pyramids in which the clusters hang; those great bunches, white or purple, really satisfy my idea both as to aspect and taste. We can buy a large basketful, half-dozen-pounds, for less than a Paul; and they are the only things that one can never devour too much of—and there is not enough short of a little too much—without subsequent repentance. It is a shame to turn such delicious juice into such sour wine as they make in Tuscany. I tasted a sip or two of a flask which the Contadini sent us for trial—the rich result of the process that I had [140] witnessed in the barrel. It took me altogether by surprise; for I remembered the nectareousness of the new cider, which I used to suck with a straw in my boyhood; and I never doubted that this would be as dulcet, but finer and more ethereal—as much more delectable, in short, as these grapes are better than puckery cider-apples. Positively, I never tasted anything so detestable—such a sour and bitter juice, still lukewarm with fermentation; it was a wail of woe, squeezed out of the wine-press of tribulation; and the more a man drinks of such, the sorrier he will be.

Besides grapes, we have for some time past had figs, and I have now learned to be very fond of them. When they first began to appear, two months ago, they had scarcely any sweetness, and tasted very like a decaying squash; this was an early variety, with purple skins. There seem to be many kinds of figs, the best being green-skinned, growing yellower as they ripen; and the riper they are, the more the sweetness within [141] them intensifies, till they resemble dried figs in everything except that they retain the fresh fruit-flavor— rich, luscious, yet not palling. We have had pears, too, some of them very tolerable; and peaches, which look magnificently, as regards size and downy blush, but have seldom much more taste than a cucumber. A succession of fruits has followed us, ever since our arrival in Florence;—first, and for a long time, abundance of cherries; then apricots, which lasted many weeks, till we were weary of them; then plums, pears, and finally, figs, peaches, and grapes. Except the figs and grapes— and I even hope to find almost as good grapes at the Wayside —a New England summer and autumn would give us better fruit than any we have found in Italy.

Italy beats us, I think, in musquitoes; they are horribly pungent little particles of Satan. I do believe the Devil multiplies himself by the million, and infests our nights in this guise. They possess strange intelligence, and exquisite acuteness of sight and smell—prodigious auda[142]city, and caution to match it, insomuch that they venture on the most hazardous attacks and get safe off. They absolutely creep into bed, and bite us in our strong holds. One of them flew into my mouth, the other night, and stung me far down in my throat; but luckily I coughed him up in halves. They are bigger than American musquitoes, and, if you crush them, after one of their feasts, it makes a terrific blood-spot. It is a sort of suicide—at least a shedding of one's own blood—to kill them; but it gratifies the old Adam to do it. It shocks me to feel how revengeful I am; but it is impossible not to impute a certain malice and intellectual venom to these diabolical insects. I wonder whether our health, at this season of the year, requires that we should be kept in a state of irritation, and so the musquitoes are Nature's prophetic remedy for some disease; or whether we are made for the musquitoes, not they for us. It is possible—just possible—that the infinitesimal doses of poison which they infuse into us are a homœpathic safe-guard against pesti[143]lence; but medicine never was ad-ministered in a more disagreeable way.

The moist atmosphere about the Arno, I suppose, produces these insects, and fills the broad, ten-mile valley with them; and as we are just on the brim of the basin, they overflow into our windows.

Villa Montauto Sept 25th, Saturday.

Una and I walked to town, yesterday morning, and went to the Ufizzi gallery. It is not a pleasant thought that we are so soon to give up this gallery, with little prospect (none, or hardly any, on my part) of ever seeing it again. It interests me, and all of us, far more than the gallery of the Pitti Palace; —wherefore, I know not, for the latter is the richest of the two in admirable pictures. Perhaps it is the picturesque variety of the Ufizzi—the combination of painting, sculpture, gems, and bronzes—that makes the charm. The Tribune, too, is the richest room in all the world; a heart, that draws all hearts to it. The Dutch pictures, moreover, give a homely, human interest to the Ufizzi; and I re[144]ally think that the frequency of Andrea del Sarto's productions, at the Pitti Palace—looking so very like master-pieces, yet lacking the soul of art and nature—have much to do with the weariness that comes from better acquaintance with the latter gallery. The splendor of the gilded and frescoed saloons is perhaps another bore; but, after all, my memory will often tread them, as long as I live. What shall we do in America!

Speaking of Dutch pictures, I was much struck, yesterday—as frequently before—with a small picture by Teniers the elder;—it seemed to be a pawn-broker in the midst of his pledges; old earthen jugs, flasks, a brass kettle, old books, and a huge pile of worn-out and broken rubbish, which he is examining. These things are represented with vast fidelity, yet with bold and free touches, unlike the minute, microscopic work of other Dutch painters; and a wonderful picturesqueness is wrought out of these homely materials, and even the figure and head of the pawnbroker have a strange grandeur.

[145] We spent no very long time at the Ufizzi, and afterwards crossed the Ponte Grazie, and went to the Convent of San Minuato which stands on a hill, outside of the Porta San Gallo. A paved pathway, along which stand crosses, (marking stations at which, I believe, pilgrims are to kneel and pray) goes steeply to the hill-top, where stands, in the first place, a smaller church and convent than that of San Minuato. The latter are seen at a short distance to the right; the Convent being a large, square, battlemented mass, adjoining which is the church, showing a front of aged white marble, streaked with black, and having an old stone tower behind. I have seen

no other convent or monastery that so well corresponds with my idea of what such structures were. The sacred precincts are enclosed by a high wall, gray, ancient, and luxuriously ivy-grown, and lofty and strong enough for the rampart of a fortress. We went through the gateway, and entered the church; which we found in much disarray, and masons at work upon the pavement. I have brought away no dis[146]-tinct idea, but remember that the tribune of the church was elevated considerably above the nave and accessible by marble staircases; that there are great arches, and a chapel with curious monuments in the Gothic style; and that there are ancient carvings and mosaic-works, and, in short, a dim, dusty, and venerable interior, well worth studying in detail. A young woman was in attendance with a key, and wished to show us the sacristy; but I had spent all my money, chiefly for an opera-glass and afterwards for some peaches, and therefore declined to incur the responsibility of a fee.

The view of Florence from the church-door is very fine, and seems to include every tower, dome, or whatever object that emerges out of the general mass.

Villa Montauto, Sept 28th, Tuesday.

I went to the Pitti Palace, yesterday, and with Una and Julian to the Ufizzi gallery to-day, paying them probably my last visits, yet cherishing an unreasonable doubt whether I may not see them again. At [147] all events, I have seen them enough for the present, even what is best of them; and at the same time with a sad reluctance to bid them farewell forever, I experience an utter weariness of Raphael's old canvass, and of the time-yellowed marble of the Venus de Medici. When their material embodiment presents itself outermost, and we perceive them only by the grosser sense, missing their ethereal spirit, there is nothing so heavily burthensome as masterpieces of painting and sculpture. I threw my farewell glance at the Venus de Medici, to-day, with strange insensibility.

The nights are wonderfully beautiful now. When the moon was at the full, a few nights ago, its light was an absolute glory, such as I seem only to have dreamed of, heretofore, and that only in my younger days. At its rising, I have fancied that the orb of the moon has a kind of purple brightness, and that this tinge is communicated to its radiance, until it has climbed high aloft, and sheds a flood of white light over hill and valley. Now that the moon [148] is in the wane, there is a gentler lustre, but still bright; and it makes the Valdarno, with its surrounding hills, and its soft mist in the distance, as beautiful a scene as exists anywhere out of heaven. And the morning is quite as beautiful in its own way. This mist, which I have so often spoken of, sets it beyond the limits of actual sense, and makes it ideal; it is as if you were dreaming about the valley—as if the valley itself were dreaming, and met you half way in your own dream. If the mist were to be withdrawn, I believe the whole beauty of the valley would go with it.

Until pretty late in the evening, we have the comet streaming through the sky, and dragging its interminable tail among the stars. It keeps brightening, from night to night, and, I should think, must blaze fiercely enough to cast a shadow, by-and-bye. I know not whether it is the vicinity of Galileo's tower, and in the influence of his spirit; but I have hardly ever watched the stars and the heavenly host with such interest as now.

[149] Villa Montauto, Sept 29th, Wednesday.

Last evening, I met Mr. Powers at Miss Blagden's; and he talked about his treatment by our government in reference to an appropriation of 25000 dollars made by Congress for a statue by him. Its payment, and the purchase of the statue, were left at the option of the President; and he conceives himself wronged by General Pierce because the affair was never concluded. Crawford, too, seems to have been somehow mixed up with the business, and to have obtained a contract for a statue of America in an underhand way, as Powers thinks, while offering to forward Mr. P.'s views for the sale of his own statue of America. I did not perceive, however, that he made out anything dishonorable on Crawford's part, but only a concealment (unnecessary, I think) that he himself had already contracted for such a statue, while proposing to assist Powers in obtaining a similar commission. As for General Pierce, he knows nothing of art, and probably acted, in this matter, by the advice of [150] the director of public works, or whatever authority it be that presides immediately over the decoration of the Capitol at Washington. No doubt, a sculptor gets commissions, as everybody gets public employment and emolument of whatever kind, from our government, not by merit or fitness, but by political influence skilfully applied. As Powers himself observed, the ruins of our Capitol are not likely to afford sculptures equal to those which Lord Elgin stole from the Parthenon, if this be the system under which they are produced. He spoke contemptuously of Crawford's works for government, as being done at a low price—hastily sketched out by the artist, and left to be modelled and put in marble by hired workmen. I wish our great Republic had the spirit to do as much, according to its vast means, as Florence did for sculpture and architecture, when it was a Republic; but we have the meanest government, and the shabbiest—and, if truly represented by it, are the meanest and shabbiest people—known in history. And yet, the less we attempt [151] to do for art the better, if our future attempts are to have no better result than such brazen troopers as the equestrian statue of General Jackson, or even such naked respectabilities as Greenough's Washington. There is something false and affected in our highest taste for art; and I suppose, furthermore, we are the only people who seek to decorate their public institutions, not by the highest taste among them, but by the average, at best.

There was also at Miss Blagden's, among other company, a Mr. Miniati, an artist in Florence, and a sensible man. I talked with him about Hume, the spiritualist, whom he had many opportunities of observing, when the latter was in these parts. Mr. Minuati says that Hume is unquestionably a knave, but that he himself is as much perplexed at his own preternatural performances as any other person; he is startled and affrighted at the phenomena which he produces. Nevertheless, when his spiritual powers fall short, he does his best to eke them out by imposture. This moral infirmity is a part of his nature; and I suggested that per[152]haps if he were of a firmer and healthier moral make—if his character were sufficiently sound and dense to be capable of stedfast principle— he would not have possessed the impressibility that fits him for the so-called spiritual influences. Mr. Miniati says that Louis Napoleon is one of the most skilful jugglers in the world, (not metaphorically, but literally,) and that probably the interest he has taken in Mr. Hume was caused partly by a wish to acquire his art.

This morning, Mr. Powers invited me to go with him and his wife to the Grand Duke's new Foundry, to see the bronze statue of Webster, which has just been cast from his model. It is the second cast of the statue; the first having been shipped, some months ago, on board of a vessel which was lost; and, as Powers observed, the statue now lies at the bottom of the Atlantic ocean, somewhere in the vicinity of the telegraphic cable. We were received with much courtesy and emphasis by the director of the Foundry, and conducted

into a large room, walled with bare, new brick, where the
statue was [153] standing in front of the extinct furnace; a
majestic Webster indeed, eight feet high, and looking even
more colossal than that. The likeness seemed to me perfect;
and, like a sensible man, Powers has dressed him in his actual
costume, such as I have seen Webster have on while making
a speech in the open air, at a mass-meeting in Concord—dress-
coat, buttoned pretty closely across the breast, pantaloons, and
boots—everything finished even to a seam and a stitch. Not
an inch of the statue but is Webster; even his coat-tails are
imbued with the man; and this true artist has succeeded in
showing him through the broadcloth, as Nature showed him.
He has felt that a man's actual clothes are as much a part of
him as his flesh; and I respect him for disdaining to shirk the
difficulty by throwing the meanness of a cloak over it, and
for recognizing the folly of masquerading our Yankee statesman in a Roman toga, and the indecorousness of presenting
him as a brawny nudity. It would have been quite as justifiable
to strip him to his skeleton as to his flesh. Webster [154] is
represented as holding in his right hand the written roll of the
constitution, with which he points to a bundle of fasces which
he keeps from falling by the grasp of his left—thus symbolizing him as the preserver of the Union. I never saw such an
expression of quiet, solid, massive strength as there is in the
whole figure; a deep, pervading energy, in which any exag-
geration of gesture would lessen and lower the effect. He looks
really like a pillar of the state. The face is very grand, very
Webster; stern and awful, because he is in the act of meeting a
great crisis, and yet with the warmth of a great heart glowing
through it. Happy is Webster to have been so truly and
adequately sculptured; happy the sculptor in such a subject,
which no idealization of a demi-god could have supplied him
with. Perhaps the statue at the bottom of the sea will be cast
up, in some future age, when this present race of man is for-

gotten; and, if so, that far posterity will look upon us as a far grander race than we find ourselves to be. Neither was Webster altogether the [155] man he looked; his physique helped him out, even when he fell somewhat short of its promise; and if his eyes had not been in such deep caverns, their fire would not have looked so bright.

Powers made me observe how the surface of the statue was wrought to a sort of roughness, instead of being smoothed, as is the practice of other artists. He said that this had cost him great pains, and certainly it has an excellent effect. The statue is to go to Boston, and, I hope, will be placed in the open air; for it is too mighty to be kept under any roof that now exists in America. It would look admirably, I think, in the centre of the Pantheon, under the circular opening of the dome.

After seeing the statue, the Director showed us some very curious and exquisite specimens of castings; such as baskets of flowers, in which the most delicate and fragile blossoms, the curl of a petal, the finest veins in a leaf, the lightest flower-spray that ever quivered in a breeze, were perfectly preserved; and the basket contained an abundant heap of such. There was likewise a pair of hands, taken [156] actually from life, clasped together as they were; and they looked like parts of a man who had been changed suddenly from flesh to brass. They were worn, and rough, and unhandsome hands, and so very real, with all their veins, and the pores of the skin, that it was shocking to look at them. A bronze leaf, cast also from the life (that is, cast first in plaister, I presume, and then in bronze) was as curious and more beautiful.

Taking leave of Powers and his wife, I went hither and thither about Florence, seeing for the last time things that I have seen many times before; the market, for instance, blocking up a line of narrow streets with fruit-stalls and obstreperous dealers, crying their peaches, their green lemons, their figs, purple and green, their delicious grapes, their mushrooms, their pomegranates, their radishes, their lettuces—but I may as well close the list at once. They use one sort of vegetable here, which I have not known so used elsewhere; that is very young pumpkins or squashes, of the size of apples, and to be cooked by boiling. They are not to my taste; but [157] the people here like unripe things; unripe fruit, unripe chickens, unripe lamb. This market is the noisiest and swarmiest centre of noisy and swarming Florence, and I always like to pass through it on that account. I went also to Santa Croce, (the church,) and it seemed to me to present a longer vista and broader space than almost any church I have seen; perhaps because the pillars between the nave and aisles are not so massive as to obstruct the view. I looked into the Duomo, too, and was pretty well content to leave it, and all the rest. Then I came homeward, and trying a new road, lost my way, and wandered far off through the white sunshine, and the scanty shade of the vineyard walls, and the olive-trees that here and there branched over them. At last, I saw our own gray battlements at a distance, on one side, quite out of the direction in which I was travelling; so was compelled to the grievous mortification of retracing a great many of my weary footsteps. It was a very hot day. This evening, I have been [158] on the tower-top, star-gazing, and looking at the comet, which waves along the sky like an immense feather of flame. Over Florence there was an illuminated atmosphere, caused by the lights of the city gleaming upward into the mists which sleep and dream above that portion of the valley, as well as the rest of it. I saw dimly—or fancied I saw—the hill of Fiesole, on the other side of Florence, and remembered how ghastly lights were seen passing thence to the Duomo, on the night when Lorenzo the Magnificent died. I smoked a cigar, too, and the air was so still that it scarcely wafted away the smoke. From time to time, the sweet bells of Florence rang

out; and I was loth to come down into the lower world,
knowing that I shall never again look heavenward from an
old tower-top, in such a soft, calm evening as this. Yet I am not
loth to go away;—impatient rather; for, taking no root, I soon
weary of any soil that I may be temporarily deposited in. The
same impatience I sometimes feel, or conceive of, as regards
this [159] earthly life; since it is to come to an end, I do not
try to be contented, but weary of it while it lasts.

I forgot to mention that Powers showed me, in his studio,
the model of the statue of America, which he wished the
Government to buy. It has great merit, and embodies the
ideas of youth, freedom, progress, and whatever else we choose
to consider as distinctive of our country's character and destiny.
It is a female figure, youthful, vigorous, beautiful, planting its
foot lightly on a broken chain, and pointing upward. The face
has a high look of intelligence and lofty feeling; the form,
nude to the middle, has all the charms of womanhood, and is
thus warmed and redeemed out of the cold allegoric sisterhood, who have generally no merit in chastity, being really
without sex. I somewhat question whether it is quite the thing,
however, to make a genuine woman out of an allegory; we
ask, who is to wed this lovely virgin? who is to clasp and
enjoy that beautiful form?—and are not satisfied to banish her
into the realm of chilly thought. But I [160] liked the statue,
and all the better for what I criticise, and was sorry to see the
huge package in which the finished marble lies bundled up,
ready to be sent to our country which does not call for it.

Siena, October 2ᵈ, Saturday.

Mr. Powers and his two daughters called to take leave of
us on Thursday evening; and at parting, I expressed a hope of
seeing him in America. He said that it would make him very

unhappy to believe that he should never return thither; but it seems to me that he has no such definite purpose of return as would be certain to bring itself to pass. It makes a very unsatisfactory life, thus to spend all the bulk of it in exile; in such a case, we are always deferring the reality of life till a future moment, and, by and by, we have deferred it till there are no future moments; or, if we do go back, we find that life has shifted whatever of reality it had to the country where we deemed ourselves only living temporarily; and so, between two stools, we come to the ground, and make ourselves a part of one or the other country only by laying our bones in [1st 161] its soil. It is particularly a pity in Power's case, because he is so very American in character, and also because, it appears to me, he profits little or nothing by the works of art around him, and, indeed, has never studied them to any great extent. The only convenience for him of his Italian residence is, that here he can supply himself with marble, and with workmen skilled to chisel it according to his designs.

We all bestirred ourselves before light, yesterday morning; and at six °clock (there being no coach within call) we left our ancient tower, and threw a parting glance—and a rather sad one—over the misty Valdarno. This summer will look like a happy one in our children's retrospect, and also, no doubt, in the years that remain to ourselves; and, in truth, though shadowed with certain glooms and despondencies, I have found it, on the whole a peaceful and not uncheerful one. It was not a pleasant morning; and Monte Morello, looking down on Florence, had on its cap, betokening foul weather, according to the proverb. We trudged on—our caravan of six—as fast as Rosebud and mamma could go, [162] and, crossing the suspension-bridge, reached the Leopoldo railway, without entering the city. We had sent our luggage before us in a contadino's cart, and found it waiting for our arrival; but there was so little time to spare, that we could but just buy our tickets and take our seats, when the train started, leaving all our ten trunks and a tin band-box behind. By some mistake—or perhaps because nobody ever travels by first-class, in Tuscany—we had received second-class tickets, and found ourselves in a long, crowded car, full of priests, military-men, commercial-travellers, and other respectable people, facing one another lengthwise along the carriage, and many of them smoking cigars. They were all perfectly civil, and made room for us as well as they could; and, bating the cigars (in which I should have liked well enough to join the other travellers,) I think I must own that the manners of this Second-class car would compare favorably with those of an American first-class one.

At Empoli, about an hour after we started, we had to change carriages, the main train proceeding to Leghorn; and in the hurry of getting out, with our [2nd 161] children, and shawls, and miscellaneous luggage, my leather-bag, containing my dressing-case, and many other precious personalities, was left behind under one of the seats. We immediately telegraphed to Leghorn to have it sent back; but, to say the truth, I hardly hoped ever to see it again, and even doubted whether the ten trunks and the tin band-box would ever come to hand, unless we returned to Florence for them. This misfortune bothered me a good deal; but, luckily, there is very little to be enjoyed in a railway-trip, at any rate; so that there is no better time for small incommodities to happen. My observations along the road were very scanty; a hilly country, with several old towns seated on the most elevated hill-tops, as is common throughout Tuscany; or sometimes, a fortress, with a town on the plain at its base; or, once or twice, the towers and battlements of a mediæval castle, commanding the pass below it. Near Florence, the country was fertile in the vine and olive, and looked as unpicturesque as that sort of fertility usually makes it; not but what I have come [164] to think better of the tint of the olive-leaf, than when I first saw it. In the latter part of our journey, I remember a wild stream, of a greenish hue, but transparent, rushing along, over a rough bed; and before reaching Siena, we rumbled into a long tunnel, and emerged from it, I believe, at no great distance from the city. At the railway-station (which is just outside of the gates) we took a cab, which, after all our losses, was pretty well heaped up with our remaining trumpery. There is one comfort in thinking of the last, long journey we shall ever take:—we can carry no luggage along with us. There will be no luggage-car, nor carpet-bags under the seats.

We drove up hill and down (for the surface of Siena seems to be nothing but an irregularity) through narrow, old streets, and were set down at the Aquila Nera, a grim-looking albergo near the centre of the town. Mrs. Story had already taken rooms for us there; and to these we were now ushered, up the highway of a dirty stone-staircase, and into a small, brick-paved parlour, dingy and forlorn. The [165] house seemed endlessly old, and all the glimpses that we caught of Siena, out of window, seemed more ancient still. Almost within arm's reach, across a narrow street, a tall palace of gray, time-worn stone clambered skyward, with arched windows, and square windows, and large windows, and small, scattered up and down its side; it is called, I think, the Palazzo Tolomei, and looks immensely venerable. From the windows of our bed-rooms we looked into a broader street, though still not very wide, and into a small piazza, the most conspicuous object in which was a column, bearing on its top a bronze wolf, suckling Romulus and Remus. This symbol is repeated in other parts of the city, and seems to indicate that the Sienese people pride themselves in a Roman origin. In another direction, over the tops of the houses, we saw a very high tower, with battlements projecting around its summit, so that it was a fortress in the air; and this I have since found to be the tower of the Palazzo Publico. It was pleasant, looking downward into the little old piazza and narrow streets, to see the swarm of life on the pavement; [166] the life of to-day, just as new as if it had never been lived before; the citizens, the priests, the soldiers, the mules and asses with their panniers, the diligence lumbering along, with a postillion, in a faded crimson coat, bobbing up-and-down on the off-horse;— such a bustling scene (vociferous, too, with various streetcries) is wonderfully set off by the gray antiquity of the town, and makes the town look even older than if it were a solitude.

We got a lunch (an omelet, some rather scrawny muttonchops, and a small flask of Montepulciano, bitter and resinous;) and soon Mr. and Mrs. Story came, and accompanied us to look for lodgings. They also drove us about town in their carriage, and showed us the outside of the Palazzo Publico, and of the Cathedral, and other remarkable edifices, which perhaps I shall speak of more at leisure, and after better acquaintance. The aspect of Siena is far more picturesque than that of any other town in Italy, so far as I know Italian towns; and yet, now that I have written it, I remember Perugia, and feel that the observation is a mistake. But at any rate, Siena is remarkably pictur[167]esque, standing on such a site, on the verge and within the crater of an extinct volcano, and therefore being as uneven as the sea in a tempest; the streets so narrow, ascending between tall, ancient palaces, while the side-streets rush headlong down, only to be threaded by surefooted mules, such as climb Alpine-heights; old stone balconies on the palace-fronts; old arched doorways, and windows set in frames of Gothic architecture; arcades, resembling canopies of stone, with quaintly sculptured statues in the richly wrought Gothic niches of each pillar;—everything massive and lofty, yet minutely interesting when you look at it stone by stone. The Florentines—and the Romans too—have obliterated, as far as they could, all the interest of their mediæval structures by covering them with stucco, so that they have quite lost their character, and affect the spectator with no reverential idea of age. Here, the city is all overwritten with black-letter; and the glad Italian sun makes the effect so much the stronger.

We took a lodging, and afterwards Julian and I rambled about the town, and went into the Cathe[168]dral for a moment, and strayed also into the Piazza del Campo, the great public square of Siena. I am not in the mood for further description now,—at least, not of public places; so shall say a word or two about the old palace in which we have established ourselves. We have the second piano, and dwell amid faded grandeur, having for our drawing-room what seems to have been a ball-room; it is ornamented with a great fresco, in the centre of the vaulted cieling, and with other frescoes covering the sides of the room, and surrounded with arabesque frameworks, where cherubs or cupids gambol and chase one another. The subjects of the frescoes I cannot make out; not that they are faded, like Giotto's, for they are as fresh as roses, and are done in an extremely workmanlike style; but they are allegories, of Fame, and Plenty, and other matters, such as I could never understand. Our whole accommodation is in similar style; spacious, magnificent even, and mouldy.

In the evening, Miss Shepard and I drove to the railway; and on the arrival of the evening train [169] from Florence, we watched with much eagerness the unlading of the luggage-van. Scores of trunks and boxes came out, but, for a long while, no sign of our missing luggage; at last, when all the rest had been delivered, first one, and then another, and in short the whole of our ten trunks and tin band-box were produced, and finally my leather bag, in which was this journal, and a manuscript-book in which I have been sketching out a Romance. It gladdened my very heart to see it; and I shall think the better of Tuscan promptitude and accuracy for so quickly bringing it back to me. We find all the public officials, whether of railway, police, or custom-house, extremely courteous and pleasant to encounter; they seem willing to take trouble, and reluctant to give it, and it is really a gratification to find that such civil people will sometimes oblige you by taking a Paul or two, aside.

Siena, October 3^d, Sunday.

I took several strolls about the city, yesterday, and find it scarcely extensive enough to get lost in; and if we go far from the centre, we soon come to silent streets, with only here and [170] there a passer-by; and the inhabitants stare from their doors and windows at the stranger, and turn round to look at him after he has passed. The interest of the old town would soon be exhausted for the passing traveller; but I can conceive that a thoughtful and shy man might settle down here, with the view of making the place a home, and spend many years in a sombre kind of happiness. I should prefer it to Florence as a residence; but it would be terrible without an independent life in one's own mind.

Una and I walked out, in the afternoon, and went into the Piazza del Campo, the principal place of the city, and a very noble and peculiar one. It is much in the form of an amphi-theatre, and the surface of the ground seems to be slightly scooped out, so that it resembles the shallow basin of a shell; it is thus a much better site for an assemblage of the populace than if it were a perfect level. A semi-circle, or truncated ellipse, of stately and ancient edifices stands around the piazza, with arches opening beneath them, through which streets con-verge hitherward. One side of the piazza is a straight line, and is oc[1st 171]cupied by the Palazzo Publico, which is as noble and impressive a Gothic structure (the English cathedrals excepted) as I have ever seen. It has not the mass of the Palazzo Vecchio at Florence, but is more striking. It has a long, battlemented front, the central part of which rises eminent above the rest, in a great square bulk, which is likewise crowned with battlements; this is much more picturesque than the one great block of stone into which the entire Palazzo Vecchio is consolidated. At one extremity of this long front of the Palazzo Publico rises a tower, shooting up its shaft high, high into the air, and bulging out there into a battlemented fortress, within which the tower, slenderer than before, climbs to a still higher region. I do not know whether the summit of the tower is higher, or so high, as that of the Palazzo Vecchio; but the length of the shaft, free of the edifice, is much greater, and so produces the more elevating effect. The whole front of the Palazzo Publico is exceedingly venerable, with arched windows, Gothic carvings, and all the old-time ornaments that betoken it [172] to have stood a great while, and the gray strength that will hold it up at least as much longer. At one end of the front, beneath the shadow of the tower, is a grand and beautiful porch, supported on square pillars, within each of which is a niche, containing a statue of mediaeval sculpture.

This great Piazza del Campo seems to be the market-place of Siena. In the morning, it was thronged with booths and stalls, especially of fruit and vegetable dealers; but, as in Florence, they appeared to melt away in the sunshine, gradually withdrawing themselves into the shadow thrown from the Palazzo Publico. On the side opposite the palace is an antique fountain of marble, ornamented with two statues, and a series of bas-reliefs; and it was so much admired in its day, that the architect, or sculptor, received the name del Fonte. I am loth to leave this piazza and palace without finding some word or two to suggest their antique majesty, in the sunshine and the shadow, and how fit it seemed, notwithstanding their venerableness, that there should be a busy crowd filling up the great,

[173] hollow amphitheatre, and crying their fruit and little merchandizes, so that all the curved line of stately old edifices helped to reverberate the noise. The life of to-day within the shell of a time past is wonderfully fascinating.

Another point—to which a stranger's footsteps are drawn by a kind of magnetism, so that he will be apt to find himself there as often as he strolls out of his hotel—is the Cathedral. It stands in the highest part of the city; and almost every street seems to run into some other street, which meanders thither-ward. On our way thither, Una and I came to a beautiful front of black and white marble, in somewhat the same style as the Cathedral; in fact, it was the Baptistery of that edifice, and should have made a part of it, according to the original design, which contemplated a structure of vastly greater extent than the actual one. We entered it (the Baptistery) and found the interior small, but very rich in its clustered columns and inter-secting arches, and its frescoes, pictures, statues, and orna-ments. Moreover a father and mother had brought their baby to be baptized; and the poor little thing, in [174] its gay swaddling clothes, looked just like what I have seen in old pictures, and a good deal like an Indian papoose. It gave one little, slender squeak, when the priest put the water on its forehead, and then was quiet again.

We now went round to the front of the Cathedral, of which it is folly to attempt a description. It is of black and white marble, with, I believe, an intermixture of red, and perhaps other colors; but time has tamed them down, so that white, black, and red, do not contrast so strongly with one another, as they may have done, five hundred years ago. The architecture is generally of the pointed Gothic style; but there are like-wise carved arches over the doors and windows, and a variety which does not produce the effect of confusion;—a magnificent eccentricity, an exuberant imagination flowering out in stone. On high, in the great peak of the front, and throwing its colored radiance into the nave within, there is a round window of immense circumference, the painted figures in which we can see dimly from the outside. But what I wish to express, and never can, is the multitu[175]dinous richness of the ornamentation of the front; the arches within arches, sculptured inch by inch, of the deep doorways; the statues of saints, some making a hermitage of a niche, others standing forth; the scores of busts, that look like faces of ancient people staring down out of the Cathedral; the projecting shapes of stone lions —the thousand forms of Gothic fancy, which seemed to soften stone, and express whatever it liked, and then let it harden again to last forever. I give it up; my description seems like knocking off the noses of some of the busts, the fingers and toes of the statues, the projecting points of some of the architecture, jumbling them all up together, and flinging them down upon the page. This gives no idea of the truth; nor, least of all, can it shadow forth that solemn whole, mightily combined out of all these minute particulars, and sanctifying the whole space of ground over which this Cathedral-front flings its shadow, or on which it reflects the sun. A majesty and a minuteness; neither interfering with the other; each assisting the other; this is what I love in Gothic architecture.

[176] We went into the Cathedral, and walked round it; but I mean to go again before sketching the interior in my poor water-colors.

Siena, October 4th, Monday.

On looking again at the Palazzo Publico, I see that the pillared portal, which I have spoken of, does not cover an entrance to the palace, but is a chapel, with an altar, and old frescoes above it. Boquets of fresh flowers are on the altar-table, and a lamp burns, in all the daylight, before the crucifix. The

chapel is quite unenclosed, except by an open-work balustrade
of stone—marble, indeed—on which the carving looks very
ancient. Nothing could be more convenient than this chapel
for the devotions of the crowd in the piazza; and no doubt the
daily prayers offered at the shrine might be numbered by the
thousand, brief, but, I hope, earnest—like those glimpses that
I used to catch at the blue sky, revealing so much in an instant,
while I was toiling at Brook Farm. Another picturesque thing,
about the Palazzo Publico, is a great stone balcony, quaintly
wrought, about midway in the front, and high aloft, with two
arched windows opening into it.

[2nd 171] After another glimpse at the Cathedral, too, I
realize how utterly I have failed in conveying the idea of its
elaborate ornament, its twisted and clustered pillars, and numberless devices of sculpture; nor did I mention the venerable
statues that stand all round the height of the edifice, relieved
against the sky, highest of all, being one of the Savior on the
topmost peak of the front; nor the tall tower that ascends from
one side of the building, and is built of layers of black and
white marble, piled one upon another in regular succession;
nor the dome that swells upward close beside this tower.

Had the Cathedral been constructed on the plan and dimensions at first contemplated, it would have been incomparably
majestic; the finished portion, grand as it is, being only what
was intended for a transept. One of the walls of what was to
have been the nave is still standing, and looks like a ruin,
though, I believe, it has been turned to account as the wall of
a palace or other edifice, the space of the never-completed nave
being now a court or street.

The whole family of us were kindly taken out, [178] yesterday, to dine and spend the day at the Villa Belvedere, with
our friends Mr & Mrs Story. The vicinity of Siena seems much
more agreeable than that of Florence, being cooler, breezier,
with more foliage and shrubbery, both near at hand and in

the distance; and the prospect, Mr Story told us, embraces a diameter of about a hundred miles, between hills north and south. The Villa Belvedere was built and owned by an Englishman, now deceased, who has left it to his butler; and its lawns and shrubbery have something English in their character, and there was almost a dampness in the grass. It really pleased me, in this parched Italy. Within the house (though the floors are homely brick, as usual) the walls are hung with fine, old-fashioned engravings from the pictures of Gainsborough, West, and other English painters. The Englishman, though he had chosen to live and die in Italy, had evidently brought his native tastes and peculiarities along with him. Mr. Story thinks of buying this villa, which, spacious as it is, and with all its furniture, may be had for about four thousand dollars. I do not know but I might be tempted [179] to buy it, myself, if Siena were a practicable residence for the entire year; but the winter in this villa, with all the bleak mountain-winds of a hundred miles roundabout blustering against it, must be terribly disagreeable.

We spent a very pleasant day, turning over books and periodicals, or talking, on the lawn, whence we could behold scenes picturesque afar, and rich vineyard glimpses, near at hand. Mr. Story is the most variously accomplished and brilliant person—the fullest of social life and fire—whom I have ever met; and without seeming to make an effort, he kept us amused and entertained, the whole day long; not wearisomely entertained neither, as we should have been if he had not let his fountain play naturally. Still, though he bubbled and brimmed over with fun, he left the impression on me that he is not a happy man; there must surely be a morbid sensibility; a pain and care, bred, it may be, out of the very richness of his gifts and abundance of his outward prosperity. Rich, in the prime of life, with a wife whom he loves, and [180] children budding and blossoming as fairly as his heart could wish; with sparkling talents, so many, that if he choose to neglect or fling away one, or two, or three, he would still have enough left to shine with;—who should be happy, if not he? It may be, that he feels his strength, in any one direction, not quite adequate to his perception, his purpose, and his longing desire; he would rather have one great diamond, than a larger bulk and weight divided among many brilliants. The great difficulty with him, I think, is a too facile power; he would do better things, if it were more difficult for him to do merely good ones. Then, too, his sensibility is too quick; being easily touched by his own thoughts, he cannot estimate what it requires to touch a colder and duller person, and so stops short of the adequate expression.

Towards sunset, we all walked out into the Podere, pausing, a little while, to look down into a well, that stands on the verge of the lawn. Within the spacious circle of its stone curb was an abundant growth of maiden-hair, forming a perfect [181] wreath of thickly clustering leaves quite round, and trailing its tendrils downward to the water which gleamed beneath. It was a very pretty sight. Mr. Story bent over the well, and uttered deep, musical tones, which were reverberated from the hollow depths with wonderful effect, as if a spirit dwelt within there, and (unlike the spirits that speak through mediums) sent him back responses profounder and more melodious than the tones that awakened them. Such a responsive well as this might have been taken for oracle, in old days.

We went along paths that led from one vineyard to another, and which might have led us for miles across the country. The grapes had been partly gathered, but still there were many purple or white clusters hanging heavily on the vines. We passed cottage-doors, and saw groups of Contadini, and contadine, in their festal attire, and they saluted us graciously; but it was observable that one of the men generally lingered on our track to see that no grapes were stolen; for there were a good many young people and children in our train, not only our own, [182] but some from a neighboring villa. These Italian peasants seem to be a kindly race, but, I doubt, not very hospitable of grape or fig. There was a beautiful sunset; and by the time we reached the house again, the comet was already visible amid the unextinguished glow of daylight. A Mr. and Mrs. Black (Scotch people from the next villa) had come to see the Storys; and we sat till tea-time, reading, talking, William Story drawing caricatures for his children's amusement and ours, and all of us sometimes getting up to look at the comet, which blazed brighter and brighter, till it went down into the mists of the horizon. Among the caricatures was one of a Presidential Candidate; evidently a man of very malleable principles, and likely to succeed.

Late in the evening (too late for little Rosebud, and even for Julian and Una) we drove homeward. The streets of old Siena look very grim, at night, and it seemed like gazing into caverns, to glimpse down some of the side-streets, as we passed, with a light burning dimly at the end of them. It was [183] about half past ten, I believe, when we reached home, and climbed up our gloomy staircase, lighted by the glimmer of some wax matches which I had in my pocket.

Siena, October 5th, Tuesday.

I have been two or three times into the Cathedral, but do not yet feel in the least encouraged to attempt a description, and probably never shall. Julian and I went thither, yesterday, towards the close of the afternoon; and while standing near the entrance, or about midway in the nave, we saw a female figure approaching, through the dimness and distance, far away in the region of the high altar; as it drew nearer, its air reminded me of Una, whom we had left at home. Finally, it came close to us, and proved to be Una herself; she had come with Miss Shepard, and was looking for objects to sketch. It is an empty thing to write down, but the surprise made the incident stand out very vividly.

The whole interior of the Cathedral is of marble, in alternate lines of black and [184] white, each layer being about eight inches in width, and extending horizontally; it looks very curiously, and might remind the spectator of a waistcoat with horizontal stripes. Nevertheless, the effect is exceedingly rich; these alternate lines stretching away, along the walls, and round the clustered pillars, seen aloft, and through the arches, everywhere, this inlay of black and white. Every sort of ornament, that could be thought of, seems to have been crammed into the Cathedral, in one place or another; gilding, frescoes, pictures; a roof of blue, spangled with golden stars; a magnificent wheel window, of old painted glass, over the entrance, and another at the opposite end of the cathedral; statues, some of marble, others of gilded bronze or wood; pulpits of carved marble; a gilded organ; a cornice of marble busts of the popes, extending round the entire church; a pavement covered all over with a strange kind of mosaic-work, in marble, wrought into marble pictures of sacred subjects; immense, clustered pillars, supporting [185] the round arches that divide the nave from the side-aisles, and, above these round arches, a clerestory of windows within pointed arches;—in fine, it seems as if the spectator were reading an antique volume, written in black-letter of a small character, but conveying a high and solemn meaning. I can find no way of expressing its effect on me; so queer, and quaint, and venerable, as I feel this Cathedral to be, in its immensity of striped waistcoat, now dingy with five centuries' wear. I ought not to say anything that might detract from the grandeur and sanctity of the blessed edifice; for these attributes are really uninjured by any of the Gothic oddities which I have hinted at.

Mamma, Julian, and I, went this morning to the Institute
of the Fine Arts, which is interesting as containing a series of
the works of the Sienese painters, from a date earlier than that
of Cimabue. There is a dispute, I believe, between Florence
and Siena, as to which city may claim the credit of having
originated the modern [186] art of painting. The Florentines
put forward Cimabue as the first artist; but as the Sienese
produce a picture by Guido da Siena, dated before the birth
of Cimabue, the victory seems to be decidedly with them. As to
pictorial merit, to my taste, there is none in either of these
hideous old painters, nor in any of their successors for a long
time afterwards. At the institute, there are several rooms hung
with early productions of the Sienese school, painted before the
invention of oil-colors, on wood, shaped into Gothic altar-
pieces; the back-grounds still retain a be-dimmed splendour of
gilding; there is a plentiful use of red; and I can conceive that
the pictures must have shed an illumination through the
churches where they were displayed. There is often, too, a
minute care bestowed on the faces in the pictures, and sometimes a very strong expression; stronger than modern artists get;
and it is very strange how they attained this merit, while they
were so inconceivably rude in other respects. It is remarkable
that all the early faces of the Ma[187]donna are especially
stupid, and all of the same type; a sort of face such as one
might carve on a pumpkin, representing a heavy, sulky, and
phlegmatic woman, with a long and low arch of the nose. This
same dull face continues to be assigned to the Madonna, even
when the countenances of the surrounding Saints and angels
are characterized with power and beauty; so that I think there
must have been some portrait of this sacred personage,
reckoned authentic, which the early painters followed and
religiously repeated.

At last we came to a picture by Sodoma, the most illustrious
representative of the Sienese school. It was a fresco, but per-

fectly well preserved; Christ, bound to the pillar, after having been scourged. I do believe that painting has never done any-thing better, so far as expression is concerned, than this figure; in all these generations, since it was painted, it must have softened thousands of hearts—drawn down rivers of tears—been more effectual [188] than a million of sermons. It is in-expressibly touching; so weary is the Savior, and utterly worn out with suffering, that his mouth has fallen apart from mere exhaustion; his eyes seem to be set; he tries to lean his head against the pillar, and is only kept from sinking down upon the ground by the cords that bind him. Really, it is a thing to stand and weep at; and yet, by nothing less than miracle, the great painter has not suffered the Son of God to be merely an object of pity, though depicting him in a state so profoundly pitiful. He is redeemed by a divine majesty and beauty, I know not how, and is as much our Redeemer as if he sat on his throne in Heaven. Sodoma, I believe, was earlier than Perugino; and neither the latter, nor any other painter, has done anything that can deserve to be compared to this.

There are some other pictures by Sodoma, among them a Judith, very noble and admirable, and full of a profound sor-row for the deed which she has felt it her mission to do.

[189] Aquila Nera, (Siena) Octr 7th, Thursday.

Our lodgings in this city had been taken only for five days, as they were already engaged after that period; so yesterday we returned to our old quarters, very narrow ones, at the Black Eagle.

In the forenoon, Julian and I went out of one of the gates, (I know not which, but the road from it leads to Florence,) and had a pleasant country walk. Our way wound downward, round the hill on which Siena stands, and gave us views of the Duomo and its Campanile, seemingly pretty near, after we had walked long enough to be quite remote from them. Sitting awhile on the parapet of a bridge, I saw a laborer chopping the branches off a poplar-tree which he had felled; and when it was trimmed, he took up the large trunk on one of his shoulders, and carried it off, seemingly with ease. He did not look like a particularly robust man; but I have never seen such an Herculean feat attempted by an Englishman or American. It has frequently struck me that the Italians are able to put forth a great deal of strength in such insu[190]lated efforts as this; but I have been told that they are less capable of continued endurance and hardship than our own race. I do not see why it should be so, except that I presume their food is less strong than ours. There was no other remarkable incident in our walk, which lay chiefly through gorges of the hills, winding beneath high cliffs of the brown Siena earth, with many pretty scenes of rural landscape; vineyards, everywhere, and olive-trees; a mill on its little stream, over which there was an old stone bridge, with a graceful arch; farm-houses; a villa or two; subterranean passages passing from the roadside, through the high banks, into the vineyards. At last, we turned aside into a road which led us pretty directly to another gate of the city, and climbed steeply upward among tanneries, where the young men went about with their well-shaped legs bare, their trowsers being tucked up till they were strictly breeches, and nothing else. The Campanile stood high above us; and, by-and-by, and very soon, indeed, the steep ascent of the street brought us right into the neighborhood [191] of the Piazza del Campo, and of our own hotel. Before going thither, we went to the Cathedral in quest of Mamma; but not finding her there, we were coming down by the Baptistery, when we met her, just on her way to the Cathedral. Julian went back with her, and I returned to the Hotel, and sat at my chamber window, from about twelve °clock till one, watching the specimens of Siena life as displayed in the Piazza Tolomei. I even noted down in pencil some of the characteristics of the moving population, and shall record them here, though they seem nowise worth it.

The Piazza Tolomei is not more than thirty yards across, and has the tall Palazzo Tolomei (a dark, stately edifice of stone, more than six centuries old) on one side, and the front of a church, adorned with two statues, on the other. In the open space of the Piazza stands a pillar, with a bronze wolf suckling Romulus and Remus on its top; and this pillar serves as a sort of centre, around which people stop a moment to talk, or perhaps sit down on its single step and pedestal. When I first looked out, there was [192] a small handcart near the pillar, containing two little flatsided barrels, moist with the wine that filled them; the handcart-man was resting himself on the pedestal. A perambulatory fruit-shop—a large board, or table, on wheels, covered with figs, grapes, peaches, pears, apples, and green lemons—likewise stood close by. A man with a bundle came and sat down beneath the pillar, likewise, another man rested a basket on the pedestal. Nobody buying any fruit, the perambulatory stall soon moves off; and there is a continual shifting of all the personages that appear on the scene of the Piazza. A priest passes; another priest, walking with a citizen; a soldier in blue uniform faced with red; another soldier; a cart, drawn by one horse, with charcoal for sale, has stopt; an old scavenger goes stooping along, with his great-basket of heterogeneous filth on his back. The charcoal cart goes off; another soldier passes; also, a priest; and there is a continual passing of citizens, women, and children; another priest passes; and another. The [193] Piazza, for one instant, is quite vacant. Then comes a priest; then a pair of gray oxen, drawing a little dung-cart; a priest; a large wine barrel, or hogshead, on a handcart; a priest; a soldier; a priest; two priests. A man sits down on the pedestal of the pillar; a priest passes; a cripple limps across the piazza; a soldier goes by; a priest, listening to the earnest talk of an old citizen; another priest with another citizen. A soldier; a priest; two young men leading a dog by a white handkerchief tied to his collar; a handcart, with potatoes for sale. A soldier. The Diligence, drawn by three horses, and guided by a postillion in a faded crimson jacket, bobbing up and down on the left-hand wheel horse. A woman passes, with a basket of figs; a priest, evidently in charge of a train of ten lads who seem to be students, and wear a peculiar costume of blue, with brass buttons. Old women pass by with broad flapt hats, of black or yellow straw; younger women in bonnets; many with heads bare, or handkerchiefs about them. Three soldiers, perhaps [194] officers go by, looking smarter than usual; another soldier; a bow-backed cripple; nine soldiers, two of them armed with musket and bayonet, and the others carrying two large baskets.

Two more priests pass. An empty cart has stopt. A soldier appears, in the jaunty little Tuscan cocked-hat and feather, most of the other soldiers having worn small caps, brimless except for the vizor in front. Two more soldiers; a little horse-cart laden with straw-covered flasks. A man, smoking a pipe, leans against the pedestal of the pillar; another soldier passes, in jaunty cocked-hat. A priest goes by; a donkey-cart; an old soldier; a cart made of wicker-work, and drawn by two gray oxen, whom a man leads with a string. A group of men lounge and sit on the step and pedestal of the pillar, which is now in shadow, the sunshine having nearly left the Piazza. Ladies, in swelling petticoats, and with fans, some of which are highly gilded, begin to appear. A priest passes; three soldiers; another soldier, with a paper in his hand, and a brisk [195] air of business; three more soldiers; a priest in company with two citizens; another priest, walking fast. A soldier; a priest and citizen; another priest. A priest, talking to a dwarfish cripple; two priests. A man, with a great basket of charcoal, stops to rest it on the pedestal. Another perambulatory fruit-shop has ap-

peared. A priest goes by, talking with a boy in military uniform; two soldiers; another soldier; a priest, talking with two
men belonging to the lower classes. The hour is about completed.

Of course, a multitude of other people passed by; but the
curiosity of the catalogue is the prevalence of the martial and
religious elements. The general costume of the inhabitants is
frocks or sacks, loosely made, and rather shabby; often, shirt-
sleeves; or the coat hung over one shoulder. They wear felt
hats, or perhaps straw. People of respectability seem to prefer
cylinder hats, either black or drab, and broadcloth frock-coats,
in the French fashion; but, like the rest, they look a little
shabby. Almost all the women wear shawls. The people [196]
generally are not tall, but have a sufficient breadth of shoulder;
in complexion, very similar to Americans; bearded, universally.
The vehicle used for driving is a little gig without a top; but
these are seldom seen, and still less frequently, a cab, or other
carriage. The gait of the people has not the energy of business
or decided purpose; everybody appears to lounge, and to have
time for a moment's chat, and a disposition to rest, reason or
none.

After dinner, I walked out of another gate of the city, and
wandered among some pleasant country-lanes, bordered with
hedges, and wearing an English aspect; at least, I could fancy
so, now that I have forgotten the hue of English verdure. The
vicinity of Siena is much more delightful, to walk about in,
than that of Florence; there being a more verdant outlook; a
wider prospect of purple mountains, though no such level
valley as the Valdarno; and the city stands so high, that its
towers and domes are seen more picturesquely, from many
points, than those of Florence can be. Nei[197]ther is the
pedestrian so cruelly shut into narrow lanes, between high
stone-walls, over which he cannot get a glimpse of landscape.
As I walked by the hedges, yesterday, I could have fancied that

the olive-trunks were those of apple-trees, and that I were in one or other of the two lands that I love better than Italy. But the great white villas and the farm-houses were unlike anything I have seen elsewhere, or that I should wish to see again, though proper enough to Italy.

Aquila Nera, October 9th, Saturday.

Thursday forenoon, we went to see the Palazzo Publico. There are some fine old halls and chapels, adorned with ancient frescoes and pictures; of which I remember a picture of the Virgin by Sodoma, very beautiful and full of expression—as likewise some other fine pictures by the same master. The architecture of these old rooms is very grand, the roofs being supported by ponderous arches, which are covered with frescoes, still magnificent, though faded, darkened, and defaced. We likewise saw an antique casket, of wood, enriched with gilding; it [198] had once contained an arm of John the Baptist—so the Custode told us. One of the halls was hung with the portraits of, I think, eight Popes and nearly forty cardinals, who were natives of Siena. I ought to have described this Palace (if at all) immediately after seeing it; for I find that the impression it made is now almost defaced.

I have done hardly any other sight-seeing, except a daily visit to the Cathedral, which I admire and love the more, the oftener I go thither. Its striped peculiarity ceases entirely to interfere with the grandeur and venerable beauty of its impression; and I am never weary of gazing through the vistas of its arches, and noting continually something that I had not seen before, in its exuberant adornment. The pavement alone is inexhaustible, being covered all over with figures of life size, or larger, which look like immense engravings of Gothic or Scriptural scenes. There is Absalom hanging by his hair, and Joab slaying him with a spear; there is Sampson, belaboring the Philistines with the jawbone of an ass; there are armed knights in the [199] tumult of battle—all done with wonderful expression. The figures are in white marble, inlaid into darker stone; and the shading is effected by means of engraved lines in the marble, filled in with black. It would be possible, perhaps, to print impressions directly from some of these vast plates; for the process of cutting the lines was an exact anticipation of the modern art of engraving. However, the same thing was done—and, I suppose, at about the same period—on monumental brasses; and I have seen impressions, or rubbings, from those, for sale in the old English churches.

Yesterday morning, in the Cathedral, I watched a woman at confession, being curious to see how long it would take her to tell her sins, the growth of a week or two, perhaps. I know not how long she had been at it, when I first observed her; but I believe nearly an hour passed, before the priest came suddenly out of the confessional, looking weary and moist with perspiration, and took his way out of the Cathedral. The woman was left on her knees. This morning, I watched another woman, and she, [200] too, was very long about it, and I could see the face of the Priest, behind the curtain of the Confessional, scarcely inclining his ear to the perforated tin through which the penitent communicated her outpourings. It must be very tedious to listen, day after day, to the minute and common-place iniquities of the multitude of penitents; and it cannot be often that these are re-deemed by the treasure-trove of a great sin. When her confession was over, the woman came and sat down on the same bench with me, where her broad-brimmed straw-hat was lying. She seemed to be a country-woman, with a simple, matronly face, which was solemnized and softened with the comfort that she had got by disburthening herself of the soil of worldly frailties, and receiving absolution. An old woman, who haunts the Cathedral, whispered to her, and she went and knelt down where a procession of priests were to pass; and then the old lady begged a crazia of me, and got a half-paul. It almost invariably happens, in church or Cathedral, that beggars address their prayers to the heretic-visitor, [201] and probably with more unction than to the Virgin or Saints. However, I have nothing to say against the sincerity of these people's devotion; they give all the proof of it that a mere spectator can estimate.

Last evening, Mamma, Miss Shepard, Julian, Rosebud, and I, all went out to see the Comet, which then reached its climax of lustre. It was like a lofty plume of fire, and grew very brilliant as the night darkened.

Aquila Nera, October 10th, Sunday.

This morning, too, we went to the Cathedral, and sat long, listening to the music of the organ and voices, and witnessing rites and ceremonies which are far older than even the ancient edifice where they were exhibited. A good many people were in the Cathedral, sitting, kneeling, or walking about—a freedom that contrasts very agreeably with the grim formalities of English churches and our own meeting-houses. Many persons were in their best attire; but others came in, with unabashed simplicity, in their poor old garments of labour; sun-burnt wo[202]men from their toil among the vines and olives; one old peasant, I noticed, with his withered shanks in breeches and blue-yarn stockings. All people, of whatever class, are wonderfully tolerant of heretics, never manifesting any displeasure or annoyance, though they must see that we are drawn thither by curiosity alone, and merely pry while they pray. I heartily wish the priests were better men, and that human nature, divinely influenced, could be depended upon for a constant supply and succession of good and pure men; their religion has so many admirable points. And then it is a sad pity that this noble and beautiful Cathedral should be a mere fossil shell, out of which the life has died long ago. But, for many a year yet to come, the tapers will burn before the high altar, the Host will be elevated, the incense diffuse its fragrance, the Confessionals be open to receive the penitents. I saw a father entering the Cathedral with two little bits of boys, just big enough to toddle along, holding his hand on either side. The father dipt his hand into the marble font of holy water (which, on its pedestal, was two or three times as high as those [203] small Christians) and wet a hand of each, and taught them how to cross themselves. When they come to be men, it will be impossible to convince those children that there is no efficacy in holy-water, without plucking up all religious faith and sentiment by the roots. Generally, I suspect, when people throw off the faith they were born in, the best soil of their hearts is apt to cling to its roots.

Raised several feet (more than a man's height, considerably) above the pavement, against every clustered pillar along the nave of the Cathedral, is placed a statue, of Gothic sculpture. In various parts of the Cathedral are sitting statues of Popes, of Sienese nativity, all of whom, I believe, have a hand raised in the act of blessing. Shrines and chapels, set in grand, heavy frames of pillared architecture, stand all along the aisles and transepts; and these seem, in many instances, to have been built and enriched by noble families, whose arms are sculptured on the pedestals of the pillars, sometimes with a cardinal's hat above, to denote the rank of one of its members. How much pride, love, [204] and reverence, in the lapse of ages, must have clung to the sharp points of all this sculpture and architecture! The Cathedral is a religion in itself; something worth dying for, to those who have an hereditary interest in it. In the pavement, yesterday, I noticed the grave-stone of a person who fell, six centuries ago, in the battle of Monte Aperto, and was buried here by public decree, as a meed of valor. I think the inscription stated that this was the first burial there.

This afternoon, I took a walk out of one of the city-gates, (I know not which, but the road soon led across the railway,) and found the country about Siena as beautiful in this direction, as in all others. I came to a little stream, flowing over a pebbly bed, and collecting itself into pools, with a scanty rivulet between; its glen was deep, and was crossed by a bridge of several lofty and narrow arches, like those of a Roman aqueduct. It is a modern structure, however. Farther on, as I wound along the base of a hill, which fell down upon the road by precipitous cliffs of brown earth, I saw a gray, ruined wall on the [205] summit, surrounded with cypress-trees. This tree is very frequent about Siena; and the scenery is made soft and beautiful by a variety of other trees and shrubbery, without which these hills and gorges would have scarcely a charm. The road was thronged with country-people, mostly women and children, who had been spending the feast-day in Siena; and parties of boys were chasing one another through the fields, pretty much as boys do in New England, of a Sunday; but the Sienese lads had not the sense of Sabbath-breaking, like our boys. Sunday with these people is like any other feast-day, and consecrated to cheerful enjoyment. So much religious observance, as regards outward forms, is diffused through the whole week, that they have no need to intensify the Sabbath, except by making it gladder than the other days.

Returning through the same gate by which I had come out, I ascended into the city by a long and steep street, which was paved with bricks, set edgewise. This pavement is common in many of the streets, which, being too steep for horses and car[206]riages, are meant only to sustain the lighter tread of mules and asses. The more level streets are paved with broad, smooth flag-stones, like those of Florence; a fashion which I heartily regret to change for the little, penitential blocks of

Rome. The walls of Siena, in their present state, and so far as I have seen them, are chiefly brick; but there are intermingled fragments of ancient stone-work, and I wonder why the latter does not prevail more largely. The Romans, however—and Siena had Roman characteristics—always liked to build of brick; a taste that has made their ruins much less grand than they ought to have been. I am grateful to the old Sienese for having used stone so largely in their domestic architecture, and thereby rendered their city so grimly picturesque, with its black palaces, frowning upon one another from arched windows, across narrow streets, to the height of six stories, like opposite ranks of tall men looking sternly into one another's eyes.

Aquila Nera, October 11th, Monday.

Again I went to the Cathedral, this morning, and spent an [207] hour listening to the music, and looking through the orderly intricacies of the arches, where many vistas open away, among the columns of the choir. There are five clustered columns on each side of the nave; then under the dome, there are two more arches, not in a straight line, but forming the segment of a circle; and beyond the circle of the dome, there are four more arches, extending to the extremity of the Cathedral. I should have said, instead of clustered columns, as above, that there are five arches along the nave, supported by columns. This Cathedral has certainly bewitched me to write about it so much, effecting nothing with all my pains. I should judge the width of each arch to be about twenty feet, and the thickness of each clustered pillar is eight or ten more; and the length of the entire Cathedral may be between two and three hundred feet; not very large, certainly, but it makes an impression of grandeur, independently of size.

It is idle to write any more on this subject. I never shall

succeed even in reminding myself [208] of the venerable magnificence of this Cathedral, with its arches, its columns, its cornice of popes' heads, its great wheel-windows, its manifold ornament, all combining into one vast effect; though many men must have labored individually, and through a long course of time, to produce this multifarious handiwork and headwork.

Leaving the Cathedral, I took a walk out of the city, by I know not which gate, but I think it may have been the one called San Viene. A road turned immediately to the left, as I emerged from the city, and soon proved to be a rustic lane, leading past several villas and farm-houses, and running into another road that issued from the Porta Romana, as I suppose it to be. It was a very pleasant walk, with vineyards and olive-orchards on each side, and now-and-then glimpses of the towers, and sombre, heaped-up palaces of Siena, and now a rustic seclusion again; for the hills rise and fall, like the swell and subsidence of the sea after a gale; so that Siena may be quite hidden within a quarter of [209] a mile of its wall, or may be visible, I doubt not, twenty miles away. It is a fine old town, with every promise of health and vigour in its atmosphere; and really, if I could take root anywhere, I know not but it could as well be here as in another place. It would only be a kind of despair, however, that would ever make me dream of finding a home in Italy; a sense that I had lost my country through absence or incongruity, and that earth, at any rate, is not an abiding-place. I wonder that we Americans love our country at all, it having no limits and no oneness; and when you try to make it a matter of the heart, everything falls away except one's native State;—neither can you seize hold of that, unless you tear it out of the Union, bleeding and quivering. Yet unquestionably we do stand by our national flag as stoutly as any people in the world; and I myself have felt the heart-throb at sight of it, as sensibly as other men.

I think the singularity of our form of government contributes to give us a kind of patriotism, by separating us from other nations [210] more entirely. If other nations had similar institutions—if England, especially, were a Democracy—we should as readily make ourselves at home in another country as now in a new state.

I forget whether I ever recorded (and therefore will record now) that our tower at Montauto measured about eighty-five feet in height from its base, on the road-side, to the top of its battlements. I think the area of its summit was about twenty-feet by thirty. The entire length of the Villa was about one hundred and forty-feet.

Aquila Nera, October 12th, Tuesday.

And again we went to the Cathedral, this forenoon; and the whole family, except myself, sketched portions of it. Even Rosebud stood gravely, sketching some of the inlaid figures of the pavement. As for me, I can but try to preserve some memorial of this beautiful edifice in ill-fitting words, that never hit the mark. This morning-visit was not my final one; for I went again, after dinner, and walked quite round the whole interior. I think I have [211] not yet mentioned the beautiful carvings of the old oaken seats round the choir, and the curious mosaic of lighter and darker woods, by which figures and landscapes are skilfully represented on the backs of some of the seats. The process seems to be the same as the inlaying and engraving of the pavement of the Cathedral, the material in one case being marble, in the other wood. The only other thing that I particularly noticed was, that, in the fonts of holy-water, at the front entrance, marble fish are represented in the depths of the basin, and eels and shell-fish crawling around the brim. Have I spoken of the rich carving of the capitals of the columns? At any rate, I have left a thousand beauties without a word. Here I drop the subject. As I took my parting glance, the Cathedral had a gleam of golden sunshine in its far depths, and it seemed to widen and deepen itself, as if to convince me of my error, yesterday, in saying that it is not very large. I wonder how I could say it.

[212] After taking leave of the Cathedral, I found my way out of another of the city-gates, and soon turned aside into a green lane, bordered on each side by a hedge; a real English lane, except that the hedges were a little more scrubby and scrawny than one usually sees them there. I had glimpses of the old brick-wall of Siena, running up hill and down, and confining the tall, rusty heap of houses within its belt. Soon, the lane passed through a hamlet consisting of two or three farm-houses, the shabbiest and dreariest that can be conceived, ancient and ugly, and dilapidated; with iron-grated windows below, and heavy wooden shutters on the windows above; high, ruinous walls, shutting in the court-yards, and ponderous gates, one of which, at least, was off its hinges. The farm-yards, so far as I peeped into them, were perfect pictures of disarray and slovenly administration of home-affairs. Only one of these houses had a door opening on the road; and that, if I remember, was the meanest in the hamlet. A flight of narrow stone-stairs ascended from the threshold to the second [213] story. All these houses were specimens of a rude antiquity, built of old brick and stone, with the marks of arched doors and windows, where a subsequent generation had shut up the lights or the accesses which the original builders had opened. Humble as these dwellings are, (though large and high, compared with rural residences in other countries,) they may very probably date back to the times when Siena was a war-like Republic, and when every house in its neighborhood had need to be a fortress. I suppose, however, prowling banditti were the only enemies against whom a defense would be

attempted. What lives must be now lived there—in beastly ignorance, mental sluggishness, hard toil for little profit, filth, and a horrible discomfort of fleas; for if the palaces of Italy are overrun with these latter pests, what must the country-hovels be!

The lane seemed to be leading me away from the city, instead of skirting along the walls; and leading me to another gate, as I at first hoped; so I turned back, and caught the first sprinklings of a show[214]er before I reached home. We are now all ready for a start tomorrow morning; our contract with the Vetturino (for seventy Tuscan scudi) having been made and signed, last week. We have fared well here at the Aquila Nera, and have been comfortable in our little brick-floored parlour and small bed chambers, that look from the third story into the bustling street. Our bill is paid (thirty-five scudi for our week's board and lodging) and the hour fixed for departure is six °clock tomorrow morning.

Radicofani, October 13th, Wednesday.

We were stirring at five, or a little after, this morning, and dressed by candle-light, having ordered breakfast at half-past five, and arranged to begin our journey at six; and, in fact, we did set out within less than half-an-hour of the time. It was a chill, lowering morning; and the rain blew a little in our faces, before we had gone far, but did not continue long. The country soon lost the pleasant aspect which it wears immediately about Siena, and grew very barren and dreary. Then it changed [215] again for the better, the road leading us through a fertility of vines and olives; after which the dreary and barren hills came back again, and formed our prospect throughout most of the day. We stopped for our dejeuner a la fourchette at a little old town, called San Quirico, which we

entered through a ruined gateway; the town being entirely enveloped within its ancient wall. This wall is far more picturesque than that of Siena, being lofty, and built of stone, with
a machicolation of arches running quite round its top, like a
cornice. It has little more than a single street, perhaps a
quarter of a mile long, narrow, paved with flag-stones in the
Florentine fashion, and lined with two rows of tall, rusty
stone-houses, without a gap between them from end to end.
The caffes were numerous, in relation to the size of the town,
and there were two taverns; our own, the Eagle, being doubtless the best, and having three arched entrances in its front,
of which the middle one led to the guests' apartments, the one
on the right to the barn, and on the left to the stable; so
[216] that, as is usual in Italian inns, the whole establishment
was under one roof. We were shown into a brick-paved room
on the first floor, adorned with a funny fresco of Aurora on
the cieling, and with some colored prints, both religious and
profane. Our dejeuner (it is the mid-day meal of Vetturino
travellers) consisted of an omelette, some boiled beef, a couple
of roast chickens, grapes, and roasted chickens, with abundance of thin red wine; a very satisfactory meal.

As we drove into town, we noticed a Gothic church, with
two doors of peculiar architecture; and while our lunch was
being prepared, we went to see it. The interior had little that
was remarkable; for it had been repaired early in the last
century, and spoilt of course. All its frescoes, if ever it had
any, are now hidden under a coat of white wash; but an old
tryptich (I think I have not spelt it correctly) is still hanging
in a chapel beside the high-altar; it is painted on wood, and
dates back beyond the invention of oil-painting, and represents the virgin, and some saints and angels, in what [217]
particular action I forget. Neither is the exterior of the church
particularly interesting, with the exception of the carving and
ornaments of two of the doors. Both of them have round

arches, deep, and curiously wrought; and the pillars of one of
the two are formed of a peculiar knot or twine, in stonework,
such as I cannot well describe; but it is both ingenious and
simple. These pillars rest on two non-descript animals, which
look as much like walruses as anything else. The pillars of the
other door consist of two figures, supporting the capitals,
and themselves standing on two handsomely carved lions. The
work is curious, and evidently very ancient, (that is, of mediæval antiquity,) and the material a red free-stone.

After lunch, Julian and I took a walk out of the gate of the
town, opposite to that of our entrance. There were no soldiers
on guard, as at city-gates of more importance; nor do I think
that there is really any gate to shut, but the massive stone
gateway still stands entire over the empty arch. Looking back,
after we had passed through, [218] I observed that the lofty
upper story of the gateway is converted into a dove-cote, and
that pumpkins were put to ripen in some open chambers, at
one side. We found a lane that led us round to the other gateway, close to the wall; and it passed near the base of a tall,
square tower, which is said to be of Roman origin. The little
town stands in the midst of a barren region; but its immediate
neighborhood seems to be fertile, and an olive-orchard,
venerable of aspect lay on the other side of the pleasant lane,
with its English hedges; and olive trees grew likewise along
the base of the city-wall. The arched machicolations, which I
have before noticed, were here and there interrupted by a
house, which seemed to have been built upon the old wall, or
incorporated into it; and from the windows of one of them
I saw ears of Indian corn hung out to ripen in the sun; and I
think somebody was winnowing grain at a little door that
opened through the wall. It was very pleasant to see the
ancient warlike rampart thus overcome with rustic peace. The
ruined gateway, by which we [219] had first entered, and

through which we now repassed, is partly overgrown with ivy.

Returning to our inn, along the street, we saw mamma sketching one of the doors of the Gothic church, in the midst of a crowd of the good people of San Quirico, who made no scruple to look over her shoulder, pressing so close as hardly to allow her elbow-room. I must own that I was too cowardly to come forward and take my share of this public notice; so I slunk away to the inn and there awaited her coming. Miss Shepard had been honored with equal attention; and, indeed, they have seldom attempted to sketch without finding themselves forthwith the nucleus of a throng.

But I am tired, sleepy, and stupid; and as we are to start at half-past five, tomorrow morning, I shall stop writing till another opportunity.

L'Aigle Noir, Viterbo, Octr 14th Thursday.

Perhaps I had something more to say of San Quirico, but the lapse of time, and intervention of other subjects, has put it out of my head; so I shall merely add [220] that there is a stately old palace of the Piccolominis, close to the church above described; it is built in the style of the Roman palaces, and looked almost large enough to be one of them. Nevertheless the basement story, or part of it, seems to be used as a barn and stable; for I saw a yoke of oxen in the entrance. I cannot but mention a most wretched team of vetturo-horses, which stopt at the door of our Albergo; poor, lean, downcast creatures, with deep furrows between their ribs; nothing but skin and bone, in short, and not even so much skin as they should have had; for it was partially worn off, leaving the back red and raw. The harness was fastened with ropes; the traces and reins were ropes; the carriage was ancient and shabby; and out of this miserable equipage there alighted an old gentleman and lady, whom our waiter affirmed to be the Prefect of Florence and his lady.

We left San Quirico at two °clock, or thereabouts; and followed an ascending road, till we got into the regions above the clouds; but I recollect little or nothing of what was remarkable along the [221] way. It is very annoying, that each successive day of travel and shifting circumstances obliterates the former day; so that, very soon, the mind gets to be either a blank or a confusion. I remember only that the landscape was very wide, but very dreary and barren, and grew more and more so, till we began to climb the mountain of Radicofani, the peak of which had been blackening itself on the horizon, almost the whole day. When we had come into a pretty high region, we were assailed by a real mountain-tempest of wind, rain, and hail, which pelted down upon us in good earnest, and cooled the air a little below comfort. As we toiled up the mountain, its upper height presented a very striking aspect, looking as if a precipice had been smoothed and squared, for the purpose of rendering the old castle, on its summit, more inaccessible than it was even by nature. This is the castle of the Robber-knight, Ghino di Tacco, whom Boccacio introduces into the Decameron. A freebooter of those days must have set a higher value on such a rock as this, than if it had been one [222] mass of diamond; for no art of medi-aeval warfare could endanger him, in such a fortress. Drawing yet nearer, we found the hill side, immediately about us, strewn with thousands upon thousands of great fragments of stone; it looked as if some great ruin had taken place there, only it was too vast a ruin to have been the dismemberment and dissolution of anything made by man.

We could now see the castle on the height pretty distinctly; it seemed to impend over the precipice; and close to the

base of the latter we saw the street of a town, on as strange and
inconvenient a foundation as ever one was built upon. I suppose the inhabitants of the village were dependants of the old
knight of the castle; his brotherhood of robbers, as they married and had families, settled there, under the shelter of the
eagle's nest. But the singularity is, how a community of people
have contrived to live and perpetuate themselves, so far out
of the reach of the world's help, and seemingly with no means
of assisting in the world's labour. I cannot imagine how they
employ them[223]selves, except in begging; and even that
branch of industry appears to be left to the old women and the
children. No house was ever built in this immediate neighborhood for any such natural purpose as induces people to build
them on other sites. Even our hotel, at which we now arrived,
could not be said to be a natural growth of the soil; it had
originally been a whim of one of the Grand Dukes of
Tuscany, a hunting-palace, intended for habitation only during a few weeks of the year. Of all dreary hotels I ever alighted
at, methinks this is the worst; but, on first arriving, I merely
followed the waiter to look at our rooms, across stone-paved
basement halls, dismal as Etruscan tombs, up dim staircases,
and along shivering corridors, all of stone, stone, stone, nothing but cold stone. After glancing at these pleasant accommodations, my wife and I, with Julian, set out to ascend the
hill and visit the town of Radicofani.

It is not more than a quarter of a mile above our hotel, and
is accessible by a good piece of road, though very steep. As
we approached the town, we [224] were assailed by some
little beggars; but this is the case all through Italy, in city or
solitude, and I think the mendicants of Radicofani are fewer
than its proportion. We had not got far towards the village,
when looking back over the scene of many miles that lay
stretched beneath us, we saw a heavy shower, apparently
travelling straight towards us over hill and dale. It seemed

inevitable that it should soon be upon us; so I persuaded my wife to return to the hotel; but Julian and I kept onward, being determined to see Radicofani, with or without a ducking. We soon entered the street; the blackest, ugliest, rudest old street, I do believe, that ever human life encrusted itself with. The first portion of it is the over-brimming of the town, in generations subsequent to that in which it was surrounded by a wall; but after going a little way, we came to a high, square tower, planted right across the way, with an arched gateway in its basement story; so that it looked like a great, short-legged giant, striding across the street of Radicofani. [225] Within this gateway is the proper and original town; though indeed the portion outside of the gate seems as densely populated, as ugly, and as ancient, as that within.

The street was very narrow, and paved with flag-stones, not quite so smooth as those of Florence; the houses are tall enough to be stately, if they were not so inconceivably dingy and shabby; but, with their half dozen stories, perhaps, they make only the impression of hovel piled upon hovel; squalor immortalized in undecaying stone. It was now getting far into the twilight, and I could not distinguish the particularities of the ugly little town, except that there were shops, a caffé or two, and as many churches, all dusky with age, crowded closely together, inconvenient, stifled, too, in spite of the breadth and freedom of the mountain atmosphere, outside the scanty precincts of this street. I never saw such a death-in-life little place; such a fossilized place; and yet the street was thronged, and had all the bustle of a city; even more noise than a city-street, because everybody in Radicofani knows everybody, and probably gos[226]sips with everybody, being everybody's blood-relation, as they cannot fail to have become, after they and their forefathers have been shut up together within the narrow precincts of a wall, for many hundred years. They looked round briskly at Julian and me, but were courteous, as Italians always are, and made way for us to pass through the throng, as we kept on still ascending the steep street. It took us but a few minutes to reach the still steeper and winding pathway, which continues from the street of Radicofani, and climbs towards the old castle.

After ascending above the village, the path, though still paved, becomes very rough, as if the hoofs of Ghino di Tacco's robber-cavalry had displaced the stones, and they had never been replaced. On every side, too, except where the path just finds space enough, there is a tremendous rubbish of huge stones, which seem to have fallen from the precipice above, or else to have rained down out of the sky. We kept on, and by-and-by reached what seemed to have been a lower [227] outwork of the castle on the top; there was the massive old arch of a gateway, and a great deal of ruin of man's work, besides the great stones which here, as elsewhere, were scattered so abundantly. Within the wall and gateway, just mentioned, however, there was a kind of farm-house, adapted, I suppose, out of the old ruin, and I noticed some ears of Indian corn hanging out of a window. There were also a few stacks of hay, but no signs of human or animal life, and it is utterly inexplicable to me where these products of the soil could have come from; for certainly they never grew amid that barrenness.

We had not yet reached Ghino's castle; and being now right beneath it, we had to bend our heads far backward to see it, standing up against the clear sky, while we were now in twilight. The path upward looked terribly steep and rough; and if we had climbed it, we should probably have broken our necks in descending again into the lower obscurity. We therefore stopt here, much against Julian's will, and went back as we came, [228] still wondering at the queer situation of Radicofani; for its aspect is, as if it had slipt off the top of the cliff and lodged at its base, though still in danger of sliding further down the hill-side. Emerging from the compact, grimy life of its street, we saw that the shower had swept by, or probably had expended itself on a region beneath us; for we were above the scope of many of the showery clouds that haunt a hill-country. There was a very bright star visible, I remember, and we saw the new moon, now a third towards the full, for the first time this evening. The air was cold and bracing.

But I am terribly, terribly sleepy; so will not describe our great dreary hotel, where we slept in a room without a window, and where a blast howled in an interminable corridor, all night. It did not seem to have anything to do with the wind out-of-doors, but to be a blast that had been casually shut in, when the doors were closed behind the last Grand Duke who came hither, and departed; and ever since [229] the blast has been kept prisoner, and makes a melancholy howl along the corridor. The dreary stupidity of this conceit proves how sleepy I am.

Sette Vene, October 15th, Friday.

We left Radicofani long before sunrise; and I saw that ceremony take place from the coupé of the vetturo, for the first time this long while past. A sunset is the better sight of the two. I have always suspected it, and have been strengthened in the idea whenever I have had an opportunity of comparison. Our departure from Radicofani was most dreary, except that we were very glad to get away; but the cold discomfort of dressing in a chill bedroom by candlelight, and then our uncertain wandering through the immense hotel, with a dim candle, in search of the breakfast room, and our poor breakfast of eggs, Italian bread, and coffee—all these things made me wish that people were created with roots like trees, so that they could not befool themselves with wandering about. In fact, travelling with a family is a bore beyond anything that can be pre-conceived. However, we had not long been on our way before the morn[230]ing-air blew away all our troubles, and we rumbled cheerfully onward, ready to encounter even the Papal custom-house officers at Ponte Centino. Our road thither was a pretty steep descent; but I have not a distinct recollection of any particular object that we saw. I remember the barren landscape of hills, with here and there a lonely farm-house, which there seemed to be no occasion for, where nothing grew.

At Ponte Centino, my passport was examined, and I was invited into an office, where sat the Papal Custom-House officer, a thin, subtle-looking, keen-eyed, sallow personage, of aspect very suitable to be the officer of a government of priests. I communicated to him my wish to pass the Custom-House without giving the officers the trouble of examining my luggage. He inquired whether I had any dutiable articles, and wrote for my signature a declaration in the negative; and then he lifted a sand-box, beneath which was a little heap of silver coins. On this delicate hint, I asked what was the customary fee, and was told that fifteen pauls was [231] the proper sum. I presume it was entirely an illegal charge, and that he had no right to pass any luggage without examination; but the thing is winked at by the authorities, and no money is better spent for the traveller's convenience than these fifteen pauls. There was a papal military officer in the room; and he, I believe, cheated me in the change of a Napoleon, as his share of the spoil. At the door, a soldier met me with my passport, and looked as if he expected a fee for handing it to me; but in this he was disappointed. After I had resumed my seat in the coupé, the porter of the Custom-House (a poor, sickly looking creature, half-dead with the mal-aria of the place) appeared, and demanded a fee for doing nothing to my luggage. He got three pauls, and looked but half-contented. This whole set of men seem to be as corrupt as official people can possibly be; and yet I hardly know whether to stigmatize them as corrupt, because it is not their individual delinquency, but the operation of a regular system. Their superiors know what [232] men they are, and calculate upon their getting a living by just these means. And, indeed, the custom-house and passport regulations, as they exist in Italy, would be intolerable, if there were not this facility of evading them at no great cost. Such laws are good for nothing but to be broken.

We now began to ascend again; and the country grew fertile and picturesque. We passed many mules and donkeys, laden with a sort of deep firkin on each side of the saddle, and these were heaped up with grapes, both purple and white. We bought some, and got what we should have thought abundance at no great price; only we used to get twice as many at Montauto. However, a Roman paul brought us three or four pounds, even here. We still ascended, and came soon to the gateway of the town of Acquapendente, which stands on a height that seems to descend by natural terraces, to the valley below. I had been walking up the hill, and being in advance of the vetturo, waited outside of the gate till it came up. French soldiers, in their bluish gray [233] coats and scarlet-trowsers, were on duty at the gate; and one of them took my passport and the vetturino's and we then drove into the town, to wait till they should be viséed. We saw but one street of the town, and that resembles those of all the towns and villages I have seen on this route; narrow, with tall, rusty, aged houses, built of stone, filthy, evil smelling; in short, a kind of place that would be intolerably dismal in cloudy England, and cannot be called cheerful, even under the sun of Italy. Beggars gathered about us, ghastly looking old men and witch-like women, childen that were never once washed in their lives;— and every woman with a child in her arms made it a plea for charity. Priests passed, and burly friars, one of whom was carrying a wine-barrel on his head. Little carts, laden with firkins of grapes, and donkeys, with the same genial burthen, brushed past our vetturo, finding scarce room enough in the narrow street. All the idlers of Acquapendente (and they were many) assembled to gaze at us, but not discourteously. In[234]deed, I never saw an idle curiosity exercised in such a pleasant way, as by the country-people of Italy. It almost deserves to be called a kindly interest and sympathy, instead of a hard and cold curiosity, like that of our own people; and it is displayed with such simplicity that it is evident no offense is intended.

By-and-by, the vetturino brought his passport and my own, with the official visé, which had cost only a half-paul apiece. We kept on our way, still ascending, passing through vineyards and olives, and meeting grape-laden donkeys, till we came to the town of San Lorenzo Nuovo, a place built by Pope Pius VI, as a refuge for the people of a lower town, which had been made uninhabitable by mal-aria. The new town (I suppose it is hundreds of years old, with all its novelty) shows strikingly the difference between places that grow up and shape out their streets of their own accord, as it were, and one that was built on a settled plan, of malice aforethought. This little rural village has gates of classic archi[235]tecture, a spacious piazza, and a great breadth of straight and rectangular streets, with houses of uniform build, airy and wholesome-looking, to a degree seldom seen on the Continent. Nevertheless, I must say that the town looked hatefully dull and ridiculously prim, and, of the two, I had rather spend my life in Radicofani. We drove through it, from gate to gate, without stopping, and soon came to the brow of a hill, whence we beheld, right beneath us, the beautiful lake of Bolsena; not exactly at our feet, however, for a portion of level ground lay between, haunted by the pestilence, which has depopulated all these shores, and made the lake and its neighborhood a solitude. It looked very beautiful, nevertheless, with a sheen of silver and a gray like that of steel, as the wind blew and the sun shone on it; and, judging by my own feelings, I should really have thought that the breeze from its surface was bracing and wholesome.

Descending the hill, we passed the ruins of the old town of San Lorenzo, of which the prim vil[236]lage on the hill-top may be considered the daughter. There is certainly no resemblance between parent and child, the former being situated on a sort of precipitous bluff, where there could have been no room for piazzas and spacious streets, nor accessibility, I should suppose, except by mules, donkies, goats, and people of Alpine habits. I remember nothing of it, as we drove past, except an ivy-covered tower on the top of the bluff, and some arched cavern-mouths that looked as if they opened into the great darkness. These were the entrances to Etruscan tombs; for the town on top had been originally Etruscan, and the inhabitants had buried themselves in the heart of the precipitous bluff, after spending their lives on its top.

Reaching the plain, we drove several miles along the shore of the lake, and found the soil fertile, and generally well cultivated, especially with the vine; though there were tracts apparently too marshy to be put to any agricultural purpose. We met now and then a flock of sheep, watched by sallow-looking and spiritless men [237] and boys, who, we took it for granted, would soon perish of malaria; though, I presume, they never spend their nights in the immediate vicinity of the lake. I should like to inquire whether animals suffer from the bad qualities of the air. The lake is not nearly so beautiful on a nearer view as it is from the hill above, there being no rocky margin, nor bright sandy beach, but everywhere this interval of level ground, and often swampy marsh, betwixt the water and the hill. At a considerable distance from the shore, we saw two islands, one of which is memorable as having been the scene of an Empress's murder; but I cannot stop to fill my journal with historical reminiscences. We kept onward to the town of Bolzena, which stands perhaps nearly a mile from the lake, and on a site higher than the level margin, yet not so much so, I should apprehend, as to free it from danger of malaria. We stopt at an albergo outside of the wall of the town, and, before dinner, had time to see a good deal of the neigh[238]borhood. The first aspect of the town was very striking, with a vista into its street through the open gateway, and, high above it, an old, gray, square-built castle, with three towers visible at the angles, one of them battlemented, one taller than the rest, and one partially ruined. Outside of the town gate, there were some fragments of Roman ruin, capitals of pillars, altars with inscriptions; these we glanced at, and then made our entrance through the gate.

There it was again, the same narrow, dirty, time-darkened street of piled-up houses, which we have so often seen; the same swarm of ill-to-do people, grape-laden donkies, little stands or shops of roasted chestnuts, peaches, tomatoes, white and purple figs; the same evidence of a fertile land, and grimy poverty in the midst of abundance, which Nature tries to heap into their hands. It seems strange that they can never grasp it. We had gone but a little way along this street, when we saw a narrow lane that turned aside from it, and went steeply upward. [239] Its name was on the corner, the Via de Castello; and as the castle promised to be more interesting than anything else, we immediately began to ascend. The street—a strange name for such an avenue—clambered upward in the oddest fashion, passing under arches, scrambling up steps; so that it was more like a long, steep, irregular pair of stairs, than anything that Christians call a street; and so large a part of it was under arches that we scarcely seemed to be out of doors. At last, Una, who was in advance, emerged into the upper air, and cried out that we had ascended to an upper town, and a larger one than that beneath.

68, Piazza Poli (Rome,) Oct[r]. 17th, Sunday.

It really seemed like coming up out of the earth into the midst of the town, when we found ourselves so unexpectedly in the upper town of Bolsena.—We were in a little nook, surrounded by old edifices, and called the Piazza del Orologio, on account of a clock that was apparent somewhere. The old castle was close by; and from its platform [240] there was a splendid view of the lake and all the neighboring hill-country. The castle itself is still in good condition, and apparently as strong as ever it was, as respects the exterior walls; but within, there seemed to be neither floor nor chamber, nothing but the empty shell of the dateless old fortress. The stones at the base and lower part of the building were so massive, that I should think the Etrurians might have laid them; and then perhaps the Romans built a little higher; and the medi-aeval people raised the battlements and towers. But we did not look long at the Castle, our attention being drawn to the singular aspect of the town itself, which—to speak first of its most prominent characteristic—is the very filthiest place, I do believe, that ever was inhabited by man. Filth was everywhere; in the Piazza, in nooks and corners, strewing the streets (miserable lanes, rather) from side to side, defiling the platform before the Castle; the filth of every day and of accumulated ages. I wonder whether the ancient Romans were as dirty a people as we everywhere find those who have succeeded them; for there seems to be something in the [241] places that have been inhabited by Romans, or made famous in their history, and in the monuments of every kind that they have raised, that puts people in mind of their earthly necessities, and incites them to defile therewith whatever temple, column, ruined palace, or triumphal arch may be nearest at hand. I think it must be an hereditary trait, probably weakened, and robbed of a little of its dirty horror, by the influence of milder ages; and I am much afraid that Caesar trod narrower and filthier ways, in his path to power, than those of modern Rome, or even of this hideous town of Bolsena. I cannot imagine anything worse than these, however. Rotten vegetables, thrown everywhere about, musty straw, standing puddles, running rivulets of dissolved nastiness—these matters were a relief amid viler objects of disgust. The town was full of great, black hogs, wallowing before every door, and they grunted at us with a kind of courtesy and affability, as if the town was theirs, and it was their part to be hospitable to strangers. Donkies (of which there were many) likewise accosted us with braying; children (little [242] imps engendered of dirt, and growing nastier every day they lived,) pestered us with begging; men stared askance at us as they stood in corners or turned against a house-wall; and women endangered us with dirty slops which they were flinging from doorways into the street. No decent words can describe—no admissible image can give an idea—of this noisome place. And yet, I remember, the donkies came up the height loaded with fruit, and with little flat-sided barrels of wine; the people had a good atmosphere—except as they polluted it themselves—on their high site; and there seemed to be no reason why they should not live a beautiful and jolly life.

I did not mean to write such an ugly description as the above; but it is well, once for all, to have attempted conveying an idea of what disgusts the traveller, more or less, in all these Italian towns. Setting aside this grand characteristic, the upper town of Bolsena is a most curious and interesting place. It was originally an Etruscan city, the ancient Volsinium, and when taken and destroyed by the Romans, was said to contain two

[243] thousand statues. Afterwards, the Romans built a town upon the site, including, I suppose, the space occupied by the lower town, which looks as if it had brimmed over and fallen from the precipitous height occupied by the upper. The latter is a strange confusion of black and ugly houses, piled massively out of the ruins of former ages, built rudely and without plan, as a pauper would build his hovel, and yet with here and there an arched gateway, a cornice, a pillar, that might have adorned a palace. Indeed, many of the houses, as they stand, may once have been palaces, and have still a squalid kind of grandeur. The whole town made me think how undesirable it is to build human habitations out of permanent materials, and with a view to their being occupied by future generations. All towns should be made capable of purification by fire, or of decay with half-a-century or so; else they become the hereditary haunt of vermin and noisomeness, and, besides, stand apart from the possibility of such improvement as is introduced into other of man's contrivances and accommodations. It is a very pretty thing, in some respects, to imagine [244] our posterity living under the same floors as ourselves; but when people insist on building age-long habitations, they incur (or their posterity do) a misfortune analogous to that of the Sibyl who asked for immortality. They build immortal houses, but cannot keep them from growing old, musty, unwholesome, dreary, full of death-scents, ghosts, murder-stains; in short, houses such as one sees everywhere in Italy, be they hovels or palaces.

The streets of this old town are the narrowest I have seen anywhere—of no more width, inded, than may suffice for the passage of a donkey with his panniers. They wind in and out in strange confusion, and hardly look like streets at all, but, nevertheless, have names printed on the corners, just as if they were stately avenues. After looking about us awhile, and drawing half-breaths so as to take in the less quantity of gaseous pollution, we went back to the castle, and descended by a path winding downward from it into the plain outside of the town-gate.

It was now dinner-time; and at our rustic albergo—a shabby old place enough, but cleaner [245] and better than could be hoped for in such a neighborhood—we had, in the first place, some fish from the pestiferous lake; not, I am sorry to say, the famous stewed eels, which, Dante says, killed Pope Martin, but some trout, and still better, some delicate little fishes, from an inch to three inches long. They are fried like white-bait, and, to my taste, were quite as good. Then, a small turkey, or part of one, and some grapes; and, with this respectable fare, a decanter of golden-hued wine, as much like weak cider as can be conceived. By-the-by, the meal was not dinner, but only our mid-day collazione. After dispatching it, we again wandered forth, and strolled round the outside of the lower town, which, with the upper one, made as picturesque a combination as could be desired. The old wall, that surrounds the lower town, has been appropriated long since as the back wall of a range of houses; windows have been pierced through it; upper chambers and loggia have been built upon it; so that it looks something like a long row of rural dwellings, with one continuous front, or back, construct[246]ed in a strange style of massive strength, contrasting with the vines that here and there are trained over it, and with the wreaths of yellow corn that hang from the windows. But portions of the old battlements are interspersed with the line of homely chambers and tiled housetops. Within the precinct of this wall, the town is very compact, and above its roofs rises a rock, the sheer precipitous bluff on which stands the upper town, the foundations of which impend over the highest roof in the lower. At one end is the old castle with its towers rising above the square, battlemented mass of the main fortress; and if we had not seen the dirt and squalor that dwells within this venerable outside, we should have carried away a picture of gray, grim dignity, presented by a long-past age to the present one, to put its mean ways and modes to shame. Mamma, Una, and Miss Shepard, all sat diligently sketching, and children came about them, exceedingly unfragrant, but very courteous and gentle, looking over their (the sketchers') shoulders, and expressing delight as they saw each familiar edifice take its place in the sketch. They are a loveable people, these Italians, as I find from almost all with whom we come in contact; they [247] have great and little faults, and no great virtues, that I know of, but still are sweet (except to the sense of smell,) amiable, pleasant to encounter, save when they beg, or when you have to bargain with them.

We left Bolsena at two °clock, and drove to Viterbo, with no noticeable incident, that I remember, except passing the gate of the picturesque town of Montefiascone, over the wall of which I saw spires and towers, and the dome of a Cathedral. I was sorry not to taste, in its own town, the celebrated wine of Est, which was the death-draught of the jolly prelate, John de Foucris. At Viterbo, however, where we dined and slept, I called for some wine of Montefiascone, and had a little straw-covered flask, which the waiter assured us was the genuine Est-wine. It was of golden colour, and very delicate, somewhat resembling still champagne, but finer, and requiring a calmer pause to appreciate its subtle delight. Its good qualities, however, are so evanescent, that (the flask continuing open) the finer flavor became almost imperceptible before we finished it.

Viterbo is a large, dirty, disagreeable town, [248] built at the foot of a mountain, the peak of which is seen through the vista of some of the narrow streets. On the evening of our arrival, we went in quest of the Cathedral, and at last found it, but only when the twilight made it impossible to see the interior. We went again in the morning; but, really, after the Cathedrals that we have seen elsewhere, the edifice is not worth a description.

It is said to be Gothic, but appears to me more in the classic style, with pillared-arches along the nave; tall, round-topt arches, supported by Grecian pillars. The antique portions of the pavement are a curious mosaic; but what chiefly interests me in this Cathedral is the murder-scene that passed in it, as long ago as the time of Henry Third; the murder of Prince Henry of England by Guy de Montfort. The piazza, before the Cathedral, is a rude and unpaved one, surrounded by old edifices, one of which is the Episcopal Palace, the doorway and front of which have some points and peculiarities of ancient architecture. We saw the hall, of noble size, where the Cardinals were sitting at the time of Prince Henry's murder, and sat nearly three years, [249] to elect Pope Gregory X. But there is no use telling things that may be found in Murray; so I shall say nothing of this, nor of the fact that, in this rude Piazza, Pope Adrian IV compelled the Emperor Frederic Barbarossa to hold his stirrup. I forget whether it was before or after this, that the Emperor had pleasantly set the Pope on an ass, with his face towards the tail.

Passing a church, in one of the streets, we saw a marble sarcophagus built into its façade, and finely sculptured with what, at a hasty glance, we took to be Meleager's boar-hunt, which is often represented on these old burial-chests; but Murray calls it a fight between a lion and a boar. This sarcophagus was doubtless once the receptacle of some old Pagan's ashes; but now it contains the dust of Galiana, a beautiful woman—the most beautiful of her day—so beautiful that she caused a war between Rome and Viterbo, in which the latter city conquered, and kept the living beauty, and still keeps her dust. But the conquered Romans stipulated, in the treaty of peace, that they should have one last look [250] at Galliana, and so her heavenly face was permitted to shed a parting gleam over them, from a window in a tower of one of the gates. This sounds like the wildest romance; but, as Murray tells it, I presume it is a historical fact.

There are more fountains in Viterbo than I have seen in any other city of its size, and many of them of very good design. Around most of them there were wine-hogsheads, waiting their turn to be cleansed and rinsed before receiving the wine of the present vintage. Passing a door-way, we saw (at least, Julian did, and told me of it) some men treading out the grapes, in a great vat, with their naked feet. It is not quite an agreeable idea, that an Italian peasant perhaps does not wash his feet from year's end to year's end, except in the wine which we are to drink. Viterbo is paved with flag-stones, in the Florence fashion, and I think it was the last place in which we found this smooth and delightful pavement. Dirt was exceedingly abundant upon it, though people were pretending to sweep it away, and succeeded so far as to raise an intolerable dust, which the wind wafted all about us. [251] The same high wind flung the spray of the fountains over us; and this, I believe, concludes all that I shall think it worth while to say about Viterbo. Among the beggars here, the loudest and most vociferous was a crippled postillion, wearing his uniform jacket, green faced with red; and he seemed to consider himself entitled still to get his living from travellers, as having been disabled in the way of his profession. I recognized his claim to the extent of a half-paul, and was rewarded with a courteous and grateful bow at our departure; the servants of the Aigle Noir, on the other hand, (being discontented with their fees) stood at the door, looking grim and sour. The same amount of fees produces a very different effect at different hotels. Two pauls at the noon collazione, and three or four after a night's lodging, is what we usually give. To beggars— after my much experience both in England and Italy—I give very little, though I am not certain that it would not often be real beneficence in the latter country. There being little or no provision for poverty and age, the poor must often suffer. Nothing can be more [252] earnest than their entreaties for aid; nothing seemingly more genuine than their gratitude when they receive it. They return you the value of your alms in prayers (which, I suspect, the Italians have generally a notion of purchasing, when they assist the poor) and say, 'God will accompany you.' Many of them have a professional whine, and a certain doleful twist of the neck and turn of the head, which hardens my heart against them at once. A painter might find numerous models among them, if canvas had not already been more than sufficiently covered with their style of the picturesque. There is a certain style of old, brickdust-colored cloak, worn in Viterbo, (not exclusively by beggars,) which, when ragged enough, is exceedingly picturesque.

We left Viterbo on Friday, the 15th, at about eleven °clock in the forenoon; and I remember nothing that I need to record, in the day's journey, unless it be that Miss Shepard and Una got out of the coach, on the ascent of a hill, and were left behind without our knowing anything about it. Rosebud, who was sitting in the coupé with us, (Julian being on the driver's seat) at [253] last wished to be put through the front window into the vetturo, and found it empty, and the door swinging open. We were then ascending a hill, which gave a view of the road far behind—and they were nowhere in sight, these poor maidens, being left to wander wide through Italy. I went back, with Julian, and at length met them, after they had walked several miles; and we overtook the vetturo in the street—a black and ugly street, of course, swarming with flies and dirty people—of Monterosi. Thence we proceeded to Le Sette Vene, where we dined and slept, after a journey of only thirty miles. There was nothing interesting at Sette Vene, except an old Roman bridge, of a single arch, which had kept its sweep, composed of one row of stones, unbroken for two thousand years, and looked just as strong as ever; though gray with age, and fringed with plants that found it hard to fix themselves in its close crevices.

The next day we started somewhere about seven °clock and drove along the Cassian Way towards Rome. It was a most delightful morning, a genial [254] atmosphere, the more so, I suppose, because this was the campagna, the region of pestilence and death. I had a quiet, gentle, comfortable pleasure, as if, after many wanderings, I was drawing near home; for, now that I have known it once, Rome certainly does draw into itself my heart, as I think even London, or even little Concord itself, or old sleepy Salem, never did and never will. Besides, we are to stay here six months, and we had now a house all prepared to receive us; so that this present approach, in the noontide of a genial day, was most unlike our first one, when we crept towards Rome through the wintry midnight, benumbed with cold, sick, weary, and not knowing whither to betake ourselves. Ah, that was a dismal time! One thing, however, that disturbed even my present equanimity a little was the necessity of meeting the Custom House at the Porta del Popolo; but my past experience warranted me in believing that even these ogres might be mollified by the magic touch of a scudo; and so it proved. We should have escaped any examination at all, the officer whispered me, if his superior had not hap[255]pened to be present; but, as the case stood, they took down only one trunk from the top of the vetturo, just lifted the lid, closed it again, and gave us permission to proceed. So we came to 68, piazza Poli, and found ourselves at once at home, in such a comfortable, cosy little house, as I did not think existed in Rome.

I ought to say a word about our Vetturino, Costantino Bacci, an excellent and most favorable specimen of his class; for his magnificent conduct, his liberality, and all the good qualities that ought to be imperial, we call him the Emperor. He took us to good hotels and feasted us with the best; he was kind to us all, and especially to little Rosebud, who used to run by his side, with her small hand in his great brown one; he was cheerful in his deportment, and expressed his good spirits by the smack of his whip, which is the barometer of a vetturino's inward weather; he drove admirably, and would rumble up to the door of an albergo, and stop to a hair's breadth just where it was most convenient for us to alight; he would hire pos[256]-tillions and horses, where other vetturini would take nothing better than sluggish oxen, to help us up the hilly roads, so that sometimes we had a team of seven;—he did all that we could possibly require of him, and was content, and more, with a buonmano of five scudi, in addition to the stipulated price. Finally, I think the tears had risen almost to his eyelids when we parted with him.

Our friends the Thompsons (through whose kindness we procured this house) called to see us soon after our arrival. In the afternoon, I walked with Rosebud to the Medici Gardens, and on our way thither we espied our former servant, Lallah (who flung so many and such bitter curses after us, on our departure from Rome) sitting at her father's fruit-stall, at the corner of Capo le Case and the Via Sistina. Thank God, they have not taken effect. After going to the Medici, we went to the Pincian Gardens, and looked over into the Borghese grounds, which, methought were more beautiful than ever. The same was true of the sky, and of every object beneath it; and, as we came homeward along the [257] Corso, I wondered at the stateliness and palatial magnificence of that noble street. Once, I remember, I thought it narrow and far unworthy of its fame.

In the way of costume, the men in goat-skin breeches, whom we met on the Campagna, were very striking, and looked much like Satyrs.

68, Piazza Poli, Octr 21st, Thursday.

As I have already described most of the prominent objects in
Rome once, there is no occasion for me to do the whole business
over again, and very likely not so well as when my impressions
were new. I have been twice to St Peter's, and was impressed,
I think, more than at any former visit by a sense of breadth and
loftiness, and, as it were, a visionary splendour and magnificence. I also went to the Museum of the Capitol; and the
statues seemed to me more beautiful than formerly, and I was
not sensible of the cold despondency with which I have so
often viewed them. Yesterday, my wife and I went to the
Corsini Palace; which we had [258] not visited before. It
stands in the Trastevere (in what seems to be the principal
street on that side of the Tiber, called the Longara) and is a
stately palace, with a grand staircase leading to the first floor,
where are situated the range of picture rooms. There were a
good many fine pictures, but none of them appear to have made
a memorable impression on my mind, except a portrait by
Vandyke of a man in point-lace—very grand and very real.
The room in which this picture hung had many other portraits
by Holbein, Titian, Rembrandt, Rubens, and other famous
painters, and was wonderfully rich in this department. In
another, there was a portrait of Pope Julius II, by Raphael,
somewhat differing from those at the Pitti and the Ufizzi galleries in Florence, and those which I have seen in England
and Paris; thinner, paler, perhaps older, more severely intellectual, but at least as high a work of art as those.

Leaving the palace (by-the-by, it has some handsome old
furniture, and gilded chairs, covered with leather cases, possibly relics of the splendor of Queen [259] Christina's time,
who died here) we strolled along Longara, and bought three

baiocchi worth of roasted chesnuts, which we ate warm, and found them a very satisfactory lunch. By the time they were disposed of, we reached Saint Peter's, and found the piazza full of French soldiers at their drill, both in the open space and among the pillars of the colonnade. We went quite round the interior of the church, and perceiving the pavement loose and broken, near the altar where Guido's archangel is placed, we pocketed some bits of rosso antico and gray marble, to be set in brooches as relics. Referring again to the Corsini palace, I know not but the most curious object there was a curule chair of marble, sculptured all out of one piece, and adorned with bas-reliefs. It is supposed to be Etruscan. It has a circular back, sweeping round so as to afford sufficient rests for the elbows, and sitting down in it, I discovered that modern ingenuity has not made much real improvement on this chair of two or three thousand years ago. But some chairs are easier for the moment, but soon betray you and grow the more irksome.

[260] We have the snuggest little set of apartments in Rome, seven rooms, including an anti-chamber; and though the stairs are exceedingly narrow, there is really a carpet on them —a civilized comfort, of which the proudest palaces in the Eternal city cannot boast. The stairs are very steep, however; and I should not wonder if some of us broke our noses down them. Narrowness of space within doors strikes us all rather ludicrously, yet not unpleasantly, after being accustomed to the naked, brick-paved wastes and deserts of the Montauto Villa. It is well to be thus put in training for the over-snugness of our cottage in Concord. Our windows here look out on a small, and rather quiet piazza, with an immense palace on the left hand, and a smaller, yet statelier one, on the right; and just round a corner of the street leading out of our piazza is the Fountain of Trevi, of which I can hear the plash in the evening, when other sounds are hushed.

Looking over what I have said of Sodoma's picture of Christ

bound, at Siena, I see that I have omitted to notice what seems to me one of its most [261] striking characteristics—its loneliness. You feel as if the Savior was deserted, both in Heaven and earth; the despair is in him, which made him say, 'My God, why hast thou forsaken me!' Even in this extremity, however, he is still divine; and Sodoma almost seems to have reconciled the impossibilities of combining an Omnipotent Divinity with a suffering and outraged humanity. But this is one of the cases in which the spectator's imagination completes what the artist merely hints at.

Mr Mozier, the sculptor, called to see us, the other evening, and quite paid Powers off for all his trenchant criticisms on his brother-artists. He will not allow Powers to be an artist at all, or to know anything of the laws of art, although acknowledging him to be a great bust-maker, and to have put together the Greek Slave and the Fisher Boy very ingeniously. The latter, however, is copied from the Apollino in the Tribune of the Ufizzi; and the former is made up of beauties that had no reference to one another; and he affirms that Powers is ready to sell, and has actually sold, the Greek [262] Slave, limb by limb, dismembering it by reversing the process of putting it together —a head to one purchaser, an arm or a foot to another, a hand to a third. Powers knows nothing scientifically of the human frame, and only succeeds in representing it (the illustration was my own, and adopted by Mr. Mozier) as a natural bone-doctor succeeds in setting a dislocated limb, by a happy accident or special Providence. Yet Mr. Mozier seemed to acknowledge that he did succeed. I repeat these things only as another instance how invariably every sculptor uses his chisel and mallet to smash and deface the marble-work of every other. I never heard Powers speak of Mr. Mozier, but can partly imagine what he would have said. By the by, Mr. M. spoke of Powers' disappointment about the $25000 appropriation from Congress, and said that he was altogether to blame;

inasmuch as he attempted to sell to the nation, for that sum, a statue which, to Mr. M's certain knowledge, he had already offered to private persons for a fifth part of it. I have not implicit faith in Mr. Mozier's veracity, and doubt not Powers acted fairly in his own eyes.

[263] Piazza Poli, October 23ᵈ Saturday.

I am afraid I have caught one of the colds which the Roman air continually affected me with, last winter; at any rate, a sirocco has taken the life out of me, and I have no spirit to do anything. This morning, however, I took a walk out of the Porta Maggiore, and looked at the tomb of the baker Eurysaces, just outside of the gate, a very queer ruin, covered with symbols of the man's trade in stone-work, and with bas-reliefs along the cornice, representing people at work making bread. An in-scription states that the ashes of his wife are likewise reposited there, in a bread basket. The mausoleum is perhaps twenty-feet long, in its largest extent, and of equal height; and if good bakers were as scarce in ancient Rome as in the modern city, I do not wonder that they were thought worthy of stately monu-ments. None of the modern ones deserve any better one than a pile of their own sour loaves.

I walked onward a good distance beyond the gate, along-side of the arches of the Claudian aque[264]duct, which, in this portion of it, seems to have had little repair, and to have needed little, since it was built. It looks like a long procession, striding across the Campagna towards the city, and entering the gate. Over one of its arches, within the gate, I saw two or three slender jets of water spirting from the crevices; this aqueduct being still in use to bring the Acqua Felice into Rome. Returning within the walls, I walked along their inner base to the church of St. John Lateran, into which I went and sat down to rest myself, being languid and weary, and hot with the sun, though afraid to trust the coolness of the shade. I do hate the Roman atmosphere; indeed, all my pleasure at getting back—all my home-feeling—has already evaporated, and what now impresses me, as before, is the languor of Rome —its nastiness—its weary pavements—its little life pressed down by a weight of death. Speaking of nastiness, the tomb of Eurysaces was strewn around with even more than the usual abundance of filthy deposits.

Quitting St. John Lateran, I went astray, as I do [265] nine times out of ten in these Roman intricacies, and at last, seeing the Coliseum in the vista of a street, I betook myself thither to get a fresh start. Its round of bricks looked vast and dreary, but not particularly impressive. The interior was quite deserted, except that a Roman, of respectable appearance, was making a pilgrimage of the round of altars, kneeling and saying a prayer at every one.

Outside of the Coliseum, on the rising ground near the arch of Constantine, a neat-looking little boy came and begged of me; and I gave him a baioccho, rather because he seemed to need it so little than for any other reason. I observed that he immediately afterwards went and spoke to a well-dressed man, and I supposed that the child was likewise begging of him. I watched the little boy, however, and saw that, in two or three other instances, after begging of other individuals, he still returned to this well-dressed man; the fact being, no doubt, that the latter was fishing for baiocchi through the medium of his child—throwing the poor little fellow out as a bait, while he himself retained his in[266]dependent respectability. He had probably come out for a whole day's sport; for, by-and-by, he went within the arches of the Coliseum, followed by the child, and taking with him what looked like a bottle of wine wrapped in a handkerchief.

Piazza Poli, Novr 2^d, Tuesday.

The weather, lately, would have suited one's ideal of an English November, except that there have been no fogs; but of ugly, hopeless clouds, chill, shivery winds, drizzle, and now and then pouring rain—much more than enough. An English coal-fire, if we could see its honest glow within-doors, would compensate for all the unamiableness of the outside atmosphere; but we might ask for the sunshine of the New Jerusalem, with as much hope of getting it. It is extremely spirit-crushing, this remorseless grey, with its icy heart; and the more to depress the whole family, Una has taken what seems to be the Roman fever by sitting down to sketch in the Coliseum. It is not a severe attack, yet attended with fits of exceeding discomfort, occasional comatoseness, and even delirium [267] to the extent of making the poor child talk in rhythmical measure, like a tragic heroine—as if the fever lifted her feet off the earth. This fever is seldom dangerous, but is liable to recur on slight occasion hereafter.

This forenoon, being sunny, though very cool for the season, I took a walk in the grounds of the Villa Borghese. They are very beautiful, with their broad, gravelled carriage-ways, and their wood-paths, which wander away beneath long vistas of sheltering boughs; their ilex-trees, so ancient and venerable, that seem to have lived for ages undisturbed, and to have no fear of the axe, and which, in the long peace of their life-time, assume attitudes of indolent repose; the stone pines, that look like green islands in the air, so high above earth are they, and connected with it by such slender length of stem; the cypresses, resembling dark flames of huge funereal candles. These wooded lawns are more beautiful than English park-scenery; all the more beautiful for the air of neglect there is about them, as if not much [268] care of man was bestowed on them, though enough to keep wildness from growing into deformity, and to make the whole scene like Nature idealized—the woodland scenes that poets dream of; a forest of Ardennes, for instance. These lawns and gentle vallies are beautiful, moreover, with fountains plashing into marble basins, or gushing like natural cascades from rough rocks; with bits of architecture, as pillared porticoes, arches, columns, of marble or granite, with a touch of artful ruin on them; and, indeed, the pillars and fragments seem to be remnants of antiquity, though put together anew; hundreds of years old, perhaps, even in their present form, for weeds and flowers grow out of the chinks, and cluster on the tops of arches and porticoes. There are altars, too, with old Roman inscriptions on them. Statues stand here and there among the trees, in solitude, or in a long range, lifted high on pedestals, moss-grown, some of them shattered, all grown gray with the corrosion of the atmosphere. In the midst of these sunny and shadowy tracts rises the stately front of the villa adorned with statues in niches, with [269] busts, and ornamental architecture blossoming in stone-work. Take away the malaria, and it might be a very happy place.

Piazza Poli, Feb. 27th, 1859. Sunday.

For some days past, there have been tokens of the coming Carnival, in the Corso and the adjacent streets; for example in the decking out of balconies with fringes and borders of red and gold; and, in the shops, by the display of masks of wire, pasteboard, silk, or cloth, some of beautiful features, others hideous; fantastic, currish, asinine, huge-nosed, or otherwise

monstrous; some intended to cover the whole face, others con-
cealing only the upper part; also, white dominos, or robes
bedizened with gold lace, and theatric splendours, displayed at
shop-windows, or flaunting before the doors. Yesterday, Una
and I came along the Corso, between one and two °clock, after
a walk, and found all these symptoms of impending merriment
multiplied and intensified; carpets and tapestries, and embroidered cloths, hanging from many of the windows; the
balconies covered with gay awnings and curtains; rows of
chairs set out along [270] the side walks, elevated a foot or
two by means of planks; great baskets full of confetti for sale
in the shops, or in the nooks and recesses of the streets; bouquets of all qualities and price. The Corso was becoming pretty
well thronged with people, but, until two °clock, nobody dared
to fling as much as a rosebud or a handful of sugar-plums.
There was a sort of holiday expression, however, on almost
everybody's face, such as I have not hitherto seen in Rome, or
any part of Italy; a smile gleaming out, an aurora of mirth,
which probably will not be very exuberant in its noontide. The
day was so sunny and bright that it made this opening scene
far more cheerful than any day of the last year's Carnival. As
we threaded our way through the Corso, Una kept wishing that
she were a boy, and could plunge into the fun and uproar as
Julian would; and for my own part (though I pretended to take
no interest in the matter) I could have bandied confetti and
nosegays as readily and as riotously as any urchin there. But
my black hat and grave Talma would have been too good a
mark for the combatants; nor was Una in [271] fitting trim;
so, much against her will, we went home before a shot
was fired.

This morning, it drizzles rain, just as it did through the
whole Carnival, last year; and very likely we shall not have
another genial day.

Piazza di Poli, March 1st, Tuesday.

The tower in the Via Portoghese has battlements and machicolations; and the upper half of it is covered with a grey,
ancient-looking stucco. On the summit, at one corner, is the
shrine of the virgin, rising quite above the battlements, and
with its lamp before it. Beneath the machicolations is a window probably belonging to the upper chamber; and there seems
to be a level space on the top of the tower. Close at hand is
the facade of a church, the highest pinnacle of which appears
to be at about the same level as the battlements of the tower;
and there are two or more stone figures (either angelic or allegorical) ornamenting the top of the façade, and, I think, blowing trumpets. These personages are the nearest neighbors of
any person inhabiting the upper story of the [272] tower, and
the sound of their angelic trumpets must needs be very loud,
in that close vicinity. The lower story of the palace extends
out, round the lower part of the tower, and is surrounded by
a stone balustrade. The entrance from the street is through a
long, arched doorway and passage, giving admittance into a
small enclosed court; and, deep within the passage, there is
a very broad staircase, which branches off, apparently, on one
side, and leads to the height of the tower. At the foot of the
tower, and along the front of the palace, the street widens, so
as to form something like a small piazza, in which there are
one or two baker's shops, one or two shoe-shops, a lottery-
office, and, at a near corner, the stand of a woman who sells,
I think, vegetables; a little further, a stand of oranges. Not
many doors from the palace entrance, there is a station of
French soldiers, and a sentinel on duty. The palace (judging
by the broad staircase, the balustraded platform, the tower itself, and other tokens) may have been a grand one, centuries

ago; but the locality is now a poor one, and the edifice itself seems to have fallen to un-[273]aristocratic occupants. A man was cleaning a carriage in the enclosed court-yard; but I rather conceive that it was a cab for hire, and not the equipage of any dweller in the palace.

68, Piazza di Poli, March 7th, Monday.

Last week, we were in full Carnival; and, the weather being splendid, the merriment was far more free and riotous than as I remember it, the preceding year. Going out in the morning, tokens of the festival were seen in baskets of flowers, for sale at the street-corners, or borne about on people's heads, while bushels upon bushels of confetti were displayed, looking just like veritable sugar-plums; so that a stranger might have thought that the whole commerce and business of stern old Rome lay in flowers and sweets.

I (as well as the rest of the family) have followed up the Carnival pretty faithfully, and enjoyed it as well, or rather better, than could have been expected; principally in the street, as a mere looker-on (which does not let one into the mystery of the fun) and twice from a balcony, whence I threw confetti, and [274] partly understood why the young people like it so much. Certainly, there cannot well be a more picturesque spectacle in human life, than that stately, palatial avenue of the Corso (the more picturesque because so narrow) all hung with carpets, Gobelin tapestry, scarlet cloths with gilded fringes, flaunting from balconies and windows, and the whole palace-heights alive with faces; and all the capacity of the street thronged with the most fantastic figures that either the fancies of folks alive at this day are able to contrive, or that live traditionally from year to year, for centuries back. To be sure, looking critically at the scene, the spectator rather wonders that the masquing scene should not be more rich and various, when there has been so long a time (the immemorial existence of the Carnival) to prepare it, and crowd it with shapes of gaiety and humor. There are not many things worth remembering;— an infinite number of clowns and parti-colored harlequins; a host of white dominos; a multitude of masks, set to an eternal grin, or with monstrous noses, or made in the guise of monkies, bears, dogs, or whatever beast [275] the wearer chooses to be akin to; a great many men in petticoats, and almost as many girls and women, no doubt, in breeches; figures, too, with huge, bulbous heads; and all manner of such easy monstrosities and exaggerations. It is strange how the whole humor of the thing, and the separate humor of each individual character, vanishes, the moment I try to grasp one and describe it; and yet there really was fun in the spectacle as it flitted by. For instance, in a large open carriage, a company of young men in flesh-colored tights and chemises, representing a party of girls surprised in the midst of dressing themselves, while an old nurse, in the midst of them, expressed ludicrous horror at their predicament; then the embarrassment of gentlemen, who, while quietly looking at the scene, are surrounded by groups of masques, grinning at them, squeaking in their ears, hugging them, dancing round them, till they snatch the opportunity to escape into some doorway; or, when a poor man in a black coat and cylinder hat is whitened all over with a half-bushel of confetti and lime dust, the mock sympathy [276] with which his case is investigated by a company of masquers, who poke their stupid, pasteboard faces close to his, still with an unchangeable grin; or when a gigantic female figure singles out some shy, harmless personage, and makes appeals to his heart, presenting him with a boquet, avowing her passionate love in dumb-show; and a hundred other nonsensicalities, among which the rudest and simplest are not the least effective. A resounding thump on the back with a harlequin's sword, or a rattling blow with a bladder, half-full of dry peas or corn, answers a very good purpose. There was a good absurdity, one day, in a figure with a crinoline petticoat, riding on an ass, and almost filling the Corso with the circumference of Crinoline, from side to side. Some figures are dressed in old fashioned garbs, perhaps of the last century, or, even more ridiculous, of thirty years ago, or in the stately Elizabethan (as we should call them) trunk-hose, tunics, and cloaks of three centuries since. I do not know that I have seen anything queerer than a Unitarian clergyman (Mr. Mountford) who drives through the Corso daily, with [277] his fat wife, in a one-horse chaise, with a wreath of withered flowers and oak-leaves round his hat; the rest of his dress remaining unchanged, except that it is well-powdered with dust of confetti. That withered wreath is the absurdest thing he could wear, (though perhaps he may not mean it so,) and so, of course, the best. I can think of no other masques, just now, but will go again, this afternoon, and try to catch some more.

The prince of Wales has fought manfully through the Carnival, with confetti and bouquets; and Una received several of the latter from him, on Saturday.

Piazza di Poli, March 8th, Tuesday.

I went with Una to Mrs. Motley's balcony, in the Corso, and saw the Carnival from it, yesterday afternoon; but the spectacle is strangely like a dream, in respect to the difficulty of retaining it in the mind and solidifying it into a description. I enjoyed it a good deal, and assisted in it so far as to pelt all the people in cylinder hats with handfulls of confetti. The scene opens with a long array of cavalry, who ride through the [278] Corso, preceded by a large band, playing loudly on their brazen instruments; and in their rear come the motley throng of masquers and merry-makers, on foot and in carriages. There were some splendid dresses, particularly contadina-costumes, of scarlet and gold, which seem to be actually the festal attire of that class of people, and must needs be so expensive that one must serve for a lifetime—if, indeed, it be not an inheritance. Clowns and zanies appear in great troops, dancing extravagantly, and scampering wildly; everybody seems to do whatever folly comes into his head; and, yet, if you consider the matter, you see that all this apparent license is kept under courteous restraint. There is no rudeness, except the authorized pelting with confetti, or blows of harlequin-swords, which, moreover, are within a law of their own; but nobody takes rough hold of another, or meddles with his masque, or does him any sort of unmannerly violence. At first sight, you would think that the whole world had gone mad; but, at the end, you wonder how people can let loose all their mirthful propensities without unchaining their mischievous ones. It could not be so in America, or in En[279]gland; in either of those countries, the whole street would go mad in earnest, and come to blows and bloodshed, were the population to let themselves loose to the extent which we see here. All this restraint is self-imposed, and quite apart from that exercised by the presence of the soldiery, who stack their arms in the Piazza del Popolo, and in the Piazza Colonna, and at every other place of vantage in the vicinity of the Corso, and would rain bullets as plentifully as confetti, in case of an outbreak.

Piazza di Poli, March 9th, Wednesday.

I stood, yesterday, an hour or so, among the people on the sidewalk of the Corso, just on the edges of the fun; they appeared to be in a decorous, good-natured mood, neither entering into the merriment, nor harshly repelling; and when groups of masquers overflowed among them, they received their jokes in good part. Many women of the lower class were in this crowd of bystanders, generally broad and sturdy figures, clad evidently in their best, and wearing a good many ornaments;— such as gold or coral beads and necklaces, combs of silver or gold (or it [280] might be, brass,) heavy ear-rings, curiously wrought, brooches, perhaps cameos or mosaics, though I think they prefer purely metallic work to these. One ornament very common among them is a large bodkin which they stick through their hair; it is usually, I believe, of silver, but sometimes it looks like steel, and is made in the shape of a sword—a long Spanish, thrusting sword, for example. Dr. Franco told us a story of a woman of Trastevere, who was addressed rudely, at the Carnival, by a gentleman; she warned him to desist, but as he still persisted, she drew the bodkin from her hair and stabbed him to the heart.

By and by, I went to Mrs. Motley's balcony, and thence looked down on the closing scenes of the Carnival. Methought the merry-makers labored harder to be mirthful, and yet were somewhat tired of their eight playdays; and their dresses looked a little shabby, rumpled, and draggled; but the lack of sunshine (which we have had, on all the preceding days) may have produced this effect. Again, all the particulars of the spectacle have glided out of [281] my remembrance. I have little or nothing to add to my previous recollections, except that the wheels of some of the carriages were wreathed round and spoked with green foliage, making a very pretty and fanciful appearance; as did likewise the harnesses of the horses, which were trimmed with roses. The pervading noise, and uproar of human voices, is one of the most effective points of the matter; but, in fine, the scene is quite indescribable, and its effect not to be conceived, without both witnessing and taking part in it. If you merely look at it, it depresses you; if you take even the slightest share in it, you become aware that it has a fascination, and you no longer wonder, at last, that the young people take such delight in plunging into this mad river of fun, that goes roaring through the heart of solemn old Rome, between the narrow limits of the Corso.

As twilight came on, the moccolletto commenced, and, as it grew darker, the whole street twinkled with lights, which would have been innumerably more abundant, if every torch-bearer had not been surround[282]ed by a host of enemies, who tried to extinguish his poor little twinkle. It was a pity to lose so much splendor as there might have been; but yet there was a kind of symbolism in the thought, that every one of those thousand twinkling lights was in charge of somebody, who was striving with all his might to keep it alive. Not merely the street-way, but all the balconies and hundreds of windows were lit up with these little torches; so that it seemed as if the stars had crumbled into glittering fragments and rained down upon the Corso, some of them lodging upon the palace-fronts, some falling on the ground. Besides this, there were gaslights burning with a whiter flame; but this illumination was not half so interesting as that of the torches, which indicated human struggle. All this time, there were thousands upon thousands of voices, shouting 'Senza Moccolo,' and mingling into one long roar. We, in our balcony, carried on a civil war against one another's torches, as is the custom of human beings, within even the narrowest precincts; but, after a while, we grew tired, and so did the crowd, apparently; for the lights vanished, one after another, till [283] the gas-lights (which at first were an unimportant part of the illumination) shone quietly out, overpowering the scattered twinkles of the mocollos. They were what the fixed stars are to transitory splendors of human life. So ended the Carnival; and I am glad it is over.

Mr Motley tells me, that it was formerly the custom to have a mock funeral of Harlequin, who was supposed to die at the close of the Carnival, during which he had reigned supreme;

and all the people, or as many as chose, bore torches at his burial. But this being considered an indecorous mockery of Popish funeral customs, the present frolic of the moccolo was substituted;—in some sort, growing out of it.

All last night, or as much of it as I was awake, there was a noise of song and late revellers, in the streets; but, to-day, we have waked up in the sad and sober season of Lent.

It is worthy of remark, that all the jollity of the Carnival is a genuine ebullition of spirit, without the aid of wine or strong drink.

[284] Piazza di Poli, March 11th, Friday.

Yesterday we went (Mamma, Miss Shepard, Julian and I) to the Catacomb of St. Calixtus, the entrance to which is along-side of the Appian Way, within sight of the tomb of Cecilia Metella. We descended not a very great way under ground, by a broad flight of stone steps; and lighting some wax tapers with which we had provided ourselves, (they were partly the relics of the Carnival,) we followed the guide through a great many intricate passages, which were mostly just wide enough for me to touch the wall on each side, while keeping my elbows close to my body; and as to height, they were perhaps from seven to ten feet, and sometimes a good deal higher. These passages were roughly hewn through what seemed to be a dark red, crumbly stone; and on either side of the passages were horizontal niches, like shelves, some long, some short, rudely dug out of the dark red wall. These were the burial places, many of them for children, others for grown people, and in some of them we saw old yellow skulls, or bones, so much decayed that it would have been [285] easy to crumble them to dust betwixt our fingers. Frequently, the form of a human body was entirely marked out in white ashes, which looked like lime, but was really all that remained of a body and skeleton, buried perhaps fifteen centuries ago. All these niches, I believe, had formerly been faced and closed in by marble slabs, on which were inscriptions to the memory of the deceased person; but scarcely any of these tombstones were now left, having been transferred to the Vatican or elsewhere. The dark, creeping, tortuous passages, sometimes slightly developed themselves into chapels, few of which (being stript of their marble-work) had much architectural pretension, though their low roofs were still covered with plaster, and sometimes painted with ancient frescoes, representing scriptural scenes. As specimens of art, they were nowise beautiful, besides being excessively dingy, and spoiled with damps and time. In one of these chapels, the guide showed us the low arch, within which the body of St Cecilia was buried, after her martyr[286]dom; and, in another, there were two stone sarcophagi, one on each side of the little chapel, and both covered over with modern glass. Holding our tapers close to this glass-cover, we saw within one of them a skeleton, quite perfect, except that it looked terribly old and crumbly; and, in the other, there lay a body, or a skeleton (for I could but dimly see it) that seemed still to retain the clothes in which it had been buried. One of the chapels was of a circular shape, and appeared to be built on a regular design, though excessively small, only two or three paces across, and seven or eight feet high; the others were merely larger burrows in the red-sandstone. Sometimes we passed beneath openings, where a draught of air and a little light came down upon us, in our cavernous wanderings; at other times, the passages seemed to tend downward, and again to creep upward. It was not, on the whole, very interesting or impressive; something like a nightmare, in which reminiscences of churches and cellars (chiefly the latter) were hopelessly intermixed and shaken up together. It was rather picturesque, when we saw the long line [287] of our tapers (for another large party had joined ours) twinkling along the dark passages; and it was interesting to think of the old inhabitants of these caverns; and it would be terrible enough, no doubt, if we could have gone astray, and for an instant fancied ourselves lost there.

We continued underground about an hour, and I can think of nothing else to record, except that, in one or two places, there was the round mark in the stone, or plaster, where a bottle had been deposited. This was said to have been the token of a martyr's burial-place, and to have contained some of his blood. After emerging from the Catacomb, we drove onward to Cecilia Metella's tomb, which we entered and inspected; but there was very little to see; nothing, indeed, but a round, vacant space, within the immensely massive, circular substance of the tomb. This interior vacancy was open at the top, and had nothing but some fallen stones and a heap of earth, at the bottom. On our way home, we entered the church of "Domine quo vadis," and looked at old fragments of the Appian Way, where our [288] Saviour met St Peter, and left the impression of his feet in one of the old Roman paving-stones. This stone has been removed, and there is now only a fac-simile engraved in a block of marble, occupying the place where Jesus stood. It is a great pity they had not left the original stone; for then all its brother-stones in the pavement would have seemed to confirm the truth of the legend.

While we were at dinner, a gentleman called and was shown into the parlour, whither Una went to receive him. We supposed it to be Mr May, but soon his voice grew familiar, and my wife declared it to be General Pierce; so I left the table, and found it to be really he. I was rejoiced to see him, though a little saddened to see the marks of care and coming age, in many a whitening hair, and many a furrow, and, still more, in something that seemed to have passed away out of him, without leaving any trace. His voice, sometimes, sounded strange and old, though generally it was what it used to be. He was evidently glad to see me—glad to see my wife—glad to see the children, though there was something mel[289]ancholy in his voice, when he remarked what a stout boy Julian had grown. Poor fellow! He has neither son nor daughter to keep his heart warm. This morning, I have been with him to St Peters, and elsewhere about the city, and find him less changed than he seemed to be, last night; not at all changed in heart and affections. We talked freely about all matters that came up; among the rest, about the project (recognizable by many tokens) for bringing him again forward as a candidate for the Presidency, next year. He appears to be firmly resolved not again to present himself to the country, and is content to let his one administration stand, and to be judged by the public and posterity on the merits of that. No doubt, he is perfectly sincere; no doubt, too, he would again be a candidate, if a pretty unanimous voice of the party should demand it. I retain all my faith in his administrative faculty, and should be glad, for his sake, to have it fully recognized; but the probabilities, as far as I can see, do not indicate for him another Presidential term.

[290] Piazza Poli, March 15th, Tuesday.

This morning, I went with my wife and Miss Hoare to Miss Hosmer's studio (in a street running out of the Via Babuino) to see her statue of Zenobia. We found the bright little woman hopping about in her premises, with a birdlike sort of action. She has a lofty room, with a sky-light window; it was pretty well warmed with a stove; and there was a small orange-tree in a pot, with the oranges growing on it, and two or three flower shrubs in bloom. She herself looked prettily, with her jaunty little velvet cap, on the side of her head, whence came frizzling out her short brown curls; her face full of pleasant life and quick expression; the upper half of her person, as usual, having quite as much the aspect of male juvenility as of young woman-hood. If you look at her as a woman, you see that her face is somewhat worn with time, thought, and struggle; but it would look very handsome and spirited as the face of a young man of twenty. She told us, the other day, by-the-by, that "her wig was growing as grey as a rat."

There were but very few things in the room; two [291] or three plaster-busts, a headless cast of a plaster statue, and a cast of the Minerva Medica, which perhaps she had been studying as a help towards the design of her Zenobia; for, at any rate, I seemed to discern a resemblance or analogy between the two. Zenobia stood in the centre of the room, as yet unfinished in the clay, but a very noble and remarkable statue indeed, full of dignity and beauty. It is wonderful that such a brisk little woman could have achieved a work so quietly impressive. She is supposed to be moving along as a captive in Aurelian's tri-umphal procession; and there is something in her air that con-veys the idea of music, uproar, and a great throng, all about her, while she walks in the midst of it, self-sustained and kept in a sort of sanctity by her native pride. The idea of motion is achieved with great success; you not only perceive that she is walking, but know at just what tranquil pace she steps, amid the music of the triumph. The drapery is very fine and abun-dant; she is decked with ornaments; but the [292] chains of her captivity hang from wrist to wrist, and her deportment (indicating a soul so much above her misfortune, yet not in-sensible to the weight of it) makes those chains a richer decora-tion than all her other jewels. I know not whether there is some magic in the present imperfect finish of the statue, or in the material of clay, as being a better medium of expression than even marble; but certainly I have seldom or never been more impressed by a piece of modern sculpture.

She showed us photographs of her Puck (which I have seen

in the marble,) and likewise of the Will o' the Wisp, both very pretty and fanciful. It indicates much variety of power, that Zenobia should be the sister of these, which would seem the more natural offspring of her quick and vivid character. But Zenobia is a high, heroic ode.

I left my wife and Miss Hoare, on their way to Mr Gibson's studio; and, on my way up the Via Babuino, I met General Pierce, with a Miss Noah on his arm, going to look at some lodgings. We have taken two or three walks together, and stray among the Roman [293] ruins, and old scenes of history, talking of matters in which he is personally concerned, yet which are as historic as anything around us. He is singularly little changed; the more I see him, the more I get him back, just such as he was in our youth. This morning, his face, air, and smile, were so wonderfully like himself of old, that at least thirty years are annihilated.

Zenobia's manacles serve as bracelets; a very ingenious and suggestive idea.

Piazza Poli, March 18th, Friday.

Una and I went to the Sculpture-gallery of the Capitol, yesterday, and saw, among other things, the Venus in her secret cabinet. This was my second view of her; the other time, I greatly admired her; now, she made no very favorable impression. There are twenty Venuses whom I like as well, or better; and there is one view of the lower part of her back which seems to me exceedingly unbeautiful. On the whole, she is a heavy, clumsy, unintellectual, and common-place figure; at all events, not in good looks to-day. Marble beauties seem to suffer the same occasional [294] eclipse that flesh and blood ones do.

We looked at the Faun, at the Dying Gladiator, and what other famous sculptures are to be seen there; but nothing had a glory round it, perhaps because a sirocco was blowing. These sculpture halls of the Capitol have always had a dreary and depressing effect on me, very different from those of the Vatican; I know not why, except that the rooms of the former have a dingy, shabby, and neglected look, and that the statues are dusty, and all the arrangements less magnificent than the Vatican's. The corroded and discolored surfaces of the statues take away from the impression of immortal youth, and turn Apollo himself into an old stone; unless at rare intervals, when he appears transfigured by a light gleaming from within. I used to admire the Dying Gladiator exceedingly; but, in my later views of him, I find myself getting weary and annoyed that he should be such a length of time leaning on his arm, in the very act of death. If he is so terribly hurt, why does he not sink down and die, without further ado? Flitting moments—imminent emergencies—imperceptible intervals between two breaths— ought not to be encrusted [295] with the eternal repose of marble; there should be a moral stand-still in any sculptural subject, since there must needs be a physical one. It is like flinging a piece of marble up into the air, and, by some enchantment, or trick, making it stick there; you feel as if it ought to come down, and are dissatisfied that it does not obey the natural law. In painting, though it is equally motionless as sculpture, there does not appear to be this objection to representing brief snatches of time; perhaps because a story can be told more broadly in picture, and so the momentary circumstance can be buttressed about with other things that give it an epoch.

Piazza Poli, March 23^d, Wednesday.

I am wearing away listlessly these last precious days of my abode in Rome. Una's illnesss is disheartening; and by confining my wife, it takes away the energy and enterprise that were the spring of all our enterprises. I am weary of Rome, without having seen and known it as I ought; and I shall be glad to get away from it, though no doubt there will be many yearnings to return [296] hereafter, and many regrets that I did not make better use of the opportunities within my grasp. Still, I have been in Rome long enough to be imbued with its atmosphere, and this is the essential condition of knowing a place; for such knowledge does not consist in having seen every particular object it contains. At any rate, in the state of mind in which I now stand towards Rome, there is very little advantage to be gained by staying here longer.

And yet I had a pleasant stroll enough, yesterday afternoon, all by myself; from the Corso down past the Church of St. Andrea della Valle, (the site where Caesar was murdered,) and thence to the Farnese Palace, the noble court of which I entered; then to the Piazza Cenci, where I looked at one or two ugly old palaces, and fixed on one of them as the residence of Beatrice's father; then, past the temple of Vesta, and skirting along the Tiber, and beneath the Aventine, till I somewhat unexpectedly came in sight of the gray pyramid of Caius Cestius. I went out of the city-gate, and leaned on the parapet that [297] encloses the pyramid, admiring its high, unbroken slope and peak, where the great blocks of marble still fit almost as closely to one another as when they were first laid; though, indeed, there are crevices just large enough for plants to root themselves, and flaunt and trail over the face of this great tomb; only a little verdure, however, over a vast space of marble, still white in spots, but prevadingly turned gray by two thousand years' action of the atmosphere. Thence I came home by the Coelian, and sat down to smoke a cigar on an ancient flight of steps under one of the arches of the Colosseum, into which the sunshine fell sidelong. It was a delightful afternoon, not precisely like any weather that I have known elsewhere; certainly never in America, where it is always either too cold or hot. It resembles summer more than anything which we New Englanders recognize in our idea of Spring; but there was an indescribable something, sweet, fresh, gentle, that does not belong to summer, and that [298] thrilled and tickled my heart with a feeling partly sensual, partly spiritual.

I believe I go oftener to the Bank than anywhere else, and read Galignani and the American newspapers; thence I stroll listlessly to the Pincian, or to the Medici Gardens. I see a good deal of General Pierce, and we talk over his presidential life, which, I now really think, he has no latent desire nor purpose to renew. Yet he seems to have enjoyed it while it lasted; and certainly he was in his element, as an administrative man, not far-seeing, not possessed of vast stores of political wisdom in advance of his occasions, but endowed with a miraculous intuition of what ought to be done, just at the time for action. His judgment of things about him is wonderful; and his cabinet seems to have recognized it as such, for, though they were men of great ability, he was evidently the master-mind among them. None of them were particularly his personal friends, when he selected them; they all loved him, when they parted; and he [299] showed me a letter, signed by all, in which they expressed their feelings of respect and attachment at the close of his administration. There appears to have been a noble frankness on his part, that kept the atmosphere always clear among them; and in reference to this characteristic, Governor Marcy told him that the years during which he had been connected with Pierce's cabinet had been the happiest of his life. Speaking of Caleb Cushing, he told me that the unreliability, the fickleness, which is usually attributed to him, is an actual characteristic, but that it is intellectual, not moral. He has such comprehensiveness, such mental variety and activity, that, if left to himself, he cannot keep fast hold of one view of things, and so cannot, without external help, be a consistent man. He needs the influence of a more single and stable judgment to keep him from divergency, and, on this condition, he is a most able and inestimable coadjutor. As regards learning and ability, he has no superior.

[300] Pierce spoke the other day, of the idea among some of his friends (and some who had had good opportunities of knowing him) that his life had been planned, from a very early period, with a view to the station which he ultimately reached. He smiled at the notion; said that it was inconsistent with his natural character, and that it implied foresight and dexterity beyond what any mortal is endowed with. I think so too; but, nevertheless, I was long and long ago aware that he cherished a very high ambition, and that, though he might not anticipate the highest things, he cared very little about inferior objects. Then, as to plans, I do not think that he had any definite ones; but there was in him a subtle faculty, a real instinct, that taught him what was good for him (that is to say, promotion of his political success) and made him inevitably do it. He had a magic touch, that arranged matters with a delicate potency which he himself hardly recognized; and he wrought through other minds so that neither he [1st 301] nor they always knew when and how far they were under his influence. Before his nomination for the Presidency, I had a sense that it was coming; and it never seemed to me an accident. He is a most singular character, so frank, so true, so immediate, so subtle, so simple, so complicated.

I passed by the tower in the Via Portoghese, to-day, and observed that the nearest shop appears to be for the sale of cotton or linen cloth. There is a woman's stall, for the sale of chestnut-meats, figs, (of the cheapest kind,) and such wares; and she seemed to have one bouquet on hand. Close by was a shop for bread and paste, under which latter head is comprised all kinds of maccaroni. The upper window of the tower was half open; of course, like all, or most, other Roman windows, it is divided vertically, and each half swings back on hinges. There was a pipe-and-cigar shop nigh.

Last week, a fritter establishment was opened in our Piazza. It was a wooden booth, erected in [2nd 301] the open square, and covered with canvass painted red, which looked as if it had stood much rain and sunshine. In front were three great boughs of laurel, not so much for shade, I think, as ornament. They were two men; and their apparatus for business was a sort of stove, or charcoal furnace, and a frying-pan to place over it; they had an armful or two of dry sticks, some flour, and, I suppose, oil—and this seemed to be all. It was Friday, and Lent besides, and possibly there was some other peculiar propriety in the consumption of fritters, just then. At all events, their fire burned merrily from morning till night, and pretty late into the evening, and they had a fair run of custom; the commodity being simply dough, cut into squares or rhomboids, or what not, and thrown into the boiling oil, which quickly turned them to a light brown colour. I sent Julian to buy some, and tasting one, it resembled an unspeakably bad dough-nut, without any sweetening. In fact, it was sour, for the Romans like their bread, and all their preparations of flour, in a state of acetous [302] fermentation, which serves them instead of salt or other condiment. This fritter-shop had grown up in a night, like Aladdin's palace, and vanished as suddenly; for, after standing through Friday, Saturday, and Sunday, it was gone on Monday morning, and a charcoal-strewn place on the pavement, where the furnace had been, was the only memorial of it. It was queer to observe how immediately it became a lounging-place for idle people, who stood and talked all day with the fritter-friers, just as they might at any old shop in the basement of a palace, or between the half-buried pillars of the temple of Minerva which had been familiar to them and their remote grandfathers.

Piazza Poli, April 14th, Thursday.

Yesterday afternoon, I drove with Mr & Mrs Story & Mr Wilde to see a statue of Venus, which has just been discovered, outside of the Porta Portese, on the other side of the Tiber. A little distance beyond the gate, we came to the entrance of a vineyard, with a wheel-track through the [304] midst of it; and following this, we soon came to a hill side in which an excavation had been made, with the purpose of building a grotto for keeping and storing wine. They had dug down into what seemed to be an ancient bath-room, or some structure of that kind; the excavation being square and cellar-like, and built round with old subterranean walls of brick and stone. Within this hollow space the statue had been found, and it was now standing against one of the walls, covered with a coarse cloth or canvas bag. This being removed, there appeared a headless marble figure, earth-stained, of course, and with a slightly corroded surface, but wonderfully delicate and beautiful; the shape, size, and attitude, apparently, of the Venus de Medici, but, as we all thought, more beautiful than that. It is supposed to be the original from which the Venus de Medici was copied. Both arms were broken off (at the elbow, I think) but the greater part of both, and nearly the whole of one hand, had been found; and [305] these being adjusted to the figure, they took the well known position before the bosom and the middle, as if the poor fragmentary woman retained her instinct of modesty to the last. There were the marks on the bosom and thigh, where the fingers had touched; whereas, in the Venus de Medici, if I remember rightly, the fingers are sculptured quite free of the person. The man who showed the statue now lifted from a corner a round block of marble, which had been lying there among other fragments; and this he placed upon the shattered neck of the Venus; and behold it was her head and face, perfect all but the nose! Even in spite of this mutilation, it seemed immediately to light up and vivify the entire figure; and whatever I may heretofore have written about the countenance of the Venus de Medici, I hereby record my belief that that head has been wrongfully foisted upon the statue; at all events, it is unspeakably inferior to this newly discovered one. This face has a breadth and [306] front which are strangely deficient in the other; the eyes are well opened, most unlike the button-hole lids of the de Medici; the whole head is so much larger as to entirely obviate the criticism that has always been made on the diminutive head of the de Medici statue. If it had but a nose! They ought to sift every handfull of earth that has been thrown out of the excavation; for the nose, and the missing hands and fingers, must needs be there; and if they were found, the effect would be like the reappearance of a divinity upon earth. Mutilated as we saw her, it was strangely interesting to be present at the moment, as it were, when she had just risen from her long burial and was shedding the unquenchable lustre around her, which no eye had seen for twenty centuries. The earth still clung about her; her beautiful lips were full of it, till Mr. Story took a thin chip of wood and cleaned it away from between them.

The proprietor of the vineyard stood by; a man with the most purple face and hugest [307] and reddest nose that I ever beheld in my life. It must have taken innumerable hogsheads of his thin vintages to empurple his face in this manner. He chuckled much over the statue, and, I suppose, counts upon making his fortune by it. He is now awaiting a bid from the Papal government, which, I believe, has the right of preemption whenever any relics of ancient art are discovered. If the statue could but be smuggled out of Italy, it might command almost any price. There is not, I think, any name of a sculptor on the pedestal, as on that of the Venus de Medici. A dolphin, or some other fish, is sculptured on the pillar, or whatever it be, against which she leans. The statue is of Greek marble. She was first found about eight days ago, but has been open for inspection only a day or two; and already the visitors come in throngs, and the beggars gather about the entrance of the vineyard. A wine-shop, too, seems to have been opened on the premises for the accommo[2nd 306]dation of this great concourse; and we saw a row of German artists sitting at a long table, in the open air, each with his tumbler of thin wine and something to eat, before him; for the Germans refresh nature ten times to another person's once.

How the whole world might be peopled with antique beauty, if the Romans would but dig!

Piazza di Poli, April 19th, Tuesday.

Genl Pierce leaves Rome this morning for Venice, by way of Ancona, and taking the steamer thence to Trieste. I had hoped to make the journey along with him; but Una's terrible illness has made it necessary for us to continue here another month, and we are thankful that this seems now to be the extent of our misfortune. Never having had any trouble, before, that pierced into my very vitals, I did not know what comfort there might be in the manly sympathy of a friend; but Pierce has undergone so great a sorrow of his own, and has so large and kindly a heart, and is so tender and so strong, that he really did us good, and I shall always love him [309] the better for the recollection of these dark days. Thank God, the thing we dreaded did not come to pass.

Pierce is wonderfully little changed; indeed, now that he has won and enjoyed (if there were any enjoyment in it) the highest success that public life could give him, he seems more like what he was in his early youth than at any subsequent period. He is evidently happier than I have ever known him since our college days; satisfied with what he has been, and with the position in the country that remains to him, after filling such an office. Amid all his former successes, (early as they came, and great as they were,) I always perceived that something gnawed within him, and kept him forever restless and miserable; nothing that he won was worth the winning, except as a step gained towards the summit. I cannot tell how early he began to look towards the Presidency; but I believe he would have died a miserable man without it. And yet, what infinite [310] chances there seemed to be against his attaining it! When I look at it in one way, it strikes me as absolutely miraculous; in another, it came like an event that I had all along expected. It was due to his wonderful tact, which is of so subtle a character that he himself is but partially sensible of it.

Well; I have found in him, here in Rome, the whole of my early friend, and even better than I used to know him; a heart as true and affectionate; a mind much widened and deepened by his experience of life. We hold just the same relation to one another as of yore; and we have passed all the turning-off places, and may hope to go on together, still the same dear friends, as long as we live. I do not love him one whit the less for having been President, nor for having done me the greatest good in his power; a fact that speaks eloquently in his favour, and perhaps says a little for myself. If he had been merely a benefactor, perhaps I might not have borne it so well; but each did his best for the other, as friend for friend.

VII

[1] Rome

Piazza di Poli, May 15th, 1859, Sunday.

YESTERDAY afternoon, my wife, Julian, & I, went to the Barberini picture-gallery, to take a farewell look at the Beatrice Cenci, which I have twice visited before. I attempted a description of it at my first visit, more than a year ago; but the picture is quite indescribable, inconceivable, and unaccountable in its effect; for if you attempt to analyze it, you can never succeed in getting at the secret of its fascination. Its peculiar expression eludes a straightforward glance, and can only be caught by side glimpses, or when the eye falls upon it casually, as it were, and without thinking to discover anything; as if the picture had a life and consciousness of its own, and were resolved not to betray its secret of grief or guilt, though it wears the full expression of it when it imagines itself unseen. I think no other such magical effect can ever have been wrought by pencil. I looked close into its eyes, with a determination to see all that there was in them, and could see nothing that might not have been in any young girl's eyes; and yet, a moment afterwards, there was the expression (seen aside, and vanishing in a moment) of a being unhumanized by some terrible fate, and gazing at me out of a remote and inaccessible region, where she was frightened to be alone, but where no sympathy could reach her. The mouth is beyond measure touching; the lips apart, looking as innocent as a baby's after it has been crying. The picture never can be copied. Guido himself could not have done it over again. The copyists get all sorts of expression, gay as well as grievous; some copies have a coquettish air, a half-backward glance, thrown allur[2]ingly at the spectator; but nobody ever did catch, or ever will, the vanishing charm of that sorrow. I hated to leave the picture, and yet was glad when I had taken my last glimpse, because it so perplexed and troubled me not to be able to get hold of its secret.

Thence we went to the church of the Capuchins, and saw Guido's Archangel, in the first chapel on the right of the entrance. I have been several times to this church, but never saw the picture before, though I am familiar with the mosaic copy at St. Peters, and had supposed the latter to be an equivalent representation of the original. It is nearly, or quite so, as respects the general effect; but there is a beauty in the archangel's face that immeasurably surpasses the copy. The expression is of heavenly severity, and a degree of pain, trouble, or disgust, at being brought in contact with sin, even for the purpose of quelling and punishing it. There is something finical in the copy, what I do not find in the original; the sandalled feet are here those of an angel; in the mosaic, they are those of a celestial coxcomb, treading daintily, as if he were afraid they would be soiled by the touch of Lùcifer.

After looking sufficiently at the Archangel, we went down under the church, guided by a fleshy monk, and saw the famous cemetery, where the dead monks of many centuries back have been laid to sleep in sacred earth from Jerusalem, and turned out of their graves, successively, as often as a new lodger comes to the sepulchral chambers. The cemetery is entirely above ground, and lighted by a row of iron-grated windows, without glass. A corridor [3] runs along beside these windows, past three or four spacious vaulted recesses, the floors of which consist of the sacred earth, beneath which the dead monks are laid asleep, and which is smoothed decorously over them, quite free from grass or weed, such as would grow even there, if pains were not taken to root them up. The arched walls of the recesses are ornamented in the strangest and horriblest way, with massive pillars and pilasters of thigh-bones and sculls, and finer tracery of the smaller bones of the human body, and knobs and embossed ornaments of the joints of the backbone, and other suitable parts of the skeleton. There is no telling how ugly and grotesque and disagreeable and laughable it is; how much ingenuity has been exerted in this queer way; and what a multitude of dead men, through how many hundred years, must have contributed to build up these great arches of mortality. The summits of the vaults are ornamented with entire skeletons, that look as if they were wrought skilfully in bas-relief; and in the side walls of the recesses there are niches, in which sit or stand skeleton monks, clad in the brown habits of the order, and labelled with their names and the dates of their decease. Their skulls looked out from under their hoods, awfully ugly; some with the mouths wide open, as if they had died in the midst of a howl which must be still screeching through eternity; mostly, they seemed to have skin or dried flesh over their skulls. The cemetery must not be conceived of as merely festooned or lined with human bones; the whole material of the structure seemed to be bones. On [4] some of the separate skulls there were names written; Padre Such-a-one, died on such a day and year; but the vast majority were built indistinguishably into the architectural pile. After all, the spectacle produced very little effect on me, and by no means edifying, so far as it went. It is rather singular, that there was no disagreeable smell, such as might have been expected from the decay of so many holy persons, in whatever odor of sanctity they may have died. The same number of living monks would not have smelt half so unexceptionably.

Piazza di Poli, May 24th, Tuesday.

At Mrs Story's, the other evening, she told a marvellous tale, on the authority of Mrs. Gaskell, to whom the personages were known. A lady, recently married, was observed to be in a melancholy frame of mind, and fell into a bad state of health. She told her husband that she was haunted with the constant vision of a certain face, which affected her with indescribable horror, and was the cause of her melancholy and illness. The physicians prescribed travel, and they went first to Paris, where the lady's spirits grew somewhat better, and the vision haunted her less constantly. They purposed going to Italy; and before their departure from Paris, a letter of introduction was given them by a friend, directed to a person in Rome. On their arrival in Rome, the letter was delivered; the person called; and in his face the lady recognized the precise reality of her vision. By the by, I think the lady saw this face in one of the streets of Rome, before the introduction took place. The end of the story is, that the husband was almost immediately recalled to England by an urgent sum[5]mons; the wife disappeared, that very night, and was recognized driving out of Rome, in a carriage, in tears, and accompanied by the visionary unknown. It is a very foolish story, but told as truth.

In an Etruscan tomb, on the Barberini estate, the form and impression, in dust, of a female figure was discovered. Not even a bone of her was left; but, where her neck had been, there lay a magnificent golden necklace, of the richest workmanship. This necklace just as it was found (except, I suppose, a little furbishing) is now worn by the Princess Barberini, as her richest adornment.

Mrs Story herself had on a bracelet, composed of, I think, seven ancient Etruscan scarabes, in cornelian, every one of which had been taken out of a separate tomb; and on one side of each was engraved the signet of the person to whom it had belonged, and who had carried it to the grave with him. This bracelet would make a good connecting link for a series of Etruscan tales, the more fantastic the better.

Hôtel des Colonies (Marseilles) May 29th, Saturday.

Wednesday was the day fixed for our departure from Rome, and after breakfast, I walked to the Pincian, and saw the garden and the city, and the Borghese Grounds, and St Peter's, in an earlier sunlight than ever before. Methought they never looked so beautiful; nor the sky so bright and blue. I saw Soracte on the horizon, and I looked at everything as if for the last time; nor do I wish ever to see any of these objects again, though no place ever took so strong a hold of my being, as Rome, nor ever seemed so close to me, and so strangely familiar. I seem to know it [6] better than my birth place, and to have known it longer; and though I have been very miserable there, and languid with the effects of the atmosphere, and disgusted with a thousand things in daily life, still I cannot say I hate it—perhaps might fairly own a love for it. But (life being too short for such questionable and troublesome enjoyments) I desire never to set eyes on it again.

We had great pother and difficulty in getting ourselves and our mountain of luggage taken to the station in season; and know not that we should have succeeded in leaving Rome, but for the good offices of Dr Appleton, who took as much as possible of the rough and tumble of the matter upon himself, out of mere kindness of heart. We bade him farewell at the railway station, at 12 °clock, and traversed again that same weary and dreary tract of country, which we passed over, in a winter afternoon and night, on our first arrival in Rome. It is as desolate a country as can well be imagined; but, about midway of our journey, we came to the seashore, and kept very near it during the rest of the way. The sight and fragrance of it were exceedingly refreshing, after so long an interval; and Una revived visibly as we rushed along, while Julian chuckled and contorted himself with ineffable delight.

We reached Civita Vecchia in three or four hours, and were there subjected to various troubles; in the first place, in getting our luggage transported from the railway to the water-side; for the people of Civita Vecchia are absolute harpies of luggage, and cannot be hindered from laying their unclean claws upon it, by any efforts of the owner. I think they are really the most pertinacious rogues in Italy, and the most ex-orbitant; and my [7] remnant of Roman silver (with which I had expected to be burthened in Leghorn and further onward) melted away as if it had been coined of snow. After shouldering our way through this difficulty, a new one sprang up; for on applying at the ticket office of the steamers, we were told that we could not be received, because my passport had not the visé of the French embassy in Rome. This signature had not been obtained, because we meant to go, in the first instance, only to Leghorn; but as I had taken a through ticket to Marseilles, with liberty of stopping at the intermediate places, the steamer-agent declared it impossible to take us without the French visé. Here was great horror and despair on my part; for I do think life would scarcely be worth having at the expense of spending one night at Civita Vecchia, and besides, in these crowded times, there was some doubt whether we could have obtained a shelter. However, the agent (who had at first put on an immitigable face, to frighten us the more, I suppose) finally intimated that the signature of the French consul at Civita Vecchia might be sufficient, if there were time to obtain it; so we sent off a commissionaire forthwith, and the passport soon came back duly viséed. I must do the steamer people, and this commissionaire, the justice to say, that they seemed to be honest men; and not only asked for no undue fees, but returned (it was the commissionaire who did this unheard of act) a slight overcharge which he had made.

All this while, while Miss Shepard and I were bothering about the passport, Mamma and the rest of the family sat in the sun, on the quay, with all kinds of bustle and confusion around them; a very trying experience to [8] Una, after the long seclusion and quiet of her sick-chamber. But she did not seem to suffer from it; and we finally reached the steamer in good condition and spirits. Mamma, Miss Shepard, Una, and Rosebud, had a state-room with four births, and Julian and I were assigned to another room, with six births in it, most of which were occupied; a hot place, too, down almost to the water's edge, and aired and lighted only by a small, round hole. We shortly left the port (which appears to be entirely an artificial harbour, built all round with stone) and I rejoiced from the bottom of my soul to see this hateful place sinking into the horizon. Dinner was served soon after our departure, (but I think only Julian, Una, and I, of our party, profited much by it,) and we had a beautiful sunset and clear calm evening, till bedtime.

I slept wretchedly in my short and narrow birth; more especially as there was an old gentleman who snored as if he were sounding a charge; it was terribly hot, too; and I got up before four °clock, I believe, and came on deck amply in time to watch the distant approach of sunrise. We arrived at Leghorn pretty early (as soon as five or six °clock, I believe) and might have gone ashore and spent the day. Indeed, we had been recommended by Doctor Franco, and had fully purposed, to spend a week or ten days here, in expectation of benefit to Una's health from the sea-air, and because he thought her still too feeble to make the whole voyage to Marseilles at a stretch. But she showed herself so strong, that the latter consideration had little weight with us, and we thought that she would get as much good from our three days' voyage as from ten days by the seashore. Moreover, mamma had a terrible headache, and we [9] all of us still felt the languor of the Roman atmosphere; and, furthermore, we dreaded the hubbub and crazy confusion of landing at an Italian port, where all Tophet is let loose upon the stranger, in the shape of custom-house officers, gens darme, commissionaires, baggage-harpies, and beggars. So we lay in the harbor all day, without stirring from the steamer; the more willingly, as we had a day of wretched experience in Leghorn, on first coming to Italy. It would have been pleasant, however, to have gone to Pisa, fifteen miles off, and seen the leaning tower; but for my part, I have arrived at that point where it is somewhat pleasanter to sit quietly in any spot whatever, than to see whatever grandest or most beautiful thing. At least, this was my mood in the harbour of Leghorn. From the deck of the steamer there were many things visible that might have been interesting to describe; the boats, of peculiar rig, and covered with awnings; the crowded shipping; the disembarkation of horses from the French cavalry, which were lowered from steamers into gondolas or lighters, by slings, and hung motionless, like the sign of the Golden Fleece, during the transit, only kicking a little when their feet happened to graze the vessel's side. One horse plunged overboard, and narrowly escaped drowning. There was likewise a disembarkation of French soldiers, in a train of boats, which rowed shoreward with sound of trumpet. The French are concentrating a considerable number of troops at this point.

Our steamer was detained by order of the French [10] government, to take on board despatches; so that, instead of sailing at dusk, as is customary, we lay in the harbour till seven of the next morning. A number of young Sardinian officers, in green uniform, came on board, and a pale and picturesque looking Italian, and other worthies of less note, English, American, and of all races; among them a Turk, with a little boy in Christian dress; also, a Greek gentleman with his young bride. At the appointed time we weighed anchor for Genoa, and had a beautiful day on the Mediterranean; and, for the first time in my life, I saw the real dark blue of the sea. I do not remember noticing it on my outward voyage to Italy. It is the most beautiful hue that can be imagined, like a liquid sky; and it retains its lustrous blue directly under the side of the ship, where the water of the mid-Atlantic looks greenish. There was no remarkable incident, that I recollect, during this day's trip; and we reached Genoa at about seven in the afternoon, or sooner, all in excellent condition. Genoa looks most picturesquely from the sea, at the foot of a sheltering semicircle of lofty hills; and as we lay in the harbour, we saw, among other interesting objects, the great Dorian palace, with its gardens, and the cathedral, and a heap and sweep of stately edifices, with the mountains looking down upon the city, and crowned with fortresses. The variety of hue on the houses—white, green, pink, and orange—was very remarkable. It would have been well to go ashore here, for an hour or two, and see the streets (we had already seen the palaces, and public buildings, and churches, at our former visit) and buy a few cheap specimens of Genoese [11] goldsmith's work; but, for my part, I preferred the steamer's deck, and therefore opposed a quiet inertness to any suggestions on Mamma's part. So the evening passed pleasantly away; the two lighthouses, at the entrance of the port, kindled up their fires; at nine °clock, the evening gun thundered from the fortress, and was reverberated from the heights; and before our steamer left the port, I went to bed. We sailed, I believe, at about eleven; for I was roused from my first sleep by the vessel's snortings and hissings, as she got under way. I slept rather better than the preceding night; and this brings us, if I mistake not, to Saturday morning.

At Genoa, we took on board some more passengers, none of them of very great interest; an English nobleman, with his lady, being of the number. These were Lord and Lady James; and before the end of our voyage, his lordship talked to me of a translation of Tasso in which he is engaged, and a stanza or two of which he repeated to me. I really liked the lines, and liked, too, the simplicity and frankness with which he spoke of it to me, a stranger, and the way in which he seemed to separate his egotism from the idea, which he evidently had, that he is going to make an excellent translation. I sincerely hope it may be so. He began the translation without any idea of publishing it, or of ever bringing it to a conclusion, but merely as a solace and occupation while in great trouble, during an illness of his wife; but he has gradually come to find it the most absorbing occupation he ever undertook; and as Mr. Gladstone, and other high authorities, give him warm encouragement, he now means to translate the [12] poem entire, and to publish it with beautiful illustrations; and, two years hence, the world may expect to see it. I do not quite see how such a man as this (a man of frank, warm, simple, kindly nature, but surely not of a poetical temperament, or very refined, or highly cultivated) should make a good version of Tasso's poem; but perhaps the dead poet's soul may take possession of this healthy organisation, and wholly turn him to its own purposes.

The latter part of our voyage, to-day, lay close along the coast of France, which was hilly and picturesque, and, as we approached Marseilles was very bold and striking. We steered among rocky islands, rising abruptly out of the sea, mere naked crags, without a trace of verdure upon them, and with the surf breaking at their feet. I have not anywhere seen such specimens of what hills would look like, without the soil that is to them what flesh is to a skeleton. Their shapes were often wonderfully fine; and the great headlands thrust themselves out, and took such hues of light and shade that it seemed like sailing through a picture. In the course of the afternoon, a squall came up and blackened the sky all over, in a twinkling; our vessel pitched and tossed; and a brig, a little way from us, had her sails blown about in wild fashion. The blue of the sea grew as black as night; and soon the rain began to spatter down upon us, and continued to sprinkle and drizzle, a considerable time after the wind had subsided. It was quite calm and pleasant when we entered the harbour of Marseilles, which lies at the foot of very fine hills, and is set among great cliffs of stone. I [13] did not attend much to this, however, being much in dread of the botheration of landing and passing through the Custom-House, with our twelve or fourteen trunks, and numberless carpet-bags. The trouble vanished into thin air, nevertheless, as we approached it; for not a single trunk or bag was opened, and, moreover, our luggage and ourselves were not only landed, but the greater part of it conveyed to the railway, without any expense to ourselves. Long live Louis Napoleon, say I. We established Mamma and Una at the Hotel des Colonies, (Rosebud too, by the way,) and Miss Shepard, Julian, and I, drove hither and thither about Marseilles, making arrangements about our journey to Avignon, whither we meant to proceed to-day. We might have saved ourselves a good deal of this trouble; but travellers, like other people, are continually getting their experience just a little too late. It was after nine, before we got back to the hotel, and took our tea in peace.

Hôtel d'Europe (Avignon) June 1st, Wednesday.

I remember nothing very special to put down about Marseilles; though it was really like passing from death into life, to find ourselves in busy, cheerful, effervescing France, after living so long between asleep and awake in sluggish Italy.

Marseilles is a very interesting and entertaining town, with its bold, surrounding heights, its wide streets, (so they seemed to us, after the Roman alleys,) its places, shady with trees, its diversified population of sailors, citizens, Orientals, and what not;—but I have no spirit for description any longer; being tired of seeing things, and still more of telling myself about them. Only a young traveller can have patience to [14] write his travels. The newest things, now-a-days, have a sort of familiarity in my eyes; whereas, in that lost sense of novelty lies the charm and power of description.

On Monday, though it began with heavy rain, we set early about our preparations for departure. I went to Rabaud, freres, & Co, Bankers, and drew £30 and thence to the American Consulate, where I found, not the Consul himself (a new appointment) but the Vice Consul, a young man whom I remember seeing on my former visit to Marseilles. He viseéd my passport for Switzerland and all Europe, and very kindly undertook to send home three trunks, which I wished to transport by sea from this port. The rest of the forenoon was spent in seeing about our luggage, and at three, or before, we took our departure from the Hotel des Colonies. It is a very comfortable Hotel, though expensive, and we dined at the Restaurant which is connected with it. This latter establishment occupies the enclosed courtyard, and the arcades connected therewith; and it was a good amusement to look down from the surrounding gallery, communicating with our apartments, and see the fashion and manner of French eating, all the time going forward. In sunny weather, a great awning is spread over the whole court, across from the upper stories of the house; there is a grass plat in the middle, and a very spacious and airy dining-saloon is thus formed.

At four °clock, we started on the railway; Mamma and Una in the first class; the rest of us in the second. Our carriage was comfortable; and we found in it, besides two other French women, two nuns. They seemed very devout, [15] and sedulously read their little books of devotion, repeated prayers under their breath, kissed the crucifixes which hung at their girdles, and told a string of beads, which they passed from one to another. So much were they occupied with these duties, that they scarcely looked at the scenery along the road, though probably it is very rare for them to see anything outside of their convent-walls. They never failed to mutter a prayer and kiss the crucifix, whenever we plunged into a tunnel. If they glanced at their fellow-passengers, it was shyly and askance, with their lips in motion all the while, like children afraid to let their eyes wander from their lesson-books. One of them, however, took occasion to pull down Rosebud's dress, which, in her frisky movements about the carriage, had got a little too high for the nun's sense of decorum. Neither of them was at all pretty, nor was the black stuff dress and white muslin cap in the least becoming; neither were their features of an intelligent or high-bred stamp. Their manners, however, or such little glimpses as I could get of them, were unexceptionable; and when I drew a curtain to protect one of them from the sun, she made me a very courteous gesture of thanks.

We had some very good views both of sea and hills, along the road; and a part of our way, I think, lay along the banks of the Rhone; but it is not worth while to try to remember the flitting panorama which one sees on a railway. By the by, at the station in Marseilles, just before we started, I bought the two volumes of the *Livre des Merveilles*, by a certain author of my acquaintance, translated into French, and printed and illustrated in very pretty style. Miss Shepard also bought [16] them, and, in answer to her inquiry for other works by the same author, the book-woman observed that she did not think Monsieur Nataniel had published anything else. The Christian name seems to be the most important one in France, and especially in Italy.

We were four hours, and more, on our journey, and arrived at Avignon in the dusk of the evening. An omnibus took us to the Hôtel d'Europe, where, on driving into the courtyard, we were received by an elderly lady in black, of brisk and kindly manners. She assigned us a suite of rooms, extending along a gallery that looks down into the court; a saloon and, I believe, four bedrooms; which number we have since diminished, to save expense, and because our hostess cannot conveniently let us have so many, in view of some races which will bring her a great crowd of guests in a day or two. We had an abundant supper of brisée beef and lamb-cutlets, and went to bed very weary; for the lassitude of Rome still clings to us, and I, at least, feel no spring of life or activity, whether at morn or eve. Neither do I sleep well; and these French beds are stuffed with wool, or some material of that kind, and have down-pillows, which are harder than a block of stone for sleeping-purposes.

In the morning, we found ourselves very pleasantly situated as regards lodgings. The gallery, above spoken of, looks down as usual into an enclosed court, three sides of which are formed by the stone-house and its two wings, and the third by a high wall, with a gateway of iron bars between two lofty stone pillars, which, for their capitals, have great stone-vases with grass growing in them, and hanging over the brim. There is a large plane-tree in one corner of the court; and creeping-plants [17] clamber up trellices, and there are pots of flowers, and bird-cages, all of which give a very fresh and cheerful aspect to the enclosure. The court-yard is paved with small round stones; the omnibus, belonging to the Hôtel, and all the carriages of guests, drive into it; and the wide arch of the stable door opens under the central part of the house. Nevertheless, the scene is not in all respects that of a stable-yard; for gentlemen and ladies come from the salle-a-manger, and other rooms of the house, and stand talking in the yard, or occupy chairs and seats there; children play about; the hostess or her daughter often appears, and talks with her guests or servants; dogs lounge about; and, in short, the courtyard might well enough be taken for the one scene of a classic-play. The Hotel seems to be a first-rate one, though such would not be indicated, either in England or America, by thus mixing up the stable with the lodging part of the house.

I have taken two or three rambles about the town, and have climbed a high rock which dominates over it, and has a most extensive view from the broad table-land of its summit; but I hardly think I shall undertake the description of these things. The old church of Avignon—as old as the times of its Popes, and older—stands close beside this mighty and massive crag. We went into it, and found it a dark old place, with broad interior arches, and a singularly shaped dome; a venerable Gothic or Grecian (for it partook of both) porch, with ancient frescoes in its arched spaces; some dusky pictures within; an ancient chair of stone, formerly occupied by the popes; and much else that would have been ex[18]ceedingly interesting before I went to Rome. But Rome takes the charm out of all inferior antiquity, as well as the life out of human beings.

This forenoon, Julian and I have crossed the Rhone, by a bridge, just the other side of one of the city-gates, which is near our hotel. We walked along the river side, and saw the ruins of an ancient bridge, which ends abruptly in the midst of the stream; two or three arches still making tremendous strides across, while the others have long ago been crumbled away by the rush of this rapid river. This bridge was originally founded, according to the legend, by St. Benedict, who received a divine order to undertake the work, while yet a shepherd boy with only three sous in his pocket; and he proved the authenticity of his mission by taking an immense stone on his shoulder, and laying it for the foundation. There is still an ancient chapel midway on the bridge, and, I believe, St

Benedict lies buried there, in the midst of his dilapidated work. The bridge now used crosses considerably lower down the stream; it is a wooden suspension-bridge, broader than the ancient one, and doubtless more than supplies its place; else, unquestionably, St Benedict would think it necessary to repair his own. The view from the river-side of this ruined bridge, grass-grown and weedy, and leading to such a precipitous plunge into the swift river, is very picturesque, in connection with the gray town, and above it the great, massive bulk of the cliff, the towers of the church, and of a vast old edifice, shapeless, ugly, and venerable, which the popes built and occupied as their palace, many centuries ago.

[19] We dined this day at the Table d'Hôte of the hotel, at five °clock, with very little company; most of the guests, I presume, dining at seven, when there is another Table d'Hôte. Our own party of six made nearly half of the company at table; and it was a very grave dinner indeed, nobody speaking a word, save in an undertone, to his nearest neighbor. The courses are not nearly so numerous as at an Italian table; a soup, some beef, fish—but I find I cannot recollect them, nor is it of much importance. Some claret, which appeared very tolerable to me, after my experience of the sour red wines of Italy, was placed on the table in liberal quantity. All the dishes were handed round separately, and it was rather essential to partake of each in order to make a hearty meal. The whole thing is far better arranged than at the Table d'Hôte of an American Hotel; and though the viands were not here half so good or so numerous, it was much easier to get a comfortable dinner.

After dinner, Una, Mamma, Julian, and I, set out on a walk, in the course of which we called at a book-seller's shop to show Una a most enormous cat, which my wife and I had already seen. It is of the Angora breed, of a mottled yellow colour; and is really a wonder; as big and broad as a tolerably sized

dog, very soft and silken, and apparently of the gentlest disposition. I never imagined the like, nor felt anything so deeply
soft as this great beast; its master seems very proud and fond
of it; and great a favorite as the cat is, she does not take airs
upon herself, but is gently shy and timid in her demonstrations.

[20] We ascended the great Rocher above the palace of the
Popes, and, on our way, looked into the old church, which was
so dim, in the decline of day, that we could not see within
the dusky arches, through which the chapels communicated
with the nave. Thence we pursued our way up the further
ascent; and standing on the edge of the precipice (protected by
a parapet of stone, and, in other places, by an iron railing)
we could look down upon the road that winds its dusty track
far below, and at the river Rhone which eddies close beside it.
This is indeed a massive and lofty cliff, and it tumbles down
so precipitately, that I could readily have flung myself from
the brink, and alighted on my head in the middle of the road.
The Rhone passes so near its base, that I threw stones a good
way into its current. We talked with a man of Avignon, who
leaned over the parapet, near us; and he was very kind in
explaining the points of view, and told us that the river, which
winds and doubles upon itself so as to look like at least two
rivers, is really the Rhone alone. The Durance joins with this
river, within a few miles below Avignon, but is here invisible.

Hotel d'Europe, June 2ᵈ, Thursday.

This morning, I went with Mamma, Una, and Julian, to the
old church of the popes, which I have two or three times mentioned already; and, this time, we allowed the Custode, or
Sacristan, or whatever the man be, to show us the curiosities
of the church. He led us into a chapel apart, and showed us the
old Gothic tomb of Pope John XXII, where the recumbent

statue of the Pope lies beneath one of those beautiful and venerable canopies of stone, which look at [21] once so light and so solemn. I know not how many hundred years old it is; but everything of Gothic origin has a faculty of conveying the idea of age; whereas, classic forms seem to have nothing to do with time, and so lose the kind of impressiveness that arises from suggestions of decay and the Past. In the sacristy, the guide opened a cupboard that contained the jewels and sacred treasures of the church, and showed a most exquisite figure of Christ, in ivory, represented as on a cross of ebony; and it was done with wonderful truth and force of expression, and with great beauty likewise. I do not see what a full length marble statue could have had, that was lacking in this little ivory figure of hardly more than a foot high. It is about two centuries old, according to our guide, and by an unknown artist. There is another famous ivory statuette in Avignon, which seems to be more celebrated than this, but can hardly be superior. I shall gladly look at it if it comes in my way. Next to this, the prettiest thing the man showed us was a circle of emeralds, in one of the holy gew-gaws, and a little bit of a Pope's skull; also, a great old crosier, that looked as if made chiefly of silver, and partly gilt, but I saw where the plating of silver was worn away, and betrayed the copper of its actual substance. There were two or three pictures in the sacristy, by ancient and modern French artists, very unlike the productions of the Italian masters, but not without a beauty of their own.

Leaving the sacristy, we returned into the church, where Una and Julian began to draw the Pope's old stone [22] chair, which stands against the wall, on the left of the high altar. There is a beast, or perhaps more than one, grotesquely sculptured on this chair; the seat is high and square; the back low and pointed; and it offers no enticing promise to a weary man. The interior of the church is massively picturesque, with its vaulted roof, and a stone gallery, heavily ornamented, running along each side of the nave. Each arch of the nave gives admittance to a chapel, in all of which there are pictures, and sculptures in most of them. One of these chapels was of the time of Charlemagne, and has a vaulted roof of admirable architecture, covered with frescoes of modern date and little merit. In an adjacent chapel, against the wall, is the stone monument of Pope Benedict, whose statue reposes on it, like many which I have seen in the Cathedral of York, and other old English churches. In another part of the church, we saw a monument, consisting of a plain slab supported on pillars; it is said to be of a Roman or very early Christian epoch. In another chapel, was a figure of Christ in wax, I believe, and clothed in real drapery; a very ugly object. Also, a figure reposing under a slab; who startles the spectator with the idea that it is really a dead person enveloped in a shroud. There are windows of painted glass (none of them ancient, I think) in some of the chapels; and the gloom of the dimly lighted church, especially beneath the broad, low arches, is very impressive.

While we were there, some women assembled at one of the altars, and went through their acts of devotion without the help of a priest; one and another of them alternately repeating prayers, to which the rest responded. The murmur of their voices took a musical tone, which was reverberated [23] by the vaulted walls.

Una and I now came out of the church; and under the porch we found an old woman selling rosaries, little religious books, and other holy things. We bought two little medals of the Immaculate Virgin, one purporting to be of silver, the other of gold; but as both together cost only three or four sous, the genuineness of the metal may well be doubted. We sat down on the steps of a crucifix, which is placed in front of the church, and Una, and afterwards Julian, began to draw the porch, of which I hardly know whether to call the architecture classic or Gothic; at all events, it has a venerable aspect, and has frescoes within its arch, said to be by Simon Memmi. After awhile, mamma (who had been drawing the pope's chair and a twisted column or two) came out of the church; and it was decided that Una, who began to feel tired, should return to the Hotel, with Julian for a protector.

Mamma, who is unweariable in sight-seeing, took me with her to visit the interior of the pope's palace, which, as I believe I have said, is right contiguous to the church, and just below it on the hill-side. The palace is now occupied as barracks, by some regiments of soldiers, a number of whom were lounging before the entrance; but we passed the centinel without being challenged, and addressed ourselves to the Concierge, who readily assented to our request to be shown through the edifice. A French gentleman and lady likewise came, with similar purpose, and went the rounds along with us. The palace is such a confused heap and conglomeration of buildings that it is impossible to make head or tail of it, or to get within any sort of a regular description. I never saw such a huge, shapeless mass of ar[24]chitecture; and if it ever had any pretense of a plan, it has lost it in the modern alterations. For instance, an immense and lofty chapel, or rather church, has had, I believe, two floors, one above the other, laid at different stages of its height; and the upper one of these floors, which extends just where the arches of the vaulted roof begin to spring from the pillars, is ranged round with the beds of one of the regiments of soldiers. They are small iron bedsteads, each with its narrow mattress, and covered with a dark blanquet; and on some of them lay or lounged a soldier; other soldiers were cleaning their accoutrements; elsewhere, we saw parties of them playing cards. So it was wherever we went, among these great, dingy, gloomy halls and chambers, which no doubt were once stately and magnificent, with pictures, with tapestry, with all sorts of adornment that the middle ages knew how to use. The windows threw a sombre light through embrasures at least ten feet thick. There were staircases of magnificent breadth. We were shown into two small chapels, in different parts of the building; both containing the remains of old frescoes, woefully defaced. In one of them there was a light, spiral staircase of iron, built in the centre of the room, as a means of contemplating the frescoes, which were said to be the work of our old friend Giotto. They looked dreary and grotesque enough to be his. Finally, we climbed a long, long, narrow staircase, built in the thickness of the wall, and thus gained access to the top of one of the towers, whence we saw perhaps the noblest landscape my eyes ever beheld; mountains, plains, and the Rhone, broad and bright, winding hither and thither, as if it had lost its way.

[25] Beneath our feet was the grey, ugly old palace, and its many court-yards, just as void of system and as inconceivable as when we were burrowing through its bewildering passages. No end of historical romances might be made out of this castle of the Popes; and there ought to be a ghost in every room, and scores of them in some of the rooms; for there have been murders here in the gross and in detail, as well hundreds of years ago, as no longer back than the French Revolution, when there was a great massacre in one of the courts. Traces of this bloody business were visible in actual stains on the wall, only a few years ago.

Returning to the Concierge's room (being a little stiff with age, he had sent an attendant round with us, instead of accompanying us in person) he showed us a picture of Rienzi, the last of the Roman Tribunes, who was once a prisoner here. On a table, beneath the picture, stood a little vase of earthenware, containing some silver coin. We took it as a hint (in the customary style of French elegance) that a fee should be deposited here, instead of being put into the hand of the

Concierge; so the French gentleman deposited half a franc, and I, in my magnificence, twice as much.

Hotel d'Europe (Avignon) June 6th Monday.

We are still here; and our life has offered few or no journalizable incidents; nor, to say the truth, am I much inclined to record them, were they ever so interesting. I have been daily to the Rocher des Doms, and have been familiar with the old church on its declivity. I think I might become attached to it by seeing it often; a sombre old interior, with its heavy arches, [26] and its roof vaulted like the top of a trunk; its stone gallery, with ponderous adornments, running round three sides. I observe that it is a daily custom of the old women to say their prayers in concert, sometimes making a pilgrimage, as it were, from chapel to chapel. The voice of one of them is heard running through the series of petitions, and at intervals, the voices of the others join and swell into a chorus; so that it is like a river, connecting a series of lakes; or, not to use so gigantic a simile, the one voice is like a thread, on which the beads of a rosary are strung. One day, two priests came and sat down beside these prayerful women, and, I think, joined in their petitions. I am inclined to hope that there is something genuine in the devotion of these old women.

The view from the top of the Rocher des Doms (*Doms*, a contraction of Dominés) grows upon me, and is truly magnificent; a vast mountain girdled plain, illuminated by the far windings and reaches of the Rhone. The river is here almost as turbid as the Tiber itself; but, I remember, in the upper part of its course, the waters are beautifully transparent. I have never seen a more powerful rush than is indicated by the swirls and eddies of its broad surface.

Yesterday was a race-day at Avignon; and apparently almost the whole population, and a great many strangers, streamed out of the city-gate, nearest our hotel, on their way to the race-course. There were many noticeable figures that might come well into a French picture or description; but only one remains in my memory—a young man with a wooden leg, setting off for the course (a walk of several miles, I believe) with prodigious courage and alacrity, flourishing his wooden leg with an air and grace that [27] seemed positively to render it flexible. The crowd returned, towards sunset; and, almost all night long, the streets and the whole air of the old town were full of song and merriment. There was a ball in a temporary structure, covered with an awning, in the place d'Horloge, and they say there is to be another race to-day, and another ball tonight. In the same public place (the principal one of the city) a show-man has erected his tent, and spread forth his great painted canvasses announcing an anaconda and a Sea Tiger to be seen. Julian paid four sous for admittance, and found that the sea-tiger was nothing but a large seal, and that the anaconda was altogether a myth.

I have rambled a good deal about the town; its streets are crooked, and perplexing, and paved with round pebbles, for the most part, which afford more uncomfortable pedestrianism than the pavement of Rome itself. It is an ancient-looking place, with some large old mansions, but few that are individually impressive; though here and there one sees an antique entrance, a corner tower, or other bit of antiquity, that throws a venerable kind of effect over the gray common-place of past centuries. The town is not over clean, and often there is a kennel of unhappy fragrance. There appear to have been many more churches and devotional establishments, under the ancient dominion of the Popes, than have been kept intact in subsequent ages; the tower and facade of a church, for instance, form the front of a carpenter's shop, or some such plebeian place. The church where Laura lay has quite disappeared, and her tomb along with it. The town reminds me of Chester, [28] though it does not in the least resemble it, and is not nearly so picturesque.

Like Chester, it is entirely surrounded by a wall; and that of Avignon (though it has no delightful promenade on its top, as the wall of Chester has) is the more perfectly preserved in its mediæval form, and the more picturesque of the two. Julian and I have once or twice walked nearly round it, commencing from the gate of Ouelle, which is very near our hotel. From this point, it stretches for a considerable distance along by the river; and here there is a broad promenade, with trees, and blocks of stone for seats; on one side the arrowy Rhone, generally carrying a cooling breeze along with it; on the other, the gray wall with its battlements and machicolations, impending over what was once the moat, but which is now full of careless, untrained shrubbery. At intervals there are round towers, swelling out from the wall, and rising a little above it. After about a half a mile along the river-side, or less, the wall turns at nearly right angles; but still there is a broad road, a shaded walk, a Boulevard; and, at short distances, are cafés, with their little round tables before the door, or small shady nooks of shrubbery; so numerous are these retreats and pleasaunces, that I do not see how the little old town can support them all, especially as there are a great many cafes within the walls. I do not remember seeing any soldiers on guard at the numerous city-gates; but there is an office in the side of each gate for levying the octroi, and old women, if I mistake not, are sometimes on guard there.

This morning, after breakfast, Julian and I crossed [29] the suspension-bridge, close by the gate nearest our hotel, and walked to the ancient town of Villeneuve, on the other side of the Rhone. The first bridge crosses to an island, from the farther side of which another very long bridge, with a timber foundation, accomplishes the passage of the other branch of the Rhone. There was a good breeze on the river, but after crossing it, we found the rest of the walk awfully hot. This town of Villeneuve is of very ancient origin, and owes its origin, it is said, to the famous sanctity of a female saint, which gathered round her abode and burial-place a great many habitations of people who reverenced her. She was the daughter of a King of Saragossa and I presume she chose this site because it was so rocky and desolate. Afterwards it had a long mediæval history; and in the time of the Avignon popes, the Cardinals, regretful of their abandoned Roman villas, built pleasure-houses here; so that the town was called Villa nuova. After they had done their best, it must have seemed to these poor Cardinals but a rude and sad exchange for the Borghese, the Albini, the Panfili Doria, and those other perfectest results of man's luxurious art, if indeed these last existed so early. And, probably, the tradition of the old Roman villas had really been kept alive, and extant examples of them, all the way downward from the times of the empire. But this Villeneuve is the stoniest, roughest old town that can be imagined; there are a few large, old houses, to be sure, but built on a line with shabby village dwellings, and barns, and so presenting little but samples of magnified shabbiness. Perhaps [30] I might have found traces of old magnificence, if I had sought for them; but not having the history of the town in my mind, I passed through its scrambling streets (paved even more vilely than those of Avignon, and strewn with loose stones besides) without imagining that princes of the church had once made their abodes here. The inhabitants appear to be peasants, or chiefly such; though, for aught I know, some of the old French noblesse may burrow in these palaces that look so much like Hovels.

A large church, with a massive tower, stands near the centre of the town; and, of course, I did not fail to enter its arched door—a pointed arch, with many frames and mouldings, one within another. An old woman was at her devotions within, and several others came in and knelt, during my stay there. It was quite an interesting interior; a long nave, with six pointed arches, on each side, beneath which were as many chapels. The walls were rich with pictures, not only in the chapels, but up and down the walls of the nave, above the arches; there were gilded Virgins, too, and much other quaint trumpery that produced an effect that I rather liked than otherwise. At the end of the church farthest from the high altar there were four columns of exceedingly rich marble, and a good deal more of such precious material was wrought into the chapels and altars. There was an old stone seat, too, of some former pope or prelate. The church was dim enough to cause the lamps in the chapels to become points of vivid light, and, looking from end to end, it was a long, [31] venerable, tarnished, old-world vista, as little tampered with by modern taste as any I ever saw.

Leaving the church, we kept on our way through the village, and emerging from a gate, went clambering and sweltering towards the Castle of St. André, which stands perhaps a quarter of a mile beyond it. This castle was built by Philip le Bel, as a restraint to the people of Avignon in extending their power on this side of the Rhone. We happened not to take the most direct way, and so approached the castle on the farther side, and had to go nearly round the hill on which it stands, before striking into the path which leads to its gate. It crowns a very bold and difficult hill, right above the Rhone, opposite to Avignon (which is so far off that objects are not minutely distinguishable) and looking down upon the long, straggling town of Villeneuve. It must have been a place of mighty strength in its day. Its ramparts seem still almost entire, as looked upon from without; and when, at length, we climbed the rough, rocky pathway to the entrance, we found the two vast round towers, with their battlemented summits, and arched gateway between them, just as perfect as they could have been, five hundred years ago. Some external defences, however, are now in a state of ruin; and there are only the remains of a tower that once arose between the two round towers, and was apparently much more elevated than they. A little in front of the gate stood a monumental cross of stone; and in the arch, between the two round towers, were two little boys at a play, and an old woman soon showed herself, but took no notice of [32] us. Casting our eyes within the gateway, we saw what looked a rough village street, betwixt old houses, built ponderously of stone, but having far more the aspect of huts than of castle halls. They were evidently the dwellings of peasantry and people engaged in rustic labor; and, no doubt, they have burrowed into the primitive structures of the castle, and, as they found convenient, have taken their crumbling materials to build barns and farm houses. There was space and accommodation for a very considerable population; but the men were probably at work in the fields, and the only persons visible were the children aforesaid, and one or two old women, bearing bundles of twigs on their backs. They showed no curiosity respecting us; and though the space, (and it is a wide one) included within the castle-rampart, seems almost full of habitations, ruinous or otherwise, I never found such a solitude in any ruin before. It contrasts very favorably, in this particular, with English castles, where, though you do not find rustic villages within the old warlike enclosure, there is always a padlocked gate, always a guide, and generally half a dozen idle tourists. But here was only antiquity, with only the natural growth of fungous human life upon it.

We went to the farther side of the castle-yard, and sat down (for lack of other shade) among some inhospitable nettles that grew close to the wall. Close by us was a great gap in the ramparts; it may have been a breach which was once stormed through; and it now afforded us an airy and sunny glimpse of distant hills. I smoked a cigar, while Julian sketched part of the broken wall, [33] which, by the by, did not seem to me nearly so thick as the walls of English castles. Then we returned through the gate, and I stopt awhile, rather impatiently, under the hot sun, while Julian drew the outline of the two round towers. This done, we resumed our way homeward, stopping, by the way, to drink from a very deep well, which, if I mistake not, was close by the square tower of Philip le Bel. Thence we went melting through the sunshine (which beat upward as pitilessly from the white road, as it blazed downward from the sky;) and before crossing the hithermost bridge, we drank a bottle of Lyons beer, at a little wayside ale-house, as the English would call it.

Hotel d'Angleterre (Geneva) June 11th, Saturday.

We left Avignon on Tuesday, about noon, and took the rail for Valence, where we arrived between four and five, and put up at the Hotel de la Poste; an ancient house, with dirty floors, and dirt generally, but otherwise comfortable enough. I remember nothing particularly of our fare, except that we drank some sparkling St Peray at dinner; it is a wine of champagny aspect, with an abundant and quick froth, and has an agreeable peculiarity of taste, at first trial. Nevertheless, we soon became cloyed with it. Valence is a stately old town, full of tall houses, and irregular streets. We found a cathedral there, not very large, but with a high and venerable interior, a nave supported by tall pillars, from the height of which spring arches. This loftiness is a characteristic of French churches, as distinguished from those of Italy. We went into one or two other churches, of which I do not find anything to say. We likewise saw, close by the [34] Cathedral, a large monument with four arched entrances, meeting beneath a vaulted roof; but, on inquiry from an old priest, and other persons, we could get no account of it, except that it was a tomb, and of unknown antiquity. The architecture seemed classic, and yet it had some Gothic peculiarities, and, at all events, it was a reverend and beautiful object. Had I written up my journal while the town was fresh in my remembrance, I might have found much to describe; but a succession of other objects have obliterated most of the impressions I received here; and, moreover, the weariness of an old traveller weighs so heavily upon me that I can no longer journalize with the same patience as formerly. Our railway ride to Valence, by the way, was intolerably hot. I have felt nothing like it since leaving America; and that is so long ago that the terrible discomfort was just as good as new. According to the system which we now regularly adopt, I took first class tickets for my wife and Una, and second class for the rest of the party; and the carriages of the second class are so much better than in England, that, except when crowded, I would quite as lief ride there as in the more aristocratic class. Very few people—almost none, indeed—seem to take first class tickets.

We left Valence at about 4, and came that afternoon to Lyons, still along the Rhone. Either the waters of this river assume a transparency in winter, which they lose in summer, or I was mistaken in thinking them transparent, on our former journey. They are now everywhere turbid; but the hue does not suggest the idea of [35] a running mud-puddle, as the water of the Tiber does. No streams, however, are so beautiful in the quality of their waters as the clear, brown rivers of New England. The scenery along this part of the Rhone (as we have found all the way from Marseilles) is very fine and impressive; old villages, rocky cliffs, castellated steeps, quaint chateaus, and a thousand other objects, that ought greatly to interest me, if I were not so very weary of being greatly interested. Rest, rest, rest! There is nothing else so desirable;

and I sometimes fancy, but only half in earnest, how pleasant it would be to be six feet under ground, and let the grass grow over me.

We arrived at Lyons at about five °clock, and put up at the Hotel de l'Univers, to which we had been recommended by our good hostess at Avignon. The day had become showery; but Julian and I strolled about a little, before nightfall, and saw the general characteristics of the place. Lyons is a city of very stately aspect, hardly, if at all, inferior to Paris; for it has regular streets of lofty houses, and immense squares, planted with trees and adorned with statues and fountains; new edifices, of great splendour, are in process of erection; and on the opposite side of the Rhone, where the site rises steep and high, there are structures of elder date, that have an exceedingly picturesque effect, looking down upon the newer town.

The next morning, I went out with Julian in quest of my bankers and of the American consul; and as I had forgotten the directions of the waiter of the Hotel, I of course [36] went astray, and saw a good deal more of Lyons than I intended. In my wanderings, I crossed the Rhone, and found myself in a portion of the city evidently much elder than that with which I had previously made acquaintance; narrow, crooked, irregular, and rudely paved streets, full of dingy business and bustle—the city, in short, as it existed a century ago, and how much earlier I know not. Right above rises that lofty elevation of ground which I before noticed; and the glimpses of its stately old buildings, through the openings of the street, were very picturesque. Unless it be Edinburgh, I have not seen any other city that has such striking features. Altogether unawares, immediately after crossing the bridge, we came upon the Cathedral; and the grand, time blackened Gothic front, with its deeply arched entrances, seemed to me as good as anything I ever saw; unspeakably more impressive than all the ruins of Rome. I could but merely glimpse at its interior; so that its noble height and venerable space, filled with dim, consecrated light of pictured windows, recur to me as a vision. But I hardly think there can be a finer old church in the world; and it did me good to enjoy the awfulness and sanctity of Gothic architecture again, after so long shivering in classic porticos. We staid only a moment; for I meant to bring my wife thither, knowing that she would feel and enjoy it far more than I.

We now re-crossed the river, and after a good deal more search, found Quisard and Co, of whom I drew fifty pounds, in the shape of, I believe, fifty seven Napoleons. This operation consumed a good deal of time; after which they sent their commissionaire to show me the way to the consul's. [37] Here it was my misfortune to find, instead of the consul, two American ladies, with whom I staid talking for above an hour, I should think, to our mutual weariness, no doubt. By and by, however, the consul came in, a Mr. White, an elderly, frank, agreeable gentleman, who received me with great courtesy when he knew my name. After all, I needed no assistance from him, my passport having been viseéd for Switzerland by the vice-consul at Marseilles; and Mr. White informed me that I needed no visée from the Swiss consul, as this little republic makes everybody welcome. He advised me, however, to get the signature of the prefet of Lyons, which would facilitate my re-entrance into France; but as time was precious, I concluded to dispense with it. Returning to our hotel, I went with Miss Shepard to the railway, where as much as an hour and a half were consumed in arranging to send four trunks to await us at Macon instead of taking them with us to Geneva. The same business would not have required five minutes, on an American railway. The French methods and arrangements in matters of business seem to be excellent, so far as effecting the proposed object is concerned,

(though I have known them fail, to my cost) but there is such
an inexorable succession of steel-wrought forms, that life is
not long enough for so much accuracy. The stranger, too,
goes blindfold through all these processes, not knowing what
is to turn up next, till, when quite in despair, he suddenly
finds his business mysteriously accomplished.

We now went back to the Hotel, and found that Mamma
and Una had gone out, under Julian's guidance, to see the
cathedral. After some time she returned in a carriage, having
met with Mrs. Sedgwick, and accompanied her to see various
interesting things in the city. We left Lyons at about four
°clock, taking the [38] railway for Geneva. The scenery was
very striking throughout the journey, but I have come to see
the nonsense of attempting to describe fine scenery. There is
no such possibility; if scenery could be adequately reproduced
in words, there would have been no need of God's making it
in reality. It is the one possible expression of the meaning
which the Creator intends to convey. So I let the hills, deep
valleys, high impending cliffs, and whatever else I saw along
the road, pass from me without an ink blot. We reached
Geneva at nearly ten °clock. It was raining fast, and we
bundled ourselves into an omnibus and came to the Hotel
d'Angleterre, where we had some tea and bread and butter,
and got to bed not long before midnight.

I have no heart any longer, as I have said a dozen times
already, for journalizing. Had it been otherwise, there is
enough of picturesque and peculiar in Geneva to fill a good
many of these pages; but really I lack energy to seek objects of
interest, curiosity even so much as to glance at them, heart
to enjoy them, intellect to profit by them. I deem it a grace of
Providence when I have a decent excuse to my wife, and to
my own conscience, for not seeing even the things that have
helped to tempt me abroad. It may be disease; it may be age;
it may be the effect of the lassitudinous Roman atmosphere;

but such is the fact. Geneva is situated partly on low flat ground, bordering the lake; and behind this level space, it rises by steep, painfully paved streets, some of which, I think, can hardly be accessible by wheeled carriages. The prosperity of the town is indicated by a good many new and splendid edifices, for commercial and other purposes, in the vicinity of the lake; but intermixed with these there are many [39] quaint buildings of a stern, gray colour, and in a style of architecture that I prefer, a thousand times, to the monotony of Italian streets. Immensely high red roofs, with windows in them, produce an effect that delights me; they are as ugly, perhaps, as can well be conceived, but very striking and individual. At each corner of these ancient houses, frequently, is a tower, the roof of which rises in a square pyramidal (or, if the tower be round, a round pyramidal) form. Arched passages, gloomy and grimy, pass from one street to another. The lower town creeps with busy life, and swarms like an ant-hill; but if you climb the half-precipitous streets, you find yourself among ancient and stately mansions, high-roofed, with a queer aspect of grandeur about them, looking as if they might still be tenanted by such old magnates as dwelt in them centuries ago. There is also a Cathedral, the elder portion of which looked exceedingly fine; but it has been adorned at some modern epoch with a Grecian portico, good in itself, but absurdly out of keeping with the edifice which it prefaces. This being a protestant country, the doors were all shut; an inhospitality that made half a Catholic of me. It is funny enough, that a stranger generally profits by all that is worst for the inhabitants of the country where he himself is merely a visitor. Despotism makes things all the pleasanter for the stranger; Catholicism lends itself admirably to his purposes.

Well; there are public gardens (one, at least) in Geneva, and hundreds of fine views, no doubt, from the heights in the neighborhood of the town. Let other travellers speak of them. Nothing struck me so much, I think, as the color of the Rhone, as it flows under the bridges in the lower town. It is absolutely miraculous, and, beautiful as it is, suggests the idea that the [40] tubs of a thousand or two of dyers have emptied their liquid indigo into the stream. When once you have conquered and thrust out this idea, it is an inexpressible delight to look down into this intense, brightly transparent blue, that hurries beneath you with the speed of a race-horse. The whole stream looks as if it might intercrystallize into sapphires, if it could only stop long enough for the process. I never saw anything so strange and beautiful as this water.

The shops of Geneva are very tempting to a traveller, being full of such little knicknacks as he would be glad to carry away in memory of the place; wonderful little carvings in wood and ivory, done with exquisite taste and skill; jewelery that seems very cheap, but is doubtless dear enough, if you estimate it by the solid gold that goes into its manufacture; watches, above all things else, for a third or a quarter of the price that one pays in England—looking just as well, too, and probably performing the whole of a watch's duty as uncriticisably. The Swiss people are frugal and inexpensive in their own habits, I believe, plain and simple, and careless of ornament; but they seem to reckon on other people's spending a great deal of money for gew gaws. We bought some of their wooden trumpery, and likewise a watch for Una, for which I paid forty dollars; and this appeared to be a high price for a Swiss watch. Miss Shepard also bought one for thirty-two dollars. Next to watches, jewelry, and wood carving, I should say that cigars were one of the greatest articles of commerce in Geneva. Cigar-shops present themselves at every step or two, and at a reasonable rate, there being no duties, I believe, on imported goods. At any rate, there was no examination of our trunks on arrival, nor any questions asked on that score.

[41] Hotel de Byron (Villeneuve) June 12th, Sunday.

At three °clock, yesterday afternoon, we left Geneva by a steamer, starting from the quay, at only a short distance from our Hotel. The forenoon had been showery; but the sun now came out very pleasantly, although there were still clouds and mist enough to give infinite variety to the mountain-scenery. At the commencement of our voyage, the scenery of the lake was not incomparably superior to that of other lakes on which I have sailed, as Lake Windermere, for instance, or Loch Lomond, or our own Lake Champlain. It continually grew more grand and beautiful, however, till at length I felt that I had never seen anything worthy to be put beside it. The southern shore of the lake has the grandest scenery; the great hills on that side appearing close to the water's edge, and after descending, with headlong slope, directly from their rocky and snow-streaked summits down into the blue waters. Our course lay nearer to the northern shore, and all our stop-ping-places were on that side. The first was Coppet, where Madame de Stael or her father, or both, were either born, or resided, or died, I know not which—and care very little. It is a picturesque village, with an old church, I think, and old, high roofed, red-tiled houses, the whole looking as if nothing in it had been changed for many, many years. All these villages (of which we stopped momentarily at several) look delight-fully unmodified by recent fashions; there is the church, with its tower crowned by a pyramidal roof, like an extinguisher; then the chateau of the former lord, half castle and half dwelling-house, with a round tower at each corner, pyramid topt; then, perhaps, the ancient town-house or hotel de [42] ville, in an open, paved square; and perhaps the largest mansion in the whole village will have been turned into a modern inn, but retaining all its venerable characteristics of high, steep-sloping roof, and antiquated windows. Scatter a delightful shade of trees among the houses, throw in a time-worn monument of one kind or another, swell out the delicious blue of the lake in front, and the delicious green of the sunny hill-side sloping up behind and around this closely congregated neighborhood of old, comfortable houses—and I do not know what more to do for the sketch. Often there was an insulated house or cottage, embowered in shade, and each seeming like the one only spot in the wide world where two people, that had good consciences and loved one another, could spend a happy life. Half-ruined towers, old historic castles—these, too, we saw. And, all the while, on the other side of the lake, were the high hills, sometimes dim, sometimes black, sometimes green, with gray precipices of stone, and often snow-patches, right above the warm sunny lake where we were sailing.

We passed Lausanne, which stands considerably upward from the lake, on the slope of the hill; the tower of its cathedral forming a conspicuous object. We mean to visit this tomorrow; so I may pretermit further mention of it here. We passed Vevay, and Clarens, which methought was more picturesque than anything we had yet seen; for now the hills had approached close to the water on the northern side, also, and steep heights rose directly above the little gray church and village, and especially I remember a rocky cliff which ascends into a rounded pyramid, insulated from all other peaks and ridges. Oh how idle to write of these [43] things! Even if I could perform the absolute impossibility of getting one single outline of the scene into words, there would be all the color wanting, the light, the haze, which spiritualize it, and moreover make a thousand and a thousand scenes out of that single one. Clarens, however, had still another interest for me; for I found myself more affected by it, as the scene of the loves of St Preux and Julia, than I often have been by scenes of poetry and romance. I read Rousseau's romance with great sympathy when I was hardly more than a boy; ten years ago, or thereabouts, I tried to read it again, without success; but I think, from my feeling of yesterday, that it still retains its hold upon my imagination.

Farther onward, we saw a white, ancient-looking group of towers, beneath a mountain, which was so high, and rushed so precipitately down upon this pile of building as quite to dwarf it; besides which its dingy whiteness had not a very picturesque effect. Nevertheless, this was the Castle of Chillon. It appears to sit right upon the water, and does not rise very loftily above it. I was disappointed in its aspect, having imagined this famous castle as situated upon a rock, a hundred, or for aught I know, a thousand, feet above the surface of the lake; but it is quite as impressive a fact (supposing it to be true) that the water is eight hundred feet deep at its base. By this time, the mountains had taken the beautiful lake into their deepest heart; they girdled it quite round with their grandeur and beauty, and being able to do no more for it, they here held it from extending any further; and here our voyage came to an end. I have never beheld any [44] scene so exquisite as this; nor do I ask of Heaven to show me any lovelier or nobler one, but only to give me such depth and breadth of sympathy with nature that I may worthily enjoy this. It is beauty more than enough for poor, perishable mortals; unless I am to live forever, it was not worth while to tantalize me so. If this be earth, what must Heaven be!

It was nearly eight °clock, I believe, when we arrived; and then we had a walk of at least a mile to the Hotel Byron, lugging along our own shawls, umbrellas, and carpet bags. I forgot to mention, that, in the latter part of our voyage, there was a shower in some part of the sky, and though none of it fell upon us, we had the benefit of those gentle tears in a rainbow which arched itself across the lake, from mountain to mountain, so that our track lay directly through this triumphal arch. We took it as a good omen, nor were we discouraged; though, after the rainbow had vanished, a few sprinkles of the shower came down.

We found the Hotel Byron a very grand hotel indeed, and a good one too, judging by the evening meal which was set before us. There was a beautiful moonlight on the lake and hills, but we contented ourselves with looking out of our lofty window, whence, likewise, we had a side long glance at the white battlements of Chillon, not more than a mile off, on the water's edge. The castle is terribly in need of a pedestal; if its site was elevated to a height equal to its own, it would make a far better appearance. As it now is, it looks—to speak profanely of what poetry has consecrated—when seen from the water, or along the shore of the lake, very like an old white-washed factory or mill.

[45] This morning, after breakfast, I walked to the Castle of Chillon with Julian, who sketches everything he sees, from a wild flower, or a carved chair, to a castle or a range of mountains. The morning had sunshine thinly scattered through it; but nevertheless there was a continual sprinkle, sometimes scarcely perceptible, and then again amounting to a decided drizzle. The road, which is built along at a little elevation above the lake shore, led us past the Castle of Chillon, and we took a side path, which passes still nearer the castle-gate. The castle stands on what may once have been a rocky island, though there is an isthmus of gravel permanently connecting it with the mainland. A wooden bridge, covered with a roof, passes from the shore to the arched entrance of the castle; and beneath this shelter, which has wooden walls, as well as roof and floor, we saw a soldier or gendarme, who seemed to act as warder. As it sprinkled rather more freely than at first, I thought of appealing to his

hospitality for shelter from the rain, but concluded to pass on. The castle makes a far better appearance on a near view, and from the land, than when seen at a distance, and from the water. It is built of stone, and seems to have been anciently covered with plaster, which imparts the whiteness, to which Byron does much more than justice when he speaks of "Chillon's snow-white battlements." There is a lofty external wall, with a cluster of round towers about it, each crowned with its pyramidal roof of tiles; and from the central portion of the castle rises a square tower, also crowned with its own pyramid, to a considerably greater height [46] than the circumjacent ones. The whole are in a close cluster, and make a fine picture of ancient strength when seen at a proper proximity; for I do not think that distance adds anything to the effect. There are hardly any windows, or few and very small ones, except the loop-holes for arrows, and for the garrisson of the castle to peep from at their windows. On the sides towards the water, indeed, there are larger windows, at least in the upper apartments; but in that direction, no doubt, the castle was considered impregnable. Trees, here and there, on the land side, grow up against the castle wall, on one part of which, moreover, there was a green curtain of ivy spreading from base to battlement. The walls retain their ancient machicolations, and I should judge that nothing had been changed, nor any more work been done upon the old fortress than to keep it in singularly good repair. It was formerly a castle of the Duke of Savoy, and since his sway over the country ceased (three hundred years, at least) has been in the hands of the Swiss government, who still keep some arms and ammunition here.

We passed on, and found the view of the castle better, as we thought, from a farther point along the road. The rain-drops began to spatter down faster, and we took shelter under an impending precipice, where the ledge of rock had been

blasted and hewn away, to form the road. Our shelter was not
a very convenient and comfortable one; so we took advantage
of the partial cessation of the shower to turn homeward, but
had not gone far when we met mamma and all her train. As
we were close by the castle entrance, we thought it ad[47]-
visible to seek admission, though rather doubtful whether the
Swiss gendarme might not deem it a sin to let us see the
castle on Sunday. But he very readily admitted us under his
sheltered draw-bridge, and called an old man from within the
fortress to show us whatever was to be seen. This latter personage was a staid, rather grim, and Calvinistic looking old
worthy; but he let us in without scruple, and forthwith
proceeded to usher us into a range of most dismal dungeons,
extending along the basement of the castle, on a level with the
surface of the lake. We first, if I remember right, came to
what he said had been a chapel, and which, at all events,
looked like an aisle of one, or rather such a crypt as I have
seen beneath a cathedral, being a succession of massive
pillars, supporting groined arches; a very admirable piece of
gloomy Gothic architecture. Next we came to a very dark
compartment of the same dungeon-range, where he pointed
to a sort of bed, or what might serve for a bed, hewn in the
solid rock; and this, our guide said, had been the last sleeping-
place of condemned prisoners, on the night before their execution. The next compartment was still duskier and dismaller
than the last; and he bade us cast our eyes up into the obscurity and see a beam, where the condemned ones used to be
hanged. I looked and looked, and closed my eyes so as to see
the clearer, in this horrible duskiness, on opening them again.
Finally, I thought I discerned the accursed beam, and the
rest of the party were certain that they saw it. Next [48]
beyond this, I think, was a stone staircase, steep, rudely hewn,
and narrow, down which the condemned were brought to
death; and beyond this (still on the same basement-range of

the castle) a low and narrow room, through which we passed, and saw a range of seven massive pillars, supporting two parallel rows of groined arches, like those in the chapel which we first entered. This was Bonnevard's prison, and the scene of Byron's poem.

The range of arches are dimly lighted by a row of narrow loop-holes, pierced through the immensely thick wall, but at such a height above the floor that we could catch no glimpse of land or water, or scarcely, I believe, at the sky. The prisoner of Chillon could not possibly have seen the little island to which Byron alludes, and which stands a little way from the shore, right opposite the town of Villeneuve. There was light enough, in this long, gray, vaulted room, to show us that all the pillars were inscribed with the names of visitors, among which I saw no interesting one except that of Byron himself, which is cut, in letters an inch long or more, into one of the pillars next to that to which Bonnevard was chained. The letters are deep enough to remain in the pillar as long as the castle stands. Byron seems to have had a fancy for recording his name in this and similar ways; as witness the record which I saw in a tree at Newstead Abbey. In Bonnevard's pillar there still remains an iron ring, at the height of perhaps three feet from the ground; his chain was fastened to this ring, and his only freedom was to walk round the pillar, around which he is said to have [49] worn a path in the stone pavement of the dungeon; but as the floor is now covered with earth or gravel, I could not satisfy myself whether this is true. Certainly six years, with nothing else to do in them save to walk round the pillar, might well suffice to wear away the rock, even with naked feet. This pillar, and all the pillars, were cut and hewn in a good style of architecture, and the dungeon arches are not without a certain gloomy beauty. On Bonnevard's pillar, as on all the rest, were many names inscribed; but I thought better of Byron's delicacy and sensitiveness for not cutting his name into that very pillar. Perhaps—knowing nothing of Bonnevard's story—he did not know which pillar the prisoner was chained to.

Emerging from the range of dungeon-vaults, our guide led us through other parts of the castle, showing us the Duke of Savoy's kitchen, with a fireplace at least twelve feet long; also the judgment hall, or some such place, hung round with the coats of arms of some officers or other, and having at one end a wooden post, reaching from floor to cieling, and having upon it the marks of fire. By means of this post, contumacious prisoners were put to a dreadful torture, being drawn up by cords and pullies, while their limbs were scorched by a fire underneath. We also saw a chapel, and, I believe, two, one of which is still in good and sanctified condition, and was to be used for religious services, our guide told us, this very day. We saw, moreover, the Duke of Savoy's private chambers, with a part of the bedstead on which he used to sleep—and be haunted with horrible dreams, no doubt, and the ghosts [50] of wretches whom he had tortured and hanged; likewise the bed chamber of his duchess, in the window of which were two stone-seats, where (right over the head of Bonnevard) the ducal pair might look out on the beautiful scene of lake and mountains, and feel the warmth of the blessed sun. Right under this window, the guide said, the water of the lake is eight hundred feet in depth; an immense profundity, indeed, for an inland lake, but it is not very difficult to believe that the mountain, at the foot of which Chillon stands, may descend then much farther beneath the water. In other parts of the lake, and not far distant, nine hundred feet and more have been sounded. I looked out of the duchess's window, and could certainly see no appearance of a bottom in the light blue water.

The last thing, as far as I remember, that the guide showed us, was a trap-door, or opening beneath a crazy old floor.

Looking down into this aperture, we saw three stone steps, which we should have taken to be the beginning of a flight of stairs that descended into a dungeon, or series of dungeons, such as we had already seen. But, inspecting them more closely, we saw that the third step terminated the flight, and beyond was a dark vacancy; three steps a person would grope down, planting his uncertain foot on a dimly seen stone; the fourth step would be into the empty air. The guide told us that it used to be the practise to bring prisoners hither, under pretence of committing them to a dungeon, and make them go down the three steps, and that fourth fatal one; and they would never more be heard of in earth, but, at the [51] bottom of the pit there would be a dead body, and in due time a mouldy skeleton, which would rattle beneath the body of the next prisoner that fell. I do not believe that it was anything more than a secret dungeon for state-prisoners, whom it was out of the question either to set at liberty or bring to public trial. The guide said that the depth of the dungeon was about forty-five feet. Gazing intently down, I saw a faint gleam of light at the bottom, apparently coming from some other aperture than the mouth of the pit, over which we were bending; so that it must have been contemplated to supply it with light and air in such degree as to support human life. Una declared that she saw a skeleton at the bottom; Miss Shepard thought she saw a hand; but I saw only this dim gleam of light.

There are two or three court-yards in the castle but of no great size. We were now shown across one of them, and dismissed out of the arched entrance by which we had come in. We found the gendarme still keeping watch on his roofed drawbridge; and as there was the same gentle shower that had been effusing itself all the morning, we availed ourselves of the shelter, more especially as there were some curiosities to examine. These consisted chiefly of wood-carvings, such as

little figures in the national costume, boxes with wreaths of
foliage upon them, paper knives, the chamois-goat, admirably
well represented, and a good many other pretty things. We at
first hesitated to make any advances towards trade with the
gendarme, because it was Sunday, and we fancied there
might be a Calvinistic scruple, on his [52] part, about turning
a penny on the Sabbath; but, from the little I know of the
Swiss character, I fancy they would be as ready as any other
men to sell not only such matters, but even their own souls,
or any smaller (or shall we say greater thing) on Sunday
or at any other time. So we began to ask the prices of the
articles, and met with no difficulty in purchasing a salad-knife
and fork, with pretty bas-reliefs of fruit and foliage carved
on the handles, and a napkin ring; the whole for six franks.
For Rosebud's and our amusement, the gendarme now set a
musical box a-going; and, as it played, a pasteboard figure of
a doctor began to pull the tooth of a pasteboard patient, lifting
the wretched simulacrum entirely from the ground, and keeping him in this horrible torture for half an hour together.
Meanwhile, Mamma, Miss Shepard, Una, and Julian, sat
down all in a row, on a bench, and sketched the mountains;
and as the shower did not cease, though the sun most of the
time shone brightly, they were kept actual Prisoners of Chillon
much longer than we wanted to stay.

We took advantage of the first cessation—(though still the
drops came dimpling into the water that rippled against the
pebbles beneath the bridge)—of the first partial cessation of
the shower, to escape, and returned towards the hotel, with
this kindliest of summer rains falling upon us most of the
way. My wife had caught a cold, the night before, but it
really seemed to be cured by the sunny raindrops of this
morning. In the afternoon, the rain entirely ceased, and the
weather grew de[53]lightfully radiant, and warmer than could
well be borne, in the sunshine. Una and I walked to the

village of Villeneuve (about a mile, or less, from the Hotel) and found a very common-place little old town of one or two streets, standing on a level, and as uninteresting as if there were not a hill within a hundred miles. It is strange what prosaic lines men thrust in amid the poetry of Nature. Nothing else of importance occurred, except that Julian bathed in the lake, under my superintendence, and tried to swim, but as yet without success; moreover, the chill water of Lake Leman has given him a cold.

At dinner, to-day, I made trial of a bottle of Swiss white wine (Yverdan, I think they call it) and found it marvellously like very meagre cider, and to say the truth, hardly worth the bottle that held it. It purported to be thirteen years old, and might grow twice as old before I should want to drink any more of it. They charge absurd prices, at the Swiss hotels, for these native wines, which cannot cost them sixpence a gallon; three or four franks for a bottle which has as huge an inward bulge at the bottom as any claret or Burgundy bottle, that holds the richest or most delicate wine of France. The hotels have not here, as in Italy and Southern France, the custom of setting before the guest, without charge, a bottle of claret or other wine, that is often as palatable as any that he finds in their list of more expensive liquors.

Hotel d'Angleterre (Geneva), June 14th, Tuesday.

Yesterday morning was very fine; and we had a pretty early [54] breakfast at Hotel Byron, preparatory to leaving it. This Hotel is on a magnificent scale of height and breadth, its staircase and corridors being the most spacious I have seen; but there is a kind of meagreness in the life there, and a certain lack of heartiness, that prevented us from feeling at home. We were glad to get away, and took the steamer on our return voyage, in excellent spirits. Apparently, it had been a cool night in the upper regions, for a great deal more snow was visible on some of the mountains than we had before seen; especially a mountain called *"Diableries"* presented a silver summit and broad sheets and fields of snow. Nothing ever can have been more beautiful than those groups of mighty hills as we saw them now, with the gray rocks, the green slopes, the white snow patches and crests, all to be seen at one glance, and the mists and fleecy clouds, tumbling, rolling, hovering, about their summits, filling their lofty valleys, and coming down far towards the lower world; making the skyey aspects so intimate with the earthy ones that we hardly knew whether we were sojourning in the material or spiritual world. It was like sailing through the sky, moreover, to be borne along on such water as that of Lake Leman; the bluest, brightest, and profoundest element; the most radiant eye that the dull earth ever opened to see Heaven withal. I am writing nonsense; but it is because no sense within my reach will answer the purpose.

Some of these mountains, that looked at no such mighty distance, were at least forty or fifty miles off, and appeared as if they were near neighbors and friends of other mountains, from which they were really still further removed. The [55] relations into which distant points are brought, in a view of mountain-scenery, symbolize the truth that we can never judge, within our partial scope of view, of the relations which we bear to our fellow creatures and human circumstances. These mighty mountains thought that they had nothing to do with one another; each deems itself its own centre, and existing for itself alone; and yet, to an eye that can take them all in, they are evidently portions of one grand and beautiful idea, which could not be consummated without the lowest and the loftiest of them. I do not express this satisfactorily, but have a genuine meaning in it, nevertheless.

We passed again by Chillon, and gazed at it as long as it was distinctly visible, though the water-view does no justice to its real picturesqueness; there being no towers nor projections on the side towards the lake; nothing but a wall of dingy white, with an indentation that looks something like a gateway. About an hour and a half brought us to Ouchy, the point where passengers land to take the omnibus to Lausanne. The ascent from the former village to the latter town is about a mile and a half, which it took the omnibus nearly half an hour to accomplish. We left our shawls and carpet-bags in the salle-a-manger of the Hotel Faucon, and set forth to find the Cathedral, the pinnacled tower of which is visible for a long distance up and down the lake. Prominent as it is, however, it is by no means very easy to find it, while rambling through the intricate streets and declivities of the town itself; for Lausanne is the town, I should imagine, in all the world the most difficult to go directly from one point to an[56]other. The town is built on the declivity of a hill, adown which run several vallies or ravines, over which the contiguity of houses extends; so that the communication is kept up by means of steep streets, and, sometimes, long, weary staircases, which must be surmounted and descended again, in accomplishing a very moderate distance. In some inscrutable way, we at last got to the Cathedral, which seems to stand on a higher site than any other in Lausanne. It has a very venerable exterior, with all the Gothic grandeur which arched, mullioned windows, deep portals, buttresses, towers and pinnacles, gray with a thousand years, can give to architecture. After waiting a while, we obtained entrance by means of an old woman, who seems to act the part of sacristan, and was then, I believe, showing the church to some other visitors.

The interior disappointed us; not but what it was very beautiful; but I think the excellent repair which it was in, and the puritanic neatness with which it is kept, does much towards effacing the majesty and mystery which belong to an old church. Every inch of every wall and column, and all the mouldings and tracery, and every scrap of grotesque carving, had been washed with a drab mixture. There were also seats all up and down the nave, made of pine wood, and looking very new and neat; just such seats as I shall see in a hundred meeting-houses (if I ever go into so many) in America. Whatever might be the reason, the stately nave, with its high, groined roof, the clustered columns and lofty pillars, the intersecting arches of the side aisles, the choirs, the armorial and knightly tombs that surround what was once the high altar, all [57] produced far less effect than I could have thought beforehand.

As it happened, we had more ample time and freedom to inspect this Cathedral, than any other that I ever was in; for the old woman consented to go away and leave us there, locking the door behind her. The others (except Rosebud, and, part of the time, Julian) sat down to sketch such portions of the Cathedral as struck their fancy; and for myself, I looked at the monuments, of which some, being those of old knights, ladies, bishops, and a king, are curious for their antiquity, and others are interesting, as bearing memorials of English people who have died at Lausanne, in comparatively recent years. Then I went up into the pulpit, and tried, without success, to get into the stone gallery that runs all round the nave; and I explored my way into various side-apartments of the Cathedral, which I found fitted up with seats for Sabbath-schools, perhaps, or possibly for meetings of elders of the church. I opened the great bible of the church, and found it to be a French version, printed, I believe, at Lille, some fifty years ago. There was also a liturgy, adapted probably to the Lutheran form of worship. In one of the side apartments, I found a strong-box, heavily clamped with iron, and having a contrivance like the hopper of a mill, by which money could be turned into the top; while a double-lock prevented its being abstracted again. This was to receive the avails of contributions made in the church; and there were likewise boxes, stuck on the ends of long poles, wherewith the deacons (or whoever the money-takers be) could go round among the worshippers, conveniently extending the begging box to the remotest cur[58]mudgeon among them all. From the arrangement of the seats in the nave, and the labels pasted or painted on them, I judged that the women sat on one side and the men on the other; and the seats for various orders of magistrates, and for ecclesiastical and collegiate people, were likewise marked out.

I soon grew weary of these investigations, and so did Julian and Rosebud, who essayed to amuse themselves with running races together over the horizontal tombstones in the pavement of the choir, treading remorselessly over the noseless effigies of old dignitaries who never expected to be so irreverently treated. I put a stop to their sport; and banished them to different parts of the Cathedral; and by and by, the old woman appeared again and released us from durance. Mamma had been drawing some curious figures of saints and monsters that adorned the arch of the northern portal; and in getting up hastily, she tripped and sprained her ancle. The pain was excessive, for the moment, but soon passed off so as to enable us to return to our hotel. Here we had a dejeuner a la fourchette, at two °clock; and drank some wine of the neighborhood, called Swiss champagne, and wonderfully resembling the genuine fluid. I had no great expectations from it, but found it a very delicate and exquisite wine, pleasanter than the champagne of France, as being lighter and less effective upon the brain. While waiting for our dejeuner, we saw the people dining at the regular table d'hôte of the Hotel; and the idea was strongly borne in upon me that the

profession and mystery of a male-waiter is a very [59] un-
manly one. It is so absurd to see the solemn attentiveness with
which they stand behind the chairs; the earnestness of their
watch for any crisis that may demand their interposition; the
gravity of their manner, in performing some little office that
the guest might better do for himself; their decorous and
softly steps;—in short, as I sat and gazed at them, they
seemed to me not real men, but creatures with a clerical
aspect, engendered out of a very artificial state of society.
When they are waiting on myself, they do not appear so
absurd; it is necessary to stand apart in order to see them
properly.

We left Lausanne (which was to us a tedious and weary
place) at a quarter before four °clock. I should have liked
well enough to see the house of Gibbon, and the garden in
which he walked after finishing the 'Decline and Fall'; but
it could not be done without some trouble and inquiry, and
as the house did not come to see me, I determined not to go
to see the house. There was, indeed, a mansion of somewhat
antique respectability, near our Hotel, having a garden and
a shaded terrace behind it, which would have answered accurately enough to the idea of Gibbon's residence. Perhaps it
was so; far more probably not.

Our former voyages had been performed in the Hirondelle;
we now (after broiling for some time in the fervid sunshine,
by the lake-side) got on board of the Aigle, No. 2. There were
a good many passengers, the larger proportion of whom
seemed to be English and American, and among the latter a
large party of talkative ladies, old and young. The voyage
was pleasant while we were protected from the sun by the
awning overhead, but became scarcely agreeable when the
sun had got so low as to [60] shine in our faces or on our backs.
We looked earnestly for Mount Blanc, which ought to have

been visible during a large part of our course; but the clouds gathered themselves hopelessly over the portion of the sky where the great mountain ought to have lifted his white peak; and we did not see it, and probably never shall. As to meaner mountains, there was enough of them, and beautiful enough; but we were a little weary, and feverish with the heat; and Mamma was in pain again with her ancle; and Julian was sick with the cold that he caught in bathing; and Una's strength of convalescence was about exhausted; and Miss Shepard, I believe, had a headache, and so, I think, had I myself, though it is so unusual a complaint with me that I hardly know it when it comes. We were none of us sorry, therefore, when the Eagle brought us to the Quay of Geneva, only a little distance from our hotel. Near as it was, however, Mamma's ancle was so bad that she had to be carried thither in a cab; and her accident, and Julian's indisposition, have kept us in Geneva a day longer than we expected, and may delay our departure still further.

To-day, I wrote to Mr. Wilding, requesting him to secure passages for us, from Liverpool, on the 15th of next month, or first of August. It makes my heart thrill, half pleasantly, half otherwise; so much nearer does this step seem to bring that home whence I have now been absent six years, and which, when I see it again, may turn out not to be my home any longer. I likewise wrote to Bennoch, though I know not his present address; but I should deeply grieve to leave England without see[61]ing him. He and Henry Bright are the only two men in England to whom I shall be much grieved to bid farewell; but to the island itself I cannot bear to say that word, as a finality. I shall dreamily hope to come back again at some indefinite time;—rather foolishly, perhaps, for it will tend to take the substance out of my life in my own land. But this, I suspect, is apt to be the penalty of those who stray abroad, and stay too long.

Hotel Wheeler, (Havre) June 22^d, Wednesday.

We arrived at this Hotel, last evening, from Paris; and find ourselves on the border of the Petit Quay Notre Dame, with steamers and boats right under our window, and all sorts of dock business going on briskly; there are barrels, bales, and crates of goods; there are old iron cannon for posts; in short, all that belongs to the wapping of a great sea-port. Our hotel seems to be the resort chiefly of merchant-captains, and passengers arriving or departing by the steamers; and the American partialities of the guests are consulted by the decorations of the parlor, in which hang two lithographed and colored views of New York, from Brooklyn and from Weehawken. The fashion of the hotel is a sort of nondescript mixture of French, English, and American, and is not disagreeable to us, after our weary experience of Continental life. The abundance of the living is very acceptable, in comparison with the meagreness of French and Italian meals; and, last night, we supt nobly on cold roast beef and ham, set generously before us in the mass, instead of being doled out in slices few [62] and thin. The waiter has a familiar kindly sort of manner, and resembles the steward of a vessel more than a landsman; and, in short, everything here has undergone a sea-change, which might admit of very effective description, if I had any spirit to write, as of yore. But I flag terribly; scenes and things make but dim reflections in my inward mirror; and if ever I have a thought, the words do not come aptly to clothe it. I may as well give up all attempts at journalizing.

So I shall say nothing of our journey across France from Geneva; nor of our five days' stay in Paris; nor of our journey thence to Havre. We came thither principally to accompany Miss Shepard, whom I put on board the Steamer Vanderbilt for New York, last evening, and who sails this morning. To-night, we ourselves shall take our departure in a steamer for Southampton, whence we shall go to London;—thence, in a week or two, to Liverpool;—thence to Boston and Concord, there to enjoy (if enjoyment it prove) a little rest, and sense that we are at home.

1858 POCKET DIARY

January

D AMP & FOGGY. This first day of the year finds us at 24, Great Russell-street, where we have been since November, awaiting the settlement of my official accounts in order to go to the continent. The delay has been much greater than I expected.

1 *Friday* Damp & foggy day. The last accts. & drafts came from Mr. Wilding. Returned the accts through Mr. Miller; and walked into the city (with Julian) to Barings, who will negociate the drafts. On our way home, called at Bennoch's, where I wrote a note to Mr. Wilding.

2 *Saturday* At about noon, went with Julian to Mr. Dallas's (U. S. Minister, 24, Portland Place) to arrange about Passport; thence walked along Oxford-st, and Piccadilly, & down into the city. Evening, Mr⁵ Lilsham came here; but I went to Princess's Theatre, & saw Pantomime, White Cat.

3 *Sunday* Wrote Journal and letters. After dinner, walked out with Julian.

4 *Monday* Forenoon, went with Julian to Barings, taking

the O'S box of private letters &c for deposit. Returning, went into Marlboro' House for a short time. After dinner, went to Bennett's, 65, Cheapside, to get Mrs. Hawthorne's watch. Bennoch spent the evening and took tea with us.

5 *Tuesday*   All got up early, & at 7 °clock, left for London Bridge station, in two cabs. Started for Folkestone at 8½, arrived at 11; left for Boulogne at 1½, arrived at 4. Left for Amiens about an hour afterwards, & arrived in about 2 hours, and put up at Hôtel du Rhin. Most bitterly cold, all the way, with a wintry aspect of country.

6 *Wednesday*   Breakfasted at about 10. Went out to see the Cathedral. Left Amiens at 1½, & reached Paris at about 5. Still desperately cold; as cold as an American winter's day. Put up at the Hôtel du Louvre, and all dined at the Restaurant of the Hôtel.

7 *Thursday*   Horribly cold. Prevented from going out in the morning by nose-bleed. Wife & Miss Shepard went to pass our luggage through Custom House. At about 2, we all went out, dined at a Restaurant, and afterwards walked to Place de la Concorde &c. Much surprised by the beauty & stateliness of Paris. Letter from Mr. Wilding

8 *Friday*   Still cold. At about eleven, went out, all of us, & visited the galleries of the Louvre, where we staid till after 3, when we went to our yesterday's Restaurant & dined. Returned to the Hôtel. Mr. Husson called; also Miss McDaniel; also Mr Fezandié

9 *Saturday*   Still cold, but rather milder. At about 11, we all walked down Rue St Honoré. Miss Mitchell called before we went out. I went to Hottinguer's bank, Rue Bergere, &

afterwards overtook the party on the Boulevards. To the church *de la* Madeleine, & saw funeral service. Afterwards through Champs Elysees to Triumphal arch, which ascended. Through Place de la Concorde, to Place Vendome, & to Restaurant d'Echelle, where dined. Home by 5 °clock

10 *Sunday* Went to the drawings & sculpture gallery of the Louvre. Dined with Mamma, Una, & Julian, at the Restaurant of the Hotel. Wrote to Russell Sturgis.

11 *Monday* Pretty early, wife, Una, Miss Shepard, & Rosebud, took omnibus for Hôtel des Invalides. Julian & I walked to American Minister's, 13, Rue Beaujon. Returning, wife, Miss Shepard, Rose, & I, took fiacre for Notre Dame. Could get no cab or omnibus to return in, were caught in the rain, & walked back. Dined at the restaurant of the Hôtel. Saw Mr. & Mrs. Pickman.

12 *Tuesday* Sunny, but exceedingly muddy. Went with Julian to the American Consul's (Mr. Spencer's) and had my passport viséd. Then we walked about the streets, to Nôtre Dame, and elsewhere. At about four, we all went to dine at the Restaurant de L'Echelle. Mamma had a bad cold to-day, owing to being caught in the rain yesterday.

13 *Wednesday* At 11 °clock, we started (with Miss Mitchell in company) from Paris, and reached Lyons at about 10 °clock P. M. A very cold and disagreeable journey. We put up at the hôtel de Provence, had a cup of tea, and went to bed.

14 *Thursday* Left Lyons at 10 °clock, and reached Marseilles at about 11, P.M., or a little earlier. Another cold and disagreeable journey; ice along the road. Put up at the Hotel d'Angleterre, near the quays.

15 *Friday*   At Marseilles. Went with Miss Shepard to the railway, about our carpet-bag, without success. Telegraphed for it. Dined at the table d'hôte of the Hotel.

16 *Saturday*   Went with Julian to Mr. Morgan's, American Consul. Afterwards with Miss Shepard to packet-boat office, & secured places for Leghorn. Afterwards to Railway station to get luggage, and saw it on board steamer.

17 *Sunday*   At about 9 A. M. sailed in Neapolitan Steamer Calabrese; very pleasant day, and warm in the sun. Coasted along the shore of the Mediterranean. Beautiful sky at sunset. I had a cold and could not enjoy it much. Wrote a little in journal, and went to bed early. Miss Mitchell is of the party.

18 *Monday*   Up about sunrise, & found the steamer approaching Genoa. We all went ashore, took a commissionaire, and went round to visit churches and palaces. Very weary. Dined at the Hotel de Croix de Malta, went on board again, & took another dinner in the steamer. Set sail after dusk. Some rain.

19 *Tuesday*   Reached Leghorn early in the morning. Went ashore, all of us. Drew £50 from Grand-more & Co, Bankers. We wandered about Leghorn, under the guidance of a Commissionaire, to get passports viséed Returned on board, & set sail about five °clock. Very beautiful evening Went to bed early.

20 *Wednesday*   Reached Civita Vecchia before daylight. At about 9, went ashore, and to the Custom House. After much bother, started in vetturino (price 3 Napoleons) for Rome. We were cheated and imposed upon, of course, & reached Rome about 11, after nearly 12 hours travel, instead

of 8. Very cold & wretched. Stopt at Hotel Spillmans, & had supper. To bed between 1 & 2.

21 *Thursday* Very cold weather. Drove about the city, to the American Minister's, the American Consul's, and in search of houses. Found one, through the agency of Mr. Shea. I feel very unwell and exceedingly miserable.

22 *Friday* Still exceedingly cold, and the most disagreeable air I ever felt. Went to Pakenham & Hooker's bank, & drew £50. Concluded engagement for house, 37, Via Porta Pinciana, at 340 scudi for four months. Very unwell, & remained shivering in our room the latter part of the day. Rosebud quite unwell. Miss Mitchell has taken apartments by herself.

23 *Saturday* Removed to our lodgings, Porta Pinciana. Cold day; & all of us half frozen at our miserable firesides. Paid master of the house 100 scudi.

24 *Sunday* Still miserably cold & frozen. On account of my cold, I did not go out. Mamma, Julian, & Miss Shepard, went out & saw the forum & Colosseum.

25 *Monday* Weather still as cold as ever. My cold much better. Went out & lost myself, but found the forum, the Colosseum, St Peter's, which I entered. Returned between 1 & 2 °clock. Miss Shepard, Una, & Julian, went out at noon. Mamma & Rosebud staid at home. Mr. & Mrs. Story & Mrs. Tappan left cards to-day; and Miss Lander called in the evening

26 *Tuesday* Still very cold; and my own cold as bad, or worse than ever. Did not go out to-day. My wife also ill, and kept her bed most of the day. Mrs. Mountford called.

27 *Wednesday*   Still very cold. My voice almost extinct. Mamma drove out with Rosebud, who has had cold and diarrhœa, and is now quite ill. I walked out for an hour or so, along the sunny side of the Corso &. Miss Shepard, Una, & Julian, go out daily.

28 *Thursday*   Still very cold. My own cold rather better. Walked out, visited St Peter's, and stumbled upon the Capitoline Hill. Baby still quite unwell. Several people called during the day, & Miss Lander in the evening.

29 *Friday*   Still very cold. Walked with wife & Rosebud (who is much better) to St Peters. They drove home, & I walked. Mrs. Bramley Moore jr, & Mr. Rakermann called; also, Mr. & Mrs. Waterston.

30 *Saturday*   Colder than ever. Walked with wife through the Corso to the Roman Forum, & to the Coliseum &c. A terribly chill wind among the arches. Also, ascended the Capitoline Hill. Found thick ice in the Forum, and a rim of icicles round a fountain near the Capitol. We rec^d letters to-day (written in October) & brought from America by Miss Hosmer.

31 *Sunday*   Colder than ever. My own cold renewed. Miss Shepard & Julian went to breakfast with Miss Mitchell; & Miss M. came to see us. The thermometer was below 20 degrees this morning.

February

1 *Monday*   Overcast & showery. Called at Mr. Hooker's bank, & read some American papers. Also, at Hôtel d'Europe

on Mr. Hamilton Fish (whom I saw) & on Dr. Hayward & Mr. G. W. Wales.

2 *Tuesday*   Walked to the Forum, the Capitoline Hill, & lost myself about the city. Found it very warm in the sun. Evening, Mr Rakemann came to give Una a music lesson. Wife indisposed, and has kept her bed all day.

3 *Wednesday*   Walked out at 10 with Rosebud along the Pincian way and to the public gardens. Quite cold, & the ground frozen. Afterwards went alone to the Forum Romanum, & smoked a cigar on a fragment of a column. The Romans were playing at pitch & toss. Very cold. Called on Mrs & Miss Story at the Barbarini palace, but found nobody.

4 *Thursday*   Went to St Peter's. On the way, met Mr. C. G. Thompson, the Boston artist. I staid a good while in St. Peter's, & think it grows larger. Coming out, saw a great sheet of ice near one of the fountains, and little Romans sliding on it. I slid too. There was a review of French soldiers in the place before St. Peters. Mr. Mrs. & Miss Fish called on us.

5 *Friday*   An overcast & rainy day. Walked out, about noon, along the Corso. Balconies and other preparations for the Carnival. The Roman streets do not seem quite so ugly & narrow as at first. Mr. Rakemann came to give music lesson in the evening, & Mr. Nichols, an American painter, made a call

6 *Saturday*   Rainy. Went with wife to Miss Lander's studio, to see her Evangeline &c. Statuette of Virginia Dare very fine. Miss L. requests to take my bust. Evening, Mr. Head, an American called.

7 *Sunday*   It has been a very unpleasant day, and I did not go out.

8 *Monday*   Overcast, and very rainy during part of the day. I went out in the forenoon, but was caught in the rain and took refuge at Pakenham & Hooker's bank, where I read Galignani & the American papers. Una, Miss Shepard & Julian went to the Sistine Chapel. We are now in the Carnival.

9 *Tuesday*   Still overcast, with gleams of sunshine. In the forenoon, went out, & visited St. Peter's. Mamma & Rosebud have gone to drive. Rec^d letter from the Barings, with statement of acct. up to Jany 1st.

10 *Wednesday*   Still cloudy & rainy. Went out this forenoon, and visited the church of St Maria Maggiore; and afterwards went to the Piazza di Monte Cavallo. Returning, met wife & Miss Shepard going to the carnival. Dr. Hayward & Mr. G. W. Wales, of Boston, have just called.

11 *Thursday*   A cloudy & rainy day. In the morning, took a walk on the Pincian Hill. Afternoon, took a carriage with wife, Julian & Rosebud, and drove for two hours along the Corso, to see the Carnival. I was not very much amused. Una & Miss Shepard were at a window, with Miss Mitchell

12 *Friday*   Morning, went to Sta Maria Maggiore's, & to the Monte di Cavallo (to see the statues of Castor & Pollux) with wife. Afterwards called at Barberini Palace, on Mrs. Story, & at Hotel d'Europe on M^r & Mrs. Hamilton Fish. Also at the studio of Mr. C. G. Thompson, the painter, and of William Story, who has become a sculptor. Julian had a severe tumble down stairs, to-day.

13 *Saturday* Forenoon, walked with Mamma thro' the Forum and past the Coliseum to the Basilica of St. John Lateran. A sunny day. Afternoon, went with Rosebud to glimpse at the Carnival.

14 *Sunday* Wrote journal. Afternoon, walked along the Pincian. Miss Mitchell dined with us to-day. A sunny day. Una, Miss Shepard, & Julian, went to the Caesars' Palace.

15 *Monday* A rainy day. At about eleven, went to Miss Lander's studio, and staid till after twelve, sitting for a bust. Afterwards, stept into the church of St Luigi de' Franchesi, for a few minutes.

16 *Tuesday* Forenoon, went with wife to the church of the Capuchins, near the Piazza Babarini; also to the church of the Sacred Heart, Pieta di Monte; also, to the church of Santa Maria del Popolo. Afterwards to Miss Lander's to sit. Afternoon, wife, Una & Miss Shepard went to balcony in the Corso, & Rosebud & I walked along the Corso to see the Carnival. Julian & Miss Mitchell went to the Baths of Caracalla.

17 *Wednesday* Morning, went with wife to St Peter's to see Pope & cardinals. Wife admitted to Sistine Chapel. I not, for lack of dress-coat. Went into the statuary department of the Vatican. Afterwards, sat to Miss Lander. Home about 3, & wife an hour after. Mrs. Story called.

18 *Thursday* Went out in the morning, and walked to the forum, & along the Via delle Rupe Tarpeia &c. Looked into one or two churches. Drew £50 from the bank. Hugh Bright called. I called at Mr. Thompson's studio. Afternoon,

walked on the Pincian &c with Julian. Evening, Mr. & Mrs. Thompson called.

19 *Friday*   A bright, cool day. After breakfast, went with wife to Sta Maria dei Angeli.

20 *Saturday*   In the morning, walked to Saint Peter's. At two °clock, went with wife to the Barberini Palace. Thence went to Rospigliosi Palace, & saw Guido's Aurora. Went into the church of St Andrea a Monte Cavallo.

21 *Sunday*   In the forenoon, walked through the Port del Popolo, and along the shore of the Tiber; afterwards, to the Pantheon, & church of St Ignazio. Returned home, & at 1 °clock, set out with wife to St Peter's, to hear Vespers. As they began too late, we came away without hearing them.

22 *Monday*   After breakfast, walked out along the Corso &c. Returned, & after twelve, went with wife to the Museum of the Capitol. Afterwards visited the Mamertine Prisons. Left wife in the forum, & went to call on Mr. J. P. Kennedy, at Hotel d'Europe. Found him unwell, & just returned from a drive. Mr. Rakerman called in the evening, & played on the piano.

23 *Tuesday*   Crossed the river by the Ponte Sisto, & returned by the Island; thence rambled past the palace of the Caesars &c &c, through the gate of San Sebastiano, & into that of St Giovanni.

24 *Wednesday*   Rainy day. Staid within doors. Began to-day upon a lot of wine, price 3 scudi & 2 pauls.

25 *Thursday*   Went with wife to see the picture-gallery of the Borghese Palace.—Very damp & chilly weather.

26 *Friday*   Forenoon, went out on the Pincian, & rambled a little about the city. Evening, Mr. T. Buchanan Read & Mr. G. W. Wales called, but were not admitted.

27 *Saturday*   A very rainy day. Took only a short walk, up the Quirinal Hill.

28 *Sunday*   A very rainy day. More so than I have seen since leaving America. Have not been out to-day. We have not had a really pleasant day since last Sunday.

March

1 *Monday*   A showery day. Morning, went with wife to picture-gallery of the Capitol. Afterwards, I walked to the Forum & along the Appian way, leaving wife at the Capitol.

2 *Tuesday*   An overcast day, inclining to rain. Forenoon went with wife & Miss Lander to Mr. T. B. Reade's studio, & looked at some of his pictures. Had a sitting for bust at Miss Lander's

3 *Wednesday*   Una's 14th birth-day, which we celebrated by driving with the whole family to the tomb of Cecilia Metella, the Scipios, Columbaria &c. Miss Mitchell & Miss Lander dined with us.

4 *Thursday*   A rainy morning. At about ½ past 11, went to Miss Lander's studio, & had a sitting for bust. Then read the newspapers, at Pakenham & Hooker's Bank. Staid within doors the rest of the day; but towards sunset, it became perfectly clear and pleasant

5 *Friday*   Showery weather. Walked with Rosebud on the Pincian. At 3 °clock, had a sitting at Miss Lander's for bust.

6 *Saturday*   Showery weather. After breakfast, walked along the Corso, & to the forum. At 12 or 1, went with wife & Una to Sciarra Palace; afterwards to Mr. Nichols' painting-room, where we met Miss Lander

7 *Sunday*   Windy & cold, with threats of rain. Wife, Una, & Miss Shepard went to Church of Minerva, the Pantheon, & afterwards to St. Peters. Baby & I walked out along the Pincian, & thence to the Corso, & home by Fountain of Trevi. Julian went to breakfast with Miss Mitchell.

8 *Monday*   Cool & windy. Forenoon, Mamma, Una, Julian & I, went to the sculpture galleries of the Vatican.

9 *Tuesday*   Forenoon, went with wife to the Doria Palace. Afterwards to Miss Lander's to sit for bust. Mr. Reade called in the evening, & invited me to dinner on Friday

10 *Wednesday*   Morning, walked on the Pincian, & along the Corso. Afterwards to Miss Lander's. Met Mr. & Mrs. Daubeny there.

11 *Thursday*   An ugly day. Went to Mr. Thompson's studio; afterwards to Crawford's studio, Negroni Villa.

12 *Friday*   Sat for bust at Miss Lander's. At 6 °clock went to dine at Mr. T. B. Reade's. Present, Mr. Gibson, Mr. Rogers, Mr. Thompson, Mr. Mozier, Mr. Terry, Mr. Caldwell, Mr. Hooker, &c &c &c—ten or twelve in all.

13 *Saturday*   Cloudy & showery day. About 2 °clock, sat

for bust. Afterwards went to Mr. Aker's Studio, with wife, Una, & Julian

14 *Sunday* In the forenoon, walked out with Rosebud on the Pincian. Had a bad cold, and spent the rest of the day in the house. Miss Lander called, & spent the evening.

15 *Monday* Cool & rather unpleasant weather. Still troubled with a cold. Forenoon, walked out along the Corso, and to the Bank, where read newspapers. Then home for the rest of the day.

16 *Tuesday* A bright, cool day. Walked out in the morning, & drew £50 from the bank. Staid in the rest of the day, on account of a cold. Wife & Una went to the Palace of the Caesars.

Had a wretched night with cold and fever, for which took four cold baths, and received some benefit therefrom.

17 *Wednesday* Bright, pleasant, but rather cool. Lay in bed till nearly eleven. Wife, Una, Julian, & Miss Shepard, have gone to the baths of Caracalla. At nearly 3, Rosebud & I have just returned from a walk on the Pincian. Left letters to be posted for F. Bennoch & H. Wilding.

18 *Thursday* Bright & pleasant. At about noon, went with Mamma to the Temple of Vesta &c. Thence crossed by Ponte Rotto and went to St. Peter's by right bank of the Tiber. Left Mamma at St. Peters to see the Cardinals, and got home before 5.

19 *Friday* Morning, walked to the Forum, Colosseum, &c &. and found it very hot in the sun. Returned home about 12 ½, & at 2, went with Mamma to call on the Mountfords

(out) the Waterstons (found them in) the Daubenys (out) & the Westons (in). Met Miss Shepard & Rosebud, & went with them to call on Miss Mitchell, after which, took Rosebud to walk on Pincian

20 *Saturday*   Sat for bust at Miss Lander's.

21 *Sunday*   Walked with wife & all the family to the Coliseum &c. Miss Lander was of the party.

22 *Monday*   A bright, rather cool day. At about ten, went with Mamma to Miss Lander's, & thence to the Vatican Sculpture Gallery, where we staid till 3. Afterwards went into St. Peter's & thence home. Mr Akers called in the eve^g, & took Miss Shepard, Una, & Julian to the Coliseum.

23 *Tuesday*   Wife, Una, Rosebud, & I, breakfasted at W. Story's, Barberini Palace. Afterwards Mamma & I went to lunch at the Misses Weston's, & thence to the Castle of St Angelo, & thence to Pamfili-Doria Villa. Home after six.

24 *Wednesday*   Went with Julian to Braschi Palace; afterwards to Miss Lander's, & sat for bust.

25 *Thursday*   Wrote a note to Mr. Cass. Went to Hooker's bank and read newspapers. About 12, we all went to the Villa Ludovisi, & stayed till after 3. Miss Weston called after our return.
Mr. Cass has sent us three sets of tickets for the Holy Week.

26 *Friday*   Went with my wife to St Peter's, and saw the Pope pray at the Chapel of the Holy Sacrament &c.

27 *Saturday*   Took a walk to the gate of San Paolo, and

saw the Pyramid of Caius Cestius. Evening, Miss Lander & Miss Mitchell called.

28 *Sunday* Wife, Una, & Miss Shepard, went to St Peter's, to see the ceremonies of Palm Sunday. Julian, Rosebud, & I, walked on the Pincian in the morning, & spent the rest of the day at home.

29 *Monday* Morning, walked on the Pincian. Afternoon, went to the Sculpture Gallery of the Capitol, the Forum &c &. Mr. Akers called in the evening.

30 *Tuesday* Walked on the Pincian, & afterwards to Miss Lander's, to sit for bust. Wife came during the sitting. Afterwards, we called at Mr. Reade's studio, & at Mr. Mozier's. Mr. Akers called in the evening, & went with Una & Miss Shepard to see Saint Peter's by moonlight.

31 *Wednesday* Morning, walked on Pincian, & afterwards read newspapers at the Bank. Letter from Ticknor, dated Boston, March 10th. Wife, Una, & Miss Shepard went to St. Peters. Rosebud & I walked on the Pincian, & afterwards went to Miss Landers, & sat for bust. She declares the clay-model finished.

April

1 *Thursday* Wife, Una, & Miss Shepard, went to St. Peter's to see ceremonies of Holy Week. I staid at home with Rosebud, &, being a showery day, did not go out.

2 *Friday* Showery. Morning, walked to the Forum, Coliseum, &c &c. Mr. Mozier the Sculptor called in the evening.

3 *Saturday*   Went with wife & Rosebud to Miss Lander's; afterwards to Miss Hosmer's, & to Mr. Akers' Studio.

4 *Sunday*   Wife, Una, & Miss Shepard drove early to St Peter's, to see ceremonies of Easter Sunday. At about 9, I took Rosebud to Miss Weston's, & afterwards went with Julian to St. Peter's. Staid there a short time, & then Julian & I went to Janiculum Fountain & home over Ponte Rotto. Eve^g, we all went to see Illumination of St. Peters from Monte Cavallo. Being ill with a cold, I came away soon. Mr. Akers & Miss Lander dined with us to-day, but I was not at table

5 *Monday*   Much indisposed with cold & fever. Staid at home all day, and did not go out to witness Fireworks in the evening. Miss Mitchell called, & also Mr Akers in the evening to go with the ladies to fireworks. A letter from Bennoch to-day.

6 *Tuesday*   Cold getting better. Forenoon, went to the Bank & read papers. Afternoon, went with wife and the rest to the Medici Villa, on the Pincian. Then called at Mr. Thompson's studio, & at Mr. Storey's.

7 *Wednesday*   Forenoon, went to Miss Lander's, who put the final touches on the bust. Wife, Una, & Rosebud, went this afternoon to make calls. I walked on the Pincian. Mr. Akers, jr. called, this evening

8 *Thursday*   All of us except Julian went to the Sculpture Gallery of the Capitol. Afterwards to the Palace of the Conservatori, & saw Bronze Wolfe &c &c Finished to-day the lot of wine which we began Febr^y 21$^{st.}$—lasting six weeks & 1 day.

9 *Friday*—Forenoon, went with wife & Rosebud to the

Medici Gardens on the Pincian. Afternoon, the whole family went to the Pontifical Palace (Monte Cavallo,) & afterwards into the Pontifical Gardens. Miss Lander & Mr. Read called in the evening.

10 *Saturday*—Morning, smoked on the Pincian, & afterwards went with wife & Rosebud to Miss Lander's. Thence to Mr. T. B. Reade's studio, & aftewards to Mrs Ward's, at Hotel de Londres. Miss Mitchell called in the evening.

11 *Sunday* Afternoon, we all went to call on Miss Mitchell, who is on the eve of leaving Rome, for Florence & home. Afterwards, walked with Julian on the Pincian. Miss Lander called & spent the evening.

12 *Monday* Morning, walked & smoked on the Pincian. Afterwards, went to St Peter's, where wife, Una, & Julian met me; and we went to the Stanze of Raphael, & the Sculpture Gallery of the Vatican.

13 *Tuesday* Forenoon, went to the Bank, and drew £50, of which paid Miss Lander 20 scudi. Afternoon, walked in the Medici Gardens with Rosebud. Mamma, Miss Shepard, Una, Julian, & Rose, have been at the Borghese Palace. Evening, Miss Lander called, after all but me had gone to bed.

14 *Wednesday* Rainy the early part of the day. Afternoon, walked with Julian to the Forum, and went down into the excavations.

15 *Thursday* A pleasant day. Morning, walked with Rosebud on the Pincian &. At 1 °clock, went with wife & Una to the Colonna Palace. Left them in the Corso, and went to

walk & smoke on the Pincian. Miss Lander dined with us; her farewell visit before returning to America

16 *Friday*   Forenoon, went with wife to the Academy of St Luke's, and afterwards to the Church of San Pietro in Vincoli, to see Michael Angelo's Moses.

17 *Saturday*   Morning, sent letter to Ticknor, through Pakenham & Hooker. All the family then went to Villa Borghese, & returned between 4 & 5 P.M. Eve^g Mr. Akers called.

18 *Sunday*   Miss Shepard and Julian set out at 6 ½, this morning, on a walk along the shore of the Tiber, out of Gate del Popolo, & returned at about 2. Afternoon, I walked out of the Salara Gate, round the base of the city wall, to the Gate del Popolo, & home by the Pincian.

19 *Monday*   We all spent the day, between twelve and three, at the Sculpture Gallery of the Vatican. I afterwards went into St Peters.

20 *Tuesday*   Walked to the Forum, Coliseum &c &c Afternoon, Miss Bremer called. Wife and I afterwards went to the church in Piazza de Popolo, & saw Raphael's angels; to Mr. Bartholomew's sculpture studio; to Mr G. L. Browne's Studio, & saw his beautiful Swiss & Italian landscapes.

21 *Wednesday*   Morning, walked with Rosebud on the Pincian, & then went to Bank to read papers. Saw Mr. T. B. Reade, who gave me two volumes of his poems. Mr. Nichols, the painter, & Mrs. Page called in the evening.

22 *Thursday*   Morning, walked with Rosebud on the

Pincian. Afterwards, went with wife to the Picture & Sculpture galleries of the Capitol, where we met Miss Bremer. I bought a hat, in the Roman fashion.

23 *Friday* Morning, walked on the Pincian, & afterwards read papers at Bank. Evening, wife & I set out at 9 on a walk to the Forum, Coliseum, Capitol &c &c, by moonlight. Returned at about 11 ½.

24 *Saturday* Morning, the whole family went to the top of St. Peters. Afterwards went to the picture gallery of the Vatican, and to the mosaic manufactory. Mr Akers called in the evening.

25 *Sunday* Bright & warm weather. The whole family staid within doors all day.

26 *Monday* Morning, wife, Una, & I, went to Mr. Akers's studio, and afterwards to the Sculpture gallery of the Vatican. Mr. Akers and his brother called in the evening.

27 *Tuesday* Morning, walked on the Pincian, and afterwards read papers at the bank.—At 12 ½, we all went with Mr Akers to Mr. Wilde's studio; thence to Mr. Muller's, and a young German artist's; thence to Castellane's Jeweller's shop. Wife and Miss Shepard went to Villa Albani with the Misses Weston.

28 *Wednesday* Cloudy morning. Staid in the house all day. Letters from E. P. Peabody &c. Mr. Akers called to take leave before going to America.

29 *Thursday* Walked on the Pincian; read papers at the Bank; went to the Sculpture Gallery of the Capitol, and after-

wards to the Coliseum &c. Afternoon, went with wife, Una, Julian, & Rosebud, to the Pincian. Evening, Mr. C. G Thompson called.

30 *Friday* A dull, overcast day. Morning, walked about the city. Went into Wm Story's studio. Afternoon, did nothing of importance, as usual.

May

1 *Saturday* Morning, walked about the city, & went into the Pantheon, the Church of St Agnes (Piazza Navona) & another church. Afternoon, walked with wife, Una & Rosebud, on the Pincian. Very windy all day.

2 *Sunday* Disagreeable weather. Staid in the house all day.

3 *Monday* Unpleasant weather, with showers. Forenoon went to the Bank, & read papers.

4 *Tuesday* Morning, went to the American Consul's (220, Via de Ripetta) to see about passports. Afterwards, to the Bank to read papers. Afternoon, walked with Rosebud on the Pincian

5 *Wednesday* Morning, rambled about the city, & went into one or two churches. Read papers at Bank. Afternoon, walked on the Pincian with Una.

6 *Thursday* Morning, walked about the city, & went into church of St Ignazio; at 12, to the Sculpture Gallery of the Capitol. Afterwards, read papers in Bank. Came home after two, & staid in the house the rest of the day.

7 *Friday*   Forenoon, walked a little about the city. Went with wife into W. Story's studio, to see his statue of Cleopatra, now finished in the clay. Evening, Miss Hosmer dined with us.

8 *Saturday*   Morning, wife & I breakfasted at W^m. Story's; met Mrs. Apthorp & Miss Hunter. After 3, went with Mr. & Mrs Story to call on Mrs. Jameson; afterwards to excavations, beyond the Lateran Gate, & returned about 7 ½.

9 *Sunday*   Forenoon, Mrs. Jameson called. Mamma having lain down, I received her. She invited us to come & see her in the eve^g, & me to drive out with her in the afternoon. At 4 ½ drove out with Mrs. Jameson beyond the tomb of Cecilia Metella. Returned at about ¼ of 7, & excused myself, wife &c from the evening visit.

10 *Monday*   Morning, read newspapers at the Bank. Then went to St. Peter's, and to the Sculpture Gallery of the Vatican. Staid there till about 2 ½, & then came home, after rambling through the city, Ghetto &c.

11 *Tuesday*   Discouraged by the overcast weather, and wind. Staid in the house all day

12 *Wednesday*   Pleasant weather. Mamma, Una, Julian, & I went at about 11 °clock to the Villa Albani, and staid till about 3.

13 *Thursday*   Morning, went to the Bank & read newspapers, and afterwards walked along the Corso. Afternoon, called at Mr. C. G. Thompson's studio. Thence went to the gardens of the French Academy, Villa Medici

14 *Friday*   A heavy thunder shower in the morning. At about 2, with Mamma & Una, went to the gardens of Villa Medici. Thence down into the Piazza d'Espagna & Corso, and took refuge from a shower in Monaldini's bookstore. Evening M^r & Mrs. Apthorp & Miss Hunt called.

15 *Saturday*   Morning, wife & I went to the Sistine Chapel. Afternoon, went with Mr. C. G. Thompson to inquire prices of Vetturi for Florence.
Letter to-day from Mr. Akers, dated Venice.

16 *Sunday*   A very pleasant day. Afternoon, went with wife and Julian to the Borghese Villa, & sat under the trees, beside a fountain. Evening, Mr. Nichols the painter called. Wrote letter to day to Mr. Powers, at Florence, about house there.

17 *Monday*   Forenoon, drew £50 at the Bank, & deposited 100 scudi to pay for bust as the work progresses. Read American newspapers. Then went to St. Peter's & the Sculpture Gallery of the Vatican.

18 *Tuesday*   Morning, went to the Bank, and afterwards to the Pincian Garden. Afternoon, Julian & I went with Mr. Thompson to bargain about vetturo; also visited the church of Santa Maria della Pace.

19 *Wednesday*   Morning, went to the Medici Gardens, and staid till about 12. Afternoon, went with Una, Julian, & Rosebud to the Pincian Gardens

20 *Thursday*   Rosebud's Birth-day, 7 years. Forenoon, went with wife & Julian to the Spada Palace, & to look at lodgings for next winter. Afternoon, walked in the Medici Gardens, & afterwards went with Mr. Thompson to bargain

with vetturini. Engaged a vetturino to take us to Florence, viâ Perugia, in 8 days for 100 scudi including bonamano. Mr & Mrs. Story, & Miss Hosmer called. Mamma, Una, & I, spent the evening at Mr. & Mrs. Thompson's.

21 *Friday* Morning, walked in the Medici Gardens; afterwards read newspapers at the bank. Thence to the American Consul's (Via di Ripetta) to see about Passport. After 2 °clock, Mr. W. C. Bryant called. At 7 °clock, mamma, Miss Shepard, & I (after seeking lodging for next winter) went to take tea with Miss Bremer, who lodges on the Tarpeian Rock.

22 *Saturday* Morning, walked in the Medici Gardens. Went to the bank; bought Murrays guide book at Monaldini's. Afternoon called on Mr. Bryant, at Hotel d'Europe. Later, went with Una & Rosebud to the Pincian

23 *Sunday* At 9½ went to breakfast, with Wm Story. Then walked in the Corso &c. Mr. Chapman & Miss Bryant called. Mr & Mrs. Thompson & family. Una, & I, after tea, walked on the Pincian & by the Tiber. Mrs. Story & Edith called; also Mr. Hooker. Very busy with preparations for journey.

24 *Monday* Left home between 7 & 8 °clock, A. M. with Gaetano, for Florence. He contracts to convey the whole family thither, in 8 days, for 100 scudi, including all expenses. Lunched at Castel Nuovo di Porto. Dined & spent the night at Civita Castellana.

25 *Tuesday* Started at about 5 °clock. Reached Terni between 11 & 12 °clock, & spent the rest of the day there. Prevented from visiting the falls by the rain. Stopt at the Hotel delle tre Colonne.

26 *Wednesday* A fine day. Left Terni at 6 °clock, and reached Spoleto to lunch, and Foligno to dine & sleep.

27 *Thursday* Bleak morning. Left Foligno at 6 ½ °clock, & reached Assissi to lunch. Very windy; but became pleasant in the afternoon, and was beautiful weather when we reached Perugia, where we dined and slept.

28 *Friday* At Perugia, at the Grand Hotel de France. Various rambles, this forenoon, to see churches, public edifices &c. Showery in the afternoon

29 *Saturday* Forenoon, rambled about Perugia, afternoon, started at 3 °clock, & came to Pasignano. Much infested with beggars

30 *Sunday* Left Pasignano at 6 °clock, & came to Arrezza, arriving at about 12. After lunch, wife, Miss Shepard, Julian, & I, went out to see the town. Saw Petrarch's birthplace, & Boccaccio's well. Saw the Cathedral &c. We stop at the Royal Hotel.

31 *Monday* Fine morning. We leave Arrezzo at 20 minutes after 5. Lunch at Incisa. Reach Florence after 5. Drive to Casa del Bello, not taken for us. Fail in seeing Mr. Powers. Go to Hotel. Mr. Powers calls in the evening; also, the Commissionaire of the Casa del Bello.

June

1 *Tuesday* Call with wife, Miss Shepard, & Julian at Mr Powers. Engage to take the Casa del Bello for two months at 50 dollars per month. Draw £50, by bill on Baring Brothers,

through E. Fenzi's & Co. Bank. Leave the Albergo della Fontana, & go to Casa del Bello.

2 *Wednesday*   Forenoon, walk with Miss Shepard & Una. See the Duomo &c. Buy blank book &c &c. Look at mosaics. Spend the rest of the day at home.

3 *Thursday*   Beautiful weather. Staid about the house and in the garden all day

4 *Friday*   After breakfast walked down into the city, & returned at about 10½ °clock. Did not go out the rest of the day. Warm, but very agreeable weather.

5 *Saturday*   After breakfast, walked into the city. Evening, again walked into the city with Mamma, Una, & Julian. Returning, called at Mr. Powers'.

6 *Sunday*   Beautiful weather. Staid at home all day. Towards evening, Mr. Powers called

7 *Monday*   After breakfast, called at Messrs. Plowden & French, who had notified me of letters there for me. Found it a mistake; they being for a Mr William Hawthorne. Evening, called with wife & Una on the Bryants, who are at the Hotel de New York.

8 *Tuesday*   Morning, went to the gallery of sculpture & painting at Uffizzi Palace. Mr. Bryant called while I was gone, and mamma. Just as dinner was done, Mr. R. Browning called. Evening, went to see the Brownings, at Casa Guidi, & met Mr. Bryant & daughter, Mr. & Mrs. Eckers, & Miss Fanny Howarth.

9 *Wednesday*   Mamma, Una, & Miss Shepard, went to Uffizzi gallery, & Julian to a museum. I staid at home with Rosebud. Paid (by check) 500 pauls for first month's rent, & 8 pauls for the water. Did not stir from the house to-day

10 *Thursday*   In the morning, visited (with my wife) the grand-ducal apartments at the Pitti Palace. We afterwards went into the picture-gallery, where my wife left me. Saw Miss Fanny Howarth there. Leaving the gallery, I went into the Boboli gardens. Wife, Una, & Rosebud, called to see Mrs. Browning.

11 *Friday*   Morning, went to the Uffizzi Gallery. Afterwards called at Fenzi & Co's and drew a check. On my way home, went into the Museum of Natural History.

12 *Saturday*   Morning, called at Powers' studio, with wife, and had a long talk about professional matters. Afterwards went with her to Pitti palace.

13 *Sunday*   Very warm. Staid in the house all day.

14 *Monday*   In the forenoon, went with wife to the Uffizzi Gallery. A hot day.

15 *Tuesday*   Morning, walked into the city. Stept into the duomo, and a church or two. Too hot to walk about. Mr. & Mrs. Powers called in the evening.

16 *Wednesday*   Morning, went with Miss Shepard & Una to the Uffizzi gallery. Staid at home the rest of the day. Very hot.

17 *Thursday*   Morning, went with wife to the Duomo, and afterwards to the Academy of the Fine Arts.

18 *Friday* Morning, walked into the city, to the Baptistery, the Duomo &. and afterwards to the gallery of the Pitti Palace.

19 *Saturday* Morning, went with wife to church of St. Lorenzo, & afterwards to Uffizzi gallery.

20 *Sunday* Very warm. After dinner, walked with wife, Una, and Julian, in the Boboli Gardens, and saw the sunset.

21 *Monday* Morning, went with wife to the gallery of Pitti Palace. A heavy thunder-shower.

22 *Tuesday* Ill with cold and fever. Did not go out. Wife, Una, & Miss Shepard, went to Miss Howarth's in the evening.

23 *Wednesday* Still much indisposed. Staid at home Cloudy & cool weather.

24 *Thursday* Still indisposed. Staid at home. Mr. Powers called in the evening.
Cloudy & cool weather

25 *Friday* Still unwell. Mamma &. went to Mr. Brownings. Cloudy & cool. Staid at home all day.

26 *Saturday* Rather better. Forenoon, went to the Bank, drew for £50, & left it to be checked for. Read papers. Went into the Ufizzi gallery. Evening, took cab with wife & Una, & went to Miss Blagden's at Belsguado, to spend the evening. Home at 10½

27 *Sunday* Afternoon, went with Julian to the Corso, to see the horse-race, in honor of the Feast of St. John.

28 *Monday*   Forenoon, went with wife to the church of Santa Croce, the Palazzo Riccardi &c. Afternoon, Miss Blagden took wife & Julian to see villa, outside of the city.

29 *Tuesday*   At home most of the day. At about 6. P. M. went to see the horse-race, being the winding-up of the Feast of St. John.

30 *Wednesday*   Morning, went with Julian to the Uffizi Gallery &c. Home before 12.

July

1 *Thursday*   Morning, went with wife & Una to Michael Angelo's house; not admitted. Afterwards visited Palazzo Vecchio. Thence to the Uffizzi Gallery.

2 *Friday*   Morning, went with wife to Duomo, Baptistery, &c.; and left her at Egyptian Museum   Went to Bank, drew cheque, & read Galignani.

3 *Saturday*   Forenoon, went with wife to the church of Santa Maria Novella. Afterwards, to the Uffizzi Gallery, where we saw the rooms containing bronzes.

4 *Sunday*   Evening, went with Mamma and Una to pay a visit to the Powers. A showery evening.

5 *Monday*   Forenoon, went to the Pitti Palace.

6 *Tuesday*   Forenoon, went with Mamma to the Church of the Annunziata.

7 *Wednesday*   Forenoon, went with Rosebud to Pitti

Palace, Una & Miss Shepard also. Came away with Rosebud, & went to the Museum of Natural History, where found Mamma & Julian. Home at about 1 °clock.

8 *Thursday*   Staid at home in the early part of the day. At about 4 ¼, drove with wife, Una & Rosebud, to Miss Blagden's at Bellosguado; took an outside glimpse of the villa we mean to hire. After our return, I walked into the city.

9 *Friday*   Forenoon, went with wife to the church of San Marco; afterwards to the Uffizzi Gallery.

10 *Saturday*   In the forenoon, went with wife to the picture-gallery of the Pitti Palace.

11 *Sunday*   Staid at home all day. Quite cool weather.

12 *Monday*   Staid at home till after dinner. Then walked to the Cascine. Mamma and Una took a drive with Mrs. Blagden.

13 *Tuesday*   Forenoon, with Mamma to Goodban's, the booksellers; thence to the Academy of Belles Artes. Afterwards to the Bank, drew cheque, and read Galignani. Home towards 3.

14 *Wednesday*   Staid at home all day, principally employed sketching plot of a Romance. Mild & beautiful weather.

15 *Thursday*   Forenoon, went with Mamma to Bargello, Church of the Badia, and to the Ufizzi gallery.

16 *Friday*   Staid at home all day. Slept ill, on account of a boring headache. Took a cold bath in the night, and felt better.

17 *Saturday*   Staid at home all day. Miss Howarth called in the forenoon and afternoon. I began rough draft of a Romance.

18 *Sunday*   Staid at home all day. Very warm.

19 *Monday*   Forenoon, went with Mamma to the Pitti Palace.

20 *Tuesday*   Staid at home all day. Very warm

21 *Wednesday*   In the forenoon, Miss Howarth came & sketched a crayon-portrait of me—for herself. Staid at home all day. Very warm.

22 *Thursday*   An overcast and thunderous day. Staid at home till after tea; then walked into the city as far as the Duomo, and home by way of the Ponte Vecchio.

23 *Friday*   Staid at home till evening. Then took a walk with Mamma, Una & Julian, out of the Porta Romana, to the Duke's villa, & home by Porta San Gallo.

24 *Saturday*   Forenoon, went to the Ufizzi Gallery.

25 *Sunday*   At about 1, walked towards the suspension-bridge, to meet Mamma, who had gone in quest of Julian. He had got back without seeing her. I met Mamma & returned with her. After tea, went with Una to the Boboli gardens, and afterwards over the Ponte Vecchio, & home by Ponte Trinita. Julian quite unwell & feverish with walking in the sun.

26 *Monday*   Staid at home all day. Very warm.

27 *Tuesday* Rec^d letters from E. P. Peabody &c &c. Forenoon, went to the Pitti Palace, & returned between 12 & 1. After tea, went in to see the Powers, with Mamma & Una, & sat on their terrace till nearly 10.

Miss Howarth called, just before we went, but did not see us.

A very warm day.

28 *Wednesday* Staid at home all day.

29 *Thursday* Morning, went to the Bank, drew on Barings for £50, and made arrangements about Passport. Afterwards to Or' San Michele, where met Mamma, Una, & Miss Shepard. Went with them to the Ufizzi Gallery.

30 *Friday* Staid at home all day

31 *Saturday* Morning, went to Bank, & read papers. Afterwards to Ufizzi Gallery.

August

1 *Sunday* At 10. A. M. or thereabouts, we left the Casa del Bello. Julian had preceded us to the Villa Montauto, with Bob Powers. Una and I next walked thither; and Mamma, Miss Shepard, & Rosebud (with the servant) followed in a carriage. We take up our residence at the Villa.

2 *Monday* Staid at home all day. Wife tired out, and keeps her bed. Miss Blagden & Miss Bracken call in the afternoon, and are received by Miss Shepard & Una. Also, William Story, whom I saw.

3 *Tuesday* Morning, walked into the city with Julian, & called at Mr. Powers' Studio. He is at Leghorn. Thence to the Bank & read papers Thence to Pitti Palace. Reached home about 1 °clock. Afternoon, Una drove into town with Miss Blagden & Mrs. Trollope. Mamma, Julian, & I, saw the sun set from the top of the tower.

4 *Wednesday* Staid at home all day. Una & Miss Shepard walked into town in the morning, & spent the day there.

[5 *Thursday* Entry excised.]

6 *Friday* Staid at home all day. Miss Blagden & Miss Bracken called in the evening, & saw Mamma.

7 *Saturday* Staid at home till 8, P. M. Then went with Mamma to spend the evening at Miss Blagden's. Mr. Boot & Mr Trollope were there. A cloudy & cool day.

8 *Sunday* Staid at home all day.
Major Gregory called in the evening.
An overcast and rather cool day.

[9 *Monday* Entry excised.]

10 *Tuesday* Staid at home all day.
Not very bright weather.
Major Gregory & Miss Crossman called in the afternoon. I did not see them, but Mamma did.

11 *Wednesday* Staid at home till five °clock. Then drove into town with Miss Blagden, Miss Bracken, & Mamma, and called on Mr. Kirkup, at a house by the Ponte Vecchio. Back at about 8 °clock.

12 *Thursday* Staid at home all day. After tea, climbed the tower to see the sunset; afterwards, sat out of doors, with Mamma, Una, & Julian, enjoying the starlight, till nine °clock. Saw the new moon.

13 *Friday* Staid at home all day. Mamma walked into town in the morn^g, & returned between 5 & 6. Eve^g, Mr Mackay (son of Dr Mackay, the poet) called. Letter from Mr. Thompson, Rome

14 *Saturday* Staid at home all day. At night, much tormented with musquitoes.

15 *Sunday* Staid at home all day.

16 *Monday* Staid at home all day.
Preston & Louisa Powers called at tea-time.
Mamma took a country-drive with Miss Blagden & Miss Bracken.

17 *Tuesday* Staid at home all day.
Mamma drove to town with Miss Blagden, & Una & Miss Shepard walked into town.
This night was a horrible and bloody one—the worst, so far, of the Musquito War.

18 *Wednesday* Staid at home till about 6. P.M.
Then went with Mamma & Rosebud to call on Major Gregorie &c. at Columbaia Villa.
Preston Powers came to our villa, with a letter to Una from Fanny Wrigley.

19 *Thursday* Overcast; at noon, violent wind & rain. Staid at home all day. After 6, Col. McVea called, with letter of introduction from Genl Pierce, & letters from O'Sullivan.

20 *Friday*   Set out at about 4, & walked into town, with wife & Una, & called on Col. McVea & ladies, at Hotel de New York.

21 *Saturday*   After breakfast, walked into town, called at Bank, with letter to be posted for Gen¹ Pierce. Afterwards, to Pitti Palace. Got back at 1. Mr Mackay called & took tea; and Mamma, Mr. M^cK. & I, spent the eve^g at Miss Blagden's.

22 *Sunday*   Staid at home all day.
Miss Blagden & Miss Bracken took tea, & spent the evening. Comfortably cool weather for a day or two past.

23 *Monday*   Staid at home all day.

24 *Tuesday*   Staid at home all day.
In the evening, Mamma & Miss Shepard went to attend a spiritual session at Miss Blagden's.

25 *Wednesday*   Staid at home all day.
Mamma & the children had communications with spirits through Miss Shepard, a writing medium.
Flummery & delusion.
Evening, climbed our tower and staid there in the moonlight till 10. Preston & Anne Powers came with a letter from Mr. Thompson, Rome. Answered it.

26 *Thursday*   Staid at home all day. Rainy & cool.

27 *Friday*   Staid at home all day. Preston & Anne Powers called in the afternoon. Mr. Booth & daughter in the eve^g.

28 *Saturday*   Staid at home till eve^g. Miss Shepard & Una spent the day in town. Mamma & I spent eve^g at Miss Blagden's, where were Mr. Powers, Mr. Trollope, & Mr. Boot.

29 *Sunday* Staid at home all day. Major Gregorie called after dinner.

30 *Monday* Staid at home all day.

31 *Tuesday* Staid at home all day.

September

1 *Wednesday* Staid at home all day.

2 *Thursday* After breakfast, walked with Mamma into Florence; went to Uffizzi gallery, & saw drawings. Afterwards, to museum of Galileo. Reached home between 2 & 3, leaving Mamma to rest herself in Boboli Gardens.

3 *Friday* Staid at home all day.

4 *Saturday* Staid at home all day. Eve^g, Mamma, Miss Shepard, & Una, went to take tea at Miss Blagden's.
Mamma drove into town with Miss B. in the forenoon.

5 *Sunday* Staid at home all day. Beautiful weather. Mamma sat out of doors, under a tree, much of the time.

6 *Monday* After breakfast, walked into town. Went to the Bank, & got letters from C. G. Thompson, Rome, & Genl Pierce, Geneva. Afterwards went to Ufizzi Gallery. Reached home before 2 °clock.

7 *Tuesday* Staid at home all day.
Very rainy.

8 *Wednesday*   Morning, Una & Miss Shepard went to town. An overcast day, threatening showers.

I myself staid at home all day.

At 5 °clock, Mamma, with Miss Blagden, drove to call on Major Gregory and into town.

Not very well.

9 *Thursday*   After breakfast, walked into town, visited a church or two, the Bank, the Pitti Palace, the Boboli Gardens; & home by ½ past 1.

Una, Miss Shepard, & Julian, also went to town, & returned at about 5.

Beautiful sunset, seen from the Tower.

10 *Friday*   Staid at home all day.

Mamma & Miss Shepard spent the day in town.

11 *Saturday*   Staid at home all day. Evening, Mamma & I took tea at Miss Blagdens with the British Minister &c &c &c

12 *Sunday*   Staid at home all day. Louisa & Anne Powers, and Preston P. dined & spent the day here. Mr. & Mrs. Powers and daughter Florence came in the evening.

13 *Monday*   Staid at home all day.

14 *Tuesday*   Mamma, Miss Shepard, Una, & Julian, started for Fiesole, at 7 °clock. Rosebud & I walked into town; and I left her at Mr Powers. Went to Bank & Uffizzi gallery. Returned with Rosebud at about 2. Mamma & party returned about 4. Evening, Mamma & Miss Shepard went to Miss Blagden's.

15 *Wednesday*   Staid at home all day.

16 *Thursday*   Morning, went with Mamma & Una to town   I got back about 2; Mamma & Una about 5 ½. Genl Mallette (American Consul) called. Also, Miss Bracken; also, Mr. Mackay; also, Mr. & Mrs. Powers; also, Madam Miniati, with a gentleman. Mr. Mackay staid to tea.
Beautiful weather.

17 *Friday*   Staid at home all **day**.

18 *Saturday*   Mamma, Miss Shepard, & Una, spent the day in town. I staid at home. Eve^g, Mamma went to see Miss Blagden, & I called for her at 10 ½.

19 *Sunday*   Staid at home all day.
Afternoon, measured the height of our tower, & found it about 85 feet from base to top of battlement.
Miss Howarth & Madam Tassinari called in the evening.

20 *Monday*   Morning, thick fog. At 9, Mamma & I walked to Florence; shopped, looked at mosaics. I went to Bank, afterwards joined Mamma at Ufizzi gallery. Called with her on Genl & Mrs. Mallette at Hotel de Ville. Reached home between 4 & 5. Had a terrible night with musquitoes. Drew for £50 to-day.

21 *Tuesday*   Staid at home all day.

22 *Wednesday*   Morning, walked to town, went to Bank, & afterwards to Pitti Palace. Una, Miss Shepard, & Julian, likewise went to town. M^r & Mrs Story called to-day. Dr. — (a Pole) called in the evening.

23 *Thursday*   Staid at home all day.
Gen¹ & Mrs. Mallet called. Wife saw them; I did not.

24 *Friday*   After breakfast, Una & I walked to town. Went
to Ufizzi Gallery, & afterwards to Convent of San Minauto.
Bo't Opera-glass, price 25 pauls. Home by 2 °clock.

25 *Saturday*   Staid at home all day. Una went to town in
the morning; Mamma & Miss Shepard in the afternoon.

26 *Sunday*   Staid at home all day.

27 *Monday*   Morn^g, walked to town with Julian, & went
to Bank. Afterwards, met Mamma & Una at Duomo. Bought
mosaic. Left mamma, Una, & Julian, & went to Pitti Palace.
I got home at about 2 °clock. Eve^g, mamma went to Miss
Blagden's, & I called for her at 10 °clock.

28 *Tuesday*   Morning, walked with Una & Julian to town.
Went to Bank to see about passport. Thence went to Ufizzi
gallery. All at home by 2 °clock. Spent the evening with
mamma & Una at Miss Blagden's, where were Mr. Powers
&c &c

29 *Wednesday*   After breakfast, went to town, and accompanied Mr. & Mrs Powers, and her father, to see the
statue of Webster, just cast at the foundry. Rambled about
Florence, and got home at about 2.
Evening, looked at the comet & stars from the top of our
tower.

30 *Thursday*   Morning, walked with Una & Julian to
town; went to Pitti Palace, to various shops, and to the Bank.
Drew for £10. On our way home, called on Miss Blagden.

Reached home about 2 ½. Mr. Powers & two daughters called to take leave, in the evening.

October

1 *Friday*   At 7. A.M. started by railway, all of us, for Siena; arrived at about 11, & went to Aquila Nera, where lunched. Mr. & Mrs Story called, & helped us to find a lodging, where we are established. Eve^g, went with Miss Shepard to railway, to see about baggage. All of it came safe.

2 *Saturday*   Wrote journal. Strolled about Siena &c &c &c.

3 *Sunday*   We all of us went to spend the day (beginning from 1 or 2 °clock) with Mr & Mrs. Story, at Villa Belvidere, a mile or two from the city. Dined, took tea, and were brought home after 10. P. M. A very pleasant day.

4 *Monday*   Rambled about Siena. Wife has caught a cold. Towards evening, Mr & Mrs. Black, & Mr. & Mrs Story called. Una went to spend the night at Mrs. Story's.

5 *Tuesday*   Morning, visited Belle Arti Instituto, with Mamma & Julian. Strolled about the city. A showery day.

6 *Wednesday*   Morning, removed to Aquila Nera. Julian & I took a walk out of the city. Una returned with Mr. & Mrs. Story, but went back again. After dinner, I took a walk out of another gate of the city. Strolled about the city &c &c &c

7 *Thursday*   Morning, Miss Shepard & Julian walked out to breakfast with Mr. & Mrs Story. Mamma, Rosebud, & I, went to Palazzo Publico; afterwards to Cathedral. M^r & Mrs S. came in the afternoon, & bro't Una, but took her back again.

8 *Friday*   Strolled about the city, went to the Cathedral, and a short way out of the city-gates. Afternoon, Mr. Story called. Mamma spent the day chiefly in Cathedral. Eve^g we all went out to see the comet.

9 *Saturday*   Strolled about town, to the Cathedral &c. Una came home, & brought Edith Story to spend the day. Afternoon, Julian & I took a walk out of the city, railway-gate.

10 *Sunday*   Forenoon, went to the Cathedral. Afterwards walked with baby. Afternoon, took a walk out of the city.

11 *Monday*   Went to the Cathedral; strolled about the city. Took a walk out of one gate and in at another. Mr. Story called. Una & Julian walked to Villa Borghese, Marciana, to dine with the Blacks.

12 *Tuesday*   Visited the Cathedral, strolled about the city. At mid-day, Mr. Story called. Afternoon, to the Cathedral again. Then took a walk out of the Tufi gate. Evening showery. Paid the Vetturino 35 Tuscan scudi for half journey to Rome; and the hotel keeper 35 more, in full

13 *Wednesday*   All of us left Siena, by Vettura (driven by Costatino Bacci,) at 6 °clock. Lunched at San Querico. Dined and slept at the Posta, Radicofani. Very cool weather; dismal air.

14 *Thursday*   Left Radicofani at 6 °clock; cool morning. Lunched Bolsena. Stopt for dinner and the night at L'Aigle Noir, Viterbo. Tried the Est wine of Montefiascone.

15 *Friday*   Wandered about Viterbo, visited Cathedral &c. Left Viterbo at about 11, A. M. Reached Le Sette Vene between 4 & 5; dined & slept there.

16 *Saturday* Left Sette Vene after 7, & reached Rome at about 11. Very slight examination by Customs office, at Porto del Popolo. Proceeded to 68, Piazza Poli. Then to the bank, & drew £50; paid Vetturino 42.20, balance. After dinner, walked with Rosebud on Pincian, along Corso &c. Beautiful day. Mr. & Mrs Thompson called, immediately on our arrival.

17 *Sunday* Staid at home all day and wrote journal. Mr. Thompson called before dinner, & spoke of Miss Lander. What a pity!

18 *Monday* Morn^g, wrote to Russell Sturgis about letter of credit. Went to Bank, to Pincian, to American Consul's, to St. Peter's, to Statue Gallery of the Capitol. Rec^d letter from J. T. Fields. Mr Story & Edith called; also, Mr. Hooker. Also, in the evening, Miss Hosmer.

19 *Tuesday* Morning, went to Pincian; afterwards to Bank. Along the Corso &c. Evening, Mr. Mozier called & left some newspapers. Afterwards, wife & I took a short walk by moonlight.

20 *Wednesday* Forenoon, went with wife to Corsini Palace (Trastevere) stopping into church of Andrea delle Valle &c. Afterwards to St Peters. Home by 3 or 4 °clock. American Vice Consul (Mr. Ardesson) had called

21 *Thursday* Morn^g, American Vice Consul called with permission to reside for 6 months. Mamma, Rose, & I, went to see my bust. I went to bank & read newspapers. About 6 °clock, Mr. & Mrs Story called. Showery evening, and thunder storm during the night.

22 *Friday* Rainy day. Forenoon, went to Bank, & read

papers. Staid at home the rest of the day. Much upset by the Sirocco.

23 *Saturday*   Morning, walked to the gate of Sta Maria Maggiore, saw the tomb of Eurysaces &c. Thence to St John Lateran; thence to Coliseum. The Misses Weston called.

24 *Sunday*   Disagreeable weather. A Sirocco. Staid at home all day. In the evening, went with Mamma to the Misses Weston, Palazzo Negroni. Met Mr. & Mrs Story, Mr. & Mrs. Motley, Mr (of the Edinburgh Review) & Mrs. Reeve &c &c &c. Very wet in the evening, & thunder-showery all night.

25 *Monday*   Copious showers. Began to write a Romance. At about 1 °clock, went to Bank & read papers. Went with Mr. Hooker to see his apartments, which he wishes to let to Gen¹ Pierce.
Very dull and discontented, this bad weather affecting us all unfavorably.

26 *Tuesday*   A day of cloud & showers. In the afternoon, called on Mr. Thompson at his studio. Went with him to Mr. Rogers' studio, to see bas-reliefs for bronze-door. During the forenoon, I scribbled Romance.
Una is unwell to-day.

27 *Wednesday*   Morning, scribbled romance poorly. Recᵈ letter from Gen¹ Pierce at Florence. Wrote to him. Went to Bank & read papers; thence to American Consul's to see about letters for Gen¹ Pierce. Thence to St Peter's.
Una seriously ill; feverish. Mamma sits up with her to-night.

28 *Thursday*   Scribbled Romance ineffectually. Went to

the Bank, and walked on the Pincian. Una much indisposed. Afternoon, walked with Rosebud to Coliseum &c. Doctor Franco came to see Una in the even^g; also, Mr & Mrs. Story called.

A letter from Mr Tucker (Consul at L'pool) and Mr Wilding, to-day

29 *Friday* Staid at home all day. Una is little or no better. Doctor Franco came in the forenoon, and again in the evening. Very bad weather. At about 10, P. M. went to Dr. Franco's, to ask directions about medicine. Found him not at home. Mr Rakerman called to-day.

30 *Saturday* Very dark and rainy morning. Una is considerably better. Doctor Franco came at about 9 °clock. I staid at home all day. Afternoon & evening, Una not so well. Dr. Franco came again, & Mr Hooker called.

31 *Sunday* Very disagreeable weather. I staid at home. Mr Thompson called. Una alternately worse & better through the day; and Dr. Franco came three times. Una is taken to another chamber.

November

1 *Monday* Letter from Barings, inclosing credit for £300. Dr. Franco came at about 10. Una decidedly has Roman fever, but not violently. Forenoon, went to Bank, & read papers. Walked to St. Peter's. Doctor Franco came during the day, & at about 9. P. M. In the evening, Una's fever somewhat subsides.
Very cool weather, cloudy, a sprinkle of rain.

2 *Tuesday*   Una has passed a quiet night. Dr. Franco comes at about 9. Very cool, bright morning. At about noon, I went to the Bank, & afterwards took a walk about the ground of Villa Borghese. Dr. Franco came again at mid-day. Mr. & Mrs. Story called in the afternoon; and Dr. Franco came again at 9, P. M. Una began to take quinine to-day, but as yet with no improvement.

3 *Wednesday*   Una seems not to mend. Dr. E. came at 9 °clock. A cold, gray day. Dr. F. came again at mid-day. Una still in a smouldering fever. About dark, Mr & Mrs. Story called. Dr. F. came again at 10 P. M. The fever then subsiding, Una took quinine hourly during the night.

I did not go out, all day.

4 *Thursday*   Una has passed a comfortable night, & the fever not yet returned. Dr. Franco came at about 8. I went to the Bank, read papers, & walked along the Corso. Dr. F. came again during the day, & at about 10, P. M. Una has continued comfortable.

An exceedingly chill & disagreeable day.

5 *Friday*   Dr. F. comes at 9 °clock, & finds Una not yet quite free from the fever. The weather as disagreeable as can be. The Doctor came again in the course of the day. I did not go out.

6 *Saturday*   Una convalescent.— Dr. Franco came in the morning. I went to the Bank & to St Peters. Very cool weather. Mr Mountford called, (saw nobody) Mrs. Motley. Very cold

7 *Sunday*   Cold, bright morn^g. Una doing well; she sits up for the first time. Doctor Franco came in the forenoon.

Julian & I walked to Monte Testacchio &c &c. Towards evening, Mr & Mrs Story & Edith called to see Una.
Rainy & cold at nightfall.

8 *Monday*   Una still improving. Dr F. came at 9 °clock. I wrote notes to Mr Tucker (Consul, L'pool) & Mr Wilding. Went to Bank, and afterwards to Sculpture Gallery of Capitol. A showery day.

9 *Tuesday*—Una still convalesces. A cool, bright day.
I went to the Medici & Pincian Gardens, & to the Bank. Una removes into my study. In the evening, Miss Lander & her sister (just from America) called, and were not admitted.
Slept in my own chamber, this night; Una having removed to the next.

10 *Wednesday*   A cold, rainy day, and a fall of snow in the forenoon. Una goes on well. Dr. F. came at about 3 °clock. Sunshine in the afternoon. Miss Lander sent in a card but was not seen. Miss Hosmer called.
Staid at home all day.

11 *Thursday*   Bright, frosty morning. At about noon, walked with Mamma to Bank, & shopping &c &. Afterwards (with mamma) to Coliseum, Forum &.
We had fires to-day (for the first time) in the dining-room and parlour.
Bo't a hat $3.50

12 *Friday*   Cold, gray day. Dr. Franco came, & found Una pretty well. Mamma walked out with Rosebud. I staid at home all day. Eve^g, rec^d some letters & Longfellow's poem, bro't by Miss Lander

13 *Saturday* A very rainy day. Wrote note to Miss Lander, & took it to the Bank. Most of us (especially mamma) poisoned by the fumes of charcoal in braziers Sent for Dr Franco in the evening, but found him not at home.

14 *Sunday* Mamma better; the rest of the patients well. Dr. Franco came in the forenoon. A cloudy, warm day. Mamma & Una drove out with Mrs. Story. Mr. Thompson called. I did not go out.

15 *Monday* Showery, warm Sirocco morning. At 1 °clock, went to Bank & read newspapers. Very rainy all day.
Scribbled romance a little in the forenoon.
Bo't a load of wood.

16 *Tuesday* Still warm and wet; horribly depressing weather. At about 1, went to Bank & drew for £50. Evening, Miss Shepard went to the opera with Mr. Stone.
I have a cold.
Mr. & Mrs Geo Jones (of Georgia) called, but did not come in

17 *Wednesday* Still cloudy & showery. Some more letters, which came by Miss Lander. Having a cold, I staid at home all day.
M^r & Miss Bracken called.
Scribbled romance a little.

18 *Thursday* Cloudy, with glimpses of sunshine. My cold was troublesome, last night; rather better to-day. At about 12 ½ went out with mamma, & called on Miss Cushman (out,) on M^r & Mrs. Jones (out,) on M^r & Mrs. Motley (he in) on the Misses Weston, (at lunch so did not go in,) at the Bank, & at Mr. Thompson's studio (in.) Beautiful warm day.

19 *Friday* A day between cloud & sunshine, but warm. My cold still troublesome. Mamma drove out, with Una & Rosebud, at noon. I went to the Bank, and afterwards walked on the Pincian.

20 *Saturday* Warm morning; sunshine & cloud. At 1, walked out, went to the Bank, along the Corso, &c. Forenoon, scribbled Romance a little, as usual. Cold better.

21 *Sunday* Tremendous thunder & lightning last night. Showery morning. At about 1, Mamma drove out, with Una and Rosebud.
I staid within doors, all day.

22 *Monday* A showery day. Forenoon, I went to St Peter's, and at 12, to the Sculpture Gallery of the Vatican. Home by 2 °clock. Una being rather feverish, Dr. Franco came in the evening.

23 *Tuesday* Una pretty well. A bright morning. At about 1, I went to the Bank, and afterwards rambled about the city. The day overclouds again. Una's fever reappears. I went to Dr. Franco's at 7 ½; he was not in, but came at 10, P. M. or thereabouts.

24 *Wednesday* Cool and uncertain day. Una has past a feverish night, but is rather cooler this morning. Dr. Franco came at noon. Afternoon, I walked with Rosebud to the Pincian and the Borghese grounds. Una had a feverish day, but became more comfortable in the evening. Dr. Franco came again, after 10, P. M.

25 *Thursday* A bright morning. Una has passed a comfortable night. The Doctor came in the forenoon. Between

12 & 1, I walked with Rosebud to the Coliseum &c.; afterwards went to the Bank & read papers.

The weather has been particularly fine to-day.

26 *Friday* Sunny morning. Una seems quite restored. Dr Franco came in the forenoon. Before 2, I walked with Rosebud to the Medici Gardens, & along the Pincian.

27 *Saturday* An overcast day. At about 1, I went to the Bank; then rambled about the city. Miss Bracken called to see Una, afternoon; also, Edith Story.

28 *Sunday* A rainy morning, after a very rainy night. I staid within doors all day. Afternoon, Miss Bracken called; also Mr. Browning, Dr. Franco, Mrs. Story, M^r. & Mrs. Thompson & Cora

29 *Monday* A pleasant day. Mamma drove out with Una & Rosebud. Before 2, I went to Bank & read papers; afterwards called on Mr. & Mrs Jones, & saw the latter. (63, Corso) Then walked on the Pincian. Evening, Mr. Thompson called with Mr. Spicer, an Englishman.

Mamma is much indisposed.

30 *Tuesday* A day of half-sunshine. Mamma is rather better; Una tolerably comfortable. Before 2 °clock, I walked to the Pincian and along the Corso, with Rosebud. Mr Motley called in the afternoon.

December

1 *Wednesday* An overcast morning; and a very rainy day. Staid within doors. In the evening, and till bed-time, a thunder storm, with torrents of rain.

2 *Thursday* An overcast morning. Rain during the day. At 2, I went to the bank, and afterwards walked about the city. The Pantheon is unapproachable on account of water. Afternoon, M^r & Miss Bracken called, also, Dr. Franco.

Starlight when I went to bed.

3 *Friday* Overcast & rainy morning. After 2, I walked to the Coliseum; thence to bridge of St Angelo &c   Tiber overflows the street near the bridge. Afternoon, Mr Motley called. Evening, Miss Cushman, Miss Hosmer, & Miss Stebbins, called. Disagreeable day.

4 *Saturday* Cloudy & showery day. At noon, I went to the bank & read papers. Evening, I went to take tea at Mrs Motley's; present, Mr & Mrs Jones & daughter; Mr & Mrs Story & Edith; & Mr. Browning.

5 *Sunday* A tolerably fine day. About 2 °clock, walked out with Una (her first walk) for half an hour. Afterwards, walked with Rosebud along the Corso, to the Pincian &c. A note from Miss Lander in the evening. Wrote an answer by bearer. Dr Franco came in the afternoon.

6 *Monday* Chill, dark, rainy morning.
Una not so well to-day
It rained all day, and I did not go out.

7 *Tuesday* A bright morning. Dr F. came early & found Una in another attack of Roman fever. At 2, I went to the bank & read papers; afterwards called on the Brownings (43, Bocca di Leone) & saw Mrs. B. Afterwards walked on the Pincian, & met Mr. Story & Mr. Cranch.

This has been a fine day.

8 *Wednesday* A bright morning. Una more comfortable
Dr Franco came early. At about 2, I walked out with Rosebud,
but met the Westons, who took her to drive with them. I then
went to St. Peter's.
Dr Franco came again in the evening.
This has been a fine day.

9 *Thursday* An overcast morning. Una still in the clutch
of the Roman fever. Dr. Franco came before 10. About 2, I
went to the bank & afterwards rambled a little about the city.
Una becomes more comfortable. Mʳ & Miss Bracken called.
Dr. Franco came again in the evening.
A rainy afternoon & evening.

10 *Friday* A dim morning, with some watery sunshine.
Dr Franco came in the mornᵍ, & found Una better. At 2, I
walked to the Tarpeian Rock &c &c. Sprinkles of rain. Mʳ.
Browning called to day.

11 *Saturday* Chill, overcast mornᵍ. Doctor F came in the
forenoon, Una progressing. Between 1 & 2, I went to the
Bank, & afterwards to the Pincian; then called on Mr.
Thompson. An unpleasant day.

12 *Sunday* Dr Franco came in the forenoon, & found
Una about the same. At 2, I walked with Julian along the
Tiber to the Ponte Molle, & home by the Via Flaminia.
A fine day.

13 *Monday* A bright morning. Dr. F. came in the morning. At 12, Mamma & I went out & called at C Cranch's
studio; afterwards to the Via Babuino, Via Condotti &c &

bought Pliny; doves (in small mosaic) & a bronze lizard. I then went to the Bank & read papers. Mamma afterwards walked out with Rosebud.

Miss Bracken called. A very fine day.

14 *Tuesday*   A bright morning. At 12, Mamma drove out with Una. About 2, I walked to the Coliseum, to the Temple of Vesta, the Island of the Tiber &c. A beautiful afternoon. Mamma is taken with violent pains of a thermatic character. Dr. Franco is sent for & came in the evening. But little better at 11 ½ P.M.

15 *Wednesday*   A bright morning. Mamma rather more comfortable. Una doing well. Dr. F. came early. Rosebud not very well. Miss Shepard & Una & Rosebud drove out, for an hour, at 12. At 3, I walked on the Pincian & along the Corso. Dr. Franco came again in the evening.

This has been a fine day.

16 *Thursday*   A bright morning. Dr F. came about 10, & finds mamma rather better; Una & Rose doing pretty well. Miss Shepard, & Una & Rosebud drove out at 12. Between 1 & 2, I went to the Bank & read Galignani; afterwards to St Peters. Miss Bracken called. Mamma being no better, I went at 10 P. M for Dr. F. Not at home, but came afterwards. A fine day.

17 *Friday*   Bright morning. Dr. F. came at 10; found Mamma no better; Una & Rosebud doing well. Miss Shepard, Una, & Rosebud drove out. I staid at home till even^g; then walked to the bridge of St. Angelo. Dr Franco came in the eve^g. Patients better. A pleasant, cool day.

18 *Saturday*   Mamma better. I walked out at 10, to Bank & read Galignani, & on the Pincian. Home at 12. Dr F. had called. A cold day, sunny, but speckled with clouds.

19 *Sunday*   Bright morning. Mamma not so well, after a wakeful night. Dr. F. came at 10. At 1, I walked out with Una & Rosebud, as far as Trajan's Forum. Very cold, & no sunshine in the narrow streets. Mr Cranch called in the afternoon; also, Mrs. Thompson & Ann   In the eve^g, Julian & I went to get some homeopathic medicine. A very cold, bright evening.

20 *Monday*   An overcast day, with drizzle of rain. Dr. F. came between 10 & 11, & found the hospital in good state. Miss Shepard, at later hour, proves to be sick & feverish. At 1 or 2, I went to Bank & read American papers, & drew for £50. Dr. Franco is sent for, & comes again in the evening.
The day has been rainy throughout.

21 *Tuesday*   Sunny morning, with scattered clouds. Dr. F. came before 10, & found everybody doing pretty well. After 1, I walked with Una to Pincian, & along the Corso, Via Condotti &c.
This has been a bright & rather cool day.

22 *Wednesday*   A bright day. Dr. F came at 10, & found his patients comfortable. At 1, I walked out with Una & Julian along the Corso &c, & bought Christmas presents. Afterwards, rambled about the city with Julian.
A letter from Mrs. Mann to-day, proposing land-speculation.

23 *Thursday*   A bright morning. Dr. F. came before 10. All doing well. At 1, Mamma drove out with Una & Rosebud. At 2, I went to the Bank & read papers; afterwards strolled a little about the city.
Very delightful weather.

24 *Friday*   An overcast morning. Dr. F. did not come. Patients pretty well. Mamma & Una walked out at 1. In the morn{script}, a great quarrel with the Padrona of the house. After dinner, Julian & I strolled about the city. Bo't load of wood to-day.

25 *Saturday*   A mild, overcast morning. Dr. F. came in the forenoon. At 2 ½ Mamma & the children drove to Mrs. Story's to see Christmas tree. Miss Shepard went to St Peter's to hear silver trumpets. I staid at home till evening; then walked along the Corso &c. Clouds & a little rain to day.

26 *Sunday*   An overcast, mild morning, with some rain. Mamma not very well; Una & the rest, tolerably. After dark, I walked the length of the Corso, &c.
A mild, Sirocco day.

27 *Monday*   An overcast morning, with gleams of watery sunshine. After 1, I went to the Bank & read American papers; afterwards walked in the Borghese grounds. Daisies & other wild flowers in bloom. Very soft & pleasant weather.

28 *Tuesday*   A mild, overcast morn{script}. Some sunshine. Towards 2, I walked to the Coliseum &c   Miss Bracken called. None of the family (except Julian & myself) are well. Miss Shepard is quite ill.
A pleasant, sunny afternoon.

29 *Wednesday*   Sunny morning, a little overcast. Dr. F. came in the morning. Neither Una nor Miss Shepard are doing well. I went to the Bank, at 2, & read papers; then walked on the Pincian. Mrs. & Miss Motley called; also, Mr Sam Bridge from California. Dr. F was sent for on Miss Shepard's account, & came early in the eve{script}.

30 *Thursday*   A sunny morning. Dr. F. came before breakfast, & found Miss Shepard rather better; Una pretty comfortable. At 1, I walked out with Una to Piazza di Spagna, along the Corso &c. Afterwards with Julian to Tarpeian Rock, Sculpture Gallery of Capitol, Coliseum &c.

A pleasant day.

31 *Friday*   Cool morning, somewhat clouded. Dr. F. came. Una tolerably; Miss Shepard no better. At 12, Una drove to Mrs. Story's. I went after her, but she was to drive back with Mrs. Story   I met Mrs & Mr. Story & Mr. Motley, & walked with the two last to Ponte Nomentana; very pleasant. Miss Shepard being worse, Dr. F was sent for & came about 10, P. M.

<So ends 1858. Since Nov. 25th, I have scribbled more or less of Romance every day; &, with interruptions, from Oct. 26th.>

[On a following blank page:]

Drafts on Consular Account.

For returning allowance	$616.43
Office-rent, 1ˢᵗ Janʸ '57 to Oct. 4.	583.56
Destitute Seamen, Sepʳ Quarter	535,52
Postages, &c &c Septʳ Quarter	118,18
Despatches &c	136.56
Destitute Seamen, Octr Quar	160,89
Postages, Octr Quarter	38.79
	2190.43

The above drafts drawn on the Government of United States, Decr. 31ˢᵗ, 1857, and taken to be negociated by Baring Brothers, Janʸ 1ˢᵗ 1858.

— — —

Janʸ 9ᵗʰ. At Paris, drew on Barings, through Hottinguer & Co, for 50 Napoleons, or £40 sterling.

— — —

1859 POCKET DIARY

Rome

January

1. Saturday.

A bright, cool morning. Our chimney caught fire, & filled the Piazza with smoke. Dr. Franco came early & found Miss Shepard rather better   At noon, Una & Mamma walked out along the Corso. Afternoon, I went to St Peters. Dr Franco came again in the evening.

2. Sunday.

Bright & cool morning. Dr. F. came at about 9, & found Miss Shepard rather better than worse. At noon, Una walked out with Mamma. Afterwards, Miss Weston called; also, Mr. & Mrs. Thompson. After 3, I walked along the Pincian with Julian, met Mr. Story, & waited to see balloon go up. Balloon collapsed. Eve^g, Mr. Sam Bridge called, & Dr. Franco came.

3. Monday.

Bright & cool morn^g. Dr. F came early, & found Miss Shepard doing pretty well; Una still feverish. About 1, I went to the Bank, & afterwards walked about the city. Miss Bracken called. Dr. F came in the eve^g; and Mrs Thompson came to watch with Miss Shepard

4. Tuesday.
Bright & cool morn^g. Dr. F came early. Miss Shepard better; Una threatened with fever-fit. After 1, I walked out with mamma, a short time, along the Corso; afterwards I went to the Medici Garden & the Pincian. Evening, Mr. & Mrs Brackett called.

Mr. Albee called in the day time. Rosebud went to the Westons   Dr. F. came again in the eve^g

5. Wednesday
Cool morning, with sunshine & clouds   Dr. F. came; no great change in the patients. Una had fever to-day. After 2, I walked with Rosebud down Via Babuino, up the Corso &c. A chill day, with masses of cloud quite obscuring the sun. Dr. F. came again in the evening, & Mrs. Thompson came to sit up with Miss Shepard.

6. Thursday
Cool & bright morning. Dr F. came. Miss Shepard rather better; Una feverish. Rosebud went to spend the day at Misses Weston. At 12, I walked out & strolled about the city, it being a great festa. Most superbest weather. Afterwards walked to the Pincian. In the eve^g, Mr. and Mrs Brackett came, & the latter watched with Miss Shepard. Dr F came again.

I went to Bank & read papers in the forenoon.

7. Friday
Bright and cool morning. Dr. F. came early, & found Miss Shepard much better; Una comfortable. After 1, I walked out with Julian; went to the Palace of Caesars, Temple of

Vesta, across Ponte Rotto to Trastevere, & home by Sistine
Bridge. Mr Browning called while we were out. Dr. Franco
came in the evening.

8. Saturday

Cool & cloudy morning. Dr. F. came before 10. He considers
the patients better. The day proved to be rainy, and I did not
go out. Miss Shepard had two letters from America; Una one
from Fanny Wrigley in Yorkshire. Dr. F. did not come in the
evening. Miss Shepard has great pains, probably rheumatic.

Rosebud went to the Westons' day, & came back in the
rain.

9. Sunday

A bright, rather cool morning. Dr. F. came about 9 °clock, &
found the patients doing well. After 2, I took Rosebud to walk
along the Corso, & to the Pantheon. A bitterly cold & windy
day. Mrs. Story called. In the evening, Mrs. Brackett came
to watch with Miss Shepard.

10. Monday

A bright & cold morning. Dr. F. came; Una seems cured of
fever; Miss Shepard doing well. After 1, I went to the Bank
and read American papers; afterwards walked along the
Corso. An excessively cold, sunny day. Letter to Una from
Annie Bright. Edith Story called.

11. Tuesday.

Cold & sunny morning. Dr. F. came, & found patients about
the same. At 2, I went to walk with Julian over the Ponte
Molle, & back by way of Porta Angelica. Went into St Peters;
went astray; & rambled about the intricacies of the city, &
reached home at nearly 6. Met Miss Haworth in the street. A
cool, but pleasant day. A load of wood to-day

12. Wednesday

A bright, cold morning. At about 2, I went to the Bank, & read papers; thence went to the grounds of the Villa Borghese. A pleasant afternoon, very comfortable in the sun. Dr. Franco did not come to-day.

Mr. Bridge called in the evening.

13. Thursday

Bright & cold morning. Dr. Franco came before 10. Mrs. Motley & daughters & Edith Story called. At about 3, I went to the Sculpture Gallery of the Capitol; afterwards walked in the Forum &c. A cold day.

Una & Miss Shepard seem to be making progress.

Drank flask of Orvieto at dinner; like still champagne.

14. Friday

A cold & bright morning. Dr. F. did not come. Miss Shepard came out of her chamber for the first time. At about 2, I went to the Bank & read Galignani; afterwards went to St Peters. An excessively cold, sunny day. Miss Bracken called.

Julian went, to day, to Ponte Molle in search of fossil-shells, with Eddie Thompson &c &c

15. Saturday

A cold morning, sunny, with some clouds. Dr. F. came early. Una seems quite well; Miss Shepard likewise. The day grew cloudy; and I did not go out.

16. Sunday

A cold, cloudy morning. Una has another chill & fever-fit to day. At about 3, Mr. Browning called, & I went out to walk on the Pincian & along the Corso, with Rosebud. Meanwhile, Dr. F. came, & ordered Una more Quinine. Mr. Hooker called. A rather mild day, with sunshine & clouds.

17. Monday

A chill, overcast morning. Wife has a bad cold; Una not well; Miss Shepard tolerably. After 1, I went to the Bank & read papers, and afterwards walked along the Corso. Dr. F. came in the evening.

It began to rain, towards evening.

18. Tuesday

A rather mild, cloudy & sunny morning. Mamma no better; Una tolerably; Miss Shepard well. Dr. F. came about 11. Mamma is to lie in bed during the day. Una had another chill & fever fit. It begins to rain in the afternoon. I did not go out.

Sat up till between 12 & 1. to give Una Quinine.

19. Wednesday

A rather bright morning, & mild. Mamma better; Una comfortable. Dr. F. came at about 11. At about 2, I walked with Julian to the Baths of Caracalla, & home by St John Lateran & Sta Maria Maggiore. Very warm in the sun.

20. Thursday

A bright, cool morning. Mamma seems to be recovered. Una not well. Dr. F. did not come to day. Miss Shepard walked out for the first time. At about 1, I went to the Bank & read papers; then walked on the Pincian.

We had letters from America to-day.

It was very warm in the sun; a Sirocco, I think.

21. Friday

A chill, rather overcast morning. The Doctor came & found Una not making progress. After 2, I went out & walked to St Peters, & afterwards rambled about the city. A disagreeable day.

Mr. Bridge called in the evening

22. Saturday

A sunny, half-clouded, mild morning. Una & Mamma went out at noon. Miss Shepard also walked out with Rose, and over-exerted herself. Towards 2, I went to the Bank & read newspapers; afterwards walked to St. John Lateran & home by Coliseum &c   Warm & pleasant.

Mr. & Mrs. Brackett called in the evening.

Miss Shepard attacked with violent gastric pains in the night.

23. Sunday

A sunny & mild morning. Dr F was sent for and came to Miss Shepard. Not much better. At 11 I walked with Rosebud & Julian to the Medici & Pincian Gardens, & home along the Corso. Very pleasant, a coolish, gentle wind, but warm in the sun. Afternoon, Mr. Browning & Miss Bracken called. Una drove out with Mrs. Story. Dr. F came again in the evening.

Could not scribble Romance to-day, for the first time since Novr 25th

Mrs. Thompson & Cora called

24. Monday

Sunny morning, soon overcast. Dr. F came before 9, & found Miss Shepard rather better. Mamma is quite ill with cough and fever. Una pretty well. Mrs. Brackett called. The day proving disagreeable, I did not go out. Dr. F. came again in the evening.

25. Tuesday

Bright and mild morning. Mamma rather better; Miss Shepard doing well. Dr. F. came at about 9. Between 1 & 2, I went with Julian & Rosebud to the Borghese grounds   Una drove out with Edith Story. Dr. F. came again in the evening.

Very warm to-day, & more comfortable in the shade than in the sun. Saw a gentleman holding an umbrella over his head.

26. Wednesday

A bright & rather cool morning. Mamma better; Una not very well; Miss Shepard comfortable. Between 12 & 1, (Dr. F. having called) I walked with Una to the Forum, by way of Trajan's forum, and home by the Capitol & Corso. Warm and sunny in the forum; chill in the streets. Afterwards, I went to the Bank & read papers; thence to the Medici Gardens & smoked a cigar.

27. Thursday.

A rather dim morning. Patients neither well nor very ill After 2, I walked with Una, Julian, & Rosebud to the Medici Gardens. Dr. F. came at about 5, P.M. Julian & I went to the Post Office. Mr. S. Bridge & Mr. Robison called in the evening—Mr B. to take leave.

A warm & pleasant day.

28. Friday

A bright, rather cool morning   About 1 I went to the Bank & read papers. Returned home, & walked with Una to the Pincian. Mrs. Story took up Una in her carriage in the Via Babuino; and I rambled about the city, to the Pantheon &c The Doctor did not come to-day.

A warm & pleasant day.

29. Saturday

Bright, rather cool morning, with a few clouds. Dr. F. came in the forenoon & found us tolerably well. Between 2 & 3 I walked with Una along the Corso, & called at Mrs. G. Jones's; not in. Then we went shopping, near the Pantheon &c. After

taking Una (& Rosebud) home, I went to the Medici Gardens
& smoked a cigar.

A dim day, till the afternoon, when it grew sunny & pleasant.

30. Sunday

An overcast morning, with gleams of sunshine. The patients tolerably comfortable. Dr. F. did not come. I finished,
to-day, the rough draft of my Romance; intending to write it
over after getting back to the Wayside.

A dim day, with some rain. Did not go out.

31. Monday

Dr. F. came in the morning. Una was much indisposed
to-day. About 10, I went to Bank & read papers; thence to St
Peter's, where met Mr. Mrs. & Miss Jones; thence to the
Vatican, where I staid till 2 °clock. A dim, overcast day; a
little sun gleaming out; but looking like rain.

February

1. Tuesday

Una seems pretty comfortable. An overcast morning, very
portentous of rain. A load of wood came to-day. After 10, I
went with Julian to the Bank, drew for £50, & read papers;
thence we went to the Doria Palace & looked at pictures;
thence to the Forum, by way of the Capitol. Julian soon came
home, & I followed. Una has had chills & fever-fit.

2. Wednesday

A cloudy morning, with showers & sunny gleams. Una had
a feverish night, & seems no better. Dr. F. was sent for, &
found her in another attack of Roman fever. Between 2 & 3,

I walked to the Medici Gardens, and smoked a cigar. Quite an overcast day, & I was caught in a shower.

At bedtime, starlight.

3. Thursday

A very black & rainy morning. Una's fever-fit over. Dr. F. came; quinine, quinine. After 12, I went to the Bank & read papers. A pouring rain. Elizabeth Hoar called, from Concord, & last from Naples. A letter from Barings, enclosing their a/c with me.

I wrote (& sent through Pakenham & Hooker) a letter to J. T. Fields, Boston.

4. Friday

Dark & rainy morning. Dr F. did not come. Una tolerably comfortable. It being rainy throughout the day, I did not go out. Mʳ Cranch called (I did not see him,) and Miss Hoar (nor her,) and Mʳ Motley, whom I saw.

1 bottle Vino Santo; 1 do Frascati; ½ doz flasks Orvieto.

5. Saturday

A bright, mild, coolish morning   Una pretty well. Note of invitation from Miss Haworth; declined. At about 11, walked out with Mamma, Una, & Julian. Left Una at the Barberini Palace (Mrs. Story's) Then went to Elizabeth Hoar's (53, Via Condotti) with whom Mamma took cab for St. Peter's. Julian & I rambled about the city. Got home before 2. Mʳ Seagrave (English) called with letters from E. P. P. &c. Mrs Story called

A sunny & pleasant day.

Dr. called while Una was gone

6. Sunday

Sunny morning, with some clouds. Mamma went to Overbeck's with Miss Hoar and Rosebud. I walked on the Pincian, and afterwards along the Via Ripetta &c with Una & Julian. A dim, mild day. Una seems quite well. The Doctor did not come

7. Monday
A rather cloudy morning. After breakfast, I went to the Bank, and got a letter from Mrs. Mann for Mamma. Afterwards smoked a cigar on the Pincian. Returned home, & took Una out to walk & shop for photographs, bronzes &c. along the Corso, via Santa Croce, & Via Babuino. Afterwards, I went to the Bank & read papers. At night, I felt indisposed

8. Tuesday
A sunny morning, with a tendency to cloud. Being unwell, I lay abed late; the Doctor being here when I got up, he gave me several powders to take. Una walked out with Julian. Miss Hoar called.
At 6, Una went to dine with Miss Ward, & returned at 9 ½.

9. Wednesday
A rather dim, sirocco day. I find myself, perhaps, a little more comfortable than yesterday, but much the same. Miss Hoar called; also Mrs. Hoar; and Mamma went with them to Rospigliosi palace &c. Mrs. Story called & took Una to the Barberini palace to spend some days.
Towards night, I felt more out of order; and passed a very restless, feverish diarheetic night

10. Thursday
The doctor was sent for, and I received him in bed—the first time since my childhood. During the day, I gradually improved, & felt comparatively comfortable, though the trouble

was not removed. The doctor came again after I had gone to bed; I having risen immediately after his morning visit. Passed a pretty good night.

11. Friday

Better, this morning, but not well. The Doctor came, & left some more powders. About 11, I walked out with my wife along the Corso—very sunny, at that hour. Lay down after my return. Mrs. Thompson called—also Una & Edith Story.

I ate some dinner, which seemed not to agree with me; for I passed a restless night;—that is, almost restless.

12. Saturday

Scarcely so well, this morning An invitation from Mr. Motley to take tea—declined. In the forenoon, Mamma, Miss Shepard & Rosebud went out; Mamma called on the Doctor, who sent me a bottle of medicine; and Rosebud went with Miss S. to spend a day at Mr. Stone's. Julian went to the Ponte Molle. Afternoon, Miss Hoare called. I grew more comfortable during the day, & spent a pretty quiet night. A very fine day. Una & Edith came to see us.

13. Sunday

A misty morning, brightening somewhat later. Doctor F. came at about 10 & found me a good deal better. Mamma & I did not go out. Miss Shepard walked out with Rosebud. Miss Bracken called; also, Mr Hooker, who did not come in I drank beef-broth and ate a bird, & felt passably well.

14. Monday

A misty & chill morning. Comfortable, but not quite well. Afternoon, Mamma went with Rosebud to the Coliseum, Celian &c; the rest of the family elsewhere, & I was left alone.

Mr. Browning called & left a card; Mrs. Motley left a bouquet; & after Miss Shepard's and my wife's return, Mr. Thompson paid us a visit.

15. Tuesday

An overcast morning, brightening in the forenoon. I find myself about the same as yesterday. At about 10 ½, walked with Mamma to Barberini Palace, & left her there; then went to Bank & read papers, then walked along Corso home. Una came home with Mamma to see us, & staid two or three hours. Elizabeth Hoar called. Also, Mr Motley. I dined with the family for the first time since my illness.

16. Wednesday

A bright morning. Mamma went to Barberini Palace to see Una; & I went to the Bank. In the afternoon, Mr Motley called with Mr Cowper, a young Englishman. Mamma came home to dinner, but went back & spent the night at the Barberini Palace; Una having a fever fit.

17. Thursday

A pleasant morning, somewhat clouded. Una & Mamma came home about 10 °clock. I rec^d a letter from Genl Pierce. Went to Bank, & afterwards to the picture gallery of Borghese palace. Mamma went out with Rosebud & Miss Hoar Mrs Story called.

A very fine day.

18. Friday

A pleasant morning. Wrote to Genl Pierce. Miss Hoar called At about 11, I went to the Bank; afterwards to St Peters, and home over the Sistine Bridge. Una has had another severe chill & fever-fit to-day. Mrs & Miss Motley called. The Doctor came to see Una in the forenoon

19. Saturday

A pleasant morning. Una is tolerably comfortable. About 11, walked out with Julian, & went to the Basilica of St Paul, outside of the walls; returned between 2 & 3 °clock. The Doctor came in the evening

20. Sunday

A cool, bright, windy morning, with flitting clouds. A very cool and windy day. Miss Shepard went to St Peter's. Mrs. Story sent some papers. Una is tolerably well.

I did not go out.

21. Monday

Cold, windy, and inclining to be cloudy. Between 10 & 11, I went to the Bank, & read the American papers. Saw Miss Cushman. Got a letter for Miss Shepard. Came home & staid in the house for the rest of the day

22. Tuesday

Cool, bright, pleasant morning. Mamma, Miss Shepard, & Rosebud went out early shopping. At about 12, Mamma & I went out with Una & Julian, & called at W. Story's Studio; also at Miss Stebbins's, where we saw Miss Cushman. Afterwards walked along the Via Condotti, & left Mamma &c there. Miss Hoar called. Julian is not well to day.

23. Wednesday

A bright cool morning. Julian & the rest of us pretty well. Dr. Franco came about 9 °clock. Mamma, Miss Shepard, Una, Rosebud, & I, went out to Via Condotti &c. & looked at bronzes & photographs, & bought some. Afterwards, I went to the Bank, & smoked a cigar on the Pincian. In the evening, Julian went to the theatre, with the Thompsons, & saw Othello performed

24. Thursday

Bright, rather cool morning. Mamma went with Miss Hoar to the Ludovisi Villa, & other places. At 2 °clock, Julian & I took a walk out of the Porta Pia, & round the wall, into the gate of Sta Maria Maggiore. A rather cool day but warm in the sunshine.

25. Friday

A bright, coolish morning. After 10, I went to the Bank, & read papers; then came home, & went with Una to the Coliseum, the forum, the arch of Janus Quadrifrons, the temple of Vesta, & over the Ponte Rotto, returning by the Island of the Tiber. Shopped a little along the Corso, and reached home before 2. Mamma went with Miss Hoar to Farnesina palace. Una drove out with Miss Ward, after returning from our walk.

26. Saturday

Bright, rather cool morning. After 11, Una & I walked to the gate of Sta Maria Maggiore, thence to St. John Lateran, & home by the Coliseum, forum, & Corso. The carnival was just about to begin. Mamma was shopping &c. with Miss Hoar most of the day. Rosebud was at a window in the Corso, with Mr. & Mrs. Hoar, looking at the Carnival. Julian, in blouse and mask, was among the combatants

A very pleasant day.

27. Sunday

A cloudy, chill, & rainy morning. Una has a cold. As the day advanced, the sun came out a little. Mamma, Miss Shepard, & Rosebud, went to the Triniti di Monti to hear vespers, about five °clock. I staid at home all day

28. Monday

A cool, bright morning. About 10, I went to the Bank, & rec^d letters from Ticknor & from Mrs. Mann & E. P. Peabody. Afterwards read papers. Then went with Mamma to Miss Hosmer's studio, whom we found engaged in modelling Lady Mordaunt's nose. Returned home; & between 1 & 2, Mamma, Una, & Rosebud went to see the Carnival from a window in the Corso. Julian & I walked along the Corso; & at 4 °clock, I returned home. The rest of the family not yet arrived.

They all came home at about 6 °clock.

March

1. Tuesday

A bright, rather cool morn^g. After 10, I went to the Bank, & read papers; then walked about the city. Afternoon, Mamma & Rosebud went to see the Carnival from Miss Hoar's window; Julian to stroll along the Corso, Una to drive along the Corso with Mrs. & Miss Ward, & Miss Lily Motley. At about 4, I went into the Corso, & staid till about sunset. A great crowd.

I am troubled with a cold

2. Wednesday

Bright & cool morning. At about 10, Una & I went to call on Miss Hosmer at her studio; not in. Then we strolled about the city, & went into the Pantheon & another church   After 1, went with Mamma & Una to call on Mrs. Browning; she was engaged with a portrait-painter. Una & I went home, leaving Mamma to go on some expedition with Miss Shepard. Between 3 & 4, I went out to see the carnival, leaving Una & Rosebud at home.

Dr. Franco came in the evening

3. Thursday

Una is fifteen to-day. A bright day, with some clouds. I smoked a cigar on the Pincian, & then went to the bank. Miss Bracken called. Between 1 & 2, Mamma, Julian & Rosebud went to Miss Hoar's window in the Corso. Before 3, I went with Una to Mrs. Motley's balcony, staid a little while, left her there, rambled along the Corso, rested in the church of St Ignazio, & went back for Una in time to see the race.

4. Friday

A sunny, rather cool morning. I wrote a letter to Ticknor, & at about 11, went to the Bank. Then to the Medici gardens & smoked a cigar; then to Mr Thompson's studio. Home after 1. Elizabeth Hoar called. After 2, I walked to the Coliseum, forum &c. Una has a fever-fit to day.

5. Saturday

A pleasant morn^g. Rec^d note from Genl Pierce, at Naples. About 10, I went to the Bank, read a newspaper, & then smoked a cigar on the Pincian. Afternoon, Mamma & Rosebud went to Miss Hoar's window; Una, to drive along the Corso with Miss Jones, &c; & Julian & I to see the Carnival from Mrs. Jones' balcony. All got home after 6.

6. Sunday

A pleasant morning. Julian & Miss Shepard went to walk along the Tiber; Una went with Mrs & Miss Ward to Overbeck's studio; & Rosebud & I went to walk on the Pincian, returning along the Corso. We reached home between 12 & 1. Elizabeth Hoar called. Una has another fever-fit to-day. Miss Shepard & Rosebud went to the Medici gardens in the afternoon

7. Monday

A moist, cloudy morning Dr. Franco came at about 11. I went to the Bank, drew for £ 50, & read papers; then smoked a cigar on the Pincian. Mamma, Julian, & Rosebud, went to the window in the Corso; Una & I to Mrs. Motley's balcony. The afternoon was very sunny & pleasant. We all got home from the Carnival, from 5 to 6 °clock.

8. Tuesday

An overcast day. At about 10, I walked out with Mamma; left her at Miss Hoar's, & went to the Bank; then rambled about the city, went into the Pantheon &c. Returning, found Una suffering from chills. A letter from Mrs. Mann to-day. Between 1 & 2, Mamma & Rosebud went to Miss Hoar's window; Julian to ramble along the Corso; & at about 4, I went to the Corso; & afterwards to Mrs. Motley's balcony, to see the Moccoletto. All of us got home a little before 8.

9. Wednesday

An overcast day. Wrote a note for Gen¹ Pierce, to be dld on his arrival, & left it at the Bank. Smoked a cigar in the Medici Gardens. Mamma walked out with Una & Rosebud Julian took a ten-mile walk with Eddy Thompson. At 6, I went to dine with Mr & Mrs Story; met Mr Read, Browning &c &c; staid a little while at an evening party, & got home soon after 10.

10. Thursday

Pleasant, & rather cool morning. At 11 ½, Mamma, Miss Shepard, Julian, & I, took a carriage for the Catacomb of St Calixthius; Mr & Miss Hoar in another carriage. Spent an hour in the Catacomb, & then drove to the tomb of Cecilia Metella, where we entered. Got home at about ¼ 3. Afterwards, I went to the Medici Gardens & smoked a cigar. Una had chills & fever in our absence. A bright, windy day. While we were at dinner, Gen¹ Pierce called; just arrived at Hotel d'Europe, from Naples.

11. Friday
Bright, coolish morn\^g. Gen¹ Pierce came in, after breakfast, & we walked to St Peters; then called to see Mrs. Pierce; then went with Pierce to call on a lady at Hotel de la Minerva Mamma & Rosebud went to the Borghese palace; Una & Miss Shepard to an afternoon concert; Julian took a long walk with Eddy Thompson.

12. Saturday
Bright & cool morning. At about 11, I went to the Bank, & afterwards smoked a cigar in the Medici Gardens. Rosebud went to the Barberini Palace. Miss Shepard & Julian went to the Fountain of Egeria, beyond the walls. Mamma staid at home with Una, who had a fever-fit. At three, I walked to the Coliseum, forum &c; and on my return, found General Pierce here.
Dr. Franco came just before bedtime.

13. Sunday
Bright & cool morn\^g. Mamma & Rosebud went to the Medici Gardens; Julian & Miss Shepard to Protestant cemetery. At 12 ½ Gen¹ Pierce called, & I walked with him to the Coliseum & forum. Returned, & lunched on bread & wine. Mamma had gone to drive with Mrs. Story; she went to the Villa Pamfili-Doria. Afterwards called on Mrs Pierce. M\^r Browning & Miss Hosmer called here.

14. Monday
A pleasant, rather warm morning, with some clouds. I went

to the Bank, afterwards smoked a cigar on the Pincian, &, at about 12, drove to the Vatican with Mrs. Pierce & Miss Vandervoort, & went through the sculpture-gallery. Returned after 2 °clock. Met Mamma & Miss Hoare at the Vatican. In the evening, Dr. Appleton called. While I was out with Rosebud, Mr. Motley, Mr. Reed (of Phil[a]) & Dr. Henry called. Dr. F. came to-day.

15. Tuesday

An overcast morning. About 10, called with Mamma at Miss Hoare's, & went with her to Miss Hosmer's studio. Left them going to Mr. Gibson's, & went to Bank to read newspapers. Thence home, & did not go out for the remainder of the day. Miss Shepard received news of her father's death. Una went to an afternoon concert.

16. Wednesday

Gen[l] Pierce called after breakfast, & I went with him to the top of the Capitol-tower; afterwards to W[m] Story's studio. Afterwards to the Bank. Mamma, Una, & Julian, called at Mrs. Browning's; also at Mrs. Pierce's.—Mrs. Pickman called here. Mamma afterwards went to W[m] Story's studio with Miss Hoare & Julian.

This has been a mild, overcast day, inclining to rain

17. Thursday

An overcast morning. At about 10, called with Mamma on Mrs. Pierce. Afterwards went to the Bank; afterwards with Una to the sculpture gallery of the Capitol. Home between 1 & 2 °clock, leaving Mamma & Miss Hoare there. Rosebud went with Miss Shepard to Barberini palace. At 5, Una drove to dine at Mrs. Motley's, & returned at 10.

The day has been fitful & showery.

18. Friday

A cloudy morning, with sunny gleams. At about 11, I went with Una to call on Mrs. Pierce at Hotel d'Angleterre (not in,) and at the Hoars, where I left her with Mrs. Hoar. Thence I went to the Bank; thence home. Mamma, Miss Shepard, & Rosebud, went out in several directions. Julian & I staid at home. After 4, Gen¹ Pierce called, & I went with him to Sta. Maria Maggiore, St Andrea of Monte Cavallo &c. Una staid at Mrs. Hoares till 5 °clock

A dark, showery day

Letters from E. P. Peabody &c to-day

19. Saturday

A fair morning, but soon overcast. Gen¹ Pierce called after breakfast, & I went with him to Mʳ Sandford's (of Boston,) to Chapman's studio, to Thompson's studio; then to his lodgings at Hotel d'Angleterre, & read newspapers; then to call with him on Mʳ Stockton; then to ramble about the city. Returning home, found Mr. S. May here. Went with Mamma & Julian to call on Miss Cushman (not in) and at Page's studio.

A sunny & beautiful afternoon.

Dr. Franco came in the evening.

20. Sunday

A bright morning. At about 12, Julian & I walked out of the gate of St John Lateran, to the Excavations, stopping by the way to get some wine, bread, & eggs, at an Osteria. Returned through the same gate, but by another road, & reached home about 4 ½. Very hot in the sun.

Found Mamma suffering with a fever headache, and Una rather feverish

Mʳ Story & some other gentleman had called while I was out

21. Monday

A bright, coolish morning. At about 10, went with Julian to the Bank, & thence to the St Peter's, & the Sculpture Gallery of the Vatican (met Gen[l] Pierce by the way & turned aside to his hotel, but left him there) We came back across the ferry to the Via di Rippetta. Mamma also at the Vatican, but did not meet her. Una is feverish to-day. Dr. Franco came in the afternoon.

22. Tuesday

An overcast morning, afterwards brightening. Dr. Franco came about 9 to see Una, who is still feverish. At 10, I went to the Bank; afterwards to the Medici Gardens & smoked a cigar; thence, home. Gen[l] Pierce had called, but missed me. At 2, I went out & rambled about the city, passing St Andrew delle Valle, the Farnese palace, the Cenci Palace, the temple of Vesta, & skirted the Aventine, & to the gate of St Pauls. Home by the Colosseum. Gen[l] Pierce called in the evening.

23 Wednesday

A bright morning. I staid at home till 12; then went to the Bank, & strolled a little about the city. Miss Hoare called; & at about 3, it seems to be settling to rain. Dr. Franco has come; he finds Una better, & prognosticates favorably.

24 Thursday

An overcast morning. I staid within doors till 2. Then went to the sculpture & picture galleries of the Capitol; afterwards went to the Forum, the Velabrum, the Ponte Rotto, (stopt to see the revolving nets fish.) over to Trastevere, & back by the Island of the Tiber. Then to Portico of Octavia, St Andrea delle Valle, Pantheon, & got home by 5 ¼. Una is not comfortable to-day. A sunny & shadowy afternoon. Dr F. came. Gen[l] Pierce called in the eve[g]

25 Friday

A bright morn^g. About 10, went to the Bank, whither Julian followed me, & at 11, we went to call on Genl Pierce. Walked with him to forum, Velabrum, Ponte Rotto, Trastevere, & back by Ponte St Angelo. Afterwards went with him to Mr Tilton's studio. Home at about 2   Dr. Franco came in the afternoon. Una seems to be no better. Genl Pierce called in the evening.

26 Saturday

An overcast morning. Dr. F. came, & found Una no better. At 12, Genl Pierce called, & I went with him to Palazzo Spada; afterwards drove with him & Mrs. Pierce to Borghese Villa & about the grounds; thence to Ponte Molle & back through the Porta Angelica

27 Sunday

Overcast morn^g, brightening afterwards. Genl Pierce called at noon. Una is a little better to-day. Rosebud went to drive with Mrs. Ward. Genl Pierce called again in the afternoon. At about 4, I went to walk with Julian, to the Coliseum &c. Dr. Franco is ill, & sent another physician to see about Una; but he was not admitted to her chamber.

A bright afternoon, rather cool.

28 Monday

A bright morning. Una had an uncomfortable night, but seems better this morning. At 10, I went to the Bank, & thence to St Peter's, where I spent more than an hour. At 12, went into the sculpture gallery of the Vatican, & staid till about 2. Thence to the Bank & read some newspapers. Home a little after 3.

In the eve^g, a tailor came & took my measure for pantaloons.

29 Tuesday

A pleasant morning. Una seems a little better. Gen¹ Pierce called in the forenoon; also Miss E. Hoare. At 2, I went to the Bank & read papers; thence to the Medici Gardens & smoked a cigar; thence to the Pincian. Dr. Franco (still quite unwell) came in the evening. Miss Shepard and I went out to get some sunshine

30 Wednesday

An overcast morning; it begins to rain before noon. Mr Motley called to ask me to dinner next Saturday. Gen¹ Pierce called. Una is little or no better. Rosebud has a cough. Nobody is very well. Mrs. Thompson called. I did not go out, all day. Gen¹ Pierce called again the evening.

31 Thursday

A bright morning, rather cool, and varied with clouds. I went to the Bank & read newspapers; & after 11, went to drive with Gen¹ & Mrs. Pierce, out of the Porta Pia, to Ponte Lomentana; returning, drove round the city-wall to Porta Maggioro, & thence by the Coliseum, to the Capitol. We went in & looked at the sculptures. Returned to Hotel d'Angleterre, & Pierce & I went to a Restaurant & got a bottle of Port. Walked in the Medici Gardens. Home about 4 °clock. Dr. F. had called. Una perhaps a little better.

Rev. Mr. May called & spent the evening. Rain. A letter from H. A. Bright

April

1 Friday

An overcast morning, with dim sunshine. Wrote a long letter to Mr Bright. Elizath Hoar called. Mamma had gone out. I went to the Bank, read a paper, & then rambled about the city, into the Farnese palace—went into the Pantheon &c. A cold, windy day. Una is perhaps a little better. The Doctor came.

2 Saturday

A bright, rather cool day. Gen¹ Pierce called, & at about 10, we went to Miss Hosmer's studio (not in) & to Brown's studio. I then left Pierce & rambled about the city, to church of St. Agnes &c. Home before 12. Afternoon, Mamma walked out. The Doctor came. At 7 °clock, I went to dine at Mr. Motley's, with Mʳ Browning, Mr. Spencer Cowper, Mʳ Perkins. Home after 11.

A very cold walk home; and I caught cold.

3 Sunday

A bright day. Una no better, & much tormented with a cough. At about 2, I walked with Julian to the Coliseum, & home by the Circus Maximus & through the city. Gen¹ Pierce had called twice. The Doctor came.

A cool Tramontana, but very hot sun.

4 Monday

A bright morning. Gen¹ Pierce called. Mamma went to see the Doctor about Una. In the afternoon, I walked out with Julian to the Pincian & along the Corso. Miss Hoare called; also Mrs. Motley.

5 Tuesday

A bright morning. At 10, I went to call on Gen Pierce. He is to be presented to the Pope to-day— Afterwards, I called at the Bank, and at Mr. Story's studio (not in) & then went to Medici Gardens. Dr. F. has been here; he is alarmed about Una, & thinks her lungs are terribly diseased.

Dr. F. came again in the evening.

6 Wednesday

A dim morning. The Doctor came after breakfast. Una's state seems essentially the same. Gen¹ Pierce came, & at about 11, I drove with him, Mrs. Pierce, & Father Smith, to the Library of the Vatican. Returned at about 2. Afternoon, I took a walk with Pierce, & talked about our poor Una. Mrs. Story and Edith called. Mrs. Browning with Mrs. Eckley called. Doctor F. came again in the eve^g. He seems to think Una a little better.

This was a warm day

7 Thursday

A dim morning. Gen¹ Pierce came, also Dr. F. He thinks Una a little better. I went to the Bank, and afterwards with Julian to Mr. Story's studio. Not in. Came home at about 1, & found Mr. Story here, & Mrs. Farrar. About 3, I went out & rambled about the city till 4. The Doctor came again in the evening; so did Gen Pierce.

8 Friday

A dim morning. Gen¹ Pierce came early; so did the Doctor He seems to have very little hope. God help us! During the day, many friends, as Mr. Farrar, Mrs. Jones. Mrs. Thompson, Elizabeth Hoare, M^r. Motley, Mrs Story, called, or sent flowers and kind messages. Una lay very much in the same state. The Doctor came again late in the evening, & found her at least no worse.

9 Saturday

A dim morning. Gen¹ Pierce called after breakfast. # He finds Una no worse, & seems not quite to despair. Mrs. Farrar called. I rambled a little about the city, & went into the Sciarra Palace. Coming home, found Mrs. Ward & Mrs.

Motley here. Gen Pierce called at about 3, & I walked with him to the Pincian &c.

\# The Doctor called at about 10 ½

He called again in the evening, and found Una still no worse.

10 Sunday

A dim morning. Una seems very bright, &, when I got up, lay knitting with some long wooden needles. Mrs. Thompson called, also Gen¹ Pierce, and she asked to see them both. The Dr. came after breakfast, & says still that she is no worse. Mr. Motley called: also Mrs. Story &c &c. Mrs. Ward, &c. Also, again, Gen¹ Pierce, with whom I walked out on the Pincian &c at about 4, taking Julian along. The Doctor came again in the evening, & found Una about the same

11 Monday

A dim morning. Una has passed an unquiet night but seems about the same. Dr. F. came at about 11, & felt decidedly encouraged about her. At 11 ½, I went with Julian to the Sculpture Gallery of the Vatican. Met there Gen¹ & Mrs. Mallette &c. Afterwards went into St. Peter's. Returning, went into the Bank. Mʳ Motley called. A heavy shower of rain. Dr. F. came in the eveʳ, & found Una essentially improved.

12 Tuesday

A dim, chill morning. Gen¹ Pierce called at breakfast-time. Dr. F. came, & found Una not so well as last night. I went with Gen¹ & Mrs Pierce to the picture-gallery of the Vatican. Returned home at about 3. Mrs. Story called. Many friends sent flowers to Una. Mr. Motley called, & I walked with him along the Tiber to the Ponte Molle. Dr. F. came in the evening, & found Una neither worse nor better.

13 Wednesday

A dim morning. Dr. F came early & found Una no better.
M^r. Story called, also Mrs. Farrar; also Genl Pierce. Julian & I
went with Genl Pierce to the Castle of St. Angelo. After coming home, Mrs Story called, and I went with her, Mr. Story,
Edith, & Mr. Wild, to see the original of Venus de Medici, just
found. While I was gone, Dr. F. & another Dr. came to consult about Una. Genl Pierce called again in the evening.

14 Thursday

A dim morning. Dr. F. came after breakfast. Una had had
a quiet night. After 10, I went to the Bank; & returning home,
Genl Pierce called & we went to Mr. Story's studio &c. Miss
Shepard went with E. Hoare to see the consulting doctor
about Una, & he says that the affection of the lungs depends
on a nervous fever, & will pass away with it. In the afternoon,
I drove with Mr. Motley to the Porta Portese, & then to the
Porta Sebastiano, to see the Venus. Gen Pierce called in the
eve^r. Dr. F came, & encouraged us about Una. Began to let
my moustache grow.

15 Friday

A dim morning. At 10, I went to the Bank; then took a walk
to the Coliseum, Sta Maria Maggiore &c; then went to Mr.
Story's studio. Meanwhile, both the Doctors came to see Una,
& are encouraged, about her. In the evening, Genl Pierce
called, & I took a little stroll about the streets with him.

16 Saturday

A rather dim morning. At about 10, I walked out with
Julian & strolled about the city; afterwards, Julian went home
& I to the Barberini picture gallery. Came home about 1. Dr.
F. had been here & found Una better. Mr. Motley called; also

Eliza^th Hoare. At 4, I went to Mr. Motley's (not in,) & after-wards smoked a cigar on the Pincian   Dr. F. called in the evening, & still finds Una better.

17 Sunday

A dim morning. After breakfast, Genl Pierce called; & Julian & I went to St. Peter's with him, & saw the Pope carried in procession. Returned at 12. Both the Doctors have called, & find Una better. Mrs. Motley called; also M^r & Mrs. Story. The Doctor came again in the evening. Una is still improving

18 Monday

A bright morning. After breakfast, Genl Pierce called, & I went with him to Hotel d'Angleterre, to the Bank, to the studios of Miss Stebbins, Mr Freeman, Mr Rogers, Mr Mozier, to call on Miss Cushman &c. Afterwards to a Restaurant, & drank some Port wine &c. Home at about 2 ½. Dr. F. had called, & found Una improving. In the evening, I took a stroll with Julian, down the Via Babuino, along the Corso &c Dr. F. came again, & still finds Una doing well.

19 Tuesday

Morning between dim & bright   I went to the Bank; after-wards to Mr Story's studio (not in;) then to the Medici Gar-dens. Meanwhile, both Drs. came and found Una much im-proved. Genl Pierce & wife set out, this morning, for Venice, via Ancona. In the evening, I walked along the Corso &c. Dr. Franco came again, & found Una making progress.

A sirocco day

20 Wednesday

A dim, sirocco morning. At about 10, I strolled a little about the city, & went to the Bank. The Doctor came, & thinks Una is slowly improving. At about 3, I went with Julian to the Forum, the Celian Hill, the Coliseum &c. A languid, sirocco day, pleasant to sit down in. The Doctor did not come in the evening.

21 Thursday

A dim morning. After 10, Julian & I went to St. Peter's, & saw the Pope bless the people from the balcony. Strolled about a little, & came home about 1. Dr. F. has called, & finds Una doing, very well. A heavy, sultry, sirocco day. The Doctor did not call in the evening. Mrs. Thompson came to sit up with Una; & Mamma had a night's sleep—the first in five or six weeks.

22 Friday

An overcast, lowering morning. The Doctor came, & appears to think Una is quite free of fever, though still requiring great care. At about 3, I went with Julian to St. Peters, meaning to hear the Miserere, but was tired of waiting, & came home at about 5. In the evening, it rained. Clarke (Mrs. Story's woman) sat up with Una.

23 Saturday

An overcast morning, with sunny gleams. At about 10, I went to the Bank; afterwards to the Capitoline hill, & church of Ara Coeli. The Doctor to-day finds Una still doing well. In the afternoon, I went to the Medici Gardens & the Pincian. Mamma took a short walk out. In the evening, I went to Mr Story's to see Charles Sumner. Home at about 11.

24 Sunday

A bright morning. The Dr. came & finds Una still convalescing. After 10, Julian & I went to St Peters to hear the silver trumpets & witness the Benediction. A very great crowd. We got home between 1 & 2. At dark, Mamma, Julian, & I, went to Mrs. Story's to see the illumination of St Peter's. Returned home after 9; & I went with Miss Shepard to view it from the Pincian.

25 Monday
A bright morning. Dr. called. Una makes progress. I went to the Bank & read papers; afterwards called on Mr. May (not in) and strolled a little about the city. A warm Summer's day. In the evening, I went to the Piazza del Popolo to see the fireworks. Very beautiful. Came home at about ½ past 9.

26 Tuesday
A bright day. After breakfast, I went to the Medici Gardens & smoked a cigar; thence to the Bank & read newspapers. A letter from Barings to-day. I staid in the house the rest of the day. Mamma went out, & called at Miss Hosmer's studio. The Doctor came at about 6 °clock. Una makes steady progress.

27 Wednesday
A bright day. After breakfast, I rambled about the city, crossed to the island of the Tiber, went into church of St Bartholomew, back by Ponte Sixto; then to the Bank & read Galignani. Staid at home till evening, & then went with Julian to the Coliseum & came home over Capitol Hill. Dr. came at 6, & finds Una better & better.

28 Thursday
A bright morning. After breakfast, smoked a cigar on the Pincian & then went to Bank. About 12, Mamma went out and staid till 3 or 4. In the evening, Julian and I took a walk along the Corso &c. The Doctor did not call to-day, & Una continues to convalesce rapidly

29 Friday

A rather dim morning. After breakfast, I called at the Bank, rambled about the city, & went into the Church of the Minerve. At 2, Mamma, Julian, & I, called at Mrs Browning's; then went to Mr Rogers' studio; then went to look at & buy stereoscopic views. The Doctor came at dinner-time, & finds Una coming on bravely. A summer day.

30 Saturday

A bright morning. After breakfast I walked to the Coliseum, Caelian Hill &c, and home by the Forum & Corso. Mamma & Miss Shepard went out shopping &c. In the evening, Dr. Appleton called, with a note from Genl Pierce at Ancona; also, Mr Cranch.

The Doctor did not come to-day. Una still convalesces.

May

1 Sunday

A dim, moist morning. The Doctor came. Una steadily convalesces. Mr Sumner called with Edith Story. After 3, Julian & I walked to the Coliseum, Caelian Hill &c, & home through the Forum. Very delightful weather.

2 Monday

A dim morning, brightening into a pleasant day. At 10, Julian & I set out for St Peter's, calling at the Bank on the way. Spent more than an hour in St Peter's & then went into the Sculpture Gallery of the Vatican. Saw Mr. De Leon & wife, & kept company with them. Saw also Mr Sumner. Home at about 3. Letter had arrived from America, sent from Venice by Genl Pierce.

The Doctor did not come. Una constantly improves

3 Tuesday

A dim morning. At 10, I went to the Bank, & read papers
At 3, Mamma & Julian went with Mrs. Ward to the Villa
Albani. The Doctor came in the afternoon; Una is better &
better. It began to rain, & I staid in the house the rest of the
day & evening.

Wrote to Miss E. Hoar at Florence, & to Gen¹ Pierce at
Vienna.

4 Wednesday

A dim & showery morning. At about 12, I went to the
Palazzo Barberini to call for Mr Sumner. Not in. Thence to
Mr. Story's studio & staid about 2 hours seeing him model his
infant Bacchus. Thence, home. In the evening, I walked out
with Julian along the Corso &c

Una is getting on. The Doctor did not call

5 Thursday

A bright morning. In the forenoon, Mamma & Julian went
out shopping for photographs &c. At 1 ½ I went to the Capitol,
meaning to see the sculpture-gallery. Not being open, I went
to the Coliseum, & then to St John Lateran & Santa Croce; &
out of the gate of Santa Maria Maggiore & in at that of San
Lorenzo. Warm in the sun, but very pleasant. The Dr. came
in the evening.

6 Friday

A dim morning, with shaded sunshine. I went with Mamma
& Rosebud to look at photographs &c; afterwards went to the
Bank & read papers. Home after 12. Staid at home the rest of
the day, feeling very languid and out of sorts, probably owing
to the Roman atmosphere   Una being comfortable, Mamma
was out most of the day.

In the evening, Govr Seymour (late minister to Russia) called

7 Saturday

A dim, showery morning. At about 10, I went to the Bank & read newspapers; afterwards strolled about the city, into the Pantheon & two or three churches. I did not go out the rest of the day. Mamma drove to see the newly found Venus, & afterwards went to the Sciarra Palace, & came home in the rain with a headache &c. The Dr. did not come to day. Una goes on well.

8 Sunday

A dim morning. Mamma is quite unwell. Una comfortable. Anna Ward called; also, Edith Story; and in the afternoon, Miss Shepard & Rosebud went to St. Peter's with Mrs. Ward to hear the Vespers. I staid in the house till evening, & then walked with Julian along the Corso, the Babuino, Piazza d'Espagna &c

Mamma grew much better towards night.

9 Monday

A sunny morning, a little shaded   At 10, Julian & I went to the Bank; thence to St Peter's, & at 12 to the Sculpture Gallery of the Vatican. Staid till 2 ½, & then went out of the Porta Angelica, took some wine, eggs, bread, & cheese, at an Osteria, & came home over the ferry. A letter from E. Hoar at Florence. Dr. F came at dinner-time, & found Una doing well. In the evening, Julian & I took a walk along the Corso.

10 Tuesday

A bright morning. Una dressed herself, &, for the first time, sat in the drawing-room. Between 9 & 10, Mamma & I went to Mr. Thompson's studio; thence to the Capuccini church;

thence to Mr. Story's studio. Then Mamma came home, & I went to the Bank, & afterwards to Medici Gardens. In the evening, Mamma & I walked to the Coliseum & home by the Capitoline Hill.

11 Wednesday

A dim morning, afterwards brightening. Mamma, Julian, & I, went to the Piazza Navona & bought books; afterwards to Sta Maria della Pace, to Chiesa Nuova, to Palazzo Farnese. In the evening, Mamma, Julian, & I, walked to the Pincian, & home along the Corso. I wrote to Mr Vezey (consul at Havre) to-day, about Miss Shepard's passage home.

12 Thursday

A bright morning. After 10, I went to the Bank & read papers; thence to the Medici Gardens & smoked a cigar. At 2, Mamma, Julian & I, went to the Sculpture Gallery of the Capitol; thence to the church of Ara Coeli; thence to the Minerve; thence to the Pantheon; thence to St Ignazio. In the evening, Julian & I took a little stroll through the Piazza d'Espagna & Corso.

13 Friday

A showery morning. After 10, I went to the Bank & read papers; meanwhile came a tremendous rain. The Doctor called, & says Una can drive out in a day or two. Rain the rest of the day, & I did not go out again

14 Saturday

A showery morning, with sunshine & cloud afterwards. After 10, I went with Julian to the Bank, & drew £50. Strolled a little about the city; afternoon, went with Mamma & Julian to the Barberini picture gallery; to church & cemetery of the Capuchins; to Mr. Cranch's studio; to Monaldini's; &

to Castellani's & other jewellers' shops. In the evening, Julian & I took a stroll along the Corso &c.

15 Sunday

A dim morning, followed by a showery day. I did not go out till the evening, when Julian & I strolled a little about the city.

Very heavy rain during the night

16 Monday

A dim & showery morning After 10, I went to the Bank, thence to St Peters, & to the Sculpture Gallery of the Vatican at 12. Mamma & Julian met me there. We staid in the sculpture gallery till 3; then went into St. Peter's & staid about an hour; then walked home.

17 Tuesday

A showery morning. Before 10, I strolled a little about the city; then went to the Bank & read papers. At 6 °clock (after dinner) I walked with Julian to the Coliseum, forum, Temple of Vesta, Cenci palace &c &c   In the evening, Mr Cranch called.

Mamma went out with Rosebud in the afternoon.

18 Wednesday

A dark & showering morning; but quite bright by 10 °clock. At 11, Mamma, Julian, & I, went with Dr. Appleton to Mr. Freeman's studio; thence to Miss Hosmer's. Then Mamma took a carriage to drive out with Una; I went to the Bank & afterwards strolled about the city. Returning, found Dr. F. here, & Una not yet come back. After dinner, Julian & I walked along the Pulchrum Littus to Monte Testacchio, drank some wine from one of its grottoes, & returned by the Coliseum, Forum, &c.

19 Thursday

A bright morning. At 11, I walked to the picture gallery of the Vatican. Mamma & Julian also went in a cab. We set out to walk homeward at 2 ½. Una drove out to-day with Mrs. Story. In the evening, Julian & I walked out, passing through Trajan's forum, & along the Corso, then Via Ripetta &c &c

20 Friday

A bright morning. It is Rosebud's birth-day—8 years old. About 10, I went to the Bank; thence to Mr Story's studio. At noon, Una & Mamma drove out with Mrs. Motley. Dr. & Mrs Appleton called in the afternoon. After dinner, Mamma, Julian, & I, went to the Coliseum and ascended the ruins; thence to the Caelian Hill, & home by the Via Gregorio, the Temple of Vesta &c

The Doctor called while Mamma & I were out

21 Saturday

A bright morning. After breakfast, Mamma & I walked to the church of San Clemente, & thence to St John Lateran, by the way of the Coliseum. Saw the museum of St John Lateran. Returned between 1 & 2. Una had driven out. Afternoon, I went with Julian to the Consul's, to see about passports. After dinner, Mamma & I went to Mr Story's studio, & thence to the Pincian.

22 Sunday

A bright morning. About 2, I went with Rosebud to the Medici Gardens. Una & Mamma drove with Mrs. Eckley to the Borghese grounds. Julian went with the Thompsons to the Pamfili Doria villa. It rained a little, towards night. At 8, Mamma & I went to take tea with Mr. & Mrs. Story. Met there Mr Wilde & Mr. Browning. Came away at 11 ½.

23 Monday

A rather dim morning. At 10, I went with Julian to the Bank, & drew £ 50; thence to the Vatican, where met Mr & Miss Motley, with whom we went into St. Peter's. Came away about 3, & I called at Mr. Rogers' studio. Thence home. In the evening, Julian & I strolled out to Trajan's forum & along the Corso &c.

24 Tuesday

A bright morning. At 9 ½, I went with Julian to the Bank; there met Dr. Appleton, & went with him to get Steamer tickets for the voyage from Civita Vecchia. Afterwards, set out with Mrs. Story & Edith, to take Una to St. Peter's. Came back on account of rain. In the afternoon, I went to the Bank, & thence to pay a farewell visit to St. Peter's &c. M^r & Mrs. Motley called. Mr & Mrs. Story & Edith; M^r. Wild; Dr. Franco; Mr. Thompson; Dr Appleton.

25 Wednesday

A bright morning. Left Piazza Poli at about 11. Dr. Appleton kindly attending us to railway. Started at 12; reached Civita Vecchia at about 3, & sailed in Steamer Vatican for Leghorn. Arrived in the morning.

I drew £ 20 before leaving Rome. Una bore the journey well.

Miss Shepard & Rosebud were uncomfortable with sea-sickness, & Mamma had a bad headache

26 Thursday

Arriving early at Leghorn, we lay in the harbor all day, & did not choose to go ashore. The Steamer was detained to take government despatches. She sailed at about 7, the next morning.

Things observed during the day: the landing of soldiers and horses, &c &c &c

27 Friday

Sailed at about 7. A very pleasant and quiet day, & Miss Shepard & Rosebud were no longer troubled with sea sickness. We reached Genoa later in the afternoon. A beautiful sunset & evening, & beautiful view of the city. We sailed from Genoa (without going ashore) at about 11 at night.

28 Saturday

In the morning, we were running along the shores of France, very bold and picturesque, and (nearer Marseilles) many high & rocky headlands & islands. A squall came up with rain, in the course of the day. We reached Marseilles at about 9, & drove with Mamma & Una & Rosebud to the Hotel des Colonies. Thence Miss Shepard, Julian & I went to Custom House, passport office, & Railway, & arranged matters for our next start.

France

29 Sunday

At Marseilles. A bright day. I rambled about the streets. Una slept till 12 ½. Mamma also very tired. In the afternoon they, with Julian & Rosebud, drove out to the sea shore. We dined at the Restaurant of the Hotel. Afterwards, Mamma & I took a walk to a public garden on a height.

30 Monday

A dim morning. Heavy rain in the forenoon. I called at Messrs Rabaud, freres, & drew £ 30. Also called at American consulate, & arranged to send three trunks home to America. Spent some time with Miss Shepard at Railway bureaus &c, bothering about baggage and tickets. At 3 °clock left the Hotel des Colonies, & at 4, started for Avignon by rail; Mamma

& Una 1st class; the rest of us 2^d class. Arrived after 8, & put up at Hotel d'Europe

31 Tuesday

A pleasant morning. In the forenoon, Mamma, Julian, & I, rambled about town, went into two or three churches, & ascended the rocky hill that rises above Avignon. Dined at 3 °clock. After dinner, we walked with Julian & Rosebud about town, & on the bank of the Rhone.

June

1 Wednesday

A bright morning. After breakfast, Julian & I took a walk on the other side of the Rhone, drank a bottle of Lyons beer, & returned at about 12. Mamma went out with Miss Shepard & Rosebud; afterwards Una went with them. Dined at the table d'hote at 5 °clock. After dinner, walked to the summit of the rock, above the Pope's palace; and I threw stones from it into the Rhone

2 Thursday

At Avignon. Went with Mamma to the church, saw the pope's chair, Pope John XXII's tomb & &c. Also visited the Palace of the Popes. Showery in the afternoon

3 Friday

A showery morning. Mamma & Miss Shepard went to draw in the church; and afterwards Rosebud & I went thither & joined them. Dined at the Table d'Hote at 5. After dinner, Mamma, Una, Miss Shepard, & Rosebud, went to the Rocher des Doms   Julian & I walked along the riverside, & half way round the walls, returning by another gate.

4 Saturday

A bright morning. Mamma & Miss Shepard set out, after 9, on a drive to Vaucluse. I walked with the children about the city, & went to the Rocher des Doms. A shower came up, and we took refuge in the church. Mamma & Miss Shepard got back at about 7 °clock

5 Sunday

A bright morning. Mamma is quite indisposed. In the morning, Una & Rosebud went to the Rocher des Doms, &c to sketch. I strolled about the city. At about 2, I walked with Julian along the riverside, & round the city wall, & went into the garden of a Cafe & got some Lyons beer & Bologna sausage. Very hot in the sun. After dinner, I climbed the Rocher des Doms, & saw the sunset.

Much indisposed, at night, with fever & boring headache. Benefitted myself with aspersions of cold water.

6 Monday

A bright morning. Mamma still much indisposed. Julian & I walked to Villeneuve, & returned between 11 & 12. After-noon, ascended the Rocher des Doms with Una & Rosebud. Evening, went to see the fireworks, with Una & Julian, in the Place de Palais. Very good.

7 Tuesday

A bright morning. Mamma is very much better. At about noon, we left Avignon for Valence (by rail) where we arrived between 4 & 5, and put up at the Hotel de la Poste;—a dirty house, but comfortable enough. Drank some sparkling St Pearay at dinner; not an agreeable wine. Rambled about the town with Una

An intolerably hot day

8 Wednesday

We met Mrs Sedgwick of New York, her daughter & Mr. Childs, at our hotel. I rambled about town with Mrs Sedgwick & mamma, saw the Cathedral, an old tomb, being a square arched structure, & several other noticeable things. Started by rail at about 12, & arrived at Lyons about 4. Put up at the Hôtel de l'Univers. Dined. I walked out with Julian, but was hindered by rain.

9 Thursday

A fair morning. I went about town with Julian. Lyons a most beautiful town Saw the stately old Cathedral & some other things. Called at Quisard & Co's, & drew £ 50. Called at Mr. White's (American Consul's) & wasted much time talking with his womenkind, before he came in. Mamma went with Julian & Una to the Cathedral &c; there met Mrs Sedgwick & drove about with her. I went to Railway with Miss Shepard, to arrange about baggage. We started, after 4, & for Geneva, where we arrived at about 10. P. M, & put up at Hotel d'Angleterre. A rainy evening.

Switzerland

10 Friday

A showery morning. Before breakfast, I strolled about Geneva. In the forenoon, we all went out and bought a watch for Una; price 200 francs   Miss Shepard also bought one. We trudged a good deal about Geneva, in the course of the day, but did no especial sight-seeing.

11 Saturday

A dim morning, threatening showers. Rambled about Geneva. Miss Rachael Cushing (formerly of Salem) called to see us. At 3 °clock, we left the Hotel d'Angleterre, and took the steamer for Villeneuve at the eastern end of the lake of Geneva. Arrived here at about ½ past seven, & put up at Hotel Byron. There had been showers in the forenoon, but the afternoon and evening were very fine.

12 Sunday

An overcast morning, but less so than yesterday. After breakfast, walked with Julian to the Castle of Chillon. Mamma & the rest of the party followed & we went into the castle. Showery & sunny weather. Afternoon, walked with Una & Julian to the village of Villeneuve. Afterwards, saw Julian bathe in the lake.

13 Monday

A fine day. We left Hotel Byron & at 8 °clock took passage in the steamer for Lausanne. Arrived at 9 ½, & stopt at Hotel Faucon. Went to the cathedral and staid there about two hours, & Mamma sprained her ancle. Had a dejeuner a la fourchette at the Hotel at 2 °clock. At about 4, took the steamer for Geneva & arrived at 7 ½. Mamma's ancle had grown very painful. Julian appears to have caught cold from yesterday's bath, and is feverish. Returned to Hotel d'Angleterre.

14 Tuesday

In Geneva. Mamma's foot pretty bad, Julian not well, but improves during the day. I walked about Geneva; sought (in vain) for the American Consul; drew £ 20 from Lombard, Odier & Co. Bankers. Mont Blanc did not show himself to-day. Julian and I went to see the model of Mont Blanc & the rest of the mountains, in one of the public gardens.

15 Wednesday

A fine morning. Before breakfast, I went up on a height behind Geneva, & very doubtfully fancied I saw Mt Blanc.

Walked with Una & Julian about town. At 2 °clock, left Geneva by rail for Macon, where we arrived late in the evening, & put up at the Hotel d'Europe. Had supper & went to bed.

We liked the Hotel d'Angleterre at Geneva, better than any hotel within our experience.

Mamma's foot is better. Julian is not well, but more comfortable.

France

16 Thursday   Left Macon by express-train, at a little past 9. A sunny, dusty day. After a weary ride, arrived at Paris between 6 & 7 °clock. Drove to the Hotel de Lille & Albion, Rue Rivoli, which seems comfortable enough. Took supper, after which I walked out a little.

17 Friday   Rather pleasant, but cool morning. At about 10, I walked out with Julian in quest of my bankers—Hottinguer & Co, Rue Bergere. Returned without finding them. Went out again, & found them after much search. Drew £20. Found letters from Mrs. Mann, N. C. Peabody, Ticknor, Fields (now in London), Bennoch, &c. Mamma (who had been out with Miss Shepard) went with Julian & me to the picture gallery of the Louvre. We there met Mr. Motley. Dined at the Table d'Hote, & afterwards all except Una walked out again. Mr. & Mrs. Cranch called in the evening.

Gave Miss Shepard the money for her passage to America

18 Saturday   I wrote a note to Bennoch. Julian & I walked in the gardens of the Tuileries, & along the Champs Elysees to the Arc of Triomphe. Late in the day, Una, Rosebud, & I went to the picture-gallery of the Louvre. Mamma & Miss

Shepard spent the day chiefly in vain pursuit of a bonnet. In the evening I walked out with Julian

19 Sunday   An overcast & showery day. Went out pretty early with Mamma & Julian; looked into the church of St Germains, and then went to the Church of Notre Dame. It is still undergoing repair. Afterwards went to the Louvre, & looked at the Venus of Milo, & other sculptures, and at some of the pictures. Mrs. Green called on us after dinner. Julian & I took a short walk in the evening, along the Rue Rivoli.

20 Monday   After breakfast, strolled in the Tuillerie gardens. Went to the Bankers & drew £ 30. Took tickets (5) for our passages to London, via Havre. Mrs Green called; Mr. Stone, Miss Dustin; Mr Greene &c &c. Mamma & the rest (except myself) went to drive in the Bois de Boulogne, after dinner.
A fitful day.

21 Tuesday   Left the hotel of Lille & d'Albion, and at 12 °clock, started for Havre by rail. Arrived at 7 ½. Put Miss Shepard on board the Vanderbilt for New York; and myself & family put up at Wheeler's Hotel, close to Quay Notre Dame. Very cool weather.

22 Wednesday   Spent the day in Havre; and at about dusk, went on board steamer Alliance, which sailed at midnight for Southampton   A somewhat rough night & heavy swell in the channel. None of the family sick except Julian. We slept very scantily.

England

23 Thursday   Arrived at Southampton at about 9 ½. After

passing our things through the Custom House, went to Good-
ridge's Hotel. Spent the day in Southampton

Pleasant English weather.

24 Friday At about 9, we started for London, & arrived
at 11 ½. I went to Bennochs (leaving Mamma & the girls at
railway station) with Julian, to inquire for lodgings. Found
him well and cheerful. He directed us to Mrs Coxon's board-
ing-house, 6. Golden Square. During the rest of the day, I
took a stroll in St James' Park with Julian; & afterwards about
the street with Una & Julian.

25 Saturday After breakfast, strolled in St. James' Park,
went into Westminster Abbey & Hall. Called on J. T. Fields,
23 Northumberland St. Not in. Went to Bennoch's, 77 Wood
St. Lunched there. Walked to London Bridge, & thence returned home, very weary. A hot, sunny day. After dinner,
Fields called on us.

Late in the evening, I took a stroll.

26 Sunday A thunderstorm in the morn^g We staid in the
house during the day, which was very hot. In the evening,
Mamma, Una, Julian, & I, took a walk in Regent street &c

I wrote to Mr. Wilding, putting off our passage to America
till July 30th.

27 Monday Morning, Julian & I went to breakfast with
Mr. Fields. Afterwards, looked into the National Gallery &
found Mamma & Una there. Julian went & lunched at Mr.
Bennoch's warehouses   Afterwards we took steamer to Thames
Tunnel, & descended into it. Thence returned by steamer to
Blackfriars' Bridge. Afterwards went to St James' Park.

A very warm day.

28 Tuesday   An overcast morning. After breakfast, I walked out with Julian; went to the taylors (Mitchelhill, 20, Argyle St.); thence to the British Museum (not open,) then to the National Gallery. Came home to lunch, &, it being rainy, did not go out again. Mr. Chorley, the Athenaeum critic, called. Also, Mrs Stevens, & Mrs. Page.

29 Wednesday   An overcast morn^g, with gleams of sun. Letter from Mr. Wilding; no state-rooms to be had for July 30th. After breakfast, Julian went to British Museum; & Mamma, Rosebud, Una, & I went to the Vernon Gallery, Marlboro House. At 12 ¼, I put them into a cab to go to 77, Wood-st., & myself followed on foot. We lunched with Bennoch; Mrs. Hume being present. Coming homeward, we went into St. Paul's, & down into the crypt, & saw Nelson's & Wellington's tombs, &c. I left Mamma &c to shop in St. Paul's churchyard, & took a walk in St. James's park; thence home.

30 Thursday   A fair English morn^g. After breakfast, Julian & I went to the tailors, & then strolled about, into St James's Park &c &c. At about one, Mamma, Una, & Rosebud, set out for Blackheath, to visit Mrs. Bennoch. After 4, I went to 77 Wood St, & found Mr. Bennoch, with whom I took the rail for his residence at Blackheath. Arrived at Greenwich Station, and walked to the house. Found Mamma &c &c. there, having found their way after much difficulty We took tea there, took the rail for London a little before 9, & arrived at our boarding house before 10.

I wrote to Mr. Wilding to-day, engaging passages for August 13th.

July

1 Friday.   At 10 or 11, started from London Bridge Station with Bennoch & Fields, on an excursion with society of

Archimagi. Stopt at Lewes, looked at Castle, Priory &c. & lunched. Thence to Brighton, dined with Sir Francis Moon, & I made a speech. Thence to Arundel (Bennoch & I) where we supt & slept. A warm day.

2 Saturday   Left Arundel after 9, after seeing the exterior of the castle &c. Took the rail for Chichester, & saw the town & Cathedral. Thence to Portsmouth, arriving between 1 & 2. Took a boat & had a row in the harbour; afterwards visited the dock-yard. At about 4, took the rail for Farnboro', & met Captain Shaw there, who took us to Aldershot. Dined with N. C. Rifles, & I slept in a hut. Warm

3 Sunday   Breakfasted at the mess-room. Strolled with Bennoch about the camp. Drove with him & Captain Shaw to the residence of the latter, where we lunched & spent the afternoon. Returned to camp, & dined with the mess. To bed after 12.
A thunder storm, both this night & the preceding. Warm

4 Monday.   Breakfasted at ½ past 8. The camp all astir, preparing for an inspection of the troops. Bennoch & I went to see it. The Duke of Cambridge &c &c present. Before it was concluded, we got into cab, drove to the station, took the rail at ½ past 1, & arrived in London at about 3. At 5 ½, my wife & I went to dine with Mr. Chorley, 13. Eaton-place West. Home before 10. Warm

5 Tuesday   After breakfast, Gen¹ Pierce & Colonel Seymour called, also Mr. H. A. Bright. Mamma, Julian, & I, went at 12 to call on Mr. & Mrs. Fields, & waited till they came from the country. Lunched there. Mr. Fields has arranged with Smith & Elder for £ 600 for the new Romance. We then went to National Exhibition, where met Mr. Bright. I went

with him to the House of Commons, & afterwards to Hyde Park; thence home. Una & Rosebud went today to Mrs. Stevens. Warm.

6 Wednesday After breakfast, Julian & I set forth, & strolled cityward. Went to the Barings, got a returned letter, & drew £ 30. Went into Guildhall. Afterwards to Bennoch's where we lunched, Mr. Jerdan & two others being present. Returning, we went into St James's Park, where I smoked a cigar, & home by the palace-avenue, and Piccadilly &c. Bo't 5th Vol of Irving's Life of Washington.

Mamma has had an influenza, but is better.

A very hot day.

7 Thursday Morn^g, all of us went to Westminster Abbey, & (except Julian) went through the chapels. Also into Westminster Hall. Julian & I took a steamer & went to Chelsea, & back by omnibus. Mr. Bates called.

8 Friday Genl Pierce & Col. Seymour called early. I drove with them to the Despatch Agents, & then strolled into the city. We went to Bennoch's, & afterwards to Genl Campbell's, the U.S. Consul. Returning, I lunched at Bennoch's, & went with him to Old Bailey. Found Mr. Bright waiting for me at home. He & I went to the House of Commons, & heard part of a debate—Lord John Russell, Palmerston, Sidney Herbert &c Afterwards dined at the Wellington Then to the New Adelphi Theatre. Home at 12. Very hot. Julian went to Blackheath to-day.

9 Saturday Staid at home till after 2. Mr. Bright called, & (by his invitation) we took a cab for Waterloo Station, & thence by rail to Richmond. Dined at the Star & Garter (Mamma, Una, & Rosebud, of the party) & afterwards walked

in the Park. Took the rail homeward at 8 ½, & reached Golden Square at 9 ½. Julian returned from Mr. Bennoch's, Blackheath, at 10.

A very hot day

10 Sunday   Did not go out till after 7. Then went to the Oxford & Cambridge Club, & dined with Mr. Bright. After dinner (at about 9 ½) left the club & went with Mr. Bright to call on Mrs. Heywood, 8, Connaught Place West. Home, along Oxford and Regent street, at about 11.

Another very hot day.

11 Monday   Gen¹ Pierce called at about 11 Drove with him to Westbourne Terrace; thence to Mr. Dallas's &c. Afterwards walked with him into the city, & lunched at Bennoch's. We visited Christ Church Hospital, old Newgate, St Bartholomew's Hospital. Took cab in Holborn & drove westward. Afterwards walked with Pierce to Trafalgar Square, & left him there.

Very hot.

12 Tuesday   Mamma & the children went to Norwood & the Crystal Palace to see Gen¹ & Mrs. Pierce. Mʳ Bright called in the forenoon, & I drove with him to call on Mʳ Fields, & Sumner (not in) & afterwards to Dr. Williams' Library in the city. We lunched at an eating house; & I then went to Barings, & got some letters returned from Rome. Drew £ 50, & arranged for funds. Came home, & at 7, went to dine with Barry Cornwall. Met Leigh Hunt, Kinglake, Sumner, Fields &c.

Came home at about 11. Mamma & children had returned. Tremendously hot.

13 Wednesday   Went to the British Museum. In the afternoon, went out with Julian, took cab & called on Mr.

Chorley; not in. In the evening, Mr Bright called, & we went to the Workingman's College, where we saw T. Hughes (author of Tom Brown's Schooldays) & other persons. Home at about 11.

Awfully hot.

14 Thursday   Gen¹ Pierce called in the morn⁶. At 11, we started by Great Northern Railway, & at 7 ½, arrived at Malton, Yorkshire. Met Fanny Wrigley there, by appointment. Staid for the night at Talbot Hotel

15 Friday   Staid at Malton till 3.40, P. M. Then took rail (Fanny Wrigley in company) & came to Whitby. Mamma, Fanny, & Julian, went in quest of lodgings, leaving Una, Rosebud, & myself, at the Station. Returned at about sundown, without success. We went to the Angel Hotel; a comfortable house of the commercial class.

16 Saturday   Morn⁶, Julian & I walked on the cliffs & sands. Mamma & the others went in search of lodgings; again without success. Mamma, Una, Fanny, & Rosebud went to Lythe in a fly, to seek for lodgings but found none. Mamma & Una returned in a boat. Julian & I walked on the cliffs, on the other side of the river, & looked at Whitby church and Abbey.

17 Sunday   Mamma stayed in the house all day. Julian and I walked about a little, on the beach & cliffs.

18 Monday   We all went to Lythe on foot, along the beach, in quest of lodgings. Finding none, we returned in the same way.

19 Tuesday   A rainy morning. At about 2, I walked out with Julian in quest of Simpson & Chapman, Bankers, Grape

lane. Did not find them. We climbed up to the church & Abbey. After dinner, found the Bankers & drew £ 30. Walked on the cliffs. Sunshine & mist. Una, Rosebud, & Fanny went to the abbey. Mamma staid in the house all day.

20 Wednesday. A misty moisty morning. Rambled about the shore a little. A very dull day.

21 Thursday Dull weather In the forenoon, Mamma, Julian, & I, went to the Abbey, & obtained admittance within the ruins. In the afternoon, I walked on the cliffs and shore.

22 Friday. A dull, misty morning. Rose betimes & prepared for departure At 8 °clock, took the stage omnibus to Guisbrough; arrived at 12 ½. At 2 °clock, took the rail for Redcar, & arrived at about 3 ½. It rained almost all day. My wife & Fanny went in quest of lodgings, & found some at Mrs. King's, 120 High-st; but not available till tomorrow. Meanwhile, we went to Clarendon Hotel, near the railway, for the night.

23 Saturday Staid at the Clarendon till 2 °clock; then took possession of our lodgings, which seem comfortable. Very moist and chill weather.

24 Sunday. A bright morning. Wrote letters to Thomas Hughes, Gen¹ Pierce, Barings Brothers, Bennoch, & Geo. S. Hillard. After dinner (at 3) walked on the beach with Julian. After tea (between 6 & 7) walked on the beach with Mamma. A very pleasant day.

To day, I looked at the rough draught of the Romance, and prepared for the rewriting of it.

25 Monday Sunny morning, with some clouds. Prepared to begin writing my Romance, all the morning. At about

2 °clock, walked out on the beach. After dinner took another walk. Also, with Mamma, after tea.

26 Tuesday   Rec^d letter from Bennoch. At about 10 °clock, began the Romance in good earnest, and wrote till 3. After dinner, took a walk with Julian. After tea, took a short walk with Mamma & Una.

A very warm day

27 Wednesday   Wrote from 9 °clock till 3. After dinner, walked along the beach with Julian & Rosebud. A warm day, with cloud & sunshine

Julian went in to bathe, and avers that he swam, for the first time.

After tea, I took a long, swift walk on the beach, with Julian.

28 Thursday   An overcast day. I began to write, soon after 9, but made slow & poor progress. After dinner, took a walk along the beach, returning through the village of Coatham. Rec^d letter from T. Hughes, informing me of the death of his son. After tea, walked along the beach with Julian, & saw him swim.

29 Friday   A bright morning. Rec^d letter from Bennoch, enclosing card for dinner at St Bartholomew's. Scribbed fitfully till 2, with many idle pauses, & no good result. After dinner, walked along the beach with Rosebud & Julian, & saw Julian bathe. After tea, walked on the beach with Julian, & returned by way of Coatham.

30 Saturday   A bright morning. Rec^d letter from Henry Bright, & wrote one to R. Monckton Milnes. Wrote till nearly 3, tolerably well.

After dinner, walked with Julian along the beach, & saw him bathe. A high tide, windy, and a good deal of surf.

After tea, walked along the beach with Una & Julian, & returned by way of Coatham.

31 Sunday   Sunshine & clouds. Wrote till 2 °clock. Staid within doors till after tea, & then took a walk on the beach with Una & Julian. Julian bathed.

August

1 Monday   A bright morning. Wrote till 3, with middling success. After dinner, took a walk on the beach with Julian & Rosebud   Julian bathed. After tea, took a walk on the beach with Julian

Mamma is much indisposed with cold & chronic weariness.

2 Tuesday   A bright morning. Rec^d letter from Mr. Wilding, enclosing letters from J. R. Lowell, & N. C. Peabody. After dinner, walked with the three children on the beach. Julian bathed. After tea, walked with Julian on the beach.

Mamma has been quite ill to-day, with severe headache, but better towards night.

3 Wednesday   A bright morning. Wrote till 3 °clock. Julian went to the circus. After dinner, I walked on the beach with Rosebud Sprinklings of rain. After tea, I walked on the beach with Julian, & saw him bathe.

Una rode two hours on horseback to-day.

Mamma is better, but feeble & weary.

4 Thursday   A bright, shadowy morning Wrote till 3; a little more satisfactorily than heretofore. After dinner, took a long walk with Julian toward the mouth of the Tees. After tea, took a walk by myself.

Mamma seems rather better to day.

5 Friday   A Fair morning. Rec^d letters from J. T. Fields at Leamington. Also, from Dr. Wilkinson, London   Wrote till 3, tolerably well. After dinner, walked along the beach with Julian to Marske, & returned by the road.

Sprinkles of rain in the afternoon.

6 Saturday   A fair morning. Wrote till after 3; no great progress, but more interested as I get on. After dinner, walked on the beach with Julian, & saw him bathe. In the dusk of the evening, walked on the shore by myself.

7 Sunday   An overcast morning. Wrote till 2, then dined, & wrote an hour after dinner. A rainy afternoon. Wrote a note to Fields.

Did not go out all day.

Heavy rain at night

I wrote an hour after dinner.

8 Monday   Cloudy & inclement morning   Wrote till after 3. After dinner, took a walk with Julian & Rosebud. Julian bathed in the surf. After tea, in the dusk & moonlight, took a walk on the beach by myself. Very clear and pure atmosphere.

9 Tuesday   A bright morning. Wrote till 3. Fanny & Rosebud went to the Circus at 2. After dinner, I walked with Julian on the beach, & saw him bathe. Mamma, Una, & Julian, went to the Circus in the evening. After sunset, I took a walk on the beach, by myself.

10 Wednesday   A bright morning. Rec^d letters from G. S. Hillard at Malvern, & from E. P. Peabody, Boston. Wrote till 3. After dinner, walked on the beach with Julian, & saw him bathe. After tea, walked with Mamma, & afterwards by myself.

I enjoyed much the cool, exhilirating air.

11 Thursday   A bright morning. Wrote till 3. After dinner, walked with Julian, & saw him bathe. After tea, walked with Julian on the beach, & returned through Coatham.

Warm, dog-dayish weather.

Rec^d by post the Scouring of the White Horse, from T. Hughes.

12 Friday   An overcast day, tending to rain, but warm. Wrote from 10 till 3, not particularly well. After dinner, walked out with Julian & saw him bathe. After tea, walked with him again.

Fanny is much indisposed to-day.

13 Saturday   Sunny & shadowy morning. Wrote till 3. After dinner, walked with Julian through Coatham, & home by the beach. Saw Julian bathe. After tea, walked on the beach by myself.

Una rode on horseback to-day.

Fanny seems to be recovered.

A very warm, heavy day.

14 Sunday   A pretty fair morning. Tried to write, but could make out nothing; discouraged and depressed, & not very well. After dinner, walked with Julian & saw him bathe. At dusk, took a walk by myself.

15 Monday   An overcast morning. Wrote till 3—&c &c. After dinner, walked on the beach with Julian, & saw him bathe. After tea, walked on the beach with Mamma, & then, leaving her with Julian, took a rapid walk by myself.

16 Tuesday   A pleasant morning   At 10.40, took the rail with Julian to Middlesboro; arrived at 11. Called at Messrs. Backhouse & Co's bank & drew on the Barings for £50. Left

Middlesboro', & reached Redcar at 12. Took a walk on the beach before dinner. Again after dinner, & saw Julian bathe. Again at dusk.

Rec^d letters from E. P. Peabody, through Mrs. Coxon, to day
Wrote Barings.

17 Wednesday   A rather pleasant, rather overcast morning. Wrote till 3. After dinner, took a walk along the beach. After tea, I took a walk with Julian & saw him bathe.
Very warm.

18 Thursday   An overcast morning. Rec^d letter from Russell Sturgis, London, telling of Horace Mann's death. Wrote till 3. After dinner, walked with Julian, & saw him bathe. After tea, walked again with Julian, & returned through Coatham.

19 Friday   Rather pleasant morning. Wrote to Russell Sturgis. Wrote till 3. After dinner, took a walk with Julian & saw him bathe. After tea, took a walk by myself.
A very warm day, as well as for some days past.

20 Saturday   Very pleasant morning. Wrote till 3 ½. After dinner, walked with Julian & saw him bathe. At dusk, walked on the beach by myself
A gentleman & lady, unknown, called on me, this evening, while I was out.

21 Sunday   Rather a cool morning, with sun & cloud. Wrote till dinner, at 2, & again about an hour, after dinner. Then walked with Julian on the beach, & saw him bathe. After tea, took a walk by myself

22 Monday   A delightful morning. Wrote till after 3. After dinner, walked on the beach & met Una & Julian, who

had been to Marske. Julian bathed. After tea, walked by myself on the beach.

A most beautiful day.

23 Tuesday   A fine morning. Rec^d letter from Mrs. Mann, telling of her husband's death. Wrote till 3. After dinner, walked with Julian & saw him bathe. After tea walked with Julian, continuing the walk by myself

24 Wednesday   A fine morning. Julian & Una went on donkeys to —— castle, about 4 miles off. Una's donkey fell with her, but did no harm. I wrote till 3. After dinner, walked with Julian & saw him bathe. After tea, walked by myself.

25 Thursday   Pleasant, rather overcast morning. A note from Bennoch, endorsing one from Fields in Germany. Wrote till 3 ½. After dinner, walked with Julian & saw him bathe. After tea, walked by myself.

26 Friday   Overcast, chill, & misty morning. Wrote till 3 ½. After dinner walked with Julian, & saw him bathe. After tea, walked by myself

27 Saturday   Rather pleasant morning, afterwards more clouded. Letter from E. P. Peabody at Yellow Springs, telling of Mrs. Mann &c Wrote till after 3. After dinner, took a walk with Julian, & saw him bathe. A very high tide to-day. After tea, took a walk with Julian.

Fine day.

28 Sunday   Rather pleasant morning   Wrote till after 2. After dinner, walked with Julian & saw him bathe. After tea, walked again with Julian.

A very high tide, & fine clear day & evening.

29 Monday   Overcast morning, chill. Wrote till 3. A violent rain-storm during most of the day. Did not take my usual after-dinner's walk. After tea, it cleared up, & I walked on the beach by myself

30 Tuesday   A cool, rather pleasant, somewhat overcast morning. Wrote till 3. After dinner, walked with Julian & saw him bathe. After tea walked by myself
Cool & breezy.

31 Wednesday.   Overcast morn^g with sunny gleams. Wrote till 3. After dinner, walked with Julian & saw him bathe. A breezy day. After tea, walked by myself

September

1 Thursday   Wrote till 3.
Walked with Julian & saw him bathe. Walked by myself.

2 Friday   Wrote till 3.
Walked with Julian & saw him bathe after dinner. Walked by myself.
Mamma is indisposed to-day.

3 Saturday   Bright, rather cool morning. A letter to Una from Mrs. J. L. O'Sullivan in Lisbon. Wrote till 3. After dinner walked with Julian & saw him bathe. Cool & rather breezy. After tea, walked by myself.

4 Sunday   Bright & cool morning. Wrote till 2, when we dined. After dinner, wrote till 5 ½. Then walked with Julian & saw him bathe.

5 Monday   Bright morning.

Wrote till 3. After dinner, walked by myself along the beach towards the mouth of the Tees.

Una rode on horseback from 7 till 8. P. M.

6 Tuesday   A rainy & windy morning. Letter from E. P. Peabody &c. Wrote draft on Ticknor for $50 for my wife wedding gift to Ellen E. Peabody. Julian rode on poney back in the forenoon. After dinner, I walked on the beach.

A very pleasant afternoon.

7 Wednesday   Rather pleasant morning, somewhat overcast. Wrote till 3. After dinner, walked with Julian & saw him bathe.

8 Thursday   Pleasant morning. A note from J. T. Fields at Lucerne, Switzerland.

Wrote till after 3.

After dinner, walked on the beach with Julian, & saw him bathe.

9 Friday   A bright morning. A letter from Henry Bright.

Wrote till after 3.

After dinner, went to Coatham where was a cattle-show. Found it just closed.

Exceedingly windy.

After tea, took a short walk on the beach.

10 Saturday   Bright, windy morning. Wrote till 3. Gave Mamma the finished portion (rather more than half, I should think) of my Romance to read.

After dinner, walked on the beach by myself. Very windy & quite cool. My hat blew into the sea, & I ran in after it.

11 Sunday   Cool morning, a little overcast. Wrote till 2.
After dinner, walked on the beach with Julian, & saw him bathe.
Very pleasant.

12 Monday   Pleasant, but cool morning Wrote till 3.
After dinner, walked with Julian & saw him bathe.

13 Tuesday   Somewhat overcast morning. Wrote till 3, & also a little while after dinner.
The forenoon was rainy.
About 5, took a walk on the beach with Julian.
Chill, autumnal weather   Una & Julian rode on horseback, in the forenoon

14 Wednesday   Rather bright, cool morning. Wrote till 3.
It rained in the course of the day.
After dinner, I took a walk on the beach.

15 Thursday   Rather dull morning.
Wrote till 3.
After dinner, took a walk on beach & saw Julian bathe.
Very pleasant afternoon.

16 Friday   Cool, rather bright, breezy morning. Wrote to Bennoch, asking advice about our winter quarters. Wrote till nearly 3. After dinner, took a walk on the beach. A high wind from seaward, and a heavy surf tumbling in on the beach.

17 Saturday   Fair morning, & high wind. Wrote till 3.
After dinner, walked with Julian & saw him bathe.
Cool, but very pleasant.

18 Sunday   An overcast morning. Wrote till 2. After din-

ner, wrote again. Then took a walk with Julian, & saw him bathe

19 Monday   A bright & cool morning. Wrote till after 3. After dinner, took a walk with Julian & saw him bathe

20 Tuesday   Overcast morning.
Wrote till 3.
After dinner took a walk

21 Wednesday   Wrote till 3. After dinner, took a walk with Julian & saw him bathe.

22 Thursday   Rather pleasant, but cool. Julian & Una rode on horseback, after breakfast. Wrote till 3. After dinner, took a walk with Julian & saw him bathe.

23 Friday   Slightly overcast morning. Wrote till 3.
After dinner, took a walk on the beach with Una.

24 Saturday   Very mild & pleasant morn^g. Wrote till after 3.
After dinner, walked with Julian, & saw him bathe.
Heavy rain in the evening.

25 Sunday   Pleasant & mild morning Wrote till dinner time at 2. After dinner, again wrote till 4.
Took a walk on the beach with Julian, & saw him bathe. Windy, but pleasant.
A letter to my wife from Mrs. Mann, this morning

26 Monday   Pleasant morning, rather windy. Wrote till after 3.
In the forenoon, Julian & Una rode on horseback.
After dinner, walked with Julian & saw him bathe.

27 Tuesday   A pleasant, mild morning. Wrote till after 3.
After dinner, walked with Julian & saw him bathe.

28 Wednesday   Rather pleasant morning. A letter from
Bennoch, enclosing Cairngorm seal for Una. Wrote till after 3.
Being a rainy afternoon, I did not go out.
Rec^d a note from Miss Cust, in reference to the 'Sowle's
Pilgrimage', which she presents to me.

29 Thursday   Cloud & sunshine; rather cool & breezy.
Mamma, Una, Rosebud, & Fanny, drove to Wilton Castle &c.
Wrote till 3.
After dinner, walked on the beach with Julian, & saw him
bathe.

30 Friday   Bright morning. Wrote note to Miss I Cust.
Wrote till 3.
After dinner, walked on the beach with Julian & saw him
bathe.

October

1 Saturday   A rainy morning
Wrote till 3
After dinner, walked with Julian & saw him bathe

2 Sunday   Overcast morning. Letters from Mrs. Mann,
E. P. Peabody, Mrs. Badger &c.
Wrote till 2. After dinner, wrote till 4 ½
Walked with Julian & saw him bathe.

3 Monday   Very warm & pleasant morning. At 10.40, took
rail for Middlesboro', & drew on Barings for £60, through

Backhouse & Co. Reached home at 12 ½. Wrote to Barings. Wrote from 1 till 3; and, after dinner, wrote an hour.

Walked with Julian, & saw him bathe.

4 Tuesday   Very pleasant morning. Letters from Ticknor, E. P. Peabody, Mrs. Mann &c. Wrote till 3. After dinner took a walk with Julian & saw him bathe.

A very warm & beautiful day

5 Wednesday   Fine morning. 10 before 9, Left Redcar (all of us) and came to Leamington, viá Leeds. Arrived at about 4. Found Mrs. Malony at the station at Leamington, who came with us to our lodgings, No. 21, Bath-street.

A very pleasant & warm day.

6 Thursday   A fine day. Wrote a letter to Ticknor. At about 10 set out with Una, & walked to Warwick by the old road, & home by the new. Got back at about 1.

7 Friday   Wrote letters to G. S. Hillard, & to Bennoch. Walked a little about town.
Rather dull weather.

8 Saturday   A dull, overcast day.
In the afternoon took a short walk.

9 Sunday   A dull morning. Notes from Bennoch & Fields. Wrote till about 2. After dinner, walked with Julian in Jephson's Gardens, and afterwards on the outskirts of the town.
Wrote a note to Fields.

10 Monday   A dull morning. Wrote till 3. After dinner, walked with Una.
In the evening, Mr. Bennoch called. Spent the evening & took supper with us.

11 Tuesday   Dull morning.
Wrote till 3.
Towards twilight, took a walk.

12 Wednesday   Rather pleasant morning.
Wrote till 3.
In the afternoon walked to the outskirts of Warwick, with
Julian.

13 Thursday   Overcast morning.
Wrote till 3, and again, after dinner, till about 5.
A letter from J. T. Fields, now in Paris.
After 5, took a walk along the Newbold road.

14 Friday   A rainy morning.
Wrote till 3—the Preface of my book. It is not yet finished
by 60 or 70 pages.
About 5 °clock, walked with Julian along Tachbrook road,
& to Whitnash village

15 Saturday   An overcast, but not unpleasant morning.
Looked over manuscript of Romance till 3.
After dinner, walked with Julian to Warwick by old road,
& home by the other.

16 Sunday   A rainy morning.
A letter from Smith & Elder, Publishers, London. Also from
Madam O'Sullivan at Lisbon.
Looked over manuscript &c.
After dinner, walked with Julian on Newbold road, through
Jephson's Gardens

17 Monday   Showery morning.
Wrote till 3.

After dinner walked with Julian through Lover's Grove to Lillington.

Sent Messrs Smith Elder & Co. the manuscript of my Romance as far as page 429, by express; also, letter by post.

18 Tuesday   A rainy morning. Letters from Mr Wilding, & to Una & Mamma from Ellen Peabody. Wrote till 3 After dinner, took a walk with Julian.

19 Wednesday   Overcast morning. Letter from Smith Elder & Co. acknowledging receipt of M.S.

Wrote till 3

After dinner, walked with Julian to Warwick-castle Bridge.

20 Thursday   Pleasant morning, soon turning to clouds. Letters from G. S. Hillard, & Mr. Miller. Did not write to-day. At about 1, went to the railway station & met Hillard, who staid with us till after 2. Went to the railway to see him off.

It rained in the afternoon, & I did not take a walk.

21 Friday   Clear and cool morning. Wrote till 3. Mr. Bright came, dined, & spent the evening with us. I did not walk out

Very cool weather, & a slight fall of snow.

22 Saturday   Very cool morning; a frost last night. Did not write to day. At 12 ¼, took the rail with Mr. Bright for Rugby. Saw the school &c. Afterwards, walked with Mr. B. to Bilton Hall (a residence of Addison.) Saw the game of football in the school-close; dined with Mr. & Charley Bright at the George Hotel. Took the rail for Leamington at about 9.

23 Sunday   A cool morning. Letter from Mr. Macmillan, publisher. Mr. Bright took Una to chapel at Warwick, in a cab,

& walked back with her. He dined with us & spent the evening. After dinner, Mr B., Una, Julian, Rosebud & I took a walk through Jephson's Gardens, & to Lovers' Grove &c. Mr. B. spent the evening, with us.

24 Monday   Cool & bright morning.
Wrote till 3.
After dinner, walked with Julian to Whitnash.

25 Tuesday   Cool morning, between dim & sunny.
Wrote drearily till 3.
A heavy rain in the afternoon; so that I did not go out.
Una & Fanny Wrigley went to a lecture in the evening.

26 Wednesday   A rainy morning. Letters from Mrs. Mann & E. P. Peabody.
Wrote till 3.
After dinner took a walk.
Una & Fanny went to Mr. Mason Jones's second lecture.

27 Thursday   Rather pleasant morning. Letter from Bennoch. Wrote till nearly 3.
After dinner, walked with Julian to Warwick Castle.
Una & Fanny went to Mr. Mason Jones' lecture.

28 Friday   Dim but rather pleasant morning. A letter from John Miller.
Wrote till 3.
A letter from Mr O'Sullivan, now in Paris.
It rained heavily in the afternoon; & I did not go out.
A letter to Una from Miss Bracken, at Broadstairs.

29 Saturday   Rather pleasant morning.
Wrote till nearly 3.
After dinner, walked with Julian along the Newbold Road.

30 Sunday   Pleasant morning.
Wrote till 2.
In the afternoon, it rained heavily, & I did not go out.

31 Monday   A dim morning, boding rain.
Wrote till 3.
After dinner, walked with Julian along the Tachbrook road.
Dreamed of seeing Gen¹ Pierce.

November

1 Tuesday   A storm of wind & rain during the night;
rainy & windy morning.
Wrote till 3.
After dinner, walked with Julian towards Warwick by the
Emscote road.

2 Wednesday   A warm, showery morning.
Wrote till 3.
It rained in the afternoon; and I did not go out.

3 Thursday   Mild and pleasant morning After breakfast,
Mamma & Una walked to Whitnash.
I wrote till 3.
After dinner, took a walk with Julian.

4 Friday   Dark & rainy morning.
Wrote till 3.
After dinner, took a walk with Julian along the Whitnash
road.

5 Saturday   Rather dim morning. Letters from Mrs. Mann
& E. P. P. at Concord; and from Bennoch (London) & G. S.
Hillard, Liverpool.

A rainy day.

Towards dusk, I took a walk up & down the Parade.

I wrote till 3.

6 Sunday   Beautiful morning.

I wrote till 2 °clock, & again after dinner.

It being a rainy day, I did not go out.

Una & Julian walked to Warwick to chapel, in the forenoon, & were caught in the rain, coming home.

7 Monday   A fine morning.

Wrote till 3.

After dinner, walked by myself to Whitnash, & returned by Tachbrook road.

Una and Julian went, in the evening, to a lecture on the Electric Telegraph.

8 Tuesday   A fine morning. Letters from Mrs. Mann, & E. P. Peabody. Wrote till 5 minutes of 12, & finished the last page of my Romance. 508 manuscript pages.

Towards twilight, took a short walk with Julian.

Una, Julian, & Fanny Wrigley went to a lecture on optics in the evening.

Rain most of the day

9 Wednesday   A fine morning. Sent off my parcel of Romance to Smith Elder & Co by parcel-express; also a note to them by mail.

Walked with Una to Radford Semel; started at 10 ½ & returned between 12 & 1.

Julian breakfasted with Major Johnstone, & went with him to Whitnash.

Towards dusk, walked with Julian along Warwick road.

10 Thursday   Cool & rather pleasant morning.
In the forenoon, walked with Julian.
In the afternoon, towards evening, took a short walk by myself.
Mamma had a tooth out & many filled. She & Rosebud went to a panorama at 2 °clock.
Julian to the same, at 8. P. M.

11 Friday   A pleasant, cool morning.
A letter from Smith Elder & Co. dissenting from the title of my book.
Between 11 & 12, took a walk with Julian through Lover's Grove to Lillington &c. Home after 1.
At nearly dusk, took a short walk with Julian

12 Saturday   A fine, but cool morning. At 11, set out with Julian to walk to Warwick; market day; went into the Museum of Natural History &c. Got home at about 2.
At dusk, took a walk by myself along the Whitnash road.

13 Sunday   Cool, pleasant morning. Letters from E. P. P., & Mrs Mann. Wrote a note to Smith Elder & Co suggesting various Titles for the Romance.
A little before 5, walked with Julian along the Newbold road. Got back a little before 6.

14 Monday   Cool morning, with a slight November mist. Wrote in my Journal. Toward dusk, took a walk with Julian.

15 Tuesday   Chill, foggy, overcast morning After 4 °clock, took a moderately short walk with Julian.

16 Wednesday   Cool, pleasant morning. Letter to Una from O'Sullivan in Paris At about 12, set out with Mamma

& walked to Whitnash, returning by Tachbourne Road
A letter from Fields in Paris
About dusk, took a walk with Julian.

17 Thursday   An overcast morning.
Wrote a note to Fields.
After 4 °clock, walked by Tachborne road to Whitnash, with
Julian

18 Friday   Rather overcast morning. Letter from Bennoch.
Walked with Julian, at 11, to Warwick, & there met Mamma
& Una, who had gone by omnibus. Did some shopping, & all
walked home together, arriving before 2. After 4, took a moderate walk with Julian.

19 Saturday   An overcast morning. Letter from S. Lucas,
of 'Once a Week.' Walked out with wife, & went to the Bank,
& drew a cheque for £60, on Baring Brothers. Wrote to advise
them of it. Towards dusk, took a walk with Julian

20 Sunday   A clear, cool morning.
Towards dark, took a walk to the edge of Whitnash, with
Julian

21 Monday   Rather an overcast day. Nearly at dusk, took
a walk with Julian.

22 Tuesday   A dim, but not cloudy morning. At about 1,
went to the Bank, & rec^d £60 for my cheque. Took a walk
about town.
At dusk, took a walk with Julian along the Warwick road.

23 Wednesday   A dark, damp morning.
Towards dark, took a walk by myself; Julian following.

24 Thursday   A very pleasant day.
Mamma & Fanny went to Warwick.
Between 4 & 5, Julian & I walked to Whitnash

25 Friday   A dull & sombre morning
Towards dusk, took a short walk with Julian

26 Saturday   Showery morning, with glimpses of sun.
After 4, walked out with Una & Julian.

27 Sunday   A rather pleasant morning. Letters from Mrs.
Badger (late Miss Shepard) and E. E. Peabody, now Mrs.
How.
After 4, took a walk with Julian.

28 Monday   Cloudy & wet morning A letter from Mr.
Fields in Paris to my wife.
My wife and I answered Fields' note.
After 4, took a walk to Whitnash with Julian

29 Tuesday   A clear & cool morning. Note from Bennoch,
which I answered.
At noon, went out shopping with Mamma & Una.
After dinner, walked to the first mile-stone on the Warwick
road with Julian

30 Wednesday   A moist morning
At about 1, took a walk with Una & Rosebud.
After dinner, walked to Whitnash with Julian.

December

1 Thursday.   A moist day, with glimpses of sun.
At mid-day, walked with Una by the Tachbrooke Road to
Whitnash

Towards dusk, walked with Julian up & down the Parade.
Wrote a letter to W. D. Ticknor, to-day.

2 Friday   A bright, cool morning. A letter to Una from
Richd Manning.
At noon, took a short walk with Una.
After dinner, walked with Julian to the first mile-stone on
Warwick road.

3 Saturday   A cool & pretty clear morning After 4 °clock,
took a walk with Julian.

4 Sunday   A chill & snowy morning. Rainy pretty much
all day.
Between 3 & 4 took a walk about town with Julian

5 Monday   A rainy day.
A letter from Mrs. King, and daughter (of Redcar) to
Mamma & Rosebud.
Towards dusk, took a walk with Julian.

6 Tuesday   A clear morning.
The first proof-sheets of my Romance arrived.
Sent back the proof-sheets to Smith & Elder; likewise, a note
to them.
After 4, took a walk about town with Julian.

7 Wednesday   A clear morning.
Rec^d & sent back a package of proof-sheets.
After 4, took a walk towards Whitnash & back by the Tach-
brooke road, with Julian.
Una, Julian, & Fanny, went to a lecture on Bunyan, with
dissolving views, in the evening.

8 Thursday   A pleasant morning, but dim Rec^d letter &c from Smith Elder & Co. Rec^d & returned some proofs.
After 4, walked on the Warwick road with Julian.

9 Friday   A pleasant morning.
At about 11, walked a mile on the Warwick road with Una.
After 4, took a walk with Julian.

10 Saturday   A dim, but not cloudy morning   Letter to Mamma from Miss Hosmer, inclosed in one from Sarah Clarke At noon, took a walk up & down the Parade with Una.
Rec^d & returned a proof-sheet.
After dinner, walked up & down the Parade by myself.

11 Sunday   A dim morning.
After four °clock walked to Whitnash with Julian

12 Monday   A dark & rainy morning. A letter to Mamma from Miss Bracken in Paris. Wrote to Smith Elder & Co, proposing the "Marble Faun" as a title.
After 4, walked up and down the Parade with Julian.
A very black, foggy, and wet day.

13 Tuesday. Dark morning.
Saw Major Johnstone give Julian his last lesson in the broadsword & gymnastics.
At noon, took a walk up & down the Parade with Una.
After four, took a walk with Julian on the Warwick road.

14 Wednesday   Clear & cool morning. A letter to Mamma from Bennoch.
After 4, took a walk with Julian.

15 Thursday   A cold, clear morning. Letter to Mamma from Mrs. Mann at Concord.

After 4, took a walk with Julian

16 Friday   Dull morning. Snow on the ground.

After 4, walked out with Julian on the old Warwick road.

17 Saturday   Very cold morning; my bathing tub frozen over.

Proof-sheet from Smith & Elder; sent it back

At about 11, a telegraph from Bennoch; not coming here to-day

After dinner, walked to Whitnash with Julian

18 Sunday   Cold morning. A note from Bennoch.

After dinner, walked to Whitnash with Julian

19 Monday   An exceedingly cold morning.

After dinner, walked on the Warwick road with Julian.

20 Tuesday   Still very cold; everything frozen up.

After 4, walked to the 1st mile-stone, Warwick road, &c &c. by myself. The weather has moderated.

The Doctor came to see Rosebud for some slight ailment.

21 Wednesday   Clear & rather mild morning. Letters from Ellen & Mary Peabody.

After dinner, took a walk with Julian. Much more moderate weather.

Dr. Sutherland came again to see Rosebud. She seems better.

22 Thursday   Tolerably mild & pleasant morning.

Wrote a note to Ticknor

Also, a note to Bennoch

After dinner, walked out with Julian.

23 Friday   A foggy morning.
After dinner, took a walk with Julian

24 Saturday   A rather mild & pleasant morning.
After dinner, walked with Julian.
A barrel of oysters came from Bennoch.
After dark, we distributed our Christmas presents.

25 Sunday   A moist & sombre morning. A note from Bennoch.
Dined at four °clock. After dinner, took a walk with Julian.
After our return, we all listened to a story by Julian, on the
theme of "Sing a Song of Sixpence."

26 Monday   A dark & moist morning.
After dinner, took a walk with Julian. Very muddy.

27 Tuesday   A clear, mild, chilly morning. Letters from
Mrs Mann & E. P. Peabody.
After dinner, took a walk with Julian.

28 Wednesday   A dark & moist morning.
After dinner, walked out with Julian.

29 Thursday   A black & wet morning.
After dinner, walked with Julian.

30 Friday   A pleasant morning, but then turning to cloud
& rain.
Rec^d (and answered) a note from Fields in Paris.
Towards dusk, walked up and down the Parade with Julian.

31 Saturday   A black and wet morning.
Toward dusk, walked out with Julian.

I went to bed at 11, partly on account of a cold. The rest of the family sat up till midnight to welcome in the New Year.

[*On page following December entries*]

1859

Feb 1ˢᵗ—Drew £50

   ″   3ᵈ   Wrote to J. T. Fields

   ″ 28   Recᵈ letter from Ticknor.

Mar 4   Wrote to Ticknor

   ″   7   Drew £50.

   ″ 29   Wrote to Barings

   ″ 31   Recᵈ letter from H. A. Bright.

April 1   Wrote to H. A. Bright.

   ″ 11   Recᵈ letter from Barings, enclosing
             credit for £250

   ″ 14   Wrote to Barings

   ″ ″   Drew £50

   ″ 26   Letter from Barings, notifying remittance
             (£200) from Ticknor

May 14   Drew £50

May 23ᵈ   ″ £50

   ″ 25   ″ £20

   ″ 30   ″ £30   Marseilles

EXPLANATORY NOTES

EXPLANATORY NOTES

Abbreviations and Short Titles

References to Hawthorne's works are to the Centenary Edition (Columbus: Ohio State University Press, 1962–) with the exception of *EN: The English Notebooks,* and *Passages: Passages from the French and Italian Notebooks,* for which individual identifications are given here. In all the editorial matter that follows, library locations of letters indicate that the original manuscript texts have been quoted or cited.

ACM	*The American Claimant Manuscripts*
AN	*The American Notebooks*
Arcadian Landscape	*The Arcadian Landscape: Nineteenth-Century American Painters in Italy* (Lawrence: University of Kansas Museum of Art, 1972)
Berg	The Berg Collection, New York Public Library, Astor, Lenox, and Tilden Foundations
Bieber	Margarete Bieber, *Sculpture of the Hellenistic Age* (New York: Columbia University Press, 1955)
Bonfigli, *Guide*	F. S. Bonfigli, *Guide to the Studios in Rome, with Much Supplementary Information* (Rome: Tipografia Legale, 1860)

BR	*The Blithedale Romance*
Catalogue	*Catalogue of the Art Treasures of the United Kingdom Collected at Manchester in 1857* (London: Bradbury and Evans, 1857)
Childe Harold	Byron, *Childe Harold's Pilgrimage*
Clement and Hutton	Clara Erskine Clement and Laurence Hutton, *Artists of the Nineteenth Century and Their Works* (Boston: Houghton, Osgood, 1879)
Crane	Sylvia E. Crane, *White Silence: Greenough, Powers, and Crawford, American Sculptors in Nineteenth–Century Italy* (Coral Gables, Fla.: University of Miami Press, 1972)
Craven	Wayne Craven, *Sculpture in America* (New York: Crowell, 1968)
DAB	*Dictionary of American Biography*, eds. Allen Johnson and Dumas Malone (New York: Scribner, 1943)
DNB	*Dictionary of National Biography*, eds. Leslie Stephen and Sidney Lee (London: Oxford University Press, 1949–50)
EIHC	*Essex Institute Historical Collections*
ELM	*The Elixir of Life Manuscripts*
EN	*The English Notebooks*, ed. Randall Stewart (New York: Modern Language Association, 1941)
Fielding	Mantle Fielding, *Dictionary of American Painters, Sculptors, and Engravers* (New York: James F. Carr, 1965)
Gerdts	William H. Gerdts, *American Neo–Classic Sculpture: The Marble Resurrection* (New York: Viking, 1973)
HC	Julian Hawthorne, *Hawthorne and His Circle* (New York and London: Harper, 1903)

HSG	*The House of the Seven Gables*
Huntington	The Henry E. Huntington Library, San Marino, Calif.
JH	Julian Hawthorne
Karolik	*M. and M. Karolik Collection of American Paintings 1815–1865* (Cambridge: Harvard University Press for the Museum of Fine Arts, Boston, 1949)
McAleer	Edward C. McAleer, *Dearest Isa: Robert Browning's Letters to Isabella Blagden* (Austin: University of Texas Press, 1951)
Memories	Rose Hawthorne Lathrop, *Memories of Hawthorne*, 2nd ed. (Boston: Houghton Mifflin, 1923)
MF	*The Marble Faun*
MOM	*Mosses from an Old Manse*
Murray	[When not otherwise noted, the context will indicate which of the following volumes is quoted.] *A Handbook for Travellers in France,* 6th ed., rev. (London: John Murray, 1856). *A Handbook for Travellers in Northern Italy,* 7th ed., rev. (London: John Murray, 1858), Part I: Comprising the Continental States and Island of Sardinia, Lombardy and Venice [includes Genoa]; Part II: The Duchies of Parma, Piacenza, and Modena, North Tuscany, and Florence. *A Handbook of Rome and Its Environs; forming Part II of The Handbook for Travellers in Central Italy,* 5th ed., rev. (London: John Murray, 1858). *A Handbook for Travellers in Central Italy. Part I: Southern Tuscany and the Papal States,* 4th ed., rev. (London: John Murray, 1857). *A*

	Handbook for Switzerland, the Alps of Savoy and Piedmont, 8th ed., rev. (London: John Murray, 1858).
NH	Nathaniel Hawthorne
NHB	Randall Stewart, *Nathaniel Hawthorne: A Biography* (New Haven: Yale University Press, 1948)
NHHW	Julian Hawthorne, *Nathaniel Hawthorne and His Wife* (Boston: James R. Osgood, 1884)
Notes	Sophia Hawthorne, *Notes in England and Italy* (New York: Putnam, 1869)
OOH	*Our Old Home*
Paris Guide	*New Paris Guide for 1857*, rev. (Paris: A. and W. Galignani, 1857)
Passages	*Passages from the French and Italian Note-Books*, ed. Sophia Hawthorne (London: Strahan, 1871; Boston: James R. Osgood, 1872)
SH	Sophia Hawthorne
SI	*The Snow–Image*
SL	*The Scarlet Letter*
Taft	Lorado Taft, *The History of American Sculpture*, rev. ed. (New York: Macmillan, 1924)
Thorp	Margaret Farrand Thorp, *The Literary Sculptors* (Durham: Duke University Press, 1965)
Travelers in Arcadia	*Travelers in Arcadia: American Artists in Italy 1830–1875* (Detroit: Detroit Institute of Art and Toledo Museum of Art, 1951)
TS	*True Stories from History and Biography*
TTT	*Twice-told Tales*

Tuckerman	Henry T. Tuckerman, *The Book of the Artists: American Artist Life* (New York: Putnam, 1867)
The White, Marmorean Flock	*The White, Marmorean Flock: Nineteenth–Century American Women Neoclassical Sculptors* [introduction by William H. Gerdts] (Poughkeepsie: Vassar College Art Gallery, 1972)
Wittkower	Rudolf Wittkower, *Art and Architecture in Italy, 1600–1750*, 3rd ed. (Harmondsworth: Penguin, 1973)
WB/TT	*A Wonder Book and Tanglewood Tales*
Yankee Stonecutters	Albert ten Eyck Gardner, *Yankee Stonecutters: The First American School of Sculpture, 1800–1850* (New York: Columbia University Press for the Metropolitan Museum of Art, 1945)

3.2–4.3   Bennoch. . . . his welfare.] Francis Bennoch (1812–90) was one of Hawthorne's closest English friends; his wholesale merchant firm failed in November 1857 (see *EN*, p. 282 ff; pp. 590–91, 604–6, 615–16). NH wrote to W. D. Ticknor on January 7, 1858, "I advised him to think of going to America . . . for, you know, it [is] almost a hopeless business for a ruined man ever to recover himself in England" (MS, Berg); on March 16 he wrote to Bennoch "the first letter (except one to my bankers) that I have written since I came to Rome" to learn Bennoch's plans and prospects (MS, Virginia). Bennoch did reestablish himself, and on June 17, 1859, NH, in Paris, wrote to him of delight "to be informed of your returning prosperity" (MS, Pearson, Yale). See JH, *HC*, pp. 235–36, and Raymona E. Hull, "Bennoch and Hawthorne," *Nathaniel Hawthorne Journal*, 1974, pp. 48–74, esp. 51–52. This first paragraph was omitted by SH from *Passages*; she had included the first and last sentences of it in *Passages from the English Note-Books of Nathaniel Hawthorne* (London: Strahan, New York: Fields, Osgood, 1870), and the remainder was first published by JH in *HC*, pp. 237–38.

3.3 since we came to London] The Hawthornes and their American governess, Ada Shepard, moved from Leamington in Warwickshire on November 10, 1857 to 24 Great Russell Street, London, near the British Museum. See *EN*, p. 590.

4.1 Julian] Julian Hawthorne (1846–1934), the only son, later wrote numerous reminiscences of the family's travels on the Continent, chiefly in *NHHW, HC,* and *The Memoirs of Julian Hawthorne,* ed. Edith Garrigues Hawthorne (New York: Macmillan, 1938). For a summary see Maurice Bassan, *Hawthorne's Son: The Life and Literary Career of Julian Hawthorne* (Columbus: Ohio State University Press, 1970), chapter 1.

5.19 Rosebud] Rose Hawthorne (1851–1926), the younger daughter, wrote of her family's sojourn in Italy in *Memories*. Additional material from her first draft was used in Theodore Maynard, *A Fire Was Lighted: The Life of Rose Hawthorne Lathrop* (Milwaukee: Bruce, 1948). She married George Parsons Lathrop (1851–98) in 1871, six months after her mother's death. Lathrop, an editor of the *Atlantic Monthly* and later of the Boston Sunday *Courier,* wrote *A Study of Hawthorne* (Boston: J. R. Osgood, 1876) and edited the Riverside Edition of *The Complete Works of Nathaniel Hawthorne* (Boston: Houghton, Mifflin, 1883). Rose became a Roman Catholic, founded the Dominican Congregation of Saint Rose of Lima, and in 1901 became Mother Mary Alphonsa. She devoted the remainder of her life to nursing victims of incurable cancer.

5.24 Una] Una Hawthorne (1844–77), the older daughter, was permanently affected in health by the malaria she contracted in Rome in October 1858. Except for private music and French lessons, Una did not attend school in Europe, but received instruction from her mother and governesses. See Raymona E. Hull, "Una Hawthorne: A Biographical Sketch," *Nathaniel Hawthorne Journal* 1976, pp. 87–119; Thomas Wentworth Higginson, *Part of a Man's Life* (Boston: Houghton, Mifflin, 1900), pp. 249–70. After SH's death in 1871, Una oversaw the printing of *Passages,* and in 1872 published a manuscript draft of her father's, called

Septimius Felton in America (see the "Historical Commentary," *ELM*, pp. 583–84).

5.27   Miss Shepherd] Ann Adaline Shepard (1835–74), governess of the Hawthorne children, was born and raised in Dorchester, Massachusetts. She attended Theodore Parker's sermons; her family was interested in Transcendentalism and abolitionism, and a sister studied at Eagleswood School, New Jersey. Ada entered Antioch College at Yellow Springs, Ohio, in 1854, and was a close friend of Horace Mann, the president, and of his wife Mary, SH's sister. She concentrated her studies on French, German, and Italian, graduating in Antioch's first class in July 1857. Mann offered her the professorship of modern languages and, to further her preparation, recommended her for the Hawthornes' sojourn on the Continent. NH told Ticknor in a letter of July 30, 1857, that "it is essential to have some such person in order to give Mrs. Hawthorne the leisure and freedom which her health requires. I have tried English governesses, and find them ignorant and inefficient. Miss Shepard is to receive no salary, but only her expenses" (MS, Berg). Ada reached Paris in August 1857, and studied French while awaiting the arrival of the Hawthornes in September; when they were delayed, she joined them in Leamington in October. During her stay abroad she wrote constantly to her family and her fiancé, Henry Clay Badger (1833–94), an Antioch classmate who spent 1857–58 at Harvard Divinity School preparing to become professor of logic and belles lettres at Antioch. In July 1859 Ada returned to Dorchester and married Badger, and the two taught at Antioch until its closing in 1862. After the Civil War, Badger became a Unitarian minister, and Ada conducted a successful school for girls in Boston. At the age of 39, fearing insanity, she committed suicide by jumping from a boat off Narragansett Bay. See Robert Lincoln Straker, *Horace Mann and Others: Chapters from the History of Antioch College* (Yellow Springs, Ohio: Antioch Press, 1963); Boston *Transcript*, January 23, 1874, 1:1.

7.8–9   a mere string of gabble.] According to Ada Shepard, "Mr. Hawthorne pretends that he can't speak French, although I am sure he knows it very well; and he follows me around, when we stop at the stations or custom-house, to make me talk for him. He says he shall be dumb all the time that he is on the continent" (letter to Badger, January 5, 1858, transcript, Yale). See also note to 38.26–27.

7.15–16 Hôtel du Rhin] Described by Murray, p. 16, as "near the railway, good, clean, and cheap."

8.18–23 The Cathedral . . . lofty.] Murray, p. 17: "The proportion of height to breadth is almost double that to which we are accustomed in English cathedrals."

9.20–21 quaint and curious sculpture] Presumably the choir stalls carved from oak between 1508 and 1519 by Arnould Boulin and others, representing more than three thousand figures, many from scriptural history, named by Ruskin in 1880 "The Bible of Amiens."

9.22–24 There is not . . . modern.] Only the west rose window and the two rose windows of the north and south transepts have the original glass.

10.24 Napoleons] A piece worth 20 francs, or $4.00 in 1858. The franc was equivalent to approximately $.20. See p. 33.11. The British pound sterling was worth approximately $5.00.

11.11 Hôtel du Louvre] The *Paris Guide*, pp. 215–16: this 600-room hotel was built "on the plan of the colossal hotels for which the United States are so celebrated. It occupies a space of . . . nearly two English acres, between the rues St Honoré, de Rivoli, de Marengo, and the Place du Palais Royal. It has three courts, one of which . . . is roofed with glass, and presents a striking specimen of the progress made by modern civil architecture. . . . The comforts contrived for the inmates of this establishment are of a novel description." Electricity was used extensively.

12.23 in which Henry IV was assassinated] See note to 17.32–18.1.

13.1–2   the Tuilleries joining on to the Louvre] The connection of the emperor's residence to the old palace of the Louvre
was completed in 1853 by Napoleon III (Louis Napoleon Bonaparte, 1808–73). The Tuileries was destroyed by the Paris Com-
mune in 1871.

15.1–8   A great part. . . . to pay for.] Louis Napoleon had
begun in the early 1850s, with his prefect of the Seine, Georges
Haussmann, to rebuild Paris, with broad new boulevards and
avenues, parks and squares, and monumental public buildings.
The *Paris Guide*'s 1857 preface begins: "Paris has undergone
so many and such important alterations, as to astonish even the
resident." Opposition to the enormous cost was repressed by the
imperial government. See also note to 18.26–27.

15.21   The picture-rooms] The halls of French, Italian, and
Spanish painting. In *HC*, JH stated that his father "had little
appetite either for dinners or for works of art; he looked even upon
the Venus of Milo with coldness" (p. 248).

16.16   Childerics] Childeric I (ca. 436–81) was a semi-legen-
dary king of the Salian Franks, father of Clovis I and son of
Meroveus. His tomb, containing armor and ornaments, discovered
at his capital in Belgium in 1653, was the subject of archeological
investigations in the 1850s.

16.25   Mr. Husson] Mrs. Husson had begun teaching Una
music soon after the Hawthornes' arrival in Liverpool in 1853.
For six weeks in November and December 1854, Una lived with
Mr. and Mrs. Husson, and during that time he gave her lessons
in French.

16.26   Miss McDaniel] Frances L. (Fanny) Macdaniel (b.
1815) and her younger sister, Eunice, came with their widowed
mother from Maryland to Brook Farm and resided there during
its strongest Fourierist phase, from 1844 till its end in 1847. Her
brother Osborne assisted Albert Brisbane in editing the *Phalanx*
in New York. Eunice married Charles Anderson Dana (1819–97),
a Brook Farm leader and later editor of the New York *Sun*, in

1846. (NH sued Dana and George Ripley, in 1845, for repayment of a loan to Brook Farm.) See *Autobiography of Brook Farm*, ed. Henry W. Sams (Englewood Cliffs, N.J.: Prentice-Hall, 1958); Edith Roelker Curtis, *A Season in Utopia: The Story of Brook Farm* (New York: Nelson, 1961); James H. Wilson, *The Life of Charles Anderson Dana* (New York: Harper, 1907), p. 57. Fanny taught English to children of English and American families in Paris. She introduced Ada Shepard to Christopher Cranch, the American artist and former member of Brook Farm, in September 1857.

17.4–5   Mr. Fezandie] E. Fezandié, director of the Institution Fezandié, a "Protestant College" in the rue Balzac, an experimental school partly *pension* and partly classroom, attended by Ada Shepard in August-September 1857. The pupils were mostly English and American, of both sexes, "ranging from infancy to hoary eld," according to Henry James, who with his brothers William and Wilkinson was an *externe* there in early 1857, and who left an amusing account in *A Small Boy and Others* (New York: Charles Scribner's Sons, 1913), pp. 363–71. Henry James, Sr., sent his children to the school for the same reason that Miss Shepard sought it out: M. Fezandié was "an active and sympathetic ex-Fourierist" who had "enjoyed some arrested, possibly blighted connection in America." James described him as "a son of the south, bald and slightly replete, with a delicate beard, a quick but anxious, rather melancholy eye and a slim, graceful, juvenile wife." James remembered the school as inspired by "a bold idealism" if "quite ridiculous," and one of the teachers as "politically obnoxious to the powers that then were," full of dark hints about the police spies of the tryrannical emperor.

17.18   across the way.] I.e., in the Tuileries.

17.19   Miss Mitchell] Maria Mitchell (1818–89) was the first American woman professor of astronomy (at Vassar College), and the first woman to win an international medal (given by the king of Denmark for the discovery of a comet in 1847). The main purpose of her trip was to meet European astronomers and to demonstrate to them how photography was a tool for astronomy in America. She had arrived in Europe in June 1857 with a young Chicago lady, Prudence Swift, whose banker father lost heavily in the panic of 1857, so that the daughter soon returned home. According to Miss Mitchell's diary, she visited NH in Liverpool, August 5, 1857. The interview was brief, but they liked each other. Miss Mitchell wrote that SH told her she had opposed allowing her to accompany the family to Rome, but "Mr. Hawthorne assured her that I was a person who would give no trouble; therefore she consented." See Phebe M. Kendall, *Maria Mitchell, Her Life, Letters, and Journals* (Boston: Lee and Shepard, 1896), esp. pp. 89–92; Helen Wright, *Sweeper in the Sky: The Life of Maria Mitchell, First Woman Astronomer in America* (New York: Macmillan, 1949), pp. 107–18.

17.32–18.1   another street . . . dagger into him] The rue de la Ferronerie. On May 14, 1610 François Ravaillac, a religious fanatic, threw himself upon the king from a shop front in the narrow street.

18.8   the Rue de St Denis] The *Paris Guide*, p. 260 n., retells the legend: "St. Denis marked it out with his footsteps while walking with his head under his arm to the place where he wished to be buried."

18.16   Hottinguer & Co., the Bankers] Located by *Paris Guide*, p. 584, at 17, rue Bergère.

18.26–27   I know not why the Boulevards are called so.] The *Paris Guide*, pp. 38–39, explains that *boulevard* is derived from the French for "bulwark." The northern boulevards—des Italiens, de la Madeleine, etc.—were begun after the walls and towers of ancient Paris were pulled down about 1670. During the Second Empire, the *Paris Guide* comments, "The northern boulevards are now the pride and glory of Paris. Once its *bulevark,* they have become its ornament. Their great extent, the dazzling beauty, the luxury of the shops, the restaurants, the cafés, on or near them; the lofty houses, some of the most ornate architecture; the crowds of well-dressed persons who frequent them; the glancing of lights among the trees; the sounds of music; the incessant roll of carriages, all this forms a medley of sights and sounds anything but unpleasing to the visitor who walks the boulevards for the first time on a fine evening."

19.25 a hundred, or two hundred years ago.] Work began on the church in 1764, but it was not until 1806 that Napoleon chose the design for a "temple of glory" by Pierre Vignon (1762–1828) of a Roman peripteral Corinthian temple, the first such structure to be built since the third century. It was completed in 1843.

20.32 Rachel] Elizabeth-Rachel Felix (1821–58), the most remarkable actress of French classical tragedy of her age, died January 4 in Cannet, on the Riviera, and was buried in Paris on January 11. In 1855 she had made a long tour of the United States, during which her health was ruined.

23.8–17 Our principal object. . . . painting.] The *Paris Guide,* pp. 174–75, says of the Musée des Desseins: "Many precious specimens of the pencils of the first masters of the Italian, Flemish, French, and Spanish schools have now been abstracted from the portfolios where they were buried in useless security, and offer an ample field for the study of the artist and the amateur."

23.11 Annibal Caracci] Annibale Carracci (1560–1609), leader of the Bolognese school of baroque classicism that dominated Italian painting of the early seventeenth century (including Guido Reni, Domenichino, Albani, and Guercino). His picture *The Dead Christ Mourned (The Three Maries)* was the most popular work at the Manchester Exhibition of 1857, as NH noted (*EN,* p. 563). See also Francis Haskell, *Rediscoveries in Art: Some Aspects of Taste, Fashion, and Collecting in England and France* (Ithaca, N.Y.: Cornell University Press, 1976), pp. 96–99.

24.4–5 the English medal] A medal awarded to all troops landing in the Crimea up to September 9, 1855, the day Sebastopol was taken.

25.12–13 The galleries . . . recently prepared.] During the reign of Napoleon III, additions to the Palace of the Louvre were made, including a large wing to the riverside galleries. An elaborate inauguration ceremony had been held August 14, 1857, celebrating the "completion of the Louvre." The work is now considered a slavish academic copy of the earlier architecture and decoration.

25.28–29 poor maimed Theseus] On December 7, 1857, NH visited the ancient sculpture in the British Museum. In *EN*, p. 609, he described the "poor, maimed immortalities—headless and legless trunks, godlike cripples, faces beautiful and broken-nosed, heroic shapes which have stood so long, or lain prostrate so long, in the open air, that even the atmosphere of Greece has almost dissolved the external layer of the marble; and yet, however much they may be worn away, or battered or shattered, the grace and nobility seems as deep in them as the very heart of the stone." The *Theseus* NH refers to is the reclining figure taken by Lord Elgin from the east pediment of the Parthenon, and also identified as Dionysus, Heracles, and the personification of Mount Olympus.

27.9–10 Rue de Beaujon . . . Minister] According to the *Paris Guide*, p. 583, the residence of the envoy extraordinary and minister plenipotentiary of the United States was 13, rue de Beaujon. The address is in the eighth arrondissement, northeast of l'Etoile.

27.11–12 the Secretary of Legation] William Ransom Calhoun, of South Carolina.

27.13 Judge Mason] John Young Mason (1799–October 3, 1859), of Virginia, was minister to France from 1853 until his death, from a stroke, in Paris. He had been a congressman, a federal judge, and secretary of the navy and attorney general for Tyler and Polk.

27.25 his own troubles] There had been for some time speculation among American diplomats that Mason would be recalled by President Buchanan because of his notorious extravagance, abuse of office, indebtedness, and generally reckless and profligate way of life. It was rumored that he had suffered paralysis and "impaired intellect," and that Louis Napoleon thought him "worth-less" and treated him with "utter contempt." See *The Journal of Benjamin Moran, 1857–1865*, ed. Sarah Agnes Wallace and Frances Elma Gillespie (Chicago: University of Chicago Press, 1948), esp. pp. 148, 596.

27.29   Mr. Buchanan's inauguration.] James Buchanan (1791–1868), minister to Great Britain for Pierce from 1853 until March 1856, was inaugurated as fifteenth president of the United States on March 4, 1857. NH wrote to Buchanan on February 13, 1857, resigning his consular post as of August 31 (MS, National Archives).

30.1–3   On entering . . . repairs.] The restoration of Notre Dame by the architect Eugène Viollet-le-Duc (1814–79) was begun in the 1840s and completed in 1864.

30.11–16   a bullet. . . . Napoleon. . . . 1848.] According to the *Paris Guide*, pp. 293, 317, Monsignor Denis Affre, archbishop of Paris, attempted to stop the bloodshed of June 25, 1848, at the Place de la Bastille. He was "struck by a ball," and died the following day. The robes NH describes were worn by Pope Pius VII at the coronation of Napoleon I.

30.17   two large, full-length portraits] According to the *Paris Guide*, p. 318, one is of "M. de Quelen, the predecessor of Archbishop Affre, by [Pauline] Perdreau," and the second is of the successor to Affre, Archbishop Sibour, who was assassinated in January 1857.

30.19   image of the Virgin] A fourteenth-century statue known as *Notre Dame de Paris*.

31.26   Hotel Dieu] A municipal hospital, one building of which was located by the Seine on the south side of the Place du Parvis Notre-Dame until demolished in 1882.

32.11–12   Mr. and Mrs. Pickman] William Dudley Pickman (1819–90) and Caroline Silsbee Pickman (1819–98). He was a member of the merchant firm of Silsbee, Pickman, and Allen, of Salem and Boston, owners of some of the most famous clipper ships.

32.19 Mr. Henry Spencer] Henry W. Spencer, of New York.

32.20 51, Rue Caumartin] In the ninth arrondissement, northwest of where the Opéra now stands.

32.30–33.9 Consulting him. . . . the time comes.] On January 3 NH had discussed routes to Rome with Philip Dallas, secretary of legation in London, and with an American traveler just arrived from the Continent. The traveler "gave a fearful account of the difficulties that beset a traveller landing with much baggage in Italy, and especially at Civita Vecchia, the very port at which we intended to debark" (*EN*, p. 621). The alternate land route—from Leghorn, principal port of the Grand Duchy of Tuscany, which was controlled by Austrian troops—went through Florence.

33.10–17 there was a charge. . . . receive it.] The U.S. Congress had passed a law on March 1, 1855, placing consuls upon a salary basis and requiring that all consular fees be turned over to the government. NH was dismayed, since he had hoped to save a large amount from such charges at the Liverpool consulate.

33.20 There are whole histories] On the left is the Virgin's Door; in the center, the Door of the Last Judgment; on the right, the Door of St. Anne. They show scenes of the Death, Resurrection, and Coronation of the Virgin; the Resurrection of the Dead and Separation of the Elect and the Damned; the Annunciation, Visitation, Nativity, the Proclamation to the Shepherds, and the Questioning of the Magi by Herod. The original sculpture was done in the early thirteenth century. The twelve apostles, in the splays of the Last Judgment door, were by Viollet-le-Duc.

33.27 an island] The Ile de la Cité.

33.29 small public ground] According to the *Paris Guide*, p. 320, this is the site of the Archbishop's Palace (l'Archevêché), which was destroyed by the populace in February 1831. "The palace and dependencies were left in such a state that they were subsequently removed by order of the government, and the site is now occupied by a cheerful promenade, adorned in the center with a small Gothic fountain."

35.19–20 a column . . . Mercury] The column, to commemorate the revolution of 1830, is known as the Column of July. The statue is *The Genius of Liberty.*

36.7 Hôtel de Provence] Murray, p. 370: "H. de Provence et des Ambassadeurs, opposite the Post Office, in the Place Bellecour. . . . There is no good inn here; a new one near the Rly. Station is in progress."

36.34 Mrs. Ratcliffe's romances] NH's interest in Anne Radcliffe's *Mysteries of Udolpho* (1794) was mentioned in a letter of September 28, 1819, to his sister Louisa, along with his predilection for Scott, Smollett, and the *Arabian Nights* (MS, Morgan).

38.5–7 I wonder where . . . that very spot.] Murray, p. 376: "The bronze statue of Louis XIV in the Centre [of the Place Bellecour] was restored by Charles X."

38.26–27 it was impossible to convince the officials] In her diary of this date, Maria Mitchell noted: "Mr. Hawthorne is so thoroughly impractical and so unable to speak any other language than English, that Miss Shepard transacts all the business and settles all the bargains."

39.22–23 "arrowy Rhone."] *Childe Harold,* canto 3, stanza 71: "Is it not better, then, to be alone, / And love Earth only for its earthly sake? / By the blue rushing of the arrowy Rhone, . . . "

39.27–28 extinguishers] I.e., of candles or lamps.

40.12–13 or some town . . . miles of it] Deleted by SH in *Passages.*

40.14 Hotel d'Angleterre] Not listed in Murray. NH notes in his diary, "near the quays."

41.4 triumphal arch] Murray, p. 467, describes it as "not remarkable for elegance of design, originality of elevation, or elegance of decoration."

41.8 a large, oblong, public place] The Place de la Major.

41.12–13 some archbishop] According to Murray, p. 470, Bishop Belsunce de Castel-Moron (1671–1753) "offered a rare example of courage and piety by his intrepid intercourse with the sick in the hospitals, where, aided by pious nuns, he constantly ministered to the support and consolation of the plague-stricken inmates." The bishop's example was celebrated in Pope's *Essay on Man*, 4, 107–8. The sculptor was Marius Ramus (1805–88).

42.7–8 an attempt on the Emperor's life] In Paris, the evening before, Felice Orsini and three other Italian revolutionary conspirators had hurled powerful bombs at the imperial carriage as Napoleon and the empress arrived at the Opéra. The couple were practically unhurt, but 8 persons there were killed and 150 injured. Paradoxically, the attack increased Napoleon's sympathies for Italian independence, leading to his war against Austria in 1859.

42.24–25 a circular line of Quais] The Vieux Port.

43.25 an elevated walk, overlooking the harbor] The Parc du Pharo.

46.17 no fault to be found] According to Ada Shepard, the American consul in Marseilles told NH and her that the voyage by steamer would not be pleasant. Maria Mitchell noted in her diary for January 18: "On Sunday morning at 8 o'clock we left Marseilles for Genoa and Leghorn, uncertain what our further destination would be. Mr. Hawthorne's indecision is so great that the termination of our journey together is very uncertain."

47.18–19 an old church] Santissima Annunziata, at the end of the Via Balbi.

47.29–30 a pillar . . . from Solomon's Temple] NH was apparently without a guidebook, and misunderstood the escort. Murray, p. 105–6, describes the famous relic as a bowl, the "sacro catino," traditionally thought to be "a gift from the Queen of Sheba to Solomon, or the dish which held the Pascal Lamb at the Last Supper, or the vessel in which Joseph of Arimathea received the blood flowing from the side of the Redeemer."

48.16–17 a church . . . built . . . by a pirate] Presumably S. Matteo, in the Piazza Carlo Felice. The "pirate" would be Lamba Doria, who defeated the Venetian fleet at Scarzola in 1298, and died in 1323. The church, however, was founded in 1125 by Martino Doria, an ecclesiastic of the family, and the interior was reconstructed by order of Andrea Doria (1468–1560), the great Genoese admiral.

49.16 royal palace] The Palazzo Reale, in the Strada Balbi.

49.19–20 others which we saw] E.g., the Palazzo Durazzi, according to Ada Shepard.

49.33 a sort of pleasure-garden] Probably the public garden of Acquasola, northeast of the city and port.

50.1–4 a large yellow house . . . Dickens] The Palazzo Peschiere, where Charles Dickens lived from the autumn of 1844 till the spring of 1845, while traveling and writing *Pictures from Italy*. NH reviewed in the Salem *Advertiser*, April 29, 1846, the first part of Dickens's book, *Travelling Letters, Written on the Road* (New York: Wiley and Putnam, 1846). Dickens in this refused "to expatiate at length on famous Pictures and Statues," and NH welcomed "the richly grotesque surface of life which he here flings off to us. . . . Dickens in Rome, if the kindly fates should guide him thither, will be a phenomenon such as the city of the Caesars has never yet beheld."

50.9–10 Hôtel of the Cross of Malta] Murray, p. 91, compares this hotel with others as "also good, with table d'hôte; this house once belonged to the Order whose name it bears; forming part of it is a lofty tower, from which its inmates may enjoy a very extensive panoramic view of Genoa, its harbour, lighthouse, &c."

50.15–16 some idea of taking the rail for Pisa] Maria Mitchell recorded another version: "There was a long discussion of the question whether we would land at Leghorn and go by land to Florence, or keep on to Civita Vecchia and Rome. I dared not speak on the subject. The passengers who came on board last night are to stop here and they tried to persuade Mr. Hawthorne to stop also. Mr. Hawthorne wavered this way and that as one or another spoke. At length Una said, 'Papa, Miss Mitchell wants to go to Rome and so does Miss Shepard and so do I,' and that decided him for Rome. And so the luggage which had been taken up from the hold was ordered down again and with light hearts we went ashore for the day" (Diary, January 19, 1858). See note to 527.10–11.

50.18 a Banker's] NH's Diary specifies "Grand–more & Co." as the banker, and £ 50 as the sum drawn there.

50.21 the tomb of Smollet] See note to 36.34. Maria Mitchell commented on the visit to Smollett's monument: "Mr. Hawthorne was much the most interested in the party, in the circumstance. He so rarely shows interest in any thing that it is worthy of note" (Diary, January 19, 1858).

51.22 a vetturino] The driver of a vettura, a carriage for hire. See note to 216.8–9.

52.13 Spillman's Hotel] In the Via della Croce, near the Piazza di Spagna. SH added, in *Passages,* "the only one where we could gain admittance."

53.17–19 a suite of ten rooms . . . this house] The Palazzo Larazani, on the side of the Pincian Hill. The lease was for four months at the rate of $1,200 per annum.

54.4 that story of Alexander and Diogenes] In Plutarch's *Life of Alexander.*

54.25 French soldiers] After the abortive republican revolution of 1848, a French army restored Pope Pius IX to control of Rome and the Papal States. A garrison of 30,000 remained throughout the 1850s.

54.28–32 but old Rome . . . in and out.] These lines, adapted for *MF*, p. 325, were omitted from *Passages*, and first published in *NHHW*, p. 176.

55.3–7 Saint Peter's disappointed . . . tried] These lines, adapted for *MF*, pp. 348–49, were omitted from *Passages* and first published in *NHHW*, p. 177.

55.19 a great iron cross] Murray, p. 45: "A cross now stands in the middle of the arena; and 14 representations of Our Lord's Passion are placed at intervals around it."

56.7–15 Along these lanes. . . . magnified hovels.] These sentences were omitted from *Passages*, and first published (without mention of horse dung) by JH in *NHHW*, p. 177.

56.28–29 a regiment of French cavalry] In *Passages*, SH corrected by a footnote: "We find them to be retainers of the Barberini family, not French."

57.6–13 These fountains . . . one, for instance . . . ridiculous affair.] NH's description in *MF*, pp. 144–45, resembles this passage. The Fountain of Trevi was constructed 1732–62. Murray comments, pp. 87–88: "It was scarcely to be expected that the very questionable taste of this design would escape the criticism of [Joseph] Forsyth [1763–1815]: he calls it 'another pompous confusion of fable and fact, gods and ediles, aqueducts and sea-monsters; but the rock-work is grand, proportioned to the stream of water, and a fit basement for such architecture as a castel d'acqua required, not for the frittered Corinthian which we find there'." See *Remarks on Antiquities, Arts and Letters, during an Excursion in Italy, in the Years 1802 and 1803*, 2d ed. (London,

1816), p. 174. The architect, in *MF* called "some sculptor of Bernini's school," was Nicola Salvi (1697–1751). The sculptures of Neptune, tritons, and horses are by Pietro Bracci (1700–73). See Wittkower, pp. 439–40, 567.

57.31–33   The Egyptian obelisks . . . put . . . to shame.] Murray, p. 82: "There are no monuments of Rome of such undoubted antiquity as the stupendous obelisks which the emperors brought from Egypt as memorials of their triumphs, and which the popes have so judiciously applied to the decoration of the modern city."

58.19–20   Furness Abbey . . . Kenilworth] See *EN*, pp. 156–59 (July 13, 1855) and 569–71 (September 13, 1857).

58.29   Linlithgow Palace] See *EN*, pp. 531–32 (July 8, 1857). The architect was Sir James Hamilton of Finnart (d. 1540), "the Bastard of Arran," whose "early years were spent abroad, and he seems to have developed his great natural taste for architecture at the court of Francis I, where he resided for some time" (*DNB*). But it is doubtful that the architecture of the Roman palaces significantly influenced the French châteaux of Francis I in the first quarter of the sixteenth century. See Nikolaus Pevsner, *An Outline of European Architecture*, 7th ed. (Harmondsworth: Penguin, 1963), pp. 292–301.

59.9   this genial temperature] This apocryphal notion, repeated in *MF*, pp. 368–69, comes from Mme de Staël's *Corinne* (1807), book 4, chapter 3. Compare, e.g., Melville, *Moby-Dick*, chapter 68, "The Blanket."

59.28–60.8   If I had. . . . infinite presence.] These lines, omitted from *Passages*, were first published by JH in *NHHW*, pp. 178–79.

60.29   the Pantheon] Murray, p. 36: "This celebrated edifice is one of those relics of ancient Rome with the general appearance of which most travellers are familiar long before they cross the Tiber. . . . The proportions of its portico have been for ages the admiration of travellers, and its name has been identified with architecural beauty."

62.16 Pakenham & Hookers bank] Murray, p. xvi: "Messrs. Packenham [*sic*] and Hooker, No. 20, Piazza di Spagna, American Bankers, conduct the principal part of the business with the United States." James C. Hooker was the banker; see mention, p. 131.7. There was no Pakenham, according to Ada Shepard.

62.17 Galignani] Giovanni Galignani founded *Galignani's Messenger* in Paris in 1814, first as a tri-weekly and then as a daily newspaper for English-speaking persons on the Continent, where the stamp duty and postage made the cost of London papers prohibitive.

62.20 I walked out along the Pincian Hill] NH's favorite walk and relaxation in Rome. George Stillman Hillard (1808–79), his friend, had written in 1853: "The gardens, upwards of a mile in circuit, are laid out in rectangles and formal alleys, and divided by broad gravel walks, overhung with trees. . . . To those whose taste or temperament leads them to shun the noise of crowds and choose the soothing presence of retirement, these gardens present an attractive scene. . . . The flow of pensive thought will be interrupted only by the dash of a fountain, the rustling of a leaf, or the chirp of a bird" (*Six Months in Italy*, 14th ed. [Boston: Osgood, 1876], p. 297). Rose described playing with her father on the Pincian in *Memories,* pp. 360–62.

63.13–14 statue of Saint Peter . . . mean-looking affair.] Murray, p. 99: "The rude execution of the figure conclusively proves that it is not a work of classical times; and it seems much more likely to belong to the early ages of Christianity, when sculpture, like architecture, was copied from heathen models." The statue has been attributed to Arnolfo di Cambio (1232–ca. 1301).

63.20–21 a mosaic copy of . . . the Transfiguration] Murray, p. 100, mentions that the copy was "somewhat larger than the original painting." Frescoes, especially, were copied in mosaic because of the original painting's perishability.

63.24–25 the one glorious picture that I have ever seen.] Murray, p. 203: "The TRANSFIGURATION [1517], the last and greatest oil picture of the immortal master, and justly considered as the first oil painting in the world." Murray's description continues with a quotation from Samuel Rogers's *Italy*, and one from Luigi Lanzi's *History of Painting in Italy* (1789). American visitors typically expressed the same opinions as NH here, and chose *The Transfiguration* to represent the pinnacle of modern art as the *Apollo Belvedere* represented the pinnacle of ancient art. See Paul R. Baker, *The Fortunate Pilgrims* (Cambridge: Harvard University Press, 1964), pp. 142–47. Of the artists NH mentions, and SH in *Notes*, Raphael receives highest praise, and many others, from Raphael's teacher Perugino to contemporary nineteenth-century Americans, are placed in terms of the idealizing tradition neoclassical critics thought Raphael to have begun. Actually, *The Transfiguration*, unfinished at Raphael's death, was executed in substantial part by his pupils Giulio Romano and Gianfrancesco Penni.

63.27 monument to the Stuart family] George IV commissioned the Stuart monument, finished in 1819, which represents the entrance to a mausoleum guarded by genii and, says Murray, pp. 100–101, honors "the memory of JAMES THE THIRD, CHARLES THE THIRD, and HENRY THE NINTH, KINGS OF ENGLAND,—names which an Englishman can scarcely read without a smile or sigh!" The sculptor, Antonio Canova (1757–1822), was the leading classicist of the early nineteenth century, and set the example for American expatriates in undeviating admiration of ancient Roman sculpture. His *George Washington* (1818–21, destroyed by fire in 1830) "contributed enormously to the establishment of sculpture as a fully developed form of art in America" (Wayne Craven in *200 Years of American Sculpture*, ed. Tom Armstrong [New York: Whitney Museum, 1976], p. 34). See also note to 72. 7–9.

64.14–15 the Carnival] In 1858, the eight days of Carnival began on February 6.

65.24 Murray tells me] Murray, p. 117: "It was founded on the highest summit of the Esquiline, A.D. 352, by Pope Liberius, and John, a Roman patrician, in consequence of a miraculous fall of snow in the month of August, which covered the precise space occupied by their basilica."

65.30 a chapel] The chapel (1585–90) of Pope Sixtus V designed and built by Domenico Fontana (1543–1607), and decorated with extraordinary sumptuousness by a team of late sixteenth-century sculptors.

66.13–15 a group in marble. . . . of peculiar sanctity.] Murray notes, p. 118, that this chapel holds the relic of "the boards of the manger in which the Saviour lay after his birth." The statues are by Arnolfo di Cambio and others.

66.29 Piazza di Monte Cavallo] The popular name of the Piazza del Quirinale.

67.7–9 I do not know . . . Praxitiles] Murray, pp. 84–85, comments that the statues "have been called Castor and Pollux by recent antiquaries. They are undoubtedly of Grecian workmanship, and, if we could believe the Latin inscription on the pedestals, they are the work of Phidias and Praxiteles. But as they were found in the Baths of Constantine, there is good reason to doubt the truth of the inscriptions; the statues are evidently centuries older than the age of Constantine, and no inscriptions of his time can be worth much as authority. Canova entertained no doubt of their Greek origin, and admired their fine anatomy and action." They are now known to be Roman copies of Greek originals of the fifth century B.C.

68.1–2 The balconies . . . join in it.] Murray, pp. xxv–xxvi, describes the Carnival: "At 2 P.M. the crowd assemble in the Corso, where the pelting with comfits, manufactured for the purpose with flour and plaster of Paris, is carried on until nightfall, all the windows and balconies being gaily decked out and filled with the *beau monde*." In *HC*, pp. 277–78, JH comments on the tone of this account in comparison with that of the 1859 Carnival, and the use of both accounts in *MF*.

68.33   our old friend Mrs. Tappan] Transcendentalist poet
and friend of Emerson, Margaret Fuller, and the Peabody sisters,
Caroline Sturgis (1819–88) had married William Aspinwall Tappan in 1847. SH had known her since the 1830s. The Hawthornes
rented the Red House on the Tappan estate in Lenox in 1850–51,
and in September 1851 a quarrel arose over the Hawthornes' right
to fruit from the orchard (see *Memories*, pp. 163–67). It was perhaps memory of this distress that caused SH to change "old friend"
to "former friend" in *Passages*. The Tappans were in Europe from
mid–1857 until 1859 or 1860. See Emerson, *Letters*, ed. R. L. Rusk
(New York: Columbia University Press, 1939), V, 86n. 148,
223, and *Notable American Women 1607–1950*, eds. Edward T.
James *et al.* (Cambridge: Harvard University Press, 1971), II,
214–15.

69.28   a baiocco] A coin worth about one American cent.

70.13   Greenwich Fair] See *EN*, pp. 289–91 (March 25,
1856), and *OOH*, pp. 234–40.

70.25   the other end of the Corso] NH added in *MF*, p. 441,
"before the palace of the Austrian embassy"; i.e., the Palazzo
Venezia.

71.21   sons of the morning] Isaiah 14:12: "How art thou fallen
from Heaven, O Lucifer, son of the morning!"

72.1   William Story] William Wetmore Story (1819–95),
sculptor and man of letters, was the acknowledged leader of the
American artists' colony in Rome in 1858. He was born in Salem,
and grew up in Cambridge, where his father, Joseph, was founder
of, and professor in, the Harvard Law School. Upon graduation
from Harvard in 1838 and from Harvard Law School in 1840, he
joined the Boston law firm of George Hillard and Charles Sumner. At that time NH resided with Hillard and met Story through
him. In 1845, at the death of Joseph Story, an associate justice of
the U.S. Supreme Court, the son—an amateur sculptor—was
chosen to execute a life-size portrait statue for his tomb in Mount
Auburn Cemetery. To prepare himself, William Story went to

Italy in 1847. On his return to Boston, he combined artistic and legal pursuits (he wrote several important books on jurisprudence) until he decided in 1851 to give up Boston for Rome, and law for art. By 1856 he and his family had settled in Italy for good. He was an accomplished poet, musician, painter, and amateur theatrical producer, and a close friend of Browning and Thackeray. Story was distinguished by having Henry James as his biographer: *William Wetmore Story and His Friends* (Boston: Houghton, Mifflin, 1903). James saw him as a "precursor" of the American cosmopolites of his own generation, one of the "light skirmishers, the éclaireurs, who have gone before." See also Taft, pp. 150–59; *Yankee Stonecutters*, pp. 33–36; Craven, pp. 274–81.

72.5 Mrs. Story] Emelyn Eldredge Story (1820–94), from a prominent Boston family, was married to William Wetmore Story in 1842. Their children were a daughter and three sons (one of whom died in childhood). See note to 146.14.

72.7–9 the ancient Greek bas-relief . . . monument in Saint Peter's.] Murray, p. 243, notes that the bas-relief was found near Tivoli. The monument is that to the Stuart family; see note to 63.27.

72.11 Mr. Hamilton Fish and family] Hamilton Fish (1808–93), from New York City, was a lawyer, congressman, governor, and senator. He and his wife, Julia Morris Kean Fish (1817–87), and their five daughters and three sons, were in Europe for two years, from August 1857 to June 1859, traveling in noticeably grand style. They had a letter of introduction to NH from Franklin Pierce (Mrs. Fish to Pierce, June 16, 1857; MS, Library of Congress). Fish was later secretary of state in the Grant administration; see Allan Nevins, *Hamilton Fish* (New York: Dodd, Mead, 1936), chapter 4.

72.11–12 Hotel d'Europe] The Hotel d'Europa in the Piazza di Spagna, center of the Anglo-American community in Rome, was described by Murray, p. viii, as "good and comfortable, but expensive."

72.12–13 Mr. C. G. Thompson] Cephas Giovanni Thompson
(1809–88), painter of landscapes, portraits (e.g., Longfellow,
Bryant) and copies of old masters, was born in Middleboro, Massachusetts, son of a portraitist. He painted NH's portrait in Boston
in 1850 (see *AN*, pp. 491–99; NH to Fields, January 12, 1851,
MS, University of Virginia). Thompson was in Rome from 1852
until his permanent return to New York in June 1859 (see NH
to Ticknor, May 23, 1859, MS, Berg). James Jackson Jarves, a
severe critic of American artists in Rome, declared: "no one of our
artists has brought back with him from Italy a more thorough
knowledge of the old masters, technically, historically, and aesthet-
ically, than C. G. Thompson" (*The Art-Idea* [1864], ed. Benjamin
Rowland, Jr. [Cambridge: Harvard University Press, 1960], p.
180). Compare Anna Jameson's opinion, p. 209, below. See also
Tuckerman, pp. 490–91; *DAB*; Metropolitan Museum of Art,
Nineteenth-Century America: Paintings and Sculpture (New
York: New York Graphic Society, 1970), no. 63; Karolik, p. 489.
The Thompsons were among the Hawthornes' best friends at
Rome, as NH's diary attests; see also pp. 216, 218–21, and 489,
below.

72.19 a small Madonna by Raphael] Probably the *Staffa Ma-
donna*, or *Connestabile Madonna* (1504), now in the Hermitage,
Leningrad, but until 1871 owned by Count Scipione Connestabile
Staffa of Perugia. The Thompson copy was owned by William
Cullen Bryant.

72.30 a sitting statue of Cleopatra] By the time of the first
public showing of this statue at the London Exhibition of 1862,
it was already well known to the public through NH's praise of
Story in the preface to *MF* and detailed appreciation in chapter
14, "Cleopatra." It was thereafter considered Story's masterpiece.
As Taft comments, p. 153, "It is a little uncertain whether it was
Story or Hawthorne who made 'Cleopatra.' "

72.31–32 thin and worn . . . gray, but] Omitted by SH from
Passages, along with the following sentence. Published in *HC*,
p. 287. See the Historical Commentary.

73.1–2   a poet . . . a sculptor] SH added "a musician" to this list in *Passages*.

73.4–6   a beautiful statue . . . simplicity.] *Marguerite*, a work of the early 1850s, now in the Essex Institute, Salem.

73.20–21   a statue of Hero] *Hero Waiting for Leander* (1852), sold to William Douglas of New York.

73.31   The statue of his father] *Joseph Story* (1852–54), now in the Harvard Law School.

74.26   a marble Pieta] Murray, p. 114, notes this as "a good Pietà by A[ntonio] Montauti" (died ca. 1740).

75.12–13   Corregio's picture] SH corrected to "Leonardo da Vinci's" in *Passages*. Correggio (1494–1534) did not paint a Last Supper.

75.30–31   the one spot in Aladdin's palace] "Aladdin and the Magic Lamp" in the *Arabian Nights*. Apparently a favorite incident for NH: see, e.g., *SL*, p. 103, and *MOM*, pp. 172, 481. Longfellow referred to it in his elegy "Hawthorne, May 23, 1864," in *Flower-de-Luce* (1866): "Ah! who shall lift that wand of magic power, / And the lost clew regain? / The unfinished window in Aladdin's tower / Unfinished must remain!"

76.25   Hillard commemorates him] In *Six Months in Italy*, Hillard devoted a paragraph of his description of the Piazza di Spagna to this beggar, "one of the most noted personages in Rome" (1876 ed., pp. 295–96). NH in *MF*, p. 111, called the beggar "Old Beppo, the millionaire of his ragged fraternity."

77.26   Miss Lander's studio] Louisa Lander (1826–1923), of Salem, was the daughter of ship captain Edward Lander, a great-granddaughter of the merchant Elias Derby, and a distant relative of the painter Benjamin West. She studied sculpture, and completed a bust of her father before going to Rome in 1855 to study with Thomas Crawford (see p. 129 below). She saw the Hawthornes frequently after their arrival in Rome (see the 1858 diary, January 25 ff.), and by April had finished the clay model for a bust of NH which he pronounced, in a letter to Ticknor, "excellent. . . . Even Mrs. Hawthorne is delighted with it"; he cites the praise of John Gibson and Fredrika Bremer for the work, and adds his own for the artist: "I like her exceedingly" (April 14, 1858; MS, Berg). The Hawthornes left for Florence, and Miss Lander for New England, to seek new commissions for her work (see Frederic A. Sharf ," 'A More Bracing Morning Atmosphere': Artistic Life in Salem, 1850–1859," *EIHC*, XCV [1959], 160–62); the bust remained, as was a frequent practice, in the hands of workmen who were to translate the cast into marble. But sometime after the Hawthornes saw the finished work on October 21, two weeks before Lander's return, their opinion of it and of the artist were radically altered, for reasons difficult to establish. Writing to Fields the following February, NH notes the opinion of "friends" that the bust is "not worth sixpence," although he still will pay for it: "she did her best . . . " (NH to Fields, February 11, 1860; MS, Huntington). JH later enlarged upon this: "the bust . . . looks like a combination of Daniel Webster and George Washington," and explained the change as due to interference by a presumptuous third party, an American "man of culture," a "critic" who, visiting Lander's studio in her absence, ordered rectification of "errors in the modelling of the lower part of the face" on his own responsibility (*NHHW*, p. 183). It is possible that annoyance at the ruined likeness accounts for the ensuing rejection of Lander: the Hawthornes refused to see her again when she returned to Rome; refused, "for reasons unnecessary to mention," to "communicate with the lady" at all, for any purpose (NH to Fields, cited above); finally SH entirely omitted all reference to her in *Passages*. It is also possible, however, that the Hawthornes' *volte face* was at least partly related to some unrecorded scandal that seems to have hovered over Miss Lander at this time. She apparently angered some influential members of the English-speaking community at Rome, for an informal "court of inquiry" headed by William Story was soon followed by Lander's permanent return to New England and relative obscurity. See Craven, pp. 332–33, and John L. Idol, Jr., and Sterling Eisiminger, "Hawthorne Sits for a Bust by Maria Louisa Lander," *EIHC*, CXIV (1978),

207–12. The bust was left in Lander's keeping for display at the Dusseldorf Gallery in New York in 1860 (see *Cosmopolitan Art Journal,* IV [March 1860], 31), was returned to the Hawthornes in Concord, and is now in the Concord Free Public Library.

78.4–5 "Virginia Dare"] a statue of the first English child born in America, completed in 1859. For its history, and reproductions of it, see Gerdts, *The Great American Nude: A History in Art* (New York: Praeger, 1974), pp. 14–15; *The White, Marmorean Flock* (unpaged).

79.2–3 the horses in the race] Murray, p. xxvi: "The amusements of each afternoon [of the Carnival] end with a horse-race. The horses have no riders, but are urged on by balls and plates of metal, covered with sharp spikes, suspended from their backs."

79.6 in the Via di Ripetta] Actually, at the southern end of the Via della Scrofa, the continuation of the Via di Ripetta.

79.16–17 Domenichino . . . Guido] Domenico Zampieri (1581–1641), a prominent follower of the Carracci in Rome, was considered a major representative for neoclassicism through the seventeenth, eighteenth, and nineteenth centuries. Murray, p. 146, comments on the two frescoes in Saint Cecilia's chapel: "These interesting works, though somewhat theatrically treated, are good examples of Domenichino's peculiar style of composition and colouring." He goes on: "The fine copy over the altar, of Raphael's St. Cecilia, now in the Gallery at Bologna, is by *Guido.*" NH does not mention the paintings in S. Luigi de' Francesi that are now most celebrated, those of Caravaggio. For Guido Reni (1575–1642), see also notes to 80.25–26 and 92.14–15.

79.25–26 the Capuchin church] I Cappuccini, or S. Maria della Concezione.

80.16–23 where the dead man. . . . vacant bed.] NH noted the scene in a close paraphrase of Murray, p. 136.

80.25–26 pictures and frescoes by Guido and Domenichino]

Guido Reni's *St. Michael Trampling the Devil,* the most celebrated painting in the church, is described at length in Murray,
p. 135. NH saw the mosaic copy of it in St. Peter's a few days
later; see p. 100.3–5. Murray, p. 135, notes: "The Ecstasy of St.
Francis, by *Domenichino,* in the third chapel on the rt., was
painted gratuitously for the ch. A fresco by *Domenichino,* formerly
in the convent, representing the death of St. Francis, has been recently placed here."

81.21–22 convent of French nuns] Murray, p. 170, notes that
Trinità dei Monti "now belongs to a convent of nuns of the Sacré
Cœur, who devote themselves to the education of young females,
and is the most frequented institution of the kind in Rome." In
the postscript to *The Marble Faun* Hilda reveals, "I was a prisoner
in the Convent of the Sacré Cœur" (*MF,* p. 466).

82.13–14 Daniele da Volterra . . . the Descent from the
Cross] Daniele da Volterra (1509–66) was a disciple of Michelangelo. His mannerist interest in institutionalizing and standard-
izing the High Renaissance style made his considerable reputation
from the seventeenth to the nineteenth century. Murray, p. 170:
the *Descent from the Cross* was "considered by Poussin to be the
third greatest picture in the world, inferior only to Raphael's
Transfiguration, and to the Communion of St. Jerome of Domenichino." Murray goes on to quote at length a reverent appreciation
by Luigi Lanzi. Other pictures by Daniele in Trinità dei Monti
included an *Assumption,* a *Presentation in the Temple,* and a
Massacre of the Innocents.

82.21–22 on a spot where Nero . . . phantoms.] Murray, p.
153: "S. Maria del Popolo . . . founded, it is supposed . . . on
the spot where the ashes of Nero are said to have been discovered
and scattered to the winds. The tradition states that the people
were constantly harassed by phantoms which haunted the spot,
and that the ch. was built to protect them from these supernatural
visitants."

82.25–26 frescoes, oil pictures . . . famous men] Murray, p.
154: "The Chigi chapel, the 2nd on the l., dedicated to the Virgin

of Loreto, was erected and decorated from the designs of *Raphael*."
He mentions as painters of the frescoes Pinturicchio and Giovanni
da San Giovanni; of oil paintings, Carlo Maratti, Annibale Carracci, Caravaggio, and Sebastiano del Piombo; of sculptures, Andrea de Sansovino, Algardi, Lorenzetto Lotti, and Bernini.

83.16   the extinguishing of the tapers] See notes to 504.5 and
504.22.

85.7–8   Wolsey's hat . . . Manchester Exhibition] See *EN*, p.
548 (July 26, 1857).

85.29   **the ex–queen of Spain.**] Maria Cristina de Borbon
(1806–78), daughter of Francis I, king of the Two Sicilies, was
queen of Spain from 1829 until 1833 as fourth wife of Ferdinand
VII; at his death in 1833 she became regent for her daughter Isabella II (1830–1904), but was forced to give up the regency in
1840. SH in *Passages* changed "ex–queen" to "queen."

85.34   Scala Sancta] Properly, Scala Santa. Corrected by SH
in *Passages*.

86.13–14   the Apollo, and the Laocoon, and the torso of
Hercules] The *Apollo Belvedere*, the *Laocoön*, and the *Torso Bel-
vedere* ("generally supposed to represent Hercules") are described
by Murray, pp. 184–88, with appropriate quotations from *Childe
Harold* and references to the judgment of Winckelmann. For
American tourists the *Apollo* and *Laocoön* ranked with the *Dying
Gladiator* of the Capitoline Museum and the *Medici Venus* in the
Uffizi at Florence as the most awesome examples of classical genius
in sculpture. See Baker, *The Fortunate Pilgrims*, pp. 146–47.

86.17–19   Most of these . . . I had seen] In 1822 Augustus
Thorndike gave the Boston Atheneum plaster casts of celebrated
ancient statues, including the *Apollo Belvedere*, the *Laocoön*,
the *Medici Venus*, the *Capitoline Venus*, the *Borghese Gladiator*,
the *Torso of Hercules*, *Diana*, the *Hermaphrodite*, the *Discobo-

lus, the *Little Apollo* [*Apollino*], and the *Capitoline Antinous*. See Mabel Munson Swan, *The Atheneum Gallery 1827–1873: The Boston Atheneum as an Early Patron of Art* (Boston: Boston Atheneum, 1940), p. 134. In "The Ghost of Doctor Harris," a sketch of 1856, NH recalled the reading room of the Atheneum as "a spacious hall, with the group of the Laocoön at one end, and the Belvidere Apollo at the other" (*Nineteenth Century*, XLVII [January 1900], 89).

87.10   Tarpeian Way] The Via della Rupe Tarpeia.

87.22–33   But the fact is . . . as other people.] SH's sense of propriety led her to omit from *Passages* "and along . . . ancient wall," "or they will . . . nastiness," and "and, in my opinion . . . as other people."

88.26–27   Fountain of the Termini] Now the Fontanone dell' Acqua Felice. The sculptor of the *Moses,* Prospero Bresciano (or Antichi), did not live to complete the fountain, which opened in 1587. Murray notes, p. 88, that he "is said to have died of grief at the ridicule excited by his performance."

88.34   Piazza di Termini] Now the Piazza di S. Bernardo.

89.31–32   martyrdom of Saint Sebastian . . . mosaic copy.] Murray, p. 148: "This ch. contains several large and fine paintings which were once altar-pieces in St. Peter's, where they have been replaced by copies in mosaic . . . amongst them the most celebrated is the St. Sebastian" by Domenichino.

90.12   Carlo Maratti] (1625–1713). The leading painter of the late baroque period in Rome, he restored Raphael's frescoes in the Vatican.

90.13   Salvator Rosa] (1615–73). He was, for the eighteenth and nineteenth centuries, with Claude Lorrain the most influential of landscape painters. His pictures epitomized the sublime, as Claude's did the beautiful. See Samuel H. Monk, *The Sublime* (New York: Modern Language Association, 1935), chapter 9.

EXPLANATORY NOTES

90.13–16   Saint Bruno, by Houdon. . . . Washington] Jean-
Antoine Houdon (1741–1828), the first neoclassical sculptor, did
this statue during an early, more baroque phase (1764–68).
Murray, p. 147: "It is recorded that Clement XIV. was a great
admirer of this statue: 'It would speak,' he said, 'if the rule of his
order did not prescribe silence.'" Houdon's *George Washington*
(1788–92; Virginia State Capitol, Richmond) "was not only important for American sculpture as a major modern work, admired
by all who saw it, but it also served as a model for more images of
Washington than any other life portrait" (Gerdts, p. 13).
Houdon's original bust of Washington was begun on his visit
to Mount Vernon in 1785.

90.27   Fontana Paolina] The Fontanone dell' Acqua Paola
(1610–14), by Flaminio Ponzio (1559–1613), on the Janiculum.
Murray, p. 87: "The most abundant, and perhaps the most imposing, of all the Roman fountains. . . . The style of the fountain
is not in the best taste, but the effect of the water can hardly be
surpassed. The view from this fountain over the whole of Rome
and the Campagna is very fine."

92.4–11   a picture of Christ. . . . a very remarkable picture.]
Painted by Dürer in 1506, reportedly in five days. The ugliness of
the doctors was frequently mentioned by critics and tourists.

92.14   Raphael's Fornarini] The *Fornarina*. This portrait of a
woman naked to the waist was traditionally supposed to be of
Raphael's mistress Margherita, the baker's daughter ("la fornarina"), though the subject has recently been identified as the
Sienese lady Margherita di Francesco Luti, and the artist is considered to be Giulio Romano. The story of Raphael's love for the
coarsely beautiful common woman was notorious during the
Romantic period, provoking pictures of the artist and his mistress by
Ingres and others.

92.14–15   Guido's portrait of Beatrice Cenci] This is perhaps
the one painting in Rome that most impressed NH. Murray, p.
243, describes it as "one of the most celebrated portraits in Rome.

• 746 •

According to the tradition, it was taken on the night before her execution; other accounts state that it was painted by Guido from memory after he had seen her on the scaffold." SH in *Notes*, p. 212, rhapsodizes: "And now we sat down before Beatrice Cenci! at last, at last! after so many years' hoping and wishing. This is a masterpiece which baffles words. . . . " More recently scholars have come to doubt both that Guido painted the portrait and that it represents Beatrice Cenci. Hans Tietze and J. P. Richter attribute it to Francesco Albani (1578–1660), Arthur McComb claims that "it probably represents a Sibyl." See McComb, *The Baroque Painters of Italy* (Cambridge: Harvard University Press, 1934), pp. 26, 31. Cesare Gnudi, *Guido Reni* (Florence: Vallecchi, 1955), does not mention it. The legend associating the Barberini painting with Guido and Beatrice grew up in the late eighteenth century and reached the peak of its popularity in the 1850s. See Corrado Ricci, *Beatrice Cenci* (London: Heinemann, 1926), chapter 32.

94.19 Guido's Aurora] Murray, p. 262: "one of the most celebrated frescoes in Rome. . . . The composition is extremely beautiful, and the colouring brilliant beyond all other examples of the master. A large mirror has been so arranged as to enable the visitor to view the fresco with greater facility."

94.34–95.1 Christian's tremulous glimpse of the Celestial City.] Near the end of the first part of Bunyan's *Pilgrim's Progress*, ed. James Blanton Wharey, 2nd ed., rev. Roger Sharrock (Oxford: Clarendon Press, 1960), pp. 122–23: Christian and Hopeful "essayed to look, but the remembrance of . . . [hell] made their hands shake; by means of which impediment they could not look steadily through the [perspective] Glass; yet they thought they saw something like the Gate, and also some of the Glory of" the Celestial City. See page 278, below.

95.1–2 pictures by Domenichino, Rubens] Murray, p. 262, mentions "a large and fine picture of Adam and Eve in Paradise after the Fall, by *Domenichino*; . . . The Triumph of David, by *Domenichino*; 13 pictures of the Saviour and the 12 Apostles, by *Rubens*, many of them copies."

95.2   other famous painters] The names mentioned by Murray, p. 262, are Ludovico Carracci, Guido, Van Dyck, Daniele da Volterra, Poussin, Cigoli, and Passignano.

95.21   St. Andrea] Bernini's S. Andrea al Quirinale (1658–70), which he considered one of his most perfectly realized conceptions.

96.5–6   the Great Carbuncle] NH's tale "The Great Carbuncle" was first published in *The Token and Atlantic Souvenir* (Boston: Charles Bowen, 1837), pp. 156–75. See *TTT*, pp. 149–65.

96.14–16   the house . . . in Rome] Milton was in Rome for two months in the fall of 1638; he was frequently a guest in the palace of the Cardinal Barberini.

98.29–34   the frescoes . . . instead of frescoes.] Murray, p. 144, says of S. Ignazio: "Its magnificence is not in the best taste, but is interesting from its excessive ornament. The paintings of the roof and tribune are by *Padre Pozzi,* and are remarkable for their perspective." Padre Andrea Pozzo (1642–1709), *Allegory of the Missionary Work of the Jesuits* (1691–94).

99.7–8   one of Bernini's absurd fountains] There are two fountains by Bernini in the Piazza Navona: the *Four Rivers Fountain* (1648–51) and the *Fontana del Moro* (1653–55). See notes to 148.30–31 and 196.26.

99.10–11   the poor battered torso of Pasquin] Murray, p. 89, explains that the *"Piazza di Pasquino,* at the angle of the Braschi Palace, near the Piazza Navona . . . derives its name from the well-known torso . . . a mutilated fragment of an ancient statue found here in the 16th centy., and considered to represent Menelaus supporting the dead body of Patroclus. . . . Baldinucci, in his Life of Bernini, tells us that it was considered by that sculptor the finest fragment of antiquity in Rome. It derives its modern name from a tailor called Pasquino, who kept a shop opposite, which was the rendezvous of all the gossips of the city, and from which their satirical witticisms on the manners and follies of the day obtained a ready circulation. The fame of Pasquin is perpetuated in the term *pasquinade*, and has thus become European; but Rome is the only place in which he flourishes."

100.3–7   Guido's picture . . . celestial.] See note to 80.25.

101.7   a fountain] In Murray, p. 89, called the *Fontana del Campidoglio*.

101.19–21   busts of the Caesars . . . eighty-three] Murray, p. 235: "Around the room are arranged 83 busts of the Roman emperors and empresses in chronological order, a collection of great value, presenting us the portraits of some of the most remarkable personages in history."

101.21–22   a bust of Julius Caesar, in the British Museum] See *EN*, p. 242 (September 29, 1855): "Julius Caesar was there, too, looking more like a modern old man than any other bust in the series. Perhaps there may be a universality in his face that gives it this independence of race and epoch."

102.11   the Dying Gladiator] This statue was ranked first in perfection by American tourists, before the *Apollo Belvedere* and the *Laocoön*, according to Baker, *The Fortunate Pilgrims*, p. 146. Murray, pp. 232–33, describes it at length, quoting *Childe Harold*, canto 4, stanzas 140–41, and the sculptor John Bell (1811–95): "It is a most tragical and touching representation, and no one can meditate upon it without the most melancholy feelings. Of all proofs this is the surest of the effect produced by art. . . . The forms of the Dying Gladiator are not ideal or exquisite, like the Apollo; it is all nature, all feeling." This statue is now generally known as the *Dying Gaul* or *Dying Trumpeter*; it is a Roman marble copy of a bronze original from Pergamon, made probably after 228 B.C. by an artist identified by Pliny as Epigonos; see Bieber, p. 108.

102.28   statue of Antinous] The *Antinous* of the Capitol is described by Murray, p. 233, as an "exquisite statue" of "exceeding beauty." Antinous, the favorite of the Emperor Hadrian, drowned himself in the Nile in 130 A.D., and was decreed a god by the emperor. The *Faun of Praxiteles* is listed in Murray as in place next to the *Antinous,* but NH did not apparently notice it until his fifth visit, on April 22. See p. 178, below.

104.14–19 A multitude . . . guilt and suffering.] Compare Murray, pp. 77–78: "It is hardly possible to imagine a more horrible dungeon. Admitting that these are the Mamertine prisons, it must have been in this cell that Jugurtha was starved to death; that the accomplices of Catiline were strangled by order of Cicero; and that Sejanus, the minister of Tiberius, was executed."

105.19 Mr. J. P. Kennedy] John Pendleton Kennedy (1795–1870), from Baltimore, Whig politician and historical romancer, was in Europe for a tour from August 1857 until October 1858. Despite his family's Virginian aristocratic, slaveholding traditions, Kennedy held liberal views on slavery and its spread to the West: on several occasions he was denied election as senator from Maryland because of his lukewarm advocacy of slavery. His specific views on the "Kansas difficulty" are not known. President Buchanan on February 2, 1858, had submitted to the Congress the constitution proposed for Kansas at Lecompton in 1857, a proslavery document that had already been repudiated by Kansas voters. Presumably Kennedy's "settlement" would have involved compromise between proslavery and Free Soil forces in the Congress. See the biographies of Kennedy by Edwin M. Gwathmey (1931) and Charles H. Bohner (1961), and David M. Potter, *The Impending Crisis, 1848–1861* (New York: Harper and Row, 1976), chapter 12. For more on Kansas, see p. 222 and note to 222.30–33.

106.1–3 the site of my Town Pump . . . prints.] NH's sketch "A Rill from the Town-Pump" was first published in the *New-England Magazine,* VIII (June 1835), 473–78. The sketch begins with a stage direction and footnote identifying the scene as the corner of Essex and Washington Streets, in Salem (see *TTT,* p. 141.)

107.7–9 covering them up . . . babes with leaves.] The ballad "The Children in the Wood" in Percy, *Reliques,* Series 3, Book 2, number 18.

108.24–25 the Porta Latina . . . entered Rome] According to Murray, p. 7, it was through the adjoining Porta Asinaria that Belisarius first entered Rome.

109.7 a street . . . with the Corso] The Via della Fontanella, now called the Via di Fontana Borghese.

109.10–11 an immense edifice] The architects were Martino Longhi the Elder (d. 1591) and Flaminio Ponzio.

109.29 One beautiful hall] The Stanza degli Specchi.

110.19 Prince Borghese] Marcantonio V (1814–86). After his death, bankruptcy in 1891 forced the sale of the library and art of the palace; in 1902 the state took over the Borghese gardens as a public park, and the casino houses many of the art treasures.

111.9–112.8 A quarter part. . . . not from within.] Murray, pp. 245–47, considers of special importance Raphael's *Entombment* and his portrait of *Cesare Borgia*; Francia's *St. Stephen*, and a *Madonna*; Correggio's *Danaë*; Sebastiano del Piombo's *Christ at the Column*; Domenichino's *Cumæan Sibyl* and *Chase of Diana*; Albani's *The Four Seasons*; and Titian's *Three Graces* and *Sacred and Profane Love*.

111.34–112.5 Francia . . . prayers upon canvas.] Francesco Francia (1450–1517) was represented in the Borghese Collection by a *Virgin and Child*, with a half-figure of St. Anthony; a *Madonna and Saints*; *St. Stephen*; and a *Madonna and Child in a Rose Garden*. In *Passages* SH added a parenthesis after "class of subjects": Christs and Madonnas. Francia was reputed to have died of envy of Raphael.

112.10–16 Dutch and Flemish pictures. . . . taste.] Murray, p. 247, mentions Van Dyck's *Christ on the Cross*, and *Entombment*; Potter's *Cattle*; Rembrandt's *Boors on the Ice*, and portrait of *Marie de Medicis*; Rubens's *The Visitation of St. Elizabeth*; Tenier's *Boors Drinking*; and portraits by Holbein, Dürer, and Cranach. Many Amercian tourists disapproved of Dutch and Flemish genre and naturalistic painting, and considered it inferior to Italian Renaissance painting of religious subjects. See Neil Harris, *The Artist in American Society: The Formative Years, 1790–1860* (New York: Braziller, 1966), pp. 136, 362. For NH's first appreciation of Dutch masters, see *EN*, p. 556.

112.25   St Gesu] Properly, Il Gesù. The architects were Giacomo da Vignola (1507–73) and Giacomo della Porta (ca. 1537–1602).

113.4   a picture over the altar] Murray, pp. 141–42, identifies this as the *Presentation of the Infant Saviour in the Temple*, by Alessandro Capalti (1817–68).

113.8–9   the great ball of lapis lazuli] Murray, p. 142: "The marble group of the Trinity is by Bernardino Ludovisi [ca. 1713–49]: the globe below the Almighty is said to be the largest mass of lapis lazuli known."

113.27   face in the Museum] The bust of Julius Caesar in the Hall of Emperors of the Capitoline Museum.

114.24–25   the Rape of Europa, by Paul Veronese] Murray, p. 228, notes: "a repetition of the picture in the Ducal Palace at Venice."

115.2   Garofalo] Il Garofalo (Benvenuto Tisio, 1481–1559), a Ferrarese follower of Raphael whose reputation has declined in the last hundred years. His paintings in the Capitoline Gallery included a *St. Catherine*, a *Holy Family*, a *Madonna in Glory*, a *St. Lucia*, an *Annunciation*, a *Madonna and Child in Glory*, a *Madonna with Certain Doctors of the Church*, and an *Adoration of the Magi*. See note to 124.19.

115.4   Maria Sublegras] Maria Felicia Subleyras, née Tibaldi (1707–70), a miniaturist, was married to the painter Pierre Subleyras (1699–1749). The spelling "Sublegras" is used in Murray, p. 227.

115.20 Curtius] Mettus Curtius, legendary Roman hero of the fourth century B.C., according to Livy rode his horse into the chasm to demonstrate that Rome's greatest treasure was a brave man.

115.30 talma] A cape named for the French actor François Joseph Talma (1763–1826).

116.7–8 Palace of the Caesars . . . a convent] Murray, pp. 26–27: "The first palace of the emperors on the Palatine was erected by Augustus, on the site of the houses of Cicero, Hortensius, Cataline, and Claudius. . . . standing nearly in the centre of the hill, is the *Villa Spada* or Palatina, known also as the *Villa Mills*, from an English gentleman of that name to whom it once belonged; it has now passed into the possession of a community of French nuns."

116.27 the tomb of Cecilia Metella] According to Murray, p. 63, it was "erected more than 19 centuries ago to the memory of Cæcelia Metella, daughter of Quintus Metellus, who obtained the surname of Creticus for his conquest of Crete, B.C. 67."

118.13 a battlemented wall] See note to 208.12–14.

118.26–32 The posthumous fate. . . . after her death.] These dry observations seem to respond to the effusive romantic speculations about the dead lady in *Childe Harold*, canto 4, stanzas 99–103, quoted by Murray, p. 64.

120.28–30 another similar one . . . few years ago.] Murray, p. 73, says this columbarium is "called improperly that of the Liberati of Pompey," and that a third columbarium nearby was discovered in 1853.

122.13 Mammoth Cave] In Kentucky.

123.7 the Temple of Honor and Virtue.] So Murray, p. 31, but SH in *Passages* changed it to the Temple of Virtue and Honor.

123.13   some frescoes] Murray, p. 31: "The paintings on the walls, representing events in the life of Christ, S. Cecilia, &c., are curious frescoes of the 11th century."

123.21–22   but Murray—a highly essential nuisance] Murray, p. 31: "*Temple of Bacchus*, or of the *Camenœ*, most doubtful designations given to a ruin near the pretended Grotto of Egeria."

123.33   Palazzo Laza—] See note to 53.17–19.

124.6–7   Raphael's Violin Player] Now attributed to Sebastiano del Piombo, *The Young Violinist* was later acquired for the Rothschild Collection, Paris.

124.8   Vanity and Modesty] Now attributed to Bernardino Luini (ca. 1480–1532) and in the Rothschild Collection, Paris. See Angela Ottino della Chiesa, *Bernardino Luini* (Novara: Agostini, 1956), fig. 153.

124.11–12   Joanna of Aragon] NH saw *Giovanna d'Aragona* in the Doria-Pamphili Palace three days later; see p. 125. This portrait is now considered a copy of one in the Louvre by Giulio Romano (?1499–1546), perhaps from a design by Raphael. See Angela Ottino della Chiesa, *The Complete Paintings of Leonardo da Vinci* (New York: Abrams, 1969), p. 114; S. J. Freedberg, *Painting of the High Renaissance in Rome and Florence* (Cambridge: Harvard University Press, 1961), I, 345–46, and plate 431; John Pope-Hennessy, *Raphael* (New York: New York University Press, 1970), p. 294.

124.13   Titian's Bella Donna] Now attributed to Palma Vecchio (Jacopo Palma, ca. 1480–1528), *The Portrait of a Lady* was later acquired for the Rothschild Collection, Paris, and is now in the Thyssen Collection, Lugano.

124.16   Gainsborough's Lady Lynedoch] Better known as *The Honorable Mrs. Thomas Graham* (1777). Since 1859 in the National Gallery, Edinburgh. NH saw it at the Manchester Exhibition in 1857 (*Catalogue*, p. 84).

124.17–18   two Madonnas by Guido] These paintings were Magdalens, as corrected in *Good Words*, XII (1871), 436, but not in *Passages*. In *Notes* SH describes them, pp. 262–63: "the Magdalen delle Radice, and the other much like it." *The Magdalen of the Cross* is now in the Capitoline Gallery, and the other in the Palazzo Corsini (Galleria Nazionale d'Arte Antica).

124.19   several pictures by Garofalo] Murray, p. 263, notes the *Samaritan at the Well*, a small *Noli me tangere*, the *Adoration of the Magi*, and a hunting scene (queried, as a questionable attribution). SH first saw a painting by Garofalo in the Borghese Gallery on February 25; she immediately found his work "immortal," and on March 1 his *Annunciation* in the Capitoline Gallery was superior to "all I have yet seen, even Murillo's" (*Notes*, pp. 239, 248).

124.25   fairly made out.] Here SH added a note in *Passages*: "I cannot refrain from observing here, that Mr. Hawthorne's inexorable demand for perfection in all things leads him to complain of grimy pictures and tarnished frames and faded frescos, distressing beyond measure to eyes that never failed to see everything before him with the keenest apprehension. The usual careless observation of people both of the good and the imperfect is much more comfortable in this imperfect world. But the insight which Mr. Hawthorne possessed was only equalled by his outsight, and he suffered in a way not to be readily conceived, from any failure in beauty, physical, moral, or intellectual. It is not, therefore, mere love of upholstery that impels him to ask for perfect settings to priceless gems of art; but a native idiosyncrasy, which always made me feel that 'the New Jerusalem,' 'even like a jasper stone, clear as crystal,' 'where shall in no wise enter anything that defileth, neither what worketh abomination nor maketh a lie,' would alone satisfy him, or rather alone not give him actual pain. It may give an idea of this exquisite nicety of feeling to mention, that one day he took in his fingers a half-bloomed rose, without blemish, and, smiling with an infinite joy, remarked, 'This is perfect. On earth a flower only can be perfect.'"

125.13   the Apollo Belvidere] The *Apollo* is now known to be a Roman marble copy, probably of a Greek bronze original. Some scholars speculate that the original was by Leochares, a contemporary of Praxiteles; others suspect a first century B.C. origin.

125.17   the Laocoon] By the Rhodian sculptors Agesander, Polydoros, and Athenodoros in the late second century B.C. Since it was found in 1506 on the Esquiline where Pliny described its placement in the home of the Emperor Titus (*Natural History*, 36), it is seen as the original statue and not a copy. In neoclassical taste the *Laocoön* complemented the *Apollo Belvedere*: the *Apollo* exemplified harmonious beauty; the *Laocoön*, sublime tragedy.

125.30   the Doria Pamfili palace] Murray, p. 255, describes it as "the most magnificent perhaps of all the Roman palaces."

126.20–23   a bust of the present prince Doria . . . Talbot family] By Pietro Tenerani (1787–1869), a leading pupil of Thorvaldsen.

126.26   Sebastian del Piombo] Sebastiano del Piombo (1485–1547), a Venetian painter, was deeply influenced by Michelangelo, and was an outstanding portraitist.

126.26–27   other portraits and busts of the family] Velazquez's portrait of Pope Innocent X (ca. 1650) is now considered the most important picture in the gallery. There is a bust of Innocent X by Bernini, busts of other Pamphilis by Algardi, and a portrait of Gianetto Doria by Bronzino.

127.8   landscapes of Claude's] Claude Lorrain (1600–82), *The Repose on the Flight into Egypt; Landscape with Mercury Stealing the Cattle of Apollo; The Sacrifice in the Temple of Apollo on the Island of Delos* (ca. 1672); *Landscape with Diana, Hippolytus, and Aricia; The Landscape of the Mill, with the Marriage of Isaac and Rebecca* (ca. 1647).

127.10   those in the British National Gallery] See *EN*, pp. 293 (March 26, 1856) and 615 (December 8, 1857). *The Embarkation of St. Ursula* (ca. 1646); *Landscape of the Mill, with the Marriage of Isaac and Rebecca* (copy of the Doria picture); *Embarkation of the Queen of Sheba* (1648); *Classical Landscape* (1673).

128.5 his wife] May Ogden Thompson (b. ca. 1822), sister of the actress and playwright Anna Cora Ogden Mowatt.

129.6 Crawford's Studio] Thomas Crawford (?1813–57) was the first American sculptor to settle in Rome. The son of Irish immigrants, he was first apprenticed to a woodcarver in New York City. He was employed as a stonecutter by the sculptor John Frazee about 1832, and was able to go to Rome in 1835, where he studied sculpture under the influence of Thorvaldsen. A prolific workman, Crawford became well known in the 1840s to the American public; his studio in Rome was a "shrine to travellers" before most of the other sculptors NH met had come to Rome. He died of cancer of the eye in London on October 10, 1857, leaving many projects unfinished. See Taft, pp. 72–91; Craven, pp. 123–35; Crane; Thorp; Robert L. Gale, *Thomas Crawford: American Sculptor* (Pittsburgh: University of Pittsburgh Press, 1964).

129.8–22 principally portions. . . . enough.] Crawford's bronze monument of Washington (1850–57) was commissioned by the state of Virginia for Richmond. The design included an equestrian statue of Washington atop a pedestal; at the lower level pedestrian statues of six famous Virginians: Thomas Jefferson, Patrick Henry, George Mason, John Marshall, Thomas Nelson, and Andrew Lewis. Before his death Crawford completed Washington and his horse, Jefferson, and Henry. His models of Mason and Marshall were cast by Randolph Rogers (1825–92), who later executed the Nelson and Lewis statues and allegorical figures around the base, completing the entire work in 1869. See Gale, *Thomas Crawford*; Crane; and Millard F. Rogers, Jr., *Randolph Rogers: American Sculptor in Rome* (Amherst: University of Massachusetts Press, 1971), chapter 6. NH's unenthusiastic response was unusual, but one contemporary who shared it was James Jackson Jarves in *The Art-Idea*, p. 213.

129.22–24 casts of statues . . . personages] Probably figures for *The Progress of American Civilization* (1855), for the Senate pediment, east front, U.S. Capitol, including a soldier in Revolutionary uniform, a schoolmaster, schoolboy, mechanic, merchant, Indian chief, Indian wife, and Indian boy.

129.24–27   some ideal statues . . . Flora] *Boy Playing Marbles* (1853), *Orpheus* (1839), *Adam and Eve* (1855), and *Flora* (1853); reproductions in Gerdts, nos. 163, 9, 35, 53. Crawford's *Orpheus* was his first statue; it was championed by Charles Sumner, who promoted subscriptions for its purchase by the Boston intelligentsia. Upon its arrival a special building was constructed near the Boston Atheneum, where it was exhibited with great fanfare in the spring of 1844. This was the first one-man sculpture show in the United States.

131.5   Mr. T. B. Reades'] Thomas Buchanan Read (1822–72), artist and poet, had begun his career in Cincinnati. He lived in Boston and Philadelphia in the 1840s, and in Florence and Rome in the 1850s. He kept an apartment in the Palazzo Torlonia, and was known as an excellent host. Read's poetry was admired by the Brownings, Leigh Hunt, Rossetti, Landor, Patmore, and Thackeray. He painted portraits of Robert and Elizabeth Barrett Browning in 1853. See [H. C. Townsend], *A Memoir of Thomas Buchanan Read* (Philadelphia, 1889); *Travelers in Arcadia*, p. 58; *Yankee Stonecutters*, p. 70; John R. Tait, "Reminiscences of a Poet-Painter," *Lippincott's*, XIX (1877), 307–21; David Howard Dickason, *The Daring Young Men: The Story of the American Pre-Raphaelites* (Bloomington: Indiana University Press, 1953), pp. 26–32.

131.6   a party composed of painters and sculptors] NH's diary records the presence of C. G. Thompson, Joseph Mozier (see p. 153, below) Luther Terry (see p. 227), Randolph Rogers, and Holme Cardwell (b. 1820).

131.7   Mr. Hooker] See note to 62.16.

131.9   Mr. Gibson] John Gibson (1791–1866), born in Wales (which accounts for NH's remark about his accent), came to Rome from Liverpool in 1820 at the urging of the sculptor John Flaxman;

he studied with Canova and Thorvaldsen, and was considered their successor by his American colleagues. He frequently repeated his principle in art: *"Whatever the Greeks did was right"*; see Lady Eastlake, ed., *Life of John Gibson, R.A.* (London: Longmans, Green, 1870), p. 128. Murray, p. 268: *"John Gibson, R.A.,* No. 4, Via della Fontanella, between the Via Babuino and the Corso. First amongst our countrymen resident in Rome is this distinguished sculptor, who merits the high praise of having united the styles of the two greatest sculptors of modern Rome, Canova and Thorwaldsen: most of his works are in England, but models of all will be found in his studio." Bonfigli, *Guide,* lists his principal works as two statues of Queen Victoria, a *Pandora,* a *Wounded Amazon,* a *Cupid Drawing an Arrow from His Quiver,* and a *Psyche Carried by Zephyrs.*

131.31   about India] The nationalist uprising by native soldiers, sepoys, of the Bengal army of the East India Company began in early 1857. Later that year the sepoys captured Delhi and Cawnpore and besieged Lucknow. By March 1858 the British, supported by loyal Indian troops, recaptured Delhi and Cawnpore, and relieved the long siege of Lucknow.

133.10–11   Thorwaldsen—"The Clay . . . the Resurrection."] Bertel Thorvaldsen (1770–1844), the Danish neoclassical sculptor, was in Rome from 1797 until 1838. Influenced by Canova, he in turn influenced Greenough, Crawford, and Powers. The dictum quoted is also attributed to Canova.

134.5   the Frangipanis] A powerful Roman family of the thirteenth century who converted a number of classical buildings and monuments into fortresses and castles. NH follows the text of Murray, p. 53.

134.23–24   a modern roof] Murray, p. 42: "The entablature has entirely disappeared, and the roof has been replaced by an ugly covering of red tiles."

135.16   Horatius Cocles] A legendary Roman hero of the sixth century B.C. Murray, p. 10, says of the Pons Sublicius, "It was upon this bridge that Horatius Cocles withstood the army of Porsena till the Romans had succeeded in breaking it down behind him." See Livy, *History of Rome*, 2, 10. T. B. Macaulay's popular poem on this incident was in his *Lays of Ancient Rome* (1842).

136.33 Niagara] NH visited Niagara Falls in 1832 and recorded a similar disappointment in "My Visit to Niagara," *New-England Magazine*, VIII (February 1835), 91–96. See *SI*, pp. 281–88.

137.20–21 *Indulgentia . . . et vivis*] "Full and eternal indulgence for both the dead and the living."

138.28–31 Perseus. . . . Apollo] Murray, pp. 185–86: Canova's *Perseus* and *The Two Boxers* "were brought here when the ancient statues were carried off to Paris [by Napoleon I]; the Perseus was placed on the pedestal of the Apollo [Belvedere], and obtained the name of the Consolatrice. On the restoration of the Apollo and the Laocoon, the Perseus and the boxers were ordered to remain here, in opposition to the wishes of Canova, who felt that they would challenge comparison when standing by the side of those masterpieces of ancient art."

139.19 Mr. & Mrs. Daubeny] Mr. Daubeny may be Charles Giles Bridle Daubeny, M.D. (1795–1867), professor of botany and rural economy at Oxford, who had written extensively on volcanoes in Italy. Another possibility is Henry Daubeny, M.D. (1820–87), an English physician who in 1865 published a pamphlet, *The Climate of San Remo as Adapted to Invalids*. There is also a chance that he may be Charles William Dabney (1823–70), of Boston, U.S. consul at Fayal, Azores.

139.20 the Waterstons] Robert Cassie Waterston (1812–93), a Boston Unitarian minister born in Maine, and Anna Cabot Lowell Quincy Waterston (1812–99), daughter of the wealthy lawyer Josiah Quincy (1772–1864), mayor of Boston from 1823 to 1828 and president of Harvard from 1829 to 1845. Both NH and SH had known them since the late 1830s; see *AN*, p. 70, and SH to her brother George, May 21, 1839 (MS, Berg). NH's letter to

SH of April 14, 1844, suggests that Waterston was the model for
Mr. Smooth-it-away in "The Celestial Rail-road" (MS, Huntington). The Waterstons were traveling with their seventeen-year-old
daughter, Helen, who died in Naples in the summer of 1858.

139.21–22 Miss Pickering] Mary Orne Pickering (1805–86),
daughter of John Pickering (1777–1846), an eminent lawyer and
philologist, and granddaughter of Colonel Timothy Pickering
(1745–1829) (both in *DAB*).

139.24 Miss Bremer] Fredrika Bremer (1801–65), the Swedish novelist, had visited the Hawthornes in Lenox, probably in 1851
(see *AN*, pp. 296, 633). Her *Two Years in Switzerland and Italy*,
trans. Mary Howitt (London: Hurst and Blackett, 1861), does not
mention her several meetings with the Hawthornes in Rome. See
page 177 for NH's memory of what she had written of him, quoted
in the note to 177.22–27.

139.29 Thackeray] William Makepeace Thackeray (1811–63)
is mentioned several times in *EN*, but NH never made the occasion
to meet him in England. The Storys knew Thackeray well in Rome
during the winter of 1853–54; see *The Letters of William Makepeace Thackeray*, ed. Gordon N. Ray (Cambridge: Harvard University Press, 1946), III, 330–31 n. 260, 341, 359, 464–66; Gordon
N. Ray, *Thackeray: The Age of Wisdom 1847–1863* (New York:
McGraw-Hill, 1958), pp. 225–30.

139.31–140.1 the story of Bluebeard] Story's poem "Blue
Beard's Cabinets" in his *Graffiti d'Italia* (New York: Scribner,
1868), was written after 1856. NH's only use of the character was
a momentary one in *MF*, p. 219.

140.15 the great hall] The frescoed ceiling (1633–39) of the
Gran Salone is by Pietro da Cortona (1596–1669). For an account
of his use of illusionistic foreshortening to convey an intricate allegorical, mythological, and emblematic program, see Wittkower,
pp. 250–53.

141.15 the Palazzo Galizin] Named for the Russian princely
family Galitzine.

141.16 the Misses Weston] Caroline (1808–82), Anne Warren (1812–90), and Emma Forbes Weston (1825–88), were daughters of Captain Warren (ca. 1780–1855) and Nancy Bates Weston (1785–1839), of Weymouth, Massachusetts. Their elder sister, Maria Weston Chapman (1806–85) was a leader of the abolitionist movement, and "one of the most remarkable women of the age." Caroline and Anne had been schoolteachers in Massachusetts; they were close friends of William Lloyd Garrison and were officers in various antislavery societies. Emma, the youngest sister, was described by Garrison as "warmly interested in the anti-slavery cause." Their maternal uncle, the London banker Joshua Bates, provided for their education and travel in Europe. Since 1848 they had spent much of their time in Paris and Rome. See the biography of Maria Weston Chapman in *Notable American Women*, ed. Edward T. James *et al.* (Cambridge: Harvard University Press, 1971), and Garrison's *Letters*, eds. Walter M. Merrill and Louis Ruchames (Cambridge: Harvard University Press, 1971), II, 57, 209, 717; III, 626; IV, 612.

143.6 where Beatrice Cenci . . . execution.] NH apparently did not consult Murray, p. 68, which refers to some small cells "in one of which the custode will have it that Beatrice Cenci was confined—more probably her brothers."

143.14 her mother-in-law] Actually her mother, Lucretia Cenci, who was executed with Beatrice in 1599.

143.16 Benvenuto Cellini] Cellini (1500–1571), in his *Autobiography*, described his imprisonment in 1537 by Pope Paul III for allegedly stealing jewels entrusted to him by Pope Clement VII. Modern guidebooks point out that he was more likely incarcerated in a larger room containing a fireplace and opening on the court, since he mentions melting wax and metals in his cell.

143.27–31 Archangel Michael. . . . to be stayed.] Murray, p. 66: "At the close of the 6th century, according to the Church tradition, while Gregory the Great was engaged in a procession to St. Peter's for the purpose of offering up a solemn service to avert the pestilence which followed the inundation of 589, the

Archangel Michael appeared to him standing on the summit of the fortress, in the act of sheathing his sword, to signify that the plague was stayed." The statue, by the Flemish sculptor Pieter Verschaffelt (1710–93), was erected in 1753.

143.34 Ardea, and Corioli] Settlements south of Rome, near the sea. Ardea was the capital of Turnus, of the *Aeneid*, and Corioli (now Monte Giove) is associated with Coriolanus.

144.2–3 frescoes by I forget whom] The Sala del Consiglio, by Pierino del Vaga (1500–1547).

144.32–34 If we are to believe . . . shot the constable.] Charles, duc de Bourbon (1490–1527), constable of France, was killed as his army sacked Rome. According to Cellini's *Autobiography* he and two of his friends fired their arquebuses through a thick fog and shot a figure who later was identified as the constable. See note to 163.30–31.

146.14 Edith Story and her two little brothers] Edith Marion Story (1844–1917) was the same age, 14, as Una. In 1876 she married Marchese Simone Peruzzi, a distinguished Florentine and retired soldier. Thomas Waldo Story (1854–1915) and Julian Russell Story (1856–1919) later attended Eton and Oxford and became a sculptor and a portrait painter respectively. Another son, Joseph, born in 1847, had died in 1853.

147.3 Villa Ludovisi] The villa, its casinos (except that housing Guercino's *Aurora*), and grounds were demolished in 1887 for urban development, and the works of art became the Ludovisi Collection in the Museo delle Terme (the National Museum).

147.8 gardens of Sallust.] Murray, p. 80: "The gardens of the Vigna Barberini, in the Via di Porta Pia, enclose. . . . vestiges of the luxurious palace of the historian Sallust, the favourite retreat of Nero, Nerva, Aurelian, and other emperors. It was destroyed by Alaric, and little now remains but traces of foundations."

147.12   colossal head of Juno] The *Ludovisi Hera* or *Juno*, a first-century A.D. Roman sculpture.

147.16–17   the face of Penelope . . . Telemachus.] SH corrected this in *Passages* to: "the face of Penelope (if it be her face) in the group supposed also to represent Electra and Orestes." Murray, p. 299, refers to "the celebrated group considered by Winckelmann to represent Orestes discovered by Electra, bearing the name of a Greek sculptor, Manelaus son of Stephanus." The group is still conventionally known as *Orestes and Electra*, though recent historians speculate that it perhaps represents a mother and son (which makes NH's idea more plausible). The work dates from ca. 10 A.D. Menelaus was pupil, not son, of Stephanus. Their style was academic imitation of fifth-century B.C. models, presaging nineteenth-century neoclassicism.

147.18–19   the groupe of Arria and Pœtus] Murray, p. 299, identifies the "group called Pætus and Arria, or the Gaul slaying his wife, considered by Winckelmann to represent Canace receiving the sword sent by her father Æolus." The group is now known as *The Gaul Killing Himself and His Wife*; it is a Hellenistic work done in Pergamon ca. 230 B.C.

148.16   the Aurora of Guercino] Guercino (1591–1666), *Aurora* (1621–23). "The very antithesis of Guido's fresco in the Casino Rospigliosi" (see above, p. 94); "an extraordinary freedom of handling" (Wittkower, p. 88). SH's comment compares with NH's: "It is rather harsh-looking after Guido's, but upon patient study, there is found great beauty and expression in it" (*Notes*, p. 178).

148.30–31   a groupe by Bernini] *The Rape of Proserpina* (1621–22), now in the Borghese Gallery. The daring freedom of Bernini's baroque ingenuity was not in favor with nineteenth-century neoclassical taste. See notes to 95.21 and 99.7–8.

149.10   the Pope] Pius IX (Giovanni Mastai-Ferretti, 1792–1878), universally known as Pio Nono, reigned from 1846 until

1878, the longest pontificate in history. Beginning as a liberal, swayed by Mazzini's nationalism, after 1848 he turned authoritarian and conservative. Metternich characterized him as "warm of heart and weak of intellect." See E. E. Y. Hales, *Pio Nono* (New York: Kenedy, 1954), p. 67.

151.9   Monte Testaccio] JH recalled in *HC*, p. 321: "Another walk of ours was to the huge, green mound of the Monte Testaccio; it was, at that period, pierced by numerous cavities, in the dank coolness of which stores of native wines were kept; and they were sold to customers at the rude wooden tables in front of the excavations, in flasks shaped like large drops of water, protected with plaited straw."

151.14   Saddleback mountain . . . Lenox.] Compare *AN*, pp. 87, 106.

153.17–18   Mr. Mozier] Joseph Mozier (1812–70), born in Vermont, lived in Ohio as a young man, and was a successful businessman in New York until 1845, when he retired to Florence to study sculpture. He later opened a studio at Rome, where he remained for the rest of his life. Murray, p. 268, lists him: "*Mozier*, an American artist, No. 54, Via Margutta . . . has acquired some celebrity for his statue of Pocahontas." Most of his works were "ideal" figures inspired by contemporary literature, the Bible, and classical mythology. See *DAB*; Taft, pp. 109–12; Tuckerman, pp. 590–91; *Yankee Stonecutters*, p. 69; Clement and Hutton.

153.19–31   We found a figure. . . . into himself.] Gerdts gives reproductions of versions of *Pocahontas, The Wept of Wishton-Wish* (derived from Cooper's romance of 1829), *Boy Mending a Pen,* and *The Prodigal Son.*

154.7   the French Academy . . . there in plaister.] SH noted in *Passages,* "we afterwards saw it in the Medici Casino." See NH's diary, May 13, 1858. The French Academy, founded in 1666 by Louis XIV, was established in the Villa Medici by Napoleon in 1803.

154.33 Greenough] Horatio Greenough (1805–52), the "first American sculptor" (in that he was the first to devote his entire professional life to the art), was born in Boston. He went to Rome in 1825 after graduating from Harvard. His first major work, other than portrait busts, *Chanting Cherubs* (1829–31), was commissioned in Florence by James Fenimore Cooper, who proposed that the group be based on two singing *putti* in Raphael's *Madonna del Baldacchino* in the Pitti Palace. Greenough's colossal seated statue of *George Washington* (1832–41), commissioned by the U.S. Congress for the Capitol rotunda, was based on contemporary reconstructions of Phidias's statue of Zeus for the Temple of Elis in Olympia, which had been destroyed in the fifth century A.D., though the head was modeled on Houdon's portrait bust of Washington. Mozier's view of Greenough's talent as a theorist on aesthetics is generally held today; see Greenough, *Form and Function*, ed. Harold A. Small (Berkeley: University of California Press, 1947); Richard P. Adams, "Architecture and the Romantic Tradition: Coleridge to Wright," *American Quarterly*, IX (1957), 46–62. See also Taft, pp. 37–56; Craven, pp. 100–111; Crane; Thorp; and Nathalia Wright, *Horatio Greenough: The First American Sculptor* (Philadelphia: University of Pennsylvania Press, 1963).

155.4–157.11 From Greenough. . . . sisters might.] Omitted by SH from *Passages*. Published by JH in *NHHW*, I, 259–62, with several significant omissions and revisions: 155.7–8 "His developements . . . very curious" is omitted; 155.14 "Margaret's" and "her" become "——'s"; 155.25 "hymen" becomes "man" (probably a misreading); 155.29 "except it were purely sensual" is omitted. A more complete and accurate text, taken from the unpublished transcript by Norman Holmes Pearson, appeared in Malcolm Cowley, ed., *The Portable Hawthorne* (New York: Viking, 1948), pp. 594–97.

This passage has been, from the American publication of *NHHW* on November 14, 1884, to the present, the most famous —or better, notorious—moment in NH's Italian journalizing. It created, as the Boston *Transcript* put it in a review on November 28, 1884, 6:1–4, a "profound stir in literary circles" that became in two months a war of insults between JH and Fuller's surviving friends, principally Thomas Wentworth Higginson, Christopher Cranch, and the Clarkes. Much of the passage, particularly the last half paragraph, was quoted in several important American reviews, among them those in the *Transcript*; the New York *Tribune* (November 16, 4:5–7); the New York *Times* (November 23, 6:1–2); the *Critic*, V (December 13, 1884, pp. 277–78, by Richard Henry Stoddard); the *Nation*, XXXIX (December 18, 1884), 525–26, by George Edward Woodberry; and the *Independent*, XXXVII (January 1, 1885), 10–11, also by Stoddard. Early reviews tended to agree with the *Transcript*'s editorial opinion (November 15, 6:1) that "of all Margaret Fuller's contemporaries none has shown so much insight into character in general as Hawthorne, and his judgment of her, severe as it is, wonderfully reconciles all the others. . . . It is not a pleasant solution of the riddle, but it is better to know precisely what sort of Isis is behind the veil." Stoddard, in the *Critic*, quoted the end of the passage to show how NH's style was "painful in its intense power."

The counterattack was begun in the *Transcript* of December 12 (4:4) by a letter of Sarah Clarke, who was not only one of Fuller's closest friends but had been in Rome in 1850, shortly after her shipwreck. Miss Clarke characterized Mozier's account as "the rubbish of studio gossip" and appealed to letters by Emelyn Story and William Henry Hurlburt in *Memoirs of Margaret Fuller Ossoli*, ed. R. W. Emerson, W. H. Channing, and J. F. Clarke (Boston: Phillips, Samson, 1852), II, 281–93, 320–30, to confirm the propriety of Fuller's conduct and Ossoli's noble standing and intelligence. Sarah Clarke turned attention to JH by closing her letter with a comparison of JH to SH as editors: "The son, it seems, has not shown the qualities that distinguished his mother," who "wisely omitted things not characteristic of [NH's] genius or his normal temper." JH responded in a letter to the *Transcript* on January 2, 4:4. He called Fuller "a dismal fraud," Ossoli a "handsome animal," and claimed that his mother had consulted him before deciding to omit the passage: "We concluded . . . that it should be published, if at all, only when a complete biography was written." Meanwhile, James Freeman Clarke had written at length to the *Independent*, a New York weekly friendly to Unitarianism, on January 1, pp. 11–12, adding Emerson, Frederick Henry Hedge, Horace Greeley, and even Carlyle to the defenders of Fuller his sister had invoked. Probably remembering SH's preface to *Passages from the English Note-Books*, Clarke described NH's notebooks as "all sorts of hints, and suggestions, as they occurred to him, as the grounds for future imaginative characters," and therefore "the last thing he himself would ever have thought of printing." The *Transcript* promptly reprinted Clarke's letter on January 2, and on January 9 published two letters, one from Christopher Cranch, who had been in Rome with Fuller, and the other anonymous (probably by Mrs. Cranch; see Leonora Cranch Scott, *The Life and Letters of Christopher Pearse Cranch* [Boston: Houghton Mifflin, 1917], p. 352). Cranch suggested that JH's motive was "the much wider sale" scandal about Fuller would give to his book. (Osgood had announced a second printing on December 11.) On the tenth the *Literary World* printed a long, emotional statement by Frederick T. Fuller, her nephew, with quotations from Margaret's diary to show the kindness and nobility of her character. Not content with this defense, Frederick Fuller reminded the public of NH's attack on Margaret through the character of Zenobia in *BR*, and called the author's character into question by recalling his crucifixion of Upham as Judge Pyncheon in *HSG* and his disrespectful portrait of the old inspector in "The Custom-House."

By this time JH was on the defensive, and Higginson, whose biography of Fuller had been published six months earlier, sought to administer the *coup de grace* through his anonymous review of *NHHW* in the *Atlantic Monthly*, LV (February 1885), 259–65, which was published by January 15. He compared JH to the son in a primitive tribal ritual who murders the father when the latter has outlived his usefulness. Rather than defend Fuller, Higginson questioned NH's acumen in judging Mozier's credibility (JH had omitted the cautionary word "curious" at the outset of the passage, and SH's omission of Mozier's name did not reveal NH's questioning of his veracity later in these notebooks; see below, p. 493): Mozier was "a very poor type of scandal-monger," and NH's "mental processes were unsteady and fragmentary, however brilliant, and it was only when he transformed them into the final form of art that the result became great." Higginson's most effective attack, however, was on JH for not mentioning the names

of James T. Fields and George P. Lathrop in *NHHW*. JH was
now clearly perceived in "literary circles" as a man of many prejudices and animosities (see the *Critic*, January 17, p. 30; the
Boston *Transcript*, January 20, 3:1; the *Independent*, January 29,
p. 11, which described the *Atlantic* review as a "sharp and ex-
emplary discipline" for JH). JH replied to Clarke and Cranch in
the *Transcript* on January 16, 4:4, describing Margaret Fuller as
a Pharisee, and repeated that charge in replying to Higginson in
the *Transcript*, February 5, 4:4. His style became more strident
as he was pressed. Cranch fired another round, on February 10,
along with shots from W. C. Burrage and an anonymous correspondent (Emelyn Story, if Cranch is correct; *Transcript*,
6:2-3). Cranch claimed that the whole incident had tarnished
NH's reputation: "Hundreds of readers . . . are beginning to
feel that they must make large discount of their former esteem
of this author as a friendly and fair-minded critic." Here the
debate ended.

Perhaps the comment most suggestive of contemporary taste
was in an editorial of the *Literary World* on January 10, in the
issue that printed Frederick Fuller's piece. The writer apparently
wished to quiet the animosity that was to follow: "Both Hawthorne
and Margaret Fuller were in some respects abnormal and un-
healthy growths of their kind . . . the genius of each ran into
eccentricities, and when eccentricities meet, they clash. . . . Some
things, some words, are best forgotten. . . . Let us hold fast to
what is pleasant and good to keep, and let the rest go."

Biographers of Fuller and Hawthorne, however, did not forget,
and the controversy came into focus fifty years later, in the
extravagant speculations of Oscar Cargill's "Nemesis and Nathaniel
Hawthorne," *PMLA*, LII (1937), 848-61, which was provoked
in part by Katherine Anthony's *Margaret Fuller: A Psychological
Biography* (New York: Harcourt, Brace, 1920). Cargill was
criticized by Austin Warren in *PMLA*, LIV (1939), 615-18,
and by William Peirce Randel in *American Literature*, X (1939),
472-76.

The renewed interest in Fuller brought about by feminist critics
and historians of the 1970s has reopened the incident. Now
Fuller's supporters extol her sexual freedom rather than her
propriety as mother and wife. The frankness of NH's analysis of

her feelings (in part suppressed by JH) must be considered as well as the typical Victorian moralism in his final sentence. Ann Douglas in *The Feminization of American Culture* (New York: Knopf, 1977) characterizes NH as "vicious" (p. 266), and Bell Gale Chevigny in *The Woman and the Myth: Margaret Fuller's Life and Writings* (Old Westbury, N.Y.: Feminist Press, 1976) describes the passage as NH's "malignant virtuosity" (p. 416). Barbara Welter, however, in *Dimity Convictions: The American Woman in the Nineteenth Century* (Athens: Ohio University Press, 1976), pp. 80–81, quotes NH's last sentence and comments: "Hawthorne was inclined to forgive her trespasses, since they were sins of the flesh, so much less serious to him than the sins of the intellect."

Doubtless the passage has not yet exhausted its power to draw comment from readers.

155.6 she having been an inmate of his] When Fuller returned to Florence in September 1847 from a tour in northern Italy, she collapsed from physical and emotional fatigue. She was taken in by Mozier and his wife for several days, and nursed back to health.

155.8 Ossoli's family] Giovanni Angelo Ossoli (1821–50) came from an ancient family of modest fortune, which for generations had been in the service of the papacy. His father, Marchese Filippo Ossoli, a Vatican official, died in 1848, leaving four sons (of whom Giovanni was the youngest) and two daughters. The oldest brother was the papal functionary for one of the regions of Rome, and secretary to the pope's privy council. The other two brothers were colonels in the papal guard. The older sister was married to the Marchese de Andreis, and the younger was married to a man named MacNamara and lived in Ireland. See Joseph Jay Deiss, *The Roman Years of Margaret Fuller* (New York: Crowell, 1969).

155.13–18 Ossoli himself. . . . a gentleman.] Fuller described Ossoli as "a person of no intellectual culture" in a letter published in *Memoirs of Margaret Fuller Ossoli*, II, 314–15. In another letter she said, ". . . he is entirely without what is called culture, educated by a tutor and that tutor an old priest. . . . I think he never used to go through with a book; nature . . . he has spelled thoroughly" (quoted by Paula Blanchard, *Margaret Fuller: From Transcendentalism to Revolution* [New York: Delacorte, 1978], p. 327). Another letter: "His mind has little habitual action, except in a simple natural poetry that one not very intimate with him would never know anything about" (Perry Miller, ed., *Margaret Fuller: American Romantic* [Garden City: Doubleday, 1963], p. 313).

155.18–23 At Margaret's . . . the wrong side.] Mozier apparently confused Ossoli with "one Germano, a poor and dishonest Italian whom Margaret had befriended until he was proved an imposter." Mozier took Germano into his studio in Florence, possibly at Margaret's request, until he learned that the work he claimed as his own he had bought cheaply. This information comes from an unpublished letter of Moncure Conway; see Chevigny, *The Woman and the Myth*, p. 417. But Mozier did allow "Giovanni to try his hand at modeling in his studio." See Madeleine B. Stern, *The Life of Margaret Fuller* (New York: Dutton, 1942), pp. 472–73.

155.23–31 He could not. . . . charm of womanhood.] Norman Holmes Pearson has speculated that the conversation between Hilda and Kenyon about Miriam's affection for Donatello in *MF*, p. 105, is NH's later, more temperate answer to this "riddle": "As Hawthorne discussed, as he must have discussed, the matter with the Storys and the Brownings, who had known them both, he would have discovered a more admirable side to the young nobleman, a social charm which they never seem to have found wanting, and an idealism which led to his casting off the conservatism of his family to ally himself with the liberal party of Italy" (*The French and Italian Notebooks of Nathaniel Hawthorne*, Ph.D dissertation, Yale University, 1941, p. lxxxix).

156.16 History of the Roman Revolution] Fuller had begun to write an account of the revolution as early as its outbreak in

February 1848. She planned to finish the book, which she described to correspondents as the most important work she had yet attempted, in Florence in the autumn and winter of 1849–50. She attempted unsuccessfully to arrange its publication in England. One reason for her return to America in the spring of 1850 was to find a publisher. Mozier was in Florence throughout the Ossolis' stay there. Fuller certainly claimed to bring the manuscript with her aboard the ship. After the ship was wrecked off Long Island and the Ossolis drowned, looters scattered or destroyed most of the papers that were washed ashore; the precious manuscript was not found.

157.12 Miss Hosmer] Harriet Goodhue Hosmer (1830–1908), from Watertown, Massachusetts, was raised like a boy by her widower father. Intending from an early age to be a sculptor, she studied anatomy in St. Louis before going to Rome in 1852 with the actress Charlotte Cushman. After seeing her work, Gibson gave her studio space; she became his favorite pupil and colleague until his death, following his neoclassical principles closely. She was a good friend of the Brownings, and of visiting royalty—the prince of Wales, the czar of Russia, the empress of Austria—and even of Pope Pius IX. Murray, p. 268, lists her studio among those that might be visited by tourists: "*Miss Hosmer,* a very talented young American lady, and one of the very few pupils of our great sculptor Gibson, adjoining whose studio she has also hers, and where her principal works may be seen." See *Harriet Hosmer: Letters and Memoirs,* ed. Cornelia Carr (London: John Lane, 1913); Taft, pp. 203–11; Craven, pp. 325–30; Thorp, pp. 79–88; John L. Idol, Jr., "Nathaniel Hawthorne and Harriet Hosmer," *Nathaniel Hawthorne Journal* 1976, pp. 120–28.

157.15–33 A Venus and a Cupid. . . . depth of tint.] Gibson's *Tinted Venus* (ca. 1850) is the best known of his controversial colored statues. He used colored wax, in emulation of ancient Greek practice. SH in *Notes,* pp. 266–67, gives a lively and humorous account of her confrontation with Gibson on an earlier occasion. For a reproduction of Gibson's Venus, see Gerdts, *The Great American Nude,* p. 85.

158.11   my wife (whom she already knew)] SH, according to *Notes*, p. 265, had visited Gibson's and Hosmer's studios on March 10.

158.29   Beatrice Cenci] Commissioned for the Mercantile Library of St. Louis, and completed in 1855. For reproductions, see Taft, p. 205; *The White, Marmorean Flock*, fig. 2. That Hilda in *MF*, who seems partly based on Miss Hosmer, should have painted a copy of Guido Reni's *Beatrice Cenci*, may have been suggested by this statue.

158.29–31   a monumental design . . . quiet sleep.] The monument to Mlle Judith Falconet (1857–58), in S. Andrea delle Fratte, Rome. This tomb for a sixteen-year-old English girl is the only commission gained by an American sculptor for a Roman church. Murray, p. 129, mentions the "beautiful recumbent figure." For a reproduction see *The White, Marmorean Flock* and Gerdts.

158.32   a Puck] *Puck on a Toadstool*, 1856, her most popular piece, of which at least thirty replicas were made, and which earned her about $30,000. Reproductions are in *The White, Marmorean Flock*, catalogue no. 5; Metropolitan Museum of Art, *Nineteenth-Century America: Paintings and Sculpture* (New York: New York Graphic Society, 1970), no. 102.

161.9   Mr. Akers] (Benjamin) Paul Akers (1825–61), from a village in Maine, turned from an early interest in mechanics to portrait sculpture in Boston, where he did a bust of Longfellow among others. In 1852–53 he was in Florence; in 1854–55 in Washington he did busts of Franklin Pierce and Edward Everett. He was in Rome from 1855 till April 1858, when bad health forced his return to America. NH's diary records thirteen meetings with Akers in March and April; Akers suggested NH's writing to Hiram Powers to rent the Casa del Bello in Florence for June and July (NH to Powers, May 16, 1858; MS, Yale). It has been argued that Akers was the prototype of Kenyon in *MF*. In his preface to *MF*, NH mentions Akers's bust of Milton and a statue of a Pearl-Diver for reproductions see Gerdts. See also Craven, pp. 281–84; Tuckerman, pp. 612–19; Leila Woodman Usher, "Benjamin Paul Akers," *New England Magazine*, n.s. XI (December 1894), 460–68.

162.4–5 a bust of Cato the Censor] In the Hall of Illustrious Men (poets, philosophers, statesmen). Cato (234–149 B.C.), an austere, courageous statesman, is best remembered for his writings on methods of farming, and his demand that Carthage be destroyed.

162.17 the bronze she-wolf suckling Romulus and Remus] *The Bronze Wolf* of the Capitol, discussed by Murray, p. 225, with a quotation from *Childe Harold*, canto 4, stanza 88. Now identified as an Etruscan work of the late sixth century B.C. The suckling infants were added during the Renaissance.

163.30–31 when the soldiers . . . floors.] Murray, p. 207: "A few years after [Raphael's paintings] were completed they were seriously injured during the sack of Rome by the Constable de Bourbon, whose troops are said to have lighted their fires in the centre of the rooms." The sack of Rome occurred in 1527. See note to 144.32–34.

164.22–25 the frescoes . . . by other artists.] Actually, the ceiling and walls of the Stanza delle Segnatura are by Raphael, and several of the frescoes are completely autograph works.

164.31–165.5 the little chapel. . . . window.] NH follows closely the information in Murray, pp. 212–13.

165.8–9 It would have . . . hidden.] The first of NH's many disparaging remarks about medieval and early Renaissance frescoes. The subjects of Fra Angelico's frescoes are the lives of Saints Stephen and Laurence. They are dated 1447–49.

165.21 we ourselves possess them] SH was wont to decorate the family residence with engravings and plaster casts of statuary. See *NHHW*, I, 279, 286, 367–71.

165.25 On reference to Murray] Murray, p. 177, states, "Each coved roof of the 13 arcades contains 4 frescoes connected with some particular epoch of Scripture history, executed from Raphael's designs by Giulio Romano, Pierino del Vaga, Pellegrino da Modena, Francesco Penni, and Raffaelle del Colle."

166.3 The Minerva Medica] A Roman copy of a bronze *Pallas Athena* of the end of the fifth or beginning of the fourth century B.C. Described by Murray, p. 183, as "one of the finest draped statues in Rome." Close by in the Braccio Nuovo is a copy of Praxiteles' *Faun*, considered inferior to that in the Capitoline Museum. See note to 178.24.

166.21 the excavations] Murray, pp. 23–24, describes "the wide open space occupied by the Basilica Julia" as recently uncovered after its location had been discovered in 1834. The Column of Phocas was excavated in 1813, at the time when Byron wrote "Thou nameless column with the buried base!" (*Childe Harold,* canto 4, stanza 110), quoted by Murray.

167.30 we saw some . . . master-pieces.] Murray, p. 250, says of the Palazzo Colonna's picture gallery: "once the most considerable in Rome, [it] has been much reduced by division amongst members of the family; it still contains some fine works. . . ."

168.5 noble portraits] Van Dyck, *Don Carlo Colonna* and *Lucretia Colonna*; Holbein, *Lorenzo Colonna*; Titian, *Onofrio Panvinio* (now known as *Portrait of a Franciscan*); Guercino, *Moses*, and *The Angel Gabriel*.

168.7–8 Rubens and other forestieri] Rubens's *Assumption*, and *Joseph and His Brothers*. The other foreign painters, chiefly of landscape, include Claude, Poussin, Philips Wouwerman (1619–68), and Herman van Swanevelt (1600–1655).

168.24 pictures in fresco] Murray, p. 252: "the roof is covered with frescoes relative to the deeds of the Colonna family; the largest, in the centre by [Giovanni] Coli [1636–81] and [Filippo] Gherardi [1643–1704], represents the Battle of Lepanto [1571]."

169.3–4   some ancient . . . in themselves] Murray, p. 252: "The *Great Hall* or *Gallery* . . . one of the finest in Rome, is ornamented with ancient statues, none of which are of any merit."

169.6   two cabinets] Murray, p. 252: "On one side of this hall is a handsome cabinet, with 27 bas-reliefs in ivory, executed by the German artist [Dominicus] Steinhart [1655–1712], and copied from Michel Angelo's Last Judgment in the Sistine Chapel, and from 26 of Raphael's subjects in the Loggie."

169.20   in the Via Bonella] The Accademia is now located in the Palazzo Carpegna near the Fountain of Trevi.

170.4   two, or more, by Guido] *Bacchus and Ariadne*, a ceiling fresco; *Fortune*, now in the Pinacoteca of the Vatican.

170.18–19   pictures by Titian, Paul Veronese and other artists] Murray, p. 273, mentions "*Paolo Veronese*, Vanity, personified by a lady looking at herself in a mirror; *Titian*, Vanity, a recumbent naked figure." Also mentioned are Veronese's *Susanna* and Titian's *Saviour and Pharisee* (a work not now thought to be Titian's).

170.24   Calypso and her nymphs] Properly, *Callisto and the Nymphs*; now considered a copy. Murray, p. 275: "it is a fine, but not very delicate picture to look on."

171.11   Moses] By Michelangelo (c. 1515).

171.28   Hope, by Guido] Murray, p. 162; "perhaps the most beautiful of his smaller works."

173.14–18   The entrance-hall . . . to decline.] Murray, p. 296: "This magnificent room, the ceiling of which, painted by Mario Rossi [1731–1807] in the last century, represents the arrival of Camillus at the Capitol, is paved with ancient mosaics of gladiators and combatants in the amphitheatre, discovered in

1834. . . . As a work of art this mosaic has little pretensions, and dates probably from the latter part of the 3rd century."

173.23 a Faun] Murray, p. 298, "Copy of the Faun of Praxiteles." See note to 178.24.

175.2 Canova's statue of Pauline] Pauline Bonaparte as *Venus Victrix*, 1805–8.

175.10 some works of Bernini] *Aeneas and Anchises* (1618–19), *David* (1623), *Apollo and Daphne* (1622–25).

175.18 Hillard's description] George Hillard, in *Six Months in Italy*, p. 247: "In mere technical dexterity and manual skill, this group excels any thing of the kind I have ever seen. It is a miracle of manipulation. It is such a work as would, beforehand, have been pronounced an absolute impossibility, and, as it is, we look at it with a sort of incredulous wonder as if there must be some trick about it, and it could not be what it purports to be. The manner in which the flesh passes away into foliage is something quite indescribable, and remains a mystery after careful examination. Such a work would have been esteemed very remarkable if cut out of pine wood, but, wrought as it is in marble, it appears rather the result of magic than of mortal tools and fingers."

176.6 G. L. Brown] George Loring Brown (1814–89) of Boston, "Claude" Brown or "the American Claude," studied in London and Paris in the 1830s and made copies of Claude's landscapes to sell in America. In the *New-England Magazine*, IX (December 1835), 398, Park Benjamin, the editor, suggested that NH's sketch, "A Night Scene" therein published from the uncollected "Sketches from Memory" (see *SI*, pp. 304–5), might become a subject for "young Brown, whose promise is as great as the hopes of his friends" (*MOM*, p. 649). Brown was in Italy from 1840 until 1859. Murray, p. 269, lists him among "several eminent painters from the United States . . . settled at Rome: *G. Brown*, No. 7, Vicolo de' Alberti, off the Via del Babuino, landscapes." However, Brown's most important pictures seem to have been painted after his return to America: *The Bay of New York*

(1860) was presented to the Prince of Wales by some New York businessmen, and *The Crown of New England* (1861) was purchased by the Prince of Wales. See *Travelers in Arcadia*, pp. 18–20; *Arcadian Landscape*, nos. 4 and 5; Karolik, pp. 145–53; Tuckerman, pp. 346–54; Albert ten Eyck Gardner and Stuart P. Feld, *American Paintings: A Catalogue of the Collection of the Metropolitan Museum of Art* (New York, 1965), I, 275–77.

177.7 Mr. Bartholomew's studio] Edward Sheffield Bartholomew (1822–58), of Connecticut, learned bookbinding and dentistry before turning to painting and then to sculpture. He came to Rome in 1850, where he did a number of portrait busts of Americans, as well as ideal mythological and literary statues. He became ill in the spring of 1858 and moved to Naples, where he died in May. *Eve Repentant*, one of his best known works, was sent to the Wadsworth Atheneum in Hartford after his death, along with a statue of Sappho, a bust of Diana, and other works. See Craven, pp. 319–21; Taft, pp. 194–96; Tuckerman, pp. 609–12; H. W. French, *Art and Artists in Connecticut* (Boston: Lee and Shepard, 1879), pp. 112–18; and reproductions of the *Eve* and the *Sappho* in Gerdts, nos. 34, 117.

177.22–27 Miss Bremer. . . . mouth and chin.] NH was remembering a passage from Miss Bremer's *The Homes of the New World: Impressions of America*, trans. Mary Howitt (New York: Harper, 1853), II, 597: "I spent one evening with Hawthorne, in an endeavor in converse. But, whether it was his fault or mine, I can not say, but it did not succeed. I had to talk by myself, and at length became quite dejected, and felt I know not how. Nevertheless, Hawthorne was evidently kind, and wished to make me comfortable—but we could not get on together in conversation. It was, however, a pleasure to see his beautiful, significant, though not perfectly harmonious head. The forehead is capacious and serene as the arch of heaven, and a thick mass of soft dark brown hair beautifully clustered around it; the fine, deep-set eyes glance from beneath well-arched eyebrows like the dark but clear lakes of the neighborhood, lying in the sombre bosom of mountain and forest; the nose is refined and regular in form; the smile, like that of the sun smiling over the summer woods; nevertheless, it has a bitter expression. The whole upper part of the countenance is classically beautiful, but the lower part does not perfectly correspond, and is deficient in decided character."

178.11–12   a very beautiful face . . . by Vandyke.] From one of two double portraits: *The Painters Lucas and Cornelius de Wael; The Engravers Peter de Jode Senior and Junior.*

178.13   Paul Veronese's Rape of Europa] a copy; see note to 114.24–25.

178.24   the faun of Praxitiles] Murray, p. 233, describes the statue as "a repetition of the FAUN OF PRAXITELES. We have already noticed others in the Vatican; this is the most beautiful of all, and in Carrara marble; it was found in the Villa d'Este at Tivoli." Murray notes copies of the *Faun* in the Braccio Nuovo and the Gallery of Statues, in the Vatican (pp. 183, 190), and in the Camera del Fauno of the Villa Borghese (p. 298), as NH noticed on his visit of April 17 (see pp. 173–174, above). On his first visit to the Capitol, February 22, NH apparently did not notice the *Faun*, focusing his attention on the *Dying Gladiator*, the statue for which the Hall was named: see p. 102, above. The statue has been identified as a copy of a bronze by Praxiteles (ca. 370–ca. 330 B.C.), since Pliny's *Natural History*, 34, 69, mentioned a "celebrated Satyr, called by the Greeks 'world-famous'," by Praxiteles. Nearly 150 copies exist. Many modern scholars accept it as a copy from Praxiteles; see Bieber, pp. 17–18. But doubts are raised by Gisela M. A. Richter, *The Sculpture and Sculptors of the Greeks*, 4th ed. (New Haven: Yale University Press, 1970), p. 205: "If the original was by Praxiteles it was probably one of his later works: for the picturesque composition, the almost exaggerated curve of the body, with the foot of the fixed leg placed behind that of the supporting leg, and the personal element in the conception—a mingling of human and animal qualities—are different from the serene and detached Praxitelean creations. This very picturesqueness, which heralds the Hellenistic period, made the statue an appropriate garden figure and may account for its popularity in Roman times." Ironically enough, the "earliest copy known to us of the famous marble *Faun* of Praxiteles" is now in the Bowdoin College Museum of Fine Arts, a marble torso dated ca. 300 B.C. See S. Lane Faison, Jr., *A Guide to Art Museums of New England* (New York: Harcourt, Brace, 1958), p. 48.

179.7-12 Mr. Gibson's. . . . beforehand.] See note to 157.15–33, and Gerdts, *The Great American Nude*, p. 84.

179.8 Mr. Nichols] Abel Nichols (1815–60), of Danvers, Massachusetts, was in Florence and Rome from 1849 until 1858, where he painted landscapes and copies of Old Masters. Murray, p. 269, lists him among the American painters at Rome: "*Nicholls*, 4, Vicolo dei Greci, landscapes." W. C. Bryant, in a letter from Rome of May 17, 1853, wrote: "Nichols has very successfully transferred the calm glow of Claude's landscapes into some fine copies which he is making" (*Letters from the East* [New York: Putnam, 1869], pp. 237–38). SH had visited his studio in Salem in 1838, and may have known him well in the 1830s and 1840s (letter to Elizabeth Peabody, May 4, 1838; MS, Berg). See *The Arcadian Landscape*, no. 33; Mary Eliot Nichols, "Abel Nichols, Artist," *Historical Collection of the Danvers Historical Society*, XXIX (1941), 4–31.

180.8 Bernini's sculptures] The sculptures of the Fountain of Trevi are by Pietro Bracci. See note to 57.6–13.

180.14-16 the possibility . . . interview.] In Mme de Staël's *Corinne* (1807), book 4, chapter 6, Corinne first seats herself by the fountain to express her grief at the impending loss of Lord Nelvil, her lover. She sees the reflection of her face in the water; then he arrives and sees first her reflection, and then his own next to hers. The lovers are reconciled. Using the present entry in *MF*, p. 146, NH (apparently without consulting *Corinne*) wrote: "Corinne, it will be remembered, knew Lord Nelvil by the reflection of his face in the water."

181.30 temple of Minerva] The Temple of Minerva Chalcidica, a ruin described in Murray, p. 35: "Architects still regard it as the most perfect model of the Corinthian order."

182.32 Byron's description] *Manfred*, act 3, scene 4, lines 8–41;

Childe Harold, canto 4, stanza 128. Compare Hillard, *Six Months in Italy*, p. 194: "As a matter of course, everybody goes to see the Colosseum by moonlight . . . "

183.29–33 The architecture . . . pile of material.] Michelangelo created new façades for the existing Palazzo del Senatore and Palazzo dei Conservatore, and designed a third palace for the piazza, as well as the patterned pavement, the pedestal for the statue of Marcus Aurelius, and the ramp leading up the hill. His other architectural works in Rome include the upper story of the Farnese Palace, the church of S. Maria degli Angeli, and the Porta Pia. He was the architect of St. Peter's basilica during 1546–64.

185.23–26 I have made . . . dome] Murray, p. 106, describes a circular gallery at the top of the drum of the cupola.

185.32 the Transfiguration] The painting by Raphael; see note to 63.24–25.

186.4 the new church of St Paul's] S. Paolo fuori le Mura, a fourth-century church largely destroyed by fire in 1823. Murray, p. 122: "The series of portraits of the popes in mosaic have been already completed round the transept; they include all those who occupied the Papal Chair down to John IV., most of whom have been acknowledged as saints by the Church. . . . These portraits are executed at the mosaic establishment at the Vatican."

186.10–11 a holy family of Raphael] It is uncertain what picture is meant here, since there is and was no *Holy Family* by Raphael in Rome; possibly it is the *Holy Family* (1518) in the Louvre.

186.11 the Sybils] Guercino's *Persian Sibyl*, in the Capitoline Gallery, and Domenichino's *Cumaean Sibyl*, in the Borghese.

186.26 three Murillos] Bartolomé Esteban Murillo (1617–82); Murray, p. 202, lists *The Return of the Prodigal Son* and *The Marriage of St. Catherine of Alexandria with the Infant Christ*, "a lovely picture. Both these paintings were recently presented to Pius IX. by the Queen of Spain. An inferior work, the Adoration of the Shepherds, lately placed in this room, is attributed to the same master."

186.32   the picture was worthy of its fame] See note to 63.24–25.

187.6 the Communion of St Jerome] Murray, p. 202: "This magnificent work, the undoubted masterpiece of Domenichino, is generally considered second only to the Transfiguration of Raphael." The painting is dated 1614.

188.6   Mr. Wilde] Hamilton Gibbs Wilde (or Wild; 1827–84), portrait, landscape, and genre painter, was described by Tuckerman, p. 486, as effective in his "command of the richer combinations of color . . . [in his] *genre* and architectural pieces . . . novel and pleasing memorials of the land of song [Italy], which American travellers have, within a few years, brought home as trophies of native talent." Wilde studied in Europe in 1846 and in 1858–59. His work was exhibited at the annual Boston Athenaeum Gallery exhibitions eight times between 1853 and 1869. He is mentioned in the letters of Browning, Story and Mrs. Story, and Charles Sumner. See Gertrude Hudson, *Browning to his American Friends: Letters between the Brownings, the Storys, and James Russell Lowell 1841–1890* (London: Bowes and Bowes, 1965). See also Henry James, *William Wetmore Story* . . . , II, 46, 114, 124, 130, 176, 181.

188.29   Muller] Probably Rudolf Müller (1802–85), from Basel, who had resided in Rome since 1838, after working in Paris, Naples, and Greece. Bonfigli, *Guide*, p. 85, lists his studio at 95, Via del Lavatore. English and Russian tourists were the most frequent buyers of his watercolors of Italian and Greek landscapes with ruins and classical monuments; his work is preserved in museums in Basel and Zurich. See Ulrich Thieme and Felix Becker, *Künstler-Lexicon* (Leipzig: Seemann, 1931).

189.11   English water-color artists] On August 14, 1857, NH visited the gallery of watercolors at the Manchester Exhibition; he did not comment on any particular artists or pictures (see *EN*, p. 558). According to the curator of this gallery, Edward Holmes, "the practice of this branch of the fine arts is so much followed in England . . . that we generally look upon this as peculiarly a national school of art" (*Catalogue*, p. 177). Exhibited were 969 drawings, of which 85 were by J. M. W. Turner. The other artists most represented were George Cattermole (1800–1868), David Roberts (1796–1864), and the Pre-Raphaelite William Holman Hunt (1827–1910).

189.22   German artist] There was no German painter listed in the vicinity of the Via del Lavatore in Bonfigli's *Guide*.

190.12   Castellani] Murray, p. xxii: "Castellani, No. 88, Via Poli, is of European celebrity for his reproductions from the Etruscan models. . . . It is impossible to surpass in taste and beauty some of his works. On the stairs leading to his show-room are placed several specimens of antique sculpture discovered on the spot and on the site of one of his villas. Castellani is celebrated amongst the Roman nobility for his taste in setting diamonds and precious stones, most of which, and amongst the most magnificent in Europe, have passed through his hands."

191.17–20   he has a pipe . . . by his side.] JH published this statement in *HC*, p. 235, and commented: "Both in his notes and in his romance [*MF*, p. 8] he makes the same mistake as to the pose of the figure. . . . Of course, the left arm, the one referred to, is held akimbo on his left hip." *HC* also included on pp. 325–26 the lines "the whole person. . . . unsophisticated man" of 192.2–18.

192.21   the Ara Coeli] NH's Hilda "climbed the hundred steps of the Ara Coeli" (*MF*, p. 346). Murray, p. 134, notes of Edmund Gibbon that it was here, "as he himself tells us, . . . 'on the 15th of October, 1764,' as he 'sat musing amidst the ruins of the Capitol, while the barefooted friars were singing vespers,' that the idea of writing the Decline and Fall of the city first started to his mind."

192.29–193.6 The room. . . . statues.] The Faun of Praxiteles was in the Hall of the Dying Gladiator; the adjacent Hall of the Faun held another faun found in Hadrian's villa. The other statues NH lists were in the Hall of the Dying Gladiator (Murray, pp. 232–34). *MF*, p. 6, revising this passage, follows Murray more accurately, referring to "the Amazon" rather than "a Minerva," and to "the Lycian Apollo."

194.9–10 the name of the first one] Possibly S. Eustachio.

195.18 a Revival] The "Great Awakening" of 1858 had begun in New York the previous autumn, about the time of the stock market crash. It was characterized by daily noontime interdenominational prayer meetings. The prominence of laymen, the urban setting, the nonsectarian emphasis, and the extensive publicity provided by the secular press made this a new kind of revival, and a model for those to follow. The most intense phase, as the movement spread into New England and throughout the country to small towns and the countryside, was from February to June 1858. See Timothy L. Smith, *Revivalism and Social Reform: American Protestantism on the Eve of the Civil War* (Nashville: Abingdon, 1957; New York: Harper, 1965).

196.26 the fountains] The sea monsters are part of Bernini's *Fontana del Moro*; his central fountain, the *Four Rivers*, has personifications of the Nile, Danube, Ganges, and Plata. See also notes to 99.7–8 and 148.30–31.

197.31 the house] I.e., brothel.

198.2–4 a range of chapels . . . out of the marble.] Murray, p. 125: "The entrance and 3 splendid chapels form the arms of the Greek cross; they are decorated with statues and large bas–reliefs by [Alessandro] Algardi [1598–1654]; the latter scarcely merit the praises bestowed on them." The architect was Francesco Borromini (1599–1667).

199.13 Mrs. Jameson] Anna Brownell Jameson (1794–1860), English popular writer on art and literature: *Sacred and Legendary Art* (1848), *Legends of the Monastic Orders* (1850), and *Legends of the Madonna* (1852), to be completed by *The History of Our Lord* (1864), were "reissued again and again in England and in the United States and . . . provided popular reading for the cultivated tourist who required just such a well bred, informative and impeccably correct guide to the development of artistic appreciation" (Clara Thomas, *Love and Work Enough: The Life of Anna Jameson* [Toronto: University of Toronto Press, 1967], p. 176). Mrs. Jameson had been in Massachusetts in 1837–38 and there became acquainted with Catherine Sedgwick, Dr. William Ellery Channing, and Washington Allston. She had been a friend of the Brownings since before their marriage, and had met the Storys through them. According to Thomas, she was in Rome for a year during 1857–58. For a brief assessment of her place in the history of art criticism, see John Steegman, *Victorian Taste: A Study of the Arts and Architecture from 1830 to 1870* (Cambridge: MIT Press, 1971; first published, 1950), pp. 186–87.

199.16   Mrs. Apthorp and Miss Hunter] Eliza Henshaw Hunt Apthorp (1817–1903) and Sarah Henshaw Hunt (1815–95), of Boston, were in Europe from 1856–60. They were accompanied by their mother, Sarah Swift Henshaw Hunt, widow of Ebenezer Hunt Jr. of Northampton, Massachusetts; by Eliza's husband and son, Robert East Apthorp (1811–82), a philanthropist, supporter of abolition, and friend of Emerson, and William Foster Apthorp (1848–1913), later music critic of the Boston *Transcript* (see *DAB*). The sisters were parishioners and close friends and correspondents of Theodore Parker. They were in Rome in 1858, and in Berlin and Dresden (with young Henry Adams) in early 1859. From June till October 1859 they were in Montreux, with Parker, who had come to Europe in an unsuccessful attempt to recover from tuberculosis, and they were with him in Rome from October till April 1860, shortly before his death. See John Weiss, *Life and Correspondence of Theodore Parker* (New York: Appleton, 1864), I, 291–309; II, 190, 264, 285, 297, 328–418 *passim*; John White Chadwick, *Theodore Parker: Preacher and Reformer* (Boston: Houghton Mifflin, 1900), pp. 312–14; *The Education of Henry Adams*, chapter 5.

200.29   Monaldi's bookstore] Monaldini, 80 Piazza di Spagna;

according to Bonfigli, *Guide:* "a large assortment of Books in different languages, and general Stationery."

201.1 San Stefano.] Murray, p. 356: "Immediately beyond where the modern road [to Albano] intersects the Via Latina, and in the space between them upon the farm of the *Arco Travertino,* or *del Corvo,* excavations have been made during the last few months which have led to the discovery of some most interesting sepulchral monuments of the age of the Antonines . . . and of the Basilica of St. Stephen, founded in the pontificate of St. Leo in the 5th century."

206.25–26 Michael Angelo's statue of the Savior] *Christ* (1521), in S. Maria sopra Minerva.

206.34 Murray] Murray, p. 319: "On the floor of the ch. is a marble slab, with a fac-simile of the foot-marks of our Saviour, which are said to have been left upon the block of the road pavement on which he stood; the original, in black lava, is preserved amongst the most precious relics of the neighboring basilica of San Sebastiano."

207.11–17 In a chapel. . . . most of his works.] Murray, p. 167; "the chapel of St. Sebastian, in the S. aisle, designed by Ciro Ferri [1634–89], has a recumbent statue of the saint by Antonio Giorgetti [d. 1669], after his master, Bernini." In her *Sacred and Legendary Art* (London: Longmans, 1848), Mrs. Jameson described this statue as "perhaps the finest thing ever designed by Bernini." It is now thought to be the work of Gioseppe Giorgetti in 1672, from his brother's design. See Wittkower, p. 317 and note.

208.12–14 the gray, battlemented . . . years ago.] Murray, p. 64: "Adjoining the tomb are the extensive ruins of the Caetani fortress. As early as the beginning of the 13th century the Savelli family had converted the ruin into a stronghold; the Caetanis, before the close of the same century, obtained possession of it, and built those towers and battlemented walls which now form, from many points of view, a ruin scarcely less picturesque than the massive tomb itself." The name is spelled either Gaetani or Caetani.

209.9 Gibson] Gibson's bust of Mrs. Jameson is in the National Portrait Gallery, London. Clara Thomas describes it as "a forbidding piece of work" (*Love and Work Enough*, p. 213).

210.4 Mr. Cass] Lewis Cass Jr. (?1814–78), minister resident of the United States to the Pontifical States from 1854 until November 1858, had his office in the Palazzo Braschi, at the Piazza di Pasquino. His father was the former U.S. senator from Michigan, secretary of state in the Buchanan administration.

210.25 I do not recall any of the Sculpture] Murray, p. 293, lists "a repetition of the Faun of Praxiteles" among many others.

210.28 This is said . . . Laocoön.] This judgment by J. J. Winckelmann in *The History of Ancient Art*, trans. G. Henry Lodge (Boston: J. R. Osgood, 1880), book 12, chapter 1, sections 15–16, is quoted in Murray, p. 294.

211.12–17 among which . . . religious man.] Murray, p. 294, describes a Perugino painting in 5 compartments of the "Adoration of the infant Saviour by the Virgin with saints, the Crucifixion, the Magdalen, and an Assumption" (1491).

211.18 a small bronze Apollo] A copy of the *Apollo Sauroctonos* (Lizard-Slayer) by Praxiteles, according to Pliny, *Natural History*, 34, 70. The supposition of Winckelmann (*The History of Ancient Art*, book 9, chapter 3, section 17), has been abandoned by modern scholars; see, for example, Bieber, p. 18; A. W. Lawrence, *Greek and Roman Sculpture*, rev. ed. (London: Cape, 1972), p. 188.

213.4 the story of Meleager] See note to 485.22.

213.12 bas-relief of the discovery of Achilles] In the third of the Halls of the Urns, according to Murray, p. 230.

213.15 Pelieus] Properly, Peleus.

214.10–11 pictures by Perugino . . . Sacred History] Frescoes of the lives of Moses and Christ by Perugino, Botticelli, Domenico

Ghirlandaio, Cosimo Roselli, and Luca Signorelli, contracted for by Pope Sixtus IV in the 1480s.

215.4–20 I fear I am. . . . perception of them.] In a letter to Louisa Hawthorne, October 26, 1843, SH reported that NH "abominates . . . the 'Michael Diabolic' frescoes (as he calls them)" that she had put on the walls of the Old Manse (MS, Berg).

215.21–216.6 In the lower. . . . Chapel.] Murray, pp. 175–76, retells the story of the major-domo Biagio's objection to Pope Paul III about the nudity of the figures. NH seems to respond in his last sentence to this general comment in Murray, p. 174, on the Sistine Chapel ceiling: "No language can exaggerate the grandeur and majesty of the figures, which are subservient to the general plan, and carry out the sublime idea which presides over it, even in the minutest details."

216.8–9 veturrinos . . . Florence.] Murray, *North Italy*, p. 517: "*Vetturini* to Rome [from Florence] may be always met with. The journey by way of Arezzo, Perugia, and Terni, occupies five days in summer and six in winter, sleeping each night at a good inn; by way of Siena, one day less; the fare for a single person, including living and expenses, from 12 to 15 dollars (2 *l*. 14s. to 3 *l*. 7s. 6d.). Families having their own carriage may hire four horses for the journey by either road, including tolls and barriers, exclusive of living, or *buonamano*, which is about 30 fr. for the whole journey, at about 16 to 18 napoleons (320 to 360 fr.). [In April 1857 a large, comfortable carriage accomodating 6 persons and a servant, between Rome and Florence, cost by way of Perugia 500 fr. and 30 for buonamano, the journey being performed in 6 days—hotel expenses not included.] The prices of vetturini conveyances have much increased in late years." Murray's *Rome*, p. xii, comments: "*Vetturini* abound at Rome, but their charges have of late been very high, especially after the Easter festivities, when . . . a decent *vetturino* carriage with 4 good horses can scarcely be procured for less than 20 [napoleons] by the Siena road to Florence, and 25 by Perugia, employing respectively . . . 4 and 5 days."

216.13–217.5   Mr. Thompson. . . . of his palace.] This legend is given in [William M. Gillespie], *Rome as Seen by a New Yorker in 1843–4* (New York: Wiley and Putnam, 1845), pp. 48–49. See p. 498. NH had retold a remarkably similar anecdote about Oliver Cromwell in *Biographical Stories for Children* (1842); see *TS*, p. 252.

217.16–17   the colossal statue of Pompey] The legend that Caesar was murdered in front of this particular statue is cautiously endorsed by Murray, p. 264: "This noble figure has been regarded for about 300 years as the identical statue which stood in the Curia of Pompey, and at whose base 'great Caesar fell.'" Murray quotes *Childe Harold*, canto 4, stanza 87, and Sir John Hobhouse's lengthy note to this stanza, which concedes that the red stain in the marble is not blood, but concludes: "At all events, so imposing is the stern majesty of the statue, and so memorable is the story, that the play of the imagination leaves no room for the exercise of the judgment, and the fiction, if a fiction it is, operates on the spectator with an effect not less powerful than truth."

218.11–12   the Judith of Guido] According to Murray, p. 265, *Judith with the Head of Holofernes*. Probably a copy of a painting now called *Salomé with the Head of the Baptist*, which was earlier in the Colonna Palace and is now in the Ringling Museum, Sarasota, Florida. See Gnudi, *Guido Reni* (Florence: Vallecchi, 1955), pp. 88–89.

218.12–13   a copy . . . in the Boston Atheneum] In 1833 John Watkins Brett, an English collector, exhibited a number of pictures at the Boston Atheneum, including "Judith with the Head of Holophernes, by Guido Reni," which, according to the catalogue, "had been purchased in Italy for 1200 guineas and formerly hung in the Colonna Palace." This painting was acquired by exchange for the Atheneum Gallery in 1837, at which time it was still considered an original. See Swan, *The Atheneum Gallery*, pp. 95, 127.

218.13–14   many portraits . . . by the same.] A portrait of

Cardinal Bernardino Spada, and a painting of the *Rape of Helen* (a copy of the picture in the Louvre).

218.15 portraits . . . by Titian] Murray, p. 265, mentions a "Portrait of Cardinal Fal. Spada" and "A good Portrait of Cardinal Spada," but calls attention to the "doubtful authenticity" of "the greater number" of pictures in this gallery. These works are not mentioned in Francesco Valcanover, *All the Paintings of Titian* (New York: Hawthorn, 1964).

218.16 good pictures by Guercino] A portrait of *Cardinal Bernardino Spada.* Murray also mentions a *David,* a *St. John the Evangelist,* a *Santa Lucia,* and a picture of the *Death of Dido.*

220.1 to Florence, via Perugia] Murray's *Central Italy,* p. 229, says of the route: "this beautiful road is longer than that by Siena, but surpasses it both in picturesque and in historical interest, and the inns are in general better."

220.8 contract] The agreement with Gaetano Gazzari, dated May 20, is in the Berg Collection.

220.14–221.26 In the evening. . . . finished pictures.] Omitted by SH from *Passages,* and first published by JH in *NHHW,* II, 186–88.

220.17 Mr Ropes] Joseph Ropes (1812–85) of Salem, was known there as a portrait painter and author of essays on "Linear Perspective" (1850) and "Progressive Steps in Landscape Drawing" (1853). His presence in Rome in 1858 is apparently not recorded other than by NH here; he later spent more than ten years in Italy, beginning in 1863, and returned to America about 1876 to exhibit his landscapes at the Centennial Exposition in Philadelphia. See *The Arcadian Landscape,* no. 35; Tuckerman, p. 567; H. W. Belknap, *Artists and Craftsmen of Essex County Massachusetts* (Salem: Essex Institute, 1927), p. 12; Frederic A. Sharf, "'A More Bracing Morning Atmosphere': Artistic Life in Salem, 1850–1859," *EIHC,* XCV (1959), 151.

220.19   Mr. Rothermel] Peter Frederick Rothermel (1817–95), from Philadelphia, a portraitist and historical painter in the older Romantic tradition, was in Rome from 1856 to 1859. His best-known works done there are *King Lear and Cordelia* (now in the Philadelphia Museum) and *St. Agnes* (now in the Soviet Union). See *DAB*; Tuckerman, pp. 437–38; Clement and Hutton. JH removed his name in *NHHW*, II, 186; possibly he recalled that NH had used the name in *The Ancestral Footstep*, in a passage written on April 14, 1858 (see *ACM*, p. 10).

221.30   Mr. W. C. Bryant] William Cullen Bryant (1794–1878), poet and editor of the New York *Evening Post*, had been in Europe since June 1857, with his wife Frances (ca. 1797–1866), his daughter Julia (1831–1907), and Julia's friend Estelle Ives. He had been a close friend of the Sedgwick family of Stockbridge, Massachusetts, since 1820. Bryant's appearance of weariness was caused by nursing his wife during her four-month illness with cholera in Naples during the winter of 1858. In the previous autumn the party had traveled through Spain, from Burgos to Madrid to Malaga. Bryant wrote descriptive letters to his newspaper that were collected in *Letters of a Traveller, Second Series* (New York: Putnam, 1859). See Parke Godwin, *Biography of . . . Bryant* (New York: Appleton, 1883) and Charles H. Brown, *William Cullen Bryant* (New York: Scribner, 1971).

222.30–33   I introduced the subject of Kansas . . . opposition.] Since NH's conversation on Kansas with J. P. Kennedy on February 23, the U.S. Senate had adopted the proslavery Lecompton Constitution for Kansas on March 23, but on April 1 the House had voted a substitute resolution to resubmit it to the Kansas voters. The conference committee's compromise, the English Bill, tied a new referendum on the constitution to a reduced land grant for Kansas; this bill passed both houses by narrow margins on April 30, and was widely considered a victory for the Buchanan administration and the cause of slavery. See Potter, *The Impending Crisis, 1848–1861*, chapter 12. Bryant, who had come to oppose slavery strongly in his editorials, had joined the Republican party in 1855. In a letter of May 18, 1858, he had commented on the Kansas situation before learning of the administration's "triumph" of April 30: "I have been watching with interest the proceedings of Congress in the Kansas affair, but, the moment the House agreed to a Committee of Conference with the Senate, I took it for granted that a majority for the Lecompton constitution had been brought over. The question is settled before this time; but, as my newspapers from New York are only to the 24th of April, they leave the matter yet in the hands of the Committee. Whatever Congress may do, the Free State Party are destined eventually to triumph." See Godwin, *Bryant*, II, 110.

222.34   Sumner] Charles Sumner (1811–74), of Boston, was a senator from Massachusetts from 1851 until his death. Ardently opposed to slavery, he had spoken in the Senate on "the crime against Kansas" in May 1856, proposing immediate admission of Kansas as a free state and attacking the character of, among others, President Pierce and Senator Andrew P. Butler of South Carolina. Butler's cousin, Congressman Preston S. Brooks, thereupon assaulted Sumner in the Senate, striking him on the head many times with a cane. For more than three years Sumner sought to regain his health, moving from one resort to another. He was in Europe from March until November 1857; Bryant met him in Paris on June 16, and wrote of his condition in a letter very similar to NH's record here. See Godwin, *Bryant* II, 96–97. Sumner made another trip to Europe in May 1858 to consult physicians and to rest at resorts. When he arrived in Rome in April 1859 he was much improved. NH saw him on April 23 and May 2, according to his diary. See David Donald, *Charles Sumner and the Coming of the Civil War* (New York: Knopf, 1960). NH had known Sumner since about 1840; Sumner was George Hillard's law partner at the time of NH's residence in Hillard's home. Sumner supported in the Senate Pierce's appointment of NH as consul to Liverpool. On May 23, 1855, NH wrote to him, urging his attention to the shameful situation of American seamen (MS, Houghton), but Sumner did not reply. On January 31, 1857, NH wrote to William D. Ticknor, complaining: "Had he busied himself about this, instead of Abolitionism, he would have done good service to his country and have avoided Brooks's cudgel" (MS, Berg).

225.12–13 come home to everybody's business and bosom] An adaptation of Francis Bacon's Epistle Dedicatory to the Duke of Buckingham for his *Essays* (1625).

226.11 the court-yard of a palace.] Augustus J. C. Hare, *Walks in Rome*, 16th ed. (London: George Allen, 1903), I, 97: "Near the courtyard of the [Caffarelli] Palace there existed till 1868 a court, represented as the scene of the murder in Hawthorne's 'Marble Faun' or 'Transformation.' The door, the niche in the wall, and all other details mentioned in the novel, were realities. The character of the place is now changed by the removal of the boundary wall and formation of a new road."

227.26 Mrs. Chapman] The wife of John Gadsby Chapman (1808–89). He began his career as a portraitist in Virginia, studied at the Pennsylvania Academy, and was in Italy briefly in 1828 and 1830–31. Mrs. Frances Trollope, in *Domestic Manners of the Americans* (London: Whittaker, Treacher, 1832), p. 175, praised a painting of Hagar and Ishmael that he brought back as "the best picture by an American artist I have met with." He lived in Rome from 1848 until 1884. Murray, p. 269, lists him among the "eminent painters" from America: "*Chapman*, 135, Via Babuino, landscape painter and author of a good work on 'the Elementary Principles of Art.'" Among his best-known works were *The Baptism of Pocahontas* (later in the U.S. Capitol) and *Sunset on the Campagna*. NH visited his studio on March 19, 1859; see diary. See *DAB*; Tuckerman, pp. 216–22; *The Arcadian Landscape*, no. 7; Crane, *passim*; Karolik, pp. 157–59.

227.27 Mr Terry] Luther Terry (1813–1900), from Connecticut, came to Rome in the 1830s and remained until his death. His studio was in the Via Margutta; he painted "large canvasses representing religious and allegorical subjects," according to his daughter Margaret, Mrs. Winthrop Chanler, in her *Roman Spring: A Memoir* (Boston: Little, Brown, 1935), p. 4. Bonfigli, *Guide*, mentions *The Departure of Tobias*, *The First Meeting of Miranda and Ferdinand*, and *The Parting of Romeo and Juliet*. In 1861 Terry married Louisa Ward (1823–97), widow of Thomas Crawford, the sculptor; see Louise Hall Tharp, *Three Saints and a*

Sinner (Boston: Little, Brown, 1956), pp. 271–76. See also Tuckerman, p. 451; *Travelers in Arcadia*, pp. 59–60.

228.9 Mr Twisden] Edward Turner Boyd Twisleton (1809–74), a barrister and minor politician, and a scholar and archeologist, was said to have sat on more commissions than any man in England. He came to Boston in 1851 to examine "our institutions for education," according to Richard Henry Dana, Jr., who was impressed by Twisleton's conversation; see *The Journal of Richard Henry Dana Jr.*, ed. Robert F. Lucid (Cambridge: Harvard University Press, 1968), p. 463. In Boston he met and married in 1852 Ellen Dwight (1828–62), daughter of Edmund Dwight (1780–1849), a manufacturer and member of the Massachusetts Board of Education. Her uncle, the literary historian George Ticknor, was a frequent guest at the Twisletons' home in Hyde Park, London, in 1856–57. The Twisletons were close friends of the Richard Monckton Milneses, the Brownings, and the Storys. NH could have heard of Twisleton from George Ticknor, whom he met in a train to Liverpool, August 29, 1857. See *EN*, p. 560; G. S. Hillard and A. Ticknor, eds., *Life, Letters, and Journals of George Ticknor* (Boston: Houghton Mifflin, 1909), II, 400.

228.16–19 Lord Ellenborough's . . . emasculate them! !] Edward Law, first earl of Ellenborough (1790–1871), was minister for Indian Affairs in 1858, and president of the Board of Control of the East India Company, which was shortly to be dissolved by Parliament because of its inadequate government of India. George Ticknor and Twisleton (who was born in Ceylon) took part in a conversation about the sepoy mutiny at a breakfast given by Monckton Milnes in London on July 19, 1857 (*Life . . . of George Ticknor*, II, 373). On the sepoys, see note to 131.31.

228.25–26 'Niobe all tears.'] *Hamlet*, I, ii, 149. Compare *AN*, pp. 254, 618.

230.3 a mean people] SH added in *Passages*: "(though our landlord is German)."

230.27–28 'city of the soul,'] *Childe Harold*, canto 4, stanza 78.

232.2 Flaminian Way] This is "the old and direct road" from Rome to Civita Castellana, which, according to Murray, p. 276, "has fallen into disuse since Pius VI opened the post-road through Nepi, in order to unite the two great roads from Florence, by Siena and Perugia." NH followed the new road in returning to Rome in October.

234.2–3 Byron . . . on the bend] Murray, p. 275, quotes *Childe Harold*, canto 4, stanzas 74–75: ". . . the lone Soracte's heights display'd, / Not *now* in snow, which asks the lyric Roman's aid / For our remembrance, and from out the plain / Heaves like a long-swept wave about to break, / And on the curl hangs pausing."

237.19–24 Soracte kept us . . . final.] NH here echoes Murray, p. 271: "Soracte gives a new feature to the landscape, and continues for the rest of our road to Rome to be a prominent object. From its great height it appears much nearer than it really is, and seems to follow the traveller, so extensive is the circuit which the road makes round it."

237.30–31 field of the cloth of gold.] A locality near Calais where in 1520 Henry VIII of England and Francis I of France met for the purpose of arranging an alliance. The name reflects the splendid pageantry of this event.

240.16 Cascade of Terni] Murray, pp. 269–70, spends two pages of description of the falls, with detailed information to direct travelers to the best vistas; Murray quotes *Childe Harold*, canto 4, stanzas 69–72, devoted to the falls.

244.2 Murray] P. 267; the pass on Monte Somma is "3738 feet above the sea."

245.16–22 the lions. . . . fact.] Murray, p. 267, mentions the "local tradition of Hannibal's repulse": "It is a plain arch, with a device of the middle ages, representing a lion devouring a lamb," but NH probably means by "to see the lions," "to see the sights worth seeing"; see OED, "lion," 4.

246.4–5 the little temple . . . Pliny.] Murray, p. 264, notes "the small ancient temple supposed to be the one described by Pliny," and quotes *Childe Harold*, canto 4, stanzas 66–67. See Pliny the Younger (62–113 A.D.), *Letters*, 8, 8.

248.13–15 This church . . . much injured] S. Domenico. The modernization by white-wash was after an earthquake. See note to 254.2–19.

248.27–28 St. Mary within the Walls] S. Maria infra Portas. NH's remarks about the frescoes are puzzling, probably because he accepted the fanciful claims of the doorkeeper. SH said in *Notes*, p. 307, "All about the church were frescoes saved from the general whitewash, some of which were well worth study." The painter is Pier Antonio Mezzastris (1430–1506), a collaborator of Niccolo da Foligno. Bernardino Pintoricchio (ca. 1454–1513), a follower of Perugino, is represented in Spoleto and Spello, the towns visited just before and after Foligno, as well as in Perugia, where NH wrote this entry. Neither Giotto nor Cimabue are thought to have worked in this church; Cimabue, who may have been Giotto's teacher, would hardly have assisted him.

251.24–25 an old church] S. Chiara, according to SH, *Notes*, p. 308.

251.26 melancholy frescoes] In the face of NH's aversion, Murray, p. 255, presents Assisi with enthusiasm: "No traveler who takes an interest in the history of art, who is desirous of tracing the influence which the devotional fervour of St. Francis exercised on the painter of the fourteenth and fifteenth centuries, will fail to visit [Assisi]. . . . Assisi is the sanctuary of early Italian art, and the scene of those triumphs of Giotto to which Dante has given immortality" (in *Purgatorio*, 11, 94).

252.6–9 My wife, Una . . . early Italian art] In *Notes*, pp. 308–10, SH records their visit to S. Francesco, both lower and upper churches. Her comment on the frescoes, then attributed principally to Giotto and to Cimabue, is: "With what wonderful devoutness these ancient masters painted! They pray, they adore

God, they deny themselves, they live gloriously,—all with their pencil. They painted religiously, and there is an expression in the face and figures nowhere else found, excepting in Raphael, who imbibed so deeply the spirit of these men, and was their last expression."

254.2–19 St Mary. . . . merit.] According to Murray, p. 255, this church was rebuilt after the earthquake of 1832; "the church is remarkable for a very large fresco, of the Vision of St. Francis, painted in 1829 by *Overbeck*." Johann Friedrich Overbeck (1789–1869) was the most important of the German "Nazarene" painters, and he influenced the English Pre-Raphaelites.

254.6 small old chapel] Known as the Portiuncula.

254.13 Lo Spagna.] Lo Spagna (Giovanni di Pietro, ca. 1450–ca. 1528), a painter born in Spain, and associated with Perugino and Raphael. According to Murray's 1850 edition these frescoes, of the first Franciscan Saints, were "very much injured" (p. 265). Modern scholars doubt the attribution of them to Lo Spagna.

254.15–17 a fresco . . . the Assumption of the Virgin.] See p. 258.18–23 for NH's correction of this. In *Passages* SH corrected the parenthetical phrase to "on the pediment of the chapel," and in *Notes*, p. 311, remarked, "Over the arch of its [the chapel's] façade, Overbeck has painted a famous fresco of the Vision of St. Francis." She did not correct NH's title for the painting, presumably because it is, in effect, an Assumption.

255.22 a church] S. Domenico, according to *Notes*, p. 314.

256.7–8 (S. Luigi, I believe,)] Corrected on 260.6–7: the Cathedral of S. Lorenzo.

256.27–29 Raphael . . . Perugino.] Pietro Perugino, named for the city, his adopted home, was favored by nineteenth-century classicist taste as the teacher of Raphael. Murray, p. 245, speaks with some awe of "the influence of the school of Umbria on the genius of Raphael, whose early powers were first developed here under the instruction of Perugino." Perugino's painting in the Cambio includes six sibyls, six prophets, and "philosophers and warriors of antiquity, with allegorical figures of the different virtues above them" (Murray, p. 250). The decoration was probably begun in 1497 and completed soon after 1500. Raphael may have assisted Perugino here; see Pope-Hennessy, *Raphael*, pp. 129–30.

257.9–10 a pupil of Perugino.] Giannicola di Paolo Manni (?1470–1544); in 1519.

258.18 painting of Overbeck's, mentioned above] See note to 254.15–17.

258.27 pictures by Fra Angelico] The *Perugia Triptych: The Virgin and Child Enthroned with Angels between Saints Dominic, Nicholas of Bari, John the Baptist, and Catherine of Alexandria* (1437), now in the Galleria Nazionale dell' Umbria, Perugia. Described at length by SH in *Notes*, pp. 314–16.

258.30 Gothic monument . . . Benedict 12th] The monument, in the manner of Giovanni Pisano, was of Benedict XI (1303–4), who died by poisoning. Murray, pp. 246–47, describes it as the "great treasure" of the church, and as "justly considered by [the art historian Leopoldo] Cicognara [1767–1834] as one of the finest works of the revival in sculpture."

259.6–13 San Pietro in Martyre, . . . picture by Perugino.] Properly, S. Pietro Martire. The other church is of the Benedictine monastery, S. Pietro de' Casinensi; the picture there is described by Murray, p. 248, as "an exquisite Madonna and Child between two angels . . . by *Perugino*, a work of so much beauty that it has been attributed to Raphael."

259.26 Paul de Kock's novels] Paul de Kock (1794–1871) was a popular and prolific novelist of Parisian middle-class life, better known abroad than in France itself. NH read his books for relaxation at the Old Manse, although SH had heard that they were "abominable"; see SH to her mother, March 6, 1845 (MS, Berg).

260.9–11 beautiful fountain . . . with angels] Usually considered more noteworthy than the statue of Julius III is the fountain designed by Fra Bevignate in 1274, with marble sculptures by Nicola Pisano and his son Giovanni.

260.11–17 a bronze statue. . . . his presence.] Murray, p. 250, identifies the statue as by Vincenzio Danti in 1555: "The citizens erected this statue to Julius III. in gratitude for his restoration of many of their privileges, which were taken from them by Paul III. after their rebellion against the salt-tax." Later the statue was moved from the Piazza Danti to the steps of the cathedral, facing the Piazza S. Lorenzo, where it had originally stood.

262.20 the Lake of Thrasimene] The scene of Hannibal's victory over the Romans in 217 B.C.

265.2 The inn at Pasignano] Murray, p. 241, describes this inn as "very indifferent."

266.21 the Sanguinetto] Murray, p. 241, quotes *Childe Harold*, canto 4, stanza 65: ". . . a brook hath ta'en— / A little rill of scanty stream and bed— / A name of blood from that day's sanguine rain; / And Sanguinetto tells ye where the dead / Made the earth wet, and turn'd the unwilling waters red."

266.26 Bloody Brook, in Deerfield] Captain Thomas Lothrop and more than sixty members of his company were ambushed and slain by Indians in 1675, during King Philip's War, at "Bloody Brook" in South Deerfield, Massachusetts, on the Connecticut River.

266.32–267.6 The tower. . . . fathom.] Murray, p. 239, describes the battle at some length, quoting Sir John Hobhouse's note to the fourth canto of *Childe Harold*. The village is named Torre in Murray and Tuoro sul Trasimeno on more modern maps.

267.12 Saragota or Monmouth] Battles of the American Revolution in upstate New York, 1777, and in New Jersey, 1778.

267.19 Byron] *Childe Harold*, canto 4, stanza 64–65, quoted in Murray, p. 241.

268.3 Tuscan Custom House] According to Murray, p. 238, this was located at the village of Ossaja. See note to 361.6.

268.9 Cortona] Cortona, described by Murray, p. 236, as "one of the most ancient of the 12 cities of the Etruscan league," was located a mile up the mountain from the road to Arezzo.

268.30–31 Petrarch's house] Murray, p. 234, "The most remarkable house in Arezzo is that in the Sobborgo del'Orto, close to the Cathedral, in which *Petrarch* was born on Monday, July 20, 1304. A long inscription, put up in 1810, records the fact; the room shown as the scene of his birth has retained no trace of antiquity."

269.20 a well which Boccaccio has introduced] Immediately after the description of Petrarch's house quoted above, Murray continues, p. 234: "Close to it is the well near which Boccaccio has placed the comic scene of Tofano and Monna Ghita, his wife." See the *Decameron*, seventh day, fourth story.

269.34 my own Town Pump] "A Rill from the Town-Pump," *TTT*, pp. 141–48.

270.8 as far as England, as far as India] NH's sketch was much reprinted and widely distributed by temperance groups.

270.19–20 we left her with Miss Shepard] According to SH, *Notes*, pp. 333–34, she and Ada Shepard visited the cathedral and the church of S. Maria della Pieve.

270.22–31 We found. . . . Italian windows.] Murray, p. 231, comments of the cathedral: "its brilliant painted windows were executed early in the sixteenth century by Guillaume de Marseilles

. . . a French Dominican monk. The tall lance windows of the Tribune have been compared and even preferred to the 'Five Sisters' of York Minster, and another in the s. wall near the w. end, representing the Calling of S. Matthew, was so highly prized by Vasari, that he says 'it cannot be considered glass, but rather something rained down from heaven for the consolation of men.' " SH quotes Vasari's statement in *Notes*, p. 333, but not from Murray.

271.19–20   the rape of their ancestresses] The legend of the rape of the Sabine women to supply wives for the womanless followers of Romulus.

271.23   a bottle of Monte Pulciano] A famous wine grown at the town of Montepulciano, south of Arezzo, near the road from Siena to Rome.

273.12–14   A pre-Raphaelite . . . Exhibition] John Everett Millais (1829–96), *Autumn Leaves* (1856), now in the Manchester City Art Gallery. According to the *Catalogue*, p. 102, this painting was among those exhibited by "modern masters." In *EN*, p. 550 (July 28, 1857), NH describes his reaction to this painting, among others by the Pre-Raphaelite school: "I remember a heap of Autumn leaves, every one of which seems to have been stiffened with gum and varnish, and then put carefully down into the stiffly disordered heap."

278.8–10   the Celestial City . . . Mountains.] See note to 94.34–95.1.

278.12–13   residence of some great noble] According to Murray, p. 229, this is the Villa di Torre à Cona, "the grounds of which command fine prospects."

278.27–29   Thank Heaven . . . this country!] Leopold II (1797–1870), grand duke of Tuscany from 1824 until 1859, was a cousin of Emperor Franz Josef I (1830–1916) of Austria. In 1849 the grand duke had fled from the Florentine revolutionaries to Gaeta, where he joined the pope; a few months later he was restored by Austrian troops. He had granted a constitution and democratic political processes in 1848; these were abolished in favor of a mild despotism in 1852.

278.32   Mr. Powers] Hiram Powers (1805–73) was the most famous American artist of his time, at home and abroad. Born in Woodstock, Vermont, he moved with his family in 1818 to Cincinnati. At the age of 18 he went to work as a mechanic in a clock and organ factory, and at that time became interested in sculpture, working first in beeswax. He attracted the patronage of Nicholas Longworth, who encouraged him to go to Washington in 1834, where he modeled portrait busts of Chief Justice Marshall, President Jackson, and John Calhoun. He went with his family to Italy in 1837, and took up permanent residence in Florence. According to Murray, p. 521, his studio was at Via della Fornace 2539. For biographies of Powers, see Crane, Craven, Taft, Thorp; Donald Martin Reynolds, *Hiram Powers and His Ideal Sculpture* (New York: Garland, 1977), and "The 'Unveiled Soul': Hiram Powers's Embodiment of the Ideal," *Art Bulletin*, LIX (1977), 394–414.

278.33–34   found him too much engaged] According to JH, Powers "had promised to engage lodgings for us, but he had not expected us so soon" (*HC*, p. 336).

279.21–22   the fisher-boy . . . the bust of Proserpina] *The Fisher Boy* (1846) and *Proserpine* (1839). Reproductions are in Gerdts. The half-bust of Proserpine was the most popular of all neoclassical sculptures by American artists: well over one hundred are known to have been made (and are listed in Reynolds's *Hiram Powers*, pp. 1070–75).

279.27   a bust of Mr. Sparks by Persico] Luigi Persico (1791–1860) came to America in 1818, gained acclaim as a sculptor for his bust of LaFayette in the mid-1820s, and in the next two decades did busts of Nicholas Biddle, John Quincy Adams, and (in 1834) Jared Sparks (1789–1866), the Harvard president and historian, and former editor of the *North American Review*. Persico's pedimental sculptures for the Capitol in Washington are still in place. See Craven, pp. 64–65. When Sparks's colleagues at Harvard commissioned a new bust in 1854, Hiram Powers was engaged to make it. Sparks proposed that this work be modeled after Persico's, but his friends (perhaps with Powers's advice) insisted on a fresh study from life. Accordingly Sparks went to Florence in the autumn of 1857, where Powers spent a month and fourteen sittings preparing the plaster cast; the work was finished and sent to America on October 8, 1858. It was placed in Memorial Hall in Cambridge. Powers wrote that no portrait-bust in his studio had ever attracted more attention. See Herbert D. Adams, *The Life and Writings of Jared Sparks* (Boston: Houghton, Mifflin, 1893), II, 477–78; Crane, p. 249.

279.30–31   image of Mr. King, of Alabama, by Clark Mills] Clark Mills (1810–83) was a native of New York State who became an ornamental plasterer in South Carolina in the 1840s. He learned portrait-bust sculpture without assistance, working from plaster life masks; his rather primitive, naturalistic bust of John C. Calhoun was considered a work of genius in Charleston, and led to the patronage of John Preston, whose brother had assisted Powers to go to Florence and set up his studio there. Mills was best known for his heroic equestrian statue of Andrew Jackson, which was unveiled in 1853 with great fanfare in Washington, and is now in Lafayette Square. Powers's contempt was presumably based not only on Mills's self-taught approach and lack of aesthetic finesse, but on the fact that Mills had been commissioned to erect Greenough's *Rescue* group in Washington after Greenough's death, and was considered to have botched the composition. See Craven, pp. 166–74, and Tuckerman, pp. 583–86. William Rufus DeVane King (1786–1853) was U.S. senator from Alabama almost continuously from 1819 until 1853, when he became Franklin Pierce's vice-president.

280.9–15   An appropriation . . . Washington.] On March 3, 1855, Congress voted a resolution "to enable the President of the United States to contract with Hiram Powers for some work of are executed or to be executed by him, and suitable for the ornamentation of the Capitol," and appropriated $25,000. Because Powers would not return to America to negotiate, and because the government would not accept his *America* for the entire sum, the matter was not contracted until January 28, 1859, when Powers agreed to create statues of Franklin and Jefferson for $10,000 apiece. See Crane, pp. 241–42. Compare below, pp. 431–32 and note. In 1853 Congress appropriated $50,000 for a colossal equestrian statue of Washington by Clark Mills, whose statue of Jackson had just been unveiled. See Craven, pp. 171–72.

281.2–17 a statue of Washington. . . . actual work.] Commissioned in 1848 by the Louisiana legislature for the statehouse at Baton Rouge for $10,000 and finished in 1855; destroyed during the Civil War. Powers was sensitive about the derision Americans had heaped on Greenough's partially nude statue of Washington.

281.20–32 California. . . . 'auri sacra fames.'] Powers had begun this statue as early as 1850, hoping to sell it to the state of California or the city of San Francisco, but it evoked no enthusiasm there or in Washington. In 1858 he sold it to William B. Astor of New York, who in 1872 gave it to the Metropolitan Museum. The quotation ("cursed lust for gold") is from Virgil, *Aeneid*, 3, 57.

281.33 Mrs. Powers] Elizabeth Gibson Powers (b. 1812), a native of Cincinnati, married Powers in 1832. They had nine children, seven of whom were born in Florence.

282.33 an English lady] In *Passages* SH added "the Countess of St. George" and removed the reference to her husband.

284.13 Ponte Carraja] the Ponte alle Carraia.

284.24–285.3 The streets are delightful. . . . sake than here.] SH wrote to her sister Mary Mann on June 7 that NH "did not live in Rome," but "he is now himself again, as he was in the first summer in Concord at the Old Manse" (MS, Boston Public Library).

285.8 one immediately thinks of the Pantheon] This comparison is suggested by Murray, p. 536.

285.14–15 the famous bronze doors] "The gates of Paradise," the east doors of the Baptistery, by Lorenzo Ghiberti, 1425–50.

NH saw the cast at the Crystal Palace on November 15, 1857 (*EN*, p. 603).

285.18–19 my third or fourth visit] NH's diary mentions only a visit on June 2.

286.9 high and narrow windows] The side-aisle windows, by Francesco Talenti in 1355–58.

286.13 a wreath of circular windows] Seven fifteenth-century windows designed by Donatello, Ghiberti, Uccello, and Castagno. The subjects are the *Coronation of the Virgin*, the *Nativity*, the *Presentation in the Temple*, the *Agony in the Garden*, the *Pietà*, the *Resurrection*, and the *Ascension*.

286.18–19 The 'dim, religious light' that Milton speaks of] "Il Penseroso," lines 159–60; "And storied windows richly dight, / Casting a dim religious light."

287.7–8 (like General Washington's . . . small-clothes)] In Powers's statue; see p. 281 above.

287.26–27 a bronze equestrian statue] By Giovanni Bologna (1529–1608) in 1587–95.

287.29 David, by Michael Angelo] 1501–4. Since 1873 in the Accademia; replaced in 1905 by a copy in the piazza.

288.7–9 Benvenuto Cellini's . . . Crystal Palace.] 1545–54. See *EN*, p. 603 (November 16, 1857).

288.30–289.7 This front was once. . . . finished now.] Murray, p. 530: "[The] façade subsisted till the sixteenth century, having been adorned with statues by the best masters, including Donatello, when in 1558 it was destroyed by the Proveditore, Benedetto Uguccione, for the purpose, as he professed, of re-erecting it in the then modern style; and so eager was he to effect the demolition, that instead of detaching the precious marble, which might have been employed again, the facing was plucked off so rudely and hastily that, according to a contemporary, not a slab on a column was left entire." The cathedral was begun on a plan conceived by Arnolfo di Cambio in 1294–1302. A new façade, by Emilio de Fabris (1808–83), was built between 1875 and 1887.

289.21 the Campanile] Begun by Giotto, continued by Andrea Pisano, and completed in the 1350s by Francesco Talenti.

291.17 bust of Caracalla] In the Uffizi; see p. 295.

291.21 that of Cato the Censor] In the Capitoline Sculpture Gallery; see p. 162.

291.26 Mr. Harte] Joel Tanner Hart (1810–77), from Kentucky, gained success and fame at an early age as a sculptor of busts of General Cassius Clay, Andrew Jackson, and Henry Clay. He came to Florence in 1849 and lived there until his death. During the mid-1850s he invented a "pointing machine" for transferring the forms and proportions of a head directly into clay, reducing the time for making a portrait bust by two-thirds. Powers criticized the machine for making art too mechanical. See Craven, pp. 197–200; *Yankee Stonecutters*, pp. 65–66; J. Winston Coleman, Jr., *Three Kentucky Artists: Hart, Price, Troye* (Lexington: University of Kentucky Press, 1974), pp. 1–23; Albert ten Eyck Gardner, *American Sculpture: A Catalogue of the Collection of the Metropolitan Museum of Art* (Greenwich, Conn.: New York Graphic Society, 1965), pp. 7–8.

292.4–10 We asked him. . . . Gibson's friends.] Extracts from Powers's letter on the tinting of sculpture were given in the London *Athenaeum*, no. 1365 (December 24, 1853), 1559–60. Powers asserted that form is the vehicle of expression in art, and that color is only an accompaniment. On his wax figures, see p. 337 and note to 337.20.

293.18 the Bryants] They had left Rome on May 28, on their way through northern Italy to Paris and England and return to America in September.

293.18 Hotel de New York] Murray, p. 514: "on the Lung'Arno: some complaints have been made of late of the attendance and charges; table-d'hôte at 5 pauls."

293.19 Mrs. Browning] Elizabeth Barrett Browning (1806–61), considered by many contemporaries the greatest woman poet ever to write in English, had come to Florence in 1847 with Robert Browning after their marriage and their escape from her tyrannical father in London. The Casa Guidi or Palazzo Guidi, where the Brownings had lived most of the time since 1847, is located between Via Maggio and Via Mazetta, in sight of the Pitti Palace. See p. 300.7–8 and note thereto.

293.21 the Uffizzi Gallery] The Hawthornes' stay in Florence came during a period of neglect and deterioration for the Uffizi. In 1864, after Tuscany had become firmly allied with the new kingdom of Italy, the museum was reorganized and the collection presented in a more orderly, logical way.

293.26–29 some busts of the princes . . . his own wig.] Members of the Medici family who contributed to the collections. The sculptors included Nicodemo Ferrucci (?1574–1650) and Francesco Curradi (1570–1661).

294.6–8 Here are Giotto . . . a hundred others] The enthroned Madonnas of Cimabue and Giotto had not yet been brought to the Uffizi; see note to 322.25. The pictures NH thought to be by them in the Uffizi are now ascribed to their followers. SH mentions twice a triptych by Fra Angelico in the Uffizi of *Madonna and Child Surrounded with Angels in Choir* (*Notes*, pp. 356–57, 373); this is the Linaiuli triptych (1433), now in the Museo di S. Marco. Neither Fra Filippo Lippi's *Madonna and Child* (ca. 1455) nor any of the several Botticellis in the Uffizi receive further mention by NH or SH.

294.13–17 a large, dark, ugly picture . . . entrance.] Passignano (Domenico Cresti, 1560–1636), *Our Lord Burdened with the Weight of the Cross.*

294.24 a bust of Pompey the Great] Possibly the bust with head in porphyry, a modern work, in the Hall of Niobe, described in the 1860 catalogue of Emilio Burci and Giorgio Campari, I, 45.

296.21–22 a copy of the Laocoon] By Baccio Bandinelli (1493–1560), a Florentine rival of Michelangelo.

296.29–32 unfinished bas-relief . . . ago.] Known as the *Pitti Tondo* or *Pitti Madonna* (ca. 1506), this piece was transferred to the Bargello in 1864.

297.4–8 a beautiful picture . . . on the shore.] *A Seaport with the Setting Sun* (1644). This picture resembles Claude's *Embarkation of St. Ursula* and *Embarkation of the Queen of Sheba;* see note to 127.10.

297.8–9 Landscapes by Rembrandt] *Mountain Landscape* (ca. 1630–35), by Hercules Seghers (ca. 1589–ca. 1638). This picture, presented to the Uffizi in 1839 by Baroness Maria Hadfield Cosway as a work of Rembrandt, has been attributed to Seghers since 1871.

297.9–10 fat Graces . . . by Rubens] *The Three Graces* (1620–23) and *Venus and Adonis* (1601–10), later in the Akademie, Düsseldorf.

297.10–12 brass pans . . . by Mieris] David Teniers the Elder (1582–1649), *An Old Chemist in His Laboratory;* David Teniers the Younger (1610–90), *An Old Man Caressing an Old Woman in an Inn, A Physician with a Bottle in his Hand;* Gerard Douw (1613–80), *A Schoolmaster* (1660–65), *The Pancake Seller* (1650–55); Franz van Mieris (1635–81), *A Charlatan, A Young Woman Asleep, The Painter with his Family* (1675), *The Aged Lover, The Meal, The Drinkers.*

298.6–15 I felt a kind. . . . her body.] Murray, p. 586, comments: "The countenance of the Medicean Venus is amongst its highest excellences, and gives an elevated character to the whole figure. . . . She is evidently solicitous to discover whether she is observed. Yet the look does not indicate the timid modesty of a young girl, but the dignified anxiety of a noble married lady in such circumstances. Combining this with the position of the arms, it is impossible to conceive more feminine purity than the statue displays: it may be called its motive."

299.1–2   a painted Venus by Titian . . . lustful.] The *Venus of Urbino* (1538) or another reclining Venus by Titan (Uffizi no. 1431).

299.3   the room of the Venus] The Tribune.

299.6   several by Raphael] *The Madonna of the Goldfinch, Portrait of Julius II, Portrait of a Young Woman, St. John in the Desert*; the *Fornarina* (a copy of the portrait in the Barberini Palace in Rome; see note to 92.14), then attributed to Raphael, but now to Sebastiano del Piombo.

299.12   Mr. Robert Browning's] Browning (1812–89) was much less well known than his wife until after her death. NH had met the Brownings on July 11, 1856, at a breakfast party given by Richard Monckton Milnes. His conversation with each of them was brief. He and Browning exchanged appreciation of each other's work; Browning mentioned that *BR* was the book by NH he admired most, and NH wondered why to himself. Mrs. Browning brought up their friendship with the Storys, and with Margaret Fuller, and her interest in spiritualism. See *EN*, pp. 381–83. The close and long friendship of the Storys and the Brownings is fully recorded in Hudson, *Browning to his American Friends*. A more general account is Louise Greer, *Browning and America* (Chapel Hill: University of North Carolina Press, 1952).

299.30–32   They are to leave Florence . . . summer.] The Brownings planned to spend the summer on the French coast in order that a change of air might help Elizabeth to regain her strength. They left Florence on July 1, spending most of the summer in Le Havre, returning to Florence in October, and then traveled by vettura to Rome in late November. NH's diary records frequent visits between the families in the winter and spring.

300.7–8   'Casa Guidi Windows.'] A long poem by Mrs. Browning, published in 1851, containing, according to the advertisement, "the impressions of the writer upon events in Tuscany of which she was a witness"—the democratic uprisings of 1847 and 1848 and the Austrian repression of 1848–49. There were many public demonstrations outside the Pitti Palace, the residence of the grand duke, that could be seen from the Casa Guidi. In *Passages*, SH changed the text to give Mrs. Browning as author of the poem.

300.11–12   a church close by.] S. Felice.

300.14   his little boy, Robert] Robert Wiedemann Barrett Browning (1849–1912). Spoiled by his mother, who kept him in curls till her death, and then spoiled by his father, he did not succeed at Oxford. He became a mediocre painter and sculptor, and made his home in Italy.

300.16   diminutive of Appennine] Browning denied this explanation after it was published in *Passages*: "That mistake of Hawthorne's—or rather of Hawthorne's informant—has long amused me. There was never any sort of allusion to the Apennine (statue, or the mountains' self) in the diminutive 'Penini,'—which was simply the little fellow's first attempt at pronouncing his own second Christian name of Wiedemann—the maiden-name of his Grandmother—by which it was at first proposed that he should be called to the avoiding the ambiguous 'Robert'" (Browning to Frederick J. Furnivall, May 14, 1882, in *Browning's Trumpeter: The Correspondence of Robert Browning and Frederick J. Furnivall, 1872–1889*, ed. William S. Peterson [Washington: Decatur House, 1979], p. 53).

301.22   Mr. Milnes's] Richard Monckton Milnes (1809–85), later first Lord Houghton; politician, patron, critic, man of letters, and renowned host. He had met NH in Liverpool in September, 1854. See also note to 299.11.

301.33   Mr. & Mrs. Eckers] David Eckley (b. 1820), a wealthy Bostonian, was the grandson of Dr. Joseph Eckley (1749–1811), pastor of the Old South Church from 1779 to 1811. He and his wife, Sophia May Tuckerman Eckley (1822–74) lived many years in Europe. She was a sister of the poet Frederick Goddard Tuckerman, and a cousin of Louisa May Alcott. She was Mrs. Browning's most intimate friend in 1858–59, showering her with adulation and gifts. A medium, she played upon Mrs. Browning's addiction to spiritualism. Late in 1859 apparently Elizabeth discovered that Sophia had "cheated" her and their friendship ended. In 1860 Mrs. Eckley published a book of travels about the East, *The Oldest of the Old World*. When she called with Mrs. Browning on the Hawthornes in Rome on April 6, 1859, NH spelled her name correctly in his diary. See McAleer, pp. 31, 295, 314; Katherine H. Porter, *Through a Glass Darkly: Spiritualism in the Browning Circle* (Lawrence: University of Kansas Press, 1958), pp. 57–68; Samuel A. Golden, *Frederick Goddard Tuckerman* (New York: Twayne, 1966), pp. 22, 154.

302.1 Miss Fanny Howarth] Euphrasia Fanny Haworth (1801–83), English poet and author, met NH in Liverpool on August 23, 1853, little more than a month after his arrival from America. See *EN*, pp. 15, 626. She had been a friend of Browning's since the 1830s, and is the "Eyebright" of *Sordello*.

302.21–23 told a story . . . fifty years.] A celebrated incident in the early history of the spiritualist fad. In June 1850 the Fox sisters, whose "Rochester rappings" had begun interest in spiritualism in America, came to New York to confront a skeptical public. At a demonstration at the home of Rufus Griswold, attended by Bryant, Cooper, George Bancroft, Horace Greeley, Nathaniel Parker Willis, George Ripley, and others, the sisters (or the spirit) correctly knocked fifty times when asked how long ago Cooper's sister Hannah had died, and rightly guessed the cause of her death as a fall from a horse. Ripley's long report in the New York *Tribune* of June 8, 1850, contributed much to the girls' popularity. See Slater Brown, *The Heyday of Spiritualism* (New York: Hawthorn, 1970), pp. 115–16; Howard Kerr, *Mediums, and Spirit-Rappers, and Roaring Radicals: Spiritualism in American Literature, 1850–1900* (Urbana: University of Illinois Press, 1972), p. 7. According to Kerr, NH was the first American writer of note to make serious literary use of mesmerism and spiritualism;

he summarizes the development of NH's attitudes (pp. 56–65). For a more recent and fuller general discussion, see Taylor Stoehr, *Hawthorne's Mad Scientists: Pseudoscience and Social Science in Nineteenth-Century Life and Letters* (Hamden, Conn.: Archon, 1978), pp. 168–82.

302.24   Mr. Hume] Daniel Dunglas Home (pronounced Hume, 1833–86), American medium, born in Scotland, had discovered his powers at the age of seventeen. After demonstrating them at a number of séances in Massachusetts, Connecticut, and New York, Home went to Europe in 1855. On July 23, 1855, the Brownings attended his performance at the home of John S. Rymer in Ealing, near London. After placing the poet's garland on Mrs. Browning's head, Home enraged Browning by suggesting that Browning jealously wished to be crowned himself. Browning, totally unconvinced by the performance, asked unsuccessfully for a second séance, and showed his anger when Home came to call a few days later. Browning's eventual revenge was the poem "Mr. Sludge, 'the Medium' " (1864), written probably in Florence in 1859–60. Many versions of this incident circulated in London, and in Florence, which Home visited later in 1855. NH had discussed Home with Dr. J. J. Garth Wilkinson, a spiritualist, in London, in December 1857 (*EN*, pp. 616–17). See Porter, *Through a Glass Darkly*, and Jean Burton, *Heyday of a Wizard: Daniel Home the Medium* (London: Harrop, 1948).

303.10   so cool, so calm—so bright] George Herbert, "Virtue": "Sweet day, so cool, so calm, so bright, / The bridal of the earth and sky."

303.11–14   He has a great loss . . . reach America.] Frances Bryant had been close to death in Naples with cholera during the spring of 1858, but she did not die until 1866. Shortly after her death Bryant made a sixth trip to Europe.

305.16–18   The collection . . . I have seen] Murray, p. 598: "the collection of pictures . . . formed somewhat later than the *Uffizi Galleria*, has become the finest of the two."

305.32–34   The most beautiful. . . . engravings, and copies]
Murray, p. 600: "The sweetest of all his Madonnas, if not the
grandest. Nature, unsophisticated nature, reigns triumphant
throughout this work, highly sought for, highly felt, and
most agreeably rendered."

306.15   the Three Fates of Michael Angelo] Actually by Francesco (or Cecchino) Salviati (1510–63), a pupil of Andrea del
Sarto. See Filippo Rossi, *The Uffizi and Pitti*, trans. Richard
Waterhouse (London: Thames and Hudson, 1966), p. 286; Frederick Antal, *Classicism and Romanticism with Other Studies in
Art History* (New York: Harper and Row, 1973), p. 165. SH
recalled in *Notes*, p. 369, the copy given to Ralph Waldo Emerson
in the 1830s by the artist William Allen Wall, whom Emerson
had known in Florence. The picture hung for the rest of Emerson's life in his study. See Emerson, *Journals*, (1909–14), III, 97;
Journals and Miscellaneous Notebooks (1960–) VIII, 523 n. 16.
It was mentioned by a number of British and American visitors:
among them, Mrs. Trollope, George Hillard, and Bayard Taylor.

307.3   'Keep the heights I gain,'] Wordsworth, *The Excursion*,
IV, 138–39: "And the most difficult of tasks to *keep* / Heights
which the soul is competent to gain." These lines recur frequently
in Emerson's journals.

308.8   three thousand years ago] Actually the Venus is a
Roman copy of a late Hellenistic work, probably of the third century B.C. See Bieber, p. 20.

308.15–16   their Venuses, their Greek Slaves, their Eves] Gibson's *Tinted Venus*, Powers's *Greek Slave* (1843) and *Eve
Tempted* (1842). The *Greek Slave* was by far the most famous
sculpture produced by an American in the nineteenth century. Influenced by the Venus de' Medici, it represented a modern incident
in the Greek War of Independence (1821–30): the captivity of a
chaste, virtuous Greek woman by the infidel Turks, who are selling
her at auction. Thus nudity and Puritan morality were not in conflict, and the statue was immensely popular throughout Great
Britain and the United States. It was also considered relevant to

the conflict over slavery in America, and was called "American art's first antislavery document in marble." NH saw the *Greek Slave* in the Egyptian Hall in London on August 6, 1856, and disliked it, condemning its nudity (*EN*, p. 393).

309.4 Messrs Emmanuel Fenzi & Co] Murray, p. 519: "Pal. Uguccione, in the Piazza Gran Duca."

309.19–22 I think Murray . . . character.] Murray observes, p. 604: "The models in wax are interesting. The more ancient by *Zummo*, a Sicilian, who executed them for Cosimo III, principally represent corpses in various stages of decomposition. The greater number are more strictly speaking, anatomical, and display every portion of the human body with wonderful accuracy. They embrace also many representations of comparative anatomy, a branch much increased of late years." The artist was Gaetano Giulio Zumbo (1656–1701).

310.10–11 the face . . . that of an idiot.] Compare the judgment of Sir Kenneth Clark in *The Nude: A Study in Ideal Form* (1956; New York: Doubleday Anchor Ed., 1959), p. 134: "The line of the body tapers up to the tiny, Praxitelean head, with the vapid elegance of a Victorian fashion plate." See also the note to 517.9.

311.13 busts of Proserpine and Psyche] *Proserpine*, 1839; *Psyche*, 1849. Reproductions in Crane, pp. 188, 237.

312.6 the reigning Grand-duchess] Maria Antonia (1814–98), daughter of Francis I, king of the Two Sicilies, became the second wife of Leopold II of Tuscany in 1833. Powers's bust was done in 1846. Reproduction in Crane, p. 210.

313.6 Contemplation] According to Richard P. Wunder, *Hiram Powers: Vermont Sculptor* (Taftsville, Vt.: Countryman Press, 1974), p. 29, *La Penserosa* "was eliminated from the collection of the New York Public Library a few years ago and has since apparently been lost." The statue was made in 1856 for James Lenox of New York (Craven, p. 120). See Gerdts, pp. 116–19.

313.8 'rapt look commercing with the skies.'] Milton, "Il Penseroso," lines 38–40: "With even step and musing gait, / And looks commercing with the skies, / Thy rapt soul sitting in thine eyes."

313.19–20 a little baby's hand] Powers's daughter Louisa, done in Florence, 1839; some thirty copies were made. Reproduction in Gerdts.

314.33–34 Judith . . . by Allori] Cristofano Allori (1577–1621).

315.2 two peasant Madonnas by Murillo] The *Madonna of the Rosary* (ca. 1650) and *Madonna with the Infant Christ Standing* (1650–60).

315.6–7 Salvator Rosa . . . seaward] There were three seascapes by Rosa in the Pitti, dating from the 1640s: the *Seascape of the Towers*, the *Seascape of the Port*, and *Seascape*.

315.7–8 Rubens . . . mountain and plain.] *Peasants Returning from the Fields* (1637) is of the plain of Flanders; *Landscape with Ulysses and Nausicaa* (1635) is a mountainous scene.

317.23–318.5 Dutch paintings. . . . a flower] Dutch and Flemish still lifes in the Uffizi included works by Jan Davidsz. de Heem (1606–83/84), *Fruits, oysters and utensils, Different varieties of flowers*; Rachel Ruysch (1664–1750), *Fruits and Flowers, Flowers in a basket*; Maria van Osterwick (1630–93), *A vase of flowers, with fruits and insects*; Otho Marcellis (1613–73), *Plants, flowers, insects and serpents*; Nicholas Verendael (1659–1717), *A vase of flowers*; Jan van Kessel (1626–79), *Fish and Fruits*; Abraham Mignon (1640–79), *Fruits*.

318.8–9 a picture of Venus . . . Cupid's head] Giovanni da San Giovanni (Giovanni Mannozzi, 1592–1636), *Venus combing Cupid*.

318.11–12 Judith, by Bordone] Now ascribed to Palma Vecchio and not to Paris Bordone (1506–71).

318.17–18　Bacchus, astride on a barrel, by Rubens] *Bacchus with a Cup in His Hand* (1637–40).

318.21–22　Madonna's face . . . in her lap] In *Passages*, SH added "by Raphael" after "face," and changed "lap" to "arms."

320.16　Chantrey . . . Washington] Sir Francis Chantrey (1781–1841), English neoclassical sculptor of portrait busts and statues, made *George Washington* (1826) with Washington wearing a Roman toga over contemporary dress. The statue, in the Massachusetts State House, was described by NH, with an accompanying engraving, in the *American Magazine of Useful and Entertaining Knowledge*, II (June 1836), 402. See Arlin Turner, *Hawthorne as Editor* (University, La.: Louisiana State University Press, 1941), pp. 137–38. See Gerdts, pp. 100–101; Craven, pp. 69–70. NH had seen Chantrey's work in Salisbury Cathedral and in the Taylor Institute, Oxford (see *EN*, pp. 359, 414).

320.19–20　Washington, and . . . Daniel Webster.] *Daniel Webster*, a bronze statue made by Powers in 1857, is now on the State House lawn in Boston. Powers wrote to Edward Everett, March 2, 1859: "You say that one of the criticisms of my statue of Mr. Webster is the baggy pantaloons! I copied them from his own placed upon a figure, life size of Mr. Webster, which I had prepared to dress up in his own suit which you sent out to me" (quoted in Craven, pp. 119–20). See NH's comment, pp. 433–34 below. On the statue of Washington, see note to 280.9–15.

321.11–12　I have had this perception myself] Compare *The Ancestral Footstep*, characterizing the villain Eldredge, written on May 15, 1858: "Taste seems to be a department of moral sense; and yet it is so little identical with it, and so little implies conscience, that some of the worst men in the world have been the most refined" (*ACM*, p. 74).

321.21–24　a little picture . . . hardly bear to look at.] Neither Cristofano Allori (see note to 314.33–44) nor Alessandro Allori (1535–1607) nor Francesco Albani (1578–1660) painted this subject. In *Passages* SH deleted the parenthesis and inserted "by Zucchero." There are in the Uffizi small Mannerist paintings (50 x 38 cm.) of *The Golden Age* and *The Silver Age* that were thought to be by Federico Zuccari, or Zucchero (1542–1609); more recently they have been ascribed to Jacopo Zucchi (1541–89). See Sergio Negrini, *The Uffizi of Florence and Its Paintings* (New York: Arco, 1974), p. 88, and Antal, *Classicism and Romanticism*, p. 63 n. 2.

322.12   my record of a former visit.] See p. 286.1–4.

322.13   the monument of Giotto . . . bas-relief] By Benedetto da Maiano (1442–97).

322.15–16   fresco of a knight . . . one John Hawkwood] The fresco was painted on the wall by Paulo Uccello (1397–1475) in 1436, and transferred to canvas in 1845. Sir John de Hawkwood, an English professional soldier, stormed the defenses of Pau in 1359 and progressed across southern France to his career in the factional wars of Italy (*DNB*). He was *condottiere* for the safety of Florence from 1382 until his death in 1394. Murray, p. 532, gives an extended account of his service.

322.25   Giotto, Cimabue, and others] Cimabue, *Enthroned Madonna and Child* (ca. 1280, originally in S. Trinità); Giotto, *Enthroned Madonna and Child* (1310, originally in the Ognissanti convent). These pictures were moved to the Uffizi in 1919. NH's description is apparently of a series of small panel pictures from the sacristy of S. Croce, representing the lives of Christ and St. Francis. These were thought to be by Giotto, but are the work of his assistant Taddeo Gaddi (ca. 1300–1366).

323.11–12   a picture . . . of the Adoration of the Magi] Gentile da Fabriano (ca. 1370–1427) painted the *Adoration of the Magi* (1423) as an altarpiece for the Strozzi Chapel in S. Trinità. It was moved to the Uffizi in 1919.

323.27   Fra Angelico] According to Murray, pp. 605–6, the Academy showed the *Descent from the Cross*, the *Last Judgment*,

Entombment, and nine other paintings. These are now in the Museo di S. Marco in Florence.

324.5–15 Perugino. . . . Christ, dead . . . on his mother's knees.] This *Pietà* (1495) is considered one of Perugino's most characteristic works. See note to 371.15–19. In *Passages* Sophia inserted at the end of this passage "A Pietà."

324.15–20 The most inadequate . . . prettily painted, nevertheless.] NH continued to hold a poor opinion of Carlo Dolci (1616–86); see pp. 371–72 below.

324.24–325.6 These pictures. . . . holier light.] The *Last Judgment* (ca. 1431) was done for S. Maria degli Angeli, the *Deposition* (ca. 1443) for the Strozzi Chapel of S. Trinità, and the *Lamentation* (1436) for the Confraternity of S. Maria della Croce. These are all now in the Museo di S. Marco, Florence.

325.10 St. Lorenzo] A pioneer work of Renaissance architecture, begun in 1418 by Filippo Brunelleschi (1377–1446).

325.31 pulpits] Not medieval, but the last major work of Donatello, in 1460–70, in which he renewed the tradition of the carved pulpit.

326.2–7 Murray says . . . pavement.] NH paraphrases Murray, p. 553.

327.11–328.17 But the statue. . . . before it.] Lorenzo de' Medici, duke of Urbino. Murray, pp. 553–54, quotes an appreciation by Richard Westmacott (1775–1856), an English student of Canova (see NH's comment on his statue at Kenilworth, *EN,* p. 571): "He is represented absorbed in thought. . . . The general action is one of perfect repose and the expression that of deep meditation. It is impossible to look at this figure without being forcibly struck with the *mind* that pervades it. For deep and intense feeling it is one of the finest works in existence. . . . It has been well observed of this statue, that it has no resemblance to the antique, but it rivals the best excellences of the ancients in expression."

328.10–11 At the Crystal Palace . . . space.] *EN*, p. 603 (November 16, 1857): " . . . a sitting statue by Michael Angelo of one of the Medici, full of dignity and grace, and reposeful might."

328.18 the Medicean Chapel] The Cappella dei Principi, begun in 1603 by Giovanni de' Medici, Alessandro Pieroni, Matteo Nigretti, and Bernardo Buontalenti; a distinctly conservative structure in relation to baroque architecture generally.

328.25–26 a series of brilliant frescoes . . . years ago.] Murray, p. 555: "The roof . . . is covered with frescoes executed between 1828 and 1837, by the late director of the Academy, Pietro Benvenuti." The frescoes were designed by Anton Raphael Mengs in 1772.

329.15–17 No, I mistake; the statue is of John de Medici . . . a soldier.] NH apparently corrected himself after consulting Murray, p. 557. The statue of Giovanni delle Bande Nere, founder of the grand-ducal dynasty, by Baccio Bandinelli (1493–1560), was originally in the Palazzo Vecchio, and was placed in the piazza in 1851.

333.31–32 those of Rubens . . . Rosa's] See notes to 315.6–7, 7–8.

334.11 I looked again . . . Michel Angelo's Fates] See note to 306.15.

337.20 'Infernal Regions,'] In 1828 Joseph Dorfeuille had a "Western Museum" in Cincinnati, and he hired Powers as manager and as inventor of automata and wax effigies. According to Thomas Adolphus Trollope, *What I Remember* (London: Bentley, 1887), I, 176–77, his mother suggested representing one of the *bolgias* of Dante's *Inferno*. For the scene Powers made lifelike waxworks and "all sorts of automatic contrivances that groaned and emitted smoke and rattled chains" (*Yankee Stonecutters*, p. 29). The show was immensely popular. See Mrs. Frances Trollope, *Domestic Manners*, chapter 7; Johanna Johnston, *The Life, Manners, and Travels of Fanny Trollope* (New York: Hawthorn, 1978), pp. 78–81.

338.19   Miss Blagden] Isabella Blagden (?1816–73), English poet and novelist, came to live in Florence in 1849. A writer of no talent, she was best known as hostess to Anglo-American tourists and friend of Anglo-American residents, particularly the Brownings. From 1856 to 1861 she lived in the Villa Brichieri, on Bellosguardo. She suggested to the Hawthornes that they spend August and September in the Villa Montauto, near her home. See SH, *Notes*, p. 410. After Mrs. Browning's death she maintained a regular monthly correspondence with Browning until her own death. See McAleer.

338.25   Mr. Trollope] Thomas Adolphus Trollope (1810–92), older brother of Anthony, lived in Florence from 1843 until his death. He wrote novels, historical works about Italy, and an entertaining autobiography, *What I Remember*. See note to 337.20.

338.25–26   Mr. Boot of Boston and a young daughter] Francis Boott (1813–1904), amateur singer and composer, had taken his infant daughter Elizabeth (1846–88) from Boston to live in Florence after the death of his wife in 1847. Boott's sister had married Henry Greenough, the sculptor's brother. Later Henry James based Gilbert and Pansy Osmond in *The Portrait of a Lady* on Frank and Lizzie Boott. See James, *Notes of a Son and Brother* (New York: Charles Scribner's Sons, 1914), pp. 475–83; Leon Edel, *Henry James* (Philadephia: Lippincott, 1953–1972), I, 259–60; II, 111–12; William James, *Memories and Studies* (New York: Longmans, 1911), pp. 63–72; *Baker's Biographical Dictionary of Musicians*, 5th edition, 1971.

338.28   Miss Blagden's companion] Annette Bracken (b. 1834) shared expenses at the Villa Brichieri with her relative Isa Blagden. Her mother, Mary Egerton Smith Bracken, and her brother

William, traveled extensively. All three were friends of the Brownings, and "Willy" was a particular friend of Pen Browning. Annette later married a Genoese portrait painter. See McAleer.

338.31   Sir Lytton Bulwer] Edward George Earle Lytton Bulwer-Lytton (1803–73), the novelist and dramatist, later first baron Lytton of Knebworth, best remembered as author of *The Last Days of Pompeii*. Miss Blagden was a close friend of his son Robert Lytton (1831–91), who had lived in Florence since 1852 as an unpaid attaché to the British legation, wrote poetry under the pseudonym Owen Meredith, and was later to become viceroy of India.

339.2   a portrait of his wife] Commissioned for Sophie Eckley, who bequeathed this and a companion portrait of Browning to him in 1874, the painting was by the Florentine Michele Gordigiani (1835–1909). It is now in the National Portrait Gallery, London. See Grace Elizabeth Wilson, *Robert Browning's Portraits* . . . (Waco, Texas: Baylor University, 1943), pp. 65–69.

339.7   Page] William Page (1811–85) is the only American painter mentioned in these notebooks who receives any account in most mid-twentieth-century histories of American Art. He is best remembered as a genre painter of the 1840s, but at that time he had earned extravagant praise for portraits, among them those of W. W. Story's father and of James Russell Lowell and his wife. During eight years in Boston, Page developed idealistic aesthetic theories under the influence of Emerson and Lowell. In 1850 he went to Florence, where he copied portraits by Titian and discussed artistic intentions and Swedenborgian teachings with Hiram Powers. In Rome in 1852 he painted a much-admired portrait of the American actress Charlotte Cushman. After November 1853 the Brownings lived in Rome directly above the Pages at 43, Bocca di Leone. They soon became close friends. Page painted Browning's portrait in the spring of 1854 as a gift for Mrs. Browning. Both considered the picture "marvelous," "wonderful," and "perfect"; but because of Page's experiments with glazing and undertoning in a desire to imitate Venetian coloring, it soon began to darken. Browning had wanted to exhibit it at the Royal Academy in London in 1855, but Dante Gabriel and William Rossetti apparently refused to hang it. Nevertheless, the Brownings continued to encourage Page and to promote his work until his return to America in 1860. The portrait became almost totally obscure until cleaned in 1949. It is now in the Browning Library at Baylor University, Waco, Texas. See Joshua C. Taylor, *William Page: The American Titian* (Chicago: University of Chicago Press, 1957).

339.23   Mrs Trollope] Frances Trollope (1780–1863), novelist and travel writer, whose *Domestic Manners of the Americans* is generally critical of Americans and American institutions. At this period, she was a recluse from social life.

340.23–24   a Bourbon, of the Naples family] See note to 312.6.

342.10   our street] According to Murray, p. 613, the Teatro Goldoni was in the Via S. Maria. The Casa del Bello, however, was in the Via delle Fornaci, which is now the Via de' Serragli.

342.13–14   church of Santa Croce . . . worthies.] Murray, p. 539: "Almost from its foundation this church became the favorite place of interment of the Florentines; and it has been appropriately designated as the 'Westminster Abbey' and the 'Pantheon' of Florence."

342.15–19   The piazza . . . well into operation.] Murray, p. 546: "The democracy of Florence established its power in the Piazza di Santa Croce, in the year 1250. . . . The goodmen . . . assembled here, with the determination of taking the power into their own hands, which they accomplished without the lightest resistance. . . . With this revolution dated the free institutions and liberties." See note to 414.19–20.

342.20–23   the façade of one of the houses . . . laid on.] Palazzo dell' Antella, Piazza S. Croce No. 21, with murals completed in twenty days in 1619 by twelve painters under the direction of Giovanni da San Giovanni.

342.23–28   The front of the church . . . doing something.]

The facade was completed in 1863 by Nicola Matas, based on a seventeenth-century neo-Gothic design, and was consecrated in the presence of Pope Pius IX.

343.16–22 the first monument. . . . pyramidal form] The design was by Vasari. Of the three figures, *Sculpture* was by Valerio Cioli (1529–99), *Painting* by Battista Lorenzi (1527–94), and *Architecture* by Giovanni dell' Opera (Giovanni Bandini, 1540–99). The bust of Michelangelo was by Lorenzi.

343.24 a modern work] By Stephano Ricci in 1829.

343.27 tomb of Alfieri . . . owed him.] By Canova in neo-classic style, completed in 1810.

343.29–30 Her own monument] The duchess of Albany was Louisa Maximilian Caroline Stuart (1753–1824), who married Charles Edward Stuart, the Young Pretender (1720–88), in 1772, and was the mistress of the poet Vittorio Alfieri (1749–1803). She is buried in the Castellani Chapel.

343.32 not many years after his death.] According to Murray, p. 540, this monument was raised in 1787. Machiavelli died in 1527.

344.3 Raphael Morghen] (1758–1833), a copper engraver, who tirelessly reproduced the masterpieces of Raphael and other artists of his period.

344.7 Galileo] His tomb in the Noviziata Chapel dates from 1737.

344.10 put to death] SH in *Passages* substituted "imprisoned for life."

344.29–345.8 some of those horrible. . . . the very same.] In *Passages* SH changed "horrible" to "distressing." The Bardi and Peruzzi chapels are the surviving masterpieces of Giotto's later period, and profoundly influential on the development of European painting. The Bardi *Scenes from the Life of Saint Francis* and the Peruzzi *Scenes from the Lives of Saint John the Baptist and Saint John the Evangelist* were painted in the 1320s, white-washed in 1714, and uncovered, badly restored, and completely repainted between 1849 and 1863. (Another restoration in 1958–63 revealed the original work.) SH remarks in *Notes*, p. 405: "Here I was again glad and Mr. H. desperate; for they had all been white-washed over, and only lately brought to view by a zealous priest; and so they were injured and then repaired and patched. . . . Can this child-like, unconscious grandeur ever again be found in art?" Other chapels in S. Croce have frescoes by an unknown follower of Cimabue, and by members of the school of Giotto, e.g., Bernardo Daddi, Taddeo and Agnoldo Gaddi, Maso di Banco. Ruskin's enthusiastic account of Giotto's frescoes was published in *Mornings in Florence* in 1875.

346.30–32 grew to be a church . . . I forget.] NH remembered the story with Murray's help, on his next visit. See note to 351.10–20.

346.34–347.2 great statues of Saints . . . Greek art.] Donatello (1386–1466), *St. Mark* and *St. George*; Lorenzo Ghiberti (?1381–1455), *St. John the Baptist*, *St. Matthew*, and *St. Stephen*; Nanni di Banco (d. 1421), *Four Crowned Martyrs*, *St. Philip*, and *St. Eligius*. These statues, made between 1411 and 1429, began the new great figurative style of the Renaissance, leading to the revolution in painting begun by Masaccio. Twentieth-century historians see these works as combining vestiges of late Gothic with "manifestoes of a new classicism." See Frederick Hartt, *History of Italian Renaissance Art*, 3rd ed. (Englewood Cliffs, N.J., and New York: Prentice-Hall and Abrams, 1975), pp. 131–32. For NH's later thoughts, see p. 351.4–9 and p. 404.6–11.

347.3 Riccardi palace] Now usually known as "Medici-Riccardi," the Riccardi, built in 1444–60 by the architect Michelozzo Michelozzi (1396–1472), was the prototype of Florentine Renaissance palaces. Via Larga is now Via Cavour; the other street is Via dei Gori.

348.6–11 frescoes of the Giotto. . . . two artists.] Benozzo Gozzoli (1420–97) was an assistant of Fra Angelico. His fresco here, *The Procession of the Magi* (1459), is his masterpiece.

348.15–19 a frescoed cieling . . . perfectly happy] Luca Giordano (1621–1705), a Neapolitan baroque artist, painted the *Apotheosis of the Medici Dynasty* and a *Cycle of the Life of Man* in 1682–83. This work is described by Wittkower, p. 309, as "a grand allegorical pageant glorifying the reign of the Medici dynasty with a dazzling élan and strikingly fresh and vivid colors."

348.25–26 the historian of Italy] Francesco Guicciardini (1483–1540) was the author of a *History of Italy* from 1494 to 1532. A coldly analytical writer, he was also a prominent statesman, described by his contemporaries as a venal and grasping seeker of power, more cynical and corrupt than his contemporary Niccolo Machiavelli (1469–1527). Guicciardini's private papers and manuscripts were opened to the public in 1857, raising his reputation as a historian and darkening judgment of his character.

350.18–21 one of Raphael's Madonnas . . . playing . . . it itself.] NH's description could fit Raphael's *Madonna of the Goldfinch* (1506), but it fits better *The Madonna Adoring the Christ Child* (1520), by Correggio. In *Passages* SH changed "Raphael's" to "Correggio's." She may be suspected of not allowing an implied criticism of Raphael from NH's pen. See p. 424.22–29.

350.21 Michael Angelo's Madonna] *The Doni Madonna* (ca. 1504).

350.21–22 William Ware] (1797–1852), a clergyman originally from Hingham, Massachusetts, and the Harvard Divinity School, pastor of the First Congregational Church, New York, and former editor of the *Christian Examiner*, in *Sketches of European Capitals* (Boston: Phillips, Sampson, 1851), pp. 118–20, describes Raphael's Madonnas as "at most and best, beautiful young women, as in the Seggiola of the Duke's Palace, but nothing more; no religious elevation, no peculiar sanctity, no holy and divine abstraction—no prophetic glancing of the soul into the future. This was reserved as the task of a loftier genius even than the divine Raffaelle. . . . It is a picture of the Holy Family, by Michael Angelo . . . the whole picture is in the Virgin Mother. She sits as in solitude, though in the midst of many; the young child, with one arm thrown round her in an endearing manner, soliciting attention;—but she heeds him not—still she sits alone—raised, apparently, above all earthly objects and thoughts—her face turned to heaven, her eye looking intently upward as if it reached into heaven;—yet a melancholy overspreads the face, as if while rapt out of herself by the moral glory of the unfolding ages, there was not concealed from her heart—a prospect in the distance of Calvary and the cross. The language of the face, while exalted is also truly feminine and deeply sad. It was to me incomparably the noblest female head, for that subject, I ever saw in art, and the only one worthy of the theme."

351.10–20 It appears. . . . plague.] Murray, p. 567: "This sanctuary commanded so much veneration, that, in 1348, the year of the great plague, described by Boccaccio, the offerings amounted to 35,000 golden florins." NH's description is generally indebted to Murray. See the *Decameron*, first day, first story.

351.23 Palazzo Buonarotti] Now called the Casa Buonarotti. The house became a public museum in 1858, after the death of Cosimo Buonarotti, the last member of the family. The house contains works of art by Michelangelo.

352.11–25 We came back. . . . sluggishness of mind.] This palace was the residence of the chief of police (and therefore used as a prison) until 1859, when the Museo Nazionale was installed here to house sculptures and small works of art from the overcrowded Uffizi. SH omitted this paragraph from *Passages*.

353.20 Ghirlandajo] Ridolfo Ghirlandaio (1483–1561), son of the more famous Domenico (see p. 359 below), *The Holy Family with Evangelists* and *The Annunciation*, heavily renovated in 1841. In *Notes* SH spends two pages (416–18) admiring these frescoes.

353.27-30 The Custode . . . little girl.] NH's memory (or interest) apparently failed him here. SH in *Passages* changed "and along some passages" to "into a smaller room"—the Studiola of Francesco I—and rewrote the latter part of the sentence to read: "among whom was one Carolina, an intelligent and pretty child and Bianca Capella." NH may be confusing "the famous" Catherine de' Medici (1519–89), Queen of France, with Caterina de' Medici (1593–1629). If so, SH further confused the situation by changing the name to Carolina. Bianca Capello was the mistress and later the second wife of Francesco I. She was the subject of a blank verse tragedy by the Hawthornes' Florentine acquaintance Elizabeth Clementine Dodge Kinney (1810–89), published in New York by Hurd and Houghton in 1873.

354.5 immense frescoes] By Giorgio Vasari (1511–74) and others, between 1567 and 1571.

354.6–8 Statues . . . round the hall] Michelangelo, *Victory* (1527–28); Giovanni Bologna, *Apollo* (1570); Bandinelli, statues of the Medici family (1540s).

354.11 Faneuil] Faneuil Hall in Boston, known as "The Cradle of Liberty."

355.13–14 This colonnade . . . cloister.] Murray, p. 561: "The walls of a cloister extending from the rt. of the facade are composed of arches, under each of which is an ancient tomb."

356.13 a fountain or a tomb] According to Georg Kauffmann, *Florence: Art Treasures and Buildings* (London: Phaidon, 1971), p. 253, "a fountain was restored in 1859."

356.16–18 These were painted . . . ground.] In *Passages* SH omitted this sentence; in *Notes*, p. 431, she mentioned "curious pictures of events in the Old Testament, by Uccello and Dello, with a good deal of force and utmost *naïveté*." Paulo Uccello (1397–1475) did frescoes of *The Creation* (1431) and *The Flood* (ca. 1445–47). His contemporary Dello Delli may have done some of the others. NH's, and perhaps SH's, error in dating these may come from confusing Uccello's work with that of Turino

Baldese (d. 1348), who first painted Old Testament frescoes in the cloister.

357.1–13   the ancient Chapter House. . . . thieves.] Better known as the Spanish Chapel. In *Notes*, pp. 431–32, SH identifies the frescoes as by Taddeo Gaddi and Simone Memmi (now known as Simone Martini; see p. 539 below). Actually they are by Andrea da Firenze (active ca. 1343–77), and represent the *Sufferings and Imitation of Christ*. SH omitted from *Passages* the sentence "I could not . . . two thieves."

358.12–29   Fra Angelico's pictures. . . . what they were.] SH in *Notes*, p. 433, identifies one of these reliquary panels as the *Madonna of the Star*. The other two are *The Annunciation and Adoration of the Magi* and *The Coronation of the Virgin*. They were moved to the Museo di S. Marco in Florence in 1868. Their authorship by Fra Angelico is questionable; John Pope-Hennessy, *Fra Angelico*, 2nd ed. (London: Phaidon, 1974), pp. 224–25, attributes them to the artist's workshop, and dates them ca. 1434.

358.16–17   "apples of gold in pictures of silver."] Proverbs 25:11.

358.31–32   great black crucifix . . . either of them.] Presumably the crucifix now in the Gondi Chapel, traditionally attributed to Brunelleschi in ca. 1410, according to the anecdote told by Vasari in his biographies of Brunelleschi and Donatello.

359.4   frescoes by Orgagna] Orcagna (Andrea di Cione, ca. 1308–68) did only the altarpiece in this chapel. The frescoes are now attributed to his brother, Nardo di Cione, and dated in the 1350s. See SH's admiring description in *Notes*, pp. 433–34.

359.18   frescoes by Ghirlandaio] Domenico Ghirlandaio (1449–94), the most popular Florentine fifteenth-century painter for nineteenth-century taste (over Botticelli, Masaccio, and Piero della Francesca, for example), painted these frescoes of the lives of the Virgin and St. John the Baptist from 1485 to 1490 with the help of pupils, possibly including Michelangelo.

359.30–360.2 We next saw. . . . gold ground.] Murray, p. 561: "At the end of the rt.-hand transept is the *Capella dei Rucellai*, in which is the celebrated picture, by *Cimabue*, of the Virgin seated on a throne with the infant Saviour on her lap, and three angels on each side, painted upon a gold ground. It shows a marked improvement in drawing beyond the art of the time, and, when produced, it excited the highest admiration. While the painter was employed upon it, Charles d'Anjou passed through Florence, and was taken to see it; none had then seen the picture, but, profiting by the King's admission, all Florence followed; and, such was the wonder excited and pleasure given by it, that the quarter in which Cimabue lived acquired the name of *Borgo Allegri*, which it long retained. When completed the picture was carried from Cimabue's house to the church in triumphal procession." Actually, Murray (following Vasari's "Life of Cimabue") is mistaken here: the *Rucellai Madonna* (1285) is by the Sienese master Duccio di Buoninsegna (ca. 1255–1318). This painting is now in the Uffizi.

360.22–24 church . . . precincts.] Murray, p. 566, describes the French and Austrian occupations; the French ruled during the First Empire, and the Austrians after the republican uprisings of 1848.

361.6 Paul] A silver coin worth two-thirds of a lira, or an American dime, or a little more than five English pennies.

361.11 John of Bologna's Mercury] Made in 1564–65; now in the Bargello (Museo Nazionale).

361.19 Perseus] See p. 288 above.

361.24 the Wrestlers, the Knife-sharpener] Ancient Hellenistic sculptures in the Tribune. NH did not mention them on his first visit (see pp. 293–99 above) because of his overriding interest in the *Venus de' Medici*, but SH was impressed by *The Slave Whetting His Knife* (*Notes*, p. 353).

362.3–10 On the corner. . . . to my eyes.] The Palazzo

Grifoni (now called Riccardi-Mannelli) is misnamed Antinori in most annotations of "The Statue and the Bust," which was first published in *Men and Women* (1855). The statue of Ferdinando dei Medici (1549–1608) was begun by Giovanni Bologna and completed by his disciple Pietro Tacca (1577–1640) in 1608. The bust was, of course, only legendary. The poem may have had a special interest for NH, author of "Wakefield" and "Rappaccini's Daughter." See p. 413.

362.12–13 pillared arcades . . . his scholars.] Brunelleschi designed the foundling hospital on the east side of the piazza in 1419; most of the other arcades, dating from the sixteenth and seventeenth centuries, were designed to harmonize with his work.

362.16–17 frescoes of Andrea del Sarto and others] Andrea del Sarto (1486–1530), *Scenes from the Life of San Filippo Benizzi* (1509–10), *The Voyage of the Magi* (1511), and *The Birth of the Virgin* (1514). The other frescoes, from the same period, are by Jacopo Pontormo, Rosso Fiorentino, and Francesco Franciabigio. The glass enclosure was added in 1833.

363.15–16 Bandinelli . . . interesting] Cellini and Bandinelli contended bitterly for the patronage of Grand Duke Cosimo I dei Medici in 1545. According to Cellini's *Autobiography*, Bandinelli impeded work on his *Perseus*.

363.18–24 This church. . . . rubbish.] NH here paraphrases Murray, p. 546.

364.9–10 It was built . . . Pietro de Medici] Murray, p. 548: "The Chapel of the Annunziata . . . was built in 1448, at the expense of Pietro dei Medici, from the designs of *Michelozzo*." Murray is in error; the donor was Piero de' Medici (1414–69), not his grandson Pietro (1471–1503).

364.18–25 In the inner. . . . see it.] Murray, p. 548: "The wealth lavished here is in honour of a miraculous fresco of the Annunciation, by *Pietro Cavallini* according to Vasari, but painted by angels according to popular belief. As much as 8000 l. sterling has been recently expended on a new crown for the Virgin in this miraculous picture. It is probably of the latter half of the 14th century, and has not much merit as a work of art." Another version of the legend attributes it to a monk named Bartolomeo in 1252; the actual author of the fourteenth-century fresco is unknown.

366.10–11 the new attempt to lay the electric cable] The first attempt to lay the telegraphic cable between Ireland and Newfoundland, promoted and directed by the American manufacturer Cyrus Field, failed in August 1857; his second attempt, begun June 10, 1858, also failed, the cable-layer *Niagara* returning to port in Ireland on July 5. A third attempt succeeded on August 5, 1858, but the current faded out within a few weeks. It was not until 1866 that a lasting cable was successfully laid. There is no record of Powers being consulted. See Samuel Carter III, *Cyrus Field: Man of Two Worlds* (New York: Putnam, 1968). NH referred to the cable in the first entry of *The Ancestral Footstep* on April 1, 1858: "If only those two parts [of the story] could be united across the sea, like the wires of an electric telegraph" (*ACM*, p. 6).

366.19–31 He told an anecdote. . . . intuitive faculty.] Powers was proud of the commission, early in his stay in Washington in 1835, to make a portrait bust of Andrew Jackson at the White House. "The occasion was to be throughout Powers's career, a treasured memory and an anecdote often repeated with varying embellishments for the entertainment of dozing tycoons who, seeking marble immortality, ascended the model's dais in his Florentine studio" (*Yankee Stonecutters*, p. 29).

366.31–34 I have heard . . . his auditor.] Franklin Pierce (1804–69), fourteenth president of the United States, had been NH's close friend at Bowdoin. He served with the army during the Mexican War as a brigadier general. NH owed his opportunity to live in Europe to Pierce's appointment of him to the Liverpool consulate in 1853, in reward for the presidential campaign biography NH wrote in 1852. Both NH and Pierce became enthusiastic supporters of Jackson while in college. Pierce's first public speech, in 1828, advocated Jackson's candidacy for president, and his career was tied to Jackson for several years thereafter.

366.34–367.2   President Buchanan . . . to another.] NH entertained Buchanan twice in Liverpool, in April 1854 (NH to Ticknor, April 30, 1854; MS, Berg), and in January 1855 (EN, pp. 99–100); and saw him in London several times in September 1855 (EN, pp. 220 ff.) Buchanan had known Jackson from the presidential election of 1824 until the latter's death in 1845.

367.7–8   Raphael's picture of Pope Julius II.] NH may be thinking of one of two portraits in Florence, one in the Uffizi and one in the Pitti. See note to 299.6. According to Murray, p. 587, "at Florence no one doubts that *both* are originals." NH later saw another version in the Palazzo Corsini in Rome; see p. 490.22–27.

368.4–6   the architectural character . . . century] The façade is by Gioacchino Pronti (1777–78).

368.14–16   statues of medieval date . . . bas-reliefs] The sculptural works in the S. Antonino Chapel, by Giovanni Bologna and his assistants Francavilla, Portigiani, and Susini, date from 1578 to 1589.

368.16–17   an old wooden crucifix by Giotto] Attributed to Giotto by Vasari, but now considered a work of one of his remote followers.

368.20–22   a very ancient and hideous . . . forgetting it.] An eighth-century Roman mosaic of the Virgin represented in the costume of a Byzantine empress, with imitation mosaic saints and angels added in 1609.

368.22–25   Savonarola . . . Ducal piazza.] Murray, pp. 559–60, devotes a long paragraph to Girolamo Savonarola (1452–98).

368.27   St. Anthony] St. Antoninus (1389–1459), archbishop of Florence and founder of the Convent of S. Marco.

368.29 some old frescoes] By Passignano and Alessandro Allori in the 1580s.

369.1–5 a large cloister. . . . of the cloister] S. Antonino. Fra Angelico, *Christ on the Cross Adored by St. Dominic, St. Dominic, St. Peter Martyr Enjoying Silence, St. Thomas Aquinas, Pietà,* and *Christ as Pilgrim Received by Two Dominicans.* Dated 1438–46. In *Passages* SH changed "Fra Angelico" to "the angelic friar."

369.22–25 a great frescoe. . . . large as life.] *Crucifixion with Attendant Saints* (1441–42).

369.26–370.1 the figures upon. . . . incompetency.] Murray comments, p. 559: "All these figures are nearly upon one plane: the colouring is clear and bright, the drawing timid and incorrect. The expression of the countenances disappoints as to strength, but there is purity and thoughtfulness in the heads."

371.1–2 a woman "in the straw."] A woman in childbirth.

371.4 for the second time] See June 17, 1858, pp. 322–25.

371.9–12 There is what . . . after.] Murray, p. 605: "Buffalmacco, a very curious picture, bearing the date of 1316, relative to Sta. Umilita of Faenza." Buffalmacco's dates are 1262–1340.

371.12–13 Adoration . . . Fabriano] See p. 323.11.

371.15–19 Three pictures by Perugino. . . . since.] Compare 324.5–15. SH in *Notes,* pp. 454–56, mentions a Pietà, and a Deposition (1504; painted with Filippino Lippi).

371.28–372.23 I looked again. . . . this picture.] See 324.15–20 above. SH in *Notes,* p. 464 (July 23, 1858), mentions that NH called Carlo Dolci "Sweet Charles."

372.27 a statue of Saint Matthew, by Michael Angelo.] Ca. 1506; thought to reflect his reaction to the discovery of the Laocoön group in Rome in January 1506.

373.4–5 the Bargello] Compare 352.11–25.

373.20–25 an old chapel. . . . portrait of Dante.] The Podestà
Chapel. The frescoes, ca. 1330–40, are by assistants of Giotto,
including Maso di Bianco, Puccio Capanna, and Taddeo Gaddi.
They depict the lives of St. Mary Magdalene and St. John the
Baptist, Hell, and Paradise. Dante's portrait was recognized in the
Paradise; see p. 392 below. Murray, p. 578, indicates that attempts
at restoration of the portrait of Dante have led to its being "almost
completely ruined." See note to 392.17–18.

374.3–5 two or three Gothic tombs . . . them.] Identified
by SH as by Mino da Fiesole (1429–84) in *Notes*, p. 457. The
subjects are Count Ugo of Tuscany (d. 1001) and Bernardo
Guigni.

374.13–14 the finest . . . of Fra Lippo Lippi.] This is the
judgment of Murray, p. 550, and of SH in *Notes*, p. 457. The
artist, however, is Filippino Lippi (1457–1504), son of Fra Lippo
Lippi. The subject is the *Apparition of the Virgin to St. Bernard*.

374.21 Luca della Robbia] (1400–1482).

374.33–34 we admired anew . . . Mercury] See p. 361,
above.

375.2–3 a bronze bust . . . Cellini] The bust is of Cosimo I
(1547), as noted by Murray, p. 597, and also by SH in *Notes*, p.
458. In *Passages* she omitted the parenthesis showing NH's uncertainty.

375.21 sketching out a Romance] In *Passages* SH explicitly
identified *MF*.

375.23–24 little heart for journalizing and describing new
things] NH's diary mentions visits to the Pitti on July 19 and
to the Uffizi on July 24. SH recorded the first, and her own visits
to S. Maria del Carmine (Masaccio frescoes, Brancacci Chapel),
S. Trinità (frescoes by Ghirlandaio, Sassetti Chapel), Orsanmichele, and the Corsini and Guadagni palaces, in *Notes*, pp. 459–72.

375.31　The bridegroom] In *Passages* SH added: "son of the Countess of St. G——"; Ada Shepard identified him as "young Lord Selby, the son of the Pope's Chamberlain." Mgr. George Talbot (1816–86) was the chamberlain of Pius IX.

377.2　A Madonna of Raphael's] *The Madonna of the Grand Duke* (1505), bought by Ferdinando II of Tuscany in 1799. See p. 403.

377.11　Perugino's pictures] SH mentions, *Notes*, p. 454, that NH had seen in the Pitti Gallery the *Lamentation over the Dead Christ* (1495). See 402.33–34 below. Also in the Pitti were a *Saint Mary Magdalen* and an *Adoration of the Holy Child*, and in the Uffizi, *Madonna and Child with Two Saints* (1493).

378.1　Master Bob] Robert Powers, described by JH (who was 12) as "a few years older than I" in *HC*, pp. 336–37.

378.13–14　a manufacturer of organs] In the mid-1820s while working in Luman Watson's clock factory in Cincinnati, Powers "invented a new reed that could be tuned by twisting a screw" (Crane, p. 174).

379.2–9　We reasoned high . . . we possess.] Probably this idea had been discussed by NH and Melville in the Berkshires in 1850 or 1851.

379.29　Villa Montauto] In *Passages* SH added "Monte Beni."

382.33　Galileo's tower] The Torre del Gallo, celebrated in Milton's description of the moon in *Paradise Lost*, 1, 287–89: "whose orb / Through optic glass the Tuscan artist views / At evening, from the top of Fesole."

383.4–7　it lacked only water. . . . it is seen.] NH seems to be recalling the "Red House" in Lenox, with its clear view of Lake Mahkeenoc (Stockbridge Bowl) to the south.

387.4　another subject for sculpture] Probably the *Libyan*

Sibyl, which was exhibited with *Cleopatra* in London in 1862, and shared the fame of that statue.

387.6–8   his sketches . . . recovered.] *Roba di Roma* (Boston: Ticknor and Fields, 1862), first published serially in the *Atlantic Monthly* in seven installments, from April 1859 through June 1860.

387.28–30   the pillar . . . of the Immaculate Conception] The Immaculate Conception was proclaimed in December 1854 by the pope on his sole authority, a precedent for the dogma of Papal Infallibility of 1870. The tall column in the Piazza di Spagna was surmounted with a statue of the Virgin in 1856.

388.1–2   Lord Clifford] Hugh Charles Clifford, seventh Lord Clifford of Chudleigh (1790–1858), had resided for several years in the neighborhood of Tivoli, near Rome. He died at Rome on February 28, 1858, of the effects of a wound in the ankle (*DNB*).

390.29   Mr. Kirkup] Seymour Kirkup (1788–1880) had studied to be an artist in his youth, and had been the friend of Blake and Haydon. He lived permanently in Italy from about 1820; he was present at the funerals of Keats and Shelley. He became in time a tourist attraction for the English and Americans visiting Florence, for his relics and his mine of anecdotes and stories. His spiritualist activities are described in Porter, *Through a Glass Darkly*, and in Giuliana Arton Treves, *The Golden Ring: The Anglo-Florentines, 1847–1862*, trans. Sylvia Sprigge (London: Longmans, Green, 1956), pp. 56–61. See also McAleer, p. 15 n.8; David Robertson, "Weave a Circle: Baron Kirkup and his Greatest Friends," in *From Smollett to James: A Festschrift for Edgar Johnson* (forthcoming).

392.17–18   Giotto's fresco of Dante] Kirkup took credit for discovering the portrait, but the project was apparently initiated by the American poet and scholar Richard Henry Wilde (1789–1847) and the Anglo-Italian Giovanni Aubrey Bezzi. They enlisted Kirkup's assistance because of his antiquarian knowledge. Shortly after the whitewash was removed from the fresco and the likeness of Dante was discovered on July 21, 1840, Kirkup surreptitiously made his sketch, and it became valuable when efforts to restore the painting did not succeed very well. After Wilde's death, Kirkup began to take all the credit for initiating the project. The painting is now generally attributed to the school of Giotto; by 1962 it had become unrecognizable, according to Kauffmann, *Florence*, p. 330. The fullest account of the incident is Edward L. Tucker, *Richard Henry Wilde: His Life and Selected Poems* (Athens: University of Georgia Press, 1966), pp. 57–58. Murray, p. 578, mentions the "faithful tracing" of the fresco by "Mr. Kirkup, our countryman."

393.12   This child's mother] Regina Ronti (1837–56) was considered by Browning and others a fraud; according to Austen Henry Layard, "a more transparent case of imposture" than her spiritual communications "it would have been difficult to imagine." See Treves, *The Golden Ring*, p. 59. In editing this paragraph for *Passages*, SH increased greatly the impression of NH's skepticism.

393.18   that potentate communicated] Czar Alexander I of Russia (1777–1825). The last years of his reign were marked by increasing popular embitterment toward him because of his reactionary policies, leading to the speculation that his death was from poison.

393.24   the child of Mr. Kirkup] Browning wrote to Isa Blagden of Kirkup: "—he is as much Imogen's father as I am— but what use in beginning the inventory of his absurdities?" (McAleer, p. 352).

394.8–9   the child . . . into a Romance] Kirkup, the girl, and her kitten did contribute to NH's conception of *The Dolliver Romance* in 1864. *See* ELM, p. 580. Kirkup's appearance in chapter 28 of *MF* is noted by Helen Rose Selkis Mahan, *Hawthorne's The Marble Faun: A Critical Introduction and Annotation* (Ann Arbor: University Microfilms, 1966; Ph.D. dissertation, University of Rochester, 1966), p. 412; Richard H. Rupp, ed., *The Marble Faun*, by Nathaniel Hawthorne (Indianapolis: Bobbs,

Merrill, 1971), pp. 243–44; Kerr, *Mediums, and Spirit-Rappers, and Roaring Radicals*, p. 62.

394.31–32   Lady Catherine Fleming] Lady Katherine Elizabeth Cochrane Fleming (d. 1868), wife of John Browne Willis Fleming (1815–72), and daughter of the naval hero Lord Admiral Thomas Cochrane, tenth earl of Dundonald (1775–1860) (*DNB*).

395.7   Trelawney] Edward John Trelawny (1792–1881), adventurer and author, published his autobiographical *Adventures of a Younger Son* in 1831. He is best remembered for his friendships with Shelley and Byron, and *Recollections of the Last Days of Shelley and Byron* (1858). He tells in *Recollections*, section 21, of arriving in Missolonghi soon after Byron's death, and of uncovering his embalmed body to discover that "both his feet were clubbed, and his legs withered to the knee" (ed. J. E. Morpurgo, [New York: Philosophical Library, 1952], pp. 165–66). Byron had concealed the cause of his lameness, which had caused much speculation. Trelawny said that it was a withered Achilles' tendon. His explanation is now considered unreliable; see Leslie A. Marchand, *Byron: A Biography* (New York: Knopf, 1957), p. 1238.

396.5   a good Italian incident . . . in Vasary] This apocryphal incident is recorded in Giorgio Vasari's *Lives of the Most Eminent Painters, Sculptors, and Architects* (1550), trans. Gaston DuC. DeVere (London: Warner, 1912–14), III, 103–4. Vasari's account is retold in M. Valery [Antoine Claude Pasquin, 1789–1847], *Historical, Literary, and Artistic Travels in Italy*, trans. C. E. Clifton (Paris: Baudry, 1842), p. 367. NH's version comes directly from Valery. In fact, Andrea del Castagno died in 1457, at the age of 36, four years before Domenico Veneziano. In *Passages* SH changed "Vasary" to "Valery."

397.4–6   Mr. Powers related . . . at his house.] In the autumn of 1855. See note to 301.22–23.

397.9   Countess Cotterel] Sophia Augusta Tulk Cottrell, wife of Count Henry Cottrell, an English artist and member of the household of the last duke of Lucca, from whom he received his title. They were close friends of the Brownings from 1847 onward.

397.32–33 Mr. Kinney] William Burnet Kinney (1799–1880) had been U.S. minister to the court of Sardinia at Turin from 1850 until 1853. He and his wife Elizabeth (whose child by her first marriage was the poet and critic Edward Clarence Stedman) then moved to Florence, where they lived for a time in the Casa del Bello. For an account of her diary, see Lewis Leary, " 'The Congenial Few': An Expatriate Diary, 1854–1855," in James Woodress, ed., *Essays Mostly on Periodical Publishing in America: A Collection in Honor of Clarence Gohdes* (Durham: Duke University Press, 1973), pp. 22–34. See note to 353.27–30.

399.13–14 Mary Runnel] In *NHHW*, I, 31–35, JH tells the story of Mary Rondel. After NH's death Julian came into possession of a copy of Sidney's *Arcadia*, brought to America by Major William Hathorne in 1630. In it the name "Mary Rondel" was found with that of Daniel Hathorne, NH's grandfather, with other indications of a liaison between them. Old residents of Salem told Julian that about 1755 Daniel was in love with Mary but the affair ended unhappily, and that she died soon afterward. JH speculated that NH had not read the *Arcadia* for twenty years previous to Miss Shepard's spirit messages, and that "it is impossible to suppose that there was any collusion between him and the medium on that occasion." But there is reason to question JH's identification of Mary Rondel with Mary Runnel. In her journal of August 24, SH described that evening's séance: "Mary Runnel said she was Mr Boott's friend & could help him . . . " (MS, Berg).

402.33–34 some sketches . . . by Perugino] The *Lamentation*. See note to 377.11.

403.8–10 Raphael shows . . . especial Madonna] See p. 377.2.

403.13 designs for frescoes, I think, in the Vatican] In *Notes*, p. 481, SH identifies the Vatican frescoes as *The Expulsion of Heliodorus* and *The Release of St. Peter from Prison*.

404.1   San Michele] Orsanmichele. See pages 346, 351.

404.6–11   Within stand statues. . . . it means something.] See pp. 346.34–347.2 and note thereto.

404.12   crazias] A copper coin worth one-eighth of a paul, or a little more than one American cent.

405.18   the Museum of Natural History] See p. 309, above.

405.21–22   a colossal statue of Galileo] By Aristodemo Costoli (1803–71). The Tribune was erected by Grand Duke Leopold II in 1840 (Murray, p. 604).

407.22–25   The gate of a city . . . painter or writer.] See also p. 412 below.

408.32   Sir John Hawkwood's painted effigy] See p. 322.15–16 and note.

409.2–3   the scene of . . . attempted assassination] Murray, p. 533: "It was in [the Ancient Sacristy] that *Lorenzo de' Medici* took refuge when he escaped the daggers of the Pazzi." Lorenzo was wounded in the cathedral during the Pazzi conspiracy of 1478.

409.5   Bank] See note to 309.4. Murray, p. 580, says of the Palazzo Uguccione: "Its design has been attributed to Raphael, and Michael Angelo, but with the greatest probability to the latter; it is now occupied by Messrs. Fenzi and Hall, the well-known bankers."

409.7   a letter from General Pierce] Having failed to win Democratic renomination in 1856, Franklin Pierce retired from the presidency in March 1857. With his wife he began an extended trip in November. They spent the winter of 1858 on the island of Madeira, and in the spring proceeded to tour Portugal, Spain, France, and Switzerland. On March 28 Pierce wrote to Horatio Bridge, "I dwell with much satisfaction upon the prospect of meeting Hawthorne and of passing perhaps a few months with

him at some agreeable place on the Continent" (MS, Bowdoin).
NH's diary, September 6, notes that Pierce's letter to him came
from Geneva.

409.23   Greater things] In *Passages* SH explained "Greater"
by adding "[larger]".

410.1   Ponte Grazie] The Ponte alle Grazie; corrected in
Passages by SH.

412.24   I have already described this church] See pp. 362–65.

412.25–27   the profuse gilding . . . in oils] The ceiling was
decorated by Pietro Giambelli in 1664–69, from a design by
Volterrano (Baldassare Franceschini, 1611–89), who also painted
the *Assumption and Coronation of the Virgin* (1676–83). SH
omitted this description from *Passages*.

413.28–31   the bronze statue . . . after all.] Compare with
362.3–10.

414.19–20   I wonder . . . Croce!] See p. 342.

414.23   Andrea del Sarto's pictures] Eighteen paintings, in-
cluding three Annunciations, two Assumptions of the Virgin, three
Madonnas, two Holy Families, a Lamentation, a Dispute of the
Holy Trinity, two scenes from the life of Joseph, and a St. John
the Baptist. NH may be influenced by Browning's "Andrea del
Sarto," in *Men and Women* (1855). See p. 428.

414.30–31   the minute accuracy . . . fruit and flowers] See
pp. 297, 315.

417.14–15   Christ spoke . . . rose from the dead."] Luke
16:31.

417.20   Major Gregorie] Major Charles Gregorie (1791–1858)
died on October 10, shortly after the Hawthornes' departure from
Florence.

417.21   Mrs Crossman] Mrs. Annie Crossman was Major Gregorie's widowed sister (McAleer, p. 16).

417.24   Mrs. Baker . . . written statement] Mrs. Eric Baker, née Georgina Crossman, lent NH a translation of a popular Italian story, *Veronica Chivo*, by Domenico Guerrazzi (1804–73), which NH found "outrageously passionate," though perhaps tolerable to the Italian taste (NH to Mrs. Baker, August 27, 1858; MS, St. Lawrence). Mrs. Baker in 1862 provided Browning with a manuscript source for *The Ring and the Book* (McAleer, p. 127). The "written statement of her experiences with a ghost" is in D. D. Home, *Incidents in My Life* (New York: Carleton, 1863), pp. 127–34.

419.1–2   an incident . . . at the Old Manse] In a letter to her mother of February 28, 1843, SH mentioned that "our ghost has been twice lately. Once he pushed my shoulder at midnight when I was awake, and once he coughed and groaned" (MS, Berg).

419.12   Dr Harris] Thaddeus Mason Harris (1768–1842), pastor of the Unitarian church in Dorchester, Massachusetts, from 1793 to 1836. NH told the story of Harris and the Atheneum in Liverpool in 1855, and wrote it down for Mrs. John Pemberton Heywood on August 17, 1856 (*EN*, pp. 106, 634 n. 148); it was first published in 1900 as "The Ghost of Doctor Harris" in *The Nineteenth Century*, XLVII (1900), 88–93, and reprinted in *The Living Age*, CCXXIV (February 10, 1900), 345–49.

419.20   Mrs. Hillard] Susan Tracy Howe Hillard (1808–79), daughter of Judge Samuel Howe of Northampton, Massachusetts, married George Hillard in 1835.

419.26–420.10   we saw (for the second time). . . . in marble] See pp. 326–28.

421.26–29   The Custode showed . . . finely done.] SH in *Notes* gives more detail: "We were first shown the earliest manuscripts of the Pandects of Justinian. . . . We saw also, in the same case, the famous earliest manuscript of Virgil; and the

Decameron, much interlined, with many notes on the margin; Cicero's epistles, copied by Petrarch; Aristotle, in a dozen folios; Horatius Flaccus, with an autograph of Petrarch, showing it to have been his property; an old Evangel from Trebizond, and beautiful colored contemporaneous portraits of Petrarch and Laura, as illuminations in the Canzoniere" (p. 495).

424.23–30   the picture of the nativity. . . . her child.] See note to 350.18–21.

424.33   Enthronement . . . Andrea del Sarto] Presumably *The Madonna of the Harpies* (1517).

424.34   the Dancing Faun] One of the Hellenistic statues in the Tribune, along with the *Venus de' Medici*, the *Wrestlers*, and the *Knife-Sharpener*.

428.6–9   the frequency . . . art and nature] See p. 414.

428.15–23   a small picture. . . . strange grandeur.] David Teniers the Elder, *An Old Chemist*. Compare note to 297.10–12.

428.30   smaller church and convent] The Franciscan convent of S. Salvatore del Monte.

430.21   the comet] Donati's Comet, named for Giovanni Battista Donati (1826–73), who had discovered it in Florence on June 2, 1858. "Each day after sunset the mighty and brilliant comet of Donati stretched itself across the valley in a great fiery arch, and remained in view till near morning" (JH, *NHHW*, II, 198). The comet came nearest to the earth on October 10. Its period has been calculated to be approximately two thousand years.

430.30–431.27   he talked about his treatment. . . . workmen.] See p. 280.9–15 and note. After great pressure from friends of Powers in 1853, Montgomery C. Meigs (1816–92), who was in charge of decoration of the Capitol, sent identical letters to Powers and Crawford requesting them to submit designs for the sculptured pediment of the extension of the building. Meigs suggested that the two work together; both refused, Crawford because he wanted to pursue his own ideas, and Powers because he was deeply offended that Crawford was considered his equal. Crawford went ahead to plan his *Progress of Civilization* group, and to offer the entire group for $20,000; Powers wanted $20,000 for his *America* alone. Powers had priced himself out of the market, and he refused further involvement with the pediment. In petulant correspondence with friends in America, he accused Crawford of plagiarizing his *America* in the rendition of *Liberty*. Powers's friend Edward Everett, in an effort to bypass Meigs, approached President Pierce; in 1855 Pierce offered to appoint a committee to judge the "fitness and value" of *America*. NH noted Powers's complaint in a letter to Pierce, October 27, 1858, repeating his supposition that Pierce "acted by deputy," and suggesting that Pierce "set yourself right with him . . . for he is a good and sensible (though very sensitive) man, as well as a great artist" (MS, New Hampshire Historical Society). Finally, in 1859 President Buchanan contracted with Powers for statues of Franklin and Jefferson; *America* was not mentioned. See Crane, pp. 239–42; Gale, *Thomas Crawford*, pp. 108–16.

432.1   equestrian statue of General Jackson] By Clark Mills. See note to 279.30–31.

432.8   Mr. Miniati] George (or Giorgio) Mignaty (1824–95), a Greek living in Florence, was a painter of historical subjects. He helped James Jackson Jarves, the Bostonian, to assemble his collection of medieval and Renaissance paintings; it was substantially complete by the summer of 1858. The collection was eventually sold to Yale University. Mignaty somehow knew the location of many valuable old pictures, and he was a clever restorer. See Francis Steegmuller, *The Two Lives of James Jackson Jarves* (New Haven: Yale University Press, 1951), p. 134; Treves, *The Golden Ring*, p. 71. Jarves apparently did not meet NH in Florence. He may not yet have returned from America, or he may have been unavailable socially because of his quarreling with his wife at this time; see Steegmuller, p. 162.

432.23–25 the interest he has taken . . . a wish to acquire his art.] After six months in Italy in 1855–56, Home went to Paris. He had become a Roman Catholic in Rome, and had given up his séances for one year's time. But when summoned by Louis Napoleon in February, 1857, his powers restored, he gave a series of famous performances in the Tuileries; throughout 1857 his conquest of the French court and his favor with the Empress Eugénie were favorite subjects for the European and American press. Louis Napoleon was considered a good amateur magician.

432.27–28 bronze statue of Webster] See note to 320.19–20.

432.30–31 a vessel which was lost] The *Lucy Francis* was not lost but finally arrived in Boston in early 1859 after a passage from Leghorn of 105 days. See Crane, p. 247.

435.31–32 on the night when Lorenzo the Magnificent died.] At the death of Lorenzo, April 8, 1492, "the agitation of the public mind was increased by a singular coincidence of calamitous events. . . . For three nights, gleams of light were said to have been perceived proceeding from the hill of Fiesole, and hovering above the church of S. Lorenzo, where the remains of the family were deposited" (William Roscoe, *The Life of Lorenzo de' Medici*, 8th ed. [London: Bohn, 1846], p. 333).

436.10 model of the statue of America] See note to 430.30–431.27.

437.20 at six °clock] Murray, p. 177: "The [railway] traveller, by leaving Florence early, will arrive at Siena before 11 A.M."

437.31 the Leopoldo railway] Murray, p. 177: "The station of the Leopoldo Railway at Florence is outside and close to the Porta al Prato, the gate leading to the Cascine."

438.14–15 At Empoli . . . Leghorn] Murray, p. 177: "the line is the same as that to Pisa and Leghorn . . . as far as Empoli, from where the branch to Siena ascends the Val d'Elsa."

439.1–8 In the latter. . . . trumpery.] Murray, p. 182: "From Poggibonsi the railway follows the valley of the Staggia nearly to the source of the river: the ascent is very rapid, being about 750 feet in a distance of 16 m. . . . 2 m. before arriving at Siena the railroad enters a tunnel nearly a mile long (1661 yards), pierced in the hill of San Dalmazzo. . . . A mile beyond this tunnel we arrive at the *Siena* Stat., close to the newly opened Porta di San Lorenzo, which leads into the principal streets of the city."

439.14 the Aquila Nera] Described by Murray, p. 183, as "good, but in a more remote situation [than the Hotel Royal], but nearer the Cathedral and other sights."

439.15 Mrs. Story] NH had written to Mrs. Story on September 29 suggesting that she meet the Hawthornes at the hotel, at her leisure, rather than at the railroad station (MS, Berg).

439.25 Palazzo Tolomei] Begun in 1208, the oldest private palace in Siena. The column with the wolf was erected in 1260 to commemorate the victory over Florence at Montaperti. According to legend Senus, the founder of the city, was the son of Remus.

440.14 Mr. and Mrs. Story came] The Storys had first summered in Siena in 1857 (Henry James, *William Wetmore Story and His Friends*, II, 3).

442.1 bringing it back to me] SH added in *Passages*, in parentheses: "It was left behind, under one of the rail carriage seats."

443.27–30 antique fountain . . . del Fonte.] Murray, p. 191: "The *Fountain*, called the *Fonte Gaja*, gave the name 'della Fonte' to *Jacopo della Quercia* [1371–1438], who executed the marble bas-reliefs, representing various subjects of Scripture history, now unfortunately damaged."

444.7 the Cathedral.] Begun in the twelfth century and completed in 1382. The façade, with its remarkable sculptured figures, was designed by Giovanni Pisano (ca. 1250–ca. 1328) under French Gothic influence.

446.8 toiling at Brook Farm] Compare *BR*, pp. 65–66: "Pausing in the field, to let the wind exhale the moisture from our foreheads, we were to look upward, and catch glimpses into the far-off soul of truth"; and NH to SH, May 4, 1841 (MS, Huntington): "All the morning, I have been at work under the clear blue sky, on a hillside. Sometimes it almost seemed as if I were at work in the sky itself; though the material in which I wrought was the ore from our gold mine [manure pile]."

448.3–13 It may be. . . . adequate expression.] Omitted by SH from *Passages*, but the last two sentences were published by JH in *HC*, p. 287. See the Historical Commentary.

449.6–7 Mr. and Mrs. Black] Charles Christopher Black (1809–79), curator of the South Kensington Museum in London, and from 1863 to 1869 provisional assistant keeper of the Victoria and Albert Museum, lived in Italy for many years, where he carried out special commissions for these museums. He wrote a life of Michelangelo (1875), and translated a French study of arms and armor (1870).

449.7 the next villa] The Villa Marciana.

450.18–19 pulpits of carved marble] The masterpiece of Nicola Pisano (ca. 1206–80) in 1265–68, is described by SH in *Notes*, pp. 501–2.

451.1–2 the Institute of the Fine Arts] Now the Pinacoteca Nazionale.

451.8 a picture by Guido da Siena] Murray, p. 189, mentions "the celebrated Madonna by *Guido da Siena*, with the date 1221, nineteen years before the birth of Cimabue, on the strength of which the Sienese claim the honor of being the earliest school of art." Earlier, p. 184, Murray more cautiously characterizes the school of Siena as "in antiquity . . . nearly equal to that of

Florence." The picture was located in the church of S. Domenico, but it is now in the Palazzo Pubblico. Guido da Siena is unknown beyond the signature and date of the Madonna. Some authorities now judge it likely that the picture dates from as late as 1280.

451.13 early productions of the Sienese school] Including Guido da Siena, *Virgin and Child* (1262); Duccio, *Madonna of the Franciscans* (ca. 1290–95); Ambrogio Lorenzetti, *Maestà* (1330s). SH in *Notes*, p. 502, showed no greater interest: "We saw pictures in tempera from 1200 to those in oils in 1500. Very quaint Madonnas and holy Infants, all evidently from some sacred type, perhaps Greek—with long noses, low foreheads, small eyes, and interminable fingers, with the babe always mature in expression."

451.33 a picture by Sodoma] Murray, p. 185, describes "the magnificent fresco of Christ bound to the column [1514], one of the finest productions of the second period of the Siennese school." The school of Siena, Murray notes, p. 184, "declined until the time of Sodoma [1477–1549], a follower of Leonardo da Vinci, whose merits were so great that he was employed on the decorations of the Vatican and the Farnesina Palace in Rome." SH admired Sodoma's paintings in Siena greatly, and concluded (*Notes*, p. 511) that "Sodoma is more like Raphael than any other painter, I think." Jeffrey Meyers, *Painting and the Novel* (New York: Barnes and Noble, 1975), p. 6, attacks "the philistine and provincial" NH for praising "the 'touching' spirituality of the aptly named 'Sodoma',", citing Vasari's account of the painter's sexual aberration and depravity.

452.17 Sodoma . . . was earlier than Perugino] Sodoma followed Perugino (1445–1523) by one generation. SH has it correct in *Notes*, p. 506: "Sodoma was after Perugino, and broke free from the hard line of previous schools."

452.28–29 one of the gates . . . to Florence] The Porta Camollia.

454.1–456.4 I even noted. . . . about completed.] Omitted

by SH from *Passages*, with the bracketed comment: "Here follow several pages of moving objects." JH noted in *HC*, p. 355: "My father, according to a common custom of his, sat for an hour at the window one day and made a note of every person who passed through the little square, thus getting an idea of the character of the local population not otherwise obtainable."

454.7　a church] S. Cristofano.

457.9–10　a picture of the Virgin by Sodoma] SH in *Notes*, p. 509, identifies this as a Madonna and Child.

457.18–19　eight Popes . . . Siena.] Murray, p. 191, reports "eight popes and thirty-nine cardinals."

460.34　Monte Aperto] Montaperti. See note to 439.25.

463.9–10　which gate . . . San Viene.] Perhaps the Porta S. Marco, at the southwest corner of the city.

470.22　castle of the Robber-knight] Murray, p. 196, mentions "the ruined castle of Ghino di Tacco, the robber-knight, whose seizure of the abbot Clugny when on his way to take the mineral waters of Tuscany, is celebrated by Boccaccio." See the *Decameron*, tenth day, second tale.

471.14　our hotel] Murray, p. 196, describes this inn as "lately improved—but exorbitant, *if the prices are not agreed upon beforehand*—and the best sleeping-place for the first night from Siena."

472.29　everybody in Radicofani] Murray, p. 196, says that Radicofani "contains nothing to attract attention, except the wild dress and appearance of its inhabitants."

474.11–17　a blast howled. . . . the corridor.] Murray, p. 196, mentions that the inn's "vast range of apartments, with their high black raftered roofs, and the long passages, were considered by Mr. Beckford a fitting scene of a sabbath of witches." See William Beckford, *Italy* (London: Bentley, 1834), I, 226.

475.12–476.10   At Ponte Centino. . . . to be broken.] Murray, p. 197, describes "*Ponte Centino*, the Papal frontier station and custom-house, on the left bank of the Elvella, near the point where that torrent and the Siele fall into the Paglia. Passports are signed here but persons travelling by diligence are not annoyed by an examination of their luggage . . . [neither are] those travelling by post or vetturino, on the administration of a small fee, or provided they have obtained a *lascia passare*."

479.1–2   two islands . . . murder] Murray, p. 199: "The two small islands, the largest called *Bisentina*, and the smallest *Martana*, are picturesque objects from the hills. The latter is memorable as the scene of the imprisonment and murder of Amalasontha, queen of the Goths, the only daughter of Theodoric and the niece of Clovis; she was strangled in her bath, A.D. 535, by the order or with the connivance of her cousin Theodatus, whom she had raised to a share in the kingdom."

481.32–482.1   It was originally . . . statues.] This fact is recorded by Murray, p. 198, on the authority of Pliny, *Natural History*, 34, 16. The city was taken by the Romans in 280 B.C.

483.6–7   the famous stewed eels . . . Pope Martin] NH follows Murray, p. 199, who mentions that the lake's eels "are commemorated by Dante, who says that Pope Martin IV killed himself by eating them to excess," and quotes *Purgatorio* 24, 20–24, in the original. J. Chesley Mathews, "Hawthorne's Knowledge of Dante," *University of Texas Studies in English*, No. 20 (1940), p. 161, chastized NH for forgetting "that Dante neither mentioned the Pope's name nor stated that stewed eels killed him." Commentators on Dante are agreed, however, that NH's information is correct.

484.16–19   I was sorry . . . John de Foucris.] Murray, p. 200, explains that Bishop Johann Fugger's monument is in Montefiascone, where he died, "caused by his drinking too freely of the wine to which he has given such extraordinary celebrity." The wine's name, *est*, came from the bishop's valet's custom of writing *est* (*it is good*) on the wall when he had approved the wine. Johannes de Foucris is the Latin version of the bishop's name, on his epitaph as given by Murray.

485.1–3   It is said to be Gothic . . . pillars.] Murray, p. 201: "The *Cathedral*, dedicated to San Lorenzo, is a Gothic edifice, built on the site of an ancient temple of Hercules."

485.13–19   But there is no use. . . . towards the tail.] Murray, pp. 201–2, retells these events in detail, quoting Dante, *Inferno*, 12, 115–20 on Guy de Montfort and Prince Henry, but does not mention the emperor's setting the pope on an ass.

485.20–486.2   Passing a church. . . . fact.] Murray, p. 203, gives this information about the church of S. Angelo in Spata, dating Galiana, "the Helen of the Middle Ages," at 1138.

485.22   Meleager's boar-hunt] In Greek mythology Meleager, son of King Oineus of Kalydon, did battle with the great boar sent to ravage the county by the goddess Artemis. The story is told in Ovid's *Metamorphoses*, book 8. NH had taken an interest in this myth in *EN*, p. 107 (April 12, 1856), when describing a germ of *The Ancestral Footstep*: "It would be something similar to the story of Meleager, whose fate depended on the firebrand that his mother had snatched out of the flames." The Fates had announced at his birth that he would live until the brand burned. After he killed the boar, Meleager quarreled with his mother, and she threw the brand into the fire, killing him.

487.30   Le Sette Vene] This place does not appear on modern maps. Murray, p. 277, describes it as "a large and good inn, certainly the best between Civita Castellana and Rome, being 16 miles from the former and 22 miles from the latter. . . . The vetturini very properly prefer Sette Vene as a resting-place to either Monterosi or Baccano."

488.28–29   68, piazza Poli] Near the Palazzo Castellani and the Fontana di Trevi. See p. 491.18–33.

490.14   Longara] Via della Lungara.

490.20–21   portraits by Holbein, Titian, Rembrandt, Rubens]
Murray, pp. 253–54, lists Hans Holbein the Younger, *Henry VIII of England* (1539); Titian, *Cardinal Alessandro Farnese;*
Rubens, *St. Sebastian.*

490.23–27   a portrait of Pope Julius II . . . as those.] See p.
367.7–8. NH is mistaken; the Corsini portrait is a copy of that
in the Pitti. NH does not mention seeing this picture in *EN.*

490.30   Queen Christina's] Christina of Sweden, who lived
from 1662 until her death in 1689 in the Palazzo Riario, on the
site of which the Palazzo Corsini was built in the eighteenth century. NH wrote a brief account of her in his 1842 *Biographical Stories for Children*; see *TS*, pp. 275–83.

493.11   the tomb of the baker Eurysaces] Erected in the first
century B.C. Discovered in 1838.

495.12–13   to sketch in the Coliseum] Changed by SH in *Passages* to "in the Palace of the Caesars, while Mrs. S—— sketched
the ruins." Ada Shepard reported that on Sunday October 24
she and Una had spent the day in peaceful isolation in the ruins
of the Palace of the Caesars. Una caught a severe cold there, and
by the following Thursday was afflicted by a raging fever.

496.5   a forest of Ardennes] Apparently a reference to the
forest of Arden in Shakespeare's *As You Like It.*

496.23   Feb. 27th, 1859. Sunday.] A letter from Rome in the
New York *Times* for April 4, 1859, "by Pericles," dated February
26, comments: "HAWTHORNE I frequently see in the street,
swinging along with a sort of land-measuring pace, smoking, and
occasionally looking out from under his shaggy brow, and otherwise timorous face. He avoids all society, and is said to be engaged
on some new work, the subject of which is not even known by his
wife."

496.27   masks] This was the first carnival since the revolution
of 1848 at which full masks were allowed.

498.2–499.5 The tower in the Via Portoghese. . . . in the palace.] Omitted by SH from *Passages*; published by JH in *HC*, pp. 360–62. See p. 216, above.

499.7–15 the weather. . . . flowers and sweets.] This passage, omitted by SH from *Passages* because of its use in *MF*, was published by JH in *HC*, pp. 283–86, along with subsequent omissions from *Passages* at 499.30–501.18 and 502.6–26.

501.10 Mr. Mountford] William Mountford (1816–85) was born in England and came to the United States in 1849. After being a Unitarian minister, he retired in Cambridge, Massachusetts. He was an early convert to spiritualism. He wrote several books on religious subjects, notably *Euthanasy; or, Happy Talk toward the End of Life* (Boston: Crosby and Nichols, 1848). In 1853 he had married the heiress Elizabeth Boardman Crowninshield (1804–84), a cousin of NH's onetime friend Mary Silsbee.

501.19 The prince of Wales] Albert Edward, later King Edward VII (1841–1910) was in Rome, as "Baron Renfrew," from late January till late April 1859. He visited the pope and many "duly approved English sojourners," including Browning and Gibson, and the American John Lothrop Motley. At the outbreak of war in April, he was hastily taken away by a British ship. See *DNB*.

501.22 Mrs. Motley's] Mary Elizabeth Benjamin Motley (1813–74), sister of Park Benjamin, the poet, editor, and reviewer, and wife of John Lothrop Motley (1814–77), the historian. SH had known her since the early 1830s in Boston. The Motleys were married in 1837, and NH and SH had gone together to visit them soon thereafter; see SH to her father, February 9, 1838 (MS, Berg). The Motleys had spent most of the 1850s in Europe, while he was preparing *The Rise of the Dutch Republic* (1856) and *The History of the United Netherlands* (1860–68). They were in England for most of 1858, arriving in Rome for the winter in early October.

503.12 Dr. Franco] Una's physician during her long illness

of 1858–59. He is first mentioned in NH's diary on October 28, 1858. Murray, p. xviii, lists him first among the "Homeopathic Physicians" at Rome: "Dr. Franco, a Maltese, No. 81, Via della Croce, is the principal practitioner in this line at Rome, and speaks English—he is much employed by the Roman nobility, and foreigners resorting to Rome."

504.5   moccolletto] The *festa dei moccoletti*, festivity of the little tapers. Murray, p. xxvi, describes this concluding ceremony of the carnival: "The diversions end on the evening of Shrove Tuesday, with the *Moccoli*, when every one in the windows and in the streets appear with tapers, and endeavour to blow out the lights of each other."

504.22   'Senza Moccolo,'] Literally, "without taper." JH recalled in *HC*, p. 282: " '*Senza moccolo!*' was the universal cry; young knights-errant, singly or in groups, pressed their way up and down, shouting the battle-cry, and quenching all lights within reach, while striving to maintain the flame of their own."

507.28   Mr May] Samuel Joseph May (1797–1871), born in Boston, and brother-in-law of Bronson Alcott, was pastor of a Unitarian church in Syracuse, New York, 1845–67. He had been from 1842 to 1845, at the request of Horace Mann, principal of the girls' normal school in Lexington, Massachusetts. He was a prominent abolitionist, prohibitionist, and advocate of women's rights. He had arrived in Rome from Naples on March 7, and was to leave for Florence in late April, joining Elizabeth Hoar's party there for a tour of Switzerland. See J. P. Quincy, *Memoir of Samuel Joseph May* (Boston: Roberts, 1873).

507.29   General Pierce] NH's diary records correspondence with Pierce, who was in Geneva in August and September, 1858, and in Florence in October. On March 5, 1859, NH received a letter from Pierce from Naples.

508.5   neither son nor daughter] Pierce's three sons had died, one in infancy, one at the age of four, and the third at the age of eleven in a railroad accident two months before Pierce's inauguration as president. Pierce's ineffectiveness as president is attributed in part to his and his wife's grief at their loss.

508.11 candidate for the Presidency] Pierce did not seek the Democratic nomination in 1860, in spite of the importunities of his friends.

508.22 Miss Hoare] Elizabeth Hoar (1814–78), a member of a leading family in Concord, had been one of SH's closest friends during the Hawthornes' residences there. She had been engaged to Emerson's brother Charles, who died suddenly in 1836. (SH made a medallion of his profile in 1840, as a gift to Elizabeth.) She left for her first voyage to Europe in October, 1858, accompanied by her brother Edward Sherman Hoar (1823–93) and their neighbor Elizabeth Hallett Prichard (1822–1917). After touring England and France they came to Italy in November. Edward and Miss Prichard were married in Florence on December 28. The Hoars left Rome on April 27 to travel northward and eventually return to America in September 1859. For letters of Miss Hoar to SH of May and June 1859, see *Memories*, pp. 366–68. For much of the information in this note I am indebted to Mrs. Elizabeth Maxfield-Miller.

508.23 a street running out of the Via Babuino] Via della Fontanella.

508.24 Zenobia] *Zenobia, the Queen of Palmyra, in Chains* (1859). This is the "noble statue" by Miss Hosmer that NH speaks of "stealing" for *MF*, in the preface to that romance. A counterpart of Story's *Cleopatra* and *Libyan Sibyl*, *Zenobia* was received with high praise in America and England (where it was assumed to be the work of John Gibson). Taft comments on how NH's praise is based on the statue's literary suggestiveness rather than any sculptural quality. Jarves, in *The Art-Idea*, p. 220, earlier made a similar observation. For reproductions see Taft, p. 209; Gerdts, no. 138; *The White, Marmorean Flock*, catalogue no. 6.

509.9–10 a cast . . . her Zenobia] According to a letter of 1864 from Lydia Maria Child to the Boston *Transcript*, the features of Zenobia "were copied from an ancient coin of the Queen of Palmyra. . . . [Miss Hosmer searched] libraries to find every allusion to her, whether historic or romantic." NH had seen the *Minerva Medica* in the Vatican Sculpture Gallery the previous April. See p. 166. See Harriet Hosmer, *Letters and Memories,* pp. 191–92.

509.34–510.2 photographs of her Puck . . . fanciful.] See p. 158.33. *Will o' the Wisp* was a companion piece to *Puck.* For a reproduction, see Gerdts, no. 167.

510.8 Miss Noah] Possibly a relation of Mordecai Manuel Noah (1785–1851), an editor and politician who had been prominent in the Democratic party, and U.S. consul in Morocco and Algiers.

511.8 Apollo] SH in *Passages* added a footnote: The Lycian Apollo.

512.14–15 St. Andrea della Valle] Best known for its frescoes by Domenichino and Lanfranco. Murray, p. 130: "This ch. is supposed to stand on the site of the Curia of Pompey, and very near to where Caesar fell."

512.16 Farnese Palace] Murray, p. 257: "the architecture of this palace is beyond all doubt the finest in Rome. . . . Nothing can surpass the solidity of the construction" by Antonio da Sangallo (1483–1546), Giacomo da Vignola (1507–73), and Michelangelo.

512.17 the Piazza Cenci . . . Beatrice's father] Murray, p. 249: "The ancient residence of the family stands partly on the site of the Theatre of Balbus, near the western entrance to the Ghetto. . . . The palace, an immense and gloomy pile of massive architecture, was for many years deserted and left without doors or windows or any sign of human habitation, to tell, as forcibly as a building could, the record of crime: it seemed to have been stricken with the curse of which Beatrice Cenci was the victim. Within the last few years, however, it has been made habitable, and a part of it was long occupied as a studio by the celebrated German painter Overbeck. . . . Its position in the most obscure quarter of

Rome, and its gloomy aspect, are perfectly in accordance with the atrocities perpetuated within its walls." Compare *MF*, pp. 387–89.

512.20–31   Aventine . . . Coelian] Among the hills southeast of the Capitoline, described by Murray, p. 2, as "almost uninhabited . . . covered with vineyards or gardens, and . . . a few convents and villas."

513.27   Governor Marcy] William L. Marcy (1786–July 4, 1857) was secretary of state in the Pierce administration. Born in Southbridge, Massachusetts, he moved to Troy, New York, where he pursued a career in Democratic politics. He was governor of New York from 1833 to 1838, and secretary of war from 1845 to 1849 under Polk. Marcy's handling of foreign affairs was one of the few successful aspects of the Pierce administration, and at his death Marcy was considered an abler statesman than either Pierce or Buchanan.

513.30   Caleb Cushing] (1800–1879), lawyer and politician from Newburyport, Massachusetts. As Whig congressman (1835–43) and brigadier general in the Mexican War, 1847, Cushing antagonized transcendentalists, abolitionists and opponents of "Manifest Destiny." He was attorney general in the Pierce administration. His erudition in the law, and many other subjects, was well known. The most famous characterization of him was Lowell's in *The Biglow Papers*, No. 3 (1847): "General C. is a dreffle smart man: / He's been on all sides that give places or pelf; / But consistency still wuz a part of his plan,— / He's been true to *one* party, an' thet is himself."

515.27   like Aladdin's palace] See note to 75.30–31.

516.5   a statue of Venus] The London *Times* correspondent reported from Rome on April 16 (*Times*, April 22, 1859, 8:5): "The interest of the artistic portion of the community in politics has this week been suspended by the discovery of a remarkably beautiful statue of Venus, in Parian marble. Possessing very high merit, it is pronounced by some connoisseurs to be as fine as the Venus de' Medici. Eminent sculptors, while more moderate in their praise, still speak of it as being very beautiful, as being of Greek art. It will settle a very disputed point, and lead probably to the correction of a great error in the repairs made by Bernini in the Venus de' Medici. It will be remembered that Bernini has so adjusted her arms that, while bent over the bosom and the lower part of the body, they do not touch it in any part. In the new statue the marks of the fingers on the right thigh and on the left bosom are plainly visible. The head, too, I should say, is some what larger than that of the Venus de' Medici. The head has been broken off, as also the two arms, but the only parts missing are the left hand and wrist and the fingers of the right hand, all of which may be easily supplied, as enough exists to show the perfect form of every limb of the body. Undoubtedly it is a great find, and crowds are rushing down to see it." The correspondent of the New York art magazine the *Crayon*, VI (August 1859), 252, reported from Rome on May 14 that the head had been fastened on the shoulders and the statue placed on a pedestal for show in a small building near the ruins of the Baths of Caracalla.

517.9   that head . . . the statue.] See pp. 298, 310–11, 316. William Story remarked to Ada Shepard in Siena that he found the Venus de' Medici's expression insipid, and that he would like to knock her head off.

517.32   making his fortune by it.] The *Crayon*, VI (September, 1859), 279, reported: "The statue of Venus, lately found in Rome, and which is said to be the most beautiful antique statue that has been exhumed for a hundred years, has become the property of a Russian."

518.19–20   I had hoped . . . along with him] Plans for travel to Venice, Milan, Geneva, and Paris had been made as early as February (NH to Fields, February 3, 1859; MS, Huntington). Ada Shepard recorded that in March Pierce asked the Hawthornes to accompany his party through Venice to Germany, but NH remained undecided. On April 18 Dr. Franco urged that Una remain in Rome another month.

520.4–5   I attempted . . . a year ago] See p. 92, above.

523.3   Mrs. Gaskell] Elizabeth Cleghorn Gaskell (1810–65), the English novelist, had met the Storys in 1855 or earlier, and had visited them in Rome in 1857. See Anne Henry Ehrenpreis, "Elizabeth Gaskell and Nathaniel Hawthorne," *Nathaniel Hawthorne Journal* 1973, pp. 89–119 (especially 110–12), for a conjecture on how this tale may have influenced *MF*, chapter 43.

524.26   Dr Appleton] Benjamin Barnard Appleton (1815–78), M.D. Harvard, 1839, an American physician from Boston, who had lived in Italy with his consumptive wife since the early 1850s. He had been a parishioner of Theodore Parker; during Parker's last illness in Rome and Florence from October 1859 till May 1860, Dr. Appleton treated his consumption and was his friend and confidant. See John Weiss, *Life . . . of Theodore Parker*; List of Subscribers, Twenty-Eighth Congregational Society, Boston, April 1848.

524.28–29   the railway station] The railroad from Rome to Civita Vecchia had been opened a few weeks earlier.

527.10–11   a day of wretched experience] See note to 50.15–16. At that time Maria Mitchell wrote in her diary of the confusion and anxiety caused when the guide led the Hawthorne family astray from herself and Ada Shepard. They met finally in the street, to everyone's relief.

527.20   the disembarkation of horses] A passing allusion to an event of great concern to tourists and travelers throughout the spring of 1859: the war for control of Italy that opposed the French and Sardinians to the Austrians. French troops began arriving in Italian ports in late April 1859, and during the next month 100,000 disembarked. The first decisive battle, at Magenta on June 4, was won by the French; and after another major French victory at Solferino, in late June, an armistice was signed. Travel in northern Italy was disrupted from April until July.

527.22–23   hung motionless . . . Golden Fleece] Compare "The Golden Fleece," in *Tanglewood Tales*, 1853; see *WB / TT*, pp. 364–65.

527.33   Sardinian officers] The Kingdom of Sardinia included the entire Piedmont, its capital being at Turin and its principal port Genoa.

529.1   more passengers] Ada Shepard mentioned "Mrs. Greenough, the sculptor's wife," probably meaning Sarah Dana Loring Greenough, wife of Richard Greenough (1819–1904), brother of Horatio. Sarah Greenough was originally from Boston, and was a resident of Florence. Ada Shepard also noted a number of Italian refugees from Naples, which was then in the throes of revolution against the despotic King Ferdinand II, whose jails had been full of political prisoners.

529.3   Lord and Lady James] Sir John Kingston James (1815–93) published his verse translation of *Jerusalem Delivered* in 1865. Another volume of verse, *Day Dreams, to Which Are Added Some Translations from the Italian*, was privately printed in 1879.

529.15–16   Mr. Gladstone] William Ewart Gladstone (1809–98) was chancellor of the exchequer in 1859, in the cabinet of Lord Russell. He later was prime minister, beginning in 1868. Gladstone published *Studies in Homer and the Homeric Age* in 1858. His knowledge of James's poetic endeavors does not appear to be recorded.

530.19–20   Hotel des Colonies] Not mentioned in Murray.

530.22   Avignon] After deciding not to stay at Leghorn, as Dr. Franco had recommended, NH planned to spend several days at Avignon. Avignon's popularity for discriminating tourists had been furthered by the travel writings of Mérimée (1835), Stendhal (1838), and, especially, by Dickens's *Pictures from Italy* (1846).

531.14–15   the Consul . . . the Vice Consul] The new consul was Alexander Derbes, a naturalized American appointed from Louisiana. The deputy consul, who viséed NH's passport, was Charles Chevrier.

532.27   *Livre des Merveilles*] NH's *A Wonder Book* was published by Hachette in Paris in 1858 in a translation by Léonce

Rabillon: *Le Livre des Merveilles: Contes pour les Enfants, Tirés de la Mythologie*. It was in a series called "la Bibliothèque Rose Illustrée." SL was the only other of NH's works already translated into French, by Emile Forgues in 1853.

533.3 Hôtel d'Europe] Described by Murray, p. 438, as "excellent; attentive landlord." Built in the sixteenth century, the edifice was purchased by the widow Pierron in 1799, and soon became known as one of the most excellent hotels in Europe. The Brownings, with Mrs. Jameson, had rested several days there on their first journey to Italy together in 1846. The hotel is still extant.

533.4 an elderly lady in black] Identified by Ada Shepard as Madame Pierron; presumably a descendant of the hotel's founder.

534.12 The old church of Avignon] Notre-Dame-des-Doms, built in the twelfth century. The popes lived in Avignon from 1309 to 1377.

534.16–17 ancient frescoes] See note to 539.2–3.

534.24–25 the ruins of an ancient bridge] The Pont St. Bénézet, also known as the Pont d' Avignon (as in the popular song). The legend says that Pierre Bénoit or Bénézet, a twelve-year-old shepherd of Savoy, was ordered by Christ to build the bridge on September 13, 1177, a day the sun was eclipsed. In 1185 or 1186 he died, and was buried in the newly completed bridge. In 1669 a flood swept away eighteen of the twenty-two arches, disclosing, the legend says, the boy's body. It was reburied in the Church of the Celestines.

535.10–11 a vast old edifice] The Palace of the Popes, built between 1335 and 1365, was used as a barracks between 1822 and 1906, and was not frequently visited by tourists. See p. 539.

536.30–31 the old Gothic tomb of Pope John XXII] John XXII (Jacques d'Euse, 1249–1334) began his reign in 1316. The tomb was completed in 1345. It was hacked to pieces in 1789, and when restored during the reign of Louis Philippe, the lost body and the effigy were replaced by those of an unknown bishop.

537.9–10 figure of Christ, in ivory] Probably the figure made in 1659 by Jean-Baptiste Guillermin (1622–99) for the confraternity of the Pénitents Noirs of Avignon; now in the Musée Calvet in Avignon.

537.16 another famous ivory statuette] A fourteenth-century ivory Virgin, kept in a safe in the sacristy of the chief church at Villeneuve-lès-Avignon, across the Rhone. See p. 545.

537.24–25 two or three pictures . . . French artists] Probably including a fifteenth-century Adoration by an unknown Avignon painter, and a portrait of an old man by Louis Le Nain (ca. 1593–1648).

538.6–7 the stone monument of Pope Benedict] Benedict XII (Jacques Fournier), pope from 1334 to 1342.

538.7–8 like many . . . Cathedral of York] On his first visit to York Minister, May 8, 1856, NH had noted "very few monuments, and these seem to be of ecclesiastical people. I saw no armed knights asleep on the tops of their tombs" (*EN*, p. 347). On his second visit, April 13, 1857, he noticed tombs of archbishops and "many interesting monuments, of prelates, and other old dignitaries" (*EN*, p. 454).

539.2–3 frescoes within its arch . . . Simon Memmi.] Simone Martini (1284–1344), a Sienese painter known in the nineteenth century as Simone Memmi, went to the papal court at Avignon about 1340. NH had seen his work in Florence and Siena. The subjects of his frescoes in the portico include a Redeemer with six flying angels, and a Madonna of Humility.

540.4–8 old frescoes. . . . friend Giotto.] Matteo Giovannetti da Viterbo (died after 1367), a pupil of Simone Martini, painted frescoes in the St. Michel and St. Martial chapels, probably about 1344–45. Some frescoes were deliberately mutilated by soldiers of the garrison, who sold fragments to curious travelers.

540.17–25 No end of historical romances. . . . years ago.] Murray, p. 440, describes the torture chamber of the Inquisition and the tower still stained with "streaks of human blood," from which "no less than 60 unfortunate and innocent persons, females as well as men, were massacred by a band of democrats more savage than wild beasts, in October 1791. The prisoners were dragged from their cells, and poignarded or struck down in the door; but in the blind haste of the ruffians, it is believed that some of their victims were precipitated from above before life was yet extinct; but to finish this deed of infamy, quicklime in large quantities was thrown down over them upon the mangled heap of dead and dying. The actual scene of these atrocities is no longer visible, the tower having been floored and fitted up." A similar account is given, with more on the Inquisition and the horrific history of the palace, by Dickens in *Pictures from Italy* (1846); ed. David Paroissien (New York: Coward, McCann and Geohegan, 1974), pp. 54–58.

540.28   a picture of Rienzi] Niccolo Gabrini, known as Cola di Rienzi (1313–54), Italian reformer, came to Pope Clement VI in Avignon ca. 1342, seeking to restore the millennial rule of Christ in Rome. In 1344 he went to Rome and prepared a revolution against the aristocracy that succeeded in 1347, when he was elected tribune of the people. Corrupted by power, he was excommunicated and expelled from Rome in 1348. He was imprisoned at Avignon in the Palace of the Popes in 1352; the new pope released him, and he returned to Rome, where he was killed by a mob. Bulwer-Lytton's popular romance, *Rienzi, or the Last of the Tribunes*, was published in 1835.

541.4   We are still here] NH had planned to leave Avignon on Monday, June 6, and to stop that night at Valence on the way to Lyons; but SH had been very unwell the day before, and continued so on Monday. The party became anxious about the time remaining for travel in Switzerland.

543.1   The church where Laura lay] Presumably the Church of Ste. Claire, in which Petrarch first saw Laura, in 1327. The church was destroyed during the French Revolution.

543.10   the gate of Ouelle] The Porte de l'Oulle.

543.13   the arrowy Rhone] See note to 39.22–23.

544.4   Villeneuve] Villeneuve-lès-Avignon.

544.5   female saint] This saint, and the source of NH's account, have not been identified. In the sixth century the Benedictine abbey of St. André was founded on Mt. Andaon, and the village that grew up around it took its name. In the thirteenth century the monks, supported by the king, established a new town, Villeneuve.

544.16   if indeed . . . so early.] Omitted by SH from *Passages*. NH's second thoughts were prudent: the Roman villas did not exist until the seventeenth century.

545.21–22   Philip le Bel] Philip IV of France (1268–1314) built the tower named for him (see page 547) in 1302, but the adjoining Fort-St. André was not begun until 1366. Philip created the first Avignon pope in 1305.

547.17   Hotel de la Poste] Murray, p. 430, comments: "outside the wall; not at all bad, with some pretension to English comforts; not dear, and very civil people."

547.20   St Peray] NH apparently followed Murray's advice, p. 430: "Try here the sparkling St. Peray, an excellent wine, not inferior to Champagne."

547.24   a cathedral] St. Apollinaire, built in the eleventh and twelfth centuries.

547.29–548.3   We likewise saw . . . antiquity.] Murray describes, p. 430: "On the N. side of the Ch. . . . a singular building, known as the *Le Pendentif*, of classical architecture, erected 1548, as a monument to the family Mistral, whose arms are still visible on it. It is . . . the first of its kind erected, and regarded as a type in architecture. In the rusticated space occupying the sides, carvings of monstrous birds may be discovered."

548.22–25 Either the water . . . former journey.] See pp. 47–48.

549.5 Hotel de l'Univers] Murray, p. 370, comments: "Rue de Bourbon, not very good, though an English landlord."

549.32 the Cathedral] St. Jean, begun in the twelfth century. Murray, p. 372, remarks that "the painted glass windows are remarkably fine."

550.15–16 two American ladies] In NH's diary identified as the American consul's "womenkind."

550.18 a Mr. White] Joel W. White, of Bolton, Connecticut, consul at Lyons, 1857–60.

550.22–26 Mr. White informed. . . . into France] Murray, *Switzerland*, p. xi: "The rule in France is, that if a traveller has left France 10 days he requires a fresh visa to re-enter it; and this rule is now always enforced. But in all matters relating to passports, much probably depends upon the caprice of the individual gendarme. . . . No visas are required by Switzerland, but a passport is asked for at Geneva."

551.9 Mrs. Sedgwick] Elizabeth Dana Ellery Sedgwick (1799–1862), originally from Newport, Rhode Island, was a cousin of Dr. William Ellery Channing and widow of Robert Sedgwick (1784–1841), a New York lawyer, brother of the novelist Catherine Maria Sedgwick. Mrs. Sedgwick and her daughter Elizabeth Ellery (1824–98) had been in Europe for two years, hoping that the air of Switzerland would restore the daughter's delicate health; but late the previous summer she had also suffered a paralysis of the legs, Ada Shepard reported, and was still taken about in a chair. At this time the ladies were accompanied by Elizabeth's fiancé, Francis James Child (1825–96), Boylston professor of rhetoric at Harvard, who had published his first collection of English and Scottish Ballads in eight volumes in 1857–58. The Hawthornes had encountered them at Valence the day before (see NH's diary). Elizabeth later recovered, and married Child in August 1860.

551.21–22   Hotel d'Angleterre] Murray, p. 144, comments: "on the quay, good," but apparently not as good as three others previously described.

552.21–25   There is also . . . prefaces.] Murray, p. 146, says of the cathedral, "its fine Corinthian portico added on the outside is a blemish where it is placed, but its interior possesses interest as a very early and uncorrupted specimen of the Gothic of the 11th century."

553.1–11   Nothing struck me. . . . this water.] Murray, p. 145, comments: "The intensely blue colour of the water of the Rhone, alluded to by Byron, is certainly very remarkable, and resembles nothing so much as the discharge of indigo from a dyer's vat." See pp. 39, 545, and "The Prisoner of Chillon," XIII.

554.17–19   The first was Coppet . . . very little.] NH seems to have read Murray, p. 156, inattentively: "[The Chateau of Coppet] was the residence of Madame de Stael the author, as well as of her father, the French minister Necker." Necker died at Coppet in 1804. Madame de Staël was born and died in Paris. Ada Shepard noted that *Corinne* was written at Coppet.

555.33–556.6   Clarens, however . . . imagination.] NH's memory of reading *La Nouvelle Héloïse* (1761) was likely sharpened by Murray's quotation, pp. 161–62, of several stanzas (canto 3, stanzas 99–102, 104) from Byron's *Childe Harold* that evoke Rousseau's theme. NH recorded his first reading of "Rosseaus' Eloisa" in an undated letter written when he was sixteen, sent probably to his sister Elizabeth (MS, Essex Institute).

557.6   Hotel Byron] Murray, p. 164: "A comfortable *Pension*, on the lake, table-d'hôte liberal, and great cleanliness and civility; rooms lofty and airy: charge 7 fr. a day."

558.7   "Chillon's snow-white battlements."] Quoted in Murray, p. 163, from Byron's "Prisoner of Chillon," VI.

558.26–29   It was formerly . . . government] Murray, p. 163: "At length, in 1536, the Swiss wrested the Pays de Vaud from the hands of Charles V of Savoy. . . . Chillon was the last place which held out for him."

560.4   Bonnevard's prison] François de Bonnivard (1496–1570) was imprisoned from 1530 to 1536 for conspiring to establish a republic. He was released by the Bernese.

560.5   Byron's poem] "The Prisoner of Chillon" (1816).

560.21   a tree at Newstead Abbey.] See *EN*, p. 490 (May 29, 1857).

565.4   "*Diableries*"] According to Murray, p. 170, this should be "Diablerets."

566.11   Hotel Faucon] Murray, p. 158: "Good and quiet."

566.12   the Cathedral] Built 1175–1275, it was to be much restored by Viollet-le-Duc in 1873–79.

569.15   the house of Gibbon] Murray, p. 159, does not make a visit to Gibbon's house inviting: "Both it and the *garden* have been entirely changed. The wall of the Hôtel Gibbon occupies the site of his summer-house, and the *berceau* walk has been destroyed to make room for the garden of the hotel, but the terrace overlooking the lake, a lime and a few acacias, remain." This information alludes to Gibbon's description in his *Autobiography* of the moment at which he completed *The Decline and Fall of the Roman Empire*, on June 27, 1787.

570.19   Mr. Wilding] Henry V. Wilding (d. 1872), NH's clerk in the U.S. consulate at Liverpool, was later vice-consul. He is characterized in *OOH*, pp. 35–36. Accounts and drafts from him had been the last obstacle to NH's departure for the continent; see NH's diary, p. 575, and memorandum, p. 629.

570.27   Henry Bright] Henry Arthur Bright (1830–84), of Liverpool, partner with his father in an international shipping firm, and amateur man of letters, was introduced to NH by Longfellow in 1852, and became a close friend soon after NH's arrival in Liverpool in 1853. See *DNB*; *Happy Country, This America: The Travel Diary of Henry Arthur Bright*, ed. Anne Henry Ehrenpreis (Columbus: Ohio State University Press, 1978).

571.1 Hotel Wheeler] Murray's comment on this hotel, p. 62: "on the Quai Notre Dame, near the steamers."

572.3–4 thence, in a week . . . to Boston and Concord] As his diary indicates, NH decided in London on June 26 to defer departure from Liverpool from July 15 to 30. There being no accommodations available for the sailing of the thirtieth, he requested passages on August 13. But after his conversation with James T. Fields on July 5, he decided to stay in England to finish *MF*, thus securing English copyright, and to see the romance through the press.

575.8 Mr. Miller] John Miller, of Covent Garden, London, dispatch agent of the U.S. legation. His duty was to seal the bags and get them to the post or boats. NH mentions visiting the agency during his first visit to London, September 8, 1855 (*EN*, p. 207).

575.9 Barings] Baring Brothers & Co., 8 Bishopgate Street, London, NH's bankers, had been founded by Sir Francis Baring (1740–1810). The Americans Joshua Bates and Russell Sturgis had become leading partners in the house.

575.12–13 Mr. Dallas's] George Mifflin Dallas (1792–1864), from Pennsylvania, was U.S. minister to Great Britain from 1856 to 1861. A lawyer, he had served as mayor of Philadelphia, U.S. senator, attorney general of Pennsylvania, vice–president under Polk, and minister to Russia.

575.16 Pantomime, White Cat.] A fantasy (first performed in 1842) by James Robinson Planché (1796–1880), who created numerous similar stage versions of fairy tales for the Christmas and Easter seasons.

575.17 Wrote . . . letters.] The letters preserved are those to Henry Bright (MS, Pearson, Yale), and Coventry Patmore

(MS, Boston College). NH asks Bright to help Wilding procure a new job if the new American consul were to force his resignation. NH thanks Patmore for the gift of a volume of his poems.

576.1　O'S] John Louis O'Sullivan (1813–95) and Susan Kearny Rodgers O'Sullivan. He had been among the Hawthornes' closest friends since he was editor of the *Democratic Review*, 1837–46. O'Sullivan was U.S. minister to Portugal from 1854 to July 1858. SH and her daughters had spent the winter of 1854–55 in Lisbon and Madeira with the O'Sullivans. O'Sullivan had been in London in March 1857; see NH to Bennoch, March 17, 1857 (MS, Virginia). See *HC*, pp. 133–38.

576.3　Bennett's] William Cox Bennett (1820–95), a poet as well as a watchmaker. NH met him in September 1855 (*EN*, p. 222).

577.8　Russell Sturgis.] Russell Sturgis (1805–87), son of Russell Sturgis (1750–1826), a Boston manufacturer and merchant, was a senior partner in the banking firm of Baring Brothers.

578.4　Mr. Morgan's] George Washington Morgan (1820–93), from Ohio, was U.S. consul at Marseilles, 1856–58, U.S. minister to Lisbon, 1858–61, and later a Civil War general and congressman.

579.4　the American Minister's] See note to 210.4.

579.4　the American Consul's] See note to 615.22.

579.5　Mr. Shea.] Murray, p. ix: "Mr. Shea, No. 11, Piazza di Spagna, has been recommended as careful, intelligent, and trustworthy, by a great number of persons who have employed him in the business of house agency, of recent introduction at Rome."

580.12　Mrs. Bramley Moore jr,] Daughter-in-law of John Bramley-Moore (1800–1886), developer of the port of Liverpool and M.P. for Liverpool, whom NH met in 1853 or 1854 (see *EN*).

580.12   Mr. Rakermann] Louis (or Ludwig) Rakemann, a pianist originally from Bremen, a pupil of Thalberg, who had lived in America many years before. On the occasion of his first concert Rakemann was acclaimed as "unquestionably the best pianist that has ever played in Boston" (Boston *Post*, November 7, 1839). He had been living in Italy for most of the 1850s, giving occasional concerts in London and elsewhere; see *Dwight's Journal of Music*, August 7, 1858, p. 152. He had given lessons to Una in Madeira in 1856 (Una to Elizabeth Peabody, April 22, 1856; MS, Berg), and he was to play for her on her birthday in Rome, March 3, 1858; see *Notes*, p. 256. His younger brother Frederick, also a concert pianist, was in the 1840s a good friend of Longfellow, G. W. Curtis, and J. S. Dwight.

581.1   Dr. Hayward] George Hayward (1791–1863), Boston surgeon and professor of clinical surgery at Harvard, 1835–49, spent several years in Europe and acquired a continental reputation as a surgeon.

581.2   Mr. G. W. Wales.] George Washington Wales (1815–96), a Boston merchant, was a patron of C. G. Thompson and a founding trustee of the Boston Museum of Fine Arts.

581.18   Miss Fish] Presumably Sarah (b. 1838), the eldest daughter of Hamilton and Julia Fish.

581.27–28   Mr. Head] An American, a recent graduate of Hamilton College in New York, who had brought a letter of introduction to Ada Shepard from an Antioch classmate.

583.14   Pieta di Monte] Properly, Trinità dei Monti.

583.27–28   Hugh Bright] Hugh Meyler Bright (1839–66), brother of NH's Liverpool friend, Henry Arthur Bright.

584.8   St Andrea a Monte Cavallo.] S. Andrea al Quirinale.

586.8   Church of Minerva] S. Maria sopra Minerva, described by SH in *Notes*, pp. 267–69, as "the only Gothic church in Rome."

586.23   Mr. Rogers] Randolph Rogers was born in New York and grew up in Ann Arbor, Michigan. He was a drygoods clerk in New York City in 1848 when he exhibited a bust of Byron and other figures. On that basis his employers financed two years' study in Florence and Rome. He returned to Rome in 1855 and lived there the rest of his life. NH first saw his "bas-reliefs for bronze-door" on October 26, and praised them in the preface to *MF*. Rogers's "Columbus Doors," 1855–60, for the Rotunda of the U.S. Capitol, were done in close imitation of Ghiberti's doors for the Baptistery in Florence. See Taft, pp. 159–70; Craven, pp. 312–19; and Millard F. Rogers, Jr., *Randolph Rogers*.

586.24   Mr. Caldwell] Holme Cardwell (b. 1820), English sculptor from Manchester, was in Rome for several years after studying in London and Paris. His studio was located at 20, Piazza di Spagna. He produced portrait busts and genre groups such as *The Good Samaritan, Cinderella, A Huntsman with a Wounded Stag,* and *Sabrina,* from Milton's "Comus" (which was exhibited in 1856 at the Royal Academy in London). See Bonfigli, *Guide,* p. 42; Thieme-Becker, *Künstler-Lexicon* (Leipzig: Seemann, 1931), V, 590–91.

587.19–20   Left letters . . . Wilding.] The letter to Bennoch begins: "This is the first letter (except one to my bankers) that I have written since I came to Rome" (MS, Virginia). The letter to Wilding has not been recovered.

588.17   Braschi Palace] In the Piazza di Pasquino, housing the office of the American minister, Lewis Cass, Jr.

589.16   Ticknor] William Davis Ticknor (1810–64) was a cousin of the literary historian George Ticknor; he was NH's publisher and close friend, who held his power of attorney while the author was abroad. More than 160 of NH's letters to him during the period 1851–64 are extant; 146 are published in *Letters of Hawthorne to William D. Ticknor 1851–1864* (Newark, N.J.: Carteret Book Club, 1910), and a number are in Caroline Ticknor, *Hawthorne and His Publisher* (Boston: Houghton Mifflin, 1913).

589.23   I staid at home] NH wrote the first surviving segment of "The Ancestral Footstep" on this day. See *ACM*, pp. 3, 497.

590.22–23   Mr. Akers, jr.] Charles Akers (1835/36–1906) was a brother of Paul Akers, the sculptor, with whom he studied in Rome in 1857–58; in 1860–61 he helped his dying brother complete a bust. He later lived in New York, and made medallions of Emerson, Longfellow, and Holmes, and a crayon portrait of Lowell. See Charles Akers, "Personal Glimpses of Our New England Poets: From an Artist's Autobiography," *New England Magazine*, n.s., XVII (December 1897), 446–56; Clement and Hutton.

591.7   Mrs Ward's] Anna Hazard Barker Ward (1813–1900) of Boston, daughter of Jacob Barker (1779–1871), a prominent lawyer, politician and entrepreneur of New York and New Orleans. Her husband, Samuel Gray Ward (1817–1907), American agent of Baring Brothers of London after 1850, wrote on Italian art and literature for the *Dial*, and had much furthered Emerson's artistic education. Mrs. Ward, whom SH had known since the early 1830s, was one of Margaret Fuller's closest friends, and was admired by Emerson for her beauty and grace. The Wards lived in Lenox 1844–50 (see *AN*, p. 293). Anna Ward was in Europe from May to October, 1856, and SH saw her briefly in Liverpool; see NH to Mrs. Ward, October 9, 1856 (MS, Massachusetts Historical Society). When she returned to Europe with her husband and children in the spring of 1858, she was suffering from a nervous illness and was on the verge of conversion to Catholicism; see Emerson to Arthur Hugh Clough, May 17, 1858, in *Emerson-Clough Letters*, eds. Howard F. Lowry and Ralph Leslie Rusk (Cleveland: Rowfant Club, 1934), and note to 642.17.

592.20   Raphael's angels] Murray, p. 154, explains that in the mosaic of the creation of the heavenly bodies within S. Maria del Popolo, "each planet is represented under the guidance of a guardian angel."

592.26   Mrs. Page] Sophia Candace Stevens Hitchcock Page (1826–92), third wife of the American painter William Page. She had married Page in October, 1857, following the death of Steven Hitchcock and Page's divorce. NH had met her brother, Henry Stevens, the American bibliographer, in London in April, 1856 (*EN*, p. 326. See also note to 678.6). She had lived in 1854–55 in Paris, where she wrote for the New York *Tribune* over the signature "An American Woman in Paris." The Pages were close friends of Abel Nichols and his wife Florence. Page's portrait of her (1861) standing in front of the Coliseum is one of his best-known works. See Joshua C. Taylor, *William Page: The American Titian* (Chicago: University of Chicago Press, 1957), pp. 156–58; Charles Capen McLaughlin, ed., *The Papers of Frederick Law Olmstead* (Baltimore: Johns Hopkins University Press, 1977–), I, 91–93.

593.24   E. P. Peabody] Elizabeth Palmer Peabody (1804–94), SH's sister.

594.11–12   Staid in the house all day.] NH began to write daily "The Ancestral Footstep." Except for May 8, he wrote usually 1,000 to 2,000 words per day, until May 19.

595.18   Ghetto] See *MF*, p. 388.

596.13–14   Wrote letter . . . about house there.] The letter begins, "Our friend Mr. Akers had given me reason to hope that you would take the trouble to make some negotiations on my behalf, about a suite of apartments in Florence" (MS, Pearson, Yale).

596.21–22   the church of Santa Maria della Pace.] Near the Piazza Navona. Best known for Raphael's frescoes of the *Four Sibyls* above the Chigi Chapel.

597.12   Murrays guide book] *A Handbook for Travellers in Central Italy. Part I: Southern Tuscany and the Papal States.*

599.16–17   Messrs. Plowden & French] Bankers located in the Via Legnaioli, according to Murray, p. 519.

602.14   Egyptian Museum] In *Notes*, p. 426, SH describes trying to find, in the Via Faenza, "the building in which is the

Cenacolo of Raphael. After some straying, we found it, and then Mr. H. left me; for he said he could not look at a fresco today." The building, known as the Cenacolo di Fuligno, was then part of the Convent of S. Onofrio. The *Last Supper* (1490) is now attributed to Perugino and his assistants. SH described the Egyptian Museum, then in the same building (pp. 428–29); it contained objects recovered by the Tuscan expedition of 1828–29 led by Ippolito Rossellini.

603.14   the Cascine] The public garden outside the Porta al Prato, on the western edge of Florence.

603.16   Goodban's] Murray, p. 519: "Edward Goodban, in the Via de Legnaioli, No. 4183 (opposite the Café Doney), agent for these Handbooks, is well provided with works on art, and with maps and books useful for travellers in Italy, photographic views, &c.; and will procure all modern Italian and other books."

604.15–16   the Duke's villa] The villa of Poggio Imperiale.

604.18–19   the suspension-bridge] Ponte S. Leopoldo, on the western edge of the city.

607.6–7   Mr Mackay] George Eric Mackay (1835–98), poet and journalist, later used the pseudonym George Eric Lancaster. His father, Charles Mackay (1814–89), poet and journalist, was editor of the *Illustrated London News* from 1852 to 1859; NH met him in London on August 1, 1856 (*EN*, p. 311).

607.13   Preston & Louisa Powers] Preston Powers (1843–1904), named after his father's patron, Senator William C. Preston of South Carolina, became his father's pupil in 1868, and exhibited statues at the Royal Academy in 1892 and the Chicago World's Columbian Exposition in 1893. His sister Louisa was born ca. 1839.

607.25   Fanny Wrigley.] The Hawthornes' English nurse and housekeeper from the summer of 1855 to October, 1856, and from March to December, 1857. She had accompanied SH and her daughters to Portugal, and expected to go to Rome with the family, but her father's sudden death forced her return to her home in Yorkshire. She rejoined the Hawthornes July 14, 1859 in Malton, Yorkshire.

608.20 Anne Powers] Born ca. 1838, in Florence.

610.16 the British Minister] Richard Bickerton Pernell Lyons, later second baron and first earl Lyons (1817–87), was appointed to Florence in 1853 and became envoy in 1858. From December, 1858, to 1865 he was British minister in Washington, and from 1867 to 1887, ambassador to France (DNB).

610.19 Florence] Florence Powers (1846–63).

611.3–4 Gen¹ Mallette] E. J. Mallett, from New York, had just arrived as U.S. consular agent at Florence.

611.15 Madam Tassinari] Mary Thornton Tassinari (1819–95), daughter of Sir Edward Thornton, English diplomat, and wife of Giovanni Tassinari (1805–92), chamberlain to the grand duke of Tuscany.

611.25 Dr. —(a Pole)] Dr. E. G. G. Grisanowsky (1824–88) held a Ph.D. from Königsberg (1845), and had been in diplomatic service briefly; he received his M.D. from Heidelberg in 1855, and thereafter practiced medicine in Italy. He attended Mrs. Browning in Siena in 1859.

615.13 J. T. Fields.] James Thomas Fields (1817–81), Hawthorne's close friend, had become a junior partner in the publishing firm of William D. Ticknor and Company in 1843; the partnership became Ticknor and Fields in 1854. Fields may have met NH as early as 1839. He gave an account of their relationship in Yesterdays with Authors (Boston: J. R. Osgood, 1872).

615.22 Mr. Ardesson] The signature of Antoine Ardisson, a Frenchman, had appeared on U.S. consular dispatches from Rome since 1846; as consuls came and went, he kept the archives in his own home. In 1861 he applied for the consulship, but the appointment was made to William Dean Howells, who diverted to Venice and was succeeded by W. J. Stillman. Murray, p. xx, notes Ardisson's second occupation: "M. Ardisson, a Parisian, American vice-consul, gives lessons in French and Italian, 222, Circo di Ripetta." The address of the consulate is given as 220.

616.9 Mr. (of the Edinburgh Review) & Mrs. Reeve] Henry Reeve (1813–95) was editor of the *Edinburgh Review* from 1855 to 1895. He was the first English translator of Tocqueville's *Democracy in America* (1835–40). Christina Georgina Jane Gollop Reeve was a daughter of George Tilly Gollop, a translator of Schiller and of German works of biblical scholarship. Reeve's journal notes that "the Motleys, Storeys, and Westons were at Rome, and very hospitable. Saw Mr. Hawthorne at the Westons'" (*Memoirs*, ed. John Knox Laughton [London: Longmans, Green, 1898], I, 396). Motley described Reeve as "a good-humoured, tall, large Englishman; Mrs. Reeve is intelligent and literary" (*Correspondence*, ed. George W. Curtis [New York: Harper, 1889], I, 233).

616.24 Wrote to him] NH urges Pierce to arrive in Rome in time for the Carnival in February, Pierce having decided not to spend the whole winter there (MS, New Hampshire Historical Society).

617.5 Mr Tucker] (Nathaniel) Beverley Tucker (1820–90), from Virginia, a journalist in Washington, D.C., was NH's successor as U.S. consul in Liverpool from 1857 to 1861. He was later emissary of the Confederacy to Great Britain and France.

619.11 her sister] Possibly either Elizabeth Rebecca Lander (b. 1814) or Sarah West Lander (1820–72). Sarah wrote popular fiction for children about major cities of the world, including Rome. According to a letter of their father to H. W. Longfellow, October 12, 1859, his daughters "Louisa & Eliz. were on a visit to Mrs. Pierce"—presumably before the Pierces' return to America in July 1859—"& would soon return to Rome to resume work." See Carl L. Johnson, *Professor Longfellow of Harvard* (Eugene:

University of Oregon Press, 1944), p. 106. This letter also indicates that one of the Lander sisters was married to a man who lived in St. Petersburg.

619.27   Longfellow's poem] *The Courtship of Miles Standish and Other Poems* (Boston: Ticknor and Fields, 1858), was published October 16, with the print order doubled from ten thousand to twenty thousand copies.

620.15   Mr. Stone.] Remembered by JH seventy years later as "a rich and handsome man, about forty-five, a banker in Paris, a favorite in society, and often with us in Rome" (letter to William L. Reenan, 1929). SH's diary, June 21, 1859 (MS, Berg), identifies the Stone children as "Minnie and Harry." NH wrote to Una, May 16, 1860, after conversation with the Motleys in London: "Poor little Minnie Stone died of diptheria at Rome, last winter. They have also lost their baby which was born there. We had wonderful luck in getting out of Rome alive" (MS, Huntington).

620.17   Mr. & Mrs. Geo. Jones (of Georgia)] George Noble Jones (1811–76), of Savannah, descendant of the settler Noble Jones, and his wife Mary Wallace Savage Nuttall Jones (1812–61), a Savannah heiress. They were accompanied by their daughter Sarah Campbell Jones (1843–1925) and a young son.

620.22   M^r . . . Bracken] William Bracken, uncle of Annette, who was with her in Rome for the winter. His address was 88, Via delle Quatro Fontane. See McAleer, pp. 23–26.

620.26   Miss Cushman] Charlotte Cushman (1816–76), American actress, was considered the greatest Lady Macbeth of her time in Great Britain as well as in America. She had come to Rome in 1852 with Harriet Hosmer, whom she had championed, as well as other "emancipated females." She visited the Hawthornes in Liverpool, where her sister Susan Cushman Muspratt lived, in December, 1853, and met them by chance in the Lake Country in July, 1855. After retiring from the American stage, she returned to Rome in the fall of 1858 and lived at 38, Via Gregoriana, near

Trinità dei Monti, with Emma Stebbins, her latest protegée. The New York *Times* letter from Rome by "Pericles," dated February 26, 1859, singled her out (with NH and Motley): "Miss Cushman has taken a house for five years. She gives most agreeable entertainments, and adds to them a most interesting feature in her own spirited musical recitation." See Joseph Leech, *Bright Particular Star: The Life and Times of Charlotte Cushman* (New Haven: Yale University Press, 1970).

622.13   Cora] Cora Thompson was born ca. 1844, and named for her aunt, the actress and playwright Anna Cora Mowatt (1819–70).

622.18   Mr. Spicer] Probably Henry Spicer (d. 1891), a playwright and adapter of contemporary French plays, who had also written *Sights and Sounds: The Mystery of the Day; Comprising an Entire History of the American "Spirit" Manifestations* (London: Bosworth, 1853). Anna Mowatt had performed the heroine in his drama *The Lords of Ellingham* in 1849.

623.8   Miss Stebbins] Emma Stebbins (1815–82), from New York, had been a painter for several years when she took up sculpture in 1857, prompted by the success of Harriet Hosmer. She went immediately to Rome, where she studied with Paul Akers, and in 1858 met Charlotte Cushman, whose close friend and biographer she became. Gerdts reproduces two of her works of 1859, *Industry* and *Commerce* (nos. 170–71). See *Yankee Stonecutters*, pp. 71–72; Taft, p. 211; Craven, p. 333; Tuckerman, pp. 602–3; Emma Stebbins, ed., *Charlotte Cushman: Her Letters and Memories of Her Life* (Boston: Houghton, Osgood, 1878).

623.27   Mr. Cranch.] Christopher Pearse Cranch (1813–92), a distant cousin of SH through the Palmer family, was a graduate of Harvard Divinity School and a minor Transcendentalist poet and caricaturist before turning to landscape painting in 1841. Cranch and his family spent three years in Italy in the 1840s, and in 1852 lived briefly in the Red House at Lenox, which the Hawthornes had recently vacated. They lived in Paris from 1853 to 1863, Cranch spending the winter of 1858–59 in Rome. Ada Shepard had visited them in Paris in August, 1857. See *DAB*; *Travelers in Arcadia*, no. 37; Leonora Cranch Scott, *The Life and Letters of . . . Cranch* (Boston: Houghton, Mifflin, 1917), pp. 234–42 (letters from Rome, 1858–59).

624.27 Via Babuino, Via Condotti] Streets leading to the Piazza di Spagna, center of trade and business, especially for the international community of Rome.

625.1 Pliny] Presumably the *Natural History* of Pliny the Elder (23–79 A.D.), which contains in books 35–36 a history of ancient art.

625.7 the Island of the Tiber] Site of three ruined temples, to Aesculapius, Faunus, and Jupiter, and of the church of S. Bartolomeo in Isola; also called the island of S. Bartolomeo.

625.8 pains of a thermatic character] SH had been afflicted since childhood with chronic neuralgia and migraine headaches.

626.8 Ann] Anna Cora Thompson.

626.25 Mrs. Mann] Mary Tyler Peabody Mann (1805–87), SH's sister and wife of Horace Mann (1796–1859).

627.27–28 Mr Sam Bridge] Samuel James Bridge (1809–84), a cousin of NH's friend Horatio Bridge, had been principal appraiser at the Boston Custom House from 1841; in 1853 he was appointed appraiser-general of the Pacific Coast, supervising California, Oregon, and the Washington Territory. When that office was abolished in 1862, he retired and spent the remainder of his life traveling. See William F. Bridge, *An Account of the Descendants of John Bridge, Cambridge, 1632* (Boston: J. S. Cushing, 1884).

634.8–9 Mr. and Mrs Brackett] A couple from Chicago, who came to Ada Shepard on December 11 with a letter of introduction from a classmate of hers who was teaching in Chicago. The Bracketts had stayed at M. Fezandié's in Paris. See note to 17.4–5.

634.10   Mr. Albee] John Albee (1833–1915), poet, lecturer at
the Concord School of Philosophy in the 1880s, and author of
Remembrances of Emerson (1901). In the *Unitarian Review*,
XXIII (May, 1885), 427–28, Albee described coming to the
Hawthornes' building to inquire about an unnamed person, and
knocking at their door. NH came to the door and gave him the
necessary information. Actually, Albee had come to deliver a
package of letters to Ada Shepard, who was unable to see him
because of her illness. Ada described him as a very timid young
man.

634.25   watched with Miss Shepard.] Ada Shepard wrote to
her fiancé that Mrs. Brackett was very kind to her during her
illness.

635.23   Annie Bright.] Anna Bright (b. ca. 1840), sister of
Henry Bright, was a friend of Una, who met her in Liverpool in
February, 1854, and visited her several times.

636.20   Eddie Thompson] Edmund Francis Thompson (b. ca.
1846) was the son of C. G. Thompson and a friend of Julian. He
was later a captain in the U.S. Army. See *HC*, pp. 266–71.

639.15   Mr. Robison] Mr. Robinson, an American about
twenty years old, from Buffalo, New York, had made Ada
Shepard's acquaintance en route to Europe and had escorted her
in Paris. He was to study at the University of Heidelberg. His call
on her in Rome came during her recovery from illness, when she
had gone to bed early. He apparently did not call a second time.

641.10–11   I wrote . . . a letter to J. T. Fields] NH describes
the family's "dismal time" in Rome, and his shutting himself up
"for an hour or two, almost every day, [to] come to close grips with
a Romance which I have been trying to tear out of my mind" (MS,
Huntington; excerpt in *Yesterdays with Authors*, p. 84).

641.24–25   Mr Seagrave] Possibly Mr. Seabury, from New
Bedford, first mate of the *Ariel*, who had become acquainted with
Ada Shepard during her voyage to Europe. She described him to

her fiancé as a rough though kindly sailor, who showed a fatherly affection for her. He visited her in Paris in September, 1857, and is mentioned in a letter she wrote in Rome on February 2, 1859.

641.30–642.1   Overbeck's] See note to 254.2–19. According to Bonfigli, *Guide*, p. 84, Overbeck's studio was located at 9, Via del Olmo, near S. Maria Maggiore. "Several pictures in water colours, generally representing religious subjects, are to be seen in his Studio."

642.10   via Santa Croce] Properly, Via della Croce.

642.17   Miss Ward] Anna Barker Ward (1841–75), later Mrs. Joseph Thoron. Mrs. Anna Ward had apparently been in Europe since meeting with the Hawthornes the previous April; SH noted in a letter to Elizabeth Peabody, January 8, 1859, that she was in Rome (MS, Berg). Her husband, Samuel G. Ward, and three of their children had apparently returned to Boston, but she had remained with her daughter Anna. Mrs. Ward's nervous and religious problems had continued, but SH remembered that she came to visit Una every day during the height of her fever, although normally unable to go upstairs (SH to Elizabeth Peabody, July 3, 1859; MS, Berg). See also Emerson, *Letters*, V, 142–44, 169.

644.15   Mʳ Cowper] The Honorable Spencer Cowper, who edited in 1865 the *Diary of Mary Countess Cowper, Lady of the Bedchamber to the Princess of Wales, 1714–1720*. NH was later to dine with him at the Motleys'; see entry of April 2.

647.5–6   Lady Mordaunt's] Caroline Sophia Murray Mordaunt (ca. 1815–1913), daughter of the Right Reverend George Murray (1784–1860), bishop of Rochester, and widow of Sir John Mordaunt (1808–45).

647.17   Miss Lily Motley.] Elizabeth Cabot Motley (b. 1840) was later married to Sir William Vernon Harcourt and to Captain Thomas Poynton Ives.

647.25 portrait-painter] Field Talfourd (1815–74) drew companion portraits of the Brownings, now in the National Portrait Gallery, London. See McAleer, p.31, and Grace Elizabeth Wilson, *Robert Browning's Portraits* . . . (Waco, Texas: Baylor University, 1943), pp. 56–58. The Hawthornes had met Talfourd on their voyage to Europe in 1853; see *Memories*, p. 222. NH was to see him again in London (NH to SH, May 17, 1860; MS, Huntington).

648.10 I wrote a letter to Ticknor] NH describes his plans for travel, return to the Wayside, and revision of *MF* at home, and mentions "another Romance ready to be written," presumably *The Ancestral Footstep* (MS, Berg; published in *Letters to Ticknor* [Newark, N.J.: Carteret Book Club, 1910], II, 73–77).

650.7 Mrs. Pierce] Jane Means Appleton Pierce (1806–63), of Amherst, New Hampshire, had married Franklin Pierce in 1834.

650.8 Hotel de la Minerva] Murray, p. viii: "*Albergo della Minerva*, in the Piazza della Minerva, behind the Pantheon, much frequented by French and R.C. ecclesiastics."

651.2–3 Miss Vandervoort] Probably Mary Vandervoort. Pierce wrote from Capri to his friend John Hatch George on December 30, 1858, that he and his wife had in Florence "made the acquaintance of two agreeable Americans, a brother and sister named Vandervoort, of New York" (MS, New Hampshire Historical Society). The Vandervoorts accompanied the Pierces to Naples and then to Rome. The Pierces much appreciated Miss Vandervoort's fluency in French. In 1860 she was with them for five months in Nassau, Bahamas; see Roy Franklin Nichols, *Franklin Pierce: Young Hickory of the Granite Hills* (Philadelphia: University of Pennsylvania Press, 1958), p. 511. She is apparently the Miss Mary Vandervoort JH describes as a longtime resident of Dresden, who suggested that SH and her children come to live there in 1868; see *Memoirs*, ed. Edith Garrigues Hawthorne (New York: Macmillan, 1938), pp. 181–82. Her brother is apparently the James Vandervoort who wrote to Pierce in Brussels from

Carlsbad, Bohemia, on June 22, 1859, inquiring about Mrs. Pierce's health (MS, Library of Congress).

651.6 Mr. Reed (of Phil^a)] William Bradford Reed (1806–76), lawyer and professor of American history at the University of Pennsylvania, was appointed first plenipotentiary minister to China in 1857. He negotiated the Treaty of Tientsin, in 1858, securing the same rights for the United States as those won by the British and French from the Chinese, and legalizing the opium trade. Reed left China in November, 1858, and returned to America by way of Europe.

651.6 Dr. Henry] Caleb Sprague Henry (1804–84), clergyman, professor, and author, had been in early life a Congregationalist minister in Massachusetts and Connecticut. In 1836 he was ordained an Episcopal priest. He was professor of philosophy and history at New York University from 1839 to 1852. Besides publishing lectures and addresses, and editing the *New York Review* and the *Churchman*, Dr. Henry translated from the French the works of Cousin, Bantain, and Guizot.

652.3 Hotel d'Angleterre] In the Via Bocca de Leone, near the Via Condotti.

652.14 Mr Sandford's (of Boston,)] Milton L. Sanford, a wealthy Bostonian, uncle of Kate Field (1838–96), later a famous journalist and lyceum lecturer. Mr. and Mrs. Sanford, childless themselves, brought Kate to Europe in January 1859. In Florence she became an intimate of Anthony and Thomas Adolphus Trollope, Landor, and the Brownings. SH's diary recorded that on March 22 Mr. Sanford and Miss Field called and were not received, presumably because of Una's illness (MS, Berg). See Lilian Whiting, *Kate Field: A Record* (Boston: Little, Brown, 1899).

652.15 to Thompson's studio] NH had written to Thompson, a few days earlier, in response to Thompson's desire to see Pierce: "It will be quite proper for you to call on Genl Pierce, and I am sure he will be very glad to see you; but, if you prefer it, I will call with him at your Studio—where, indeed, I had already spoken to him of going. I want you to know him, because I am sure you will like him" (MS, St. Lawrence University).

652.17 Mr Stockton] John Potter Stockton (1826–1900) of New Jersey, U.S. minister to the Pontifical States from November 1858 until 1861, and later senator from New Jersey.

652.19–20 Page's studio.] William Page. Murray, p. 269: "Page, 39, Via Babuino, an American painter, chiefly of portraits." See note to 339.7.

653.26 the Velabrum] A hollow at the foot of the Palatine Hill.

654.5–6 Mr Tilton's] John Rollin Tilton (1828–88), from New Hampshire, a close friend of William Story, had kept a studio in the Barberini Palace since 1855. American and English travelers bought his pictures of famous Italian sites as souvenirs of their trips. His *Venetian Fishing Boats* and *Rome from Mount Aventine* were purchased by the Corcoran Gallery in Washington. See James, *William Wetmore Story and His Friends*, II, 127; *The Arcadian Landscape*, no. 39; Tuckerman, pp. 558–59; James Jackson Jarves, *The Art-Idea*, p. 179.

655.28–29 Wrote a long letter to Mr Bright.] An extract copied by Bright, on the "horrible state of things" in the relations between merchant seamen and officers, is published in *NHHW*, II, 152.

656.10–11 Mr Perkins] Charles Callahan Perkins (1823–86), art critic, was a grandson of the Boston philanthropic merchant James Perkins, who contributed much to the Boston Atheneum. He had lived several years in Florence; there he had been much influenced by Alexis-François Rio, the historian of Christian art. In 1859 Perkins was studying etching and preparing his first book, *Tuscan Sculptors* (1864). He is probably the author of an article in the Boston *Transcript*, November 24, 1884, 6: 1–3, on "Pre-Raphaelitism and Rubens," in which "the writer remembers twenty-six years ago telling Mrs. Hawthorne to study Botticelli and Bellini as the greatest types of their respective schools, with Mantegna for classic."

657.4 Father Smith] Rev. Dr. Bernard Smith, O.S.B. (1812–92), born in Ireland, was vice-rector of the Irish College in Rome from 1850 to 1855. He was much involved in the establishment of the North American College in Rome; when it opened, December 8, 1859, he was its first superior, with the title of pro-rector, until the arrival of the first rector from America in March, 1860. Father Smith was agent for twenty-one American Catholic bishops, and was a semi-official guide to Rome for prominent English-speaking visitors such as the prince of Wales, President Pierce, and NH, among others, according to R. F. McNamara, *The American College at Rome, 1855–1955* (Rochester, N.Y.: Christopher Press, 1956), p. 702.

657.15 Mrs. Farrar.] Eliza Ware Rotch Farrar (1791–1870), widow of John Farrar (1779–1853), professor of mathematics and natural philosophy at Harvard from 1807 to 1836. Mrs. Farrar lived in England until 1819, and became Professor Farrar's second wife in 1828. SH had known her since the early 1830s. She wrote several books for children, and *Recollections of Seventy Years* (Boston: Ticknor and Fields, 1865).

659.7 another Dr.] Dr. Liberali, 69, Via della Frezza; also a homeopathic physician.

660.13 Mr Freeman] James Edward Freeman (1808–84), born in Nova Scotia, a genre painter and close friend of the sculptor Crawford, came to Rome in 1836 and stayed until his death. See Freeman's *Gatherings from an Artist's Portfolio* (New York: Appleton, 1877); Crane, *passim;* Gale, *Thomas Crawford,* p. 101; Tuckerman, pp. 414–18. Freeman had served as American consul in Rome during the siege of the city in 1849. See Taylor, *William Page,* p. 120. His studio was located at 68, Via di Capo le Case (Bonfigli, *Guide,* p. 65).

663.25 Mr. De Leon] Edwin De Leon (1818–91), of South

Carolina, U.S. consul general at Alexandria, Egypt, from 1854 to 1861. A lawyer and editor, he became a Confederate diplomatic agent in Europe during the Civil War. He recalled his friendships with Dickens, Thackeray, Tennyson, and NH in *Thirty Years of Life in Three Continents* (London: Ward and Downey, 1890).

664.7–8   to Gen¹ Pierce at Vienna.] NH informs Pierce that the Hawthornes will "probably be forced to give up our proposed tour in Germany." He expects to be able to leave Rome with Una "in a fortnight, or perhaps in ten days" (MS, Pearson, Yale).

664.12–13   his infant Bacchus.] *Bacchus and Panther*, completed in 1863.

664.20   Santa Croce] The Basilica of S. Croce in Gerusalemme, a Roman imperial palace converted in the fourth century into a church, and finally redecorated in the eighteenth century in the baroque style.

665.1   Govʳ Seymour] Thomas Hart Seymour (1808–68), had been governor of Connecticut from 1850 to 1853, after having served as colonel in the Mexican War. His friend Franklin Pierce appointed him U.S. Minister to Russia (1853–58); after resigning that position he traveled for several months in Europe.

666.8   Chiesa Nuova] The popular name of S. Maria in Vallicella, a church near the Ponte S. Angelo. This church is best known for three paintings by Rubens, frescos by Pietro da Cortona, and the adjoining oratory by Borromini.

666.10   Mʳ Vezey] W. H. Vezey, of Pennsylvania.

667.28   the Pulchrum Littus] A quay on the Tiber at the mouth of the Cloaca Maxima, built of large blocks of travertine, and dating possibly from the period of the kings.

668.19   the church of San Clemente] on the Esquiline Hill, near the Baths of Titus. Murray, p. 137: "One of the most interesting and unaltered early Christian edifices in Rome."

670.22   a public garden on a height] Probably the Parc du Pharo.

672.3   Vaucluse.] Fontaine-de-Vaucluse, eighteen miles from Avignon, source of the river Sorgue. Murray, p. 443, says that "it is incumbent on all travellers to perform this 'sentimental journey' not only on account of Petrarch and Laura, but because Vaucluse itself is a striking scene." Vaucluse was a place of retirement and spiritually active relaxation for Petrarch. According to Ada Shepard, NH did not wish to visit it.

673.29   Miss Rachael Cushing] Rachel Cushing (1807–90), daughter of Thomas C. Cushing (1764–1824), publisher of the Salem *Gazette* from 1790 to 1823. SH had known her since the early 1820s.

674.24–25   sought (in vain) . . . Consul] The U.S. consul until 1859 was Nathaniel Bolton of Indiana. He was then relieved by William Fell Giles of Maryland. SH's diary recorded that the American consul called on the Hawthornes on the next day (MS, Berg).

675.15   17 Friday] SH recorded in her diary this day: "Met Mr. Parker at Minerve's"; and on the 18th: "Mrs. Theodore Parker & Mrs. Stephenson [called]." Theodore Parker (1810–60), accompanied by his wife, Lydia Dodge Cabot Parker (1813–80), and their friend Miss Hannah Stevenson, had arrived in Paris on June 13 from London, and left on the nineteenth for Switzerland, where he hoped to recover from tuberculosis.

675.19   N. C. Peabody] Nathaniel Cranch Peabody (1811–81), SH's brother, a homeopathic pharmacist in Boston. He and his family occupied the Wayside from the Hawthornes' departure in 1853 until Mary Peabody Mann and her children moved there after Horace Mann's death. See note to 688.11, and Margaret M. Lothrop, *The Wayside: Home of Authors* (New York: American Book, 1940), pp. 96–99.

675.22 Mr. Motley] Motley and his family left Rome June 1 and arrived in Paris June 3, traveling by express train from Marseilles. He wrote to his mother: "We were driven out of Italy by the war" (*Correspondence*, I, 322).

675.24 Mrs. Cranch] Elizabeth De Windt Cranch, originally of Fishkill, New York. She married Christopher Pearse Cranch in 1843. She was a friend of Margaret Fuller and of the Brownings.

675.26 I wrote a note to Bennoch.] Asking him to recommend "any respectable lodgings in the neighborhood of London" (MS, Pearson, Yale).

676.4–5 the church of St. Germains] St. Germain-l'Auxerrois, Place du Louvre, in which are buried many painters, sculptors and architects who had in earlier centuries lived in the Louvre.

676.8 Mrs. Green] Anna Blake Shaw Greene (1817–78) of Boston, daughter of the wealthy merchant Robert Gould Shaw (1776–1853). Her brother, Francis George Shaw (1809–82), was intimately connected with the progress of Brook Farm. With her sister-in-law Sarah Blake Sturgis Shaw, Anna Shaw was a visitor at the Old Manse in 1843; she was later a neighbor of the Hawthornes in Lenox, living near the Samuel Wards and her sister-in-law Caroline Sturgis Tappan. See *Memories*, pp. 59, 79, 143–44; *AN*, pp. 649–50.

676.13 Mr Greene] William Batchelder Greene (1819–78), Anna's husband, after two years at West Point had fought in the second Seminole War between 1839 and 1841. In Florida he experienced a religious conversion. After leaving the army, he was for a short time at Brook Farm. He graduated from the Harvard Divinity School in 1845, was minister of a Unitarian church in Brookfield, Massachusetts, and published a pamphlet, *Transcendentalism* (West Brookfield, Mass.: Oliver S. Cooke, 1849), dedicated to Emerson. He was an unorthodox Transcendentalist who debated Alcott and disputed Dr. William Ellery Channing in meetings at Elizabeth Peabody's bookshop. He published a number of works on religion and on economics and mathematics, and brought many of them together as *Socialistic, Communistic, Mutualistic, and Financial Fragments* (Boston: Lee and Shepard, 1875). Greene lived in Paris from 1853 to 1861, as his father, Nathaniel Greene (1797–1877), also did from 1849 to 1861. Nathaniel was a newspaper editor, and postmaster of Boston (1829–40, 1845–49). See George Willis Cooke, *Historical and Biographical Introduction to the Dial* (Cleveland: Rowfant Club, 1902), II, 117–28; Louise Hall Tharp, *The Peabody Sisters of Salem* (New York: Pyramid, 1968), p. 210 ff.

677.23–24   breakfast with Mr. Fields.] In his diary Fields recorded that NH "talked nervously about his new romance, the muscles of his face twitching, and with lowered voice; he thought some time he might print his journal also. . . . " NH also suggested that Fields rent the Villa Montauto during his planned stay in Florence the following winter (James T. Fields, *Biographical Notes and Personal Sketches* [Boston: Houghton, Mifflin, 1882], p. 60).

677.26–27   Thames Tunnel] The first underwater tunnel in the world was designed by Marc Isambard Brunel (1769–1849). It was begun in 1825 and completed in 1843, but at such ruinous expense that its approaches were not developed for railroad traffic until 1869. In the 1850s it was only a pedestrian walkway between Rotherhithe and Wapping, and a night shelter for London's homeless. NH and JH had walked through it in September, 1855; see *EN*, pp. 232–33, and *OOH*, pp. 245–51.

678.5–6   Mr. Chorley, the Athenaeum critic] Henry Fothergill Chorley (1808–72) became music and literature critic of the *Athenæum* in 1833. He had reviewed six of NH's books; it was his favorable notice of three tales by NH in the 1835 *Token* that much pleased and encouraged NH (letter to Elizabeth Hawthorne, January 25, 1836; MS, Essex Institute). See *NHB*, p. 34. Chorley in 1852 characterized NH as "the highest, deepest, and finest imaginative writer America has yet produced" (*Athenæum*, July 10, 1852, p. 742). On the present meeting, NH's first with Chorley, see *NHHW*, II, 223–24. For further correspondence of SH and

NH with Chorley, in regard to his less favorable review of *MF*, see *Memories*, pp. 467–71; *NHHW*, II, 244–48.

678.6   Mrs Stevens] Mary Newton Kuczynski Stevens (b. 1819 in Lincoln, England), wife of the American bookman Henry Stevens (1819–86), whom NH had met in London in April 1856 (*EN*, p. 326). She was the widow of Count Vincent Kuczynski and a descendant of Sir Isaac Newton.

678.10–11   Vernon Gallery, Marlboro' House.] A collection of some two hundred pictures, most by contemporary English painters, presented to the nation in 1847 by Robert Vernon (1774–1849), who had made a fortune as contractor of horses to the British army during the Napoleonic Wars. The collection was later moved to the South Kensington Museum, and in 1876 to the National Gallery. NH had enjoyed his previous visit in July, 1856 (*EN*, p. 389).

678.13   Mrs. Hume] A friend of Bennoch's who kept a school for girls at Clifton Villa in Shirley, two miles from Southampton. The Hawthornes stayed with her for two weeks in June and July, 1856, after SH's return from Portugal.

678.27–28   I wrote . . . August 13ᵗʰ.] NH wrote on July 6, probably to Wilding, to cancel the steamer berths he had engaged for August 13 (letter sold by Sotheby, March 14, 1968).

678.31–679.1   society of Archimagi.] The Society of Noviomagus, a social club elected from the membership of the Society of Antiquaries. The name derived from a Roman city in Kent excavated in 1828. The society conducted an annual outing on the first Saturday in July. It invited to its meetings distinguished authors, artists, scientists, inventors, travelers, and the like. "The governing and peculiar rule of the society is that a speaker shall say what he does not mean, and mean what he does not say. This rule gave rise to much 'fun' " (S. C. Hall, *Retrospect of a Long Life* [New York: Appleton, 1883], p. 599. See also William Jerdan, *Autobiography* (London: Arthur Hall and Virtue, 1853), IV, 32–34.

679.2 Sir Francis Moon] Sir Francis Graham Moon (1796–1871), a printmaker and fine-art publisher, who had reproduced some of the finest works of David Wilkie, Edwin Landseer, David Roberts, and other contemporary British artists (*DNB*).

679.10 Captain Shaw] Of the North Cork Rifles. He had been the host of NH and Bennoch in April, 1856, when they visited Aldershott camp.

679.20 The Duke of Cambridge] George William Frederick Charles, second duke of Cambridge (1819–1904), grandson of George III, general and commander-in-chief of the army. NH described his appearance on a previous visit to the camp in April 1856 (*EN*, p. 297).

679.28–29 Mr. Fields has arranged . . . new Romance.] Pierce reported to Bridge on September 11, 1859 (MS, Bowdoin): "I was with Hawthorne in Rome daily, and our arrangements were made to return together. But when he reached England he was offered £600 to allow his forthcoming book to be published there. It was a proposition gratifying to his pride & agreeable enough to his purse and was of course accepted— As he could not be ready to cross the Atlantic till late in the season, I advised him, in view of Una's rather delicate health, to remain till next Spring, which he has concluded to do."

679.30 National Exhibition] Identified as the Royal Academy by SH's diary (MS, Berg). There was no officially titled "National Exhibition" in London at this time. The Annual Exhibition of the Royal Academy (popularly known as "the Exhibition") and the National Gallery continued to "jostle" each other in shared quarters at Trafalgar Square (*Times*, February 10, 1859). NH apparently compacted their names as well.

680.6 Guildhall] See NH's descriptions in *EN*, pp. 379–80, 598–99.

680.7 Mr. Jerdan] William Jerdan (1782–1869), editor of the *Literary Gazette* from 1817 to 1850, a friend and encourager of many distinguished authors. NH met him with Bennoch in Liverpool in 1853 and in London in July, 1856. He is characterized in *EN*, pp. 282–83. See also *DNB*.

680.9–10 Bo't 5th Vol. . . . Washington.] Washington Irving, *The Life of George Washington*. The fifth and concluding volume was published July 2 by Bohn in London.

680.16 Mr. Bates] Joshua Bates (1788–1864), born in Weymouth, Massachusetts, had lived in London and had been a partner with Baring Brothers since 1826. By the 1850s he was head of the firm, and probably the most influential foreigner in private life in Great Britain. He was the principal founder of the Boston Public Library in 1852. His wife, Lucretia Augusta, was a cousin of his partner, Russell Sturgis (*DNB, DAB*).

680.19 Genl Campbell's] Robert Blair Campbell (d. 1862), U.S. consul in London from 1854 to 1861, had been commissioned general of South Carolina troops in 1833. He had also served as congressman from that state. NH had met him in London in September 1855.

680.23–24 a debate— . . . Sidney Herbert &c] The debate included consideration of the state of affairs in Italy. Lord John Russell (1792–1878), foreign secretary, and Henry John Temple, third viscount Palmerston (1784–1865), prime minister, answered questions on this topic. Sidney Herbert (1810–61), secretary of state for war, also spoke briefly. See *Hansard's Parliamentary Debates*, Third Series, CLIV (1859), 862–946.

681.8 Mrs. Heywood] Mrs. John Pemberton Heywood of Norris Green, Liverpool, was an aunt of Henry Arthur Bright, and a distant cousin of William E. Gladstone. Her husband was a banker; they kept a residence in London. NH had been their guest for dinner on several occasions.

681.22 Dr. Williams' Library] Daniel Williams (?1643–1716), a nonconformist divine and benefactor (for example, of Harvard

University), left provision in his will for a building to hold his extensive library. This building, in Red Cross Street, was for many years "the headquarters of London dissent." The library was moved in 1864, and now is in University Hall, Gordon Square, W.C. Among its possessions are the original minutes of the Westminster Assembly and a death mask of Oliver Cromwell (*DNB*).

681.25–26   Barry Cornwall] Pseudonym of Bryan Waller Procter (1787–1874), poet, playwright, and lawyer. After an exchange of letters in 1851 and 1852 (*NHHW*, I, 440–41), Procter called upon NH in Liverpool in June 1854 (*EN*, p. 62), and introduced NH by letter to Leigh Hunt in October 1855.

681.26   Leigh Hunt] Leigh Hunt (1794–August 28, 1859), poet and essayist. For NH's memorable description of their meeting in October, 1855, see *EN*, pp. 254–56.

681.26   Kinglake] Alexander William Kinglake (1809–91), lawyer and historian, now mainly remembered as author of *Eöthen; or, Traces of Travel Brought Home from the East* (1844), one of the best Victorian travel narratives. He was to write *The Invasion of the Crimea* in eight volumes (1863–87).

682.2   T. Hughes] Thomas Hughes (1822–96), lawyer and social reformer, anonymously published *Tom Brown's School Days,* the most famous account of Victorian public school life, in April, 1857; there were five printings in the next nine months. Hughes was a principal sponsor of the Working Men's College, Great Ormond Street, London, where he taught and was to be principal from 1872 to 1883 (*DNB*). Henry Bright recalled that Hughes sang "The Tight Little Island" on this occasion (letter to NH, September 8, 1860, in *Memories*, p. 465), and that Hughes read Tennyson's "The Grandmother's Apology" to his adult students (letter to JH, in *NHHW*, II, 223).

682.21   Whitby church and Abbey.] The original abbey was founded by St. Hilda in 657. It was ravaged by the Danes in 867, and refounded by the Benedictines in 1087. Here NH found the name of Hilda, one of the principal characters in *MF*.

683.21–23 Wrote letters . . . Hillard.] Those to Bennoch and Hillard have been recovered. NH describes Redcar for Bennoch (MS, Virginia). He proposes that Hillard stop there if he is to tour Scotland (MS, Berg).

684.27 R. Monckton Milnes.] Henry Bright had written to NH on July 29, 1859 (MS, Berg), "Monckton Milnes is bringing on the ship-cruelty question in the House on the 2nd, August, & he wishes you very much to send him a few lines relative to the matter." Milnes' speech in the Commons is summarized in *Hansard's Parliamentary Debates*, Third Series, CLV (1859), 871–82.

685.13 J. R. Lowell] Lowell (1819–91) was editor of the *Atlantic Monthly* from its inception in November, 1857, until 1861. The letter mentioned by NH is not included in the *Letters of James Russell Lowell*, ed. Charles Eliot Norton (New York: Harper, 1894), or in *New Letters of James Russell Lowell*, ed. M. A. DeWolfe Howe (New York: Harper, 1932). However, in Lowell's letter to Emerson, July 18, 1859, he wrote, "If you should see Hawthorne before I do, will you put in a good word for the Atlantic. He brings home a honey-bag, I hear" (*New Letters*, p. 97).

686.2 Dr. Wilkinson] James John Garth Wilkinson (1812–98), homeopathic physician, translator and biographer of Swedenborg, and advocate of spiritualism, was a friend of Emerson and of Henry James, Sr. NH met him in December, 1857, just before leaving England, when Wilkinson introduced him to Coventry Patmore, and attended the Hawthorne children for the measles (*DNB*).

686.11–12 Wrote a note to Fields.] NH reports slow progress on *MF*, and regrets that Fields has chosen to visit Switzerland rather than Scotland. He plans to winter in Leamington (MS, Collection of Arnold Whitridge).

687.5 the Scouring of the White Horse] A sentimental novel published by Hughes in 1859. The story is of an urban white-collar worker's prejudices against rural life, and how an idealized country parson and squire teach him faith in democracy and Christianity.

688.11 Horace Mann's death.] On August 2, 1859, in Yellow Springs, Ohio, the seat of Antioch College. See note to 675.19.

689.9 —— castle] Wilton Castle, baronial seat of the Bulmer family. It was rebuilt in the early nineteenth century.

690.20 Mrs. J. L. O'Sullivan in Lisbon.] John O'Sullivan had been replaced as U.S. minister to Portugal in July 1858, but he and his wife and mother continued to live in Lisbon.

691.7 Ellen E. Peabody.] Ellen Elizabeth Peabody (1836–1906) daughter of SH's brother Nathaniel, married George Phineas How of Concord on November 3, 1859.

694.4 Cairngorm seal] A seal made from a yellowish precious stone found in the highlands of Scotland.

694.6 Miss Cust] Katherine Isabella Cust edited William Caxton's translation (1483) of Guillaume de Guileville, *The Booke of the Pylgremage of the Sowle*, published in London by Basil Montagu Pickering, 1859. In 1858 Miss Cust had edited a work by Nathaniel Hall comparing Guillaume de Guileville's *Pilgrimage of Man* to Bunyan's *Pilgrim's Progress*.

694.22 Mrs. Badger] Ada Shepard married Henry Clay Badger on August 30, and joined the faculty of Antioch College for the 1859–60 academic year.

695.13 Wrote a letter to Ticknor.] NH is "within a fortnight of finishing" *MF*, but will not send it to Smith and Elder until Fields returns from the continent. The family will probably spend the winter in Leamington (MS, Berg).

695.16 Wrote . . . to Bennoch.] NH asks that Bennoch tell Fields, on his return to London, that the Hawthornes are in Leamington. He expects to come to London soon after *MF* is finished (MS, Virginia).

695.23 Jephson's Gardens] Described by NH in *EN*, pp. 566–67 (September 11, 1857). Henry Jephson (1798–1878),

M.D. Glasgow 1827, settled in 1828 in Leamington and built a large and lucrative practice, his patients coming from all parts of Great Britain and from the Continent to take the Leamington waters internally and externally. In 1848 a statue was erected and the public gardens were called after his name.

695.24   Wrote a note to Fields.] Fields was in Paris. NH reports his progress on *MF*, and alternate titles from which Fields may select after reading the romance. NH proposes, "we had better all go home together," the next spring or summer (MS, Huntington; excerpt in *Yesterdays with Authors*, p. 85).

696.23   Madam O'Sullivan] Mary Blackburn Rowly O'Sullivan, mother of John Louis. NH sent her a copy of *MF* shortly before her death in May, 1860; see *HC*, pp. 136–37.

697.23–24   Bilton Hall (a residence of Addison.)] A large house and manor near Rugby purchased by Joseph Addison (1672–1719) in 1713. NH had admired Addison's prose since his boyhood, when he had written a weekly newspaper called the *Spectator* (*New England Quarterly*, IV (1931), 288–330. He had previously visited Addison's residences in London and Lichfield, and his grave in Westminister Abbey (*EN*, pp. 282, 151, 220; *OOH*, p. 130).

697.25   Charley Bright] George Charles Bright (1840–1922), a cousin of Henry Bright, was a student at Rugby. His father, Richard Bright (1789–1858), was an eminent pathologist; nephritis is called "Bright's disease" in his honor. Charles became M.D. at Oxford in 1875.

697.27–28   Letter from Mr. Macmillan, publisher.] Alexander Macmillan (1818–96), head of Macmillan and Company, Cambridge and London, who was to bring out the first issue of *Macmillan's Magazine* in November, 1859. The company had published the very successful books of Thomas Hughes, beginning with *Tom Brown's School Days* in 1857. See note to 682.2.

698.16   Mr. Mason Jones'] (Thomas) Mason Jones, an orator

and politician, gave lectures at the Leamington Public Hall on October 25, 26, and 27. The subjects were Richard Brinsley Sheridan, John Wesley, and Edmund Burke.

699.26   E. P. P.] Elizabeth Palmer Peabody.

700.27   Major Johnstone] JH recalled "an old Peninsula veteran, Major Johnstone, who trained me in the use of the broadsword, and who, during the pauses of the encounter, used to regale us with anecdotes of Spain, Waterloo, and Wellington" (*NHHW*, II, 266). His further recollection of the major is in *HC*, pp. 369–70.

701.9–10   A letter . . . title of my book.] See the discussion in Claude M. Simpson, "Introduction," *MF*, pp. xxv–xxvii.

701.24   Wrote in my Journal.] This entry and six others, from February to May, 1860, written in England, and one written in Maine in 1862, were edited by SH for *Passages*. The English 1859–60 journal entries will be included in the Centenary edition of *The English Notebooks*.

702.1   Tachbourne] I.e., Tachbrook. NH was not secure in the name, which he also wrote "Tachborne" as on November 17.

702.5   Wrote a note to Fields.] "Leamington is not so desirable in winter as in summer," and after Christmas the Hawthornes may move to Bath or to Devonshire (MS, Huntington; excerpts in *Yesterdays with Authors*, p. 86). They moved to Bath on March 22, 1860, and stayed until sailing from Liverpool on June 16.

702.13   S. Lucas] Samuel Lucas (1818–68), literary reviewer for the London *Times* and editor of *Once a Week*, an illustrated periodical begun by Bradbury and Evans in July, 1859, to fill the gap caused by the discontinuance of Dickens's *Household Words*. (Dickens, however, had already founded *All the Year Round*.) Lucas twice wrote to NH soliciting contributions, on November 5 and 17 (*NHHW*, II, 233–35).

703.14   My wife and I answered Fields' note.] Fields had suggested that SH write for the *Atlantic Monthly*. NH praises "her narrative and descriptive epistles to her friends; but I doubt whether she would find sufficient inspiration in writing directly for the public" (Transcript, Hawthorne-Fields Letterbook, Harvard College Library).

703.16–17 Note from Bennoch, which I answered.] NH will not come to London at present unless called by business, because his experience of London in the late autumn of 1857 was unpleasant. He expects Bennoch to come to Leamington in ten days (MS, Virginia).

704.2 Wrote a letter to W. D. Ticknor] NH suggests "Saint Hilda's Shrine" as the American title of *MF*. He asks Ticknor to pay any bills for repairs of the Wayside that Mrs. Mann may request (MS, Berg; published in *Letters to Ticknor*, II, 84–87).

704.4 Richd Manning] Richard Clarke Manning (1830–1904), son of NH's uncle Robert Manning (1784–1842), and Una's first cousin once removed.

704.19–20 a note to them] NH is concerned about the publishers' choice of title. He asks that the manuscript be preserved for a friend who has requested it, Henry Bright (Transcript, Pearson; MS, collection of Mrs. Reginald Smith).

704.27 dissolving views] Pictures produced on a screen by a magic lantern, one picture being caused gradually to disappear while another gradually appears on the same field (*OED*).

705.8 Sarah Clarke] Sarah Anne Clarke (1808–96), a landscape painter and portraitist who was in the 1830s SH's closest friend among American artists. She was a sister of the Unitarian minister James Freeman Clarke. She had studied with Washington Allston, and was in Europe in 1850, 1853, and 1855–56, when she visited SH in Liverpool.

706.21 Mary Peabody] Mary Cranch Peabody (1837–1917), daughter of SH's brother Nathaniel.

706.24   Dr. Sutherland] A local physician. According to SH's diary (MS, Berg), Rosebud's ailment was a sore throat.

706.26   Wrote a note to Ticknor] NH has rejected the publishers' proposal to call *MF* "The Transformation; or, the Romance of Monte Beni" (MS, Berg; published in *Letters to Ticknor*, II, 87–88).

706.27   a note to Bennoch] NH is disappointed that Bennoch has been unable to visit, and expects him "immediately after Christmas" (MS, Virginia).

707.23   Rec^d (and answered) a note from Fields] Fields will be traveling soon to Italy; he proposes to return to America the following May, but NH will not be ready until July (MS, Huntington; excerpts in *Yesterdays with Authors*, p. 88).

EDITORIAL APPENDIXES

HISTORICAL COMMENTARY

T HIS IS the first complete publication of Hawthorne's
French and Italian notebooks, which he began on his
arrival in Paris on January 6, 1858, and concluded on
the day of his departure from Havre for England, June 22,
1859. They are an extension of notebooks he had kept in
England from 1853 to 1857: the first entry begins at the foot
of page 112 of the seventh English volume. The continental
notebooks consist of 863 manuscript pages, or somewhat less
than two hundred thousand words, of which all but a hundred
pages were written between January and October, 1858, before Hawthorne's daughter Una became seriously ill. The
English notebooks, written over four and a half years, are
less than twice as voluminous, containing 1,508 manuscript
pages, or approximately three hundred forty thousand words.

The notebooks for the first ten months of 1858—a record
mainly of travel, of visits to churches, museums, and other
cultural monuments, and of conversation with American
and English expatriates and tourists—are the most sustained
and detailed journalizing of Hawthorne's life. He had begun
in England in the summer of 1855 to make extensive use
of his notebooks for his family's vacation in Leamington and
its environs; that September, in London for the first time, he

made twenty entries for the month, and filled 115 pages. During the remainder of his stay in England, he continued in the springs and summers to write at a more or less steady pace. But on arrival in France, and then in Rome for the winter and spring of 1858, he journalized in greater detail than ever before, most in May and June in Rome and Florence and the cities between them, and less in the summer, when he was making a first draft of *The Marble Faun*; his use of the journal increased in September in Florence and in October on the return to Rome by way of Siena.

Before arriving on the Continent he had never kept a journal in the winter, for during that season he habitually wrote for publication. The bulk of the narrative portions of the American notebooks—the excursions to Maine in 1837 and to the Berkshires in 1838, the Old Manse journal of 1842, "Twenty Days with Julian & Little Bunny" in 1851—were written in the months of July and August. But Hawthorne had good reasons to change his habit in January 1858: he had just escaped from a prolonged and distasteful involvement with the finances of the Liverpool custom house; he had saved enough money to live as a gentleman for at least two winter seasons in Rome, with the prospect of summer travel to Florence and other cities of Italy; his wife's health, which had suffered from the damp English climate, could be expected to improve in the warmth and sunshine of Italy; and for her, Italy's treasures of art represented a chance for the fulfillment of a lifetime's dream of study and appreciation.

In April 1852, after contracting to buy the Wayside for $1,500 from Mrs. Bronson Alcott, Hawthorne had written to his friend Grace Greenwood: "I have bought a house in Concord, deeming it better to do so, on the whole, than to spend the money in going to Italy, although I do not yet give up that long-cherished idea. It is best, perhaps, to keep it by way of a second youth, wherewith to gladden my late declining age."[1] The opportunity presented itself sooner than expected, however. With Franklin Pierce's nomination for president the following June, and Hawthorne's offer to write a campaign biography, the possibility of a European consular post soon became a reality. As soon as he was awarded the consulship at Liverpool, he began to think of spending four years there, coinciding with Pierce's term, and then "a year in Italy before returning."[2]

It was Sophia Hawthorne who had most cherished the idea of living in Italy. In 1824, at the age of fifteen, she had begun to study drawing, and had read *Corinne*, Mme de Staël's fictionalized guidebook to the art of Rome. Like many other young women of the 1820s and 1830s, she conceived a passionate longing for Italy. This longing was doubtless fed by reading Anna Jameson's *Diary of an Ennuyée* (1826) and other imitations of *Corinne*; thirty years later she would have the chance to meet Mrs. Jameson in Rome.[3] Sophia's interest in art, and her considerable talent, led her into the company of artists in Boston; and in May 1832 the dean of American painters, Washington Allston, came to her house to see and praise a landscape she had painted in imitation of Salvator Rosa. As Louise Hall Tharp explains, "He recreated for her the glamour of his student days abroad and described the long discipline an artist must undergo."[4] A few months later, after reading the "Tour through Italy and Switzerland" of Edmund Dorr Griffin, she wrote excitedly to her sister Elizabeth, "Oh *why not live in Rome*. . . . Pack up—Betty—& let us be off—& live in Rome—the eternal—imperial 'Mother of dead

1 April 17, 1852, MS, Berg.

2 Hawthorne to Mrs. Horatio Bridge, May 18, 1853, MS, Bowdoin.

3 Louise Hall Tharp, *The Peabody Sisters of Salem* (1950; New York: Pyramid, 1968), p. 41; Ellen Moers, "Performing Heroinism: The Myth of Corinne," in Jerome H. Buckley, ed., *The Worlds of Victorian Fiction* (Cambridge: Harvard University Press, 1975), pp. 338–39.

4 Tharp, *The Peabody Sisters of Salem*, p. 61.

empires'—the city of the soul—the retreat of the arts & graces— the garden of Nature—for three or four years!"[5] But she had to trade this dream for a brief career in Boston as a copyist and illustrator (she contributed the frontispiece to the special edition in 1839 of Hawthorne's *The Gentle Boy*). After their marriage, it was her practice to fill the various Hawthorne residences with copies of paintings, busts, and statuary— Madonnas and Sibyls by Michelangelo, Leonardo, and Raphael, landscapes by Claude and Rosa, statues by Thorvaldsen, Canova, and Thomas Crawford—so that their children grew up in an atmosphere saturated with culture.[6] It is not surprising that shortly after their arrival in Rome Sophia sent off a triumphant announcement to Elizabeth, which should "have the effect at least of the bell of St. Peter's—or the cannon of St. Angelo." In spite of "the utter and hopeless misery of cold . . . I am in Rome—Rome, *Roma*—I have stood in the Forum, & beneath the Arch of Titus at the end of the Sacra Via. I have wandered about the Coliseum, the stupendous grandeur of which equals my dream & hope, & I have seen the sun kindling the open courts of the Temple of Peace, where Sarah [Clarke] said years ago—that my children ought to play. . . ."[7]

It is difficult to believe that Hawthorne felt the same kind of exultation. For him a more generalized sense of the past, which he had indulged in his English notebooks, was joined with impatience at time's power to fade and decay works of art. He was fifty-three years old when he came to Rome, and he had dealt little with Europe and its artistic heritage in his fiction.[8] Such references as there are to Italy and Italian cul-

[5] September 5, 1832, MS, Berg.

[6] Julian Hawthorne, *Nathaniel Hawthorne and His Wife* (Boston: James R. Osgood, 1884), I, 279, 286, 367-71.

[7] N.d. [February? 1858], MS, Berg. For Sarah Clarke, see Explanatory Note to 705.8.

[8] See Christof Wegelin, "Europe in Hawthorne's Fiction," *ELH*, XIV

ture come in works written after meeting Sophia in 1837. And in view of the "second youth" he told Grace Greenwood he hoped to find in Italy, it is understandable that Arthur Dimmesdale is invited by Hester Prynne to find a new life "in pleasant Italy," and Clifford Pyncheon proposes in "a low, self-communing voice" to leave the dismal House of the Seven Gables to live in "Paris, Naples, Venice, Rome."[9] Hawthorne's duties in Liverpool had become onerous, and before his first year was out he was writing to Horatio Bridge to propose that "we might form a little colony amongst ourselves" in Italy, "and see our children grow up together." The agitation over slavery in America made him shrink from his native land: "If it were not for my children, I should probably never return, but after quitting my office, should go to Italy, and live and die there."[10] Italy in his mind took on some of the same utopian prospect that Brook Farm had fifteen years earlier. In the winter of 1854–55, he became concerned about a law recently passed by the U.S. Congress that reduced consular incomes, and considered resigning in 1856, "for," he

---

(September, 1947), 219–45; Nathalia Wright, *American Novelists in Italy* (Philadelphia: University of Pennsylvania Press, 1965), p. 152. The following references to Italy occur in Hawthorne's tales and romances previous to *The Marble Faun* (pages are of the Centenary Edition): *Twice-told Tales*, pp. 155, 194, 261, 268; *Mosses from an Old Manse*, pp. 91–128 ("Rappaccini's Daughter"), pp. 173, 269, 307, 408, 478–88 ("A Virtuoso's Collection"); *The Snow-Image*, pp. 63, 207; *The Scarlet Letter*, p. 197; *The House of the Seven Gables*, pp. 111, 162, 176, 188, 193, 198, 200, 203–4, 286, 292–95; *The Blithedale Romance*, p. 103.

[9] *The Scarlet Letter*, p. 197; *The House of the Seven Gables*, p. 111. In a letter to Longfellow, January 12, 1839, MS, Houghton, Hawthorne had announced a "presentiment" that he would one day be in the Mediterranean area. And at some later time, Horatio Bridge had planned to "eject from office" Longfellow's friend George Washington Greene, the American consul at Rome, "for thy husband's benefit," Hawthorne reminded his wife in a letter of August 26, 1843; MS, Huntington. And again, in March 1845, when Hawthorne was seeking a government position at Salem, John O'Sullivan recommended him to George Bancroft for —among other posts—consulships at Marseilles, Genoa, and Gibraltar (Julian Hawthorne, *NHHW*, I, 284).

[10] March 30, 1854, MS, Bowdoin.

wrote Bridge, "I can live economically in Italy, and pursue my literary avocations as well there as elsewhere."[11] To Ticknor he was more cautious: "I shall spend a year on the Continent, and then decide whether to go back to the Way Side, or to stay abroad and write books."[12] Sophia's health suffered during this winter of 1855, and Hawthorne considered taking her to Rome before the next one. But he decided to continue in Liverpool while the position was profitable, and sent Sophia, Una, and Rose to Lisbon, to stay with the O'Sullivans, from October 1855 to June 1856. Upon her return Sophia had decided—so he reported—"with great certainty that she can safely spend another winter in England," thereby allowing him to serve out his four years, and to accumulate a "pile . . . large enough to enable me to live, in Italy, on the interest."[13] Now more positive than ever, he announced to Ticknor: "I mean to settle in Italy. My business, such as it is, can be carried on just as well there as in America, and I will get you to sell the place [the Wayside] in Concord. But this need not be done quite yet."[14]

On February 13, 1857, the day he sent his resignation (effective August 31) to President Buchanan, Hawthorne wrote to Ticknor that he looked forward to Italy, where, "perhaps, I shall begin to be a literary man again." But by now a new plan had entered his mind: "It is a pity I can not take advantage of my residence in England to publish something while I remain here, and to secure the English Copyright."[15] By April he had decided that "I shall leave the consulate joy-

11 December 14, 1854, MS, Bowdoin.

12 January 19, 1855, MS, Berg. He went on to mention "the germs of a new Romance" that he apparently already planned to write in Italy, "The Ancestral Footstep."

13 Hawthorne to Bridge, June 20, 1856, MS, Bowdoin; to Ticknor, August 15, 1856, MS, Boston College.

14 November 10, 1856, MS, Boston College.

15 MS, Berg.

fully, but England with some regret; for it is a good country to live in, and if I were rich enough, I doubt whether I should ever leave it for a permanent residence elsewhere."[16] Italy he saw as Sophia's second youth, rather than as his own: "I shall rejoice, on her account, when we get to the Continent. For myself, I should be well content to spend the remainder of my days in England."[17] By the summer he seems to have reconsidered his literary intentions. Looking over his English journal of several hundred pages, he began to appreciate the record as a work of art in its own right: It would be "delightful to the public" because it was written with "so free and truth-telling a pen"; but of course it was "too spicy," "too full and free ever to be published."[18] This writing seems to have given him the sense of freedom that he had yearned for in Italy. He wrote to Bridge in September, enthusiastic about his plans for immediate departure for Paris: "I doubt much whether I do anything more than observe and journalize, while I remain abroad."[19] He felt the same in November, in spite of frustrating delays: "I shall have so much to see, while I remain in Europe, that I think I must confine myself to keeping a Journal."[20] The satisfaction of journalizing in England included descriptive writing, appreciation of landscapes and old buildings and historic sites, but also such social success—parties, outings, breakfasts, under the guidance and sponsorship of his friends Bennoch and Bright—as Hawthorne

[16] Hawthorne to Ticknor, April 24, 1857, MS, Berg.

[17] Hawthorne to Ticknor, January 2, 1857, MS, Berg.

[18] Hawthorne to James T. Fields, September 9, 1857, MS, Houghton; to Elizabeth Peabody, August 13, 1857, MS, Berg; to Francis Bennoch, June 13, 1857, MS, Virginia. As early as April 14, 1857, Hawthorne wrote in his journal: "I have really made it a matter of conscience to keep a tolerably full record of my travels, though conscious that everything good escapes in the process" (*English Notebooks*, ed. Randall Stewart [New York: Modern Language Association, 1941], p. 456).

[19] September 17, 1857, MS, Bowdoin.

[20] Hawthorne to Ticknor, November 5, 1857, MS, Berg.

had never enjoyed before. He found that sketching the personalities of his new acquaintances engaged his faculties and
challenged his creative powers. He looked forward to more
such encounters with the Anglo-American communities of
Rome and Florence.

The departure for the Continent was delayed from September to January: Hawthorne's chief clerk, Henry Wilding,
became seriously ill, and was unable to settle the outgoing
consul's accounts with the United States government; the
financial crash of 1857, which forced some English banks to
close, exacerbated the problem. Hawthorne was congenitally
restless and impatient about both finances and the mechanics
of travel. His mood darkened. He wrote to Elizabeth Peabody:
"I am weary, and, if it were not for Sophia and the children,
would like to lie down in one spot for about a hundred years."[21]
Similar notes of depression and emotional entropy were to
recur on the Continent, and for the remainder of his life. As
if to confirm his fears of committing himself as a writer to
the strange and possibly incomprehensible cultures and languages of France and Italy, the weather changed at the
moment of the Hawthornes' crossing the Channel. A mild
December in London turned into the coldest winter in twenty
years in Paris and Rome. Speaking of Amiens, his first city in
France, he put his disappointment into his journal: "If the
cold had not been such as to dull my sense of novelty, and
make all my perceptions torpid, I should have taken in a new
set of impressions and enjoyed them very much. As it was I
cared little for what I saw."

But the weather was not, finally, important. Clearly Hawthorne felt out of his element in Europe. He had discovered
in England that the very privacy of his journal gave him the
greatest satisfaction. To give an exact record of his impres-

---

[21] [October 9,] 1857; in Moncure Conway, *Life of Hawthorne* (London:
Walter Scott, 1895), p. 156.

sions sometimes meant putting down his quirky reactions, or his boredom and indifference, or his impotence to express what he wanted to express. When such unsatisfactory or disturbing moments occurred infrequently, the journal could absorb them. When they became, as they often did in France and Italy, the norm of his reactions, his only alternatives were silence or the dogged determination to keep on writing regardless. As he tried to write about Marseilles while the steamer pitched its way through the Mediterranean toward Italy, Hawthorne noted the evanescence of novelty in descriptive writing, "the fleeting aroma of a new scene." "And it is always so much pleasanter to enjoy this delicious newness than to attempt arresting it, that it requires great force of will to insist with oneself upon sitting down to write." When there was no pleasure (as there often would not be), he would find writing much more difficult, no matter what the weather.

Thirty years later, William Wetmore Story, the Bostonian sculptor resident in Rome, recalled Hawthorne's arrival there in January, 1858: "Hawthorne had just liberated himself from the consular galleys at Liverpool, and was rejoicing in his freedom. He had come to Rome only to give his family—particularly his wife, and their daughter Una, both devoted to art—a pleasant excursion. For himself, he had little knowledge of art, and no taste for ruins; and it was to be some time before he should take Rome seriously."[22] The notebooks qualify the easy tone of this reminiscence, just as the facts of cultural history were to qualify so many of Story's impressions. Even before his arrival in Rome, Hawthorne had found it impossible not to take the world of art seriously, and had found himself the more "perfectly miserable," as he put it in Genoa, "the better worth seeing are the things" that his limited "receptive capacity" forced him to reject. From this point till the

[22] Conway, *Life of Hawthorne*, p. 161.

end of the journals in Havre eighteen months later, Hawthorne's keynote is this plaintive and insistent self-criticism.
Finally, he was reduced to inventing excuses to his wife
(whose enterprise and energy were relentless), and "to my
own conscience, for not seeing even the things that have
helped to tempt me abroad."

The decade of the 1850s was the flood tide of American
interest in Italy as a museum. Hawthorne himself remarked
in a letter to Ticknor, March 4, 1859, that "there are said to
be 1500 Americans now in Rome."[23] During 1858, nearly two
thousand Americans visited Florence. Most of these tourists
and temporary residents had little interest in Italian social
institutions and political developments; they had come to
appreciate—and, in the cases of the artists, to copy or
imitate—the spirit of classical antiquity and of the Renaissance. Guidebooks and travelers' accounts made the museums
and churches familiar to the armchair traveler, and those
who may have arrived without such preparation were soon
attracted to them. As one minister wrote, "It is impossible
to live in Italy long without becoming at least a profound
amateur in the fine arts."[24] Nevertheless, there was some
reaction against this worship, especially by English novelists
and poets—among them Thackeray, Browning, Patmore, and
Clough, who sometimes saw Rome not as Byron's "city of the
soul" but as a picturesque, even squalid modern city. Dickens
announced at the beginning of his *Pictures from Italy*: "There
is, probably, not a famous Picture or Statue in all Italy, but
could be easily buried under a mountain of printed paper
devoted to dissertations on it." He would not add to the pile,
he emphasized. Hawthorne's description of Italy is repre-

[23] MS, Berg.

[24] Paul R. Baker, *The Fortunate Pilgrims: Americans in Italy, 1800–
1860* (Cambridge: Harvard University Press, 1964), pp. 3–5, 123. See
chapter 6, "The World of Art," and especially pp. 149–50, for a succinct
analysis of American attitudes toward Italian art.

sentative of this realistic reaction,[25] except that, unlike Dickens, Hawthorne felt obligated to give his impression of every picture and statue. Of course, Sophia was with him, setting down her own notes on "the illustrious works of the Great Masters."[26] They spent many quiet evenings together on either side of their dining room table, putting down separate records of the day's observations.

For the four months of their first stay in Rome, Hawthorne's strongest feeling, beyond complaints of the cold, was disillusionment with himself and his contemporary artists. He was entertained by Thomas Buchanan Read in mid-March, where he had a conversation with John Gibson, the leading English sculptor, but was not impressed by Gibson or by any other painter or sculptor present. "Possibly, they can only express themselves in their own art, and what poets say in words, they must say in marble."[27] His round of visits to galleries and churches brought him, by April, to "wonder whether other people are more fortunate than myself, and can invariably find their way to the inner soul of a work of art. I doubt it; they look at these things for just a minute, and pass on, without any pang of remorse, such as I feel, for quitting them so soon and so willingly. I am partly sensible that some unwritten rules of taste are making their way into my mind; that all this Greek beauty has done something toward refining me, who am still, however, a very sturdy Goth." Since it was soon after this that he found the germ of his next romance in the Faun of the Capitoline, he may have felt that

[25] Charles Dickens, *Pictures from Italy* (1846: ed. David Paroissien [New York: Coward, McCann, and Geohegan, 1974]), p. 36; Mario Praz, *The Hero in Eclipse in Victorian Fiction*, trans. Angus Davidson (London: Oxford University Press, 1956), Appendix II, "Rome and the Victorians."

[26] Sophia Hawthorne, "Preface" to *Notes in England and Italy* (New York: G. P. Putnam, 1869).

[27] The sources of inspiration for the Anglo-American neoclassical sculptors were actually almost exclusively literary.

the necessary refinement had come. But on leaving Rome for Florence he professed a "strange affection," a "sad embrace" of farewell by the city where "the intellect finds a home . . . more than in any other spot in the world." On the other hand, the inner soul of the work of art, he discovered with Guido's portrait of Hope, is found not by analysis of the intellect but by a "trusting simplicity" in the viewer.

As he proceeded with his family through the Umbrian and Tuscan hill towns, Hawthorne was disturbed by his uncertainty about the roles of intuition and intellect in the understanding of art. This journey, "one of the brightest and most uncareful interludes of my life," was marked at Assisi with his turning away from the faded frescoes of San Francesco— "the sanctuary of early Italian art" according to Murray's guidebook—to admire the landscape, in which "God expressed himself" to men, intending that it should not "be translated into any tongue save His own immediate one." Believing this idea, the writer was relieved of any responsibility or any sense of accomplishment.

Of course he did not want to believe it; he went on writing in Florence, which seemed on first view a delightful contrast to Rome: "I can hardly think there can be a place in the world where life is more delicious for its own simple sake than here." He looked forward to "assuage and mollify myself a little, after that uncongenial life of the Consulate, and before going back to my own hard and dusty New England." In July he began to sketch the plot and a rough draft of *The Marble Faun*. In the course of leisurely visits to the Uffizi, he concluded cheerfully that though he still knew nothing of pictures, "in a year's time, with the advantage of access to this magnificent gallery, I think I might come to some little knowledge." But painting, he decided, was more dependent than other arts on a "mysterious something" beyond the intelligence of the viewer to express. He could "toss brilliant words by the handful," but the result would be to leave out "everything that really characterizes" a masterpiece like the *Madonna della Seggiola* or Michelangelo's statue of Lorenzo de' Medici. A great picture is "a great symbol, proceeding out of a great mind; but if it means one thing, it seems to mean a thousand, and often opposite things." For reasons like this, in spite of "an impulse to be at work" in the middle of June, he was "kept idle by the sense of being unsettled." Florence was not home. It provided a sense of remoteness from America that he had long desired,[28] but not the "monotony" of "an eventless exterior life" to allow him to "live in the world within." He could not deal with "the brilliant succession of novelties" that Europe continued to offer, and we can assume that he held back in drafting *The Marble Faun* from attempting to deal with them.

If Hawthorne in his tower at the Villa Montauto wished to retreat from both America and Europe to his own fund of literary resources, he could not help contrasting himself with other artists. At the scene of the battle of Thrasimene, he remarked on Byron's success in *Childe Harold*, "wonderfully impressing his own perception of the subject on the reader. Whenever he has to deal with a statue, or ruin, a battle-field, he pounces upon the topic like a vulture, and tears out its heart in a twinkling so that there is nothing more to be said." A similar insight came to him about Benvenuto Cellini, as he passed the houses of the goldsmiths on the Ponte Vecchio, after admiring the gems in the Uffizi. These works were of "minute magnificence. . . . You must sharpen your faculties of observation to a point, and touch the subject exactly on the right spot; or you do not appreciate it at all. . . . It would have been a ticklish affair to be Benvenuto's fellow-workman within such narrow limits." He sometimes conceived a similar awe of Hiram Powers, who in the notebooks is his principal

---

[28] Hawthorne to Fields, September 3, 1858, MS, Huntington.

partner in conversation in Florence. Powers, like Herman Melville seven years earlier, would speculate with Hawthorne about everything familiar or cosmic; but Hawthorne could not escape the conclusion that Powers's extreme jealousy of all other sculptors "between the inclusive extremes of Phidias and Clark Mills" made him, for all his fame, of the same sort as the American sculptors he had met in Rome. And he concluded that Powers had profited little from the art of Florence, having "hermetically sealed" himself from the atmosphere of Italy, even though he had lived there twenty years without interruption. Powers was really, Hawthorne agreed with Mrs. Powers, a Yankee mechanic curiously displaced. William Story reappears in the notebooks in October in Siena, where Hawthorne took his measure as he had not in Rome the previous spring. For all his manifold talents, his aristocratic charm, and his assimilation of Italian culture, Story "stops short of an adequate expression" because "his sensibility is too quick," his imaginative processes "too facile." Hawthorne shrewdly saw that the problems he had wrestled with since arriving in France were not real to Story, and now Story was that much less real to him. Siena itself seemed, more than Florence now, a place where "a thoughtful and shy man might settle down," but he concluded that "it would be a kind of despair that would ever make me dream of finding a home in Italy." He wrote of missing American democracy, but for the reader of the notebooks his obsession with his inability to describe the cathedral of Siena must seem as important.

Upon returning to Rome he found it "more beautiful than ever," but was not inclined to describe it again. Within a week even the pleasure of recognition had evaporated, and he saw Rome not as a home but as a place of "nastiness . . . its little life pressed down by a weight of death." On October 25 he turned his attention to *The Marble Faun.* On the twenty-fourth Una had contracted malaria in the Palace of the Caesars, and his concern for her long illness kept him from his journal. His last journal entry for four months, written on November 2, describes a walk in the park of the Villa Borghese. This entry, and those that follow beginning with the Carnival in February and March, were written apparently with the romance in mind, for he later levied heavily on the Roman journal of March to May.

For knowledge of Hawthorne's activities in the winter of 1858–59, we are largely dependent on the pocket diaries he kept for those years, which are here published for the first time. The daily entries are brief, usually twenty to forty words; they describe in telegraphic style the activities of the family, the weather, and the names of people they saw. There are almost daily comments on Una's state of health throughout the winter, and on the illnesses of Sophia and Ada Shepard, the governess; there are a few brief references to the rough draft of *The Marble Faun*. After finishing the draft, Hawthorne wrote to Fields that in spite of "so much domestic trouble, I take some credit for having sternly shut myself up for an hour or two, almost every day, and come to close grips with a Romance which I am trying to tear out of my mind."[29] The diaries describe his frequent "rambles" and "strolls" about Rome, apparently not with intent to visit specific places but to observe the activities of the people. For a few days in February, Hawthorne himself was confined to bed with an intestinal disorder and fever and was attended by the doctor— for "the first time since my childhood," he noted. He became more convinced of the "lurking poison in the atmosphere" of Rome, and resolved to leave "this pestilential city" as soon as Una's condition would permit.[30]

[29] February 3, 1859, MS, Huntington.

[30] Hawthorne to Ticknor, March 4, 1859, MS, Berg. For an analysis of Hawthorne's ambivalent attitude toward Rome, see Terence Martin, "Hawthorne's Public Decade and the Values of Home," *American Literature*, XLVI (1974), 141–52.

The winter social season, to which Sophia had so much looked forward, was the most brilliant and exciting in years for the Anglo-American community. The painter Christopher Cranch wrote to his wife from Rome on January 20: "Every evening this week past has been occupied with visits or parties. . . . Last Wednesday evening the Storys gave us a great ball in their palatial rooms. . . . Wednesday was a party at Miss [Charlotte] Cushman's, her first reception in her new apartment in the Via Gregoriana."[31] The Hawthornes attended none of these. As Sophia put it in a letter to Elizabeth Peabody describing Una's and Ada's illnesses: "No Rome this winter for us so far. . . . No society for me this winter."[32] Without her, Hawthorne was usually unwilling to go into society. To C. G. Thompson he wrote, declining an invitation, that Sophia was unable to go out in the evening, and "as for myself, I suffer under a native and inherent incapacity for making visits."[33] Sophia's need to stay at home and care for Una was a cause of his weariness and listlessness, he wrote in the notebook on March 23: "It takes away the energy and enterprise that were the spring of all our enterprises."

In early March, Hawthorne's gloom and despondency were interrupted by the happy arrival of Franklin Pierce, his old friend and the man who had made his sojourn in Europe possible. After an initial shock of recognition of "something that seemed to have passed away out of him, without leaving any trace," Hawthorne was surprised to find that Pierce began to bring him a second youth: "He is singularly little changed; the more I see him, the more I get him back, just such as he was in our youth. This morning his face, air, and smile, were

---

[31] Leonora Cranch Scott, *The Life and Letters of Christopher Pearse Cranch* (Boston: Houghton, Mifflin, 1917), pp. 238–39.

[32] January 8, 1859, MS, Huntington.

[33] [March 12, 1859?,] MS, St. Lawrence. For a reporter's observations on Hawthorne at this time, see the Explanatory Note to 496.23.

so wonderfully like himself of old that at least thirty years are annihilated." By his sympathetic presence during Una's last and most critical bout with malaria, Pierce almost saved her husband's life, Sophia thought. Hawthorne was oblivious of Pierce's failures as president; nevertheless, his portrait of Pierce is one of the literary triumphs of the notebooks. He understood the "magical touch" of momentary success of the politician "that arranged matters with a delicate potency which he himself hardly recognized." It seems that for the extremely self-conscious Hawthorne, Pierce was a complementary self, whose life seemed "planned from a very early period, with a view to the station which he ultimately reached."

Hawthorne left Rome with mixed sentiments. He felt he knew the place better than Salem, that it was "strangely familiar," and that he had gained a love for it. He had expended many words on this most fully and often described of cities, and now he did not "wish ever to see any of these objects again, though no place ever took so strong a hold of my being." The Hawthornes left Rome as the war between Sardinia and Austria was beginning, but he took only the vaguest interest in these events. France seemed to him "busy, cheerful, effervescing," but the pages devoted to it were perfunctory, the weary observer being still more weary of telling himself about his observations. Beautiful scenery and historical associations aroused his interest at times in France and Switzerland, but he gave up entirely in Paris, and in Havre he decided to journalize no more. During the following twelve months in England, he wrote in the notebook only seven times. He used the book a final time in August 1862, on a tour in Maine with Julian, for a brief description of Yankees mobilizing for war. The motive for journalizing, so strong at the outset of the family's continental adventure, and sustained with increasing misgivings throughout his encounters with Italian culture, had been largely lost by the time of departure from France.

II

In London on June 27, 1859, Hawthorne had breakfast with his publisher, James T. Fields. In the course of discussing his plans for revising and completing *The Marble Faun*, he told Fields, as the latter noted, that he "might print his journal also."[34] It is not clear whether he referred to his English notebooks, which he had entrusted to Henry Bright and would recover in a few days, or to the just-completed record of his life on the Continent, or to both. Lacking his preliminary plans and drafts for *The Marble Faun*, we do not know how much use he planned to make of the descriptive and travel portions of the Italian notebooks in the romance. We do know that the romance is pervasively indebted to the notebooks.[35] Nine-tenths of the chapters include material directly from the notebooks, and some chapters are largely adapted from them: "An Æsthetic Company," "The Owl-Tower," "Scenes by the Way," "Pictured Windows," "Market-Day in Perugia," "The Emptiness of Picture-Galleries," and "A Scene in the Corso." From the notebooks Hawthorne used mainly the entries written in Rome during his first month there, including the Carnival; those gallery observations from about the time of his discovering the statue of the Faun; scenes in Foligno, Perugia, and Passignano; the first days in the Villa Montauto in August; the second Roman Carnival; and his revisiting of favorite places in Rome later in the spring of 1859. Much remained in the notebooks that might have been published in magazine articles, such as his conversations with, and verbal portraits of, such well-known contemporaries as Anna Jameson, Fredrika

[34] James T. Fields, *Biographical Notes and Personal Sketches* (Boston: Houghton, Mifflin, 1882), p. 60.

[35] See the appendix "Cross-References with *The Marble Faun*."

Bremer, John Gibson, Elizabeth and Robert Browning, Thomas Adolphus Trollope, William Story, and Hiram Powers; but there is no further record of an intention by Hawthorne to publish any of it.

After his death in 1864, Sophia Hawthorne prepared editions of her husband's notes, working first in close consultation with James T. Fields and his wife Annie. *Passages from the American Note-Books* was published in the fall of 1868. At that time Sophia quarreled with Fields over the percentage of royalties due her, and she completed her work on the English and the French and Italian volumes without his assistance.[36] In her correspondence with Fields, the only reference to the continental notebooks is a progress report in 1867: "I have still six and a half volumes of English notes to copy, besides all the Italian, which are not absorbed into the Marble Faun."[37] The quarrel was still unresolved when Mrs. Hawthorne and her children sailed to Europe in October, 1868. She stopped in New York to discuss her situation with her cousin, the publisher George Palmer Putnam, and contracted with him for publication of her own notes on England and Italy. She may have contemplated placing Hawthorne's remaining posthumous books with Putnam, as well; but after negotiation between her sister Elizabeth and Fields, she decided in January, 1869, to continue with Fields. She was then in Dresden, where the Hawthornes lived until July, 1870.

Mrs. Hawthorne's journal for 1869[38] reveals that she completed copying Hawthorne's English notebooks in June, and that she spent a month in July and August making her own

[36] See Randall Stewart, "Editing Hawthorne's Notebooks: Selections from Mrs. Hawthorne's Letters to Mr. and Mrs. Fields, 1864–1868," *More Books*, XX (September 1945), 299–315, and "Mrs. Hawthorne's Quarrel with James T. Fields: Selections from the Letters to Fields by Mrs. Hawthorne and Elizabeth Peabody," *More Books*, XXI (September 1946), 254–63.

[37] March 23, 1867, MS, Boston Public Library.

[38] In the Berg Collection, New York Public Library.

Italian journal ready for Putnam. She then reread *The Marble Faun*. After reading proof of her own book in October, she recorded on November 1: "I began to copy my husband's Continental journals." She referred frequently to this copying throughout November and the first half of December, characterizing it once as "my beloved MSS." Unfortunately, her journal for 1870 (if she kept one) is not available, and the only documentation concerning the notebooks is two letters to William Story. On January 2, she wrote requesting his permission to retain his name in full and "the records about" him. She assured Story that he was "often mentioned, *of course*, in the highest terms," and that she had received similar permissions with regard to the English notebooks from Robert Browning and Coventry Patmore.[39] Story's reply was encouraging, but Mrs. Hawthorne wrote again, on May 1, enclosing copies of some paragraphs from a notebook that troubled her because "they refer to the more intimate characteristics which I dared not venture to keep unless with your leave."[40] These are probably Hawthorne's discovery in Rome of "a vein of melancholy" in Story (p. 229.6–12, above) and in Siena of his "morbid sensibility" (pp. 447.29–448.13). As had been her policy with the earlier notebooks, Sophia edited the passages to delete any suggestion of inadequacy or unhappiness in Story.

On May 11, 1870, Sophia and Una traveled from Dresden to London to read proof of *Passages from the English Note-Books*, which was to be published in June simultaneously by Strahan and Company, London, and by Fields, Osgood, and Company, Boston. Their return to Dresden was brief, for by

[39] MS, University of Texas, Austin. A similar letter concerning the English notebooks from Sophia to Mrs. Samuel Carter Hall, June 13, 1869, observed, "Of course Mr Hawthorne could only speak of you in the kindest way, and it is so much more interesting to have names instead of initials or blanks"; MS, Boston Public Library.

[40] MS, University of Texas, Austin.

the end of July they were installed, with the help of Francis Bennoch, at 5 Shaftesbury Terrace, Kensington, London, where on the following February 26 Sophia Hawthorne died. Probably most of the editing was finished by the fall of 1870, but not all. Rose joined her mother and sister in London late in the year, and it was no doubt on the basis of her recollection that her husband, George Parsons Lathrop, stated in his introductory note to the Riverside Edition that the French and Italian notebooks "were transcribed for publication by Mrs. Hawthorne, at London, in the winter of 1870–71."[41] There is every reason to believe that Sophia Hawthorne completed the editing, without assistance from Una.[42]

Students of Hawthorne are well aware of his wife's efforts to protect and embellish his reputation by presenting his notebooks not as he had written them but as she thought he would have revised them for publication.[43] She was torn between a desire to keep his memory private and the economic necessity of presenting all his writings to the public. "Above all things," she had written to Fields, "I would be loyal to what Mr. Hawthorne would approve. I had rather starve than do what he might think an impropriety."[44] In deciding what to omit, she began with that which had been previously published. As she had with the English *Passages* and *Our Old Home*, she com-

[41] (Boston: Houghton, Mifflin, 1883), X, 7.

[42] The ascription of the editing to Una by Jacob Blanck (*Bibliography of American Literature* [New Haven: Yale University Press, 1955–]) and others is apparently only based on the time between Sophia's death and the first book publication in November, 1871.

[43] See Claude M. Simpson, "Historical Commentary" to the Centenary Edition of *The American Notebooks* (Columbus: Ohio State University Press, 1972), pp. 687–90; Randall Stewart, "Introduction" to *The English Notebooks*, pp. ix–xxii. The discovery of Mrs. Hawthorne's corrections and suggestions in the manuscript of *The Marble Faun* reveals that her edition of the French and Italian notebooks was her second attempt at influencing the public's perception of Hawthorne's experience in Italy. See Fredson Bowers, "Textual Introduction" to the Centenary *Marble Faun*, pp. lxv–lxx.

[44] January 30, 1868, MS, Boston Public Library.

pared the French and Italian notebooks to *The Marble Faun*, and omitted from her copying some seventy passages that had been used in the romance. More than a hundred similar passages remained in her copy.[45]

By 1869 Sophia had become an experienced copyist and editor. She no longer tried to change Hawthorne's manuscript physically, by scissoring out parts of pages or inking over words that she wished to delete. Except for one instance early in the continental journal, concerning apparently Julian's indecorous behavior in the Louvre (p. 25), she did not tamper with what Hawthorne had written in his notebook. But her copy varied considerably, as with the previous notebooks, from what she read on his page. She knew that his diction and phrasing in the notebooks were more relaxed, informal, and colloquial than he allowed in his published works. For instance, the Venuses he saw in the Borghese Gallery are "naked" (p. 111); those he describes in "The Emptiness of Picture-Galleries" are "nude." On first view in the church of the Capuchins, the dead monk's feet "stuck forth" (p. 80); in the romance they "protrude." In passages used in the romance that she did not delete, we find that occasionally Mrs. Hawthorne makes the same change that her husband had (she apparently did not consult the text of *The Marble Faun*); "imagine" (p. 48) becomes "conceive"; "homes" (p. 60) becomes "houses"; "great" (p. 253) becomes "huge"; "pot" (p. 384) becomes "vase." But as often, in the same passages, she makes a change that Hawthorne did *not* make in writing *The Marble Faun*. In Sophia's text "intense" (p. 48) becomes

[45] She may have consciously kept some passages that had served *The Marble Faun*, for in her "Preface" to the English notebooks she remarked: "It seemed a pity not to give these original cartoons fresh from his mind, because they are so carefully finished at first stroke" (*Passages from the English Note-Books* [Boston: Fields, Osgood; London: Strahan; both 1870], p. viii [both editions]). Her text reduces the length of the continental notebooks by approximately twenty thousand words, or a little more than ten percent.

"excessive"; "little" (p. 60) becomes "small"; "awfully" (p. 253) becomes "immeasurably"; "made" (p. 384) becomes "modelled." In the notebook the city of Assisi is "old and strange" (p. 253); in the romance it is "ancient and strange"; in her edition Sophia made it "old and singular." Generally, her imposition of a tone of propriety and genteel conventionality considerably exceeded Hawthorne's own tendencies in that direction, and readers of her text of the notebooks were presented with a less colorful and realistic account than her husband wrote. He saw the pope walk "with a sort of dignified waddle" (p. 150); her text makes that a "dignified movement." (Of course, Pius IX was still alive in 1871.) But her cautious changing of private attitudes to public ones is consistent, it should be repeated, with the use of the notebook in *The Marble Faun*. Describing the Laocoön on March 23, 1858, Hawthorne concluded that "Heaven will not help" the struggling human figures; in the romance Kenyon observes the group and speculates that Laocoön will be strangled "if no divine help intervene." Sophia's change in the notebook creates a similar modification of Hawthorne's initial reaction: "Heaven alone can help them."

Mrs. Hawthorne had expressed the hope, in her preface to *Passages from the English Note-Books*, that all the notebooks would "dispel an often expressed opinion that Mr. Hawthorne was gloomy and morbid. . . . He saw too far to be despondent, though his vivid sympathies and shaping imagination often made him sad in behalf of others." For this reason, and by her acceptance of contemporary standards of taste, she tried to present him in as cheerful and dignified an attitude as possible. This meant toning down his initial reaction to Rome: she consistently changed "stink" and "filth" to "dirt" and "rubbish," and "smell" to "odor." References to such activities as paying money, sleeping, dressing, eating, drinking, and smoking, were regularly excised from the record, as were those to minor mishaps and illnesses. It had been Sophia's policy from the beginning of her stewardship to suppress references to herself,[46] and to other members of the family. When Hawthorne and Julian took their own direction in sightseeing, not accompanying "Mamma and her party" to a given church or gallery, Sophia suppressed the separation. She allows the children to appear occasionally enough to give the implication of Hawthorne's benevolent concern as father, but only then with the modest diminution of their names to initials. Sophia herself and Ada Shepard, the governess, are most frequently removed. She wanted to give an opposite impression from Hawthorne's statement on the journey from Siena to Rome: "In fact, travelling with a family is a bore beyond anything that can be pre-conceived"; and from his preference not to revisit Genoa: "I . . . therefore opposed a quiet inertness to any suggestions on Mamma's part."

Mrs. Hawthorne's decisions about the publishing of names in the notebooks had given her trouble since she had allowed Jonathan Cilley to appear in the extracts from the American notebooks in the *Atlantic Monthly*. She wrote letters to eminent people, such as Story, Browning, and Patmore, whose names she wished to include, even if that meant editing what was said about them. She established three alternatives: a name might be presented in full, or an initial or dash might be used, or the person might be omitted completely. Her choices are interesting. Some American artists appear in full: Story, Thompson, Brown, Akers, Wilde, Chapman, Terry, Powers. Those who appear by initial are Bartholemew, Mozier, Hosmer,[47] and Page. Ropes and Rothermel do not appear at all. Most American tourists appear only by initial: Maria

---

[46] See her letter to Fields, October 4, 1865, MS, Boston Public Library; Stewart, "Editing Hawthorne's Notebooks," p. 301.

[47] Sophia had second thoughts; on April 3, 1858, Miss Hosmer appears only as a dash, but on May 23 her entire name is retained.

Mitchell, Caroline Tappan, John Pendleton Kennedy, Charles Sumner, even William Cullen Bryant. When the Motleys appear in Rome for the second winter, Mrs. Hawthorne changes a reference to "Mrs. Motley's balcony" to "Mr. Motley's balcony." She removed all mentions of Anna Jameson from the passages published in the British periodical *Good Words*, but later restored them to the book version. Louisa Lander's misfortune with her bust of Hawthorne led Sophia to expel her entirely from the text.

As a lifelong student of art and Italy, Sophia was able to improve and correct a number of expressions in the notebooks. In her copy pictures became frescoes, a story a piano, an arcade a loggia, a desk a prie-dieu, a room a saloon, a chapel a sacristy. She removed definitions of such terms as Pietà and Nativity. She corrected Hawthorne's mistaken attributions of *Casa Guidi Windows* and of Leonardo's *Last Supper*. She corrected the names of Roman roads and churches. If Hawthorne could not remember a name, she supplied it. In all these matters she placed her own knowledge and taste between the reader and the Hawthorne who had put his impression into the notebook. In her preface to the English *Passages*, she had tried to prepare the reader for the eccentricities, irreverencies, and boredom that the notebooks contained: "Throughout his journals it will be seen that Mr. Hawthorne is *entertaining*, not *asserting*, opinions and ideas. He questions, doubts, and reflects with his pen, and, as it were, instructs himself. So that these Note-books should be read, not as definite conclusions of his mind but often merely as passing impressions. Whatever *conclusions* he arrived at are condensed in the works given to the world by his own hand, in which will never be found a careless word." In the French and Italian journals, one passage led her to insert a page-long editorial note: Hawthorne had complained, in recording his visit on March 10, 1858, to the Sciarra Palace, of grimy pictures and tarnished frames, and

Mrs. Hawthorne attributes his displeasure not to inattention to the pictures themselves but to his "native idiosyncrasy," his "exquisite nicety of feeling" that led him to experience "actual pain" at all imperfections and failures of beauty.

The notebooks frequently express Hawthorne's uncertainty and dissatisfaction. Sophia removed on several occasions such "careless words" as "I think" or "I believe." As a traveler going to Italy and returning to England the following year, Hawthorne often described his first impressions with a naïveté that Sophia must have found disconcerting, for on some twenty-five occasions she removed statements such as "I never saw anything . . . so glorious and gorgeous as the Madeleine," or "I found it [a church in Genoa] more magnificent than anything I had before seen or imagined." In some fifty cases she suppressed Hawthorne's comments about his own writing: how he could not describe a place or sight, or had forgotten what needed to be said, or was too tired or bored to comment on matters that in themselves deserved his attention.

Mrs. Hawthorne edited these journals in Europe. She did much of the work in Dresden, "Florence on the Elbe," a favorite residence for British and American tourists who wished to study masterpieces of the High Renaissance and seventeenth century in its Picture Gallery of Old Masters. Johann Joachim Winckelmann, the leading exponent of neoclassical taste, had begun his studies in Dresden, in the gallery and in the Cabinet of Antiquities. Nowhere outside Italy would Hawthorne's lack of reverence have seemed more noticeable. Sophia was careful to tone down a number of his negative comments,[48] and to remove a few homesick references to the superior beauty of American or English scenery or institutions.

---

[48] One perhaps typical instance is Hawthorne's humorous wish, after seeing the tomb of Galileo in Santa Croce, that "every sculptor might be at once put to death, who shall hereafter chisel an allegoric figure." Sophia soberly changes the sculptor's fate to imprisonment for life.

But she was too honest to remove many other passages that might be taken to be provincial in Hawthorne. Her own health was failing. She must have realized that some reviewers would take the book to task, but she nevertheless went ahead with its publication.

Excerpts of the *Passages from the French and Italian Note-Books* appeared in Strahan and Company's magazine *Good Words* as "First Impressions of France and Italy," in eleven monthly installments from January to November 1871. This text was a shortened version of Sophia's copy of the entries from January 6, to June 13, 1858, with some entries from April and May completely omitted. The magazine editors may have chosen the text, or have collaborated with Sophia or Una in choosing it. Una apparently read proof for Strahan's edition of *Passages*, which was published November 18, 1871, in two volumes, and sold for 24s. The American edition, by James R. Osgood and Company, was announced for October,[49] but was not published until February 29, 1872, also in two volumes, at $4.00. The first American printing was of 1,500 copies, in uniform binding with the other volumes of Hawthorne's work published by Osgood. His children's royalty was $.40 per copy. A second impression of 280 copies was not needed until 1874; a second edition was published in 1876. By 1880 a total of 5,691 copies had been printed, considerably fewer than for either the American or English notebooks.

In his two biographies of his father, Julian Hawthorne published a number of passages that his mother had omitted.[50] He printed thirty-one quotations from the French and Italian journals in 1884, and twenty-two more in 1903, repeating five from the earlier book. These included passages that had been incorporated into *The Marble Faun* and descriptions

[49] *Literary World* (Boston), II (September 1, 1871), 61.
[50] *Nathaniel Hawthorne and His Wife* (Boston: James R. Osgood, 1884); *Hawthorne and His Circle* (New York: Harper, 1903).

or fragments of descriptions of people. He stirred up an old controversy by printing in 1884 Hawthorne's portrait of Margaret Fuller; he also then restored Louisa Lander to the record. In 1903, he restored significant (and unchivalrous) details to Hawthorne's portraits of Anna Jameson, Fredrika Bremer, and William Story. In 1929, Newton Arvin used the manuscripts to prepare a selection, *The Heart of Hawthorne's Journals,* and restored some of Hawthorne's original phrasing, but as frequently allowed Sophia's changes to stand.[51] In 1941, Norman Holmes Pearson made a complete transcription of the manuscripts, with an extensive introduction and notes, as a doctoral dissertation at Yale University; his work, though never published, was generously made available to many interested scholars, and it represents the beginning of modern critical study of these notebooks. The present edition constitutes a new transcription and annotation.

III

The first review of the serialized "First Impressions" in *Good Words* appeared in *Lippincott's* in April, 1871.[52] The opinion set forth there was characteristic of those to follow in singling out Hawthorne's individuality and "his power of refreshing commonplaces." Unlike "enthusiastic travellers" who reinforce "old illusions," he was able "to *disinvest* himself of all instilled conceptions previously to laying solid foundations for a structure of his own." Most reviewers, both English and American, of *Passages,* located the center of interest in the book's revelation of Hawthorne's originality of mind and personality; the *Independent* even concluded that these

[51] Boston: Houghton Mifflin. See the review by Randall Stewart, *New England Quarterly,* II (1929), 517–21.
[52] VII (April 1871), 452.

notebooks provided superior illustration of the author's character than the previous volumes.[53]

In placing such emphasis, several reviewers recalled Mrs. Hawthorne's statement in her "Preface" to Passages from the English Note-Books that Hawthorne's journals were "originally designed for his own reference only," and that she had refused to comply with the demand for a biography, since he had wished that there be none; the notebooks would serve in its place. Most reviewers accepted what was offered, but the Examiner questioned the editor's judgment in publishing as much as she had, since "a great deal of trivial matter" was included. The Examiner also called attention to Sophia's note to the entry of March 10, 1858, about Hawthorne's dislike of Italian picture frames, to comment that it did "not mend matters." Lathrop, who had married Rose Hawthorne shortly before writing his review, quoted Sophia's preface and note with approval. James, Howells, and the London Times noticed Hawthorne's comment on the frames, but not the note.

Several reviews mentioned the passages about the Marble Faun of the Capitol that remained in the text. The Athenæum and the Boston Advertiser also pointed to William Story's anecdote of the wife whose body had been "chemically resolved" into the stone of a ring, and Hawthorne's comment,

[53] This discussion of Passages from the French and Italian Note-Books draws upon the following reviews and notices: Appleton's Journal, VII (April 6, 1872), 388; H. A. P. [i.e., Alexander H. Japp], Argosy, XIII (January, 1872), 109–15; Athenæum, no. 2301 (December 2, 1871), 717–18; [William Dean Howells,] Atlantic Monthly, XXIX (May, 1872), 624–26; Boston Daily Advertiser, March 2, 1872, Supplement, 1:5–7; Boston Evening Transcript, March 2, 1872, 3:2, and March 16, 1872, 3:1–2; British Quarterly Review, LV (January, 1872), 256–57; Eclectic XV (April, 1872), 506; Examiner, no. 3331 (December 2, 1871), 1196–97; Harper's, XLIV (May, 1872), 934; Independent, XXIV (February 1, 1872), 8:5–6; Lippincott's, IX (May, 1872), 605–7; London Times, January 13, 1872, 4:1; London Quarterly Review, XXXVIII (April, 1872), 253–55; [Henry James,] Nation, XIV (March 14, 1872), 172–73; George P. Lathrop, St. Paul's, IX (January, 1872), 311–13; Spectator, XLIV (March 23, 1872), 371–72; Westminster Review, XCVII (January, 1872), 230–31.

"I think I could make a story on this idea"; The *London Quarterly Review* recalled Hawthorne's interest in Story's expansion of the story of Bluebeard. For the most part, however, it was implicitly recognized that the purpose of these notebooks was primarily to record impressions and not to store up ideas for new tales.

There was general praise by American and English reviewers alike for Hawthorne's portraits of his contemporaries, painted, as Howells put it, "with that firm, delicate touch, and that certain parsimony of color which impart their pale charm to the people of Hawthorne's romances." Miss Bremer, the Brownings, and Mrs. Jameson were most often mentioned. Sophia had done her editing well. But in the case of Powers, Sophia's judicious deletions may have led the *Athenæum*, the *Westminster Review*, and Howells to conclude that the opinionated sculptor had overwhelmed Hawthorne's "faith in his own discrimination"; *Lippincott's*, however, found Hawthorne's "taking off of Powers . . . capitally sly."

The English notebooks had been received on both sides of the ocean as full of relaxed and sympathetic humor. None of the reviews of the continental notebooks makes such a comment. Howells remarks, "It is odd that his humor did not help him to be more amused by the droll rascality and mendicancy with which a foreigner's life in Italy is enveloped." Praise for Hawthorne's sincerity and frankness in describing his Italian experience replaced appreciation of his playful, detached attitude in his earlier notebooks. English reviewers who admired his originality and genius nevertheless decided that in his criticism of art and culture Hawthorne "did not rise much above the level of the average American tourist," as the *Athenæum* put it. The *London Times*, more discriminating, concluded that "when Hawthorne only does his best to admire, conscientiously trying to be contented to follow the multitude, he is sometimes as commonplace as need be. When either his heart or his senses are touched, he expresses himself in language always fresh and suggestive, and often eloquent." The *British Quarterly Review* remarked that "most readers will be surprised to find Hawthorne confessing a defective appreciation of works of art, which is infinitely better than a whole volume of cuckoo admiration." The *Spectator* and the *Westminster* were also sympathetic to Hawthorne's "struggle in his mind . . . between his sense of what was proper to be seen and his indifference to the sight." Hawthorne dared, to his credit and unlike many contemporaries, to confess to the world his inconstancy of taste. Only the *Examiner* and Edith Simcox in her review of *Septimius* in the *Academy*[54] gave Hawthorne the lambasting Sophia might have feared: Simcox found the judgments in the notebooks always either conventional or false, and the writing marked by a "childish docility." The *Examiner* recognized that Hawthorne's indifference to the drawings in the Louvre was shared by many visitors to that museum, but found such a confession "hardly to have been looked for from a man of taste." On balance, the British press, which had been mostly unfriendly to his discussions of art in *The Marble Faun*, gave Hawthorne a more generous reception on his own terms than his editor and heirs probably could have hoped for.

In America questions of taste were less refined. *Harper's* conceded that other books dealt more profoundly with Italy and its galleries, but preferred Hawthorne to all others "for a companion with whom to spend a month of summer afternoons or winter evenings in Rome." The *Eclectic* concluded that "if ever the Eternal City had a born interpreter we should say that interpreter is Hawthorne." The most sophisticated and searching American reviewers were, we might expect, Hawthorne's successors in the art of fiction, Henry James and

---

[54] III (November 1, 1872), 405.

William Dean Howells.[55] Howells had already published *Venetian Life* and *Italian Journeys*; James had returned from fifteen months in Europe in 1870, and was eager to go back for a longer residence later in 1872. Both noticed (as had the *London Times* and the *Spectator*) that Hawthorne preferred the landscapes of George Loring Brown to those of Claude, and that he enjoyed C. G. Thompson's pictures equally with the Old Masters. Both were touched and embarrassed by Hawthorne's "simplicity," and by the pervasive tone of doubt, shrinking, misgiving and mistrust in the notebooks. James saw him walking about "bending a puzzled, ineffective gaze at things, full of a mild, genial desire to apprehend and penetrate, but with the light wings of his fancy just touching the surface of the massive consistency of fact about him, and with an air of good-humored confession that he is too simply an idle Yankee *flâneur* to conclude on such matters." Howells picked up a word Hawthorne had used twice (pp. 256, 350) to identify with Hawthorne's alienation: "We suppose that his doubt that he was not *bamboozling* himself when he admired an old master, is one that has occurred, more or less remotely to most honest men under like conditions." James found "dignity" in the "sturdy candor" of his confession to "indifference, to ignorance and weariness." And in spite of his opinions about nudity in sculpture and the value of Giotto and Cimabue, Howells concluded that Hawthorne's "journals might be read with greater instruction upon art than many critical works."

For both Howells and James these notebooks manifested quintessentially American qualities, and summarized the integrity and the blessed amateurism as well as the provinciality of the preceding generation of American writers. James goes

[55] James's review is reprinted in *The American Essays of Henry James*, ed. Leon Edel (New York: Vintage, 1956); Howells's is reprinted as an appendix to Clara Marburg Kirk, *W. D. Howells and Art in His Time* (New Brunswick: Rutgers University Press, 1965).

to the heart of the matter when he says of Hawthorne that "he looks at things as little as possible in that composite historic light which forms the atmosphere of many imaginations." He concludes, however, that Hawthorne's is a "rich simplicity," and "we seem to see him strolling through churches and galleries as the last pure American—attesting by his shy responses to dark canvas and cold marble his loyalty to a simpler and less encumbered civilization." This sense of Hawthorne helps explicate James's well remembered statement, in a letter of the same time: "It's a complex fate, being an American."[56]

T. W.

[56] James to Charles Eliot Norton, February 4, 1872; James, Letters, ed. Leon Edel (Cambridge: Harvard University Press, 1974–), I, 274.

TEXTUAL COMMENTARY

Manuscript Copy-Texts for the Centenary Edition

HAWTHORNE recorded the journey with his family from England to their Italian sojourn and back again in seven journals and two pocket diaries. The first of the notebooks begins with an entry of October, 1857, in England, and the last one continues after the entry of June 22, 1859, in France, with English notes dating from November 14 to May 16, 1860, and an American note added on August 15, 1862. In the present text, the continuity of the European record is carried from the first entry at Paris, January 6, 1858, to the final one at Havre, June 22, 1859.[1] The pocket diaries, however, are presented as integral units in this first publication. The 1858 diary includes the first four days of January before the Hawthorne's departure from England, and the 1859, the months in England when Hawthorne did not keep an English journal while working on printer's copy of *The Marble Faun*.

[1] Sophia Hawthorne's edition of the journals, *Passages from the English Note-Books*, in 1870, included details of Hawthorne's last meeting with Francis Bennoch, taken from the first journal entry at Paris. Randall Stewart, in editing *The English Notebooks* in 1941, halted at the London entry of January 3, 1858, omitting the notes of 1859 and 1860—which Mrs. Hawthorne included in *Passages from the French and Italian Note-Books* in 1871. The Centenary editors propose to return the English material to a new edition of *The English Notebooks*.

The French and Italian Notebooks

1. October 1857–January 3, 1858, in England; January 6–24, in France and Italy. A notebook measuring 8 ⅞ by 7 ⅛ inches, of 96 leaves, the first and last glued to endpapers; inscribed from the second leaf to the end and paged by Hawthorne 1–189, the final page being the recto of the leaf glued to endpaper. The first French entry begins three lines from the foot of page 112. The following recto is numbered 114 in error, and 114 is repeated on the verso; similarly, a recto is numbered 132 in error for 131, with the verso correctly numbered 132 (Morgan MA 587).

2. February 3–March 10, 1858. A notebook measuring 8 ½ by 7 ⅛ inches, 60 leaves remaining in the binding after previous use and abuse. Inscribed inside the front cover is "N. Hawthorne / Boston U.S.A. / July 7. 1853." At the front, a flyleaf and eight leaves were excised, and at the back the final leaf was torn out and a flyleaf torn off to a stub. The remaining leaves are inscribed and paged by Hawthorne 1–101, 101–102, 102–103, the last on a flyleaf that holds on the verso, reversed, a note of June 22, 1855, by Sophia Hawthorne. Inside the back cover are childish scrawls (Morgan MA 588).

3. March 11–April 22, 1858. A notebook measuring 8 ⅜ by 6 ⅜ inches, of ruled paper inscribed and paged [1]–88 by Hawthorne, who marked 43 as 41, in error (Berg).

4. April 25–May 29, 1858. A notebook measuring 9 ⅞ by 7 ½ inches, the paper of inferior quality. Initial and terminal leaves glued to endpapers. Inscription begins on recto of the second leaf, and is paged by Hawthorne [1]–83, 86–94 (Morgan MA 589).

5. June 2–July 2, 1858. A notebook measuring 8 ¾ by 5 ⅞ inches, of lined paper. Inscribed and paged by Hawthorne

[1]–113, 108^A–113^A, 114–129, 129^A (Huntington HM 302).

6. July 4, 1858–April 19, 1859. A notebook measuring 8 ⅝ by 6 ⅛ inches, with faintly lined paper. The pages are erratically numbered by Hawthorne [1]–129, 140–310, with errors: 161 repeated for 163, 171 for 177, 301 followed by a second 301, no 303, 307 followed by second 306, no 308 (Morgan MA 590).

7. May 15–June 22, 1859 (Europe); November 14, 1859–May 16, 1860 (England); August 15, 1862 (America). A notebook measuring 10 ¼ by 7 ½ inches, of faintly lined paper, in 8 gatherings of 12s. Inscribed and paged by Hawthorne 1–62 for European entries, and continuing at 62 with English notes through 79. The verso of 79 is blank; there follow inscribed pages numbered [1]–4, holding a Hawthorne note at West Gouldsborough, Maine. The remainder of the book is blank, but with eight leaves cut out of the final gathering (Morgan MA 591).

The 1858 and 1859 Pocket Diaries

1858. *Renshaw's Diary and Almanac for 1858*, published by John Renshaw and Company, London. A pocket book measuring 5 ¾ by 3 ⅝ inches, with twelve almanac pages preceding the diary space. Headings for the diary pages hold the year and month; horizontal lines divide each page into three areas with date and day at upper left. The first three days of the week are on versos and the following three days on rectos; Hawthorne crowded entries on the rectos to leave room for Sunday entries. At the end, he wrote on a blank page two January 1858 memoranda of accounts. The excision of ⅓ leaf removed the entry of August 5, recto, and that of August 9, verso. It is not known why or by whom the cutting was done (University of California, Berkeley, A 8).

1859. *Agenda Perpetuel*, printed by L. Tinterlin, Paris. A pocket book measuring 4 ⅞ by 3 ⅛ inches, leaves 4 ¾ by 2 ⅞ inches. The heading for the first entry page is "Janvier 1850" (altered to 1859 by Hawthorne), and thereafter only the months are printed. The book has four divisions with title pages for quarters of the year, as, "Premier Trisemestre." The unlined pages are designed for two entries, each headed by date at the left, church calendar day at the center, and at the right the number of days past and number remaining in the year. Hawthorne used spaces between these imprints to write the day of the week, as on April 9: "9. Sat Sᵉ Marie, egyp. urday 99–266." On a blank page at the end of the book he entered financial notes (Berg).

A Note on Editorial Practices

The inscription of these notebook and diary manuscripts indicates distractions by place and company—the entries being made variously in hotels or rented quarters—that led to miswritings, and some unsystematic correction and other alteration by Hawthorne when he later consulted the texts. In this first edition of the complete manuscripts, a clear text is presented that retains Hawthorne's inconsistencies and idiosyncrasies. Emendation is directed at inadvertent errors that could create confusion and at unacceptable variant forms resulting from careless inscription.

Emendations of substantives. These include (1) additions necessary to sense: "Julian & staid" becomes "Julian & I staid"; "Miss &" becomes "Miss Shepard &"; "better than hotel" becomes "better than any hotel"; (2) elimination of dittography: "we we" becomes "we"; (3) correction of patent slips in spelling, as of "Faun-blod," "Oxfor,"—and the careless omission or addition of a pen stroke, as for "columes," "Atar," "mortherly"; (4) correction of miswritten construction such as "home at" for intended "at home"; (5) normalization of end-line anomalies such as "stu-|io" and "indis-|sposed." All substantive changes are recorded in the list of Editorial Emendations.

Emendations of accidentals. All Centenary changes in punctuation are noted in Editorial Emendations; these include the addition of missing elements in pairs of quotation marks, as at 73.27; the occasional addition or deletion of punctuation, as at 16.25–26 and 457.28; or replacement of one mark by another, as at 125.11. Periods are supplied for journal sentences lacking them, and are listed in Editorial Emendations. Periods are not supplied after jottings in the diaries that lack them.

Inconsistencies and anomalies preserved. These include (1) inaccurate accents, as "Viá, "Trinitá," "Dejeûner," and lack of diacritical marking, as "a la fourchette," "facade," "Macon"; (2) hybrid titles, as "Piazza d'Espagna," "hotel of Lille & d'Albion", and spellings influenced by foreign language: "cieling," "groupe," "batallion"; (3) inconsistency in compounding: "today," "to-day," "to day"; "medi-æval," "medi-æval"; (4) unbalanced punctuation with parenthetical phrases: "Mr. Cranch called (I did not see him,)" and "Between 12 & 1, (Dr. F. having called)"; apostrophe use with possessive singular: "Brownings' " "James' " (6) doublet or triplet spellings of surnames and place names, as "Hoar," "Hoare," "Boot," "Boott," and "Uffizi," "Uffizzi," and "Ufizzi"; (7) forms acceptable in Hawthorne's time: "recal," "perhap," "century-box," "centinel," "poney," "scull," "ancle," "texture" (for "textile"); and (8) an apparent coinage (conscious or unconscious), "wapping," drawn from Wapping, in London. The variant forms are retained in the established text unless normalization seems justified on the authority of the dictionary that Hawthorne used, *A New Critical Pronouncing Dictionary of the English Language* . . . *By an American Gentleman* (Burlington, N.J.: Allinson, 1813). The *Oxford English Dictionary* is the standard for establishing usage current in Hawthorne's time. Hawthorne inscribed many surnames after only hearing them: as "Eckers," "Howarth," "Hume," and "Twisden." These spellings are kept, and the persons are identified in the Explanatory Notes.

Centenary format discards double underlining, presumably a location device, of entry headings; headings are here placed apart above the entries, and the headings of diary entries are also discretionary.

L. N. S.

EDITORIAL EMENDATIONS
IN THE COPY-TEXT

Every editorial change from the copy-text is listed here. For each entry, the Centenary reading is at the left of the bracket and the rejected reading follows the bracket. A vertical slash | indicates the end of a manuscript line. In recording punctuation emendation, a wavy dash ∼ represents a word after the bracket, and a caret ∧ indicates the absence of a punctuation mark.

THE FRENCH AND ITALIAN NOTEBOOKS

6.3	a little more or less] little more less
7.8	speech] *omit*
9.19	numerous] nunerous
14.12	monotonous] mon- | onous
16.16	Bourbons] Bourbon's
16.25–26	Liverpool,] ∼∧
18.10–11	martyrdom] matyrdom
18.22	Napoleons] Napoelons
19.26	it] *omit*
19.27	building] build-|
19.29	it.] ∼∧
21.6	Triumphal] Trumphal
24.1	week] weeks
26.23	of] of|of

29.9	collections] col-	ections
29.19	occurring] occurying
30.9	of] of	of
31.9	imagine] im-	gine
31.21	bosom.] ~∧
31.24	other,] ~∧
32.11	accosted] ac-	customed
34.31	lodging] lodgding
35.34	with hardly] with a hardly
36.7	Hôtel de Provence] hôtel de Proence
38.7	spot.] ~∧
39.3	it.] ~∧
39.29	vineyards] vineyard
40.24	gardener] gard-	er
41.11	in an attitude] in attitude
42.7	an] omit
43.11	Marseilles] Marsilles
45.9	grasshoppers] grashopperes
45.29	interesting] intrerseting
48.13	magnificence] magnifence
48.27	casket] caket
49.8	stateliest] staliest
49.31	vault-like] vault∧	like
53.2	Wednesday.] ~∧
53.17	malignancy] maglignancy
54.8	shade.] ~∧
54.23	monuments] monments
55.11	noonday] noon day
56.15	meanest] meansest
56.29	cavalry] calvalry
57.8	one,] ~∧
62.3	heresy] heresay
62.14	pity] party
65.7	yore.] ~∧
67.14	enlivened] entivened
67.14	Carnival] Carnivil
67.17	festivities.] ~∧
68.32	ladies.] ~∧
72.25	has] *omit*

73.1	lawyer,] ~∧
73.20	of a] of of a
73.27	represent?"] ~?∧
76.17	gravity.] ~∧
77.19	for] for for
79.7	Medici] Medic
84.17	wife] *omit*
84.22–23	elsewhere] elsewere
85.7	generally.] ~∧
88.8	with] with with
89.3	quartered] quarterred
90.11	frescoes] frescooes
93.31	tree,] ~∧
95.11	rosiest] rosest
96.24	cities.] ~∧
96.26	my] *omit*
96.31	like] liked
97.9	rod] road
99.32	in] *omit*
101.32	it] it it
105.17	chapel.] ~∧
111.33	Saviour.] ~∧
112.11	Potter,] ~∧
116.6	far as the] far the
117.30	nor] nore
118.6	think so] think to so
118.20	have] *omit*
120.2	a] *omit*
120.28	another] other
120.32	had.] ~∧
122.33	one] once
124.23	varnished.] ~∧
128.19	the] the the
130.32	precipitate] precipatate
131.3	together.] ~∧
132.26	says] say
133.29	place,] ~∧
134.31	ruin.] ~∧
135.1	patches of brickwork] patches brickwork

136.25	myself to] myself to to
137.19	inscription] incscription
138.12	iridescence] irredescence
139.25	24] 25
142.13	dead.] ~∧
142.19	earth.] ~∧
143.14	mother-in-law] ~ - ~∧~
144.22	long as the] long the
144.30	gates] gate
145.19	hot-houses.] ~ - ~∧
148.12	gateway] gate∧|way
150.19	kneeled] kneeld
152.2	Caius] caius
154.28	seems really to] seems to really to
160.15	perceive] percive
161.7	same evening we] same we
161.16	departed.] ~∧
163.4	pierced] piercd
163.19	in] in in
164.27	wherever] where-|ever
165.5	entered] enterered
169.8	Last] last
170.30	vanished.] ~∧
171.1	elsewhere] elswhere
171.8	columns] columes
171.20	an] a
171.22	we were there] we there
173.3	northerly] mortherly
174.8	existence] existance
175.31	foliage,] ~∧
178.2	responses.] ~∧
178.32–33	faun-blood] faun-blod
179.7	Gibson's] Gibson
181.28	Ultor] Ult-|tor
182.7	waiting] wait-|ting
182.12	viewing] view-|
188.26	genius.] ~∧
190.12	jeweller's] jewellers
192.2	incapable] incable

193.22	carriages] carriage
193.25	wear] war
193.26	families] familes
197.28	week's] weeks
199.9	vanishes.] ~∧
201.26	have] *omit*
202.4	inner] inmer
207.6	tidings.] ~∧
208.34	pronounced] pronouced
209.29	and,] ~;
210.6	long,] ~∧
210.12	Casino] Ca-|asino
210.30	to] *omit*
211.23	ornamental] ormental
211.24	Coffee-house] Coff-house
212.22	artificially] ar-|ficially
213.17	enters] entres
213.21	much.] ~∧
214.5	is] *omit*
214.10	one] *omit*
215.18	inexorable] inexporable
218.5	intellectual] intelectual
219.1	vetturinos] vetturino's
220.13	buonamano.] ~∧
220.25	souled] sould
220.27	scrupulously] scrupoulously
222.12	quality] quali-|ity
223.7	irremediable] irremediably
223.14	in] in in
225.10	course] couse
227.6	by-the-by] ~∧~ - ~
227.23	former] latter
228.9	gentleman),] ~)∧
231.19	Peter's] Peters
232.11	though the] though their the
232.15	fresh] freesh
234.18	from] from from
234.34	I] I I
235.13	caused,] ~;

239.5	living.] ~∧
240.29	accommodations] accomodations
242.17	stood.] ~∧
243.26–27	to the] to his the
244.4	passengers)] ~,
245.4	mezzo-baioccho] mezzo-baiocch
246.4	is] has
246.27	situation] sit-|ation
249.7	cosa'] ~∧
251.10	sky.] ~∧
252.30	rocky] rockly
253.27	without.] ~∧
254.3	spacious one] spacious ones
254.7	its] is
256.16	one] ones
257.24	lingered] lingerered
258.5	through] though
258.23	Francis.] ~∧
259.28	shoes] Shoes
260.16	exigency] exagency
262.1	before] befor
262.5	piano,'] ~',
262.24	banks] barks
263.24	perceiving] peceiving
263.33–34	persevering] perservering
265.3	tall,] ~∧
265.11	course] couse
265.20	anticipation] anticpation
266.25	Its] It
269.27	around] aroud
270.27	of] *omit*
270.31	windows.] ~∧
271.18	than] than than
273.21	arcades] acades
273.23–24	picturesquely] picturesqu-|ly
273.27	imaginary] imginary
273.28	Wherever] Whereever
274.18	not] not not
275.4	one] *omit*

277.13	dead?"] ~?'
278.16	in] in in
280.8	ought] aught
285.7	within and out] within out
285.14	Baptistery] Babtistery
285.27	thrown] thown
286.15	inefficiency] ineffiency
287.9	Peter's] Peters
288.29	work] ~∧
289.2	Uguccione,] ~∧
290.19	friendly] frienly
290.30	intelligence] inteligence
291.8	American] Amerian
291.32–33	recognize] recgnize
293.7	little] lit-|
294.23	families] familes
301.1	Brownings] Browngs
301.8	fingers] finger
302.21	successful] succes-|ful
304.14	frescoed] frecoed
310.31	than] then
311.13	continued] con∧|tued
311.31	is] omit
312.26	illustration] il-|ustration
313.31	much as forty] much forty
315.13	one] omit
319.17	away] a-|away
322.10	Peter's] Peters
324.34	devils] devil's
325.28	chapels] chapes
325.28	are dark] and dark
327.10	house-room] ~ - ~∧
331.16	looking] look-
333.20–21	engaged] engged
333.24	side of] side of of
337.29	it is so] it so
338.5	the] the the
338.28	companion,] ~∧
341.2	thousand] thousan

345.12	Altar] Atar
346.23	abbreviated] abrreviated
346.26	look] looks
354.6	Michael] Michaell
356.30	were] *omit*
358.2	where strangers,] where, stranger,
361.13	an] *omit*
367.7	Raphael's] Raphaels
370.25	the shrine.] ~ ~$_\Lambda$
376.12	petitionary] petionary
377.2	Raphael's] Raphaels
377.5	Madonnas] Madonna's
377.18	evening] eve-|nig
380.18	battlemented] batlemented
385.21	cultivated] cutivated
385.29	Yankees.] ~$_\Lambda$
386.27	another] a-|other
386.28	people.] ~$_\Lambda$
387.11	classifying] classyfying
387.22	meet] meek
391.4	an] *omit*
391.28	as] *omit*
391.30	think of] *omit*
391.31	to raise] raise
396.6	Thursday.] ~$_\Lambda$
398.17	spirits.] ~$_\Lambda$
406.10	there always] there is always
407.9	for a] for a a
407.30	vegetables] vegetable
408.16	street] ~,
413.17	Cloth] ~,
417.22	one of the] one the
418.29	benevolent] benevo-|ent
419.14	Athenaeum] Athanaeum
421.26	us] as
422.2	By-the-by] ~$_\Lambda$~ - ~
422.3	Laura] Laua
423.2	quality] quatity

424.29	representation] repsensation
424.33	"and] ∧∼
427.18	infinitesimal] infinitesmal
436.10–11	wished the Government] wished Government
437.29	caravan] carvavan
438.1	leaving] lea-|ing
439.13	through] throgh
439.29	wolf] wolfe
440.4	just as] just as as
441.3	reverential] revential
441.31–32	manuscript-] manscript-
444.12, 15	Baptistery] Babtistery
446.27	turned] tuned
446.29	street.] ∼∧
446.35	foliage] folige
447.13	buying] byying
448.33	lingered] lingerered
449.8	Storys] Stories
450.1	be] *omit*
451.26	phlegmatic] phelgmatic
453.32	Baptistery] Babtistery
454.9	serves] of-|serves
454.11	perhaps] perphaps
454.26	heterogeneous] heterogenous
457.28	life] ∼,
458.16	but I] but I I
458.26	iniquities] inquities
461.12	precipitous] precpitous
463.19	a] *omit*
466.16	week's] weeks
467.16	a] *omit*
468.26	interrupted] interupted
473.29	it,] ∼;
476.21	in] *omit*
476.25	vetturino's] vetturinos
477.27	Nevertheless] Neverthess
478.2	of silver] of a silver
478.2	of] *omit*

481.33	Etruscan] Etrusan
482.1	a] a a
483.22	constructed] construct-|ted
483.27	-tops.] - ∼∧
486.2	tells] tell
486.11	year's . . . year's] years' . . . years'
486.16	as to raise] as to raise as to raise
487.3	more] *omit*
490.19	Vandyke] Vanddyke
490.21	Rembrandt] Rembrand
490.27	those.] ∼∧
492.23	third.] ∼∧
499.15	sweets.] ∼∧
499.17	faithfully] fathfully
500.20	embarrassment] embarassment
500.30	presenting] present∧|ting
503.19	merry-makers] merry-makes
507.26	were] are
508.27	warmed] wamed
509.7	as] as as
512.29	but] by
514.14	long and] ∼,∼
516.18	there] their
517.29	innumerable] inumerable
521.34	floors] floos
523.25	been,] ∼;
524.6	Marseilles)] ∼,
525.16	been] *omit*
526.15	by] *omit*
527.12	been] *omit*
532.20	them from] them one from
533.17	-purposes.] -∼∧
533.22	lofty stone] ∼ - ∼
534.31	shepherd] shep-|ard
535.33	Angora] Angola
536.22	to] *omit*
538.18	especially] esepecially
541.15	at] it
542.19	anaconda] an-|conda

543.4	picturesque.] ~∧
544.6	gathered] gatherered
544.31	French] Frech
551.10	left Lyons] left at Lyons
551.23	midnight.] ~∧
551.34	situated] sit-|ated
552.3	carriages.] ~—
552.12	houses] house
552.13	of] *omit*
558.30	here.] ~∧
559.2	a] *omit*
559.11	Calvinistic] Calvanistic
560.1	castle)] ~,
560.1	room] *omit*
563.17	patient,] ~∧
564.22	often as] often as as
565.13	we] we we
567.9	pillars,] ~∧
567.21	for] form
570.3	have] *omit*
570.13	therefore,] ~∧
570.23	been] *omit*
571.30	to Havre] from Havre
572.6	home.] ~∧

THE 1858 POCKET DIARY

576.22	eleven] elven
581.11	Called] Caled
582.5	bank] banks
582.27	studio] stu-|io
583.17	I] *omit*
586.8	Pantheon] Panhtheon
586.14	9 *Tuesday*] 2 *Tuesday* [*entry inscribed on wrong page but printed date not corrected*

586.17	10 *Wednesday*] 3 Wednesday [*entry inscribed on wrong page but printed date not corrected*]
589.18	Rosebud & I walked] Rosebud & walked
590.6	Julian & I went] Julian & went
590.13	evening] eve-|ing
597.7	After] Afer
597.17	Una & I, after] Una &, after
598.5	weather] whether
598.12	beggars] baggers
599.14–15	Towards evening,] ~,~,
603.12	at home] home at
605.3	in to] into
605.22	at home] home at
606.21	Major] Majory
614.27	Reached] Reaced
626.9	homeopathic] homoepathic

The 1859 Pocket Diary

639.29	grounds] gronds
641.10	through] thrugh
647.14	Farnesina] Farnsina
652.6–7	Julian & I staid] Julian & staid
665.7	Mamma drove] ~, ~
668.5	Julian & I walked] Julian & walked
670.2–3	Miss Shepard] Miss
670.8	we] we we
673.10	A fair] a fair
673.18	for Geneva] & for Geneva
675.5–6	than any hotel] than hotel
678.10	Rosebud,] ~∧
681.5–6	the Oxford] the Oxfor
683.10	betimes] bitimes
683.11	to] *omit*
685.25	satisfactorily] satisfacortily
687.11	indisposed] indis-|sposed

688.8	I took] & took
695.8	Redcar] Recar
695.27	evening &] eveing &
701.24	a walk] a a walk
703.3	Julian & I walked] Julian & walked

WORD-DIVISION

1. *End-of-the-line Hyphenation in the Centenary Edition*

Possible compounds hyphenated at the end of a line in the
Centenary text are listed here if they are hyphenated within
the line in the copy-text. Exclusion from this list means that
a possible compound appears as one unhyphenated word in
the copy-text. Also excluded are hyphenated compounds in
which both elements are capitalized.

6.21	slender-stemmed	114.8	picture-rooms
7.23	mutton-cutlets	115.19	bas-reliefs
7.31	dressing-operations	125.27	forty-four
7.32	dining-room	132.33	stone-mason
27.20	meal-times	134.19	garden-house
37.25	to-and-fro	135.10	suspension-bridge
37.27	inner-court	142.22	fellow-slumberers
41.27	narrow-streeted	145.34	weather-beaten
44.21	semi-circular	146.22	country-residence
50.4	pleasure-garden	148.5	country-seat
54.20	mean-looking	149.25	ill-mannered
56.11	white-washed	151.4	dark-brown
64.28	willow-twigs	158.4	straight-forward
68.28	non-combatants	158.8	side-pockets
84.27	jack-boots	159.17	small-tooth
84.30	wide-awake	164.7	battle-field
109.15	picture-rooms	171.11	side-aisles
111.15	altar-pieces	173.34	orang-outang

504.7	torch-bearer	555.3	time-worn
507.20	paving-stones	557.16	white-washed
527.7	custom-house	558.32	rain-drops
542.3	race-course	559.23	sleeping-place
542.18	sea-tiger	567.26	side-apartments
544.11	pleasure-houses	572.1	To-night
552.18	high-roofed	636.19	fossil-shells

2.   End-of-the-line Hyphenation in the Copy-Text

The following possible compounds are hyphenated at the ends of lines in the copy-text. The form adopted in the Centenary Edition, as listed below, represents Hawthorne's predominant usage as ascertained by other appearances or by parallels within the copy-text.

THE FRENCH AND ITALIAN NOTEBOOKS

5.24	sea-sickness	46.27	sunrise
5.29	wash-bowls	47.8	cab-drivers
5.31	brandy-|and-water	53.21	fireplaces
7.22	dining-room	56.4	alley-like
7.25	bedtime	56.6	corner-wise
8.4	court-yard	60.33	half-heathenish
13.4	dining-place	65.18	side-aisles
13.19	mutton-chops	68.34	re-passed
19.12	half-dome	80.26	side-chapels
21.19	cake-and-candy	95.32	red-veined
23.8	pencil-drawings	96.18	railways
27.21	arm-chair	111.6	thousand-fold
34.7	mud-pudding	115.13	to-day
35.5	a-light	115.32	roll-call
36.18	staircase	118.5	head-stone
39.6	castle-wall	119.14	re-entered
45.20	drawing-room	120.3	semi-circular

132.23	finger-ends	286.11	daylight
134.9	bas-reliefs	289.22	mediæval
146.2	canal-like	301.5	drawing-room
149.19	side-aisle	301.14	akin
161.2	city-gate	301.15	common-place
162.6	ugly-tempered	314.4	lifetime's
171.3	two-foot	321.6	swallow-tailed
171.8	side-aisles	323.17	sword-hilt
175.16	roundabout	324.29	worm-eaten
181.27	weather-stained	326.1	mediæval
184.20	mosaic-work	326.6	high-altar
188.22	forest-ground	330.19	twenty-millionth
197.8	wheelbarrows	332.8	outspread
199.27	scull-cap	333.19	scarlet-damask
202.9	bas-relief	334.4	eyelids
211.25	semi-circular	334.11	to-day
224.2	lady-like	334.17	last-mentioned
228.22	headache	352.13	stone-staircase
233.25	staircase	360.18	side-aisles
235.10	wayside	361.33	blackbird
235.34	sleeping-chambers	366.15	bell-wire
237.1	mediæval	369.6	four-sided
237.9	fig-tree	369.13	tomb-stones
243.5	wayside-inn	371.31	fair-haired
243.21	strongholds	382.9	frame-work
244.15	hill-tops	393.23	death-bed
248.5	white-washed	397.10	lady-like
248.22	one-legged	401.26	to-day's
260.24	common-place	404.12	cake-shop
267.23	battle-field	408.4	guard-room
269.16	birth-place	408.8	to-|and-fro
270.6	tea-kettles	411.2	bas-reliefs
272.2	female-head-|dress	411.10	goldsmiths
272.13	door-steps	413.31	copper-captain
272.31	rose-trees	418.1	bed-chamber
275.6	staircase	418.5	staircase
276.17	roundabout	426.20	fruit-flavor
276.34	copper-shower	438.6	commercial-\ \ \ \ \ \ travellers
280.31	twenty-year		
283.4	willow-tree	438.31	mediæval

445.19	Cathedral-front	493.13	stone-work
446.10	midway	494.22	well-dressed
446.28	never-completed	495.6	within-doors
455.3	handcart	497.4	shop-windows
457.3	apple-trees	500.25	half-bushel
462.3	stone-work	514.31–32	chestnut-meats
465.24	stone-stairs	515.29	charcoal-strewn
469.25	vetturo-horses	516.13	bath-room
472.31	blood-relation	516.19	earth-stained
474.1	hill-side	526.9	sick-chamber
474.5	hill-country	533.27	bird-cages
477.15	vineyards	535.31	book-seller's
479.19	ill-|to-do	550.26	re-entrance
484.1	long-past	562.19	forty-five
486.25	half-paul		

THE 1858 POCKET DIARY

584.27	picture-gallery	612.15	passport
593.6	moonlight	616.20	bas-reliefs
594.17	passports	618.6	to-day
598.15	birthplace	618.9	mid-day
601.9	thunder-shower	621.18	reappears
602.5	horse-race		

THE 1859 POCKET DIARY

663.14	to-day	691.4	horseback
671.27	river-side	691.20	cattle-show
673.26	sight-seeing	692.11	horseback
677.8	boarding-house	693.25	horseback
678.20	Blackheath [1st]	704.6	mile-stone
679.9	dock-yard	705.10	proof-sheet
679.12	mess-room	706.10	to-day
688.6	overcast		

3. *Special Cases*

The following possible compounds are hyphenated at the ends of lines in both copy-text and Centenary Edition. Words appear here in the adopted Centenary form which is obscured by line-end hyphenation:

9.14	century-box	349.1	horse-race
50.21	burial-place	418.20	twenty-seven
59.17	overwhelmed	423.32	life-long
91.23	gateways	440.8–9	street-cries
99.30	slant-wise	458.29	straw-hat
162.6	strong-willed	515.31	chestnut-meats
217.9	court-yard	521.17	archangel
226.28	court-yard	525.9	water-side
243.27	door-steps		

ALTERATIONS IN THE MANUSCRIPTS

This listing takes account of all alterations in Hawthorne's manuscripts except for undeciphered deletions and the simple mending of letters or words without alteration. Hawthorne's practice in deletion was to wipe out wet ink with a finger, and to cancel dry inscription with straight pen strokes. For brevity of listing, *over* is used to mean "in the same space" and *above* and *above caret*, "interlined"; the presence of a caret is always noted. Empty brackets signify one or more undeciphered letters; letters within brackets are conjectural on some evidence although not wholly certain. Sophia Hawthorne's editing is noted where it infrequently occurs.

THE FRENCH AND ITALIAN NOTEBOOKS

3.21	we] over wiped-out 'he'
4.19	Paris, by] over wiped-out 'Boulogne'
5.9	were] 'h' of original 'where' cancelled
5.25	Rosebud] 'Rose' over wiped-out 'Baby'
6.28	an] above caret
6.30	(as] parenthesis cancels comma
6.33	they] added in margin

6.34	Weary] 'W' over 'Ti'
7.15	advised on] over wiped-out 'directed by'
7.25	and] over wiped-out 'under'
7.34	see the] 'the' mended from 'this'
8.6	three-cornered] 'three-corn' over wiped-out 'cocked hats'
8.10	outlandishness] 'ness' above caret
8.13	have] above caret
9.21	rich] 'r' over wiped-out 'b'
9.25	Cathedral] 'C' mended from 'c'
9.33	former] over wiped-out 'latter'
10.8	crucified] 'cruci' over wiped-out 'image'
10.11	were] 'w' over wiped-out 's'
10.12	on the] 'on t' over wiped-out 'in al'
11.12	the] over wiped-out 'our'
11.15	candle] above caret
12.14	London] 'L' over 'P'
13.1	but] over wiped-out 'not'
13.1	to] over wiped-out 'the'
13.3	is] over wiped-out 'are'
13.5	where] over wiped-out 'into'
13.7	a waiter] the article over wiped-out 'the'
13.26	human gore] above caret and cancelled 'it'
13.27	Place] 'P' over 'p'
14.15	Moorish] 'M' over 'm'
15.4	years] over wiped-out 'days'
15.32	elder] 'l' over 'd'
16.15	reclaim] 're' cancelled by spiraling stroke typical of SH
16.17	Henrys] 'rys' over 'ries'
17.20	a] over 'an'
17.31	a rock] the article over wiped-out 'the'
18.7	rumbling] 'rumb' over wiped-out possible 'crumbl'
18.13	could not] 'not' added later, in margin
18.20	within] 'with' over wiped-out possible 'of'
18.20	by] preceded by wiped-out parenthesis
18.31	us] mended from 'me'
20.15	were a] 'r' of original 'ar' wiped out, leaving the article

20.17	as] above caret
20.21	to see a] over wiped-out 'when the [ ]'
20.25	a cocked . . . sword,] above caret
20.28	not] above 'in'
20.31	at whose] 'at w' over wiped-out 'whose'
21.18	provision] 'p' over possible 'ch'
22.8	round] 'ro' over wiped-out 'ar'
23.12	Rubens] 'Ru' over 'and'
23.13	Dutch] over wiped-out 'or wha'
23.27	not] above 'think'
24.2	for] over wiped-out 'an'
24.32	and encrusted] 'and' over wiped-out 'with e'
24.34	stand] a terminal 's' was wiped out
24.34	groups] 's' mended from 'es', possibly by Sophia
25.1	sarcophagi] 'ph' over 'gi'
25.18	statuary—] dash cancels comma
26.12	which] preceded by cancelled 'all'
26.27	XVI—] dash cancels semicolon
26.32	the] preceded by a single word or two short words cancelled with spiral overmarking by Sophia
26.33	galleries,] followed by three-quarters line cancelled with spiral overmarking by Sophia
27.2	another chill, raw day] 'er' over 'a', 'day' preceded by cancelled 'ev'
27.14	in a morning-gown] above caret
28.5	said] over wiped-out 'remarked'
28.29	think] above caret
28.32	Minister] over wiped-out 'Judge'
29.13	transitorily] preceded by wiped-out 'to'
29.26	her] over 'and'
30.9–10	It was the sacristy.] preceded by an asterisk, the sentence was added above 'a Chapel, where'
30.15–17	A mistake. . . . shown.] preceded by an asterisk, the two sentences were added above 30.13–14 'floor . . . vestments'
31.11	gold and] 'and' above caret
31.24–25	we . . . do.] above caret that covers possible original punctuation after 'other'
31.27	pointed arches] over wiped-out 'vaulted entrance'

32.4	bookseller] a second 's' within the word cancelled
32.16	is] above caret
33.3	an] over wiped-out 'the'
33.7	Vecchia] second 'c' over wiped-out 'h'
33.27	an] above caret
34.6	saw] above caret
34.14	I had not time] 'have' inscribed above 'time' in afterthought, from reading preceding 'had' as 'did'
34.23	race] preceded by two cancelled letters
35.19	surmounted] 'surm' over wiped-out 'with'
36.18	staircase] 'stair' above 'case'
36.27	length,] comma cancels semicolon
36.31	passage] 'pas' over wiped-out 'corr'
37.4	own] over wiped-out 'sle'
37.21	hole] mended from 'holes'
37.22	over] 'o' over wiped-out possible 'at'
38.3	which is] 'is' over wiped-out 'st'
38.5	Place] 'P' mended from 'p'
38.12	a fog] the article over wiped-out 'the'
38.15	et] over wiped-out 'and'
38.18	sleeping] 'sl' over wiped-out 'dep'
38.26	as registered] 'as regis' over wiped-out 'that had'
38.24	much] over wiped-out 'care'
39.9	a mile] 'a' over wiped-out possible 'at'
39.14	which] 'w' over wiped-out 'that'
39.18	blue] 'bl' over wiped-out 'col'
39.23–24	did not] over wiped-out 'only parte'
39.25	that we] 'th' over wiped-out 'of'
39.29–30	Still going] 'Still' over wiped-out possible 'Also' and 'going' over possible 'we'
40.8	plaster] 'i' of 'plaister' cancelled
40.15	go] over wiped-out 'back'
40.22	and] followed by wiped-out comma
41.11	as] over wiped-out 'of'
41.22	city—] dash cancels comma
41.28	or] above caret
42.1	be] over wiped-out 'the'
42.16–17	conspicuous] initial 'c' over wiped-out 'p'

42.34	warm] 'wa' over wiped-out 'hot'
43.2	steel—] dash cancels comma
43.2	exhilarating] first 'a' mended from 'i'
43.6	hand;] semicolon cancels comma
43.11	which] 'w' over wiped-out 'of'
43.14	water] 'wa' over wiped-out 'cl'
44.9	another] 'an' above caret
44.9	after] 'af' over wiped-out 'the'
45.17	Places] 'P' over 'p'
45.18	several of] over wiped-out 'many of wh'
45.19	set] over 'the'
45.21	like] above caret
45.23	hear] 'h' over 'al'
45.30	(which] parenthesis cancels comma
46.9	a crowd] 'a' over wiped-out 'a'; 'cro' over wiped-out 'least'
46.10	a] above caret
47.25	were] above caret
48.26	Perhaps] 'er' mended from 'e'
49.28	what] 'w' over 'to'
50.17	steamer] 'ste' over wiped-out 'boat'
51.9	walked] 'w' over wiped-out 'sat'
51.16, 20	Vecchia] second 'c' over wiped-out 'h'
51.33	structure] 's' over 'a' of wiped-out 'ba'
52.1	strongly] 's' over wiped-out 'of'
52.4	feed our] 'feed' over wiped-out 'change'; 'o' over wiped-out 'h'
52.5	along] 'a' over wiped-out 't'
54.20	between] over wiped-out 'with'
54.30	shape] over wiped-out possible 'that yet'
58.1	city—] dash cancels comma
60.3	is] above 'all'
60.8	his] over wiped-out 'their'
60.8	infinite Presence] above 'his . . . church'
60.10	an] above 'agony'
63.9	unexpected] 'un' above caret
63.21	framed] above 'within'
65.15	row] above caret
65.25	precisely] 'pre' over 'mar'

66.14	with] above caret, in a different ink
67.6	chance—] dash cancels comma
67.23	has] above caret, in a different ink
68.30	missiles] above cancelled 'weapons'
70.27	his] over wiped-out 'its'
71.4	masque] above cancelled 'show'
71.18	on] above caret
72.33	saw him] 'him' above caret
73.29	it] above caret
74.17	it, and] 'it' above comma, in different ink
77.29	of] added below 'want'
77.30	plaster] 'i' of 'plaister' cancelled
78.4	may] 'm' over wiped-out 'p'
78.13	acting] 'a' over wiped-out possible 'f'
79.1	were] above caret
79.1	killed] 'we' added above in false start, not cancelled when 'were' was added before preceding 'several'
79.10	looking] over wiped-out 'and we'
80.2	see—] dash cancels comma
80.6	woollen frock] over wiped-out 'a frock of'
80.6	head] above uncancelled 'face'
80.7	to] above 'leave'
80.18	has been] 'has' above caret
83.8	a resounding] 'a' above caret
84.22–23	elsewhere] MS 'elsewhere'; second 'e' above caret
84.32	any] above caret
86.32	Peter's] 't' mended from 's'
88.4	them] above caret
89.3	quartered] MS 'quarterred' followed by wiped-out comma
91.10	suddenly] 'su' over 'pe'
92.29	an] above caret cancelling 'a' in constricted space
93.14	Fornarina] terminal 'a' mended from 'i'
93.16	—ready . . . money,—] above caret
96.6	fiery gem] 'fiery g' over wiped-out 'rose gem'
96.28	getting] preceded by cancelled 'soon'
97.9	rod] 'a' of 'road' cancelled
97.27	side-long] above caret

99.28	(which] parenthesis cancels comma
100.26	Capitol] 'C' over 'c'
103.28	flight of] over wiped-out 'staircase'
104.15	or] over 'and'
106.10	not] above caret
106.20	close] terminal 'st' cancelled
106.30	Circus] followed by cancelled 'and'
107.11	away] 'the' of 'the way' cancelled and 'a' prefixed to 'way'
107.23	right] above cancelled 'left'
107.28	left] above cancelled 'right'
108.4	Columbaria] 'C' over 'c'
109.13	a part of] above caret
109.25	thrown] over wiped-out '[ ] into'
109.25	like] 'k' over 'g'
109.29	away] above cancelled 'down'
110.18	and value] above caret that cancelled a period
111.13	it] above caret
111.26	on] above caret
111.33	Saviour] 'iour' over wiped-out 'ior'
112.7	ever] over wiped-out 'them'
112.11	Teniers] above caret misplaced before comma after 'Potter'
112.25	on] above caret
113.31	a river] 'a' above caret
114.15	Nevertheless] preceded by cancelled 'Nevertheless'
115.17	you] added in margin
116.1	echoes of the] above caret
117.29	trump] above cancelled 'day'
118.14	six] above caret and cancelled 'five'
118.22	had] above caret
119.4	castle] above caret and cancelled 'fortress'
119.12	but] followed by cancelled '[ ] doing'
120.3	about] above 'a'
120.6	rising to] above caret
120.28	another] 'an' added later
121.13	feet] above caret
121.17	rows in] 'in' over 'on'

122.9	of] above caret
122.29	been] above caret
122.31	dark] over wiped-out 'black'
123.27	the waters of] above caret
123.33	Laza—] Hawthorne later wrote 'Lazarini' in pencil in top margin.
124.8	Leonardo] preceded by cancelled 'Corregio's'
124.11	by] 'b' over 'of'
124.12	Aragon] above cancelled 'Naples'
128.6	of] over 'from'
128.19	productions of the] above caret
129.20	me] above caret
131.4	with] above caret
133.18	can] terminal 'not' cancelled
133.30	mass is] 'is' above caret
134.31	(and] parenthesis cancels comma
135.8	vicinity] 'v' over 'to'
136.17	be—] dash cancels semicolon
137.27	lizards] 'l' over 'L'
139.18	whom] above caret
140.10	interest] terminal 'ing' cancelled
140.24	cloth] above caret
141.14	own] above caret
143.4	room—] dash cancels comma
144.8	by] over 'to'
149.27	St] over 'his'
149.29	away] over wiped-out 'back fr'
150.1	caps] 'c' over wiped-out 'p'
150.6	good] 'g' over wiped-out 'C'
150.16	known] over wiped-out 'felt'
152.12	it stood] 'it' above caret
154.14	in him] 'in' above caret, in a different ink
154.19	from] over 'to'
155.1	taken] followed by cancelled 'taken'
155.20	Mr. Mozier] preceded by cancelled 'Margaret eve'
157.4	But] 'B' over wiped-out possible 'S'
157.19	of both] 'of' above caret
158.12	on] above caret

158.26	enough] above caret
159.12	took] 't' crossed later, in a different ink
159.23	to beg] 'to' above caret
161.7	same evening] 'same' above 'next' of cancelled 'next evening (Monday)'; 'evening' is restored
162.5	been] followed by cancelled 'of'
163.19	standing in] above caret and uncancelled 'in'
165.6	frescoes of sacred] over wiped-out 'sculptures presenting'
165.18	coved] above cancelled 'vaulted'
166.29	forming] 'for' over wiped-out 'as f'
167.6	the slabs] 'the' over wiped-out 'crack'
167.11	buy;] semicolon cancels comma
167.23	not] above caret
167.27	the feudal system] above caret
167.34	been] above caret
168.3	the pictures] 'the' followed by cancelled 'm'; 'pictures' above caret
168.5	noble] over wiped-out 'excelle'
168.17	heraldic] 'her' over wiped-out 'cert'
168.21	splendid] over wiped-out 'brilliant'
168.26–27	polished, and arranged] above caret; followed by wiped-out 'in'
168.27	in square] 'in sq' over wiped-out 'ranged'
169.5	result] 'resu' over wiped-out 'effec'
169.9	and of] 'of' above caret
169.11	I] preceded by cancelled 'that'
171.16	very] over wiped-out 'great'
171.31	indeed—] dash cancels comma
171.32	picture—] dash cancels comma
173.30	as well] 'as w' over wiped-out 'might'
174.8–9	beautifully] 'ly' added in a different ink
175.32	great urns and vases,] above caret that inadvertently covers comma after 'foliage'
176.10	Italy] preceded by cancelled 'talking'
176.12	by] followed by cancelled 'by'
177.6	herself] 'her' over possible 'it'
177.19	be] above caret
177.26	my] over wiped-out 'the ap'

177.28	person] 'per' over wiped-out 'app'
177.29	a huge] 'a' preceded by wiped-out 'h'
180.25	ascertain] over wiped-out 'discover'
180.30	one] above 'looks'
181.13	fragments] over wiped-out 'parts'
181.19	some] over wiped-out 'the'
183.31	architectural] 'archi' over wiped-out 'works'
184.13	by any] 'by' above caret
184.14	our residence] 'by' added above, between the two words, in error, but not deleted when later 'by' was inserted (in a different ink) before 'any' in the line above
185.5	a man] over wiped-out 'the Custo'
185.6	a door] 'a' above caret, in a different ink
185.10	winding] 'indi' over wiped-out 'ithin'
185.13	by] over wiped-out 'through'
186.4	of] the 'o' over wiped-out 'f'
186.17	innumerable] 'in' over wiped-out 'd'
187.6	dying Saint] over wiped-out 'half-dead'
187.34	it] above caret
188.31	went] followed by cancelled 'went'
189.6	who] above caret
191.17	it] above caret
192.3	nor] 'no' over wiped-out 'and'
193.19	as] over wiped-out 'as it'
193.21	and] over wiped-out 'as it'
193.27	mostly] over wiped-out 'but [ ]'
194.15	before] 'b' over wiped-out possible 'f'
194.20	dome] 'd' over wiped-out 'f'
196.24	there] 'r' over 'y'
197.33	her] above caret
198.9	pray] over wiped-out possible 'be d'
199.30	her] followed by cancelled 'her'
200.8	one] above caret
200.27	through] over 'out of'
201.7	were] above caret
201.14	there] above caret
201.17	to] above caret
201.30	one of its] 'of' covers original 'its'

202.4	Christians] 'C' over 'c'
203.8	long] over 'tough'
203.9	should] followed by cancelled 'not'
203.9	not] above caret
203.31	the] mended from 'those'
204.13	dread] over 'horror' and then added above for clarity
205.6	be] over 'one'
207.10	cieling,] over 'roof,'
209.17	of the] 'of' over wiped-out 'that'
210.23	them] above caret
211.28	rare] above cancelled 'curious'
212.4	during] over wiped-out 'as long as'
212.23	at its] over wiped-out 'its ba'
213.7	the rush] over wiped-out 'with dyin'
213.21	to] above caret
213.22	16th] mended from '15th'
213.26	enough] above caret
213.31	are] over wiped-out 'were'
215.8–9	far beneath] 'far be' over wiped-out 'beneath'
216.26	monkey] 'n' over 'k'
216.26	lest] preceded by cancelled 'up'
218.1	is] above caret
218.23	in] above caret
222.3	He] over wiped-out 'I pre'
222.4	as a] 'as' above caret
222.30	Kansas] 'Kan' over wiped-out 'Sla'
223.33	some] over wiped-out 'pag'
224.12	his] over wiped-out 'her'
225.23	Campagna—] dash cancels comma
225.27	Miss Bremer] over wiped-out 'she asked them'
227.1	meet] followed by cancelled 'her'
229.5	be] above caret
230.7	the Italians,] above caret
230.16	Piazza] 'P' over wiped-out 'pi'
230.22	great] over wiped-out 'deep'
230.27	her here] 'her' above caret
231.5	bringing] 'bri' over wiped-out possible 'giv'
231.11	never] 'n' mended from 'm'

231.25	move] over wiped-out 'drive'
232.18	have] 'v' over 'd'
232.20	of] over wiped-out 'that'
233.26	cieling] over wiped-out 'roof with'
233.29	a valley] 'a' above caret
233.32	he] 'h' over wiped-out 'w'
234.1	entirely] over wiped-out 'quite'
234.30	is] over wiped-out 'was'
235.24	by a] 'a' over wiped-out 'the'
236.19	laborers] 'la' over 'per'
237.8	verdure] 'ver' over wiped-out 'foliag'
237.21	it] above caret
237.27	one] 'o' over 'e' of wiped-out 'the'
237.34	the] followed by cancelled 'the'
238.11	each] 'ea' over wiped-out 'his'
238.16	boy] above caret
239.17	frowning] 'fro' over wiped-out 'look'
239.22	at] over 'in'
239.27	shops as] over wiped-out 'houses with'
239.34	through] over wiped-out 'at the b'
240.18	being] over wiped-out 'having'
241.1	breakfast] 'brea' over wiped-out 'dinn'
241.33	us] above caret
242.8	inhospitable] 'inh' over wiped-out 'not'
242.14	as] above caret
242.22	are] above caret
242.24	objects] 'o' over 's'
242.25	one of] over wiped-out 'a great'
243.3	to] above 'cover'
243.3	cover] followed by cancelled 'to'
243.4	perhaps] preceded by cancelled 'in'
243.12	right] over wiped-out 'quite'
243.18	commanding] 'co' over wiped-out 'hei'
244.11	beside] above cancelled 'along'
244.15	through] 'th' over wiped-out 'of'
244.15	between] over wiped-out 'among'
244.27	window-] 'win' over wiped-out 'high'
245.18	force] 'fo' over wiped-out 'ent'
245.26	and . . . us] above caret

245.31	it was] 'it' above caret
246.13	brighten,] 'n,' added over original terminal 'r'
246.16	fertility] 'li' over 'ty'
246.24	city] over wiped-out 'town'
246.31	the road] 'the' above caret
246.32	evidently] over wiped-out 'no road'
246.33	a crown] 'a' above 'crown'
247.3	my] 'm' over wiped-out 'd'
247.18	whole] above caret
247.18	exceeding] terminal 'ly' cancelled
247.26	the] 'e' over wiped-out 'at'
247.29	we] above caret
248.21–22	spots of the white] 'spots of the w' over wiped-out 'the white plaister'
248.32	Pinturrichio] 'h' mended over 'c'
249.10	we] over wiped-out 'he'
249.13	we] 'w' over wiped-out 'h'
249.33	of the] over wiped-out possible 'stood'
250.14	mountain] terminal 's' wiped out
252.22	which] above caret
253.14	susceptible] 'c' over wiped-out 'p'
253.16	than] above caret
253.20	grow] followed by cancelled 'up'
254.22	Gaetano] 'Ga' over 'we'
255.3	landscape] over wiped-out 'language to'
255.15	therefore] final 'e' over wiped-out 'ed'
255.20	edifices] 'es' over wiped-out 'ices'
255.21	Miss] over 'and'
256.1	had] 'h' over 'y'
256.2	in some] followed by cancelled 'in some'
256.29	Perguino] 'Peru' over wiped-out 'Raph'
256.30	so] over wiped-out 'the'
257.16	headless] 'head' over wiped-out 'neck'
258.22	side-walls] originally 'sides of the'; 'of the' wiped out, 'es' of 'sides' mended to 'e' and hyphen and 'walls' added
258.22–23	This . . . Francis] added in space at end of paragraph and along right margin
259.5	seeing] 'see' over wiped out 'the'

259.28	show:] colon altered from period
260.3	an] 'n' added to 'a'
260.3	open] over wiped-out 'stone g'
260.6	old] 'l' over wiped-out 'f'
260.9	piazza] over wiped-out 'place'
260.9	large and] over wiped-out 'beautiful'
260.10	consisting of a] over wiped-out 'carved all round'
260.11	Within] second 'i' mended from 'o'
260.32	extent] above caret
261.16	A] 'n' of original 'An' cancelled
261.18	loaded with] 'loaded w' over wiped-out 'followed b'
262.9	its] over wiped-out 'be'
262.26	we] over wiped-out 'the'
262.28	airy] over wiped-out 'heig'
263.11	boat,] comma cancels period
264.5	Yet] over 'And'
264.19	white] 'w' over wiped-out 'sh'
266.19	by its] over wiped-out possible 'squee'
266.25	slain] over 'Rom'
266.26	company] over wiped-out 'multitude'
266.27	massacred] 'ma' over wiped-out 'sla'
266.33	is] over 'are'
267.3	have] above caret
267.19	English] over 'Romans'
268.28	space] preceded by cancelled comma
270.6	there,] a caret was inserted after 'there' but no alteration inscribed; followed by deleted 'back when my hand touched the iron handle,'
270.6	fill] above cancelled 'boil'
270.19	her] over wiped-out 'here'
270.20	to our] 'our' over 'the'
271.1	him] 'them' deleted and 'him' added above
271.12	made] 'm' over wiped-out 'th'
275.16	plastered] 'i' of 'plaistered' cancelled
275.19	women's] over wiped-out 'others'
276.1	(growing] parenthesis over dash inscribed over original comma

276.1	narrower)] 'nar' over wiped-out 'oth'; parenthesis over wiped-out dash
276.3	vendita] preceded by cancelled single quote
276.24	a] over 'to'
277.1	these] mended from 'them'
277.1	were] above caret
277.3	persons—] 'per' over wiped-out 'beg'; dash cancels comma
277.12	swarm] over wiped-out 'crowd'
278.5	out] over wiped-out 'that'
278.18	train of gigantic] over wiped-out 'gigantic trai'
278.21	From] preceded by wiped-out 'F' at left margin
278.26	fee] mended from 'few'
279.3	house] above caret
279.14	Florence.] period cancels comma
279.15	say] preceded by cancelled 'to'
280.10	work] 'w' over wiped-out 'sc'
280.33	no] above caret
281.24	fig-leaf] 'af' over 'ves'
282.13	at] above caret
283.10	temptation] above cancelled 'addition'
283.19	tolerable] 't' mended from 'f'
285.22	Florentine] 'F' over wiped-out 'f'
285.26	to] above caret
285.26	capacity] second 'a' over 'ic'
285.30	mosaic] 'mos' over wiped-out 'large'
286.6	vast] 'v' over wiped-out 'g'
286.8	dome-covered] hyphen and 'covered' above caret
287.11	of] over 'and'
288.28	plastered] 'i' of 'plaistered' cancelled
289.16	in adorning] above caret
291.7	by] 'b' over 'f'
291.31	what others] 'what' followed by wiped-out continuation 'ev', 'o' inscribed over the 'v'
293.17	leave] over wiped-out 'leaf'
293.24	right] above caret and cancelled 'left'
294.10	they] over wiped-out 'I'
294.14	a sense] 'a' above caret

295.5	of Caracalla] above caret
296.6	Venuses] over wiped-out possible 'Naiads'
296.15	pretty] over wiped-out 'well'
296.21	repose—] dash cancels comma
297.8	or] over 'of'
297.9	Graces] 'G' mended from 'g'
298.2	by] over wiped-out 'and'
298.16	no] above caret
298.31	the sculptor] above cancelled 'Praxitiles'
300.25	less] over 'more'
301.19	by] over 'for'
302.2–3	Liverpool] over 'London'
302.13	her poetry] 'her' preceded by cancelled 'her'
302.21	successful] MS 'succes-|ful'
303.5	her] above caret
303.6	him] above caret
303.7	taking . . . hair] above caret
303.10	may] over 'say'
303.12	soon to be] 'be' above caret
304.12	us first] 'us' above 'first'
304.15	chandeliers] 'c' over wiped-out 'f'
304.31	tread] 'tr' over 'go'
304.33	which] 'w' over wiped-out 'th'
305.9	principal] 'pri' over 'state'
306.3	a] over 's'
307.8	days ago] over wiped-out 'mornings ago'
307.11	all] over wiped-out 'the'
307.17	Boboli] second 'o' over 'b'
308.28	less] over wiped-out 'the'
309.5	is] above caret
310.6	it] 'i' over 'a'
311.12–13	his two] 'his t' over 'the g'
311.29	them] above caret
312.8	royal] 'r' over 'q'
312.18	is—] dash cancels comma
312.33	benevolent] 'nevolen' over 'neficent'
313.5	heretofore] 't' over wiped-out 'f'
314.12	plaster] 'i' of 'plaister' cancelled
314.22	an] 'a' over wiped-out 'A'

314.24	to make] 'to' over wiped-out 'the'
316.8	too—] dash cancels comma
316.21	that the] 'e' over 'is'
319.15	long] over wiped-out 'they'
320.26–27	in a] 'a' over wiped-out 'the'
321.5	him] above caret
321.14	men] above caret
321.22	Albano] Sophia Hawthorne added an asterisk above this name to call attention to 'Zucchero' which she added in left margin
321.33	all] above caret
323.8	large] 'e' over wiped-out 'ely'
323.11	picture (] parenthesis cancels comma
325.5	quench] over possible 'put o'
325.6	Fra Angelico] over wiped-out 'Michael'
325.21	other] over wiped-out 'general'
326.3	(who] parenthesis cancels comma
326.5	posterity] over wiped-out 'successo'
326.16	left] over wiped-out 'right'
326.17	with] over wiped-out 'the'
327.6	Morning] above caret and cancelled 'Day'
327.6	sufficiently] over wiped-out 'like'
327.14	vindicate for him] above caret and cancelled 'justify'
327.17	one] over wiped-out 'the'
327.18	thigh.] period cancels comma
327.19	it] above caret
329.10	Michael Angelo] above caret
330.19	or the] terminal 'y' of 'they' cancelled
331.12	side] above cancelled 'shore'
331.20	of it] above caret
333.15	pedestals of] 'of' above caret
333.20	was] followed by cancelled 'was'
333.31	could see] above caret
334.24	spectators] over wiped-out 'pic'
337.17	bone in] over 'link of'
337.32	vigor] 'v' over wiped-out 'f'
338.22	an] above caret
340.6	were] mended from 'was'

340.20	majestic] period over wiped-out semicolon
340.29	tame—] dash cancels comma
341.4	own] 'o' over 'ga'
341.9	thronged] over wiped-out 'quite'
341.15	which] 'w' over wiped-out 'the'
341.28	between] above cancelled 'through'
343.15	names] followed by cancelled 'that are'
343.19	design] above caret
343.22	marble] over wiped-out 'pill'
344.9	Astronomy] preceded by cancelled 'some'
345.10	been] above caret
346.1	sunshine,)] parenthesis over wiped-out dash
346.22	often] above caret
346.27	them] above caret
347.16	sculptured coffins] above caret
347.24	excel] preceded by cancelled 'it'
348.20	out] above caret
350.7	Gallery.] period cancels comma
350.8	It was] over wiped-out 'being'
352.17	stood] over wiped-out 'wat[ ]'
353.28	hung] over wiped-out possible 'adorned'
356.12	arched] 'ed' added after inscription of following word
356.21	its] over wiped-out 'h'
356.28	monumental] 'mo' over wiped-out 'tombs'
359.2	accessible] 'acce' over wiped-out 'acess'
359.9	white-wash;] semicolon cancels period
360.31	Verde.] period cancels comma
361.15	fling himself] over wiped-out 'take flight'
362.13	After] 'Af' over 'As'; 'ter' over wiped-out 'you'
362.30	if] above caret
363.12	memorial-] above caret
363.26	were] above 'there'; accepted alteration, but possibly may be in hand of JH rather than NH
364.10	since.] period cancels semicolon
364.19	Annunciation] above caret and cancelled 'Virgin'
364.21	providing] 'provi' over wiped-out 'the pro'
364.23	as] over wiped-out 'for'
364.32	inscriptions] 'inscri' over wiped-out 'memor'

365.4	be] over wiped-out 'the'
365.12	crucifix] followed by wiped-out comma
365.23	steam] over wiped-out 'any'
365.33	gas] 's' over wiped-out 'ss'
366.17	ballad] above caret
366.21	will] over wiped-out 'in'
367.27	improbable] 'i' over wiped-out 'p'
368.1	Saturday] 'Sa' over 'Fri'
369.19	Chapter] 'C' mended from 'c'
369.34	not] over wiped-out possible 'th'
370.3	produce] 'e' over wiped-out 'es'
371.24	Perugino] over 'Cherubine'
372.13	of a] 'a' over wiped-out 'of'
372.16	satire] 's' over wiped-out 'st'; 'ire' mended from 'ue'
373.14	an] over wiped-out 'th'
374.2	twilight] preceded by wiped-out 'in'
375.10	were] followed by cancelled 'were'
377.26	the upper] 'the' above caret
378.5	(as] parenthesis cancels comma
378.6	are] above caret
378.29	in great] 'in' above cancelled 'his'
378.32	(at least] parenthesis cancels comma
380.29	Powers] over wiped-out 'and p'
381.10	original] 'orig' over wiped-out 'was'
381.30	is some] 'is' over wiped-out 'was'
382.7–8	a great] 'a' over 'an'
383.2	avenue] above cancelled 'line'
383.14	hue] mended from 'hues'
383.17	and barren] above caret
383.18	half-] above caret
383.30	floor] 'or' over wiped-out 'wer'
383.31	vaulted] above caret
383.32	walls] over wiped-out 'two lat'
384.17	him anywhere] 'self' of original 'himself' wiped out, and 'anywhere' added
384.19	him] above caret
387.2	(in reply] over wiped-out 'that he had'
387.30	be] above caret

388.25	Magdalen] 'g' mended over 'd'
389.16	mist—] dash cancels comma
390.3	yellow moss] originally 'yello moss'; 'moss' wiped out and 'w' and 'moss' added
391.21	Monte] 'M' over wiped-out 'the'
392.9	in] above caret
392.22	profile] over 'portrait'
393.26	had] above caret
394.13	dark] over wiped-out 'old'
397.10	hands] preceded by cancelled 'pair of'
398.4	felt] followed by cancelled 'as'
398.4	as] above caret
399.27	(Miss] parenthesis cancels comma
404.6	very] 'v' over wiped-out 'bea'
404.21	—all] dash cancels period
404.24	street-cries] 'cries' mended from 'cry'
405.8	intellectual;] semicolon cancels period
406.23	would] above caret
407.21	of] above caret
407.22	a] above caret
408.29	were] 'h' after 'w' cancelled
409.13	are] above caret
409.25	a] over wiped-out 'of'
409.30	are] above caret
409.31	impend] 'en' over wiped-out 'erf'
412.30	presume—] dash cancels parenthesis
413.18	sale] 'le' over 'il'
414.6	and ours] above caret
414.8	life.] period cancels comma; followed by wiped-out 'ex'
414.8	inhabited it;—] originally 'inhabited;—'; 'it;' inscribed over original semicolon
416.27	one] above caret
417.4	and] 'a' over wiped-out 'of'
419.29	Giulian] 'G' mended from 'J'
421.9	pages of] 'of' over wiped-out 'from'
422.9	however—] dash cancels comma
425.28	never] above 'devour'
426.27	were] above caret

428.24	no] over 've'
429.25	all] above caret
431.25	price—] dash cancels period
433.7	Concord—] dash cancels period
435.11	to go] 'to' above 'go'
435.29	fancied I saw] 'I' above caret
436.22	virgin?] question mark cancels comma
437.20	(there] parenthesis cancels comma
438.17	leather-] over wiped-out 'containing'
438.32	castle] over wiped-out possible 'fort'
440.21	towns] above caret
440.31	in the] 'the' above caret
440.34	far] over wiped-out 'the'
441.32	in which I] 'in' above cancelled 'I'
443.9	there] above caret
443.15	Publico] above cancelled 'Vecchio'
444.5	point—] dash cancels comma
444.13	according] terminal 'ly' wiped out
444.15	(the] parenthesis cancels comma
445.11	express] terminal 'ed' wiped out
445.18	sanctifying] 'ing' above caret
447.11	had] above caret
448.1	many,] above caret
448.7	many] above caret
448.18	trailing] 'ing' above caret
449.7	(Scotch] parenthesis cancels comma
451.28	when] added above 'the'
452.10	from] over wiped-out 'by'
452.23	7] over '5'
453.14	strong] 'str' over wiped-out 'than'
453.14	ours] preceded by cancelled 'h'
453.16	with] above caret
454.13	little] over wiped-out 'small'
455.16	Two] preceded by wiped-out 'Two' in left margin
455.18	caps] over wiped-out 'brimless'; preceded by wiped-out comma
455.33	of] over wiped-out 'stops'
458.25	day after day] followed by cancelled 'to listen'
459.7	of] above caret

460.10	(which] parenthesis cancels comma
465.5	yesterday] preceded by cancelled 'in'
468.4	rest] above caret and cancelled 'rest'
470.13	Radicofani] 'c' over original 'f'
470.20	and] over wiped-out 'away'
471.1	saw] over 'heard' and then added above for clarity
471.34	us] above caret
472.10	like] above caret
472.22	there] above caret
473.4	and winding] above caret
473.26–27	to see] 'to' above caret
474.23	it] above caret
476.24	duty] over wiped-out possible 'duty'
477.22	one] above caret
478.2	that] 't' over 'of'
478.5	breeze] 'bree' over wiped-out 'wind'
479.21	figs] MS 'figs,' followed by cancelled 'peaches' but the comma inadvertently left after 'figs'
480.24	(miserable] parenthesis cancels comma
481.15	(of which] parenthesis cancels comma
482.28	anywhere—] dash cancels comma
484.5	(the sketchers')] above caret
484.33	description.] period cancels comma
485.6	Henry Third] over 'the reign of' which was added above cancelled 'the Crusade'
486.2	a] mended from 'an'
486.16	away] above caret
486.29	amount] over wiped-out 'fees pr'
490.1	Piazza] mended from 'Piaza'
490.16	rooms] period cancels comma
491.15	or] over wiped-out 'th'
491.24	us] above caret
491.29	left] over wiped-out 'right'
495.6	could] above caret
496.14	of] above caret
497.18	any] mended from 'in'
505.30	fingers.] period cancels comma
506.10	roofs were] over wiped-out '[ ] roofs'
507.26	dinner] preceded by cancelled 'a'

508.13	country] above cancelled 'contrary'
509.17	moving] preceded by cancelled 'led alon'
509.31	of] above caret
512.32	ancient] 'a' over wiped-out 'fl'
515.3	course,] comma cancels parenthesis
516.14	cellar-] above caret and cancelled 'hollow'
519.15	it] above caret
520.20–21	(seen . . . moment)] parentheses cancel commas
520.22	of] above 'a'
521.23	of] above caret
521.27	fleshy] 'le' over 'el'
521.29	been] above caret
522.26	Padre] 'p' over 'F'
523.10	lady's] mended from 'ladies'
524.20	(life] parenthesis cancels comma
525.7	in three] 'in' over wiped-out 'aft'
525.34	the] followed by cancelled 'the'
526.2–3	returned] mended from 'retained'
528.17	a] mended from 'an'
528.19	houses—] dash cancels comma
528.20	orange] 'ora' over 'whit'
528.32	hissings] 'h' over 'a'
529.11	idea] above caret
529.18	illustrations] preceded by cancelled 'translations' and inadvertently uncancelled semicolon
534.6	thus] mended from 'this'
535.12	many] over possible 'five'
536.4	cat is] 'is' above caret
536.13	look] above caret
536.22	as to look like] originally 'as like like'; 'look' added later above cancelled first 'like'; 'to' is a Centenary emendation
537.12	full] over wiped-out 'great'
537.21	as if] 'as' above caret; 'if' mended from 'is'
538.18	especially] MS 'esepecially,' 'p' over 'c'
538.24	which was] 'which' added above, and 'w' added before 'as' in a different ink
540.6	as] 'a' over wiped-out 'f'

543.15	and] 'nd' above caret, in a different ink
543.25	a great] 'a' above caret
545.1	door—] dash cancels comma
545.26	crowns] 'n' above caret, in a different ink
546.8	soon] over possible 'slowly'
546.24	solitude] 'soli' over possible 'such'
546.34	sunny] above canceled 'sunny'
547.8	was] over wiped-out possible 'stood'
547.9	(which] parenthesis cancels comma
548.18	aristocratic] second 'a' over 't'
548.21	Valence] above cancelled 'Avignon'
548.25	They] 'T' over 't'
549.18	as] over wiped-out 'I'
551.8	time] above 'she' in different ink
553.20	whole of] 'of' above caret
554.20	which—] dash cancels comma
554.29	town-house] 'town-' above caret
555.9	an] above caret, in a different ink
557.14	As it now is] 'now' added, in margin
558.2–3	and from] over wiped-out 'and the'
559.6	whether the] 'er' (at left margin) over 'the'; 'the' over 'Swiss'
560.16	one] over wiped-out 'the'
561.14–15	was to be] over '[ ] good'
561.31	appearance] 'ap' over wiped-out 'bot'
563.13	pretty] 'y' mended from 'ily'
568.3	in the] 'in t' over wiped-out 'amid'

THE 1858 POCKET DIARY

575.8	Returned] 'Re' over 'W'
575.14	Passport] 'P' mended from 'p'
575.16	White] preceded by cancelled 'Harlequin,'
577.18	viséd] 'd' over 'ed'
577.20	de L'Echelle] 'L' over 'de' and then 'de' interlined with a caret
577.21	P.M.] above 'or'

578.13–14	approaching] 'appro' over wiped-out 'entering'
578.25	Vecchia] second 'c' over wiped-out 'h'
578.28	We] over 'The'
578.29	about] 'a' over wiped-out 'at'
578.29	instead] 'ad' over 'd'
579.4	American] 'n' over 'ns'
579.7	Still] over 'Cold'
579.10	340] '4' over '6'
579.25	left] over 'called'
579.25	cards] 'car' over wiped-out 'to-'
580.2	Rosebud] 'Ros' over 'Una'
581.10	on] over 'at'
581.16	one] preceded by inked-out 'th'
582.1	has] 'h' over 'w'
583.10	St.] 'St' over 'Lui'
583.12	with wife] above caret
583.15	Popolo] 'P' over 'p'
583.22	Went] 'We' over 'Less'
584.11	Returned] 'Re' over 'At'
584.19	Rakerman] 'k' over 'ck'
584.21	Crossed] preceded by cancelled 'Rainy. Staid within doors all day.'
584.25	Rainy] preceded by cancelled 'Forenoon, went to Mr Hooker's bank, & read the American'; 'Ra' over 'Wen'
585.10	Hawthorne in error skipped a verso holding printed headings for first three days of March. He saw his oversight and returned to preceding recto on Thursday, March 4, then utilized preceding verso: see two following entries.
585.10	1 *Monday*] '1' inscribed over printed '8', and the entry preceded by 'This page is misplaced. See the next but one preceding.' Dates correspondingly changed for Tuesday and Wednesday from printed '9' and '10' to '2' and '3'.
586.12	8 *Monday*] '8' inscribed over printed '1', and the entry preceded by '(See next page but 1)', but

	dates not correspondingly changed for following Tuesday and Wednesday.
587.22	with Mamma] 'M' over 'm'
587.28	the Mountfords (out)] above caret
588.3	on Miss] 'o' over 'i'
592.5	Moses.] followed by uncancelled beginning of 'M', perhaps false start for next entry.
592.13	base of] 'of' over 'to'
592.27	Rosebud] 'R' over 'U'
594.5	Went] 'W' over 'Af'
594.9	Pantheon] 'e' over 'o'
595.1–2	city. Went with] period mended from comma and 'Went w' over wiped-out 'to the Ba'
595.5	wife & I] above caret
595.14	from] 'f' over possible 'O'
595.22	I] mended from '&', and '&' added in left margin
596.3	Piazza] 'Pia' over 'Cor'
596.13	Powers] 'Po' over 'at'
597.11	Morning] 'M' over 'A'
598.3	morning] 'mo' over partially wiped '& ra'
598.13	Left Pasignano] 'Left P' over wiped-out 'Fore-noon'
598.19	minutes after] 'a' over ascender, possibly of 'l'
599.1	Fenzi's] 'i' mended to cancel a following 'o'
599.22	Bryant] 'Bry-|' over 'Pow'
600.5	visited] 'vi' over 'w'
602.15	Galignani] 'G' over 'n'
603.6	Bladgen's] 'la' mended from 'ala'
603.7	After our] 'After' over wiped-out '[ ]f[ ]'; 'our' over wiped-out 'towa'
604.2	afternoon] over 'after supp'
608.1	with] 'wi' over '&'
609.18	C.] 'C' over 'G'
611.18	joined] 'joi' over wiped-out 'call'
612.16	2] over 'c'
612.26	and] 'd' over 'to'
613.7	Eve^g] 'Ev' over 'w'
613.21	After] followed by cancelled 'I'
613.26	came in] followed by cancelled 'Friday'

614.6	Story.] period over wiped-out 'to'
614.7	railway] 'w' over 'y'
614.9	baby] second 'b' over 'y'
614.12	Villa] 'V' over beginning of 'M'
615.11	Pincian] 'P' over 't'
619.11	America)] parenthesis cancels comma
619.20	Afterwards (with] parenthesis cancels comma
620.3	Sent] 'S' over 's'
620.17	Jones] 'J' over 'G'
622.15	Rosebud] 'Ro' over 'Jul'
622.20	day] 'da' over wiped-out 'hal'
622.21	Before] 'B' over 'O'
622.21	clock] initial 'c' over 'o'
623.16	with] 'w' over wiped-out 'to'
623.17	along] 'alo' over wiped-out 'the C'
623.19	Franco] 'F' over 'S'
625.2	Mamma afterwards] 'M' over 'A'
625.13	& Rosebud] above caret
626.11	& 11] '&' over 'a'
627.3	morn^g] 'g' over 'il'
627.5	day] above 'to-|'
627.11	An] over 'Ov'
628.14–16	So . . . 26th.] excised; transcript on following MS leaf is headed "Cut from preceding page:" and subscribed with initials of George P. Lathrop and "Mar 22, '74"

The 1859 Pocket Diary

633.1	1859] print mended by pen from '1850'
633.4	Saturday] over 'Sunday'
635.2	M^r] over 'Dr'
639.19	1] over '2'
642.15	walked] 'alk' over 'en'
642.17	Mrs.] 'rs' over 'iss'
645.21	Condotti] 'do' over 'otti'

647.26–27	Between] 'B' over 'At'
649.10	left] 'le' over possible 'at'
656.10	Cowper] 'w' over 'o'
656.11	after] 'af' over 'be'
657.27	#He] '#' above caret, keying to interpolation below
658.3	#The Doctor] '#' above caret, as cross reference to similarly marked sentence above
661.1	(not] parenthesis cancels comma
661.23	Una] above caret
664.21	Maria Maggiore] above cancelled 'Lorenzo'
667.28	Littus] 'L' over 'l'
671.23	Monday] 'Mon' follows cancelled 'Mon'
672.26	a dirty] 'a' over 'd'
673.24	francs] 'c' over 'k'
676.11	£30] '3' mended from '5'
676.26	slept] over 'asleep'
678.10	Rosebud] above caret
680.25	Adelphi] 'l' over 'p'
680.28	a cab] 'a' over 'th'
681.14	old] added at left margin preceding 'Newgate'
682.3	School] 'S' over 's'
682.10	Friday] 'Fri' over 'Thurs'
682.16	Saturday] 'Sat' over 'Fri' but 'ur' not added before 'day'
682.20	Una] over 'Rose'
682.22	Sunday] 'Sun' over 'Sat' and 'ur' cancelled
682.24	to] above caret
687.19	Tried] follows cancelled 'Tried'
692.6	him] above caret
693.1	again.] period over wiped-out 'till'
695.8	before 9, left] '9' squeezed into left margin and 'L' mended to 'l'
696.13	the] 'th' over 'fin'
696.25	on] over 'to'
698.4	evening] followed by wiped-out period
700.19	on] 'n' over 'f'
701.27	Wednesday] 'Wed' over 'Tues' but 'nes' not added before 'day'

702.4   Thursday] 'Thur' over 'Wed' but 'nes'
             not cancelled before 'day'
702.8   Friday] 'Fri' over 'Thurs'
702.13   Saturday] 'Sat' over 'Fri' but 'ur' not added
             before 'day'
709.13   May 14] '4' over '5'

CROSS-REFERENCES WITH
THE MARBLE FAUN

Page references are to the Centenary Edition. Asterisks mark Mrs. Hawthorne's omissions of Notebook entries from *Passages from the French and Italian Note-Books*.

Miriam, Hilda, Kenyon, Donatello

The Marble Faun	The French and Italian Notebooks	
5	192–93	Statues of Capitoline sculpture gallery*
6	192	View from a gallery window*
8–10	178, 191–92	The Faun*

The Faun

16–17	511	The Dying Gladiator*
18	203, 213	Figures on sarcophagus

CROSS-REFERENCES WITH "THE MARBLE FAUN"

SUBTERRANEAN REMINISCENCES

The Marble Faun	The French and Italian Notebooks	
24–26	505–6	Catacomb of St. Calixtus*

THE SPECTRE OF THE CATACOMB

| 30 | 489 | Man in goat-skin breeches |

MIRIAM'S STUDIO

| 37 | 72 | Bas-relief in a palace |
| 44 | 318 | Judith and Holofernes |

THE VIRGIN'S SHRINE

51	498	Hilda's piazza*
51	514	Roman matron, selling chestnuts, figs, and bouquets*
51–52	216	The shrine and the lamp
54	78	American female artist's (Miss Lander's) freedom in Rome*
59	315	Copyists of a single work
60	306	"That inestimable something"

BEATRICE

| 64–66 | 92–93*, 521, 520 | Guido's Beatrice Cenci |

THE SUBURBAN VILLA

CLEOPATRA

The Marble Faun	The French and Italian Notebooks	
123	281	Nakedness in sculpture
123	209	Clothing in sculpture
123	179	Sculpture stained with tobacco juice
123–24	308	Modern statues and quicklime
124	154–55	Greenough unimaginative
125	73	Characteristics of Kenyon's (Story's) Cleopatra
126	177	Cleopatra like a tigress (see also *The Marble Faun*, pp. 377–78)

AN ÆSTHETIC COMPANY

131–32	78	Rome's attraction for artists
132	220	Jealousies of artists*
133	176	Magical landscapes (of G. L. Brown)
133	131	The poet-painter (T. B. Read)
133	128	The angel and St. Peter (C. G. Thompson)
134	293	Color makes chaste marble nude
136	292	Waxwork and sculpture
136	153–54	A modern group (Mozier's) as indestructible as the Laocoön
137–38	221*, 402–3	Drawings by Old Masters

A Moonlight Ramble

The Burial Chaunt

The Dead Capuchin

The Medici Gardens

Miriam and Hilda

THE TOWER AMONG THE APENNINES

The Marble Faun	The French and Italian Notebooks	
214–15	381	Tower of Monte Beni (Montauto)
215	390	Ivy, lichens, and moss*
215	380	The tower and the residence*
217	382–83	Galileo's tower
219	140	The rooms in Blue Beard's castle

SUNSHINE

223–25	484	Wine of Monte Beni (Est)
226	345	Frescoes of Monte Beni (Santa Croce)

MYTHS

242	237	The fig tree married to the vine
243	448	Trailing maidenhair

THE OWL-TOWER

252–53	390–92	English necromancer (Kirkup)
253–54	381	The famous monk's (Savonarola's) imprisonment*
254–55	390	Owls in the tower*

THE OWL-TOWER

ON THE BATTLEMENTS

DONATELLO'S BUST

The Marble Saloon

The Marble Faun	The French and Italian Notebooks	
277	384	The locked chapel
278–79	174	Marble saloon at Monte Beni (Casino of the Villa Borghese)

Scenes by the Way

290–91	272–73	Women seen on the road
291	273	A Pre-Raphaelite artist's subject
291–92	274	Vines growing on fig-trees
292	473	Walls converted to farm houses
292–93	468, 483	Houses built into town walls
293	476	Ugly village houses
293–94	271–72	Characteristic scenes in villages
294	472	Closeness of society in walled towns
294	273	A bough stuck up before a wineshop
295	430	Mist in a valley
295	274	Mist seen as light
295–96	243	Comparison of Italian to New England villages
296	273	Time-stained old houses
296	250–51	Instruments of crucifixion hung on crosses
297	243	Various situations of shrines

Pictured Windows

300	243	Mountain scenery
300–301	274	Stream bed and stone bridge

PICTURED WINDOWS

The Marble Faun	The French and Italian Notebooks	
301	246	Description of hilltop towns
301	253	Age and durability of the towns
301–2	482	Disadvantages of building permanently*
302–3	253	City (Assisi) as fossil and as birthplace of art (see also *The Marble Faun*, p. 258)
303	251–52	Frescoes wretchedly bedimmed
304	256	Painted windows
305	286	Milton's "dim, religious light"
306	408–9	Splendor of sunshine through pictured windows
306	244–45	Begging grandsires and granddams
306–7	263–64	Beggars in Italian villages
307	246	Beggars praying to travellers

MARKET-DAY IN PERUGIA

309	254–55	Perugia seen from a distance
309	256	Perugino's magnificent frescoes
310	258	Fra Angelico's religious sincerity
310	257–58	Streets and people of Perugia
311	259*, 404, 413	The scene in the square
312–13	259–60, 450	Architecture around the square*
313–14	260	Statue of Pope Julius III*

HILDA'S TOWER

325	54	Rome as a long-decaying corpse*
325	56	Narrow, uncomfortable streets*
326	232	Rome's pull at the heart-strings
326	148	Fever lies in wait*

THE EMPTINESS OF PICTURE-GALLERIES

The Marble Faun	The French and Italian Notebooks	
335	102	Demands upon spectator
335	334	Helping out the painter's art
336	297, 350	Objects in Dutch paintings
336–37	111*–12	Italian masters not human; lack of variety in their subjects
337	93	The Fornarina and Raphael's sensuality*
339	321	Hard enamel of worldly critics
339	323	Fra Angelico's piety
339–40	452*, 491–92	Sodoma's Christ bound to a pillar
341	324	Let pictures pass to the garret of oblivion
341	126–27	The builder of a palace haunting it

ALTARS AND INCENSE

345	95–96, 113, 194	Gorgeous Roman churches (S. Andrea al Quirinale, Il Gesu, [?] S. Eustachio)
347	60	Young man before a shrine*
348	424	The Virgin worshipping the infant Saviour (by Correggio)
348–49	136, 55	Preconceptions of St. Peter's*
349	48	Church as a jewel casket magnified
349	136	Preference for the preconceived St. Peter's*
350	344	Frozen sisters of the Allegoric family

ALTARS AND INCENSE

THE WORLD'S CATHEDRAL

HILDA AND A FRIEND

The Flight of Hilda's Doves

A Walk on the Campagna

The Peasant and the Contadina

A Scene in the Corso

A Scene in the Corso

A Frolic of the Carnival

MIRIAM, HILDA, KENYON, DONATELLO

The Marble Faun	The French and Italian Notebooks	
456–58	60–61, 195–96, 198	The Pantheon and its cat*
457	285	The great Eye in the dome of the Pantheon
461	437	The exile (Powers) defers the reality of life
462	523–24	A bracelet of seven Etruscan gems*

INDEX

Note: Entries for cities include such details as bridges and streets (and, for Rome, fountains); features having interest beyond that of location are listed separately. Cathedrals, churches, palaces, and villas are grouped under those entries by order of location. For economy of space, hotels are also under a comprehensive entry.

PS 1850 .F63 v.14
Hawthorne, Nathaniel,
 1804-1864.
The French and Italian